D0769100

MARC-ANTOINE CHARPENTIER

Catherine Cessac

MARC-ANTOINE CHARPENTIER

Translated from the French by
E. Thomas Glasow

Reinhard G. Pauly, General Editor

LIBRARY MSU-BILLINGS

WITHDRAWN

AMADEUS PRESS
Portland, Oregon

Translation of this book into English was made possible in part by a grant from the French government.

Musical examples rendered by Jean-Louis Sulmon.

Numbers assigned to Charpentier's compositions in this volume (e.g., H. 425) correspond to the numbers assigned by H. Wiley Hitchcock in his catalog of the composer's work, *Les oeuvres de Marc-Antoine Charpentier: Catalogue raisonné* (1982).

Copyright © 1988 as *Marc-Antoine Charpentier*
by Librairie Arthème Fayard, Paris.

Translation copyright © 1995 by Amadeus Press
(an imprint of Timber Press, Inc.)
All rights reserved.

ISBN 0-931340-80-2

Printed in Singapore

AMADEUS PRESS
The Haseltine Building
133 S.W. Second Ave., Suite 450
Portland, Oregon 97204, U.S.A.

Library of Congress Cataloging-in-Publication Data

Cessac, Catherine, 1952–
    [Marc-Antoine Charpentier. English]
    Marc-Antoine Charpentier / Catherine Cessac ; translated from the French by
E. Thomas Glasow ; Reinhard G. Pauly, general editor.
        p.   cm.
    "Chronological table of works": p.
    Includes bibliographical references (p.   ) and indexes.
    ISBN 0-931340-80-2
    1. Charpentier, Marc-Antoine, 1634–1704. 2. Composers—France—Biography.
I. Pauly, Reinhard G. II. Title.
ML410.C433C4713 1995
782.1'092—dc20
    [B]   94-29786
                                                                        CIP
                                                                        MN

It is true that we create our own notion of the seventeenth century with our personal arsenal of thought, knowledge, and modern methods, but the works of art that have come down to us give us a notion of its essence and its aspirations.

Jean Rousset
L'intérieur et l'extérieur, 1976

Charpentier was one of the most knowledgeable and industrious composers of his day, as
one can see by the number of fine works he left.

Titon du Tillet
Description du Parnasse Français, 1727

What was the fate of our masters who zealously
admired and ardently imitated the Italian
manner of composing? Where did it lead them?
To write pieces that the public and posterity
pronounced dreadful. What did the learned
Charpentier leave to secure his memory?
Médée, Saül, and Jonathas. He might better
have left nothing.

Lecerf de la Viéville
Comparaison de la musique italienne
et de la musique française, 1704–1706

Contents

Black-and-white plates follow page 96

9

Preface

Music research often seems like a long and laborious quest, undertaken with passion, enthusiasm, and great humility. But is also entails the hope that whatever one cannot find, explain, or bring to light, may be found, explained, or brought to light by others in the future.

Such is particularly the case with Marc-Antoine Charpentier. When I began my research a number of years ago, I found myself facing a vast field of investigation, an almost virgin soil. Here was a man of uncommon discretion whose immense musical corpus was just beginning to be discovered. To tell the story of Charpentier and give an account of his multitudinous and diverse musical oeuvre, preserved for the most part in manuscript form, was an undertaking which brought great joys of discovery but which was also plagued with dead ends and at times inexplicable mysteries. What can be done about the lack or loss of documentation and eyewitness accounts? What can be done when something is difficult to affirm or prove, when the past resists close inspection or ceaselessly tempts the researcher to understand, reconstruct, and connect the slightest clues, the most infinitesimal details, to restore to our knowledge those things that have been buried by time and forgotten?

Like some other composers, Charpentier has endured much too long a period of purgatory from which, fortunately, he seems to be currently re-emerging, both in recordings and in live concert. This present volume is intended as a contribution to this important movement toward the rebirth, rediscovery, and growing interest in a composer little known to the general public and vastly underestimated.

The writing of a book is a solitary act. Nevertheless, this work could not have come into being, or taken its present shape, without the assistance of those to whom I must express my deep gratitude:

11

Philippe Beaussant, who was the first to suggest the project and who inspired me with the necessary enthusiasm to undertake it; Patricia M. Ranum, who brought to light some unpublished documents about Charpentier and took me into her confidence, manifesting the greatest interest in my work as she continued important documentary research on the Guise musical circle; and finally, Jean-Jacques Allain and the Société Marc-Antoine Charpentier, who offered me moral and financial support over several years.

Chapter 1

Charpentier's Place in History

*I was a musician, considered good by the good musicians, and
ignorant by the ignorant ones. And since those who scorned me
were more numerous than those who praised me, music brought
me small honor and great burdens.*

Epitaphium Carpentarii

Soon after his death, Marc-Antoine Charpentier fell into near-total
oblivion until the beginning of the twentieth century. Such a long
silence seems to have been, on the whole, the direct result of the
particular circumstances of the man and his music in the seventeenth century. Indeed, Charpentier's life unfolded on the margins
of the all-powerful court and the honors it could bestow. His music,
different from other French music of the day in more than one
respect, did not always enjoy the reception it deserved, since his contemporaries were neither willing nor able to appreciate fully its
originality, depth of inspiration, and emotional force.

Ignored and misunderstood by the unconditional partisans of
"French" music (which is to say, the Lullists), who had the law behind
them, Charpentier was recognized and hailed by a handful of "true
connoisseurs" and by his peers. This was also how he represented
himself in *Epitaphium Carpentarii* (H. 474), an amazing work in
which the composer dramatized his posthumous return to earth in
the form of a ghost and explained himself as follows:

> I am he who was born long ago and was widely known in this cen-
> tury, but now I am naked and nothing, dust in a tomb, at an end,
> and food for worms. I have lived enough, though too briefly in

comparison to eternity. . . . I was a musician, considered good by the good musicians, and ignorant by the ignorant ones. And since those who scorned me were more numerous than those who praised me, music brought me small honor and great burdens. And just as I at birth brought nothing into this world, thus when I died I took nothing away.

This epitaph of a composer baring his soul, looking back on his life with humility, and perhaps with a touch of bitterness, is one of the most poignant of all such gestures. The text is all the more moving since it constitutes the only psychological portrait of the composer. Indeed, those who were close to Charpentier left no account of who he was, of his relationships with his contemporaries, or of the emotions he felt or inspired. Charpentier left no correspondence or diary that might acquaint us with his tastes, his moods, and his personality. His life was unmarked by the splendid displays or excesses with which chroniclers of the day liked to entertain their readers. Only his work aroused reactions and provoked public opinion. Not the least of the composer's bad fortune was the paucity of material left for future biographers. Imagine, on the other hand, the larger-than-life figure of Jean-Baptiste Lully, whose life contrasted in every respect with that of his rival Charpentier. We must, therefore, be content with Charpentier's precious epitaph and try to understand whatever it reveals about its author.

As previously mentioned, the general tone of the epitaph is one of humility. Charpentier states unequivocally that a human being, even a creator, is of very little importance. Human life is but a brief passage, and the body returns, after death, to nothingness. This may be the attitude of a Christian, who, in the face of divine grandeur, realizes the senselessness of earthly existence and is unafraid to admit it. Jacques Bossuet, in *Sermon sur la mort*, made the same assertion: "Oh how fragile a prop is our existence! Oh how ruinous a foundation our substance! . . . How small is the seat we occupy in this world!" And yet, rising up from the very heart of this humble world view, Charpentier's text is a quiet complaint, a discreet resentment, a secret wound, as though life had not brought the composer all he had hoped for, namely, a little more glory and a little less labor and injustice.

Of whom or of what was the composer thinking? Of Lully, who thwarted his career as a dramatic composer? Of Chaperon (to whom he alludes directly in *Epitaphium Carpentarii*), appointed to the Sainte-Chapelle at a time when Charpentier had perhaps desired the post, although he did not obtain the post until twenty years later? Of the illness that prevented him from participating in the Chapelle Royale competition in 1683? Of *Médée*'s detractors?

Are we justified in regarding *Epitaphium Carpentarii* so seriously?[1] Should it be interpreted in such a literal fashion? Does this view not ignore the overall satirical and parodic spirit of the text, whose touching confession quoted above—imitating phrases frequently used in wills of the day—is only one small example? In composing that work, did Charpentier only wish to entertain and make fun of himself? In spite of the seriousness that runs through most of his work, the composer did not lack humor in certain circumstances.

Charpentier's career spanned nearly thirty-five years from about 1670 until his death in 1704. Throughout those years he never ceased to compose at the commission of important personages such as Mlle de Guise, the Dauphin, or occasional private patrons such as the painter Charles Le Brun, and to have his works performed in the most prestigious sites in Paris: the Palais-Royal, the Jesuit Église Saint-Louis, the Jesuit Collège Louis-le-Grand, and the Sainte-Chapelle. On each occasion, his compositions were tailored to the specific circumstances and performance locales. Thus he created dances and pantomimes for the actors of the Comédie-Française, tender pastorales for the singers of the Hôtel de Guise, masses and grand motets for the Jesuits, and austere chants for the convent of Port-Royal.

This brilliant and kaleidoscopic activity almost always occurred far from the powerful and splendid milieu of the court. Like every great composer of his era, however, Charpentier certainly desired an official post at Versailles; his candidacy at the Chapelle Royale competition attests to that. At court, Jean-Baptiste Lully reigned supreme. Through his talent, but also through his excessive ambition, he managed to reap all the favors of Louis XIV and to monopolize posts and privileges. Lully ruthlessly kept all other musicians (especially those of genius) from claiming what he coveted for himself alone: the supreme devotion and the recognition of his king and his adopted compatriots.

The rivalry between Lully and Charpentier has been much discussed, and the paradoxical nature of the situation has been emphasized. Of Italian origin, Lully epitomized the essence and style of French music, while Charpentier, of French stock, breathed into the music of his nation an emotion and a manner of composing learned through contact with Italy. Two composers, two countries, two esthetics were at odds; one emerged basked in glory, eclipsing the other and dooming him to an undeservedly subordinate position.

With the death of Lully in 1687, however, several questions abound. Why, with the exception of his brief foray in the Académie Royale with *Médée*, did Charpentier not try to make a name for himself at court once all obstacles had apparently vanished? Did he lack the ambition necessary to establish himself securely at the highest level? As a musician patronized by the Guise family until the death of its last descendant in 1688, the year after Lully's demise, surely Charpentier had acquired the skills needed to brave court intrigues. Yet, instead of seizing his opportunity even belatedly, he withdrew with an air of resignation, renouncing the post he had coveted in his youth, discouraged by bad luck (his illness at the time of the Chapelle Royale competition) or by Lully's tightfisted control of the theater. It is still a mystery why Charpentier never sought patrons (except for his nephew Jacques Édouard, who did not become a bookseller until around 1705), at least among some of his friends like Henri de Baussen, whom he knew from Mlle de Guise's circle and who could have engraved his works as early as 1685. Questions such as these must be answered to understand the singular fate of the greatest French composer of sacred music of the seventeenth century.

A portrait of the composer might have provided a starting point for answering these questions. We could have contemplated his attitude at the moment he posed for the artist, analyzed his facial expression, gazed into his eyes, and examined his physical traits which, while unlikely to reveal the whole truth, might have offered a foundation for speculation. But history decided otherwise: Charpentier died taking his "image" with him. No portrait has survived.[2] Again, what a cruel loss!

Though detrimental to his personal fame and immortality, Charpentier's marginal position perhaps benefitted his music. If the composer had obtained an official post at court, would he have had occasion to write his splendid masses when the king had no taste for that type of work? Would Charpentier have left us his sublime Latin oratorios, whose utterly Italian inspiration went against the fashion of the time? Would he have seized the opportunity to compose in as rich and individual a style? One need only listen to *Médée*, the only work conceived within the highly official framework of the Académie Royale, to understand the extent of that institution's constraints. Whatever Charpentier lacked in prestige, he gained in creative freedom during a long career that allowed him to express himself in diverse modes and to try his hand at all musical genres of the era, both sacred and secular.

CHARPENTIER AND POSTERITY

The first musician to be interested in exhuming Charpentier's music, which had been neglected for almost two centuries, was Camille Saint-Saëns.[3] In 1892, with a series of performances of *Le Malade imaginaire* at the Odéon in mind, Saint-Saëns published a "restoration" of the music accompanying Molière's comedy.[4] Judging that Charpentier's score needed correcting, Saint-Saëns took the greatest liberties with it, choosing to keep only certain sections intact and re-composing other passages himself.

Saint-Saëns devoted the first chapter of his book, *Au courant de la vie*, to the composer, entitling it "A Contemporary of Lully," not "Marc-Antoine Charpentier" as he should have. Lully's shadow looms as strong today as it did even then. The creator of *The Carnival of the Animals* recorded his impressions of *Le Malade imaginaire*, judged Charpentier's composition harshly, and made some incredible observations on the composer's relationship to Lully. The complete text follows:

> Concerning *Le Malade imaginaire.*
>
> My study of [the score] caused me great astonishment. There is good reason to be surprised, in fact, when one encounters charming and original ideas alongside such deplorable workmanship in an era in which manuscript correction, if not neatness, was common practice. In this case, there are none of those eccentricities since displayed by [Jean-Philippe] Rameau, no bizarre indiscretions of genius that smack of individuality. The oversights of Marc-Antoine Charpentier are crude mistakes, like a student's clumsy turns of phrase, easy to correct. Strangely enough, when the composer happened to come across a challenge—a trio for three women's voices, for example, rather difficult to write well—everything changes as if by magic: the texture becomes impeccable, although such was not the case for the simplest things.
>
> This is a mystery that is perhaps not too difficult to solve.
>
> Lully was a veritable bane on the French school; after having supplanted [Pierre] Perrin and [Robert] Cambert, who had to go into exile in England, he reigned without peer throughout his long career, leaving no room for anyone beside himself; and if

Marc-Antoine Charpentier managed to slip along in his shadow, it was because he was his son-in-law and protégé [*sic*]. There was probably no dearth of talented composers in France who were condemned to inactivity and obscurity. It is known that Lully had collaborators for the purely mechanical writing out of his five-part orchestrations: he could not have handled that enormous task alone.

There is nothing to prevent us from assuming that Charpentier, a very gifted artist whose talent nonetheless left something to be desired and whose rise was due more to favor than merit, recruited one of those anonymous practitioners as his assistant. Still another hypothesis must be considered: Lully himself might have collaborated on the music of *Le Malade imaginaire.*

Marc-Antoine Charpentier created one great opera, impeccably written from first page to last. It is conceivable that for such an important occasion, he would not have trusted his own talent for a minute, unless by dint of practicing his art he ended up learning it.

Whatever the case, there are works in Charpentier's considerable output that deserve to be known. His ideas have an attractive freshness and originality. Those marred by technical errors are easy to correct without spoiling or modernizing them; they are clearly improved by the elimination of inconsequential schoolboy's errors.

Fortunately, musicologists who were beginning to rediscover Charpentier at the time Saint-Saëns wrote this text proved a bit more serious with regard to historical fact, which Saint-Saëns treated lightly. Credit must be given to Henri Quittard and especially to Michel Brenet, who at the beginning of the twentieth century had the distinction of being the first to consider Marc-Antoine Charpentier a major figure in French music. In 1910–1914, Jules Écorcheville devoted seventy-two pages of his *Catalogue du fonds de musique ancienne de la Bibliothèque nationale* to sorting and numbering Charpentier's manuscripts. Following World War I, Lionel de La Laurencie and J. de Froberville turned their attention to the composer of *Actéon* and *La Descente d'Orphée aux Enfers.*

It was not until 1945, however, that a book embracing the life and work of Charpentier appeared: Claude Crussard's thin volume titled *Un musicien français oublié, Marc-Antoine Charpentier (1634–1704).* Interest in Charpentier's music began to extend beyond French boundaries, and a number of scholarly works were written, most of them focused on the composer's sacred music. Many of these works originated in the United States, such as the dissertations of R. W.

Lowe (1949), H. Wiley Hitchcock (1954), C. Barber (1955), D. Loskant (1957), J. P. Dunn (1962), and M. N. Johnson (1967). No study was published in France during those years.

When long-playing records appeared in the 1950s, people like Guy-Lambert or Roger Blanchard were inspired to choose and transcribe pieces for recording. As was true for the music of Claudio Monteverdi and Antonio Vivaldi, recordings revealed the richness of Charpentier's oeuvre better than any musicological essay. The first long-playing recording of the *Te Deum* (H. 146) was made in 1953, with Louis Martini conducting the Chorale des Jeunesses Musicales de France and the Orchestre de Chambre des Concerts Pasdeloup. The event was greeted enthusiastically. France had discovered one of her greatest composers. The impact of the *Te Deum* was such that television chose its overture-fanfare with trumpets and drums for the Eurovision signature theme, which signals the broadcast of important sports, cultural, and political events. In this way the entire world has come to know at least eight bars of the music of Marc-Antoine Charpentier. Over the next several years, that first recording was followed by a large number of others, conducted by Louis Martini, Jean-Paul Kreder, Jean-François Paillard, Roland Douatte, and Nadia Boulanger. Around forty works were recorded in the space of ten years.[5]

It was not until the late 1970s and early 1980s, however, after another period of near-total neglect, that a new wave of recordings appeared. Unlike the earlier recordings, the newer recordings took into account the esthetic and stylistic criteria of baroque performance practice. Michel Corboz, René Jacobs, Jean-Claude Malgoire, William Christie, and Louis Devos have also recorded the music of Charpentier. William Christie even baptized his vocal and instrumental ensemble with the title of one of the composer's pieces: *Les Arts Florissants.* Currently, like a well-merited twist of fate, Charpentier's music is enjoying a favorable upsurge in the world of recordings while attracting an increasing number of interpreters.

On the musicological front, H. Wiley Hitchcock's research on Charpentier's Latin oratorios fostered numerous articles and transcriptions of the composer's works. In 1982 the U.S. musicologist published *Les oeuvres de Marc-Antoine Charpentier: Catalogue raisonné,* an extremely valuable research tool for musicologists, performers, and anyone interested in the composer's music. In his catalog, Hitchcock compiled all the composer's works and classified them by genre. His numbering henceforth serves as reference to the composer's music, since it has proved indispensable for identifying countless pieces, notably those bearing the same title (e.g., Magnificat settings, Te Deum settings, Tenebrae lessons, Litanies, and so on).

THE WORKS

In 1704 Lecerf de la Viéville wrote: "I have not heard any of Charpentier's motets. I have searched for them without success, and apparently none is in print."[6] In fact, not one of Charpentier's sacred works was published in his lifetime. Only a very few secular works received the recognition of publication: some of the incidental music from the stage play *Circé* (H. 496), published by Christophe Ballard in 1676 along with airs from *Le Malade imaginaire*; twelve *airs sérieux et à boire* (serious airs and drinking songs), including *Le Bavolet* (excerpt from the 1679 version of *L'Inconnu*), published in the *Mercure Galant* between January 1678 and July 1695; another air, "Veux-tu, compère Grégoire," in Ballard's *Recueil d'airs sérieux et à boire de différents auteurs pour l'année 1702* (Collection of Serious Airs and Drinking Songs by Different Authors for the Year 1702); and finally *Médée*, "tragedy in music," issued by the same publisher in 1694. Except for the latter work, these publications include minor pieces not representative of Charpentier's best, especially since no religious compositions appear among them.

As for the publishers of Charpentier's music, the Ballard dynasty held a monopoly on the music printing and publishing industry in France for over two centuries. By royal privilege, the Ballards published all the great composers of their day, and the monopoly passed from father to son until 1788. The firm was located in the Rue Saint-Jean-de-Beauvais in Paris.

The other publisher of Charpentier's music, the *Mercure Galant*, was a monthly chronicle that appeared in the form of small books between three hundred to four hundred pages long. Playwright Jean Donneau, Sieur de Visé, edited the publication from 1672 to 1710. Beginning in 1677, he enlisted the collaboration of Thomas Corneille, with whom he also wrote for the stage. Throughout the pages of the *Mercure Galant*, Donneau de Visé addressed an imaginary lady of the provinces, as pretext for relating, in a light, gallant style, major and minor events not only in Paris but throughout the kingdom and even abroad. As editor of this political and literary monthly, in pursuit of current events and fashions of the day, and using the influence he acquired through his success as a writer and intriguer, Donneau de Visé won a reputation as the father of modern criticism.

The *Mercure Galant* provides an important source of information on contemporary life, especially on Charpentier's life and activities. In fact, the composer and Donneau de Visé collaborated on several successful theatrical ventures. It is probably because of their professional empathy that the playwright published the composer's airs and always mentioned him in flattering terms.

In 1709, five years after Charpentier's death, the composer's nephew and sole heir, Jacques Édouard, a bookseller and publisher, decided to publish a collection of twelve motets entitled

MOTETS
MELÊZ DE SYMPHONIE
COMPOSEZ
PAR MONSIEUR CHARPENTIER
Maître de Musique de la Sainte Chapelle de Paris.
Dédiez à Son Altesse Royale,
MONSEIGNEUR LE DUC D'ORLEANS.
Partition in—4° gravée 3.1. brochée.
A PARIS
Chez Jacques Édouard, ruë Neuve N. Dame.

AVEC PRIVILEGE DU ROY.
M.D.CC.IX.

MOTETS
WITH ORCHESTRA
COMPOSED
BY M. CHARPENTIER
Music master of the Sainte-Chapelle of Paris.
Dedicated to His Royal Highness,
MONSEIGNEUR THE DUC D'ORLEANS.
Score in quarto, engraved, and bound.
In Paris
by Jacques Édouard, New Notre Dame Street.

By royal privilege.
1709.

The dedication was as follows:

> Monseigneur, the special patronage that Your Royal Highness
> was kind enough to grant M. Charpentier, our uncle, and the
> honor afforded him by the opportunity to elaborate on the prin-
> ciples of musical composition are our justifications for the liberty
> we take in presenting you with the first collection of a portion of
> his motets. We dare to believe that Your Royal Highness will not
> refuse to accept and sponsor works which ofttimes have been a
> source of diversion to yourself. We beseech you, Monseigneur,
> to accord this favor to the memory of a man to whom you demon-
> strated much kindness during his lifetime. Thus we will con-
> sider ourselves more than fittingly rewarded for our trouble in
> bringing these works to the public and in seeking to earn, by
> dedicating them to Your Royal Highness, the honor to remain,
> with deepest respect, Monseigneur.
>
> Your very humble, very obedient,
and very meek servants,
Édouard, and Mathas

Despite its formal tone, this dedication is, in some respects,
extremely touching, both in the nephew's appeal to the kindness of
Philippe of Orleans, and in his manner of evoking the memory of
Charpentier, whom the duke had honored with his patronage and
who was once again in need. I prefer to view Jacques Édouard's decision to publish Charpentier's music not as a purely commercial venture, but as a desire to rescue the composer of Mlle de Guise from
oblivion, only five years after his death.

The *Journal de Trévoux* of August 1709 mentioned the publication of the motets, emphasizing the composer's great talent:

> Édouard has printed some *Motets of the late M. Charpentier*, one
> of the most excellent composers France has ever had. He was
> the student of [Giacomo] Carissimi. From that great master,
> Charpentier acquired the rare talent of expressing the meaning
> of words through musical tones, and of moving the listener.
> Thousands of Parisians still recall the profound effect produced
> by his music, quite different from that [music] admired only for
> the beauty of harmony that bears no relation to the words, and
> more so than that [music] whose effect depends solely on
> novelty. It is true that M. Charpentier, second to none in Latin
> music, was not equally successful in French music.[7]

If Jacques Édouard chose these smaller pieces from the immense
body of manuscripts he had inherited, it was probably because he did
not have the financial means to publish larger works. When the
collection of motets did not achieve the success that would have

enabled him to pursue the publication of other scores (implied by the phrase in the dedication, "the first collection of a portion of his motets"), Charpentier's nephew put the manuscripts up for sale:

> For sale in Paris from Sieur Édouard, bookseller, parvis Notre Dame, a book of serious motets, composed by the late M. Charpentier, music director of the Sainte-Chapelle in Paris. All the works of the composer [are] to be found [in that shop] in the form of autograph scores: masses, vespers, and motets, which were sung in the Chapelle of the king [?], all in manuscript state in M. Charpentier's hand. [The bookseller] is offering to entrust them to the care of some church choirmaster to whom this sort of work may appeal. Few musicians are unaware of the reputation acquired by M. Charpentier. The composer was Sieur Édouard's uncle, which is how he came into possession of the works.[8]

In 1727, not having found a purchaser, Jacques Édouard resolved to hand over the bulk of the manuscripts to the royal library for a modest sum, as attested by the bill of sale:[9]

> This day, 20 November, received a collection of musical manu-scripts of Sieur Charpentier, music director of the Sainte-Chapelle, Paris, who died in 1701 [?]; said collection purchased from Sieur Édouard, bookseller, nephew of the author, on behalf of the Abbé de Chancey, for the sum of three hundred livres.
>   The catalogue of these pieces of music is among the papers of the royal library.[10]

The catalog, dated 1726 and entitled "MÉMOIRE des ouvrages de musique latine et française de défunt M. Charpentier, Maître de Musique de la Sainte-Chapelle de Paris décédé en 1701 (?)" (CATALOG of the Latin and French musical compositions of the late M. Charpentier, music director of the Sainte-Chapelle of Paris deceased 1701[?]) is divided into four parts: "Partitions chiffre français" (Arabic-numbered scores), "Partitions chiffre romain" (Roman-numbered scores), "Autres cahiers de musique du même auteur" (Other notebooks of music by the same author)," and "Réflexions sur les ouvrages de musique de défunt M. Charpentier" (Reflections on the musical works of the late M. Charpentier).

The "Réflexions" consist of a text advertising the merits of Charpentier's music:

> This church music would appeal to a provincial choirmaster since those in Paris do not care to perform the works of others. Yet even today, 25 February 1726, twenty-two years after M. Charpentier's death, this music would seem fresh. Since his death, no one has possessed any copies of [this music].

In that respect, this entirely polished and ready-to-perform music might also appeal to Parisian choirmasters who might profit more from the bargain than provincial directors, who often lack instrumentalists and beautiful voices to perform a grand motet. In Paris the church music of the late M. Charpentier would enjoy the same success today as in times past because it is in a style that is still widely favored.

To judge it better, those who want to buy this music need only perform his grand motet entitled *Judicium Salomonis;* other pieces can be judged by comparison, and true connoisseurs will admit that all this music has validity today by virtue of its beautiful harmony and profound erudition. M. Charpentier's heirs have refused four thousand livres for all his works, yet they offer them for less today.

Sieur Édouard, nephew of the author, will strike a good bargain, but he desires to sell the music in a lot to a single person and use the profit for undertaking the printing of a fine new book.

Today Charpentier's autograph manuscripts are in the Bibliothèque Nationale in Paris, assembled in twenty-eight volumes under the name *Mélanges de Charpentier.*[11] Although they do not contain all the composer's works, *Mélanges* constitute the principal collection.

Chapter 2

The Early Years
in France and Italy

Charpentier, as learned as the Italians, possessed to the highest
degree the ability to set words to the most appropriate tones.
                    Journal de Trévoux, November 1704

ORIGINS

Until September 1986, Charpentier's date of birth was unknown.[1]
The first biographical account of the composer in Titon du Tillet's *La*
Description du Parnasse Français (1727), which served as reference
until the twentieth century, suggested that Charpentier was born in
1634:[2]

Charpentier, Composer
    Marc-Antoine, Parisian, choirmaster of the Sainte-Chapelle
in Paris, where he was buried after his death in March 1702, at
age 68.

In fact, Titon du Tillet was wrong about the date of Charpentier's
death. The Sainte-Chapelle registry clearly reveals the date as
follows:

Sunday, 24 February 1704
    On this day, following vespers, the treasurer called a special
assembly in his quarters on the matter of the death of Marc-
Antoine Charpentier, choirmaster of the Sainte-Chapelle, who
died this morning at seven o'clock.[3]

Although Titon du Tillet later revised his dating, it was not until the twentieth century that the date of birth was advanced to 1636.[4] In 1892, however, Michel Brenet thought that

> the date, for which there is no real means of authentication, appears to be incorrect, since it leaves too wide a gap between the composer's birth and his education, and delays the period of his greatest activity to an apparently late age.[5]

This significant remark from the earliest musicological studies on Charpentier was not taken seriously until recently. There is, in fact, a reference in which the composer Charles Coypeau Dassoucy claims to have met Charpentier in Rome.[6] Since Dassoucy was in the Italian capital between 1662 and 1669 (the last two years in prison), Charpentier also must have been there at some time during those years. The composer, then "in his youth," could not have been in his thirties, which a 1634 or 1636 date of birth would have us believe.[7] In this study, I have therefore advanced the date of his birth to approximately 1645.[8]

Thus stood my hypothesis until Patricia M. Ranum's discovery of the inventory taken after the death of Charpentier's father, Louis. That official document reveals that on 16 January 1662 the composer was "eighteen years old or thereabouts," a notarial turn of phrase inferring that he had already observed his eighteenth birthday in 1661 but had not yet reached the age of nineteen by the beginning of 1662. That would mean Charpentier was probably born in 1643.

Some of Marc-Antoine's ancestors probably held official posts in the Guise and Orléans households. The composer's father, Louis Charpentier, had inherited a house in Nivernais, duchy of the Gonzagues of Nevers, who were cousins of Mlle de Guise. Therefore, well before the birth of Marc-Antoine, the Charpentier family had come under the powerful influence of the Guise family, which explains the extraordinary patronage the composer would enjoy on behalf of Mlle de Guise, the last of her lineage.[9] Louis Charpentier was a copyist by trade, whose duties consisted of identifying forgeries as well as making transcriptions. Marc-Antoine inherited his father's calligraphic skills, as one can tell from his manuscripts.

In 1662, at age eighteen, Marc-Antoine became an orphan. A few months later, on 24 August, his elder sister Elisabeth married Jean Edouard, a dancing instructor and instrumentalist. It is not known with which teacher(s) the young Marc-Antoine began his musical apprenticeship, or if he was self-taught, but it is possible he took a few lessons from his brother-in-law after 1662. Shortly thereafter, Charpentier left for Italy.

CHARPENTIER IN ROME

Reviewer Marin Mersenne was highly critical of "ordinary choirmasters":

> One of the shortcomings of ordinary choirmasters is that their own voices are not good enough for singing and performing the florid embellishments of the airs. They do not pronounce each syllable clearly enough for their pupils performing the same things, and in a way they resemble those who try to teach the art of writing before knowing how to write well themselves. They should travel abroad, particularly in Italy, where the people pride themselves on the art of singing and on knowing music much better than the French. For although we might not approve of everything they do, there is something excellent about their arias. They bring the music much more to life than do our songsters, who surpass them in prettiness but not in vigor.[10]

Such criticism, however, could not have been aimed at Charpentier. His voice was "good enough" to allow him to participate in the performance of some of his works, and he had gone to Italy to learn that "something excellent" to which Mersenne referred.

But Charpentier was the exception. While French painters in the second half of the seventeenth century continued to make the *voyage de Rome* considered so essential to an artist's education, composers were more reluctant, less curious, or less enthusiastic about going to Italy and studying its masters.[11] Like Charpentier, Henry Desmarest, another French composer, wanted "to go to Italy to become acquainted with Italian musical taste and to achieve greater perfection in his art."[12] Lully, however, who kept an eye on Desmarest, prevented the latter from going, claiming that Desmarest "had excellent taste for French music that he would only lose in Italy."[13]

Around 1665, during Charpentier's Roman sojourn, French musicians such as Pierre de Nyert, who had also gone to Rome in 1633, no longer returned home in the hope of "adapting the Italian method to the French."[14] In 1661 the Italian-born French statesman Jules Cardinal Mazarin died, Louis XIV began his reign, and Lully was appointed Surintendant of music for the King's Chamber and became a naturalized French citizen. With Italian music henceforth banned at the French court, its supporters found themselves a minority and gathered only in private circles.

The *Mercure Galant* noted on several occasions that Charpentier "remained for three years in Rome," where he "learned music . . . under Charissimi [*sic*], considered the finest master in Italy."[15] The gazette does not specify the time frame of this Roman sojourn, so Dassoucy's account is the only basis for determining those dates.

The colorful Charles Coypeau Dassoucy (1605–1679) was nicknamed the Emperor of Burlesque by his contemporaries. In addition to his literary and musical accomplishments (he composed and played the lute), he was a vagabond, adventurer, and libertine. If the first occupations earned him modest success, the others caused serious difficulties. He dubbed poet and critic Nicolas Boileau a "constipated stoic," but had his hour of glory in 1650 when Pierre Corneille asked him to provide the music for his tragedy *Andromède*.[16] Later, Dassoucy so modestly declared, "I was the one who gave the verses of M. de Corneille's *Andromède* their soul." In the same year, Dassoucy wrote the words and music for *Les Amours d'Apollon et de Dafné* (The Loves of Apollo and Daphne), a "comedy in music."

In 1655 Dassoucy went back to the itinerant lifestyle of his youth and did not return to Paris for fifteen years. What a curious group he and his companions must have appeared—the poet-musician traveling on foot with a donkey laden with lutes, parcels of songs, and bottles, accompanied by two young page boys who sang airs of his composition during stops along the way. In July, Dassoucy met Molière and his troupe in Lyon and joined them during their tour of the south of France until February 1656. Dassoucy then visited Italy—Turin, Mantua, Florence, and finally Rome, where he arrived in 1662. After serving a two-year prison term in the Vatican on morals charges, he returned to Paris in 1669.[17] Everyone had forgotten him, and after another five-month jail term, he lived out his life in utter destitution and neglect.

In Rome, Dassoucy met the young Marc-Antoine, according to a letter Dassoucy wrote when Molière, his former traveling companion, selected Charpentier to compose the music for *Le Malade imaginaire*.[18] Dassoucy maintained that Molière had promised to employ him rather than Charpentier, and he gave vent to all his rage and frustration in this desperate letter of a man on whom fortune had just turned its back:

[H]aving been informed that contrary to the promise he had made me, [Molière] hired a youth who, if not stark raving mad, is mad enough to be pitied for having damaged the blood vessels in his brain, and who, having need of my bread and sympathy in Rome, is no more grateful for my favors than so many other vipers I nourished at my breast, which compelled me to send him this letter:

To M. Molière,

I was at once bewildered and surprised at the news I learned yesterday. I was told that you were about to give your stage play to the incomparable M.[19] . . . for the writing of the music, even though his vocal music is not compatible with your beautiful verse, and the man, who seems to have originality, is still not so original that some copy might not be found at the *Incurables*.[20] Since towering projects call for towering people, and the only thing needed to make him the greatest man of our century is a pair of stilts, you should not hesitate to make such a fine choice.[21]

In his *Biographie universelle des musiciens*, François-Joseph Fétis (1877–1878) maintained that Charpentier's desire to increase his knowledge of painting originally influenced him to travel to Rome, but that after being profoundly impressed on hearing one of Carissimi's motets, he turned his attention exclusively to music.[22] Later it was claimed that Charpentier descended from a line of painters and that he was related to Nicolas Charpentier, the king's painter, and to a Marc-Antoine Charpentier who was the "master sculptor and architect" of Tours. Such assertions are groundless as the name Charpentier was common enough at the time to cast a shadow of doubt over that sort of speculation.[23] Charpentier's real reasons for going to Rome are not known. In any case, he was probably already a fairly accomplished musician for as distinguished a figure as Carissimi to agree to give him lessons.

Whether taken to study painting or music, the *voyage de Rome*, as it was called in those days, was costly. It may have been important for those undertaking the journey to be descended from a family of artists, and it was no less crucial to be well-off or to have generous patrons to provide financial support for the venture. For example, thanks to the generosity of Chancelier Pierre Séguier, the painter Charles Le Brun and the sculptor François Girardon were able to visit the Eternal City.

Did Charpentier experience financial difficulties in Rome, as Dassoucy's account suggests? Who helped the composer during those three years? Should we presume that his visit to Rome was the first manifestation of Mlle de Guise's benevolence? The Guise family had strong ties to Italy, having spent thirteen years there in exile. During a stopover in Florence on his way back from Malta in March 1646, Roger de Lorraine, Chevalier de Guise, encountered fourteen year-old Giambattista Lulli [better known as Jean-Baptiste Lully], whom he brought back to France in fulfillment of a mission entrusted to him by the Grande Mademoiselle, namely, to "bring back an Italian . . . if he met any nice one" for the purpose of "conversing with him, [and] thereby learning the language."[24]

When Charpentier arrived in Rome, he must have been immediately struck by the atmosphere of intense musical activity. While Roman opera was on the decline (after a thriving period between 1620 and 1660), sacred music, which the major composers turned to, graced the many churches and chapels of the city. Besides the great institutions such as the pontifical choir (in the famous Sistine Chapel) and the Giulia choir of Saint Peter's Basilica, a dozen churches, including Saint John Lateran, Santa Maria Maggiore, Gesú, and Saint-Louis of the French, maintained regular choirs with a varying number of singers depending on the importance of the church. Sometimes the choirs consisted of thirty or so performers, as in the case of the pontifical choir. Certain Roman cardinals and princes, both secular and ecclesiastic (e.g., the Borgheses, Pamphilis, Orsinis, Colonnas), also maintained a corps of musicians in their households. Churches without the means of supporting a permanent chapel called on "special musicians" on important feast days.

Finally, it must not be forgotten that musical performances of oratorios played an important part in Roman religious life. They could be heard mainly in the Oratories of Santa Maria in Vallicella or the Chiesa Nuova (founded by Saint Philip Neri) and in the Archiconfraternità del San Crocifisso in San Marcello, for which Carissimi composed. The viol player André Maugars left an account of what he heard in that church one Friday during Lent in 1639:

> There is yet another type of music which is not at all in use in France. . . . It is called recitative (*stile récitatif*). The finest that I heard was in the Oratory of San Marcello, where there is a congregation of Brothers of the Holy Cross, made up of the noblest lords of Rome who consequently have the power to command all the rarest talents Italy has to offer. Indeed, the most excellent musicians take pains to be seen there, and the proudest composers covet the honor of having their works performed there and try to display the very best of their learning. This admirable

and enchanting music is heard only on Fridays during Lent, between three and six o'clock.

The church is not nearly as large as the Sainte-Chapelle in Paris, but at one end there is a spacious loft with an average-size organ, very delicate in tone and well-suited for voices. On both sides of the church, there are two small platforms, where the most excellent instrumentalists are placed. The vocal ensemble began with a psalm in the form of a motet, followed by a beautiful instrumental piece. The voices then sang a story from the Old Testament in the form of a religious drama (*comédie spirituelle*), like that of Susanna, of Judith and Holofernes, or of David and Goliath. Each singer represented a character in the story and perfectly expressed the spirit of the text. Then, one of the most celebrated preachers delivered a sermon, after which the musicians recited the gospel of the day, like the story of the Samaritan woman, of the wedding at Cana, of Lazarus, of Mary Magdalene, or of the Passion of our Lord, the singers very skillfully taking the roles of the characters described by the evangelist.

I cannot praise this musical recitative enough; one must hear it in person to appreciate its merits.[25]

At the time Charpentier met Giacomo Carissimi, his elder, the latter held an appointment at San Apollinare, the chapel of the Jesuit Collegio Germanico, then one of their greatest educational institutions and, from the late sixteenth century onward, one of the major centers of the Counter-Reformation. Carissimi officially entered that extraordinarily active musical atmosphere on 15 December 1629 and remained there until his death in 1674.

The last child of a family of humble artisans, Carissimi was born 18 April 1605 in the village of Marino near Rome and began his musical career as a chorister, then as organist in the cathedral of Tivoli. He was appointed choirmaster of the cathedral of San Rufino in Assisi before establishing himself in Rome in the service of the Jesuits. In 1637, he was ordained as a priest and received a benefice. On more than one occasion he was offered more illustrious posts than the one at San Apollinare, including successor to Monteverdi at Saint Mark's in Venice in 1643, Kapellmeister at the court of Brussels under Archduke Leopold Wilhelm in 1647, and service to Emperor Ferdinand III and his successor Leopold I. All these offers he invariably refused "with the greatest humility."

In 1649, Carissimi's oratorio *Jephte* made him famous throughout Europe. After attending performances of *Il sacrificio d'Isacco* and *Giuditta* in 1656, Queen Christina of Sweden appointed Carissimi "maestro di cappella del concerto di camera" and offered him a gold necklace with the insignia of the Académie Royale which she had founded in Rome.

Although he regularly took part in the religious activities of the Oratory of San Crocifisso by performing his oratorios, Carissimi devoted the greater portion of his activity to the many and various tasks incurred by his post at the German College, such as overseeing the musical training of the college's students, directing the education of the younger choir members, composing, and organizing the musical activities of the church of San Apollinare.

Some contemporary accounts of Carissimi's physical appearance and personality exist. According to his successor, Ottavio Pitoni, Carissimi was tall and thin, inclined toward melancholy, and he suffered from gout. He maintained very courteous relations with friends and pupils. By living modestly and simply, the former artisan's son became quite wealthy by the end of his life. After he died on 12 January 1674, his body was interred in San Apollinare.

During his lifetime and even after his death, Carissimi was considered one of the greatest composers of the seventeenth century, not only in Italy but across Europe. Even Lecerf de la Viéville, that staunch champion of French esthetics who later would never tire of criticizing Charpentier and Italian music in general, said this about Carissimi:

> I have always been convinced that he is the greatest musician Italy has produced, and a justly famous one, a man of unquestionable genius, who possesses natural simplicity and taste: in short the least unworthy opponent that the Italians can set beside Lully.[26]

It goes without saying that the latter assertion was, for Lecerf, the greatest praise that one could possibly give a composer: to be "the least unworthy opponent" of Lully!

Although all but one of Carissimi's autograph manuscripts were destroyed at the time of the suppression of the Society of Jesus [i.e., Jesuits] in 1773, a major portion of his work (masses, motets, cantatas, oratorios) is known thanks to the publication and, in most cases, the copying of scores (though some are of dubious origin), which testify to the impact of the Roman master's music on his contemporaries. Charpentier made a copy of *Jephte* for himself, with annotations for realization of the composer's figured bass.[27]

Carissimi's influence on the music of his day was a direct result of his intense teaching activities at the German College. He had many pupils, mostly young German seminarians. The most famous were Philipp Jakob Baudrexel (1627–1691), Johann Kaspar Kerll (1627–1693), Johann Philipp Krieger (1649–1727), and most importantly Christoph Bernhard (1627–1692), composer, theoretician, and pupil of Heinrich Schütz, who passed along the fruits of his Italian master's teachings to the German Protestant School. Carissimi's Italian pupils included Giovanni Paolo Colonna, organist at San Apollinare who worked principally in his native town of Bologna, and Marc-Antoine Charpentier, the Frenchman. Although apparently not a pupil at the German College, Charpentier most likely took private lessons with Carissimi. He was probably the student most profoundly influenced by Carissimi's teaching and music.

Like Mozart, who a century later at the age of fourteen copied Gregorio Allegri's superb *Miserere* from memory after hearing it in the Sistine Chapel, Charpentier (according to Sébastien de Brossard) probably did likewise for certain motets of the composer of *Jephte:*

> I was told something that is rather difficult to believe; [Charpentier] had a prodigious memory, and after he had heard any music, he could write down all its parts without error. And that is how the motets *Vidi impium, Emendemus, In melius,* and several unpublished oratorios of Carissimi appeared in France, or at least it is thus claimed.[28]

Back in France, Charpentier would write a large number of Latin oratorios inspired by Carissimi in tone and format—or, more precisely, *histoires sacrées* (sacred dramas), since neither he nor the Roman composer used the word *oratorio*.

The three years spent at the great Italian musician's side proved decisive for Charpentier: his work and life reveal a close affinity between disciple and master. Indeed, a striking number of analogies can be noted between the two greatest composers of Latin oratorios: both were private men of whom almost nothing is known; both were singers (Did Charpentier also study voice with Carissimi?); both were music directors of the most flourishing religious order of the century (i.e., the Jesuits); both were teachers; and finally, both were authors of a body of work that was essentially sacred, yet infused with a deep sense of drama.

What do these amazing parallels tell us? Are they merely the result of chance, or are they indications of kindred sensibilities and a strong influence of the Italian on the Frenchman? Probably both of the above are valid. And yet, there was one fundamental difference, namely, the effect of their music on their compatriots. While

Carissimi's music belonged to the old musical and religious traditions, Charpentier's music was a stylistic "transplantation" into an era
when the arts were extremely nationalistic. His attempt to combine
two esthetics provoked as much rejection as approval; all the
sarcastic comments concerning Charpentier by the advocates of the
French school illustrate this.

In Rome, Charpentier certainly heard the grand polychoral
masses whose elements of composition were derived from the
Venetian practice of the *cori spezzati*, best known through the works
of the Gabrielis. The gigantic dimensions of Roman churches caused
composers to increase the number of parts, which in turn resulted in
works that were just as monumental but with a pompousness and
overinstrumentation (some pieces called for as many as twelve
choirs) that sometimes made them sound indifferent and
expressionless.

Charpentier copied into a large notebook a mass for quadruple
chorus by one of the Roman composers, Francesco Beretta, entitled
Missa mirabiles elationes Maris sexdecimus vocibus del Beretta,
followed by *Remarques sur les Messes à 16 parties d'Italie* (see
Appendix 2). This long exercise in copying and analysis is one more
indication of Charpentier's keen interest in Italian music. A few years
later, he too would write a *Messe à quatre choeurs* (H. 4), clearly
inspired by Roman compositions and the only surviving example of
that genre in France. Charpentier's *Mémoire des ouvrages de
musique* mentions an "Italian mass in sixteen parts with instruments,
having a truly magnificent fugue. The composer wrote this mass in
Rome for the *mariniers*. The music is very skillfully written."[29] Was
this the *Messe à quatre choeurs* that might have been composed in
Italy, the *Missa mirabiles*, or yet another work?

Did Charpentier embark on any composition during his Italian
years? We have no proof, although it would seem natural if he did, if
only in his capacity as Carissimi's pupil. In any case, the Frenchman
set several pieces to Italian texts. Two of them are in *Mélanges:* the
very official *Epithalamio In lode dell'Altezza Serenissima Elettorale di
Massimiliano Emanuel Duca di Baviera* (H. 473), probably written
for the marriage of the Dauphine's brother in 1685, and the *Serenata
a tre voci e simphonia* (H. 472), dated the same year.

The other Italian works are pastorals (*Pastorelette del Sgr. M. Ant.
Charpentier*, H. 492, 493) and cantatas ("Beate mie pene," H. 475;
"Superbo amore," H. 476; and "Il mondo così va," H. 477). These last
three pieces can be found in collections of Italian airs and cantatas, in

which Charpentier's music is found alongside the music of Carissimi, Alessandro Stradella, Alessandro Scarlatti, and Paolo Lorenzani. There are two more Italian airs in the first interlude of *Le Malade imaginaire*, as well as an air and a chorus from the Act II divertissement of *Médée*.

The usual route between Paris and Rome passed through the Rhône valley. Some musicians liked to stop in this region of France, a busy center of musical activity. Charpentier might have been one of them, for the Musée Calvet in Avignon possesses the manuscript *Cantate française de M. Charpentier* (H. 478), though the attribution is uncertain.

RETURN TO FRANCE

Upon his return to Paris with Rome's vocal music still echoing in his ear, Charpentier probably made contacts among musicians, mainly clergymen, who were closely associated with the music of Italy. After the death of Cardinal Mazarin and the appointment of Lully as Surintendant of music for the King's Chamber, some clergy endeavored to keep the Italian tradition alive in France through performances by their choirs of the motets which some of them had acquired during their travels. Among them were Claude Nicaise (1623–1701), canon of the Sainte-Chapelle in Dijon, and René Ouvrard (1624–1694), music director of the Sainte-Chapelle in Paris, whom Sébastien de Brossard called "as fine a theoretician as a practician."

Ouvrard possessed a large collection of Italian pieces that he circulated among his friends in Paris and in the provinces. Although his own compositions are lost, it is known that he tried his hand at sacred dramas in the style of Carissimi whom he deeply admired. Nicaise, in turn, corresponded with the Italian composers he had met during his trip through the peninsula. These two men probably crossed paths in Italy at some point. Later they maintained a regular correspondence, lasting from 1663 to 1693. In a letter dated 24 February 1665 (contemporary with Charpentier's Roman sojourn), Ouvrard expressed concern about measures taken by the pope against Carissimi's music:

> Never have I received so great a surprise than when I learned
> you were in Rome on the very day that I was about to write to you
> in Dijon, after reminiscing about my trip to Rome and my hopes

to return there some day, though deciding to wait until the Holy Year. You have not exercised so much patience, Monsieur, and it appears that Rome has charms much too powerful for a spirit such as yours to endure being away from a city that is home to the arts and all the beauties capable of nourishing curious and intelligent minds. I have been led to believe that our current pope has for the past two years banned sacred dramas (*histoires en musique*), not wanting anything sung in church that is not contained word-for-word in the Holy Scriptures or the breviary. This is like cutting off the wings of the angel of music. A man who arrived in this country two months ago has told me more, namely, that Sieur Carissimi had not been able to obtain permission to publish his compositions, which I cannot believe. I hope, Monsieur, that before you return you will become informed about these things, all the more since I expect you to accomplish the work that you set out to do—to persuade M. Carissimi to give public performances of all his works, with no restrictions. I have admired everything of his since hearing [his music] during my sojourn in Rome, where I was a regular listener every feast day and Sunday.[30]

Two years later, on 10 January 1667, Ouvrard, anxious to know the opinion of Italian composers with whom Nicaise was in contact, wrote Nicaise:

For now, I content myself with sending you a printed copy of the music and words of the piece I prepared for you some time ago . . . and if you judge it worthy, you may share the music with your Italian friends, and, though it may not contain all their genius, they will perhaps appreciate the effort of my small imagination.[31]

From the early 1680s until 1706, a particularly active Italianist circle in Paris regularly gathered at the home of Nicolas Mathieu, curé of the Église Saint-André-des-Arts. It is probable Charpentier frequented those meetings hosted by the ecclesiastic, whose activities were reported by Serré de Rieux:

> *D'un pieux amateur le zèle curieux,*
> *Dans la France attira des motets précieux,*
> *Qui traçant à nos chants une route nouvelle,*
> *A nos auteurs naissants servirent de modèle.*
> *D'ouvrages renommés il forma son concert;*
> *De tous les connaisseurs il fut l'asile ouvert.*
> *Les exécutions vives et difficiles,*
> *Firent dans l'art du chant des élèves habiles;*

Et le latin offrant plus de fécondité,
Dans un tour tout nouveau savamment fut traité.
Charpentier revêtu d'une sage richesse,
Des chromatiques sons fit sentir la finesse:
Dans la belle harmonie il s'ouvrit un chemin,
Neuvièmes et tritons brillèrent sous sa main.[32]

The eager curiosity of a pious music-lover
Brought back to France some precious motets,
Which served as models for our budding composers,
In opening up new paths for our singing.
He trained his chorus with famous works;
His was an open sanctuary for all connoisseurs.
Brilliant and difficult performances
Sharpened pupils' skills in the art of singing;
And Latin, offering more fertile ground,
Was skillfully handled in its turn.
Charpentier with his well-construed richness,
Made one feel the subtleties of chromatic intervals:
In beautiful harmony he pointed the way,
Ninths and tritones shimmered under his hand.

In a note, Serré de Rieux added:

M. Mathieu, curé of Saint-André-des-Arts for several years in the last century, organized a concert every week at his home, at which was sung only Latin music composed in Italy by the great masters who had been flourishing there since 1650, namely, Luigirossi, [Pier Francesco] Cavalli, [Maurizio] Cazzati, Carissimi in Rome, [Giovanni] Legrenzi in Venice, [Giovanni Paolo] Colonna in Bologna, Alessandro Melani in Rome, [Alessandro] Stradella in Genoa, and [Giovanni Battista] Bassani in Ferrara. . . . It was thanks to the curé of Saint-André that these fine works were first heard in Paris.[33]

Nicolas Mathieu had a spacious three-floor dwelling with two rooms on each floor:[34] In

a room on the second floor overlooking the street [du Cimetière Saint-André, today Rue Suger] and the cemetery, [there were] a small organ enclosed in a walnut chest with streaks of black wood, with its bellows [and] a harpsichord of the same wood

by the manufacturer Philippe Denis. In an adjacent room, there was also an English bass viol, two French viols, a bass violin, and two violins: everything necessary for good music-making, French or Italian. Mathieu also possessed a large music library of nearly two hundred items, largely consisting of religious music. Among the Italian pieces, motets by Bassani, Melani, Lorenzani, Colonna, Francesco Foggia, and other, anonymous composers made up two-thirds of the collection. The French music included works by Lully, **Henri Du Mont, Pierre Robert, Blondel, Nicolas Bernier, André Campra, Morin, and "a bundle of motets" by Charpentier.**

Another hub of Italian music was the Eglise Sainte-Anne-La-Royale, where the Théatins had established themselves under Cardinal Mazarin in 1644. In 1675, Mlle de Guise gave eighty louis d'or to renovate their chapel. The religious circle organized its ceremonies "in the manner of Roman oratories" with the assistance of singers from the Opéra and with stage effects, advertising services by posting playbills and selling tickets.[35] This raised eyebrows among the more pious Paris circles. From 1685, the director of the Théatins' chapel was a Roman, Paolo Lorenzani, who had come to France in 1678. Much in favor with Louis XIV in spite of Lully's jealousy, Lorenzani had been appointed the queen's music director, and the king had commissioned him to bring back some fine singers from his native country. In December 1679 Lorenzani returned from Rome with five castratos who became chapel musicians. Lorenzani remained in France until 1694.

As far as we can tell, that was the state of things among the French Italianist circles with which Charpentier was very likely in touch. It should be emphasized that these clergymen were involved with sacred music, while the real forum of debate over Italianism in France was to be found in the area of secular music, particularly opera.

FRANCE, ITALY, AND MUSIC

If there is one genre in musical history that has reflected social and even political ideologies or themes at every step of its development, it is opera. Just think of Richard Wagner and, in particular, Jean-Baptiste Lully. Those two composers, at first glance different, nevertheless had a number of things in common, namely, the quest for absolute recognition and power, and the designs to create a genre whose captivating novelty would overshadow whatever had come before. Lully and Wagner cherished the dream of total spectacle which, in both cases, was accomplished most brilliantly.

Italian opera was introduced to France in the middle of the seventeenth century. At first it attracted curiosity, but later it was rejected. The French public's intense reactions were influenced not only by esthetics but by politics as well. It was the Italian minister Guilio Mazarini, naturalized French (Jules Cardinal Mazarin), who saw in the powerful charms of Italian dramatic music a formidable tool for political seduction. Later, Louis XIV's premier composer, Lully, who also was Italian and naturalized French, reversed the trend by making himself the champion of French music. Another surprising reversal involved a Frenchman and occurred when Charpentier was alternately praised and condemned for his Italianism.

While we cannot turn back the clock, it is not difficult to see that the French and Italian styles were not always the irreconcilable enemies they became in the second half of the seventeenth century. On the contrary, there was a "golden" age when both styles over-lapped and complemented each other, before national differences rose to the surface and disrupted that balance. By the end of the fifteenth century, French kings, impressed by the sumptuous enter-tainments they had witnessed during their campaigns in Italy, invited the first musicians from south of the Alps to come to the French court. Oboe, cornet, and sackbut players came, followed by string players and lutenists (e.g., Alberto Rippe at the court of François I).

It was in the field of drama (spoken as well as sung, staged as well as choreographed), however, that the Italian theatrical genius made its greatest mark on the French court ballet and later on French opera. From 1567 and for more than twenty years thereafter, the Piedmont-born Baltazarini de Belgiojoso, who Frenchified his name to Baltasar de Beaujoyeulx, was in charge of court entertainments under Catherine de Médicis. In the *Ballet comique de la Reyne* per-formed in October 1581, Beaujoyeulx achieved a synthesis of solo singing, chorus, and dance. Thus he created the court ballet, a native-French genre forged from mostly Italian elements. At the beginning of the seventeenth century, the French court ballet returned across the border and was introduced to the court of Tuscany, where it had a strong influence on Italian musical theater.

During this fruitful musical give-and-take between the two coun-tries, France discovered the expressive inflections and virtuosic ornamentation of Italian monody with the arrival of Giulio Caccini at the court of Henri IV and Marie de Médicis, whose wedding had been celebrated recently in Florence with the performance of

Jacopo Peri's *Euridice* on 6 October 1600. If Caccini's influence on the *air de cour* (the art of declamation, development of ornamentation) is apparent, the French influence on Italian artists (in particular in the area of the *chanson mesurée*) is no less so. At the same time, the arrival of Italian actors in Paris was an added attraction for the French, who soon developed an enthusiasm for the Italians' skill in blending comedy and song, for the complicated plots of their plays, and especially for their sumptuous scenery.

During the regency of Anne of Austria, Cardinal Mazarin played the most instrumental role in the invasion—the word is not an exaggeration—of Italian artists at court: the stage designer and machinist Jacopo Torelli, the composer Luigi Rossi, the librettist Francesco Buti, and the castrato Atto Melani, to mention only the most famous. Many others remained active both in their own country and in Paris. The cardinal loved music passionately since his youthful days at the Jesuit Collegio in Rome where he acted and sung. By introducing Italian opera to France, he was satisfying his own taste for the stage and singing; he also intended to win over the aristocrats and possibly the public through fabulous spectacles, such as *La Finta pazza* in 1645, *Egisto* in 1646, and *Orfeo* in 1647. Despite his intentions, France was not Italy: the wildest enthusiasts were not blinded, and reason reigned supreme. The Parisians were uneasy at first, then angry because of the enormous expenses incurred by the production of *Orfeo*. Before long, patriotic sentiment welled up against the Italian minister and his compatriots established at the French court.

Then came the outbreak of the Fronde and the exile of the royal family and Cardinal Mazarin. When the cardinal returned to Paris on 3 February 1653 after the unrest had died down, he recalled the Italian musicians who had also been obliged to flee the hostile climate of the capital. He continued to champion the art of his homeland without necessarily combining it with the French. In 1654, *Le nozze di Teti e di Peleo*—"Italian comedy in music intermingled with a ballet on the same subject"—achieved a synthesis of Italian opera and French court ballet. That work was the product of a close collaboration among artists of both countries: the composer was Carlo Caproli, the librettist Abbé Buti. The Comte de Saint-Aignan directed the ballets set to music by French composers, with the accompanying verses from the pen of Benserade. Italian singers mingled with French singers. Among the dancers were the young Louis XIV, whose presence contributed much to the production's success, and Lully, who had been appointed composer of instrumental music for the King's Chamber the year before.

Six years later, to celebrate with great magnificence the marriage of Louis XIV and the Spanish Infanta Marie-Thérèse, Mazarin planned a production of an opera by Francesco Cavalli, *Ercole amante*, composed especially for the occasion. The large theater in the Tuileries palace, designed by the architect Gaspare Vigarani, was not ready in time, so the minister decided to have another Cavalli opera, *Xerse* (composed six years earlier and less demanding in its staging), performed instead on 22 November 1660. On 7 February 1662 the completed Tuileries theater finally mounted *Ercole amante*, but Mazarin, who died on 9 March 1661, was no longer there to enjoy the theater and the music he had so persistently tried to impose on the French.

Mazarin's death marked the end of the domination of Italian music in France and the beginning of the supremacy of French music. The man who proved to be its principal spokesman, the Italian Jean-Baptiste Lully, would use the same weapons of shrewdness and seduction as his compatriot used to insure the triumph of an esthetic that was in harmony with what the French, somewhat lacking in musical identity, expected to receive. Even more than in *Xerse*, for which he had only written the dances and a few airs, Lully participated in the production of *Ercole amante*, not only by contributing some longer ballet sequences, but by having a hand in the actual staging of the spectacle. The future Surintendant was already revealing the remarkable organizational qualities that made it possible for him to have such a brilliant career.

No longer under Mazarin's yoke, the French applauded the ballets, costumes, scenery, and machinery of *Ercole amante*, while coolly receiving the music of the great Cavalli, who returned to Venice deeply humiliated. As soon as the performances ended, the Italian singers also went back to their country. Lully now had free rein. He realized that under no circumstances would he gain acceptance as an Italian. On social as well as musical grounds, he proceeded to do whatever he needed to make people forget his Florentine origins. Soon after becoming a naturalized French citizen, he married the daughter of the celebrated singer and composer Michel Lambert. Having won the esteem and confidence of the king, Lully was granted the lofty post of Surintendant of music for the King's Chamber in May 1661.

During his first fifteen years in France, Lully paid close attention to all that was happening around him. He considered how Italian music, which Mazarin had tried to establish, was incapable of pleasing the French, but he did not reject it completely. Rather he drew from it only that which seemed compatible with French thought, particularly the notion of opera to which he added features of the music of his adopted country, including declamation, dance music—all elements that he had perfectly assimilated. Showing brilliant intuitive sense, Lully gradually devised an art form developed from the court ballet by way of the comédie-ballet, which resulted in the tragédie lyrique. Everyone agreed it was the perfect expression of "good taste" and a subtle blend of clarity, simplicity, and emotion.

In 1666, while Charpentier was in Rome, Lully feared that some day the Italians might come back into favor. Thus he influenced Louis XIV to dismiss the Troupe du Cabinet made up of ultramontane artists. From then on in Paris there remained only the Italianist circles mentioned above, which posed no threat to the Surintendant. All risk of competition having been systematically eliminated, nothing and no one seemed capable of giving Lully any sort of resistance or disturbing his reign at court. At that point in history, Marc-Antoine Charpentier returned from Italy, and shortly thereafter he was asked by Molière to provide some music for Molière's comédies-ballets. For Lully, Charpentier was an unexpected rival; for Charpentier, Molière's request was the start of a career that kept him in Lully's shadow. It was also the onset of conflicting social and artistic ambitions, and the beginning of a tireless creative productivity.

CHARPENTIER, FRENCH COMPOSER?

It is striking how consistently Charpentier's contemporaries, whether in praise or in criticism of his music, equated his Italianism with his "learned" tendencies. In their ears, both were more or less the same since knowledge of the art of musical composition was a quality, or a flaw, attributable to the Italian style.

Whenever French and Italian music were compared to one another, they were always clearly differentiated and considered to be, depending on the era, sometimes complementary, sometimes incompatible. From Marin Mersenne (1636) to the Abbé Raguenet

(1702), we find the same enumeration of characteristics for each style: restraint versus expressivity, grace versus liveliness, and sweetness versus strength. According to Mersenne:

> Foreign nations do not have any [vocal music] that we can imitate satisfactorily, or, if I may say something in our favor, that we cannot surpass in some manner, particularly in terms of elegance, in delicacy and in sweetness of expression; while in clarity, accuracy, or power, Italian voices can compete with those of any other nation. In addition, they have several wonderful traits and a flair for invention missing in our singing. . . . Our songsters believe the exclamations and accents used by the Italians when singing overstate the tragic or comic effect, which is why they do not want to perform them. Nevertheless, they should imitate whatever is appropriate and excellent, since it is easy enough to moderate the exclamations and accommodate them to French grace. They should also add whatever they can that is more poignant to the beauty, clarity, and smoothness of the cadences—something our musicians do so gracefully when, having a fine voice, they have learned the art of singing from the great masters. . . . Admittedly, French airs usually lack passion because our songsters are content with tickling the ear and pleasing through prettiness, without trying to arouse the feelings of their listeners, following the subject and the meaning of the text.[36]

For Raguenet, French airs

> always aim for softness, simplicity, the flowing, and coherent; everything is of the same tone; or if there is an occasional variation, it is prepared and smoothed out so that the air remains as natural and flowing as though nothing of it had been changed at all. There is nothing bold or adventurous in it; everything about it is equal and homogeneous.
>
> On the other hand, the Italians constantly pass from major to minor and from minor to major. . . . They hold notes for so long that those unaccustomed to it cannot help but be shocked by such boldness, but before it is over they cannot admire it enough.
>
> In short, as for the appropriateness of the air to the meaning of the words, I have never heard anything quite like the music that was performed in Rome in the Oratory of Saint Jerome of Charity, on Saint Martin's Day in 1697, on the words, *mille saette*, a thousand arrows: it was an air consisting of disjointed notes, as in a gigue. The character of that air gave the soul a vivid impression of an arrow and wrought so convincingly upon the imagination that every violin seemed to be a bow, and all the bows were like so many flying arrows whose points seemed to hit upon every part of the music; it couldn't have been more ingenious or more brilliantly expressed.[37]

These writings do not display the polemical tone that characterizes later eighteenth-century texts. Their authors were nonpartisan, recognizing the virtues of both styles, even though one can sense a budding attraction for the expressive Italian air, which made the listener react more emotionally than the more subtle French air.

Admiration for Italian music, however, as expressed in *Parallèle des Italiens et des Français en ce qui regarde la Musique et les Opéra*, incited Lecerf de la Viéville, the inveterate Lullist, to pen his reaction to Raguenet's piece in *Comparaison de la musique italienne et de la musique française* (1704–1706), a veritable apology of the French style and an uncompromising criticism of the Italian.[38] For Lecerf, there could be no harmony, no possible or even desirable meeting of the two esthetics: "Let us cultivate our French spirit, let us not yield to the Italian; they are so dissimilar that it is difficult to bring them together in combination: the mixture spoils them both."[39]

Often trying to make his ideas prevail through bias and false information, Lecerf de la Viéville could be scathing in his comments about the Italians and Charpentier, whom he often considered as one and the same:

> What was the fate of our masters who zealously admired and ardently imitated the Italian manner of composing? Where did it lead them? To write pieces that the public and posterity pronounced dreadful. What did the learned Charpentier leave to secure his memory? *Médée, Saül,* and *Jonathas.* He might better have left nothing.[40]

Elsewhere, though admitting he knew little of Charpentier's work, Lecerf unrelentingly continued to malign the composer:

> I cannot understand by what miracle Charpentier could have been so expressive, that is to say natural, brilliant, and true in his Latin music, while being so harsh, dry, and excessively stiff in his French music. This is amply displayed by that wretched opera *Médée*, a collection of songs that I know, and *Jonathas*, a little opera performed at the Collège de Clermont and whose score I have recently seen. In technical knowledge, Charpentier compares favorably to the Italians, as does Colasse, and the Abbé Bernier.[41] But as inferior as the Italians are in matters of expressivity, I believe one would do them injustice by preferring Charpentier to them. And it would be a gross insult to Colasse, who is sometimes cold and awkward but excellent when at his best, and to the Abbé Bernier, whose published motets have some commendable features and whose unpublished *Te Deum* rivals Lully's setting, if Charpentier were compared to them in any area other than technical skill.[42]

If Charpentier had his detractors (we shall see with regard to *Médée* that Lecerf de la Viéville was not the only one), he also had supporters for whom his Italianism and his technical skill were two factors contributing to the formation of his own distinctive genius. Donneau de Visé, editor of the *Mercure Galant*, felt that Charpentier's sojourn in Rome provided him with "great advantages. All his works prove it."[43] Sébastien de Brossard, another Italianist musician, thought this about the influence of Italy on Charpentier:

> It is his youthful experience in Italy that a few extreme French purists, or those jealous of the excellence of his music, have seized upon quite inappropriately when criticizing his Italian taste; for it can be said without flattering him that he made use only of the good. His works display this well enough.[44]

From the *Journal de Trévoux* to *Histoire du théâtre français* by the Parfaict brothers, the name of Charpentier remained synonymous with Italian music and manifested striking originality compared to what was then generally heard in France: "Charpentier, as learned as the Italians, possessed to the highest degree the ability to set words to the most appropriate tones."[45] He made use of "harmony and technical knowledge unknown to French composers before then."[46]

These accounts and opinions about the composer's "Italian taste" and "technical knowledge" make one wonder if Charpentier was truly a French musician or an Italian-style renegade. What was it that led his contemporaries to paint such a clear portrait of a Charpentier literally "infected" by Italian esthetics? Charpentier's music holds a number of surprises. First, there is its sheer quantity to consider. His catalog numbers nearly five hundred fifty works, about a hundred of them secular, but he actually composed many more, some of his manuscripts unfortunately having been lost. No other French composer of the time was so prolific. This quantity is matched by the extraordinary diversity of his music, equally uncommon: operas, masses, motets, pastorales, cantatas, sonatas, Latin oratorios, serious airs and drinking songs, comédies-ballets, stage plays, divertissements, and instrumental *noël* settings. A musician with a great curiosity for all his era had to offer in the way of genres and languages, Charpentier, unfettered by national boundaries, left a many-faceted oeuvre that explores all fields, sacred and secular. Only the instrumental works seem slightly overshadowed by the vocal works.

Charpentier's time in Rome was spent primarily on perfecting his musical language. There he heard what he never would have heard had he stayed in France: concerted (*concertante*) masses, large poly-choral pieces, cantatas, and sacred dramas. He was in direct contact with Roman music, learning from an Italian who remained "the master" all his life and whose work he perpetuated by composing numerous Latin oratorios. If Charpentier was the first "importer" of that genre in France, he also was responsible for introducing the cantata and the sonata, genres that would flourish in France in the eighteenth century. He was also the only composer to cultivate the concerted mass, popular in Rome but totally ignored by musicians in Paris and the French court.

Charpentier, however, was not content to introduce these genres to his country. He also incorporated numerous characteristics of Italian music into his own work as a whole, including flowing melody, dramatic use of silence, chromaticism, and learned harmonies shimmering with sweet or harsh dissonances and expressive modulations. These elements were tempered by the demands of French taste, which were based on clarity and naturalness. Most of the time when one hears or reads the score of a piece by Charpentier, the shape and general aspect seem unmistakably French. Obviously, certain Latin oratorios seem less so than *Médée* or any of the Tenebrae lessons. But Charpentier was born in Paris, lived there, and composed there. He was a French musician and remained so all his life. Like Lully, he based his recitative on French or Latin declamation, he made use of the important instrumental forms of the French overture or the passacaglia, and he was fond of dance rhythms, found in both his instrumental pieces and his incidental music for the theater. Charpentier was well aware of the subtlety of the French art of singing and carried ornamentation to an extreme degree of refinement in his Tenebrae lessons.

In summary, Charpentier turned to the styles of writing he needed, styles that corresponded to what he felt and wanted to translate into music. He kindled his art with an emotion and an expressivity not always characteristic of French music, while never allowing himself to indulge in the virtuosity of Italian bel canto. A sort of precursor of François Couperin's *goûts réunis*, Charpentier created his highly personal style, infinitely rich and varied. Of him it can truly be said:

> *La musique n'est qu'une et ses mêmes accords*
> *Partout doivent former de semblables transports.*[47]

> There is only one music and her matchless harmonies
> Everywhere must create similar delight.

Although it was not written in reference to Charpentier, this couplet by Serré de Rieux most accurately describes the deep individuality of Charpentier's music.

Chapter 3

Molière and the Comédie-Française

MOLIÈRE'S COMPOSER

The program of the Palais-Royal theater on 8 July 1672 read: *la Comtesse d'Escarbagnas* and *le Mariage forcé*. After more than ten years of Molière plays at that site, it seemed as though nothing could surprise Parisians that summer evening. The performance, however, was eventful in two important ways: it marked the end of the fruitful collaboration between Molière and Lully, and it marked the theatrical debut of a young unknown composer, Marc-Antoine Charpentier. Indeed, Molière had just replaced his regular composer after what has to be termed an abuse of power on the part of Lully, who did not hesitate to sacrifice his friendship with a man of genius for his own personal ambition.

More than ten years earlier, on 17 August 1661, Molière and Lully had collaborated for the first time on *les Fâcheux*, a comédie-ballet written for the entertainment given by the Surintendant Nicolas Fouquet at his château at Vaux-le-Vicomte. In 1664, "the two great Baptistes" cemented their partnership with *le Mariage forcé*, later continuing with *La Princesse d'Élide, L'Amour médecin, George Dandin, Monsieur de Pourceaugnac,* and *Les Amants magnifiques,* and culminating with *Le Bourgeois gentilhomme* in 1670. With each play, the role of music and dance became increasingly important and more closely linked to the spoken comedy.

With *Psyché* (a "tragi-comédie and ballet" whose text was jointly written by Molière, Pierre Corneille, and Philippe Quinault) in 1671, the comédie-ballet genre leaned toward the tragédie lyrique, a genre officially created two years later with Lully's opera *Cadmus et Hermione.*

At the end of the year, on the occasion of the recent remarriage of his brother to the Princess Palatine Charlotte-Élisabeth, Louis XIV decided to offer an entertainment to his new sister-in-law, whose strong character seemed to attract him. He commissioned a comedy from Molière, *La Comtesse d'Escarbagnas,* which included a pastorale. The entire production, which was interspersed with incidental music from earlier works chosen by the king, was christened *Ballet des ballets.* On 2 December 1671 Lully and Molière were still on good terms, but Lully's desire for power and his tightening grip on the musical life of the court were about to change the course of their relationship abruptly. The circumstances can be briefly summarized as follows.

On 28 June 1669 the poet Pierre Perrin obtained from Louis XIV the privilege to establish opera academies along the lines of those in Italy, England, and Germany. Two years later, *Pomone,* written by Perrin and the composer Robert Cambert and dubbed by Saint-Évremond the "first French opera," was performed successfully in the *jeu de paume* in the Rue Mazarine. Unfortunately, poor Perrin had gone into partnership with Champeron and Sourdéac, two unscrupulous individuals, so that in spite of *Pomone's* financial success, the poet, unable to pay his creditors and artists, was thrown in prison. Sensing the French public was finally ready to accept the notion of a spectacle set entirely to music, and taking advantage of Perrin's misfortune, Lully visited the poet in jail to buy his privilege. Selling the privilege meant that Perrin could pay off his debts and regain his freedom, though the decision was not entirely up to him. Not everyone at court was Lully's friend, and some members of the court were apprehensive to see the privilege given to the Florentine. In view of these complications, Lully

> went to the king to solicit the gift with such strength and persistence that the king, fearing [the composer] might resign out of vexation, told M. Colbert that he could not do without that man in his divertissements; he had to be given whatever he wanted, which is what was done the following day, to the utter amazement of many.[1]

These few lines give some idea of the considerable influence the musician had acquired over his sovereign.

On 13 March 1672 the "privilege for Sieur Jean-Baptiste Lully, Surintendant and composer of music for the King's Chamber, to

direct the Académie Royale de Musique" was signed by Louis XIV.
Lully had obtained a monopoly on music for the stage. He was
allowed

> to establish an Académie Royale de Musique in the good city of
> Paris, consisting of whatever number and type of persons he
> deems fit, whom [the king] will choose and dismiss on the
> recommendation of [Lully], for the purpose of staging [the
> king's] performances, whenever [His Majesty] desires, of
> musical pieces to be composed both in French and in other lan-
> guages, alike and similar to the Italian academies; to serve in that
> capacity for life, and after him, his children shall be provided for
> and inherit the aforementioned duties of Surintendant of music
> for the King's Chamber, with the power to select whomever they
> feel worthy.

Moreover, it was expressly forbidden

> to perform any play set entirely to music, whether sung in
> French or other languages, without written permission from the
> aforementioned Sieur de Lully, at the risk of a fine of 10,000
> livres and the confiscation of theaters, stagecraft, scenery,
> costumes, and other things.[2]

Originally added to these Draconian conditions was a clause
stipulating that it was not only forbidden to allow any play to be
entirely set to music, but "even to stage any performance containing
more than two airs and two musical instruments without permission
in writing from Sieur de Lully."[3] This final arrangement proved
unacceptable for any playwright, and especially for Molière, whose
comédies-ballets could no longer be produced in all their glory.
Moreover, Lully's step was all the harder for the dramatist to accept
since Molière had apparently entertained the very same notion of
establishing an opera with his composer as partner.[4] On 29 March
Molière and his troupe filed a petition with the authorities:

> Today there appeared at the clerk's office at court master
> Charles Rollet, representing Jean Baptiste Pocquelain, Sieur de
> Molière; François Lenoir, Sieur de La Torillier; Charles Varlet,
> Sieur de La Grange; Philibert Gassot, Sieur du Croisy; Pierre
> Villequain, Sieur de Brye; André Hubert; Jean Pithel, Sieur de
> Beauval; and their wives, all actors in the Troupe du Roi. [Rollet]
> has declared and declares here that he has opposed and still
> opposes, until it be verified, any letters patent from His Majesty
> granting permission to Baptiste, Sieur d'Ilier, or others, the
> privilege to present dances, ballets, playing of lutes, theorbos,
> violins, and all types of musical instruments and other things, and

power to forbid anyone else to have them rehearsed or performed for reasons to be explained in due course.[5]

At the same time, Molière decided to approach the king, whose
awkward position might easily be imagined. Although entirely
devoted to Lully's cause, Louis XIV was equally attached to his
dramatist. Yet he could not go back on his promise to the Florentine.
The situation therefore became extremely delicate. Moved by
Molière's desperation, Louis agreed to strike out the clause forbidding the performance of plays having more than two airs and two
musical instruments. In spite of this concession, collaboration
between the two Baptistes was over; Molière would never again look
to Lully for assistance. Since it was impossible for the author of *Le
Bourgeois gentilhomme* to deprive his plays of music, he searched for
another composer. Was there anyone whose musical talent would not
pale in comparison to the greatest composer of the kingdom?

Under what circumstances did Molière first become acquainted
with Charpentier, then in service to Mlle de Guise?[6] What convinced Molière to entrust his stage music to a composer whose works
were mainly religious in nature? We cannot entirely rule out the possibility that Charpentier's powerful patroness recommended him to
Molière, based on the amicable ties between their families.[7]
Whatever the case, we may presume that the actor ultimately chose
Charpentier for several reasons.

Certainly the young composer lacked stage experience, although
from what we know about his subsequent career, he was probably
nurturing plans along those lines. Did Molière sense his still-
undeveloped dramatic gifts? Quite probably. Moreover, a kinship of
an esthetic nature obviously drew the two men together. The writer's
predilection for Italian comedy is well-known; he certainly would not
have been averse to working with a composer who was also partial to
the ultramontane arts.

Other, call them "extra-musical," factors probably nurtured their
collaboration. For Molière, it was a question of revenge on Lully, to a
certain extent, by substituting a composer capable of competing with
him, even making him uneasy. Molière was also alienating himself
from the king, who, after having been so loyal to him, now swore by
his favored musician. To call upon an artist who had developed somewhere other than at the French court practically amounted to a
challenge.

In any case, Molière made his decision quickly; only a few months

passed between the signing of the privilege and the first public performance of *La Comtesse d'Escarbagnas* at the Palais-Royal.
Although originally conceived in several acts (as it had been performed at court), the comedy was henceforth presented in the Palais-
Royal theater in a single act preceded by an overture. *La Comtesse
d'Escarbagnas* was followed by *Le Mariage forcé*, for which
Charpentier's incidental music (H. 494) replaced Lully's, originally
composed in 1664.

Regarding the performances in the summer of 1672 La Grange's
register wrote: "*Le Mariage forcé*, performed with *La Comtesse
d'Escarbagnas*, was accompanied by M. Charpentier's music and M.
de Beauchamps' ballets, with costumes by M. Baraillon. M. de Villiers
had a hand in the incidental music."[8]

In 1659, Charles Varlet (1635–1692), named La Grange after his
mother, joined Molière's troupe, then called the Troupe de Monsieur.
An actor and a singer, he was also the secretary, treasurer, and
spokesperson for the troupe. He kept a journal now known as La
Grange's register, which is a rich source of information on the performances and the life of the troupe. In 1682, he wrote a biography of
Molière in which he revealed his deep attachment and great admiration for the "Terence of his age."

Pierre Beauchamps (1636–1705) was the great dancer and
choreographer of the day, of whom Lecerf de la Viéville said, "No one
danced a whirligig better than he, nor could anyone choreograph
better than he." Also a composer, Beauchamps wrote the greater
share of the music of *Les Fâcheux*, while Lully composed only one
number (i.e., *Courante* of Lysandre) as his first essay with Molière.
Jean Baraillon, "regular costume designer" of the king's ballets and
Molière's troupe, contributed to the brilliance of Palais-Royal performances and court entertainments. Jean Deschamps, known as de
Villiers (1648–1701), acted and sang in numerous troupes, including
those of the Marais, the Dauphin, and Molière.

Charpentier shared with the ballet master, "for appreciation," the
sum of 264 livres, which was paid to both of them on 10 July. The composer received 11 livres for each of twelve performances that
followed until 7 August. He was also reimbursed 11 livres for each
round trip to Molière's house in Auteuil. Sometimes the two men
made the trip together, and on one trip the following incident
occurred

> witnessed by Charpentier, the famous composer, which he
> related to persons whose word is to be trusted . . . . Molière was

coming back from Auteuil with the composer. Molière gave a handout to a beggar, who a moment later stopped the carriage to say, "Monsieur, you gave me a gold piece by mistake." "Of all places to find such honesty!" cried Molière. After pausing only briefly, Molière replied, "Here, my friend, have another one!"[9]

Forced to admit that Molière did not need his assistance for the new comédie-ballet and that another composer was about to take his place, a furious Lully acted swiftly. On 12 August, only five days after the last performance of *La Comtesse d'Escarbagnas* and *Le Mariage forcé*, Lully obtained the following decree:

> His Majesty expressly forbids any troupe of French or foreign actors currently performing in Paris ... to employ in their performances any more than six singers or any more than twelve violins and instrumentalists.[10]

Molière paid no apparent attention to this measure and on 30 August revived *Les Fâcheux* with new interludes by Charpentier (this music is lost). Three more performances followed on 2 and 4 September and 4 October. On the last two dates, a payment of 22 livres was made to Charpentier to be shared with Beauchamps. The following October, the comedy *La Comtesse d'Escarbagnas* was revived; but *L'Amour médecin,* and later *Le Fin lourdaud,* were performed in place of *Le Mariage forcé.*

Since the above ordinance did not create the impact expected, nor did it discourage Molière from continuing to perform his comedies with music, Lully attacked on another front. On 20 September, a new royal privilege was issued, giving Lully permission

> to publish ... any and all the musical airs composed by him; likewise the verses, words, subjects, plots, and works to which the aforesaid musical airs are composed, without exception, and for a period of thirty consecutive years beginning with the day that each of said works is printed.[11]

Suddenly Molière found himself scandalously deprived of his own contributions, no longer having the right to make free use of the texts of his plays. No longer was there any question of remounting works to which Lully had previously added music. An entirely new work was needed for the next production of the Troupe du Palais-Royal, so Molière and Charpentier set to work. On Tuesday, 22 November, La Grange noted in his register: "Preparations have begun on *Le Malade imaginaire.*"

Since the work, as usual, was originally planned for court performance, the two authors wrote an extensive prologue in praise of the king, who had just won a military victory in Holland. The 1673 edition included the following dedication:

> After the glorious deeds and victorious exploits of our august Monarch, it is fitting that all who are concerned with writing should devote themselves to celebrating his fame or to contributing to his diversion. That is what we have endeavored to accomplish here, and this Prologue is intended as a tribute to that great Prince and as an introduction to the comedy of *Le Malade imaginaire*, which was conceived for his relaxation after his noble achievements.[12]

Expectations were shattered: the royal invitation never came. The premiere of *Le Malade imaginaire*, "a comedy combining music and dance," took place in the Palais-Royal theater on 10 February 1673. Louis XIV chose to side with Lully, who, it can be assumed, had more than a hand in alienating the king from the person who had previously amused and moved him so profoundly. Yet, more than just banning Molière at court, it is clear that Lully's real design was to foil the success of Charpentier, whose music could have bent the king's ear in a way that might have detracted from Lully's prestige.

We do not know how Charpentier felt about this exclusion. It probably affected him greatly, since it would have been his chance to have his music heard at court. Molière, in ill health and weakened by the struggles of his last years, was greatly distressed but resigned. Grimarest gives an account of what the actor said to his wife on the day of the third performance of *Le Malade imaginaire*:

> While my life has had equal shares of sadness and pleasure, I believed myself to be happy; but now that I am overwhelmed with troubles and unable to look forward to any moments of satisfaction or relief, I see it is time to give up the fight.[13]

Even so, the immediate success of the play at the Palais-Royal must have provided some consolation to the two artists. On the day of the first performance, 667 tickets were sold. Since the theater was capable of seating fifteen hundred people, many others slipped in without paying (a common occurrence in theaters of the day). The receipts for the first four performances are listed below. On the whole, 2000 livres indicates a very good night, with receipts generally averaging around 1000 livres.

Friday, 10 February	1992 livres
Sunday, 12 February	1459 livres
Tuesday, 14 February	1879 livres 10 sols
Friday, 17 February	1219 livres

Regarding the days selected for performances, Chappuzeau explained:

> It is well to note that actors only open the doors of the theater on three days of the week—Friday, Sunday, and Tuesday—except for occasional nonreligious holidays falling on days other than these. These days have been chosen wisely, Monday being the principal post day for Germany, Italy, and all the provinces; Wednesday and Saturday market and business days, when the middle class is busier than usual; and Thursday the customary day for outings, especially for schools and universities. The premiere of a play is usually given on Friday to attract larger crowds on the following Sunday after the praise it receives from word of mouth and the press. The play is performed only three days per week to allow the theater to shut down from time to time; just as daily business demands intervals, entertainments require theirs, too: *Voluptates commendat rarior usus.*[14]

Le Malade imaginaire premiered auspiciously. We know that Molière played the role of Argan.

> [O]n 17 February, the day of the fourth performance of *Le Malade imaginaire,* his [Molière's] lungs were so congested that he had difficulty playing his part. He finished it only with great effort, and the audience could easily tell that his pain was nothing less than that which he had been trying to portray on stage. Indeed, once the comedy was over, he went home promptly, where he had hardly touched his bed when the persistent cough that had been tormenting him doubled in intensity. He coughed so hard he burst a blood vessel in his lungs. When he sensed the end approaching, he turned his thoughts to heaven; a moment later, he lost his voice and suffocated within a half-hour by the quantity of blood that was escaping through his mouth.[15]

Molière breathed his last at home on Rue de Richelieu, around ten o'clock that evening.

Struck by that terrible blow, the troupe did not perform the comedy again until 3 March, giving eight more performances through 21 March. La Thorillière assumed Molière's role and, on 5 March, the king and queen attended "with their entire retinue."

At Easter, La Grange listed expenses incurred by the play:

The costs of the play *Le Malade imaginaire* were great because
of the prologue and the interludes, filled with dances, music and
props, amounting to 2400 livres. The daily expenses were great
because of 12 violins at 3 livres each; 12 dancers at 5 livres 10
s[ols]; 3 instrumentalists at 3 livres; 7 singers, male and female,
including 2 at 11 livres, the rest at 5 livres 10 s[ols]. Fees to M. de
Beauchamps for the ballets, to M. Charpentier for the music, a
share going to M. Baraillon for the costumes. Hence expenses
amounted to 250 livres per day.[16]

From this account, it would seem that Molière's troupe had
disregarded Lully's interdictions limiting the number of instrumentalists to twelve, and the singers to six. Did the king turn his head
to the infraction to make up (if we may use such an expression for
Louis XIV) for not having welcomed a court production of *Le Malade
imaginaire?* Lully remained on guard. Taking advantage of Molière's
death and the resulting confusion within the actor's troupe (some
actors left to join the Hôtel de Bourgogne troupe), Lully obtained the
Palais-Royal theater from the king for the establishment of the
Académie Royale de Musique. This was accomplished on 28 April,
the day following the premiere of *Cadmus et Hermione*. Two days
later, a new ordinance placed even greater restrictions on the
number of singers and instrumentalists allowed to perform in
theaters (no more than two voices and six violins).

Ejected from the Palais-Royal, Molière's troupe settled in the
Hôtel Guénégaud on Rue Mazarine, where they merged with the
homeless Troupe du Marais, whose theater had been closed also by
another royal ordinance. The new Troupe du Roi (still under that
name although no longer funded by the king) included nine actors
from the Marais and ten from the Palais-Royal. It opened the Hôtel
Guénégaud theater with *Tartuffe* and continued, faithful to the
memory of Molière, with performances of several of the actor's plays.

In 1674, between 4 May and 31 July, a reworked version of *Le
Malade imaginaire* was performed thirty-eight times. Charpentier
was forced to alter his composition, which he titled *Le Malade
imaginaire avec les défenses* (*Le Malade imaginaire* with interdictions), while the original version was described as "dans sa
splendeur" (in all its glory).

On 21 August the king at last attended a performance of the
comedy during the *Divertissements de Versailles* (Entertainments at
Versailles) given by the king for his entire court on returning from the
victory over Franche-Comté in 1674, a celebration lasting six consecutive days:

Third day,

The nineteenth of the same month, the king took a stroll through the Ménagerie, where he offered refreshment to the ladies of the court.[17]

After the lavish supper, His Majesty, floating down the canal in superbly decorated gondolas, was followed by music of violins and oboes in one large vessel. He lingered for about an hour enjoying the cool of the evening while listening to the pleasant concert of voices and instruments breaking through the hush of nightfall.

Following that, the king went to the end of the canal and, entering his coach, went to the theater that had been erected at the entrance of the grotto for the performance of *Le Malade imaginaire*, last work of Sieur Molière.[18]

The event was immortalized in a print by Jean Le Pautre, inserted in the account cited above. It shows the grotto's sumptuous decor (the work of Italian machinist Carlo Vigarani and the painter Barrois), with the statues of Hercules and Apollo in their niches, enormous chandeliers illuminating the stage, "pleasant shrubbery" decorating each side, the audience variously attentive and distracted, and the actors and the musicians. A person with his back to the audience directs the orchestra. Is it Charpentier?[19] If so, it might be the only representation we have of the composer, caught in action, with both arms raised, holding in his right hand the conductor's cane (a conductor's cane would eventually cause Lully's death) to mark time. The figure, however, is unidentifiable—we cannot see the face, only his function distinguishes our supposed Charpentier from the other figures represented. Looking at the print, one notices that the number of musicians seems larger than the number restricted by the royal ordinances, something Charpentier must have observed also at the work's revival at the Hôtel Guénégaud three months earlier. Was it a special favor granted for the occasion?

Le Malade imaginaire continued to be performed frequently before the public until 1680 (for a total of thirty-one times). On 11 January 1686, the troupe went again to Versailles for a single performance of the comedy. For that occasion, the work enjoyed extraordinary forces, namely, eleven dancers and seven violins. It was apparently for this performance that Charpentier conceived his "*Le Malade imaginaire* revised for the 3rd time." That version consisted of additions or replacements of instrumental airs. The general chronology of the work seems to indicate that these pieces were written a little bit earlier, around the middle of 1685, and could have been performed during the nine performances (between 15 September and 22 October) at the Comédie-Française.

On three more occasions Charpentier would be given the job of working on plays of Molière. The first was for a revival of *Le Sicilien ou l'Amour peintre* on 9 June 1679, which was followed by four more performances. Charpentier's musical portion (*Sérénade pour le Sicilien*, H. 497) is on a much smaller scale, however, than the score Lully wrote for the comedy's premiere on 10 February 1667. The text, by an unknown author and of questionable quality, was also reshaped for the revival. Nevertheless, it is easy to place Charpentier's fragments into the framework of Molière's comedy: the overture naturally at the start of the work, the air and duet of the "musicians" (there were three of them in Lully's score) in scene 3, and the dance of the "Sicilian's slaves" in scene 8.[20]

Also among Charpentier's manuscripts is an overture for *Le Dépit amoureux*, a play written by Molière in 1656 and revived on 11 July 1679. It was probably for the play's revival that Charpentier was asked to compose an overture, which turned out to be very beautiful. What is more, the composer made use of it the following year for the prologue to Pierre Corneille's *Polyeucte Martyr* (H. 498), performed at the Jesuit Collège at Harcourt.

Although *Psyché*, originally conceived as a "tragi-comédie and ballet" in 1671, was reshaped and transformed by Thomas Corneille and Lully into a tragédie lyrique in 1678, it was the first version that was given between 5 October and 28 December 1684 by the Comédie-Française: "This beautiful play, after several years of performances, still attracted throngs of admirers, because its fabulous spectacle was combined with music, *entrées de ballet*, and tragic *récits*."[21]

The following receipt, in Charpentier's handwriting and signed by him, survives to this day:[22]

> I, the undersigned, confess to having received from Monsieur de La Grange the sum of fifteen louis d'or worth one hundred and sixty-five livres for the music I composed and arranged for the play of *Psyché*, with which I leave [*sic*] the troupe,
>
> Signed this twelfth day of December one thousand six hundred eighty-four,
> Charpentier

The music, however, is lost.

Finally, we possess several adaptations (H. 460, 460a, 460b, 460c) of Sganarelle's song, "Qu'ils sont doux bouteille jolie," from *Le Médecin malgré lui.*

THE COMÉDIE-BALLET

Something should be said about the ornaments that have been added to the comedy.

The intention was to present a ballet as well. Because the number of excellent dancers was extremely limited, we were obliged to separate the *entrées* of this ballet, and it was decided to insert them between the acts of the comedy to allow these dancers time to change costumes. So as not to interrupt the play by these interludes, it was also decided to intertwine them as well as possible to the main subject and make one single unity of the ballet and the comedy, but since time was extremely short, and more than one head entered into the planning of the whole, some parts of the ballet are not as well integrated with the comedy as are other parts. This mixture, which is a novelty in our theater, has some parallels in Antiquity, and, as everyone found it satisfying, it might prove useful for other projects that could be planned in a more leisurely manner in the future.[23]

These words were penned by Molière in the preface to his first comédie-ballet, *Les Fâcheux*. That preface was the first essay about a genre which, from one work to the next, would be developed and refined until it attained its most perfect expression.

It was Molière who first had the idea of combining comedy and dance (even though it was not as novel as he would have us believe), but the success of the undertaking resulted from his collaboration with Lully, then Charpentier. One tends to forget that Molière was not only an actor, but a singer and dancer as well. Those two arts, music and dance, were very important sources of inspiration for the writer. Even if he did not compose the music for his comédies-ballets or plan the dance steps, the literary content and structure of the works are naturally imbued with those elements. That accounts for their prevailing unity and rhythm, fully in evidence only when the comedies are performed as they were originally conceived, with their "ornaments."

Lully, because of his background and in spite of his attempts to become Frenchified, still had a weakness for Italian-style comedy and farce, which he discerned in the plays of Molière. That kind of material suited his fiery temperament.

It is more difficult to understand Charpentier's connections with comedy. Unlike Molière and Lully who actively participated in the performance of their comedies, Charpentier only composed the music. Even though he later performed some singing roles in a few of his works, it is unlikely he ever was an actor by trade. Much more of an introvert than his rival, Charpentier expressed himself primarily through his music, but that did not prevent him from cultivating a theatrical "sense" nor from sometimes displaying a *vis comica* in every way as effective as his predecessor's. His contribution to the comédie-ballet, however, remained modest on the whole, since he fully collaborated on only one production, as opposed to Lully's ten. Charpentier's other compositions were written for revivals and consist only of fragments (at least that is all that remains in the manuscripts that survive).

What exactly is a comédie-ballet? As stated previously, comédie-ballet is a genre that evolved and manifested its individuality only gradually. It may be defined as a mixture of spoken plot, singing, ballet, and divertissements, which sometimes have little connection to the play (though there is always some thread tying them together, albeit artificial) yet prolong the main comedy in the same way that a fireworks display puts the finishing touch on any festive occasion. Comédie-ballet enjoyed a relatively brief existence; it was born in Molière's mind in 1661 and died with him in 1673. Besides the quality of the works it inspired, the real significance of the comédie-ballet lies in its foreshadowing of the eighteenth-century *opéra-comique*. It was the testing-ground for the tragédie lyrique, containing not only the seed but also some of the actual elements the latter genre would develop: recitatives, airs in binary form, sung dances, instrumental movements, and choruses.

La Comtesse d'Escarbagnas

The *Ouverture de la Comtesse d'Escarbagnas* and the interludes for *Le Mariage forcé* (H. 494) were Charpentier's first pieces for the stage and represent what was probably the composer's first overture *à la française.*

It should not be forgotten that it was Lully who invented, or at least systematized, the structure and language of this musical form, while making it the symbol of French style all over Europe for decades to come (e.g., in the music of Henry Purcell, George Frideric Handel, Johann S. Bach, Georg Philipp Telemann). Cultivating the spirit of ceremonial pomp and that of the dance, the "French overture" is made up of two contrasting sections. The first is moderately slow and stately, binary, basically homophonic, with dotted rhythms that conceivably derive from the alternation of long and short syllables in tragic declamation. It is usually repeated and ends on the dominant. The second section is in total contrast to the first. It is quick and light, ternary, built on imitation, and brings back the initial key. Sometimes a third part, similar to the first, but generally shorter, brings the overture to a close.

The *Ouverture de la Comtesse d'Escarbagnas* fits the latter mold exactly. It is in three parts, and the final section contains an extremely effective passage in F minor (the principal key being F major). This seems to be the only music Charpentier composed for that comedy. The other pieces (although he did not indicate for what scenes they were intended) are connected with *Le Mariage forcé*.[24] The text, however, totally unlike the text set by Lully, is not found in any of the editions of the play. Is it by Molière? If not, who wrote it? The space provided for Charpentier's music is more restricted than that space provided for Lully's music. Where the music belongs within the play is not easily discernible; in addition to the problem of the text, the manuscript groups the various pieces out of order.

The first instrumental air called "Les Maris," as well as the subsequent "Dialogue" could have been performed at the end of scene 1, a synopsis of which follows:

> Sganarelle asks Lord Geronimo's advice about whether or not he should get married. His friend tells him frankly that a man of fifty is hardly fit for marriage, but Sganarelle replies that he has made up his mind. The other man, realizing his friend's eccentricity in asking for advice after coming to a decision, urges him to get married and leaves laughing.[25]

At the start of scene 2, Sganarelle, "going to sleep in a corner of the stage, sees a vision of a woman portrayed by Mlle Hilaire." For this singer, Lully had written a "Récit de la beauté," which Charpentier replaced with an instrumental *songe*, or dream.

Scene 6 comprised an "Entrée d'Égyptiens et d'Égyptiennes" for which Charpentier substituted a sarabande sung by "bohémiennes" (gypsy girls) followed by a gigue, whose words were added to a version initially intended as an instrumental piece.[26]

In Lully's version, the next-to-last *entrée* consisted of a "charivari grotesque." Charpentier's version contains a "grotesque trio" warning the "gray-haired lovers." In the manuscript, this trio is followed by a minuet, two airs for *haute-contre* and a gavotte, which could have constituted the play's last ballet entry.[27] For some reason, Charpentier later replaced his "grotesque trio" with another, entitled "Lalala bonjour," no longer having any connection with the theme of the play but of great musical interest and irresistibly comic.

Charpentier infects us with his own sense of fun here: the text contains "neither rhyme nor reason," onomatopoeia ("tic toc, chic choc, nic noc, fric froc"), animal sounds ("oaou oaou, houpf houpf, miaou miaou, hinhan hinhan"), and references to characters of the *commedia dell'arte* ("fran fran fran pour le seigneur Gratian, frin frin frin pour le seigneur Arlequin, fron fron fron pour le seigneur Pantalon"), all forming a "lovely concert and beautiful harmony." With a twinkle in his eye, the composer was looking back ironically at Italian comedy and the strings of seventh chords and chromatic bass lines with which Italian music abounds, in particular the "lamenti," which were quite serious. Charpentier would use these writing styles often in his religious music to such expressive effect, but here he makes fun of them, turning their emotional potential inside-out, giving them an utterly comic impact. Charpentier, the great church composer, laughs at music, makes fun of himself, and surprises us when we least expect it.

Le Malade imaginaire

Charpentier's great work for Molière's troupe was *Le Malade imaginaire* (H. 495). If the play's invalid was only imaginary, its music suffered some all-too-real "*défenses*" imposed upon it, by which Charpentier was forced to make his score conform to Lully's demands, as well as to the whims of the court. The manuscript pages of *Le Malade imaginaire* contain very clear annotations from these successive rewrites: "in all its splendor," before the overture to the long prologue; "with interdictions," before the overture to the second prologue; "readjusted for the 3rd time" and "readjusted differently for the 3rd time" for the last version. Those revisions and the lack of order in the manuscript for the different musical interventions make reconstruction of the work's various stages difficult.[28] Until the twentieth century, we were also missing most of the first interlude.[29]

We shall proceed with a linear analysis of the comedy and, for each section—prologue and interludes—an account of Charpentier's score and its existing variants.

As previously stated, *Le Malade imaginaire* was supposed to have premiered at court. Molière and Charpentier had accordingly planned an "Eclogue in music and dance," an impressive prologue in honor of Louis XIV, separate from the comedy, like those of tragédie lyrique. It might not have ever been performed, since it no longer suited the occasion for the Palais-Royal production.[30] The fact remains that another prologue, much more modest and intended to take the place of the first, exists. We shall examine each of these in turn.

Prologue. The overture to the first prologue is in two sections. Its opening does not display the conventional dotted notes, but instead a fanfare-like style, "joyous and very warlike" in D major, much better-suited to the circumstances of the day, namely, the victorious return of Louis XIV from war in Holland.[31] "The setting represents a charming country scene," Charpentier wrote. Flora calls the shepherds and shepherdesses together to inform them of the king's return. All the shepherds express their joy in chorus ("Ah! ah! ah! Quelle douce nouvelle") and dance (*rondeau*).

Flora then invites Tircis and Dorilas to compete in a splendid singing "combat" celebrating "the virtuous deeds of the mightiest of kings," the winner to be crowned by zephyrs. The shepherdesses Climène and Daphné promise their love to the victor. After an "air to encourage the two shepherds to the contest," Tircis begins his song ("Quand la neige fondue enfle un torrent fameux"), first in recitative-style, then arioso. The orchestra plays a bourrée which "allows the dancers on Tircis's side to express their applause." Next is Dorilas, whose solo ("Le foudre menaçant qui perce avec fureur") mirrors the structure of Tircis's song and is followed by a repetition of the same bourrée, this time "for the dancers on Dorilas's side." The two shepherds once again deliver, in turn, an air in which each tries to outdo the other's vocal embellishments.

During the reprise of the *air du combat*, Pan, the shepherd-god, appears "attended by a group of satyrs." In a solo accompanied by two flutes, he hushes the shepherds, for

> *Pour chanter de Louis l'ntrépide courage*
> *Il n'est point d'assez docte voix*
> *Point de mots assez grands pour en traces l'mage.*

> To sing of Louis's intrepid courage
> No voice is capable enough
> And no words are great enough to portray it.

The musical depiction of the passage alluding to Icarus is particularly noteworthy in its long string of notes descending to the lowest range of the voice. The Chorus of Shepherds and Shepherdesses repeats Pan's last words, after which Flora rewards Tircis and Dorilas with crowns of flowers brought by the two zephyrs.

All join forces in a great chorus in which Charpentier contrived some subtle echo effects, single at first ("loud" and "soft"), then doubled on the name "Louis" ("loud," "echo," "second echo"). Next the satyrs, zephyrs, fauns, shepherds, and shepherdesses appear in a great *entrée de ballet* comprising two *airs de "satyres,"* one of them a minuet. This extended piece was probably never performed either at court or in public since Charpentier readapted it thirteen years later for the musicians of Mlle de Guise under the title *La Couronne de fleurs* (H. 486).

Pan's air from the prologue of *Le Malade imaginaire* ("Laissez, laissez, bergers ce dessein téméraire" changed to "Quittez, quittez bergers ce dessein téméraire") was used not only in *La Couronne des fleurs*, but in a *Petite pastorale, Églogue de bergers* (H. 479) for three male voices and two flutes, the subject of which resembles the present prologue (rivalry between two shepherd-songsters, Pan's intervention, songs in honor of the king). Two other airs ("chanson d'Alcidon" and "chanson de Lysandre"), now lost but once "in the book which began with Polchinelle's serenade from *Le Malade imaginaire*," were also part of this little pastorale, as well as "Brillantes fleurs, naissez" (H. 449) published in the *Mercure Galant* in October 1689.

The second prologue to *Le Malade imaginaire*, considerably reduced in size in comparison to the first, brings a shepherdess on stage bearing the same name, Climène, as one of the shepherdesses in the long prologue. She laments the inability of doctors to cure her heart of love's despair. This prologue was composed probably in 1674, meaning there is no real likelihood that the text is Molière's, even though it is presented as such in editions of his works.

This time "the scene is a forest. The curtain opens to the delightful strains of the orchestra." The overture in C major is now in three parts and, paradoxically, conforms more closely to the French model than to the one for the royal court.[32] It is repeated at the end of the prologue. Sandwiched between these two hearings is Climène's solo in *rondeau* form, interspersed with "ritornelles," a word Charpentier spelled in the Italian manner throughout his manuscripts.

For the production of *Le Malade imaginaire* "readjusted differently for the 3rd time" (H. 495b), Charpentier inserted at the end of the prologue an "entrée de satyres" and indicated that the air of Climène was sung by Mlle Fréville, an actress and singer engaged by the Comédie-Française in December 1684.

Then "the scene changes to a room." The comedy may now begin.

Admittedly, the first interlude is introduced in a rather artificial manner, with Toinette's response to Angélique who begs her to warn Cléante, her beloved, of the marriage that her father, Argan, has planned.

> TOINETTE: There is only one person who can do that, and that's the old usurer Punchinello, my lover. It will take some cajoling on my part, but I don't mind doing it for you.

Through the intermediary of Punchinello, Molière and Charpentier take us into the world of the *commedia dell'arte*. A summary of the 1673 livret follows: Punchinello comes after nightfall to serenade his mistress. He is interrupted first by violins, upon whom he vents his anger, and then by the Night Watch composed of dancers and musicians.

The registers contain a record of the props called for by the farce: a guitar or a lute, four muskets, four dark lanterns, four slapsticks, and a bladder.

First interlude. In his first essay in the field of comédie-ballet, Charpentier achieved a master stroke. In only a few months, he assimilated the particular flavor of the genre and rose to the level of his predecessor. As with Lully, Molière had to work in close collaboration with his new composer to achieve a perfect union between text and music.

This first interlude opens with a "fantasia" scored for four-part orchestra "played offstage." Then, after Punchinello's spoken monologue ("O amour, amour") in which he prepares to serenade his mistress, we have the first stroke of genius: the "fantasia" is repeated, but atomized, as it were, into tiny fragments by the spoken interjections of Punchinello who, losing his patience, orders the violins to stop. After the "fantasia" ends, Punchinello pretends to be tuning his lute by "imitating the sound of the instrument with his lips and tongue." Then enter the "archers" (basses in unison accompanied by two violins) who heckle Punchinello ("Who goes there?"), giving rise to a dialogue in which Molière and Charpentier indulge in an amusing repetition of words, both spoken and sung ("Me, me, me!" and "Who are you, who are you?"), producing rhythms accentuated even more by the music.

At the bidding of the first archer, "all the Night Watch enter" and "the dancing archers search for Punchinello in the darkness to catch him." A new, spirited exchange between the orchestra and Punchinello follows, ending with Punchinello's "Bang!" which "simulates the firing of a pistol." After scattering in fear, the archers return with lanterns and surround the unfortunate Punchinello, showering him with reproaches in four-part harmony ("Traitor, rascal, 'tis you then, knave, villain, rogue"). Besides its comic effect, the stringing of two- and three-syllable words lends its own rhythm to the music. To Punchinello's pleas for mercy, the chorus repeatedly answers "No!" and sentences him to a nose-tweaking (instrumental "air for the nose-tweaking") and a stick-beating ("air for the slapstick"). To make them stop, Punchinello passes out six coins, whereupon all salute him with profuse thanks and bowing ("Adieu, Seigneur Punchinello"). The scene ends with two dances (a *loure* and a chaconne).

The first interlude overflows with breathtaking vitality. Speech, acting, and singing merge and mirror each other in the most natural way, together contributing to the comic tone of the scene.

The 1674 libretto differs considerably from the earlier one: "Lord Pantalon, accompanied by a Doctor and a Trivelin, enters to serenade his mistress, singing these words [Notte e dì]. An old woman appears at the window and answers Lord Pantalon, 'Zerbinetti'." This text and the stage directions of Charpentier's manuscript (second version) again diverge, even more mysteriously:

> The fantasia is played in the wings without interruption. Punchinello enters, and when he is about to sing under Toinette's window, the violins led by Spacamond again pick up the fantasia with its interruptions.
> Spacamond beats Punchinello, then chases him, after which the violins play the archers' air, following which the Italian air ["Notte e dì"] is sung.

Both versions omit the entire scene of Punchinello and the archers, probably in deference to Lully's ban on the use of more than two singers, and include the first Italian air "Notte e dì." Why did Charpentier make no mention of the second one ("Zerbinetti") until the third version? And who wrote the words? Whatever the answer, both airs remind us that Charpentier had been in Rome and that he knew how to compose in the Italian style: with melodic ease; with the use of large intervals, repeated sequences, and a structure closer to Italian *da capo* than to the French *rondeau* (in "Notte e dì"); and with incisive rhythms, the ternary symmetry typical of certain airs in Cavalli's operas (in "Zerbinetti").

When the work was revived in 1685–1686, the vocal part of the air "Notte e dì" was transposed for *dessus*, to suit the voice of Mlle Fréville, who had joined the Comédie-Française in 1684. "Zerbinetti," originally intended for an "old woman," was given in the third version to a male singer, M. de Villiers, *haute-contre*, who was probably costumed as a woman, in the purest Italian operatic tradition.

In Act II, scene 5, Cléante and Angélique sing "a little impromptu opera" in which the two lovers appear as shepherd and shepherdess. The two performers, La Grange and Mlle Molière (i.e., Armande Béjart, the playwright's second wife), as well as other actors, were henceforth required to assume singing roles more frequently as a result of the Lullist bans on the hiring of professional singers by theatrical troupes.

An account of the vocal qualities of the two actors who sang in this scene of *Le Malade imaginaire* stated the following:

> La Molière and La Grange, who sing it, do not have the most beautiful voices in the world. I doubt if they even have much understanding of music; and although they sing by the rules, it is not their singing which attracts so much applause; instead, they know how to touch the heart and portray emotions.[33]

The music of this dialogue, encompassing recitative, arioso, and air, closely mirrors the emotions expressed with increasing ardor by the young couple.

Second interlude. The second interlude is linked much more naturally to the play than is the first. To cure his brother's ill-humor, Béralde tells him:

> I've brought along an entertainment that will chase away your ill spirits and make you better disposed to discuss what we have to say to each other. There are gypsies in Moorish dress to sing and dance for us, and I'm sure you'll enjoy it. It will do you just as much good as one of M. Purgon's prescriptions. Come with me.

Like the ceremony of the finale, it is a carnival entertainment. The "Entry of the Moors" is a tripartite overture, the last section alternating between the small and large choirs of the orchestra. Those playing solo parts are named in the manuscript: Duvivier (*dessus*), Nivelon (*haute-contre*), and Dumont (*taille*). The first, Duvivier, was violinist to the king's brother. He was engaged on 14 February 1673, the day of the third performance of *Le Malade imaginaire*, under contract with two other string players, Jean Converset and Pierre Marchand, also musicians of the Duc d'Orléans. This contract protected all three musicians from any unfavorable actions the actors might take against them.[34] Reading between the lines, we detect the increasing threat that Lully posed in the theatrical sphere and the troupe musicians' uneasiness about future measures.

After the overture to the "Entry of the Moors," a ritornello introduces the air of the first Moorish girl ("Profitez du printemps") whose refrain was sung by Mlle "Mouvant" at the premiere, and the verses alternately by Mlles Hardy and Marion. M. Poussin (*haute-contre*) performed the role of another Moorish girl. While we do not know who Mlle Hardy was, we might venture to suggest that Mlle "Mouvant" [?] was Catherine Morant, wife of the actor André Hubert. As for the third girl's identity, Marion was probably her first name, perhaps even a nickname of one of the actresses. Was she Marie Ragueneau, La Grange's wife? Louis-Joseph Poussin was not a member of the King's Cabinet, but a singer in the King's Chamber.

This light, *galant* entertainment ends with a trio and two instrumental airs accompanying the gypsies who "dance together and make the monkeys they have brought with them leap and perform." The Comédie-Française manuscript (H. 495bis) includes three more dances ("Gigue," "First Passepied," and "Second Passepied"), but it is difficult to determine for which version of *Le Malade imaginaire* they were composed.

Again, in this interlude we feel the effect of the royal decree, as the second and third versions replace the trio with a duet. In 1674 the latter was sung by Mlle Babet and M. Poussin. Like Mlle Marion, Mlle Babet was probably a nickname. She might have been Mlle Molière, Armande-Grésinde-Claire-Élisabeth Béjart, the writer's second wife, with Babet possibly being a shortened form of Élisabeth.

The performers in the third version were Mlle Fréville and M. de Villiers. For this "*Malade imaginaire* readjusted for the 3rd time," Charpentier composed a "new overture for the Entry of the Moors," shorter than the original.

Third interlude. The third interlude, or "Ceremony of the Doctors," is the crowning achievement of the entire play, not only because it blends perfectly with the spoken comedy and provides the true dénouement, but also because of the added dimension it gives the piece. A play within a play, the characters offer the entertainment to themselves; only Argan remains a laughing stock to the end—the naive, pitiful protagonist. The ceremony is certainly burlesque, but biting satire constantly rises up through the laughter.

Beneath the rambunctious carnival lies a genuine sense of derision, and behind the masks and disguises unfolds the darkest of combats, the one between life and death, in which Molière lost his last battle. The interlude owes its powerful effect to this interweaving of two levels of meaning (in which Despois and Mesnard quite correctly heard a combination of "carnival bells" and the "knell of death").

What a terrible farce, and what a cruel revenge of the medical profession which Molière had so often attacked! This time he would not be forgiven:

> While he was delivering these lines
>
> > *Grandes doctores doctrinae*
> > *De la rhubarbe et du séné,*
>
> during the "Cermony of the Doctors," he began to spit blood: having alarmed the audience and his colleagues, he was carried immediately to his dressing room.[35]

Molière had been inspired by ceremonies at the Faculté de Médecine—the processions, ceremonial vestments, solemn oaths, questions to be answered by candidates, exaggerated speeches, all of it, of course, spouted out in Latin. At the college of Montpellier, there was even musical accompaniment.

The "Ceremony of the Doctors" revives the first interlude's mixture of speech, song, and dance, though in this case the comedy derives from Molière's text, written in an absolutely hilarious, macaronic Latin. After the set is prepared and the characters enter, the ceremony unfolds in three parts with the chief physician's speech, the doctors' questioning of Argan, and the latter's initiation.

A majestic overture in two sections opens the interlude, after which the upholsterers (*air des tapissiers*) "enter and prepare the hall by setting out benches in time to the music." To the strains of a march, also stately in tone, "the whole assemblage (including eight men holding syringes, six apothecaries, twenty-two doctors, the doctoral candidate, eight dancing surgeons and two singing) enter and take their places according to rank."

The president ("Praeses") then begins his speech in Dog Latin:

> *Sçavantissimi doctores,*
> *Medicinae professores*
> *Qui hic assemblati estis*

After heaping praise on the medical profession, he presents Argan, the "Bachelierus." Short three-part "ritornelles" interrupt the harangue, giving the speaker a chance to catch his breath.

In the second highlight, each doctor asks the candidate to explain the remedy for various illnesses and Argan invariably replies:

> *Clysterium donare,*
> *Postea seignare*
> *Ensuitta purgare*

Visibly satisfied with that response, the assemblage (five-part chorus) strikes up the following refrain after each response:

> *Bene bene respondere bene bene respondere*
> *Dignus dignus est entrare*
> *In nostro docto corpore*

The tune is set syllabically with the utmost melodic, rhythmic, and harmonic simplicity, yet its comic intent is remarkably effective.

This is the first reappearance of the five-part vocal ensemble accompanied by strings since the grand prologue. The chorus included Mlles Mouvant, Hardy (both singing the same part), and Marion, and MM. Poussin, Forestier, and Frison. Frison was later to become a member of the king's music: his name is found on scores Charpentier wrote for the Dauphin.

The president then makes the Bachelierus swear allegiance, and the dancers bow before him (in the *air des révérences*) as he receives the doctor's cap. The new initiate expresses his profuse thanks—ridiculed to perfection by Molière—to all the doctors who have accepted him into their fraternity.

The chorus cheers the new doctor:

> *Vivat vivat cent fois vivat*
> *Novus doctor, qui tam bene parlat!*
> *Mille mille annis et manget et bibat*
> *Et seignet et tuat!*

> Vivat vivat for ever vivat
> Novus doctor, qui tam bene speakat!
> Mille, mille annis and manget and bibat
> And bleedat and killat!

The surgeons wish him much "pestas, verolas, fievras, pluresias, bloody effusions, and dyssenterias."

Like the chorus before it, "vivat vivat," accompanied by the clapping of the apothecaries' mortars, is simply constructed with alternating duple and triple meters.

Except for the addition in 1685–1686 of a "Second air for the upholsterers," Charpentier did not modify anything in this third interlude despite the note in the manuscript, "readjusted differently for the 3rd time." He describes the "Ceremony of the Doctors as usual." The version preserved by the Comédie-Française, however, is for four-part rather than for five-part chorus.

We cannot avoid comparing the two masterworks of Lully and Charpentier in the field of comédie-ballet. Both are plays of major importance in Molière's theater. Although written close in time to each other (1670 and 1673), *Le Bourgeois gentilhomme* and *Le Malade imaginaire* have contrasting tones, especially in the two final ceremonies, each of which is the quintessence of the entire comedy. One is pure burlesque in which Lully fully exploited his sense of comic effect and spectacle; the other is biting satire beneath a comic facade in which Charpentier proved more discreet, letting the text dominate. Whatever the circumstances of their creation, each of these two works seems to have found "its own" composer.

As for *Le Malade imaginaire* in general (which, we stress, was Charpentier's first major contribution for the stage), we have noted its great qualities in areas as diverse as the pastorale of the prologue, the tender lovers' dialogue between Cléante and Angélique, the *galant* exoticism of the second interlude, and especially the farce of the first interlude. We can only imagine the works that might have followed had the collaboration between Molière and Charpentier not been so brutally cut short only a few months after it began.

THE STAGE PLAYS

The extraordinary stage machinery of the Italian operas performed under Mazarin completely seduced the French public. The Troupe du Marais decided to exploit the new fashion for spectacular plays; thus evolved the French-style *pièces à machines* (stage plays), which rapidly became very popular. Little attention was paid to the quality of the poetry and airs, the principal attraction being the sumptuous scenery and fabulous staging. Taking his inspiration from Jacopo Torelli, the "Great Magician" as he was known in Paris, the Frenchman Denis Buffaquin became a master of the art.

Mythological subjects lent themselves admirably to scenic transformations, to the flights of gods, and to the most spectacular manifestations of nature (floods, conflagrations, etc.). Therefore, the Troupe du Marais produced plays like Chapoton's *La Descente d'Orphée aux enfers*, Boyer's *Ulysse dans l'île de Circé*, or Rotrou's *La Naissance d'Hercule*. The most famous of the plays, Pierre Corneille's *Andromède*, with music by Dassoucy, was performed on 26 February 1650:

> This tragedy with stage machinery . . . was created for the king's entertainment in the first years of his minority. The queen mother, whose every undertaking was large-scale, had it produced in the large hall of the Petit-Bourbon, where court ballets with machinery were performed. The theater was beautiful, high and deep, and His Majesty danced there in several grand ballets that were worthy of the splendor and greatness of the French court. Sieur Torelli, then royal machinist, created the effects for *Andromède*. These and the scenery were so beautiful that engravings were made of them. The great applause that this beautiful tragedy received led the Marais actors to revive it after the Petit-Bourbon was razed. The undertaking was a success and was repeated three or four times.[36]

In 1682, the French troupe revived *Andromède*, this time with a new score by Charpentier (see discussion below).

Until 1650, Pierre Corneille, author of *Le Cid* and *Polyeucte Martyr*, was strongly averse to music. Although he accepted the commission for *Andromède*, his distrust of words set to music persisted:

> I was careful to have nothing sung that was essential to the comprehension of the play, since words that are sung are so commonly misunderstood because of the confusion engendered by so many voices pronouncing them at the same time. And if their purpose was to inform the listener of something significant, that would have cast a shadow on the work as a whole.[37]

Those reservations did not prevent the playwright from returning to the genre of stage plays ten years later with *La Toison d'Or*, performed for the wedding celebration of Louis XIV. On that occasion Buffaquin outdid himself in directing the stage machinery.

Meanwhile, other writers had been adding to the repertoire of the Troupe du Marais: Boisrobert; Quinault, Lully's future librettist; and Thomas Corneille, the younger brother of Pierre, whose play

Timocrate was performed eighty times in 1656 and 1657.

In 1669, another writer joined the Troupe du Marais: Jean Donneau de Visé. Destined for an ecclesiastical career, Donneau de Visé instead manifested an interest in comedy and *galanteries*. His enormous responsibility as editor of the monthly *Mercure Galant* did not keep him from writing a significant number of plays between 1663 and 1696. A clever man with a knack for adapting his talent to the fashions of the hour, he was judged harshly by his contemporaries. La Bruyère, in his *Caractères*, rated the *Mercure Galant* as "just short of nothing," no more, no less. In their history of the French theater, the Parfaict brothers were hardly any kinder: "M. de Visé was more of a wit than a talent; he dabbled in many areas and was consistently mediocre. Suffice it to say that almost all his plays enjoyed a degree of success, without deserving it."[38] Stricken with blindness a few years before his death, Donneau de Visé was granted a royal pension of five hundred écus and an apartment in the Galeries du Louvre.

From the moment of his first tragedy with stage machinery at the Marais theater, *Les Amours de Vénus et d'Adonis,* Donneau de Visé knew the smell of success. The play was performed uninterruptedly for three months and revived in 1685 with music by Charpentier. In 1670, *Les Amours du Soleil* called for no less than thirteen scene changes and twenty-four flying machines. The following season *Le Mariage de Bacchus et d'Ariane* brought another triumph.

Circé

When the Troupe de Palais-Royal and the Troupe du Marais merged after Molière's demise, the actors of the new Hôtel Guénégaud continued to perform the great man's plays while choosing to exploit the genre of stage plays. Because of strong competition from the other royal troupe, the Hôtel de Bourgogne troupe, they needed to offer spectacles that appealed to the public and would retain the king's support. This was what motivated the two best writers of the Hôtel Guénégaud, Thomas Corneille and Donneau de Visé, to pool their talents with those of Charpentier to create a play that would surpass in magnificence everything preceding it.

At the end of the summer of 1674, *Circé* (H. 496) was completed, but the machines at the troupe's disposal proved unsatisfactory for the extraordinary effects the authors wanted to achieve. The additional cost pushed total expenses to the huge sum of 10,842 livres 17 sols. Certain actors considered this sum excessive and refused to take part in the play's production. *Circé*'s success, however, seemed guaranteed; a month before the premiere, it was referred to as "the play anticipated with such impatience that all seats have been already sold for several performances, and many foreign visitors are postponing their departure to see it."[39]

All was finally ready on 17 March 1675, and *Circé* premiered on the stage of the Hôtel Guénégaud. It was a triumph. The size of the audiences surpassed all hopes, and the play was repeated virtually without interruption until October. On the 4th of that month, Monsieur and Madame attended: "Their Royal Highnesses were marvelously pleased with this beautiful spectacle, with its extraordinary scenery, flying actors and machines."[40] Receipts totalled 23,775 livres for the first nine days and 87,475 for the entire run, more than enough to cover expenses.

Donneau de Visé later reported in his *Mercure Galant:*

> [F]or the first six weeks, the theater was filled by noon; and since no seats could be found after that, people were happy to give a half louis-d'or at the door to gain admittance, even though a *première loge* cost the same price and allowed one to be seated on the third level; . . . there would have been many more performances, if the interests of a certain individual had not cut back the number of voices.[41]

That "certain individual" was none other than Lully, of course. The play's record of expenses in the registers informs us that, besides the six violins ordinarily used, an additional six had been engaged as well as a harpsichord.[42] Hence the actors were in violation of the ordinance of 30 April 1673. The names of the instrumentalists, each of whom received 3 livres 15 sols, were Converset, Marchand, Duvivier, Du Mont, Du Fresne, and Courcelles. Marchand is also identified as the bass viol player in Charpentier's manuscript. As for the singers—Charpentier mentions seven names in his score—their number far exceeded Lully's limit. In fact, on 21 March another ordinance was issued:

> His Majesty, having been informed that contrary to his ordinance of 30 April 1673 prohibiting all actors to employ outside musicians, some of them continue to allow singers on their stage whom they consider not to be outsiders, on the pretext that they are in their employ, and thus preventing the musical stage works of Sieur Lully, Surintendant of His Majesty's music, to attain all the success expected of them, His Majesty has

ordained . . . that the aforesaid ordinance of 30 April 1673 be enforced . . . allowing only two members of said actors' troupes to sing on stage and expressly forbidding them to use any outside musicians or to hire them, on pain of prosecution.[43]

After first ignoring the interdictions, the actors were finally forced to obey, with the results Lully had intended: lower box office receipts.

Pierre Bayle, after attending a performance of *Circé*, wrote to his brother the next day, 24 June, summing up the situation quite clearly: "If Molière's troupe was permitted to perform with music and dance and whatever number of instruments it desires, *Circé* would outshine all operas that have been performed to date."[44]

Charpentier received 220 livres 10 sols for composing the music, plus 5 livres 10 sols for each performance.

The subject of *Circé*, "tragédie, embellished with machines, changes of scenery, and music, preceded by a prologue, by M. Corneille de l'Isle," was borrowed, as its author explained, from the fourteenth book of Ovid's *Metamorphoses*. The story concerns a sea nymph Scylla, whom the sea deity Glaucus falls in love with, spurning Circe. The enchantress takes revenge by transforming Scylla into a rock. Corneille added the character of "Mélicerte, beloved of Scylla, and the latter is changed into a Nereid after all her misfortune, so as to end the play with rejoicing."[45]

The dramatic situation was in this case primarily an excuse for fabulous machinery effects; indeed, spectators could marvel at plants blossoming before their eyes, mountains rising and crumbling, bronze statues that came to life and flew in the air, or deep, dark forests, wave-lashed rocks, the rising of the sun, the abduction of Glaucus by Circe in her dragon-drawn chariot, the metamorphosis of Circe's former lovers into savage beasts, and the snatching of Scylla by four cupids from four evil spirits in aerial combat with the satyrs of Glaucus in amorous pursuit of Circe's nymphs.[46]

Following the example of the Lullist tragédie lyrique, *Circé* is divided into a prologue and five acts. The text of the divertissements is by Donneau de Visé, who here exploits the *galant* style in which he excelled. The preface in the *livre de sujet* of *Circé* vaunts that

the refinement of the music, in which M. Charpentier, who has already won praise for the airs in *Le Malade imaginaire,* has in some respects surpassed himself both by the charm of his orchestral score, and by his distinguished manner of setting the words to music.[47]

Charpentier's manuscript score contains no less than twenty-two numbers and 1043 measures; it seems, however, that even more music was composed for Thomas Corneille and Donneau de Visé's play. The proof is in the edition of *Airs from the play of Circé with thoroughbass* (C. Ballard, 1676), which includes five pieces not in the manuscript, some of which had been originally planned for *Le Malade imaginaire.*

As a work of pure entertainment without any real dramatic interest, *Circé* calls on any and all devices that might attract an audience, including mythological heroes, machines, scenery, popular songs, shepherd dialogues, dancing, and pantomime. Its position among Charpentier's works (as for most of the other theater pieces about to be discussed) cannot be made without considering the public taste and style of the day.

Stage machinery, we have already mentioned, was what enthused those audiences the most. The text and music were its servants, not the reverse, as one might think today. In spite of reservations about Charpentier's contribution, his score should in no way be underestimated: the composer displayed command of a great many styles, and at times some master strokes, notably in the pantomimes of the interlude between the last two acts.

Prologue. *Circé* begins with an overture which, at first glance, seems to conform to the classical structure of the time. The first movement, binary, stately, and dotted, is in the "serious and magnificent" key of G minor. But with the second movement, in triple meter, Charpentier leaves the beaten path and treats the section homophonically, saving the imitative texture for the third movement, which is quick and binary and labeled "fugue." These last two movements are repeated (another unusual feature).

"After debates between Mars and Fortune, Fame and Love," the prologue's spoken allegory yields to Comedy and Music, assigned to the voices of M. Poussin, *haute-contre*, and Mlle Bastonnet, *haut-dessus*, singers from outside the troupe. Do we detect an ironic allusion to Lully's ordinances, when Music declares: "I would rather like to sing, but I have so thin a voice that I can hardly be heard," after which is heard a short, but charming trio of actors: "If you can tolerate us, we can help you out"?

Comedy and Music therefore decide to combine their talents in entertaining Louis. They are joined by a large five-part chorus of all the singing-actors of the troupe: Mlle Bastonnet (*haut-dessus*) and

MM. Poussin (*haute-contre*), Des Triches (*haute-contre*), La Grange (*taille*), Hubert, de Verneuil, and de Gaye (basses).

Isaac-François Guérin d'Estriché (circa 1636–1728) bore the names of both his father and mother; he is the person Charpentier referred to as "Des Triches" or "Guérin." The actor joined the Troupe du Marais in 1672 and was at the Hôtel Guénégaud at the time of the merger. In 1677 he married Armande Béjart, Molière's widow. André Hubert (d. 1700) joined the Troupe du Palais-Royal in 1664 and retired from acting in 1685. He kept the register of Molière's troupe during 1672 and 1673. Achille Varlet de Verneuil (1636–1709) was La Grange's brother. A member of the Marais theater from 1662, he was at the Hôtel Guénégaud in 1673. Jean (de) Gaye (d. 1701) sang both on stage and in the Chapelle Royale and the King's Chamber. He was in several of Lully's comédies-ballets (e.g., *Monsieur de Pourceaugnac, Le Bourgeois gentilhomme*) and operas (e.g., *Thésée, Atys, Isis*) and became known for using falsetto as well as his natural bass voice in his roles.

To the vocal choruses of *Circé* were added dances of the Arts and Pleasures, in a sumptuous apotheosis of a prologue entirely devoted, as was to be expected, to the glory of the king.

Act I. The next musical intervention occurs in Act I when two satyrs (Guérin and de Verneuil) deliver in turn their songs "Deux beaux yeux me charment," and "Un jour la jeune Lisette" in a frankly popular vein.

"As entr'acte between the first and second acts," there is a dance in *rondeau* form displaying the characteristic rhythm of the sarabande. At the end of the piece, Charpentier noted that "instead of the *rondeau* the following two airs could be played," instrumental versions of the satyrs' songs. At several other places in the *Circé* manuscript, the composer offers variants. They do not appear, however, to have been the result of Lully's interdictions, as in *Le Malade imaginaire*; they were probably due to different versions and the particular circumstances of a performance, and perhaps also to the preferences of specific actors.

Act II. In Act II, the dialogue of the shepherd Tircis and the shepherdess Silvie (the same two who witness the birth of the Christ child in the oratorio *Sur la naissance de Notre Seigneur Jésus Christ*, H. 482) transports us to the rarefied sphere of the pastorale.

The "interlude between the second and third acts" consists of a passacaille (or passacaglia). The name of this dance has a Spanish origin; it comes from *pasar calle,* meaning "to go down the street." In triple meter and in a minor key, the passacaglia is built on a more or less strict "ostinato" with variations, making it one of the favorite forms of baroque composers. The French applied the *rondeau* form to it, emphasizing even more the duality of repetition/variation that gives this dance its particular charm and great attraction. The passacaglia was already a prized feature of court ballets; it was Lully, though, who made it one of the principal orchestral movements of his tragédies lyriques. Charpentier would write one for *Médée.*

Since the passacaglia demanded both the discipline and the imagination of a composer, Charpentier was particularly comfortable with it. If the passacaglia in *Circé* is not as long as the one in *Médée* (since the play with stage machinery does not demand the same musical expansiveness as the tragédie lyrique), it is nevertheless nicely constructed.

Act III. A minuet and a bourrée for dancers in disguise "serve as entr'acte between the third and fourth acts."

Act IV. Act IV contains three airs: "Viens ô mère d'amour";[48] "Vous étonnez-vous," sung by a dryad; and "Il n'est rien de si doux," intended for a faun.

This brings us to the "pantomimes" which featured the Italian comic performers. These pantomimes consist of a series of very short fragments (from three to six measures) expressing the emotions of Circe, who is mimed simultaneously by *marcheurs* (walkers), whose steps were choreographed by La Montagne. These walkers (nine of them) were paid 3 livres per performance; La Montagne himself received 4 livres 10 sols.

Just as an artist sketches a face with a few lines of a pencil, Charpentier suggests an emotion or an attitude with a few measures. Cleverly concise, full of contrast and surprise, these pantomimes are little gems, especially within their visual context. To produce the maximum effect in the shortest amount of time, Charpentier used the most effective means of expression imaginable: leaps of a fourth ("joy"), daring modulations—to go from E-flat major to F major ("complaisance") was not common practice at the time—florid runs ("rage," "fury and quick-temperedness," "fury and despair"), and bold harmonies ending on a ninth chord with augmented fifth ("signs of weakness").

Charpentier must have been satisfied with his pantomimes. Instead of leaving a choice between two possible versions, as in every other case, here he indicated: "I opt for the pantomimes."

Act V. "There is [no music] in the fifth act." The next was intended for the "Epilogue" opening with a "prelude for the entrance of the forest divinities," followed by a great "solo of one of the forest gods" performed by Poussin, in which the refrain, "Tout aime, tout aime, tout aime," is repeated, verbatim or with variations, punctuating the entire number. A large Chorus of Forest Divinities ensued (to be repeated at the end), during which the "dancers" performed. Then the "jumpers" performed their *entrée* and joined in the final merrymaking with races, fancy steps, and perilous leaps. Also participating in the play were the "fliers" who flew about, suspended by cords.

Because of the extraordinary interest in the play and especially in Charpentier's music, Christophe Ballard published in 1676 *Airs from the play of Circé with thoroughbass* and later a series of parodies in 1695, 1696, and 1702.[49] At that time, the term *parody* referred to a resetting of new *galant* or ribald lyrics to airs then in fashion, whether dance tunes or pieces already with words. Thus, a text like *Je fais ma félicité d'une douce tranquillité* (For me happiness is sweet tranquillity) in *Circé*, Act I, was transformed into

> *Je fais ma félicité d'entamer quelque grand pâté*
> *Et d'avaler du bon vin de Bourgogne!*

> For me happiness is devouring a large pâté
> And swallowing some good Burgundy wine!

L'Inconnu

Unfazed by the difficulties that plagued the last performances of *Circé*, the same authors, Corneille, Donneau de Visé, and Charpentier, unveiled a new play on Sunday, 17 November 1676. Titled *L'Inconnu*, it was a "comedy in five acts, in verse, with a prologue in free verse, ornaments and music." About that work, Thomas Corneille said:

> After having presented in *Circé* some of the most grandiose effects for the sake of the machinery, I thought that the public would not be averse to the lighter ornaments that a *galant* subject is capable of receiving.[50]

The receipts that *L'Inconnu* brought in (2500 livres) were less than those brought in by *Circé*.[51] Charpentier was paid 11 livres 10 sols per performance. Unfortunately, the music is no longer with us. The play had a run of thirty-two performances with comparable, though much less spectacular, success than that of *Circé*.

In January 1678, the actors revived the work:

> The Troupe du Roi performing in the Faubourg Saint-Germain has remounted *L'Inconnu*, by the younger M. Corneille. This *galant* play has such exceptional ornaments that people are beginning to attend in droves, as they did three years ago.[52]

L'Inconnu was performed in October 1679 and Charpentier received 16 livres 10 sols "for additions." The play was performed again in Versailles in May 1680. In October, Donneau de Visé published an air of Charpentier's which he introduced as follows:

> Here is the *Bavolet* of M. Charpentier, which you have been so eager to see set to music, and which the Hôtel Guénégaud troupe added last season to the *galant* play *L'Inconnu*. Since a few performances of it are supposed to be given presently, after All Saints' Day, those from your province who attend will be able to tell you how much this charming song is loved.[53]

The subject of the song is the ribbon girls wore in their hair and which bobbed in the breeze as they walked. An outspoken peasant girl sings the air (H. 499a) briskly accented:

> *Ne fripez poan mon Bavolet,*
> *C'est aujordy dimanche.*
> *Je vous le dis tout net,*
> *J'ai des éplingues sur ma manche,*
> *Ma main peze autant qu'al est blanche;*
> *Et vous gagnerez un soufflet.*

> Don't steal my ribbon,
> For today's Sunday.
> I tell you loud and clear,
> I've got pins in my sleeve,
> My hand strikes as hard as it's fair;
> And you'll get slapped.

From the revival of *L'Inconnu* in 1679, the Charpentier manuscripts include an *Ouverture du prologue* (H. 499), composed initially for the prologue to *Acis et Galathée* (its title was later replaced by

L'Inconnu). It was a little opera, the remainder of which is unfortunately lost. Privately commissioned, the circumstances of the performance of this opera were reported in the *Mercure Galant:*

> This carnival season there were several sorts of entertainment, but one of the greatest was a little opera entitled *Les Amours d'Acis et de Galathée*, given several performances by M. de Rians, procureur du roi of the *ancien châtelet*, in his home and with the usual magnificence. On each occasion more than four hundred listeners assembled, and several persons of the highest quality had trouble finding a seat. All those who sang and played instruments were vociferously applauded. The music was composed by M. Charpentier, whose two airs I have already presented to you. Thus you are acquainted with his great talent. Mme de Beauvais, Mme de Boucherat, Messieurs the Marquis de Sablé and de Biran, M. Deniel, M. de Sainte-Colombe the celebrated violist, and so many others who well appreciate all the subtlety of the vocal writing, expressed admiration for this opera.[54]

The *Ouverture du Prologue d'Acis et de Galathée* (and later *L'Inconnu*) is in four sections, but only the first and third movements display any resemblance to the French-style overture. The second does not use any imitation, and the fourth, in no way a reprise of the first, exposes totally different material.

The overture is followed by other purely instrumental pieces: ballet entries for "furies," "demons," and "combatants," the latter introduced by a "fanfare for trumpets" (in defiance of Lully's bans). A "march for flutes" introduces a (lost) Chorus of Delights, followed by an instrumental air of the "delights." The rest of the score consists of airs for "nyads and dryads," "the divinity Pan," a minuet for the "delights and Flora," and a *loure* for the "satyrs."

Le Triomphe des Dames

Le Triomphe des Dames was the title of the stage play given on the stage of the Hôtel Guénégaud beginning 7 August 1676. Charpentier had a hand in the production, since he received 143 livres as "payment for the composition of the music." It is a pity this play is lost since its musical portion was probably quite significant: thirty-eight dancers and extras had been hired. The play represented a combat between French, Swiss, Venetians, and Spaniards, a ballet of games in which the kings, queens, and jacks of cards won at tennis, whist, dice, and billiards. In the last act, three quadrilles of attendants, adventurers, and faithful knights were accompanied by trumpets and drums. It is also known that Charpentier used an air from *Circé*, "Vous étonnez-vous," in Act I, and an air from *L'Inconnu*, "Si Claudine ma voisine," in Act IV.

Despite the recycling of some of the scenery from *L'Inconnu*, the production of *Le Triomphe des Dames* proved very expensive, and receipts were well below those of earlier plays. Stage plays were therefore temporarily abandoned in favor of simple comedies which, while costing less to produce, brought in excellent receipts. In *La Devineresse* (1680), Donneau de Visé and Thomas Corneille seized the opportunity to exploit the Affair of the Poisons and the ongoing trial of La Voisin; that, along with the shrewd publicity of the *Mercure Galant*, assured the play's success. It should be added that the year before La Grange had managed (with the jingling of coins) to attract the great tragedienne Champmeslé from the rival Hôtel de Bourgogne troupe.

The Hôtel Guénégaud stage no longer had much need of Charpentier, who contributed only to the revivals of Molière's *Sicilien* and *Dépit amoureux*. That hiatus from the theater permitted him the more active pursuit of religious music. In 1679 he began regularly writing motets for the Dauphin. In August, the painter Le Brun commissioned a mass for the Feast of Saint Louis. During Holy Week of 1680, Charpentier was asked by the nuns of Abbaye-aux-Bois to provide a substantial cycle of Tenebrae lessons.

THE COMÉDIE-FRANÇAISE

That same year a great event occurred in theatrical circles when Louis XIV decided to combine the two royal troupes, the Hôtel Guénégaud and the Hôtel de Bourgogne, into a single troupe under the name Comédie-Française, so "that there will henceforth be only one company in Paris to serve in his proximity at court as well as for the entertainment of the public."[55] The Comédie-Française henceforth performed daily in the Hôtel Guénégaud theater, and the Italian players, who had alternated with their French colleagues there, were relocated to the vacated Hôtel de Bourgogne. The new troupe numbered fifteen actors and twelve actresses, and gave *Phèdre* with Champmeslé in the title role as its inaugural performance.

Les Fous divertissants

On 14 November 1680 a comedy by Raymond Poisson, *Les Fous divertissants* (H. 500), with music by Charpentier in his return to the stage, was first performed. Although forgotten today, Poisson was very famous in his time. Born in 1633, he first appeared at the Hôtel de Bourgogne in 1660. He created the character of Crispin, the lackey in love with the beautiful Lisette, who used all his cunning in the service of his master. Poisson performed the role notably in *La Pierre philosophale.* Molière greatly admired the unaffected acting style of Poisson, who retired from the theater in 1685 and died at his lodging on Rue Saint-Denis on 9 May 1690. *Les Fous divertissants* was his last play and in it he took the role of M. Grognard, the old man duped in love.

The comedy was given eleven times between 14 November and 2 December. On 10 May 1681, part of the troupe went to Versailles to perform the play at court, accompanied by "8 dancers, 1 gypsy, 6 violins, 1 harpsichord, 1 musician, M. Charpentier, 2 assistants."[56] The subject of *Les Fous divertissants,* not of great dramatic interest, serves mainly as a pretext for adding songs and dances closely related to the plot, described in the synopsis as follows:

> Monsieur Grognard, doorkeeper at a lunatic asylum, is in love with a young woman named Angélique, his ward. Angélique despises Grognard and loves Léandre. The latter enters the asylum feigning insanity, and in that way sees his beloved and finds a way to abduct her. Grognard is locked up by his own lackeys.[57]

The comedy opens with an overture in which certain phrases turn back upon themselves, seeming to depict the closed-in atmosphere of the setting and the mental derangement of its occupants.

The first interlude brings on two lunatics (sung by de Villiers, *haute-contre,* and Verneuil, bass); in burlesque style, they recount their amorous adventures which make them "burn" (literally) behind bars. They are accompanied by two violins: "du V . . ." and "Bapt. . . ." While the former seems to be the Duvivier from the time of Molière, the abbreviation "Bapt. . ." remains a mystery; Baptiste, certainly, but could it have been Jean-Baptiste Lully?

After the lunatics' duet, "male and female villagers" dance, and "the chubby Cupid enters." Resigned to their sad fate, the lunatics return to their "straw mattresses to shed a torrent of tears." A "bourrée for the triumph of Cupid . . . serves as entr'acte between the first and second acts."

"In Act II, Léandre and Angélique sing airs from the opera of *Proserpine* and from *Bellérophon* (Lully's tragédie lyrique of the year before): Charpentier did not indicate which airs these were. Was this a concession to Lully's supremacy, or just an ironic stance?

The second interlude brings on "four dancing lunatics and three singers." After dances for "unchained lunatics" and "jailers," the three singing inmates (M. Guérin or M. de Villiers, *haute-contre;* M. de La Grange, *taille;* and M. de Verneuil, bass) proceed to utter nonsensical phrases simply for the pleasure of the rhyme ("Que la sotte canaille / Tempête et criaille / Jure, peste et braille"; Let the stupid hawk / storm and squawk / Swear, curse, and gawk). Each couplet begins with great bursts of laughter ("ah ah ah") while the dancers clap their hands in boisterous rhythm.

In Act III, there is an *entrée* for the actors, a tender air for Léandre, a minuet for a "gypsy girl," another tender air for Angélique, and two songs for bass (the first a drinking tune, and the second decidedly buffo).

In the final *entrée*, "the lunatics with their dolls and tambourines enter leaping," while a "mad musician" sings a strophic air about the joy of reunited lovers. Charpentier ends as he began, with a dialogue of lunatics in love, only this time with their puppet dolls. There is noticeable comic use of the two scales, C major (descending) and G major (ascending), which open this duet. As the main purpose of this work was to elicit laughter, Charpentier unleashed all his clownish spirit in a bracing and fun-filled score.

La Pierre philosophale

In 1681 Charpentier contributed new scores to two plays at the Comédie-Française. For carnival season, the composer joined forces again with Thomas Corneille and Donneau de Visé in creating *La Pierre philosophale* (H. 501), "comedy mixed with spectacle." Hoping to bring to the stage all the mystery and wonder of "the Story of the Knights of the Pink-Cross and what is called *Cabale*, or Secret Knowledge," the authors had written an unusually long, complicated plot (in five acts instead of the usual three), which did not please the public. The receipts from the premiere on Sunday, 23 February (1794 livres 10 sols) were encouraging, but they dropped in the second and last performance on 25 February to 398 livres 10 sols.

The scenic effects, however, were clever enough to kindle the audience's interest. In Act III they could see vases rise up and change into men, a grotto with a sun in the background, a tomb in the middle, and a globe of the earth below. Appearing in Act IV (the only act with music), was a

> machine composed of the four elements, with the grandeur of a Mount Parnassus. The bottom represents earth, upon which sit a male and female gnome. A bit higher is a bubbling stream of water and two water sprites of either sex. Above it is air, with two sylphs, male and female; and even higher, fire is seen, in the middle of which are two salamanders of either sex.[58]

Act V took place in the hall of a ruined, weed-infested château, with the moon and stars shining through the cracks in the roof. During a subterranean treasure hunt, the characters encountered a fiery monster. Reptiles spit flames, and a corpse dressed like a Roman senator came to life only to disappear again. It must have been difficult to make the public laugh with such sights!

Charpentier's music was written for Act IV. The scene begins with a ceremonial Chorus of the Four Elements, followed by a minuet sung by the little female gnome, a song for the male sylph, a dance of the elements, a duet for fire and water, a reprise of the first part of the opening chorus, and a "final chorus" (basically homophonic, like the first) "when the female gnome rises out of the ground," a sight that caused general amazement ("Quel éclat, quel éclat").

Endimion

On Tuesday, 22 July, *Endimion,* a tragedy by an anonymous author with incidental music by Charpentier, was performed by the French troupe. Three more performances followed immediately, plus an additional four in October.

If one compares Charpentier's score (H. 502) and the Parfaict brothers' account of the play (which was not published), it is difficult to determine clearly the relationship between the tragedy and the musical interludes, except for the presence of shepherds in both cases. Yet, while the very succinct account given in the *Histoire du théâtre français* makes no allusion to the legend of Endymion, certain musical passages are clearly drawn from it: the solo for Aurora, or the one sung by Guérin ("Heureux Endimion").

Although the "French" overture is mainly associated with Lully, Charpentier proved himself just as capable in the field as was the Surintendant; one need only hear or read each of these curtain-raisers to see whether they resemble Lully's pattern or not. The overture to *Endimion* (which is played, Charpentier specified, "before the curtain is raised") is a model of the genre, with its stately dotted rhythms, the great rising melody of the first movement, and the elaborate imitative treatment of the fugal section. The interludes consist entirely of dance movements ("fantaisie" with another remarkable fugal section, "sarabande" and "gavotte," "gaillarde," "gigue"). Most of the airs, which occur within the framework of the acts, resort to *rondeau* form.

After the *Endimion* score we find an instrumental piece entitled "Air pour des paysans dans la Noce de village au lieu de l'air du marié" (H. 503). *La Noce de village* is a little play by Brécourt (1638–1685) written in 1666. An unpretentious farce that had a great success, it was probably revived by the Comédie-Française in 1681.

Andromède

On 18 April 1682, the Académie Royale performed *Persée*, Lully and Quinault's tragédie lyrique with elaborate stage machinery. A few months later, the Comédie-Française revived Pierre Corneille's *Andromède*, the tragedy with stage machinery on the same theme as Lully's opera. Pure coincidence? Certainly not. The young Comédie-Française, feeling more and more challenged by the success of Lully's tragédies lyriques, wanted to prove that it, too, could mount great spectacles and gain public approval. While *Persée* was being performed at Versailles, the first performance of *Andromède* (H. 504) took place on Sunday, 19 July at the Hôtel Guénégaud.

The elder Corneille had ceased writing several years before (he died 1 October 1684). Nevertheless, his plays were still in the repertoire of the French troupe. The revival of *Andromède* (which, according to the editor of the 1682 libretto, "after more than thirty years has not aged a bit") was prepared with special care, evidently for reasons mentioned above. Considerable expense (nearly 13,000 livres) was incurred for the scenery and machines, and a new score by Charpentier replaced the one by Dassoucy.

The various flying machines for each of the five acts required enormous counterweights: some 3400 pounds of lead were melted down into six counterweights and eight charges, and for three days the machines were tested under the direction of Dufort, the theater's engineer and machinist. Because of the space required for the mechanical effects, the spectators who usually sat on the stage were not allowed there. What surprised the public the most was the entrance of a real horse in Act III, when the monster prepared to devour Andromeda and Perseus jumped on the winged Pegasus to rescue her:

> A person who has seen a performance of this revival has informed us how they managed to make the animal appear war-like. He was subjected to a strict fast before the performance, and this gave him a big appetite. When it was time to bring him out, a stagehand in the wings waved a basket of oats. The famished horse neighed, stamped his hoofs and reacted just as he was supposed to. Incidentally, it was Sieur Dauvilliers who played the role of Perseus. The stage business with the horse greatly contributed to the success of that tragedy. Everyone eagerly watched to see the animal's remarkable behavior, which became better with every performance.[59]

A veritable star performer, Pegasus's name was entered in the theater registers just like the names of the other actors were entered. We know that someone named Lucas took special care to groom and feed him. On 22 August, after eating too much sugar, Pegasus was given three enemas. When the production closed, the horse was given by the troupe as a reward to the actor-horserider Dauvilliers.

Although in contemporary chronicles the music seems to have been eclipsed by the special effects and the antics of Pegasus, Lully, for one, made an issue of it. On 27 July he secured a new royal ordinance to enforce the previous ordinances of 30 April 1673 and 21 March 1675, "prohibiting actors from using any more than two singing actors or actresses in their comedies."[60] An additional ban was put on the use of dancers. Performances continued neverthe-less: thirty-three by 4 October, six between 22 January and 3 February 1683, one on 20 March, and a final performance on 4 April. On 18 August 1682

> His Royal Highness came to the Foire Saint Laurent, and after-wards went to see a performance of *Andromède* by the elder Corneille. I have told you about this play, whose beauties are still drawing great crowds. The machines that are part of the scenery operate with absolute precision, and Monsieur le Dauphin seemed very pleased by them.[61]

Andromède consists of five acts and a prologue in homage to the king. For the new production, Corneille modified certain passages of his play, particularly a line in the prologue written in 1650, "Louis is the *youngest* and greatest of kings."[62] In 1682, the king by then having reached the age of forty-five, the original alexandrine was altered to "Louis is the *wisest* and greatest of kings." Similarly, "It is to you, Queen, that we owe the glory of so many great deeds," was no longer relevant, since Anne of Austria had been dead for sixteen years.

In examining Charpentier's large score, one must keep in mind that this music fell mainly within the context of spoken verses, with scenery and stage machinery constituting the primary focus of the spectacle. Corneille, as he explained in his preface to *Andromède*, conceived and structured his play on the basis of the machines:

> Each act, as well as the prologue, has its own individual set and at least one flying machine, with musical accompaniment that I employed only to satisfy the ears of the spectators while their eyes are attracted by the comings and goings of the machines or something which prevents them from paying attention to whatever the actors are saying, as in the combat between Perseus and the monster. . . . [The machines] are not incidental ornaments in this tragedy; they form the crux and the dénouement of the plot. They are such an essential part of it that not one of them could be omitted without destroying the entire edifice. . . . The beauty of the production, if you will, makes up for the lack of beautiful poetry, which you will not find in as great abundance here as in *Cinna* or *Rodogune*, because my main goal in this case was to satisfy the eye through the brilliance and diversity of the spectacle, and not to move the intellect with powerful thought, or the heart with tender emotions. This is not to say that I avoided or neglected any such opportunities; but there was so little of it that I prefer to admit that this play is for the eyes only.[63]

In view of this, we cannot discuss Charpentier's score out of context, that is, without the "reverberating" effect of the setting and the staging that accompanied it. That is why it seems appropriate here to give the reader—short of Corneille's play—enough of a description to evoke the atmosphere of a performance of a seventeenth-century stage play.[64]

The overture to the prologue, like the one in *Endimion*, uses the "serious and magnificent" key of G minor:

> At the moment the violins signal the beginning of the piece, the stage is revealed by an opening of the curtain that provokes no less surprise than delight, both by the swiftness with which it is done in view of the audience and by the able skill of the machinist, who has it lifted open on either side of the stage into the clouds by two cupids who each hold on to one half of it. . . .
>
> We see a thick forest, composed of several trees of different varieties, grouped variously in an arrangement of clumps of

earth and rock. In the background rises a mountain peak, beyond which lies the distant sea, and on the summit of the mountain the eye perceives a vast country landscape with views as far as one can see. On this height, Melpomene, the muse of tragedy, appears, and opposite her the sun is drawn in his luminous chariot by the four horses given to him by Ovid.

At the end of the prologue, Melpomene flies away in Apollo's chariot as music is played; then the god (played by de Villiers, *haute-contre*), in a stately, declamatory solo ("Cieux écoutez") punctuated by short flute ritornellos, invites all nature to glorify Louis. On the final phrase ("Louis est le plus sage et le plus grand des rois"), Apollo's voice is joined by that of a *dessus*. Charpentier does not indicate if it is supposed to be sung by Melpomene, writing only the name of the soprano, "Mlle Dyot," followed by "if desired" [?]. This unknown actress might have been Mlle Guyot (her real name was Judith de Nevers), who joined the Troupe du Marais in 1673, left the Comédie-Française in 1684, and died in 1691. The chorus (de Villiers, *haute-contre*; Guérin and La Grange, *tailles*; de Verneuil and Hubert, basses) picks up Apollo's words of praise.

Except for the four-part chorus in Act II, Charpentier only used a three-voice ensemble in *Andromède*. Either he did not have enough high voices at his disposal, or he was trying to avoid a clash with Lully, to a certain extent, by limiting his own forces. In any case, there is no reason to believe that esthetics alone determined his use of only lower voices.

The prologue's curtain closes on the flight of Apollo's chariot, after which the overture is repeated.

The scene changes:

The mass of ground and rock having vanished in an instant by an amazing device, the scene changes into a great city, whose magnificence, various orders of architecture, and the diverse construction of houses and palaces representing it, draw no less admiration than the preceding set. This is the capital city of the kingdom of Cepheus.

Its entrance is a great open portal in the center of the stage, through which can be seen the continuation of the city, and the foreground represents a public square.

In Act I, scene 3, Venus appears on a star "which approaches with such skill and naturalness, that the delightfully deceived naked eye cannot tell how she is supported or transported through the air." After she descends to musical accompaniment, the Chorus of the

King's and Queen's Attendants implore her favors ("Reine d'Eryce et d'Amathonte") and thank her for granting their wishes ("Ainsi toujours sur les autels"). The goddess turns and "goes off into the clouds, flying all the way upstage and into the flies, but so gracefully that she does not seem to move, even though she is gone."

An instrumental air in *rondeau* form serves as interlude between the acts while the scene changes:

> This is a garden of leafy bowers, beyond which are seen stone grottos. In front of the bowers [are] platforms of jasper displaying golden busts, interspersed with pedestals made of different kinds of marble. Standing on the pedestals are large gold vases filled with orange trees, flowers and fruit. Under the pedestals, as though to keep the precious trees fresh, are pools and fountains from which water falls in cascades from one into another. Between the pedestals are steps of white marble leading to an upper terrace. [The terrace], decorated with garlands of flowers and baskets on tables, extends to the rear of the stage with a great variety of gilded statues on their pedestals, creating the most magnificent and delightful garden imaginable.
>
> It is in this pleasant setting that Andromeda and her nymphs appear.

During scene 1, one of Phineus's pages intones ("without being seen") a lovely song, in ternary form ("Qu'elle est lente cette journée"), with instrumental accompaniment, and meant for Andromeda. The princess responds to Phineus through her nymph Liriope ("Phinée est plus aimé").[65] The nymph and the page sing together ("Heureux amant, heureuse amante") and are joined by the chorus in celebrating the future union of Andromeda and Phineus.

Then it is announced that Andromeda has been chosen as a victim for sacrifice to the gods. She is swept away by Aeolus and his winds, an excuse for more use of machinery in which the winds ride about on their clouds. The air titled "The Winds," with its swirling sixteenth notes in all the instruments, is not played here but during the interlude between Acts II and III, which calls for a "strange [and] quick transformation":

> The festoons, flower baskets, precious jasper, gold, and marble have turned into rocks whose haphazard mounds and crevices correspond so perfectly to Nature's whim that it seems as though she more than Art had a hand in arranging them thus on both sides of the stage. The center of [the stage] represents a vast billowing sea, with waves crashing against the terrible rocks that have been heaved on shore. There the eye is wonderfully deceived by the undulating movement of transparent crystalline

green, convincing the audience that the ocean itself has come to the stage.

No one doubts that this awesome spectacle is the dreadful manifestation of the gods' injustice and Andromeda's terrible ordeal. We see her above the clouds, when the two winds swiftly carry her and place her at the base of the fatal rock where she is to be devoured.

After Andromeda's great monologue, "Affreuse image du trépas," a lament of onlookers was supposed to be performed, but the music has not survived. The sea monster approaches, "scaly, armed with claws, and with bony protrusions." Perseus then appears in the air on his winged horse Pegasus, fights with the horrible creature, and slays it. He commands the winds to carry the princess away, then exits "after performing an admirable caracole." The shores echo with an impressive victory chant by the chorus ("Le monstre est mort"), in which the powerful homophonic texture contrasts with the more supple melodic lines of the episodes for solo voice (*haute-contre*) and duet (*haute-contre* and *taille*).

The act closes extravagantly with the arrival of "Neptune rising from the depths of the sea in a sparkling Eastern mother-of-pearl conch shell drawn by two dolphins."

For the interlude between Acts III and IV, Charpentier created an instrumental capriccio of a type rarely encountered in music for the theater, though common in keyboard literature. Italian in origin, the capriccio had always been, like the canzone or ricercare, a sort of experimental ground for composers, featuring a fugal texture and juxtaposition of contrasting tempos. Also notable in the capriccio from *Andromède* are numerous harmonic progressions.

In Act IV,

> the billowing waves of the sea suddenly sink beneath the stage, and the awful masses of rock it was thrashing give way to the magnificence of a royal palace where the great celebration for the lovers is to take place. This Doric style palace has green serpentine marble columns, whose bases and capitals are in gold. Between the columns are large statues of the same metal. In the recess is the façade of an Ionic style palace supported by pilasters of another sort of marble, whose columns, bases, and capitals are in gold, supporting their frieze, architrave, and cornice with a pediment decorated with trophies. Behind them are two large reclining figures in gold. In the distance [is] an attic representing the main part of the structure, and in the great central arcade, which is genuine, can be seen the courtyard of the royal palace of Cepheus, an extremely bright edifice, eclectic in style.

Spurned by Andromeda, Phineus asks Juno to help him. The wife of Jupiter appears out of the clouds in a superb chariot drawn by two peacocks and assures the unhappy lover of her support. Then enter King Cepheus, Queen Cassiopeia, Andromeda, and Perseus. The Chorus of Onlookers express wishes of joy to the "happy lovers." Two instrumental airs, the first a repeat of the preceding chorus, the second an "English gigue" (actually French, in ternary form but moderately paced), serve as interlude between the last two acts.

Act V reveals

> a superb Ionic-composite temple of white marble, flanked by columns fluted with Egyptian marble, all trimmed in gold. Between the columns stand large gold urns, and all the trimming of the architecture and ornamentation is likewise in gold. In the center of the stage is the temple sanctuary, with its own style of architecture, and with the same richness. The backdrop shows the continuation of the front galleries, forming a corridor in the same style.

Phineus tries to ambush Perseus, who escapes when the hero brandishes the head of Medusa and turns the assassins to stone. To announce the arrival of the gods, Mercury "appears at the top of the stage peeking through a cloud; after his speech, he jumps to the ground, then dashes back in the air and, without the slightest hesitation, flies quickly out of sight above the stage."

At the bidding of the chorus—"Chief God, hasten to appear" (from here on Charpentier uses the "joyous and very warlike" key of D major)—Jupiter enters "on his throne, shining in all its celestial brilliance, surrounded by a cloud, with Juno and Neptune at his sides." He invites the future spouses to celebrate their wedding in the heavens. All fly away, and the tragedy ends with the benediction of the populace (duet, then chorus):

> *Allez amants sans jalousie*
> *Vivre à jamais en ce brillant séjour*
> *Où le nectar et l'ambrosie*
> *Vous seront comme aux Dieux prodigués chaque jour.*

> Go forth, lovers, without jealousy;
> Live forever in that glorious realm
> Where nectar and ambrosia
> Will be lavished on you as it is on the gods each day.

La Toison d'or

The success of *Andromède* encouraged the actors to revive *La Toison d'or*, the other stage play by Pierre Corneille first produced in 1660. La Chapelle wrote a new prologue, but this time the music was assigned to Lalouette, probably because Charpentier was in poor health, having become ill in the spring of 1683.

Jean-François de Lalouette (1651–1728) had been Lully's pupil and private secretary, as well as a violinist at the Opéra. In 1677 he was dismissed by the Surintendant after boasting that he had composed the best airs in *Isis* himself. From then on Lalouette devoted himself primarily to religious music. It is known that Lully surrounded himself with musicians who "helped" him compose, so it is quite possible that Lalouette's claims were at least partially, if not totally, genuine. In this way Lully made himself another enemy, who, after having been a loyal servant of the Académie Royale, must have been delighted to compose for its rival institution.

The premiere of *La Toison d'or* took place on 9 July 1683. After an interruption due to the death of the queen, performances resumed on 15 October until 21 March of the following year.

Psyché

In autumn 1684, Charpentier, restored to health, was commissioned to work on another revival, *Psyché* (see previous discussion in this chapter under "Molière's Composer").

Le Rendez-vous des Tuileries

On Saturday, 3 March 1685, Baron staged his comedy *Le Rendez-vous des Tuileries ou le Coquet trompé*, performed ten times through 1 April. Michel Boiron, also known as Baron (1653–1729), came from a large family of actors. He entered Molière's troupe in 1670 and joined the Hôtel de Bourgogne troupe in 1673. Married to Charlotte Le Noir, daughter of La Thorillière, he retired from acting in 1691 with a pension from the king.

Le Rendez-vous des Tuileries, a comedy in three acts and a prologue, lacks a conventional plot and is a social satire on the theater world, most memorable for its witty dialogue. Charpentier composed two big orchestral pieces for the play (H. 505): an overture with a beautiful fugal section, and a chaconne.

It should be remembered that in spite of the renewal of Lully's ordinance in July 1682, the actors continued performing *Andromède* as if nothing had happened. Since the music of *Psyché* is lost, it cannot be proven if it, too, ignored the interdictions. In any case, we do know that the ordinance was renewed again on 17 August 1684, and still again on 4 September.

Angélique et Médor

Lully finally achieved what he wanted: Charpentier's last contributions to the repertory of the Comédie-Française only call for two singing voices, as stipulated by the ordinance.

For Dancourt's comedy, *Angélique et Médor*, performed on 1 August 1685, Charpentier only composed a musical dialogue.[66] Florent Carton Dancourt (1661–1725), after his studies at the Jesuit Collège at Paris, began a career as a dramatist in 1685. *Angélique et Médor* is the second of some fifty-five highly successful comedies that won him the king's recognition. Dancourt created a special comic device, which consisted of inserting a parody of another play into the comedy. In this case, it was the recent Lully opera, *Roland*, of which Dancourt made fun.

With its simple melodic lines and its totally uncomplicated harmonies, was this *Dialogue d'Angélique et de Médor* (H. 506) for one *dessus* and one *taille* meant as a parody of Lully's style? *Angélique et Médor* was performed fourteen times, until 1 September 1685.

Les Amours de Vénus et d'Adonis

In 1670, Donneau de Visé had given his first stage play, *Les Amours de Vénus et d'Adonis*, at the Marais theater. Fifteen years later, he decided to revive it:

> This play was a great success in its day, even though the machinery had neither dancing nor singing to accompany it. Since musical interludes had become expected of all plays of that type, so that they seemed naked without them, they were added, with music by M. Charpentier, who for many years had been working successfully at that sort of thing. A plaint was also added, charming all musical connoisseurs who heard it. The actors gave the work in its revised form, playing their parts perfectly to great applause, which, after six performances in one week, would have led to success, if the production had not been suspended due to the departure of the players, who were ordered to Fontainebleau for a court entertainment.[67]

The play was performed, not six times as Donneau de Visé claimed, but four, on 23, 24, 26, and 27 September 1685. *Vénus et Adonis* (H. 507) was Charpentier's last work for the Comédie-Française. Only one shepherd (bass), one shepherdess (*haut-dessus*), and the orchestra are involved in the prologue and four interludes, composed of songs (one a minuet, "Gardons-nous de livrer notre âme"), duets, and dances, including a chaconne with a fine arpeggio phrase beginning in the upper line and passing to the bass, a minuet in *rondeau* form, and a passepied. Charpentier compensated for the scanty forces by writing with greater expressivity, culminating in the shepherdess' plaint mentioned by Donneau de Visé. The plaint begins with an instrumental prelude. Not satisfied with his first effort, fine as it was, Charpentier composed a second plaint, a bit shorter, and beginning like the first with an admirable fugal passage, but in the concluding section he uses pedal points, first in the sub-dominant, then in the dominant. The shepherdess' song repeats the attractive melodic contours of the prelude, developing it with a long melisma on the word *tears*:

The instruments add their support to the plaint, now "gently," now "forcefully," extending it after the singing stops, gradually descending into the low range. This first section, which is elaborately structured (A–B–A'–postlude), is repeated, like a da capo, after a recitative episode.

The lament, a French *plainte* or Italian *lamento*, was probably the most expressive "language" of the period. In it Charpentier used stylistic devices, particularly in the area of harmony, that were unusual in the repertory we have been examining. This kind of feeling was generally reserved for prayer. A great knowledge of composition here makes up for the diminished performing forces. It is the mark of genius.

With the score for *Vénus et Adonis*, Charpentier left the Comédie-Française for good, only presenting "*Le Malade imaginaire* readjusted for the 3rd time" at Versailles on 11 January 1686. Lully had obtained what he wanted. By gradually stifling their musical productivity with his ordinances, Lully succeeded in finally discouraging the players and their composer. But the success of the tragédie lyrique also contributed to the gradual eclipse of other dramatic forms with music. In the future, the Comédie-Française would devote itself exclusively to spoken drama.

Nevertheless, for thirteen years, Charpentier resisted Lully; he challenged him with all the strength of his talent and proved his will to fight against all the strong measures imposed by the Surintendant to reign supreme in the theater. What bitterness and disillusionment Charpentier must have felt to have his creativity kept in check so tenaciously! His situation is unique in the history of Western music— a composer made to submit to the arbitrary power of one of his peers. Could a more intolerable situation be imagined?

If Charpentier's career in the theater still leaves us full of questions, we have nevertheless just seen how extensive, rich, and varied his collaboration was with the players of the Palais-Royal, the Hôtel Guénégaud, and the Comédie-Française. Even if most of his dramatic pieces cannot compete with his religious music, it is amazing to see how this modest, thoughtful, even austere man was capable of enjoying himself, indulging in the most unrestrained whimsy and the lightest diversion, and contributing to some of the most dazzling spectacles ever produced.

Furthermore, these pieces reveal a great composer of instrumental music, not only in the field of dance, but of "pure" music as well. Everything he wrote, in fact, bespeaks Charpentier's love of the theater and, we emphasize, what he might have achieved in that field unhampered by Lully's restrictions: pastorales and divertissements for the singers of the Hôtel de Guise; the Biblical opera *David et Jonathas* produced in the rarified setting of the Jesuit Collège; *Médée,* his only tragédie lyrique whose composition was possible only six years after the death of Lully. All these works prove the extraordinary fertility of Charpentier's inspiration and make us regret all the more that he was not allowed to thrive freely and completely and to earn the attention he has always deserved.

Plate 1. Patricia Ranum (1991) has suggested that an engraving by Landry, titled "The Royal Almanac of 1682" and celebrating the military victory of Louis XIV at Alsace followed by the return of the royal family to Saint-Germain-en-Laye in November 1681, may contain the only known likeness of Charpentier. King Louis XIV and Queen Marie-Thérèse stand in the center of the engraving, surrounded by the Dauphin and Dauphine on the left (also standing) and by the king's brother (the Duc de Chartres) and sister-in-law (Princess Palatine) on the right (seated). In the lower left corner of the engraving is an excerpt from *Menuet de Strasbourg* by Charpentier, and it is believed that the composer himself is holding the music with his left hand (following the custom of the time to portray an artist holding one of his works in his hands). The woman on whose lap the music rests cannot be the composer's wife (as he is not looking at her), but is believed to be Mme de Guise (only royalty dare sit in the presence of the king and queen). Bibliothèque Nationale, Paris, and the Société de Marc-Antoine Charpentier.

Plate 2. Giacomo Carissimi (1605–1674), choirmaster of the Jesuit Collegio Germanico who gave Charpentier lessons during his three-year sojourn in Rome. Bibliothèque Nationale, Paris.

Plate 3. According to Titon du Tillet, "When [Charpentier] returned to Paris, Mademoiselle gave him an apartment in her Hôtel" (Hôtel de Clisson, 58 rue des Archives). Éditions Arthaud-Giraudon.

Plate 4. Marie de Lorraine (1615–1688),
Duchesse de Guise, was Charpentier's patroness
for eighteen years. Bibliothèque Nationale, Paris.

Plate 5. The performance of Molière's *Le Malade imaginaire* on 21 August 1674 in the gardens of the Versailles château, at the entrance of the grotto. Giraudon.

Plate 6. The Dauphin (1661–1711) with his wife, Marie-Anne-Christine of Bavaria, and their three children: Philippe, Duc d'Anjou; Charles, Duc de Berry; and Louis, Duc de Bourgogne. From 1679 to 1683, Charpentier was responsible for composing the music for the Dauphin's religious services. Musées Nationaux, Paris.

QUATRIÈME CHAMBRE DES APARTEMENS.

Plates 7 and 8. The divertissement titled *Les Plaisirs de Versailles* evokes the "apartment days" inaugurated by the king in the autumn of 1682, when the court officially moved to Versailles. Bibliothèque Nationale, Paris.

SIXIÈME CHAMBRE DES APARTEMENS.

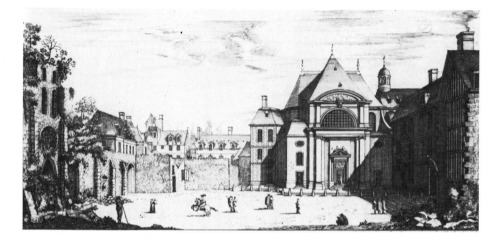

Plate 9. Port-Royal de Paris, the convent for which Charpentier composed a mass and some motets. Photothèque des Musées de la ville de Paris.

Plate 10. Fireworks at the Collège Louis-le-Grand in August 1682 celebrating the birth of the Duc de Bourgogne. Photothèque des Musées de la ville de Paris.

Plate 11. Queen Marie-Thérèse's funeral service held on 4 September 1683 at Notre-Dame cathedral in Paris. Bibliothèque Nationale, Paris.

Plate 12. The high altar of the Jesuit Église Saint-Louis on Rue Saint-Antoine in Paris. Photothèque des Musées de la ville de Paris.

Plate 13. One of the numerous attractions of the Jesuit services was the exceptional quality of the sermons, delivered by the best orators. Bibliothèque Nationale, Paris.

Plate 14. The procession of the Holy Sacrament on the feast of Corpus Christi. At the upper right, the musicians' platform. Bibliothèque Nationale, Paris.

Plates 15 and 16. Berain's decors for *Médée,* Acts I and III. Archives Nationales, Paris.

Plate 17. Philippe of Orléans (1674–1723), whom Charpentier tutored in composition in the early 1690s. Portrait by H. Rigaud. Lauros-Giraudon.

Plate 18. The Sainte-Chapelle, where Charpentier was appointed as choirboys' director on 28 June 1698. Lauros-Giraudon.

Plate 19. *Epitaphium Carpentarii*, "Amici, viatores, nolite timere." Bibliothèque Nationale, Paris.

Chapter 4

At the Court of
Mademoiselle de Guise

He lived at the Hôtel de Guise for a long time and composed some things for Mlle de Guise's musicians that were highly regarded by the ablest connoisseurs.

Mercure Galant, March 1688, p. 321

Upon the death of her grandnephew François-Joseph in 1675, Marie de Lorraine, Princesse de Joinville, Duchesse de Joyeuse, and Duchesse de Guise, known at court and in public as Mlle de Guise, became the sole representative of the illustrious House of Guise and found herself in control of an immense inheritance. Proud to be a Guise, she was respected by all, and as the last of her line, she determined to care for her family's estate and to maintain the House's reputation. Saint-Simon described her with all the respect she probably inspired in her own circle:

> Mlle de Guise . . . who lived in such splendor as a child . . . so noble and respected . . . attained great status through her estate and rank, when she assumed control of the entire House of Lorraine. Moreover she was a person of great intelligence and ability, and eminently worthy of her ancestors.[1]

A love of the fine arts and their patronage was traditional in the Guise family, who provided lodging for such writers as François de Malherbe, Tristan l'Hermite, and even Pierre Corneille, who had a room in the household between 1662 and 1664. In appreciation, the author of *Le Cid* dedicated a sonnet to Louis-Joseph on the death of his uncle, Duc Henry.[2] Other men of letters such as Donneau de Visé, the Abbé de Pure, and Boursault also frequented the Hôtel de Guise, as did Nicolas Hotman, the violist and theorbist who resided there for a few years before his death in 1663.

Henry II of Lorraine, Duc de Guise and Marie's brother, had been appointed Grand Chamberlain of Louis XIV. In that capacity he organized the king's entertainments, notably the Great Carousel of 1662. During the widespread dissemination of Italian art under Mazarin, with Lully (brought from Italy by Roger of Lorraine, another of Mlle de Guise's brothers) as one of its most active propagandists, Henry II became a staunch supporter of French music. In 1657, in ironic response to the ballet *L'Amor malato*, he produced a French ballet, *Les Plaisirs troublés*, which, despite its lavishness, did not eclipse the Italian ballet's success.

> Monsieur the Duc de Guise presented his ballet in the Louvre in the presence of the entire court. In a way it is more lavish and more beautiful than the king's [ballet], but in other respects it is vastly inferior. Monsieur le Duc was talked into it by certain jealous persons who could not tolerate the king's hiring of Italians to prepare his ballet. They hoped the king, in seeing their work, would call on their talents. The stewards of Monsieur le Duc, however, no longer wish to hand over money needed to run the household since huge sums intended for necessities were used for the ballet. All of this provides fuel for gossip and ridicule at the court.[3]

It is interesting to note that the Guises, even in artistic matters, deliberately placed themselves at odds with those in power and with the prevailing esthetic. While Italian music was in favor at court, the Duc de Guise countered with a French ballet. Later, after Lully imposed his French concept of music, Mlle de Guise supported Marc-Antoine Charpentier, a composer criticized for his Italianism. The resemblance between brother and sister ends there, however. While Henry wasted money to satisfy his passion for luxury and his taste for amorous and political adventure (his tumultuous existence carried him to the brink of ruin), Marie managed the finances of her household in a different way, consistently working to uphold the honor and the power of her dynasty.

In 1667, the nephew of Mlle de Guise, Louis-Joseph, married Élisabeth, Duchesse d'Alençon and youngest daughter of Gaston of Orléans (the king's uncle) and his second wife, Marguerite of Lorraine. With that alliance the House of Guise's former brilliance returned. In fact, when Charpentier came back from Rome and settled in the Guise residence on Rue du Chaume (today Rue des Archives, whose apartments have recently been restored), the residence was the site of great social events. One of these events, reported by Mme de Sévigné, was given the evening of 7 February 1671 in honor of the marriage of Mlle d'Harcourt to the Duc de Cadaval, which took place in the chapel of the Hôtel de Guise.

> Here is what I learned about yesterday's entertainment. All the courtyards of the Hôtel de Guise were illuminated with some two thousand lamps. The queen went first into the well-lighted and sumptuously decorated apartment of Mme de Guise; the ladies of the court were all around the queen on their knees, without distinction of rank. All forty ladies were at table; the supper was magnificent. The king entered and very solemnly observed without being seated at table. Then the company went to an upper apartment where everything was prepared for the ball. The king ushered in the queen and honored the assembled company with three or four courantes, and then returned to the Louvre to have supper with his usual entourage. Mademoiselle did not want to come to the Hôtel de Guise. That is all I know.[4]

"That is all I know," wrote Mme de Sévigné, who was not present at the event but obtained her information from second-hand reports about the extravagant supper and lights, the number of guests, the solemn attitude of the king who only opened the ball with the queen, and the absence of Mlle de Montpensier who had fallen out with Mlle de Guise (and whom she later disinherited). Not surprisingly, accounts of the evening by Marie de Lorraine and the courtiers reflect a tone of detachment. Marie's grandfather was Henri de Guise, *le Balafré* ("Scarface"), leader of the Holy League, who was murdered by order of Henry III. Her father, who was sent into exile by Cardinal Richelieu in 1631, left France with his whole family. Young Marie was deeply affected by those dozen or so years in Italy during which her father and several of her brothers died. Back in France, she would see that the remainder of her ancestors' estate was safeguarded. Even if the rivalry between the Bourbons and the Guises was no longer as violent as in the days of the Holy League, it still smoldered. By staying away from the court, Mlle de Guise asserted her wish for independence vis-à-vis the royal family. Like anyone of her rank, however, she dutifully paid homage to her sovereign whenever circumstances required it; hence, the great religious service at the Abbaye de Monmartre offered in honor of the return of the king's health in January 1687.

The brilliant lifestyle in the Hôtel in the Rue du Chaume was sadly interrupted by the death of Louis-Joseph on 30 July 1671. A power struggle followed between Mlle and Mme de Guise over the question of little François-Joseph's tutelage. After a two-year disagreement, during which time Mme de Guise lived with her son in the Palais d'Orléans (Palais du Luxembourg), the two women reached a reconciliation.[5] Élisabeth, however, remained in the palace she shared with the Grande Mademoiselle, her half-sister. In April 1672, Élisabeth's mother, Marguerite of Lorraine, dowager duchess of Orléans, died. François-Joseph followed her on 16 March 1675, only five years old. The entire family legacy then fell into the lap of Marie de Lorraine, the last descendant of Scarface.

The mark of these successive bereavements can be seen in Charpentier's *Mélanges*, the first volumes of which contain a series of funeral works: *Messe pour les trépassés à 8* (H. 2), *Motet pour les trépassés à 8* (H. 311), *De profundis* (H. 156), and *Prose des morts* "Dies irae" (H. 12).[6] Except for the *De profundis*, these pieces are lavishly scored, but we have no record of the musicians who performed them or of the circumstances in which they were first given. Could it have been following the death of Louis-Joseph, for whom a mass was celebrated in Paris on 22 August 1671 in the Église Saint-Jean and again on 20 September in the Église Saint-Didier in Champagne Province?

After Marguerite of Lorraine died, her heart was placed in the Abbaye de Monmartre where the king attended mass on 13 April 1672. On 11 May a funeral service was held in the Saint-Denis Basilique, with the "assistance of the musicians of the king's chapel."[7] On 30 July "the end of the year of the Duc de Guise was celebrated in the church of Monmartre, with all due solemnity."[8]

No contemporary source gives any details concerning the music played for the various ceremonies. Nevertheless, it is certain that Charpentier's pieces were intended for one or the other of them, and it is quite probable that some of the pieces were performed again upon the death of the young Duc de Guise, particularly the "Dies irae" to which Charpentier appended a prelude and which is now lost.

At the close of the 1660s, Charpentier's sojourn in Rome ended. Titon du Tillet informs us that "when [he] returned to Paris, Mlle de Guise gave him an apartment in her Hôtel."[9] The composer stayed there until 1687–1688, working eighteen years for Mlle de Guise and her household. Like other artists in residence in the Guise household before him, Charpentier was considered a "guest and protégé of the family" and not a "hired" musician.[10] He was given lodging and meals, cared for, and provided with a modest salary. Mlle de Guise offered him, as she likewise offered the other musicians around him, "the means of accomplishing work in tranquillity which her beneficence allows all who have the honor of being in her home to enjoy."[11]

Charpentier's attachment to Mlle de Guise and to her privileged, rich, and powerful circle, though on the fringes of the court and somewhat self-contained, might explain the curious nature of the composer's career and the many gaps in his biography. On the one hand, her generous protection permitted Charpentier to pursue his art in all tranquillity, but on the other hand it also closed certain doors to him, especially those leading to the court.

At the same time this makes it rather difficult to understand Charpentier's situation, for the composer also "belonged" to Mme de Guise, for whom he also composed. First cousin to Louis XIV, Élisabeth, unlike Mlle de Guise, assiduously frequented the court. She often visited the Carmelite nuns on Rue du Bouloir in the company of the queen and attended religious services in Saint-Germain-en-Laye, Fontainebleau, and Versailles. In the company of the king, queen, and Dauphin, she went to welcome the future Dauphine in Reims in February 1680. She offered entertainments for the baptism of the Duc de Chartres and his sister in 1676 (*Petite pastorale*, H. 479, may have been performed on that occasion[12]) and for the birth of the Duc de Bourgogne in 1682. The evidence even leads us to believe that Mme de Guise tried to establish Charpentier at the court by offering works to Louis XIV (e.g., *La Fête de Rueil*, H. 485; *Idylle sur le retour de la santé du roi*, H. 489) or by having them performed at Versailles (e.g., *Exaudiat pour le roi à 4* "Exaudiat pour Versailles,"[13] H. 180; *In festo Corporis Christi Canticum* "Grand motet pour le reposoir[14] de Versailles en présence du roi,"[15] H. 344).

Like Mlle de Guise, Mme de Guise was a devout Catholic. Saint-Simon described her as a "very pious princess devoted to prayer and good deeds."[16] Both women frequented the capital city's churches and convents, particularly the Abbaye de Monmartre whose abbess was Françoise-Renée de Lorraine, Mlle de Guise's younger sister. Marie de Lorraine and Élisabeth d'Orléans also had a common interest in pedagogical institutions. Mlle de Guise patronized the Institut du Père Nicolas Barré voué à l'Enfant Jésus whose governesses, given the responsibility of teaching poor young females, gradually established themselves throughout France. Mme de Guise manifested her benevolence in her parish of Saint-Sulpice with the creation of an academy for boys of nobility, called the Hôtel de l'Enfant Jésus.[17] Charpentier's works on the nativity theme seem to have been intended for those two establishments, especially the Latin pieces *Canticum in nativitatem Domini* (H. 393) in December 1676, *Pour la Fête de l'Épiphanie* (H. 395) in January 1677, and *In nativitatem Domini Nostri Jesu Christi Canticum* (H. 414) for Christmas 1684, all of which were performed at either Saint-Sulpice or the chapel of the Hôtel de l'Enfant Jésus on Rue de Sèvres.[18] For the Père Barré institute, Charpentier composed several pastorales (H. 482, 483, 483a, 483b) during the years 1684–1687.

In her house on Rue du Chaume, Mlle de Guise held a veritable mini-court that was at once pious, learned, and artistic. Besides the numerous "domestics" (numbering more than seventy in 1688), Marie de Lorraine surrounded herself with persons of high social standing and great cultural ability, who preserved the household's important political and economic prestige but also made it an artistic haven of the first order. The chief steward of the household was Christophe Roquette, brother of Gabriel Roquette, bishop of Autun, who exercised considerable influence over the princess. The erudite squire of the household, Roger de Gaignières, collected drawings of old monuments, documents on the history of the church, and genealogies. In 1665 Philippe Goibault Du Bois was appointed preceptor of Mlle de Guise's nephew, Louis-Joseph. A man of letters, he translated Cicero and Saint Augustine (his translations of the *Sermons of Saint Augustine on the New Testament* were published the year of his death, in 1694) and was elected to the French Academy in November 1693. He may have been the author of certain French or Latin texts used by Charpentier in his pastorales and oratorios. He was also proficient on the guitar, theorbo, and bass viol. He possibly assumed direction of the little musical ensemble at the Hôtel de Guise in 1670 and continued to direct musical performances in the years following, as implied by Mlle de Guise's letter of 11 October 1680, written when she was on an inspection trip of her lands in Champagne:

> Music does wonders, and M. Du Bois keeps so happy and so busy with it that up to now he has made no fuss about any inconvenience. I don't think he will since he takes so much pleasure in having it [music] performed most of the time.[19]

In another letter written during the course of the same trip, Mlle de Guise confided to Doctor Vallant, her house physician, about her inordinate love of music:

> I cannot keep myself from telling you how much the music being played is distracting me, to the point that I can no longer keep my mind on what I am writing. M. Du Bois got it into his head to entertain me because I have been preoccupied with business matters all day long. He has been so successful that I can't keep my mind on anything other than what I am hearing, which is causing me to make so many spelling mistakes in my letter that I don't know if you can read it.[20]

In the early 1670s, Mlle de Guise had already assembled a small group of musicians around her that was later expanded. The development of this group can be traced through Charpentier's manuscripts. It appears that the composer only had two female singers at first (*haut-dessus* and *dessus*) accompanied sometimes by one or two flutes (Cahiers 1 and 2 of *Mélanges*). A third woman's voice (*bas-dessus*) was added to the other two (in Cahier 5). The antiphon *Ave Regina coelorum* (H. 19) carries two initials ("Mlles B. et T.") referring to Élisabeth Boisseau, first chambermaid, and Élisabeth Thorin, chambermaid to Mlle de Guise.[21] *Miserere à 2 dessus, 2 flûtes et basse continue* (H. 157) dating from Holy Week 1673 is inscribed "Mlle Magdelon" and "Mlle Margot," identifying Élisabeth Boisseau (nicknamed "Magdelon") and Marguerite de la Bonnodière, maid of honor.[22] In Cahier 8 there are pieces for three male voices (*haute-contre, taille,* and bass). The following Cahiers (11–21) covering 1674–1679 include various combinations of instruments, mainly trio formations, of which Charpentier was particularly fond.

In 1684 the size of the ensemble significantly increased and the manuscripts become more informative about the singers' identities. There were eleven singers: Mlle Thorin, whom Charpentier also referred to as Mlle Isabelle ("chambermaid," *haut-dessus* or *dessus*); Mlle Brion (Jacqueline-Geneviève de Brion, "chambermaid in ordinary with the ensemble," *haut-dessus*); Mlle Talon (Antoinette Talon, "Her Highness' personal maid," *haut-dessus* or *dessus*); Mlle Guyot (Jeanne Guyot, "chambermaid in ordinary with the ensemble," *haut-dessus*); Mlle Grandmaison (Marie Guillebault de Grandmaison, "her Highness' personal maid," *dessus* or *bas-dessus*); M. Charp. (*haute-contre*); M. Anth. (François Anthoine, "musician in ordinary," *haute-contre*); M. Bossan (Henri de Baussen, "musician in ordinary," *taille*); M. Joly (*taille, basse-taille* or bass); M. Beaupuy

(Pierre Beaupuis, "musician in ordinary," *taille, basse-taille*, or bass); and M. Carlié (Germain Carlier, "musician in ordinary," bass).[23]

The abbreviation "Charp." puzzled musicologists for a long time; it is the only name, other than Anthoine ("Anth."), that the composer never wrote out in its entirety. Froberville,[24] and later La Laurencie,[25] suggested it was someone named Charpy, but no singer with that name ever seems to have been at the Hôtel de Guise. Indeed, by "Charp." Marc-Antoine Charpentier was referring to himself.[26] It was for his own countertenor voice that he wrote the roles of Actéon (H. 481), Tiburtius in *Caecilia Virgo et Martyr* (H. 413, 415), Painting in *Les Arts florissants* (H. 487), and probably (though the singer's name is not indicated) the "Umbra Carpentarii" (Ghost of Carpenter) in *Epitaphium Carpentarii* (H. 474). Who other than Charpentier could have performed his own ghost? Like his teacher Carissimi, Charpentier also sang.

The comings and goings of certain singers can be determined by the chronology of the works. Joly, for example, left the household at the beginning of 1685, Mlle Guyot and M. Anthoine did not take part in performances until late 1686. It even seems as though the latter was engaged to replace Charpentier. Only one work indicates the simultaneous presence of both singers: *La Descente d'Orphée aux enfers* (H. 488). The title role was given to Anthoine, while Charpentier created the secondary role of Ixion.[27] Charpentier stopped singing in 1687 as he was busy composing two large-scale works: in February, *Celse Martyr* was performed at the Collège Louis-le-Grand, followed by *David et Jonathas* a year later.

Mlle de Guise employed other musicians and instrumentalists whose names are missing in Charpentier's manuscripts, except for a single reference to "Loullié" [*sic*] in *La Descente d'Orphée aux enfers* (H. 488). The rest are identified in her will, in which Sieur Loüillé (Étienne Loulié, "musician in ordinary") is mentioned as well as Sieur Collin (Toussaint Collin, "musician in ordinary"), Sieur Montailly (Nicolas Montailly, "musician in ordinary"), and Mlle Manon (Anne Jacquet, "chambermaid and daughter of music," *fille de la musique*).[28]

The singers were usually accompanied by two treble viols and/or two flutes and thoroughbass. We do not know, however, who played which part. We know very little about Toussaint Collin, perhaps a relative of Didier Collin, a "master violist."[29] Montailly, a disciple of Bénigne de Bacilly, the famous singing master, composed and gave lessons to the young female singers of the household. Probably he also accompanied them on the harpsichord. The girl charmingly nicknamed Manon was really Anne-Nanon Jacquet, the sister of Élisabeth Jacquet de La Guerre. Was she a harpsichordist like her illustrious relative?

Étienne Loulié played the flute, bass viol, harpsichord, spinet, and organ. In *La Descente d'Orphée aux enfers*, he played one of the flute parts. Flutists Antoine and Pierre Pièche were the king's musicians who occasionally came to reinforce the Hôtel's modest-sized instrumental ensemble. Du Bois certainly also had occasion to direct the ensemble while playing the theorbo; *Pro omnibus festis BVM* (H. 333) and *Sonate* (H. 548) are the only two works of Charpentier that specify the use of that instrument.

Like Charpentier, most of the musicians came from families with historical ties to the Guises and the Orléans (whether they were former members of the Holy League or officers of the Guises and their allies).[30] Marie de Lorraine continued to protect the descendants of these families in the name of the House of Guise. These musicians belonged to the household's large domestic staff, having entered the Hôtel de Guise at a very early age, especially the girls. Few of them were connected to musical circles: the father of Pierre Beaupuis was a tailor by trade; Henri de Baussen's father was a Parisian "horse master," and the father of Germain Carlier held a modest position in the municipal government.[31] Their musical talent, however, encouraged Mlle de Guise to give them an opportunity to exploit it, to such an extent that the young amateurs could eventually compete with professional court musicians. Hence a sort of musical aura surrounded the House of Guise. Announcing the death of the "highly distinguished, very powerful and illustrious princess," the *Mercure Galant* declared:

> She lived her life with a sumptuousness worthy of the blood from which she sprang. She did good to many people, generously rewarded the slightest service, and attending to everything with grandeur, she even supported a group of musicians. That ensemble was so good that it can be said that the musicians of several great sovereigns do not come close to matching it.[32]

After 1688, Pierre Beaupuis, who entered the service of Mlle de Guise in 1676, and Geneviève Brion, who arrived in 1678,[33] pursued singing careers, the former with the Jesuits and the latter with the King's Chamber.

Besides Charpentier, the other important person associated with Mlle de Guise's "music" was Étienne Loulié, known chiefly as a theoretician and inventor.[34] Born in 1654, Loulié sang with the Sainte-Chapelle from 1663 to 1673 while a pupil of its choirmaster René Ouvrard, a staunch advocate of Italian music and a great admirer of Carissimi. It was from Loulié that Mlle de Guise's composer acquired an interest in the study of musical theory.

Upon leaving the Sainte-Chapelle, Loulié entered into the service of Marie de Lorraine. During his fifteen years with the household, he maintained a steady activity as an instrumentalist, teacher, and perhaps a singer and composer. Among the numerous treatises he wrote, only two were published in 1696: *Elements or Principles of Music Newly Arranged* and *Summary of the Principles of Music, with Several Lessons on Each Difficulty of These Same Principles.* Other treatises include *Two Methods for Learning How to Play the Flute, Method for Learning How to Play the Viol, Method for Learning to Read Vocal Music,* and several composition manuals.

Loulié also seems to have been responsible for preparing the scores needed for the Hôtel's concerts, which included music by Charpentier and others. At her soirées Mlle de Guise gave guests the opportunity to hear music in vogue at court, in particular that of Lully, whose music Loulié arranged for the household's musicians.

A colleague of Charpentier, Loulié was most interested in musical theory, which led him to invent things, including, for example, the chronometer, a precursor by more than a century of Maelzel's metronome. Loulié's treatise titled *Elements or Principles of Music Newly Arranged* contains the

> drawing, description and use of the chronometer, or newly invented instrument by means of which composers of music will henceforth be able to indicate the true tempo of their compositions, and their works marked in accordance with this instrument will be able to be performed in their absence as though they themselves were beating time.

Loulié also invented the sonometer, "a newly invented instrument for tuning the harpsichord," and a device for ruling music paper by hand, which Charpentier often used for his manuscripts.

Sébastien de Brossard, to whom we owe some of the rare eyewitness accounts of Charpentier, also thought very highly of Loulié, whose acquaintance he made in the early 1680s:

> Of all the musicians in Paris, he was almost the only one with whom you could discuss music intelligently. That is what led him to become acquainted with MM. Sauveur[35] and Dodart,[36] and also gave me the opportunity to gain his friendship, a very close

and sincere mutual friendship. Since we both were free of the base, foolish jealousy that impels most people in the same profession, we would discuss our discoveries openly with each other, going so far as to promise mutually that whichever of us died first would leave his memoirs to the survivor, which he did not fail to do in his will.[37]

Loulié died first, in 1702, and his papers were assembled with the writings of Brossard. Also among Brossard's writings was a copy of Charpentier's *Rules of Composition*.

Ouvrard, Loulié, Brossard, and Charpentier formed a little circle based on friendship and mutual respect, even if, contrary to what Brossard claimed, rivalry was felt from time to time. They shared a common love of Italian music (at least for three of them, who wrote in the style), and an interest in theoretical matters brought them together. They formed a community of learned and industrious musicians, who worked on the fringes of the court, but whose importance in French musical life was indisputable.

The Hôtel of the constable Olivier de Clisson, which can still be admired at 58, Rue des Archives, had been repurchased in 1553 by François de Lorraine, Duc de Guise and Marie de Lorraine's great-grandfather. The original manor was much larger (it then occupied all the land between Rues du Chaume, des Quatre-Fils, Vieille-du-Temple, and de Paradis), and it was sumptuously decorated. The austere exterior contrasted with the luxury of the apartments, furnishings, superb suites, tapestries, great paintings, magnificently framed family portraits, rich velvet furnishings embroidered in silver and gold, silver utensils with the Guise coat of arms, and jewels including the finest crystal and diamonds.

The Hôtel de Guise, like the Château de Versailles, resounded with music from morning to night: lessons, rehearsals, and concerts "almost every day."[38] There were three chapels. The "high chapel," the most beautiful of the three, where grand ceremonies were held, was decorated with paintings done in 1555 by Nicolò dell'Abbate after designs by Primaticcio. Above the windows was an Italian-like frieze depicting the three magi, one of them displaying the features of François de Lorraine. The most spacious of the chapels was in the "lower gallery"; there the entire household attended early morning mass daily. Mlle de Guise attended a private mass in the little chapel adjacent to her bedchamber. On Sundays and holidays, the "lower gallery" echoed with musical services.[39] Secular concerts took place

in the *Grand Cabinet* or "music room, adjacent to the *Grand Salon*,"
where there were "a double-manual harpsichord and six music
stands." The room also displayed numerous paintings, including "107
miniatures, depicting the story of the gospel, with copperplate
frames"; "another painting on canvas, an original Barocci, representing the Flight of our Savior into Egypt"; "another painting on
wood, an original Leonardo da Vinci, a Virgin with her infant Jesus";
"another painting on canvas, a glorious Annunciation, by Carracci";
and many others. The inventory taken after Mlle de Guise's death
also mentions the existence of incidental items tantalizingly
described:[40]

> three scented fans, five pairs of Spanish gloves, six small scented
> skins, . . . a small wine cabinet covered in morocco, with lock and
> key, holding twelve small bottles, a china cup and a little silver
> funnel, . . . five small book bags of Spanish leather.

The modern conveniences at the Hôtel de Guise were more than
simply utilitarian.

Since Charpentier's music was not written exclusively for the
Hôtel de Guise, Marie de Lorraine was able to recommend her composer to selected friends like M. de Rians.[41] She also could hold an
elaborate religious service on occasions such as the recovery of Louis
XIV from an illness. One such occasion, the solemnities at the Abbaye
de Monmartre on 20 January 1687, are described as follows:

> The joy that the king's return to perfect health caused in our
> hearts was universal. The king's loftiest and lowliest subjects,
> courtiers and citizens, all exhibited a common zeal. People were
> not content with praying and with leading others in prayer;
> everyone wanted to celebrate in accordance with one's birth,
> rank, and fortune, money being no object when it involved the
> health of one so precious to all of France. . . . Perhaps no finer
> example of this attitude was seen than that burst of munificence
> from a princess as full of zeal for His Majesty as she is generous
> and benevolent, namely Mlle de Guise. The high altar of the
> church of the Abbaye Royale de Monmartre, which she had
> chosen for offering solemn thanksgiving to God for the king's
> recovery, was so brilliantly decorated that the eye could hardly
> endure its splendor. . . . Everything was designed by M. Berrin
> [*sic*]. . . . Monsieur being seated in the choir at this ceremony, his
> presence was the reason all persons of distinction who had been
> invited were seated there. On the way out of the church one saw
> the walls, windows, and environs of the convent glowing with an
> infinite number of lights as large as torches. Everyone involved
> in the celebration appreciated the true generosity of the

princess who made it possible. She distributed many alms and earned great applause and great blessings.[42]

Totally captivated by the lavish display and by the extraordinarily radiant personality of Mlle de Guise, the chronicler makes no mention of the music played at the brilliant ceremony. From another source we learn that "the *Te Deum* was performed by excellent musicians," but its composer is not identified.[43] Was it Charpentier, who by that time seems to have written only the *Te Deum à 8 voix avec flûtes et violons* (H. 145), which was performed at the Académie de Peinture several weeks later? Or perhaps it was a work that is now lost. Were other pieces played at the Abbaye de Monmartre? Possibly one of two motets (*Gratiarum actiones pro restituta regis christianissimi sanitate anno 1686*, H. 341, or *Gratitudinis erga Deum Canticum*, H. 431) whose intimate tone would have been appropriate for a convent, no matter how sumptuously decorated it might have been.

While the *Gratiarum actiones* for two sopranos, two flutes, two violins, and continuo uses part of the text written in 1680 for the recovery of the Dauphin, the text of the *Gratitudinis erga Deum*, sung by the sisters Pièche and Frizon, the Dauphin's singers, makes no ostensible reference to the king. For what else could God have been thanked at the beginning of 1687, if not the king's victory over illness?

The *Idylle sur le retour de la santé du roi* (H. 489) was written for Mlle de Guise's singers. It seems to have been commissioned by Mme de Guise for her palace in Orléans, where a magnificent party was held on the evening of 31 January 1687.[44]

These were not the first times that Charpentier's works were performed in the two places just discussed. His very first pieces, *Leçons de ténèbres* (H. 91–93), seem to have been performed in the Abbaye de Monmartre in April 1670 in honor of the wife of Philippe of Orléans.[45] *Autre Jerusalem pour les leçons de ténèbres à 2 voix* (H. 94) might have been composed in 1672 for the same abbey, where Mlle and Mme de Guise had gone to seek solitude after the deaths of Louis-Joseph and Marguerite de Lorraine.[46] On 8 June 1673, the instrumental pieces *Pour un reposoir* (H. 508) could be heard in the palace of Mme de Guise:[47]

> The 8th and last day of the Octave of the Holy Sacrament, Mme de Guise, having offered her prayers in the church of the Barefoot Carmelites in the Faubourg Saint-Germain, went to

receive the procession of Saint Sulpice under her own roof
where she had a magnificent altar prepared, with an excellent
concert of instruments and voices.[48]

Whenever Mlle de Guise left Paris, she took along her musicians, just
like a queen. For her trip to Champagne in October 1680,
Charpentier composed *Canticum in honorem beatae Virginis Mariae
inter homines et angelos* (H. 400).[49]

The works in the last years (1684–1687) scored for the full body
of musicians (see the Chronological Table for those works indicating
the names of performers) offered a variety of genres (divertissements, pastorales, motets, Latin oratorios), yet they display common
characteristics and stand out from the rest of Charpentier's works.
Their structural unity stems from the use of a standard type of
scoring: five or six vocal parts, two treble instruments, usually viols, to
which are sometimes added two flutes, and continuo. This scoring
corresponds neither to Lully's five-part writing (the vocal distribution differs) nor to Charpentier's usual four-part writing. Its unique
instrumental, and especially vocal, color ("choral" is not the right
word, since there are only one or two singers to a part, never more) is
blended into a richly polyphonic texture, the added number of vocal
parts compensating somewhat for the thinness of the instrumental
scoring. Since the singers at the Hôtel de Guise were young, non-
professional men and women, Charpentier wrote music that suited
their youthful voices, music without great technical difficulties,
though demanding a solid technique and expression.

On 3 March 1688 Marie de Lorraine died at the age of seventy-three.
She was buried, according to her wishes, without ceremony in the
convent of the Capuchins in Paris where her mother's remains lay.
Did Charpentier honor his patroness with one last composition?
Apparently not. Mme de Guise died later in Versailles on 17 March
1696. Like her aunt, she had asked to be buried without any
ceremony in the Carmelite church in the Faubourg Saint-Jacques. It
is possible, however, that *Courtes Litanies de la Vierge à 4 voix* (H. 90)
and *Court De profundis à 4 voix* (H. 222) were intended for the
funeral of Élisabeth d'Orléans.

Upon her death, Mlle de Guise left a long will with three codicils,
which reveals the piety and generosity that characterized her life.[50]
Included in the impressive list of legatees are the names of all the

musicians who enlivened the entertainments and glorified the religious services of the House, with the exception of Joly and Charpentier.[51] How can this incredible oversight be explained?

Like Joly, Charpentier seems to have left the household in 1687 before the death of Mlle de Guise. He must have received the expected bonus at that time.[52] In 1687 Marie de Lorraine knew she was gravely ill and probably insisted, as she had already done before, on recommending Charpentier to her influential acquaintances, namely, the Jesuits, who since the end of the sixteenth century had maintained close ties with the Guises. The last descendant of her House, she did not forget that Society in her will; to them she bequeathed

> the sum of ten thousand livres, to be used according to the wishes of the Reverend Père de La Chaise, to whom she leaves paintings, china, and other possessions in the little *appartement des Hermites*, . . . asking to be remembered in his prayers.[53]

To insure the continuance of her composer's career, the pious princess established Charpentier among the Jesuits. Such was the generous benevolence of Mlle de Guise toward those who faithfully served her. That is why we cannot be surprised at the absence of Charpentier's name in her will: she could give nothing after her death that she had not already given him in her lifetime.

Chapter 5

Charpentier and the Court

When he arrived at Saint-Cloud, [the king] gave a leave of absence to all his musicians and wanted to hear those of Monseigneur le Dauphin until he returned to Saint-Germain. Every day at mass they performed motets by M. Charpentier, and His Majesty wished to hear no others, although that had been proposed to him.
Mercure Galant, April 1681

Never having known the honor of an official post, and frustrated in his theatrical ambitions, Charpentier seems to have been completely ignored by the great chroniclers of his day. Indeed, the composer did not exist as far as Mme de Sévigné was concerned, even though she devotedly attended the Jesuit sermons on Rue Saint-Antoine, or as far as Princess Palatine was concerned, although her son Philippe, Duc de Chartres, would study composition with the composer of *Médée.* For this reason Charpentier remains a musician who lived in the shadows, away from the splendors of the French court. This situation, difficult to comprehend in view of his stature as a composer, is often interpreted as simply the result of bad luck caused primarily by the ambitious Lully. Their famous rivalry, the results of which have been discussed in the chapter on the composer's collaboration with Molière and the French theater, still cannot account for all our questions about Charpentier's life and career.

Certainly, Lully found himself in absolute control at court for more than twenty-five years, though mainly in the area of secular music—religious music apparently being of much less interest to him.

112

Lully could have assumed, as Michel-Richard Delalande did later, the duties of director of the chapelle along with those of composer and Surintendant of music for the King's Chamber, but he did not. Consequently, Charpentier's desire to become one of the assistant directors of the Chapelle Royale in 1683 would not have worried him. Unfortunate circumstances, however, prevented the composer from realizing his goal.

Even though Lully had a strong influence over Louis XIV, he could not prevent the king from hearing, appreciating, and showing interest in Charpentier's music. In spite of the interdictions imposed on *Le Malade imaginaire* by the Surintendant, Louis XIV attended at least two performances of the comédie-ballet in 1674 and 1686. We also know that other pieces by Charpentier were performed at Versailles. Furthermore, in 1679 the king commissioned Charpentier to provide music for his son, the Grand Dauphin. It is also quite significant that the monarch at that time appointed an Italian, Paolo Lorenzani, as the queen's music master. By that double gesture, Louis XIV seems to have been little concerned with Lully's wish to root out all ultramontane influence from the court.

On more than one occasion Charpentier's music was connected with great events of the royal family, such as the death of Marie-Thérèse in 1683 and the recovery of Louis XIV in 1687. In spite of the sovereign's apparent favorable attitude toward the composer and the latter's important contributions to royal ceremonies, Charpentier never bore the mark of an official court musician and was never truly integrated into that illustrious society. Was it his connections with the House of Guise that make him suspect in the eyes of Louis XIV, whose confidence had its limits, the same limits seen in his political dealings?

In 1687 Lully passed away, followed one year later by Mlle de Guise. Suddenly the obstacles to Charpentier's future aspirations were gone. Nothing prevented him from following in the footsteps of Lully, or the king from exercising his benevolence by welcoming him at court. Everything seemed possible, and yet nothing, or almost nothing, changed. Charpentier waited until he was fifty before presenting *Médée*, his first and last *tragédie en musique*, at the Académie Royale. The work's semi-failure hardly encouraged the composer to renew the experiment. Why did Louis XIV not then grant him the position of assistant director of the Chapelle, which Delalande grabbed for himself even though he had already held that post for ten years? Why did the king not grant Charpentier one of the other positions that the same Delalande monopolized over the years: Surintendant in 1689, composer of music for the King's Chamber in 1690 (both left vacant by the death of Lully's son), or concertmaster of the King's Chamber in 1695? It is difficult to explain this. Yet even a composer as capable as Henry Desmarest, raised at the court and under the patronage of the Dauphine, hardly fared any better than Charpentier.

In the 1690s, Mlle de Guise's composer once again became associated with the royal family by teaching composition to the Duc de Chartres, the king's nephew. At various times in his career, then, Charpentier found himself with court connections. He had occasion to orbit around the Sun, but never to bask fully in its rays. Looking back on his life, Charpentier could only write, "Music accorded me little honor."

THE DAUPHIN'S MUSICIAN

In 1679, eighteen-year-old Louis de France finished his studies under the strict tutelage of Bishop Bossuet. As the only surviving child of Louis XIV and Queen Marie-Thérèse, the Dauphin was next in line to wear the French crown. Therefore, the king's primary concern with regard to his son was to give him the kind of education he himself had lacked. The Dauphin was first put under the care of Mme de Montausier, then the Maréchale de La Mothe, Louis XIV's former governess. At the age of seven, M. de Montausier was given charge of the Dauphin's instruction, chosen by the king for his great culture, integrity, and firmness. In 1670 Bossuet became the young prince's tutor. For ten years it was his duty

> to instruct the Dauphin in religion and the responsibilities it required, to teach him the principles of Latin by degrees as he matured, to read and discuss the great authors with him, to teach him ancient and modern history, and to acquaint him early in life with the kind of reasoning suited for a prince who must be prepared to put it into practice one day.[1]

Every day without exception, others taught the Dauphin mathematics, ancient and modern geography, the principles of geometry, and civil and military architecture. It was a strict, austere education based on the notion of duty. The Dauphin went along with this apprenticeship, though without any enthusiasm or genuine curiosity. At the end of his tutelage, Bossuet summed up the prince's education thus: "In the end, by dint of repetition, we made those three words—piety, goodness, justice—and all they implied, stick in his mind."[2]

When the Dauphin reached adulthood, it was clear that the efforts of his teachers had been totally ineffectual, and had even produced the opposite of what was intended. The prince grew more and more introverted and manifested a strong aversion for all that his tutors had tried to teach him. Almost nothing was able to cure his apathy—except for the hunt, in which he engaged almost daily, and sometimes music, particularly opera.

At the end of the 1670s, Charpentier was commissioned to compose music for Monseigneur's religious services: "As that prince had a private mass every day, [Charpentier's] duties prevented him from attending the King's [mass]. The remuneration that he received reflected one's satisfaction with him."[3]

The following year the Dauphin married Marie-Anne-Christine of Bavaria, daughter of the elector Ferdinand-Marie. The marriage was carried out by proxy on 28 January 1680 in Munich, and the real ceremony took place on 7 March at Châlons in Champagne, in the presence of the entire court.

As soon as she arrived in France, the Dauphine won over the court with her personality and wit. She combined great sensitivity and virtue with a highly discriminating taste for the arts, in particular theater and music. She knew how to draw and play the harpsichord. As she possessed a fine voice, the celebrated Michel Lambert gave her singing lessons. Guillaume Raynal, the Dauphin's dancing master, instructed her in his art, for which she demonstrated exceptional talent. One evening in January 1681 the following incident occurred:

> Madame the Princesse de Conti being ill and unable to dance her *entrées,* the king said two hours before the ballet that Madame la Dauphine should dance one of the *entrées.* He did not intend that she do it that same day. However, within an hour the Princess learned a grand *entrée* with many steps and containing more than twelve *reprises.* Thus the entire court was quite surprised to see her do in less than two hours that which a less intelligent person could not have learned in two weeks.[4]

The Dauphine quickly acquired great power. The king named her Surintendante Générale of the French and Italian theatrical companies. In 1685 she initiated a new system of allocating shares among members. She distributed roles, often swayed by personal influences, to such an extent that the careers of great actors like Baron, Raisin, and Dauvilliers were destroyed. The Dauphine does not seem to have gone against Lully's theatrical despotism, since that was the year Charpentier wrote *Vénus et Adonis*, his last score for the Hôtel Guénégaud.

We know nothing about the noble couple's relationship with Charpentier. Were his services and his compositions appreciated? Was the Dauphine happy to find such a musician at her disposal upon her arrival in France? Able to speak perfect Italian and having brought her Piedmont chambermaid Mlle Besola from Munich, could she have wished for a better composer than Charpentier, whose musical sensibilities transported her back to her homeland? Like Vienna, Munich was one of the principal centers of ultramontane art. Most of the musicians at the Bavarian court were Italians, or Germans instructed in the Italian school, following the example of Giovanni Gabrieli who lived in Munich between 1575 and 1579 or Orlando de Lasso who in 1556 settled in the Bavarian metropolis for many years after having sojourned in Italy.

For the Munich court, or at least for its elector (it is not known where the work was performed), Charpentier composed a grand Italian cantata, *Epithalamio In lode dell'Altezza Serenissima Elettorale di Massimiliano Emanuel Duca di Baviera concento a cinque voci con stromenti* (H. 473). The word *epithalamio*, although added to the manuscript after the work was composed, indicates the piece was probably written for the 1685 marriage of the Dauphine's brother, Maximilian-Emmanuel II, to Maria-Antonia, daughter of Emperor Leopold I. The groom, who succeeded his father in 1679, had a deep love of French and Italian music. In the closing years of the century he had several of Lully's operas produced at the court of Brussels.

Charpentier's cantata boasts a sumptuous instrumentation: trumpets, timpani, violins, oboes, flutes, "violone," bassoon, and harpsichord. The text is a hymn of praise to the Bavarian elector, measuring his greatness against his father and predecessor:

> *Oh del Bavaro soglio inclito herede*
> *e non minor del padre, maggior di tutti.*

> O illustrious heir of the Bavarian throne,
> No less important than the father, greatest of all.

Could this also be interpreted as a discreet allusion to the Dauphin and Louis XIV?

In October 1681, the Dauphin accompanied his father to Alsace and then on to Flanders, where he took charge of the king's army to lend support to the army commanded by the Maréchal de Créqui in the siege of Luxembourg. That military experience gave the Dauphin a taste for war. A few years later he revealed a natural inclination and great courage for war in the siege of Phillipsbourg. On his return, he passed the time at tournaments and carousels that attracted large crowds to Versailles and won him a certain amount of popularity with the people.

Though filled with respect for his father, the Dauphin did not possess his father's strong personality. Not allowed to attend all the king's council meetings until after 1691, it seems he was kept away from affairs of state and judged to have little aptitude for dealing with them. It is difficult to imagine what sort of a ruler he might have become. He died prematurely four years before the end of the reign of Louis XIV.

Charpentier seems to have worked regularly for the Dauphin in 1679 and 1682–1683. Louis XIV had several opportunities to hear his son's music ensemble and to appreciate it greatly:

> When he arrived at Saint-Cloud, [the king] gave a leave of absence to all his musicians and wanted to hear those of Monseigneur le Dauphin until he returned to Saint-Germain. Every day at mass they performed motets by M. Charpentier, and His Majesty wished to hear no others, although that had been proposed to him. They have been performing them for Monseigneur le Dauphin for the past two years.[5]

The *Mercure Galant* gives us other precious information about these musical performances, mainly concerning the musicians who participated in them:

> On Thursday, the first day of the new year, Monseigneur le Dauphin was appointed Chevalier du Saint-Esprit, with the usual ceremony.... The Prince went to the chapel of the Château of Saint-Germain and received communion from Cardinal de Bouillon. ... His musicians were heard during the mass, which was composed by M. Charpentier, whom I have so often mentioned. Mesdemoiselles Piesche displayed their beautiful voices as usual. After finishing his devotions, Monseigneur le Dauphin returned to his apartment and donned the novitiate's habit.[6]

A few months later, one could read:

> The king having given leave of absence to all his musicians, used the musicians of Monseigneur the Dauphin exclusively during the mass at which Sieur Frison [*sic*] sang every day. The accompaniment was by Sieurs Converset and Martinot, with Sieur Garnier at the organ. It is said that [the vocal ensemble] is made up of the Piesche family, because five singers are from that family, namely, two girls and three boys. During their Majesties' sojourn at Saint-Cloud, nothing was sung in the chapel that was not composed by M. Charpentier. He is so well-known, and I have referred to him so often, that I shall say no more about him today.[7]

Unlike the king, of course, and unlike the queen and the Dauphine, the Dauphin did not have his own "household": only about ten lackeys and chamber boys were exclusively assigned to him, as well as a few of the king's officers who served him on a temporary basis. Hence monseigneur had no personal musicians, at least officially, like the queen who maintained no less than ten vocalists (two of them children), seven instrumentalists, and the composer Paolo Lorenzani.

The musicians who played Charpentier's compositions belonged to the king, who "lent" them to his son whenever they were needed. As for the composer, he was then living at the Hôtel de Guise, and his duties under the Dauphin were probably the result of a recommendation by Mme de Guise, the king's cousin, who would have wanted to acquaint the court with her musician.

Charpentier's manuscripts include only two pieces expressly intended for the Dauphin: *Precatio pro filio regis* (H. 166), dated 1677, and *Gratiarum actiones ex sacris codicibus excerptae pro restituta serenissimi Galliarum Delphini salute* (H. 326), an act of thanksgiving for the prince's recovery from a grave fever contracted in the last months of 1680. Two works do not constitute a very large repertoire, especially since the first one was written two years before the start of Charpentier's regular duties under Monseigneur.

On the other hand, the *Mercure Galant* (see above) identifies the interpreters, whom we find mentioned in various places in the manuscripts.

The Piesche (Pièche) family served in the king's music for almost a century, from 1661 to 1733.[8] The father, Pierre I, was a musician in the Écurie (oboe and *musette du Poitou*), a flutist of the King's Chamber, and keeper of the Chamber's instruments from 1662 to

1689. His four sons and two daughters were also court musicians. Antoine (Pierre Antoine who died in 1704) was, like his father, a musician in the Écurie (oboe and *musette du Poitou*). Pierre II played flute in the king's cabinet from 1689 to 1723 and was keeper of the Chamber's instruments from 1689 to 1719. In 1690 he married Geneviève Brion (d. 1721), a singer for Mlle de Guise, and later for the king. Joseph was a musician in the Écurie and a flutist of the King's Chamber in 1716. Alexandre (Pierre Alexandre) was a flutist and a musette player of the King's Chamber from 1693 to 1728. Magdeleine and Marguerite Pièche were both musicians of the King's Chamber. In 1693, Magdeleine married Claude Trioche, valet of the Dauphine and the king, and later married Sébastien Huguenet, violinist with the King's Chamber and a member of the Chapelle Royale. Marguerite became the wife of Jacques Antoine de Brienne, who played flute, oboe, and the *musette du Poitou* in the Écurie.

The Pièche dynasty extended to the grandchildren: Pierre III, son of Pierre II, was keeper of the Chamber's instruments from 1719 to 1720 and flutist in the king's cabinet beginning in 1723; Jean-Joseph, son of Joseph, played flute and flageolet with the King's Chamber starting in 1716; and Marie, daughter of Pierre II and Geneviève Brion, was *demoiselle* of the king's music.

The name Pièche is found in four of Charpentier's manuscripts: *Prélude pour le Super flumina des demoiselles Pièches* (H. 170); *Seconde leçon du vendredi saint* ("The Recordare for 2 *dessus* and ritornello is in Book 2 of the demoiselles Piesches") (H. 106); "Quemadmodum desiderat cervus" (H. 174) ("Piesches" is written in the margin of folio 3); and on the introductory page of a collection of autographs containing six little motets: *Panis quem ego dabo* (H. 275); *Sola vivebat in antris* (H. 373); *Flores, flores, o Gallia* (H. 374); *Adoramus te Christe* (H. 276); *Cantemus Domino* (H. 277), and *Domine salvum fac regem* (H. 304). Both sisters are also mentioned by their abbreviated first names—"Mlle Magd . . ." (*haut-dessus*) and "Mlle Marg . . ." (*dessus*)—in four scores:[9] *Gratiarum actiones* (H. 326); *Gratitudinis erga Deum Canticum* (H. 431); *Psalmus David 12us* (H. 196); and *Psalmus David 34us* (H. 201).

According to the *Mercure Galant*, three boys in the Pièche family played in the Dauphin's music. In addition to thoroughbass, works that were apparently intended for the young prince include two treble instrument parts generally assigned to flutes. We also sometimes find a bass flute part, independent of the continuo. In two pieces Charpentier noted the first names of the instrumentalists. In a

motet, *Panis quem ego dabo* (H. 275), in which the flutists were MM.
Antoine and Joseph, the name "Pièche" inscribed on the preceding
folio confirms the identity of the two musicians. The first names
"Anth . . ." (Anthoine) and "Pierot" (Pierre) are also found in the
opera *La Descente d'Orphée aux enfers* (H. 488) for the singers of the
Hôtel de Guise. Without question, the Pièche brothers had been
invited to enrich Marie de Lorraine's orchestra.

"Sieur Frison [*sic*]" mentioned in the *Mercure Galant* appears in
certain of Charpentier's manuscripts, in connection with the two
Pièche sisters (H. 196, 201, 326, 431). Antoine Frizon sang bass and
participated in the queen's music, and later in the king's, as singer of
the Chapelle Royale and the Chamber from 1679 to 1697, the year of
his death. In 1673 he took part in the performances of *Le Malade
imaginaire* and in 1681 sang with Marguerite and Magdeleine Pièche
in Lully's *Le Triomphe de l'Amour*. Was he the same Frizon mentioned in the registers of the Sainte Chapelle, where "on 8 May 1672,
Frizon, cleric of the diocese of Avignon, is appointed *taille basse*
cleric"?[10]

The names of the continuo players ("Sieurs Converset and
Martinot, and Sieur Garnier at the organ") are not on the manu-
scripts, with the exception of Converset ("M. Convercet"); though
they are included in a heavily scored work, *Psalmus David 5tus post
septuagesimum* (H. 206) with no connection to the Dauphin's music.
Were both references to Jean Converset, officer of the music of the
Monsieur, the king's brother? Converset's son Noël, born on 25
December 1674, became a member of the Twenty-four Violins of the
King's Chamber in 1709 as bass violinist. Robert Martinot, son of
Edme Martinot, one member of the king's Twenty-four Violins, was a
lackey in the King's Cabinet and in 1717 was symphonist of the
King's Chamber. Finally, "Sieur Garnier" was quite probably Gabriel
Garnier, organist for Monsieur and later for the Chapelle, where he
succeeded Nicolas Lebègue for the "October quarter" of 1702,
remaining until 1718.

Another fact that makes it possible to identify certain pieces composed for the Dauphin's musicians is the scoring for bass flute, an
instrument rarely encountered in works of this type in that period.
Charpentier used it six times: in H. 326 and H. 196, already mentioned, as well as in *Supplicatio pro defunctis ad beatam Virginem* (H.
328) dating from 1681–1682; in a motet for the Holy Sacrament *Pour
un reposoir* (H. 523) of 1683 (the usual flute scoring is here exceptionally enriched by four-part strings); in the "Prélude pour l'été à 3

flûtes" for the *Quatuor anni tempestates* (H. 336a) written in 1685; and finally in *Les Plaisirs de Versailles* (H. 480).

Charpentier seems to have composed for the Dauphin until the late 1680s, though less and less frequently from 1683 on. The majority of the works are scored alike: vocal *haut-dessus, dessus,* and bass; two flutes sometimes with bass flute, and continuo. Two pieces mention an additional bass part entrusted to M. Bastaron. His name is indicated in H. 201, and it is very likely that he sang in H. 196. Jacques Bastaron was a court musician like his colleagues; he sang with the King's Chamber from 1703 to 1719 and with the Chapelle from 1692 to 1726, the year of his death.

Charpentier's pieces for the son of Louis XIV were meant to be performed during mass, though they are motets. In fact, the Dauphin's mass mirrored that of the Chapelle Royale, whose musical part consisted of motets played at specified points during the service. Their number varied between one and three, the second being an elevation motet and the third a *Domine salvum.*

Les Plaisirs de Versailles (H. 480) is the only scored secular work—it was usual to score music for the Dauphin. It has an additional part for *haute-contre* which it seems Charpentier, at least in the beginning, had not planned on.[11] The part was probably taken by the composer, who sang in that register.

The work was written in late 1682, the year the court officially moved to Versailles. That autumn the "Apartment Days"—Mondays, Wednesdays, and Thursdays—began, when the king invited his courtiers to a great variety of entertainments, including refreshments, gaming tables, music, and dancing. Each one of the rooms making up the Grand Apartments was reserved for one specific activity: the Diana drawing room was for billiards, the Mercury drawing room was reserved for the royal family's card games or games of chance, while the Mars drawing room accommodated other players. The Venus drawing room was where refreshments were served, including fruits, oranges, lemons, pastries, and confections. In the Abundance drawing room three buffets were set up: the middle one for hot beverages (coffee, chocolate), the other two offering liqueurs, fruit juice, sorbets, and wines. The Apollo drawing room was used for music and dancing.

> All those who have the good fortune to enter these magnificent dwellings are drawn to pleasures which, after they enter, have an even greater effect on them. Some choose one game, and others stop at another. . . . There is total freedom of speech, and people

engage in conversation with whomever they like. . . . Imagine pleasures enjoyed for four hours in surroundings reserved by such a great ruler for the courtiers' entertainment. What is more, if true pleasure consists of variety, since an overindulged pleasure becomes less enjoyable, one can change them as often as desired. When one tires of one game, one plays another. One goes to listen to music or to watch people dance. One engages in conversation; one goes to the liqueur or the refreshment room. . . . It can be said that almost all the senses find delight there, and that the spirit being quite enchanted, one can only watch, admire, and be silent; that the golden age is well represented in these apartments; and that they give a perfect idea of the realm of joy.[12]

Were the *Plaisirs de Versailles*, evoking all the entertainments of the apartments, actually played at Versailles?[13] At the end of his manuscript, Charpentier notes: "This is supposed to last an hour and a half." The time indication cannot apply to the piece itself, which is much shorter. Does it refer instead to the insertion of the work into a larger context of various festivities, like those in the apartments of Versailles?

THE CHAPELLE ROYALE COMPETITION

Under Louis XIV, music at the French court was controlled by large, rigidly structured institutions to which all musicians, whether singer, instrumentalist, or composer, dreamed of belonging. A court appointment in those days represented the ideal position, the greatest accomplishment of one's career, the highest goal one could achieve. The king's music was divided into three main departments: the Chapelle Royale for religious music, the King's Chamber for all secular genres (headed by the Surintendant), and the Écurie for outdoor ceremonial music.

The chief director of the Chapelle Royale was an ecclesiastic, a court bishop. The responsibility for the music was given to assistant directors whose duties included choosing the vocal music for the services, conducting, selecting and providing moral, religious, and musical instruction for the choirboys, and composing pieces required for ceremonies.

From 1663, Henri Du Mont and Pierre Robert shared assistant duties in the Chapelle Royale. By the time they had reached the age of a well-deserved retirement in 1683, a recruiting competition was organized for the month of April:

> The choir director positions in the Chapelle of the king being vacant, His Majesty has resolved to create four of them instead of two. He has informed all the bishops in the kingdom of this so that they may alert the choirmasters of their cathedrals to go to Versailles, to perform one of their motets there, if they feel they are talented enough to compete for the position through the beauty and strength of their music. His Majesty in any case will pay the cost of their trip if they are not accepted. In this way, the king displays his justice and generosity. Here are the names of all the musicians who have applied, listed in the order that they performed. MM. Mignon, Oudot, Dache, Lalande, Minoret, Daniëlis, Colasse, Grabus, Le Sueur, Charpentier, Lalouette, Menaut, Malet, Rebel, Salomon, Goupillet, Sevry, Jouvain, Girard, Poirier, Gervais, Desmares, Fernon, Fossart, Bouttelier, Tabaret, La Garde, Burat, Loisele, Renault, Champenois, Lorenzani, Prevost, La Grillière, Nivers.[14]

The length of the list proves how coveted the post was by Parisian, provincial, and foreign musicians alike. Very few names, however, are familiar today, and many others have been totally forgotten, such as that of poor Jacques Le Sueur from Rouen, whose audition was ridiculed by all the courtiers.[15]

After the auditions, only sixteen candidates were retained. To verify that the motet they had performed was really of their own composition,

> the applicants were lodged in a house, where for five or six days they were boarded at the king's expense, and where they spoke to no one, and each worked to the best of his ability on a psalm chosen for the competition, which was Psalm 31, *Beati quorum remissae sunt.*[16]

It was while in this "isolation booth" (as it might be called today) that Charpentier fell seriously ill and became unable to finish composing the motet. The gilded universe of the court, never before within such close reach, had opened its doors only to shut them again, even before the musician could realize the hope of crossing its threshold. The future proved even more unjust since no comparable opportunity ever developed again for Marc-Antoine. While his illness is not to be doubted, the question arises: What would have happened if Charpentier had had the opportunity to complete the competition?

Personal influence was indeed a determining factor in the final selection of four assistant choirmasters: Nicolas Goupillet, music master of the church of Meaux; Pascal Colasse, Lully's pupil and secretary; Guillaume Minoret, music master of Saint-Germain-l'Auxerrois; and Michel Richard Delalande, then organist of Saint-Jean-en-Grève. A half-century later, Claude Tannevot, Delalande's biographer, revealed that the

> Abbé Robert, who was retiring as music director of the Chapelle of the king, strongly recommended that [the king] choose M. Goupillet. The Archbishop of Reims also requested that His Majesty accept M. Minoret. Lully, who was sponsoring M. Colasse, obtained a post for him, too. All these patrons greatly extolled the merits of the three new directors, but as they were about to propose a fourth name, the king told them, "I have appointed, sirs, those whom you have presented to me. It is fitting that I select a candidate of my choice, so I pick La Lande [*sic*] for the January quarter.[17]

The mediocre Goupillet was also backed by "Mme la Dauphine, at the solicitation of M. Bossuet."[18] Later it was learned that the motets performed by Goupillet at the Chapelle Royale were, in fact, by Desmarest. The latter revealed the scandal in 1693, and Goupillet had to resign his post. Colasse remained with the Chapelle until 1708, Minoret until 1714, but it was obviously Delalande, who gradually picked up all the appointments as his colleagues departed one by one, who left the greatest stamp on the religious music of the Chapelle Royale.

In June 1683, just after the competition trials were over, "the king granted a pension to M. Charpentier," perhaps in consolation for his indisposition, but more likely in recognition of his service under the Dauphin.[19]

THE QUEEN'S FUNERAL

On 31 July 1683 Marie-Thérèse of Austria, infanta of Spain and queen of France since 1660, died at Versailles. She was interred at the Saint-Denis Basilique on 1 September with the greatest pomp and ceremony. Bossuet delivered the funeral oration and Lully's *Dies irae* and *De profundis* were performed. From August to December, funeral services were held all over France and abroad.

Charpentier, having recovered from his illness, contributed three deeply moving works for these ceremonies, among the most inspired pieces he ever composed. Was he making a special point of proving his worth after having lost the competition?

> The Carmelites in the Rue du Bouloir having held a solemn service for [the late queen] on the 20th of [December], a pontifical-style mass was celebrated by the Bishop of Auxerre and the funeral oration delivered by the Abbé des Alleurs, the chaplain of Madame la Dauphine. He measured up to everyone's expectations, and matched every glorious act of the king with an act of piety of the queen. A large number of prelates and high-ranking personages made up the assembly, and the nuns of the convent overlooked nothing in the ceremony, doubly sad for them, which would express their grief and their due respect. The music, which was deeply moving, was composed by M. Charpentier.[20]

Luctus de morte augustissimae Mariae Theresiae reginae Galliae (H. 331), a little motet for three voices (*haute-contre, taille,* and bass), two treble instruments, and continuo, might be that "deeply moving" music heard in the Carmelite convent, which the queen often visited (which is why the ceremony was "doubly sad"). Nonetheless, its chronological placement in the manuscripts suggests that it was composed in the month of August, and not December. Moreover, the use of male voices would have been inappropriate for a convent of nuns. Hence the piece performed in the Carmelite setting might today be lost.[21]

The other two works, the oratorio *In obitum augustissimae nec non piissimae Gallorum reginae, Lamentum* (H. 409) and the psalm *De profundis* (H. 189), both larger-scaled and destined for performance at the same service, would have been out of place in a convent. Where were they played? What location (certainly a prestigious one) could have accommodated their sumptuous beauties? They are not mentioned in any of the contemporary gazettes.

Both pieces call for large-scale vocal and instrumental scoring, seldom found in Charpentier's other grand sacred works: to the six-part (occasionally seven-part) vocal ensemble are added recorders (*flûtes à bec*), transverse flutes, five-part strings, and continuo. The five-part instrumental scoring suggests that *In obitum* and *De profundis* might well have been written for the musicians of the Chapelle Royale, if it were not for Lully, that is. Perhaps it was for the Jesuits. The dramatic and indeed theatrical tone of the Latin oratorio, in the same vein as funeral services that took place in the Collèges, gives credence to this theory.

A few words about the funeral ceremony are in order, the

splendors of which (meaning both the extravagance and the excess) are barely imaginable today. The official ceremony surrounding the death of great personages of the kingdom during the second half of the seventeenth century indeed was like the religious side of the *fête*, like the sacred counterpart of an operatic scene, like the apotheosis of all that theater implies, in a setting where it might be deemed inappropriate. Death, about which Bossuet wrote: "we wretched mortals refuse to acknowledge this sad spectacle, as [we refuse] the certainty of our errors," was nevertheless presented to everyone just like a theatrical production.[22] Fascination was mixed with horror in absolutely incredible liturgical displays; theater, the baroque world of illusion, reigned supreme. All the arts were present, adding their splendors: scenery, entrusted to the finest artists of the day (Berain, Le Brun); elocution, a veritable sacred dramaturgy featuring the talents of the Jesuit Bourdaloue and the funeral orations of Bossuet; and finally, music. Everything combined to honor the world's great personages, to denounce the vanity of earthly existence and to sing the praise of eternal life.

Reporters never tired of writing detailed descriptions of the decorations for funeral ceremonies. Thus we learn that in Notre-Dame, for the death of the queen, the catafalque was in the form of an urn decorated with bas-reliefs and supported by allegorical figures in white marble. Atop the urn was a pedestal; on each side of the pedestal, bronze heads of the dead were crowned with cypress branches and ornamented with bat wings, from which extended candelabra with large candlesticks. Torchères burning incense were placed at the four corners of the urn. This design, created by Jean Berain, the court artist remembered for his scenery for *Médée*, was criticized by Père Ménestrier for its lack of imagination. The latter had suggested building a stake piled high with all the silver of Versailles, to impress the spectators with the contrast between the accumulation of riches and the pointlessness of those riches in the face of death.

Yet—is it any surprise?—it was in the Jesuit church that the funeral of Marie-Thérèse inspired veritable dramas in which it is no longer just the observance of death that is staged, but death itself, generating its own dramatic structure. There was no longer any distinction discernible between the standard elements of tragedy and macabre impropriety, between reality and its representation, in short, between life and death, closely joined in a single illusion. At the Collège Louis-le-Grand on 16 August, normally a time when a tragedy was performed during the distribution of the diplomas, this is what was seen:

Instead of the magnificent stage that is constructed every year on one of the four sides of the courtyard, the church was chosen as a more appropriate location for a funeral ceremony. It is all draped in black, and at the entrance a large painting showing the Scepter of France and the Hand of Justice crossed with bones, the royal mantle covered with a shroud and crowned skulls, introduces this mournful ceremony with this inscription.

Enter and see with tears, what tragedy Death performs for us this year.

A stage built on the same spot where the [stage] of the enigmas stands each year reveals a great marble tomb, alongside which Poetry, Music, Tragedy, and Elocution weep and put down their instruments. Atop the lid of the sarcophagus is a crowned skull and two crossbones on which are written these words:

MARIA THERESIA
REGINA CHRISTIANISSIMA

And on the skull

II.
KAL. AUG.
OBIIT
1683.

And on the broken instruments of Poetry, Music, Tragedy, and Elocution, the words *JACET, JACET* are written as the echo of these fine arts amid the public mourning.

Above the tomb appears a great rainbow, seen by everyone during the funeral procession from Versailles to Saint Denis, for as the sun rose from the direction of Saint Denis, it caused a great rainbow toward the Bois de Boulogne, whence the procession emerged. The queen's soul is raised on the rainbow, symbol of the peace she finds in heaven, after having given [peace] on earth through her happy marriage to the king.

Above that, Justice and Peace place the crown of glory on the queen's soul.

Since this exhibit occurs at the time diplomas are handed out, they have depicted at three sides of the church the awards that divine justice distributes in heaven for the virtues of the queen. This is explained by the inscription placed in the back of the church.

Oh the uncertainty of human existence! When we were preparing the entertainment for the distribution of awards funded by His Majesty, divine justice had other awards to give for the virtues of the queen in heaven.

One of the professors of rhetoric will deliver a funeral oration in Latin, after which awards will be distributed in a solemn manner.[23]

The Jesuits in Rouen were also active in the theatrical observation of death. Instead of performing the usual tragedy on 13 September, the students performed another play on the death of Marie-Thérèse:

The play was divided into three parts. In the first, a few actors appeared on the regular stage, as if to begin the tragedy and the ballet, but they were prevented by the Spirit of France, who informed them of the death of the queen, and by Thémis, who commanded them to change the play that they had prepared into mournful spectacles and to join in the general grief of France. The scene changed immediately, and suddenly appeared at the beginning of the second part a second stage in mourning, on which had been built a large marble tomb. On the tomb was an urn, guarded by four weeping Cupids. Each one symbolized something different. One was extinguishing his candle with his tears; another, overcome with grief, was stabbing his heart with one of his arrows; the third was burning incense; and the fourth was throwing flowers on the tomb. Religion and Piety were at the base [of the tomb] with their symbols. Above the urn was Death, and above Death appeared Fame. She held a picture of the queen triumphing over Death, and rising toward heaven.... This unexpected spectacle at first surprised the audience, but they were even more surprised when the marble statues on the tomb, which had seemed to lack nothing but voices, began to speak after receiving Thémis' command. Each statue mourned the queen.... Their solemn verses were followed by a musical concert by Apollo and the muses.... Echoes inside the tomb answered the music. The third part was a kind of apotheosis. First the Cupids, then Apollo and the Muses, the Spirit of France, and Thémis celebrated with poetry and song the triumph of the queen in heaven.[24]

Reading the accounts of these amazing Jesuit funeral services with Charpentier's *In obitum* in mind, one cannot help but be struck, in each instance, by the similarities of the dramatic representation of death. Charpentier's work, while minus the excesses of the [Jesuit] spectacle, proceeds from the same spirit. His grandiose sacred drama also contains characters who act out the death of Marie-Thérèse: the messenger announcing the sad news to a devastated populace, the angel calling for rejoicing, and the allegorical figures of Faith, Hope, and Charity. Filled with striking contrasts, *In obitum* is just as much oratorical rhetoric as it is music. By comparison, the *De profundis* seems like a meditation on the cruel events that the sacred drama has been reenacting with no lack of assistance.

THE KING'S RECOVERY

Present at the time of the great funeral ceremonies at court, Charpentier was also present a few years later for the celebrations on the king's return to health.

Throughout 1686, Louis XIV suffered from an anal fistula for which he bravely underwent a "great operation" on 18 November, but he did not completely recover until Christmas. During the first months of the following year, rejoicing echoed throughout France.

The *Mercure Galant* was not exaggerating when it declared: "I could fill a whole volume [if I were to mention] all the *Te Deum*s that have been sung to give thanks for the king's return to health. Therefore I will mention only a few."[25] We shall do the same here by mentioning only compositions by Ludet, officer in ordinary of the king's music at the Barefoot Augustinians; by Lorenzani at the church of the Reformed Jacobins in the Rue Saint-Honoré; by Moreau, Nivers, and Desmarest at the church of the Fathers of the Oratory; by Chaperon at the Sainte-Chapelle; and by Oudot at the Église Saint-Hyppolite.

On 8 January everyone crowded into the church of the Feuillants in the Rue Saint-Honoré to hear Lully's *Te Deum* executed by 150 performers. The piece had been composed ten years before for the baptism of the eldest son of the Surintendant, Louis, whose illustrious godfather was none other than the king. On that day in January 1687, Lully directed his work while vigorously beating time with his stick, as was his custom. He injured his foot with a blow of the stick. The rest is well known; gangrene set in his leg, the infection spread through the rest of his body, and on 22 March he died. By the cruellest irony of fate, Lully encountered the ultimate obstacle to his desire for power while celebrating the return to health of his ruler, friend, and patron.

Exactly one month after the performance of Lully's *Te Deum*, on Saturday, 8 February,

> the Academy of Painting and Sculpture gave thanks to God for the restoration of the king's health in the church of the Priests of the Oratory in the Rue Saint-Honoré with great splendor. The church was decorated with rich tapestries, nine large paintings and twenty-four reliefs, and many candles.... The ceremony began with vespers after which a tribute to the king was

> delivered eloquently by Father Soanen, a priest of the Oratoire.
> Then they sang the *Te Deum* and the *Exaudiat* for double chorus
> with music composed by the Sieur Charpentier.[26]

The *Gazette de France* was probably referring to the *Te Deum à 8 voix
avec flûtes et violons* (H. 145) and to the *Exaudiat à 8 voix, flûtes et
violons* (H. 162), composed and performed for the first time in 1672,
revived in 1679 (with additional preludes) and again in February
1687. Apparently the two works were always performed together.

Charpentier's participation in the rejoicing was not limited to the
Academy of Painting and Sculpture's commission, since Mlle and
Mme de Guise also called on their musician to honor the ruler (see
Chapter 4).

Exactly two days after the performance of the *Te Deum* and *Exaudiat*
at the church of the Priests of the Oratory, *Celse Martyr* was performed at the Collège Louis-Le-Grand, and the following year *David
et Jonathas*. Charpentier's musical activities were becoming more
and more closely associated with the Jesuits, a powerful society. In
1693, however, the composer would once again try his luck at court:
with *Médée*, or (we might call it) shattered last hopes.

Chapter 6

Divertissements and Pastorales

In the seventeenth century, the term *divertissement* did not refer to any specific musical form. It was the word used to describe not only the interludes in a comédie-ballet, in certain parts of tragédies lyriques (there are some in *Médée*), and in later opera-ballets, but also in entertainments given by the king, such as the "Divertissements de Versailles" in 1674. In the latter case, the term referred to the sum total of the celebration: ballets, plays, fireworks, and so on. The divertissement could also be any short independent opera on mythological or allegorical themes. Some of Charpentier's divertissements in this category lean more specifically toward the pastorale genre.

Throughout the seventeenth century, the pastorale enjoyed great popularity in France and occupied a special position in music for the stage. To characteristics derived from the Italians (themes from classical mythology) and from the Spanish (shepherds and shepherdesses), it added supernatural elements (enchanted lands, character transformations) and a tone of *préciosité* in the spirit of the "*tendre.*"

In the beginning, the pastorale was above all a literary genre (like Honoré d'Urfé's *L'Astrée*, a sort of long pastoral novel of more than five thousand pages), which later made use of music in the form of songs or ballets. It was not until 1655 that a pastorale entirely set to music was performed at the Louvre: *Le Triomphe de l'Amour* by Charles de Beys and Michel de La Guerre. In the same period, Charles Dassoucy composed *Les Amours d'Apollon et de Daphné*. With the works by Robert Cambert and Pierre Perrin, *La Pastorale d'Issy* (1659) and above all *pomone* (1671), the form gradually began to lean toward opera. For the inauguration of the Académie Royale in

1672, Lully presented a pastorale in three acts, *Les Fêtes de l'Amour et de Bacchus*, and (despite the supremacy of the tragédie lyrique) his last piece, the heroic pastorale *Acis et Galathée* (1686), composed especially for the Dauphin, was apparently as successful as any of his operas.

In *Le Bourgeois gentilhomme* (Act I, scene 2) M. Jourdain asks, "Why is it always shepherds? You see them everywhere." The dancing master replies:

> When characters have to be made to express themselves in music, it is necessary for verisimilitude that it be done in the pastoral vein. Shepherds have always been associated with singing; and it is hardly natural, in dialogue, that princes or citizens should express their feelings in song.

If Molière himself succumbed to the fashion (as in the grand prologue to *Le Malade imaginaire*) he also created, in *La Pastorale comique*, an amusing parody of pastoral conventions that indulges in all the stereotypical amorous platitudes.

Most of Charpentier's pastorales and divertissements were intended for Mlle de Guise's singers and date from the mid-1680s, the glorious years of the Lullian tragédie lyrique. Doomed to work in the less significant genres (he would have to wait another decade to make a claim to the stage of the Académie Royale), Charpentier nevertheless found the opportunity to display a wide variety of moods, from the lightest to the most dramatic, and even to inject religious emotion into his pastorales on the nativity theme.

Besides the *Petite pastorale, Églogue de bergers* (H. 479), four other works have the word *pastorale* in their titles: *Actéon, Pastorale en musique* (H. 481); *La Couronne de fleurs, Pastorale* (H. 486); *Sur la naissance de Notre Seigneur Jésus Christ, Pastorale* (H. 482); and *Pastorale sur la naissance de Notre Seigneur Jésus Christ* (H. 483). *Il faut rire et chanter, Dispute de bergers* (H. 484) is also subtitled "pastorale." Two works have a double classification: "Opéra" and "Idylle en musique" for *Les Arts florissants* (H. 487, 487a), and "Pastorale en musique" and "Opéra" for *Actéon* (H. 481). One can see how formal classifications were far from rigid in the composer's mind.

The other pieces have no subtitles. *La Fête de Rueil* (H. 485) and *Idylle sur le retour de la santé du roi* (H. 489) are closely related to the pastorale genre since they include shepherds and shepherdesses. *Les Plaisirs de Versailles* (H. 480), like *Les Arts florissants*, includes allegorical figures. Finally, *La Descente d'Orphée aux enfers* (H. 488) is a far cry from the pastorale as well as from the divertissement; instead, it is a large dramatic work on the subject of the tragic fate of Orpheus.

LA FÊTE DE RUEIL

The length of its score and the considerable forces involved lead one to presume that the commission for this pastorale emanated from an important personage. Rueil (Charpentier wrote "Ruel") was then a little town on the outskirts of Paris, where Richelieu had built a château surrounded by superb gardens. The cardinal's first name, Armand, appears in the text. According to the chronology of works, *La Fête de Rueil* seems to have been written in 1685, the year of Richelieu's one-hundredth birthday. It therefore might very well have been composed in honor of Louis XIII's minister, and even performed at the Château de Rueil. Numerous references to peace in the text also suggest that it was destined to commemorate the Treaty of Ratisbon, signed 15 August 1684. Indeed, that event was celebrated during the summer of 1685 with great festivities, like the one organized by the Marquis de Seignelay, the son of Colbert, at the Orangerie of Sceaux on 16 July 16, during which Lully's *Idylle de Sceaux* was performed.

Charpentier's pastorale requires lavish vocal and instrumental forces: six soloists, a four-part chorus, two oboes, two transverse flutes, two piccolos, two recorders, five-part strings, and a continuo composed of bass violins, bassoons, and harpsichord. A large number of dancers appeared in various guises: "peasant boys and girls," "gypsy girls" (*Égyptiennes*), "satyrs," and "shepherds and shepherdesses."

The shepherd subject matter—Iris spurns the love of Tircis—and the praise of the king are deftly combined with dancing. Scene 3 brings on an "Égyptienne," a character type frequently seen in the comedies of the day, having nothing to do with inhabitants from the land of the pharaohs. She is a gypsy who tells Iris' fortune by reading her palm.

Charpentier takes advantage of the wide range of instruments at his disposal to individualize his characters. Recorders accompany the simple shepherds (notice the trills in the piccolos imitating bird calls in scene 1), while the transverse flutes are associated with Pan, the shepherd god, who can be viewed as an allegorical figure of the king to whom *La Fête de Rueil* was apparently dedicated.

LES PLAISIRS DE VERSAILLES

This agreeable divertissement was inspired by the soirées that Louis XIV instituted at Versailles (called "the apartments") in 1682. Having much fewer means at his disposal than in *La Fête de Rueil*, Charpentier here created a piece full of charm and humor on the subject of the pleasures of the royal residence.

A French-style overture in three sections for two flutes, one bass flute, and continuo introduces the four scenes.

Scene 1. Music (*haut-dessus*) vaunts her own charms (gorgeous suspensions on "my enchanting chords") and joyfully proclaims the devotion of the king, the "most famous of all conquerors" and "the monarch of the fleur-de-lis," to her art. The Chorus of Pleasures (*haut-dessus, dessus, haute-contre*, and bass) repeats part of her solo.

Scene 2. Conversation (*dessus*) interrupts, and Music amusingly picks a quarrel on the subject of the inexhaustible babbling of her partner, whom she haughtily scorns. After a duet in which neither allows the other to speak/sing, Music finally delivers a song ("Amour viens animer ma voix") which Conversation, somewhat tongue-in-cheek, hastens to praise. Music, more and more annoyed by the Goddess of Cackling, loses her temper when Conversation, on hearing a minuet, exclaims: "For pity's sake, not that *courante* again!" over a bass line that Charpentier rather cleverly chromaticizes. The Chorus of Pleasures ("Arrêtez, demeurez") then intervenes to prevent the exasperated Music from leaving.

Throughout the scene, Charpentier individualizes each character primarily through metrical contrasts—prevailingly ternary, slow or moderately paced, for Music, while Conversation's lines are delivered in a quick tempo (6/8, later mostly 4/8).

Scene 3. One of the Pleasures (*haute-contre*) summons Comus (bass), "God of Festivities," to reconcile the two rivals: Comus offers chocolate, wine, confitures, and pastries in vain.

Scene 4. Games (*haute-contre*) enters, proposing various forms of amusement in a delectable catalog joyfully repeated by the chorus, accompanied by the instruments.

Si les car - tes, les   dés ,l'in-no -cent trou Ma — da-me, le bil-lard, le da - mier

Conversation, finally appeased by chocolate, sings of its delights "in flats" (G minor). She then makes fun of Music in a solo ending on a long, infectious burst of laughter echoed by all the other voices: "La belle chose que voilà, ah ah ah ah ah."

Music in turn asserts that she has provoked Conversation only to get her to reveal her "playful spirit." Both characters forgive each other their mutual mockery, and all rejoice over having been able to contribute to the amusement of Louis, "the great king covered with laurels."

LES ARTS FLORISSANTS

This "opera" or "idylle en musique," like *Les Plaisirs de Versailles*, takes the form of an allegorical divertissement. The five scenes that make up the work are arranged in perfect symmetry, with scene 3— the confrontation between Peace and Discord—constituting the central axis. Before and after the scene the two characters appear separately: Discord in scene 2, and Peace in scene 4. The two outer scenes (1 and 5) are longer than the others and bring together all the allegorical figures of the arts that glorify the king and peace. The overture is in two sections, French style, for "flutes and viols." Charpentier noted that the second section should be played "tenderly."

Scene 1. Like the prologue of a contemporary tragédie lyrique, the characters, often allegorical as in this scene, pay splendid homage to the monarch. In this case, the arts (Music, Poetry, Painting, and Architecture) are represented. Charpentier vaunts his own attributes, obviously in service to the glory of Louis.

The first solo, for Music (*haut-dessus*), leads into a Chorus of Warriors that strikingly contrasts the intense, pounding beat of deadly combat with the sweet harmonies of music in soft echo. Following a "Warriors' Air," probably meant to be danced, Poetry (*haut-dessus*) sings the praises of "that invincible monarch" whose deeds "impoverish the power and beauty of words." The Chorus of Warriors repeats the last words of her solo. Painting (*haute-contre*) and Architecture (*dessus*) in turn offer their talent and art for Louis's pleasure. As though to suggest that harmony's reign will be a brief one, Charpentier repeats the Chorus of Warriors heard before.

Scene 2. "The instruments pass immediately to the prelude that follows." It is a "Terrible Din" simulated by a rapid series of repeated sixteenth notes. Music and the terrified Chorus of Arts and Warriors disperse. Discord (*taille*) bursts on the scene and strikes up a battle song, its steady rhythm carrying into the Chorus of Furies, following without a break. The instrumental "Entry of the Furies" momentarily breaks the rhythmic flow, which then returns with the still malevolent, menacing Discord.

Scene 3. Peace (*haut-dessus*) enters and soothes everyone with her song, but fails to persuade Discord to cease his acts of destruction. Peace then invokes Jupiter, who strikes the Furies with a lightning bolt and casts them into Hades, their fall represented by cascades of descending scales in the instruments.

Scene 4. In a graceful minuet, Peace celebrates her victory over the forces of evil and calls on the arts to reappear.

Scene 5. The structure of the final scene (the arts savor the return of Harmony) is built on dance movements: a chaconne and a sarabande, both in triple meter. The former was frequently used by Lully in his tragédies lyriques, and also by Charpentier (*David et Jonathas, Médée*). Based on the variation principle, the chaconne, like the passacaglia, lends itself to extensive instrumental and vocal development. When inserted in the middle of a work, generally as a sort of divertissement, it relaxes the dramatic pace; but at the end of a tragedy, it constitutes its apotheosis. The chaconne in *Les Arts florissants* continues for 260 bars, though it does not close the work. Charpentier concludes the work with a trio ("O paix si longtemps désirée"), sung by Music, Poetry, and "a warrior" whose material returns in the great Chorus of Arts and Warriors. Between the trio and chorus, Charpentier inserted a "sarabande in *rondeau* form" with a solo couplet sung by Peace.

In arranging this scene (which alone makes up almost one-half of the work) according to a structure containing so many varied elements, Charpentier still managed to give it perfect coherence.

LA COURONNE DE FLEURS

A great deal of the text of *La Couronne de fleurs* comes from the original prologue to *Le Malade imaginaire*. It is wrong, however, to attribute *La Couronne de fleurs* to Molière, who died ten years prior to the composition of this version of the pastorale.[1] What made Charpentier return to this text after so many years? Hitchcock has proposed a very'convincing theory.[2] The manuscript of *La Couronne de fleurs* is found in volume 7 of *Mélanges,* alongside the third version of *Le Malade imaginaire* which Charpentier worked on toward the end of 1685. While immersed in this work which had caused him so much bother, he must have thought again about the prologue which had not had any attention paid it by the court, perhaps never having been performed there at all. Probably with the desire to salvage that significant score, Charpentier tailored the music and text to the musical resources of the Hôtel de Guise.[3]

In *La Couronne de fleurs*, the composer preserved the D-major tonality of the grand prologue to *Le Malade imaginaire* as well as the two main characters, the goddess Flora and the god Pan. The shepherds and shepherdesses, more numerous here, have different names, and the romantic intrigues are gone.

The work is divided into three scenes preceded by an overture. In scene 1, we again see Flora inviting the shepherds to welcome the arrival of spring and the return of peace. She promises a "crown of flowers" to the one "who best sings of the glorious deeds of the famous conqueror" (Louis XIV, to be sure). A "March of the Shepherds" closes the scene. In scene 2, shepherds and shepherdesses take turns ordering nature to be quiet to allow them to present their songs.

From this point on, Charpentier adheres to the text of the prologue to *Le Malade imaginaire* (with some variants), but instead of separating each vocal entry with an instrumental ritornello, he has the chorus repeat the last words of the soloist, a device that he extends throughout nearly the entire pastorale.

A lively fanfare-prelude introduces the song of Amarande (*haut-dessus*), describing a cloudburst. Then it is Forestan's (*haute-contre*) turn to evoke "the threatening lightning bolt." The tone softens as a minuet leads into the solo for Hyacinth (*dessus*), "Des héros fabuleux que la Grèce a chantés," followed by one for Mirtil (*taille*), "Louis fait à nos temps."

Scene 3 is for Pan, which Charpentier left intact from the prologue to *Le Malade imaginaire,* apparently satisfied with it.[4] There, the shepherd god scolds the singers for daring to tackle a subject that would have intimidated Apollo himself and advises them to be silent (see Chapter 3).

The shepherdess Rosalie then sings of her disappointment over not being able to compete for the coveted crown of flowers. In view of the shepherds' sadness, Flora decides to give each one of them a flower from the crown as consolation for their undertaking. The work ends in general high spirits, once again saluting the joys of spring and the reign of Louis, master "of the world" and "of the seasons."

IL FAUT RIRE ET CHANTER, DISPUTE DE BERGERS

Charpentier seems to have had trouble choosing a title for this pastorale. He first wrote "Il faut rire et chanter, Dialogue," which he crossed out and replaced with "Il faut rire et chanter, Dispute de bergers"; he then replaced the first half of the title with the words, "Le Misanthrope." The latter, however, has no connection with Molière's play of the same name. H. W. Hitchcock thinks it might refer to a play by Baron (author of *Rendez-vous aux Tuileries*), for which the pastorale might have served as interlude.[5] In any case, whoever the author, the dull text is of very little interest. It is in the form of a dialogue between "shepherds and shepherdesses who like to laugh" and a "dejected shepherd," which Charpentier characterized basically by contrasting major and minor modes. Dances are inserted between the characters' exchanges: a "suite of breezes and whirlwinds" with its strings of eighth notes, a minuet, a "gavotte in *rondeau* form," and a concluding "gigue."

ACTÉON

Although *Actéon* is also subtitled pastorale and displays the characteristics of that genre, the work stands out from previous ones because of its much richer and more complex texture and structure, and because of its tragic ending.

The overture, which begins in the traditional French style, subsequently departs from that mold and seems like a veritable compendium of the work. It has changing meters, numerous key changes, and thematic references to the world of the hunters (nos. 3 and 5) as well as to the mournful finale (no. 4). Here is its outline:

1. (₵): D minor → the dominant of D.
2. (3): F major → A minor.
3. (6/8): D minor.
4. (2): G minor.
5. (6/8): G major → D minor.

Not only does Charpentier break the conventional mold of the overture, he gives it a dramatic function that it did not yet possess at the time. In that he was a true pioneer, since it would not be until the middle of the eighteenth century that composers ceased to treat the opera overture as exclusively decorative and started to relate it to the drama to follow.

Actéon is divided into six scenes, each governed by a specific tonality.

Scene 1 (D major: "Joyous and very warlike"). "The scene is set in the valley of Gargaphie." An orchestral fanfare-prelude subtitled "Sounds of the Hunt" introduces the Chorus of Hunters ("Allons, marchons, courons, hâtons nos pas"), whose enthusiasm is tempered by the ABA' air of Actéon (*haute-contre*) in honor of Diana ("Aimable reine des forêts").

Scene 2 (A major: "Joyous and pastoral"). Diana enters with her nymphs, all singing of the peaceful charms of nature, far from the torments of love. Then follow an arioso and air for Diana ("Ce ruisseau loin du bruit du monde"), a Chorus of Nymphs, a minuet alternating between voices (a duet for Daphné and Hyale) and orchestra, and "Aréthuse's Song" ("Ah! Qu'on évite de langueurs") in *rondeau* form in gavotte rhythm, the refrain of which is taken up by the chorus and the gavotte by the orchestra alone.

Scene 3 (D major). This scene is divided into two parts: the first consists of a long monologue for Actéon alone, expressing the conflicting emotions that stir within him. In this psychological approach toward his hero, Charpentier resorts to an extremely subtle style, full of contrasts in formal structure as well as in meter and tonality. Thus he paints a personality that is complex and contradictory, caught both on the surface and in depth, and whose innocence makes the cruel fate that destiny has reserved for him seem all the harsher.

Exhausted after the hunt, Actéon craves rest—the recitative in 4/4 in D major. After an orchestral prelude in the *sommeil* tradition, the idea of love enters his thoughts—an accompanied air ("Agréable vallon, paisible solitude"), in ¢ 3/2 in A minor. At first the young man is drawn to it, but then he abruptly turns away from it—an acceleration of tempo (passing into triple meter) and furious vocalise. Actéon then sings a hymn to freedom—an accompanied ABA air in 6/4 in A major. Suddenly he sees Diana and her nymphs; attracted by their beauty, he approaches—recitative in 4/4 in D major—discreetly—arioso in triple meter "in echo." His curiosity proves fatal—the hapless youth is caught by surprise and, despite his protestations, punished for his temerity.

Scene 4 (F major, then C minor: "Obscure and sad"). Actéon is alone again, left to his sad fate. In a pathetic recitative, broken by silences, and in which terror is mixed with despair, he powerlessly witnesses his metamorphosis into a stag. After losing all human characteristics including his voice, the orchestra expresses in its place a long plaint in C minor.[6]

Scene 5 (C major: "Lively and warlike"). This scene is in utter contrast to the previous scenes. The Chorus of Hunters returns, preceded by another "Sounds of the Hunt" that displays a certain similarity to the instrumental "air" at the end of the first scene. Everyone rejoices at having just captured the stag and the group invites Actéon to join them, ignorant of the divine punishment that has been inflicted upon their friend.

Scene 6 (A minor, C major, D minor, F major, D minor). Juno informs the hunters that the dogs have devoured Actéon transformed into a stag, and that she was responsible for it. She is thus avenged for the infidelity of her husband Jupiter.

The chorus then sinks into the deepest sorrow ("Alas, is it possible?"), which gives way to anger ("Let us raise our cries") in the "furious and quick-tempered" key of F major (note the appropriate echo effects in the setting of the line "Let the rocks echo [our cries]"), and ultimately resignation ("Actéon is no more"). In a clever retrograde structure, the composer repeats the second, then the first parts (resulting in ABCBA), concluding this great lament with the chorus, never to be consoled.

It is clear that in *Actéon* Charpentier went beyond the charm and innocuousness of the pastorale and gave us a genuine tragedy in music, whose psychological depth places it near the level of a work such as *David et Jonathas.*

ACTÉON CHANGÉ EN BICHE (H. 481A)

This second version is an adaptation (Charpentier wrote "ravaudage," mending job) of the earlier work replacing the *haute-contre* part of Actéon with a *haut-dessus* voice. There are a few melodic alterations and transpositions in the role. Other changes affect the overture, which is shorter, less interesting, and composed of only two sections, as well as the "Chanson d'Aréthuse" sung by Diana and containing a few minor changes. Finally, the Chorus of Nymphs is recast from four to five voices.

IDYLLE SUR LE RETOUR DE LA SANTÉ DU ROI

The idyll is a genre close to the pastorale. In this work, however, the shepherds only appear during the ballet interludes ("Air des bergers et des bergères" and "Entrée de bergers et de bergères"). Written after Louis XIV's recovery from his illness of 1686, the *Idylle sur le retour de la santé du roi* is in two parts. The first, in A minor, announces the news of the monarch's recovery and sings the praise of his courage in the face of suffering. The second, in A major, proposes a magnificent celebration of the event via ascending scales that burst forth in all parts like fireworks ("Qu'on lance dans les airs").

LA DESCENTE D'ORPHÉE AUX ENFERS

The Orpheus myth, which has inspired generations of composers, will always be associated with the history of opera since it inspired the first great operatic masterpiece, Claudio Monteverdi's *L'Orfeo* (1607). The poet-musician, whose singing could charm all nature, was a highly popular character for the Italians in the first half of the seventeenth century as evidenced by the following works: *Euridice* by Jacopo Peri (1600), *Euridice* by Giulio Caccini (1602), and *La morte di Orfeo* (1619) and *L'Orfeo* (performed in France in 1647) by Luigi Rossi.

Charpentier drew on two scores for the sad tale of Orpheus

braving the divinities of the underworld to lead Eurydice back to earthly life: the cantata *Orphée descendant aux enfers* (H. 471) and the little opera *La Descente d'Orphée aux enfers.* H. W. Hitchcock believes that the work as it exists in the manuscripts is incomplete, although there is nothing that proves this in my opinion.[7] At the end of Act II, Orpheus leaves the underworld, followed by Eurydice. The title of the opera, just like that of the cantata, refers to a specific episode in the story to which both acts strictly adhere. The work forms a coherent whole both musically and dramatically. Its length (1366 measures) is comparable to other pieces written for Mlle de Guise's musicians, though it is the longest. In these works intended as ornaments for the musical soirées in private households, one cannot expect the gigantic scope of the tragédies lyriques, which were performed under totally different circumstances (on stage, in theaters equipped with elaborate machinery, etc.). In any case, even if possibly incomplete, this work is one of the masterpieces of Charpentier's secular output, foreshadowing the great tragedies to come.

Certainly *La Descente d'Orphée aux enfers* was conceived for a very special evening. All Mlle de Guise's singers and instrumentalists were recruited for its performance, and indeed this was the only occasion in which both of the house *hautes-contre* appeared together: Anthoine in the role of Orpheus and Charpentier in the role of Ixion. The orchestration also calls for unusually large forces: two flutes and two tenor viols superbly interacting with Orpheus when, having arrived at the gates of Hades, he tries to move Pluto with the power of his music.

Each of the two acts of *La Descente d'Orphée aux enfers* is divided into several scenes, all preceded by an overture in two sections.

Act I. Scene 1 transports us to the world of the pastorale. The nymphs—Daphne, Enone, Arethusa, and chorus—are celebrating the couple's union by comparisons with nature (flowers, birds). Solo, duet, and chorus are agreeably linked until Eurydice, in a finely nuanced air, begs her companions not to tread on the flowers so they can be made into a crown for the hero. The light, carefree atmosphere is abruptly shattered by Eurydice's cry when she is bitten by a snake. The cry does not frighten Enone who, thinking Orpheus' wife has pricked herself on a thorn, gently teases her.

In a sudden change of key, Charpentier leaves the "joyous and

pastoral" A major for the "tender and plaintive" key of A minor, as
Eurydice collapses, mortally wounded. The music reflects her fall:
the melody sinks downward, the harmony slackens.

Eurydice dies within a few seconds. The rest ensues in rapid
succession: Orpheus' interjection, "What have I heard? What do I
see?"; the chorus "O height of grief" on a poignant ninth, seventh,
and augmented fifth chord; Orpheus again, "What! I am losing
Eurydice"; and Eurydice's farewell to life, "Orphée, adieu, I die,"
with an expressive fall of a minor third, an interval that Charpentier
would use again for the death of Créuse in *Médée,* or when David witnesses the death of his friend ("Il est mort") in *David et Jonathas.*

After a "long silence," Orpheus' *récit* begins—"Ah bergers, c'en
est fait, il n'est plus d'Eurydice" (Ah, shepherds, it is over, Eurydice is
no longer)—accompanied by a bass line of four descending notes.
Except for the meter, it is identical to the opening of the *Magnificat à
3 voix* (H. 73). Charpentier could have continued this chaconne bass,
the classic support for "lamenti," but he abandons it after two expositions in favor of an entirely free texture. The chorus repeats Orpheus'
words, followed by an "Entrée of Nymphs and Shepherds in Despair"
whose grief is represented by contorted sixteenth notes. Orpheus'
grief is expressed in the chromaticism of a recitative in which he
decides to take his life.

In scene 3, Apollo (*basse-taille*) appears in the "lively and warlike" key of C major. He interrupts his son's desperate move and con-
vinces him to go "appeal to the powers of the Prince of Shades who
reigns over the dead," saying that "your singing will soften the heart
of this tyrant of Hades." Left alone, Orpheus (back to A minor)
resolves to leave for the realm of the dead. The chorus continues
their lament, and the act ends with a reprise of the "Entry of Nymphs
and Shepherds in Despair."

Act II: Hades. After a short orchestral introduction, Tantalus,
Ixion, and Tityus bemoan their cruel fate. In the next scene, a prelude
for two viols signals the arrival of Orpheus who, accompanied by

these deep, warm-toned instruments, mitigates their suffering. As the "magnificent and joyous" key of B-flat major replaces the "furious and quick-tempered" F major, Tantalus discovers that he is no longer thirsty. Ixion's wheel stops turning and the vultures (whose hunger is now appeased) cease gnawing at Tityus. Orpheus, encouraged by the beneficial effects of his singing, continues in the key of C major, Apollo's key in Act I. The Chorus of Furies next falls under the spell, and even the "Phantoms" are bewitched and proceed to dance joyfully.

Scene 3 takes us into the "grave and pious" key of D minor as Orpheus finds himself face-to-face with Pluto (bass). Still accompanied by viols, the unhappy lover tells his sad tale to the god of Hades, his emotion choked by silence. Proserpine and the Chorus of Happy Shades, Evildoers, and Furies are moved by Orpheus' plaint. The latter repeats his song, more and more expressively, culminating in "Ah, let yourself be moved by my extreme grief." The song is repeated two more times in a tireless incantation until Pluto finally relents.

The importance of tonalities has been noted from the beginning of the discussion of this work. In this sequence, it becomes the dominant feature, making the sequence the strongest and most overwhelming section. Charpentier constructed his entire dramatic progression on what he called, in *Règles de composition*, "the differing key-feelings" (*énergie des modes*), which serve mainly "for the expression of different emotions." Thus through the key changes alone we can trace Orpheus' entreaties to the master of Hades modulating from despair to hope, the intercessions and encouragement of Proserpine and the chorus, and Pluto's inflexibility evolving into acceptance of Eurydice's departure with Orpheus. The tonal scheme is explained as follows:

Orpheus	"Eurydice n'est plus"	D minor; "grave and pious"
Pluto	"Le destin est contraire"	D minor; "grave and pious"
Proserpine and "Happy Shades"	"Ah, puisque avant le temps"	A major; "joyous and pastoral"
Orpheus	"Tu ne la perdras point"	F major; "furious and quick-tempered"
Pluto	"Quel charme impérieux"	B-flat major; "magnificent and joyous"

Proserpine and "Happy Shades, Evildoers, and Furies"	"Courage, Orphée"	F major
Orpheus	"Souviens-toi du larcin"	G major; "sweetly joyous"
Pluto	"Je cède, je me rends aimable"	D major; "joyous and very warlike"
Orpheus	"Amour, brûlant amour"	A major

In the last scene, the Chorus of Happy Shades, Evildoers, and Furies expresses its regret over Orpheus' departure, while the "Dancing Phantoms" conclude the act and the work (?) with a "gentle sarabande."

PASTORALES ON THE BIRTH OF CHRIST

In his two pastorales on the birth of Christ (H. 482, 483), Charpentier created a happy blend of the pastorale genre and the nativity celebration. The subtle combination of the sacred and the secular inspires a particular type of tone and expression, both light and meditative, playful and serious, in which the frivolity of the dance is mingled with the fervor of prayer. The shepherds, who belong to the artificial, *galant* world of the pastorale as much as they belong to Judea, come to greet the birth of the Savior. It is also interesting to note that in the first work (H. 482) Charpentier gave his shepherds the same names they were usually given in secular pastorales (Silvie, Tircis, Doris), but in the second work (H. 483), more of a sacred drama, the same shepherds' anonymity ("Troupe of Shepherds and Shepherdesses") tends to lessen the gap between the two worlds. This fusion displayed by what might be termed "Biblical pastorales" should not be viewed as sacrilegious. On the contrary, it represents the genuine sensibilities of an era in which piety was inseparable from emotion, even at the cost of drawing its spiritual energy from the temporal world.

Sur la naissance de Notre Seigneur Jésus Christ, Pastorale

This work (H. 482) begins with an exquisitely fresh overture in two sections not really in contrast to each other, despite the change from duple to triple meter. A little eighth-note motif of rising thirds in the first section, inverted in the second, is tossed around in imitation between the two treble viols and bass.

The first of the two scenes is in the form of a dialogue between Silvie (*haut-dessus*) and Tircis (*haute-contre*), who marvel at the birth of the Christ Child and the humble setting of the event. The two shepherds indulge in childlike commentary on Mary and the mystery of the Immaculate Conception. With infinite tenderness and as though in a whisper ("à demi-voix" [in half-voice] notes Charpentier), Tircis reports the words of the Angel of the Lord who explained the work of the Holy Spirit to Joseph (Matthew 1:20–21).

After a duet in which Silvie and Tircis praise the goodness of the Lord ("Que ne devons-nous pas"), a minuet forms a bridge to scene 2 in which the two shepherds announce the joyful tidings to their companions. Everyone rejoices in a lullaby-like chorus ("Le Messie est donc né"), and then alternately sing and dance to the calm and gentle rhythm of the sarabande.

Pastorale sur la naissance de Notre Seigneur Jésus Christ

A great change in tone and atmosphere distinguishes this pastorale (H. 483) from the preceding one (H. 482). Charpentier gives us two views of the same subject: one, artless and tender, in the strictest tradition of the *noël* (Christmas carol); the other, more serious and introspective, whose expressions of joy are tempered by the human desire to be saved from darkness, sin, and death.

For this pastorale, Charpentier composed three versions of the second part to totally different texts. Chronologically, the manuscripts indicate that these were not successive reworkings to improve the work, but three separate versions, each of them valid and performable, and each of them given on different Christmases between 1684 and 1686.[8]

FIRST PART. The overture to the *Pastorale sur la naissance de Notre Seigneur Jésus Christ* begins with a few terse measures of chromaticism and dissonance before relaxing into the lighter mood of the pastorale.

Scene 1. The shepherds prepare for the coming of the Savior with fervent expectation. The literary and musical content is a sort of readying of the spirit, as in a sermon. In this sense, the Elder's solemn "Écoutez-moi, écoutez-moi, peuple fidèle" should be taken quite literally. The crux of the text is based on contrasts that are admirably underscored by the music: sound is followed by silence and agitation by calm to allow light and life to emerge from "the shades of death."

We are quite beyond the naivety of the previous pastorale. To evoke the mystery of the Immaculate Conception, Charpentier drew from a section of the book of Isaiah (45:8) for the metaphor of dew falling from heaven and fertilizing the earth. There is some sublime choral writing at this point: the voices sweep downward to depict the falling of the heavenly rain, in strict homophony ("Et conçoit le sauveur du monde"). An instrumental passage (which Charpentier later used for his "Nuit" in the oratorio *In nativitatem Domini Canticum*, H. 416) gently creates a feeling of suspense and evokes the mood toward which the previous pages have been gradually leading, namely, to an ineffable point in which time and space are erased, on the edge of silence and immobility, where the Word can take on physical form.

Scene 2. An Angel appears in the splendor of the holy night. The shepherds, frightened by this voice and the sudden light, at first want to flee. The Angel allays their fears and a dialogue ensues. Assured that the hour of the Savior's birth has truly come to pass, the shepherds begin their journey to the city of David.

Scene 3. In four measures of recitative the Angel invites her "celestial companions" to praise the Lord.

Scene 4. Peace and glory are proclaimed, and a lighthearted dance ends the first part of the pastorale.

SECOND PART, FIRST VERSION (H. 483).

Scene 5. Charpentier contrasts two levels of text one after another, then simultaneously. On the one hand, an "Afflicted Shepherdess" mourns the loss of her lamb brutally killed by a wolf; on the other hand, joyful shepherds are on their way to see the newborn Christ Child. The composer set this touching parable with a clever use of major and minor, with instrumentation (alternating flutes and viols), and with dynamic markings ("very loud" for the shepherdess, "very soft" for chorus) that clearly differentiate the two levels of sound.

Scene 6. The shepherds sing a joyful syllabic chorus ("Joignons nos flûtes et nos voix"), followed by a minuet. After moralizing on the events of the night, the joyful shepherds, joined by the "Afflicted

Shepherdess," repeat the chorus and minuet. An air ensues ("C'est de l'homme aujourd'hui") in which the chorus repeats material previously sung by the solo soprano. The work ends with a "Shepherds' March" ("bourrée in *rondeau* form").

SECOND PART, SECOND VERSION (H. 483a).

Scene 5. "The Elder" welcomes the shepherds at the entrance of the manger and inspires them to praise the "newborn God." The chorus repeats his words.

Scene 6. "Shepherds and Shepherdesses in the Manger." The text contrasts the majesty of the Infant Jesus with the humble setting of the manger. In this scene we encounter the popular, childlike elements that the first part of the work completely avoided. What could be more touching than these shepherds shivering in the cold air of the manger around the warm breath of the cow and the donkey, finally realizing that only love can provide the needed warmth to combat the winter's cold? The musical setting of the manger scene displays the same popular imagery used by painters and designers through the ages.

Scene 7. The Angel once again appears to calm the shepherds' uneasiness and to invite them to rejoice on this glorious day. The shepherds do not hesitate to do so, their song mixed with radiant echo effects.

The work ends with praise to Jesus ("minuet" in *rondeau* form) and to the Virgin Mary ("bourrée" in *rondeau* form). Both orchestral dances were heard already in the first version.

SECOND PART, THIRD VERSION (H. 483b).

Scene 5. This version uses two passages from the first version.[9] Between these passages is a new episode depicting the shepherds on their way back home at sunrise ("Le soleil recommence à dorer nos montagnes"). Then the birth of Jesus, symbol of eternal light and life, is hailed in a grand *rondeau* ("Source de lumière et de grâce").

PASTORALES ON ITALIAN TEXTS

Charpentier composed two pastorales on Italian texts: *Pastoraletta Ia* "Amor vince ogni cosa" (H. 492) and *Pastoraletta italiana IIa* "Cupido perfido" (H. 493), whose date of composition is unknown.[10]

"Amor vince ogni cosa"

"Amor vince ogni cosa" considered "very good" by Sébastien de Brossard, is for five voices, two violins, and continuo.[11] Its characters include "Filli, amata da Linco" (*haut-dessus*), "Eurilla, amata da Silvio" (*dessus*), "Linco, amante di Filli" (*haute-contre*), "Silvio, amante d'Eurilla" (*taille*), "Pan, dio de pastori" (bass), and a "Choro di pastori." In this pastorale, Charpentier naturally draws on the Italian style, noticeably in the fanfare "preludio" over long bass pedals, canonic entrances and long vocalises (scene 1); in the repetition of melodic sequences in the voices and in the instruments, the ostinato eight-note accompaniment in the march, rhythmic frenzy (scene 2); in the "bel canto" style—melodic curves, ternary symmetry—of Pan's air and the final chorus (scene 6); and in the da capo form (scenes 1 and 3).

"Cupido perfido"

The second pastorale ("Cupido perfido") is shorter than the previous one. Except for Pan, Charpentier kept the same characters. After a French overture in four sections (slow-fast-slow-fast), the four scenes display the same characteristics of the Italian style observed in "Amor vince ogni cosa."

Chapter 7

The Abbaye-aux-Bois and Port-Royal Convents and the Tenebrae Lessons

The early seventeenth century saw an extraordinarily widespread religious renaissance in France, as much the result of the Counter-Reformation as of the great increase in the number of individual vocations. Parallel with the restoration of old orders returning to strict doctrines (Angélique Arnauld at Port-Royal), new institutions came into existence, either imported from abroad (e.g., Carmelites, Oratorians) or of French origin (e.g., Order of the Visitation of François de Sales and Jeanne de Chantal, the Congregation of Saint-Sulpice, the Sisters of Charity of Saint Vincent de Paul, the Society of the Blessed Sacrament). This new tide of religious feeling sparked theological quarrels. The most violent was the quarrel between the Jansenists and the Jesuits throughout the second half of the century.

Paris had lost count of its convents, some sixty of which had been established between 1600 and 1640, primarily in three sections of the city: the Marais, the Faubourg Saint-Jacques, and the Faubourg Saint-Honoré. While some orders remained strictly closed to the outside world, many convents opened their doors to aid the poor or to teach. They also offered refuge to single women and to those whose penitence required that they retire from society, whether temporarily or for life. One of the institutes best known for its educational mission was Saint-Cyr, founded near the end of the seventeenth century by Mme de Maintenon. The royal establishment was also famous for its artistic influence in drama as well as music. In 1686, Guillaume Gabriel Nivers was appointed its choirmaster and organist. He composed numerous motets written for the church services. His successor, Louis-Nicolas Clérambault, published in 1733 two volumes of *Chants et motets à l'usage de l'Église et Communauté des Dames de la Royale Maison de Saint-Cyr.* Other convents, especially at the end of the seventeenth century and the beginning of the eighteenth, called on the greatest musicians in the kingdom. For example, in addition to the famous Organ Mass *propre pour les couvents,* François Couperin composed *leçons de ténèbres* for the nuns of Longchamp, near Paris. This tendency toward music that was more attractive than the austere plainchant gradually transformed traditional services into genuinely secular concerts, scandalizing some people:

> Praise is heaped upon singers who, from behind a curtain that they pull open from time to time to smile at friends in the audience, sing a Lesson on Good Friday or a solo motet for Easter. People go to hear them at a particular convent. In their honor, the price one is normally charged at the Opera is the price paid for a seat in the church. One recognizes *Urgande* and *Arcabonne* [characters in Lully's *Amadis*] and applauds (there was applause at the Tenebrae and Assumption services, although I don't recall if it was for *La Moreau* or for *Mme Cheret*). These spectacles take the place of those which are suspended during that two-week period.[1]

The name of Charpentier, like the names of Couperin and Nivers, became associated with the music in the convents of the capital: the Carmelites in the Rue du Bouloir, the Abbaye de Montmartre (see Chapters 4 and 5), as well as the Abbaye-aux-Bois and Port-Royal.

The history of the Abbaye-aux-Bois goes back to the beginning of the thirteenth century. Under the name of "Franche Abbaye de Notre-Dame-aux-Boix," a Cistercian convent was founded by Jean de Nesle, feudal lord of Bruges, in the diocese of Noyon (Oise), in 1202. In 1655, the abbey was transferred to Paris in the Faubourg Saint-Germain, Rue de Sèvres, in the Convent of the Ten Virtues, or Annonciades, which had been founded by the Grande Mademoiselle. The Paris convent of the Abbaye-aux-Bois remained under the protection of the House of Orléans. Does that explain why the music of Charpentier was played at the Abbaye-aux-Bois while he was still in the service of Mme de Guise, the daughter of Gaston of Orléans?

The permanent establishment of the Abbaye-aux-Bois in Paris provided the occasion for an important ceremony:

On Wednesday, 10 July 1669, the Archbishop of Paris, Hardouin de Péréfixe, came to the abbey to receive the body of the virgin-martyr Sainte-Victoire, carried in procession (from the Église Saint-Sulpice) by numerous clergymen. . . . For a week, the convent's chapel observed the feast and, each day, ecclesiastics renowned for their eloquence came to deliver sermons. Heard were (among others) Father Mascaron, the Bishop of Amiens, and especially the Abbé Bossuet.[2]

The convent buildings included fifty cell-chambers, large rooms, a refectory, a large garden with fruit trees, and a courtyard with a high porte-cochère that served as the main entrance. Wishing to enlarge their monastery, the nuns acquired on 25 September 1679 a sizeable piece of land opposite them which ran parallel to the Rue de Sèvres.

The Cistercians of the Abbaye-aux-Bois favored Jansenism and strict observance of its doctrines. Their sizeable library included writings of Nicole, Arnauld, and Pascal. The nuns and their pupils alike were members of important families. Girls of nobility came to the Abbaye-aux-Bois to receive solid instruction and to learn good manners before they reached marrying age. The arts played a particularly important role. In the eighteenth century, a theater was

> built at the far end of the garden. This very elegant theater had fine scenery. It is said that grand ballets, such as *Orphée et Eurydice*, were given there, and that fifty or sixty female dancers would be selected from among the young boarders. The theater also performed *Polyeucte, Le Cid*, and *La Mort de Pompée*, which a large and distinguished audience, mostly consisting of the families, would applaud most politely.[3]

The boarders would give little concerts for the nuns as distraction from their long hours of work. Around 1778, during a Taking of the Veil Ceremony, Delalande's *Miserere* was performed.

In 1792, the twenty-two nuns of the Abbaye-aux-Bois were dispersed. Five years later, the convent house and church were sold. In the nineteenth century, the abbey was associated with the name of Mme Récamier, who occupied a modest apartment in it. Chateaubriand came to see her regularly. Today the Rue Récamier is located on the site of the church that was demolished in 1906.

In April 1680, the *Mercure Galant* described the type of music that could be heard at court and in Paris during Holy Week:

> His Majesty's music excelled as usual during the Tenebrae, which is held in the chapel of the Old Château of Saint-Germain. . . . We have also had some very beautiful music in Paris

on the same days, and people have been flocking in droves to the Sainte-Chapelle and the Abbaye-aux-Bois. What was heard at the Sainte-Chapelle was by MM. Chaperon, la Lande [*sic*], and Lalouette; at the Abbaye-aux-Bois, by M. Charpentier.[4]

Charpentier left thirty-one *Leçons de ténèbres* (no other composer of his day produced as many) for the most diverse ensembles. The music performed at the Abbaye-aux-Bois was very likely the *Neuf leçons de ténèbres* (H. 96–110), followed by *Neuf répons du mercredi saint* (H. 111–119). At the end of his manuscript, Charpentier noted: "I did not finish the others because of the change in the breviary." Indeed, modifications of the Paris breviary occurred in 1680.[5]

TENEBRAE LESSONS

The Tenebrae, or Lamentations, are services consisting of matins and initially held during the early morning hours of the *sacrum triduum* (Thursday, Friday, and Saturday of Holy Week) during which candles fixed onto a triangular frame are extinguished one by one as the first rays of the sun begin to appear. This gradual extinction of the lights symbolizes the shadows that covered the earth when Jesus died on the cross. Since the hour of matins proved rather impractical, it became customary to sing the service on preceding afternoons, namely, Wednesday, Thursday, and Friday afternoons, but the rite of the extinction of the candles was preserved.

The text set to music in the Tenebrae lessons came from the book of *Lamentations* by the Old Testament prophet Jeremiah. The book is composed of five elegies in verse describing the destruction of the temple of Jerusalem by the Chaldeans in 587 B.C. These are mournful chants in which the prophet laments not only the destruction of Jerusalem, but especially the sins that caused God to turn from the ungrateful city. The matins service of the *sacrum triduum* consists of three nocturnes, each made up of three psalms followed by antiphons, and three lessons, each with its response. It is during the course of the first nocturne that Jeremiah's book of *Lamentations* is sung. The stanzas of the first four elegies begin with the letters of the Hebraic alphabet, a feature that has been preserved in the Vulgate. The first lessons are preceded by the introductory "Incipit Lamentatio Jeremiae Prophetae" on the first day, and by "De lamentatione Jeremiae Prophetae" on the next two days. The third lesson for Saturday is introduced by "Incipit Oratio." Each lesson ends with the exhortation "Jerusalem, convertere ad Dominum Deum tuum." The complete cycle consists of nine lessons, with the text of *Lamentations* arranged as follows:

> First Thursday lesson (Wednesday) 1:1–5
> Second Thursday lesson (Wednesday) 1:6–9
> Third Thursday lesson (Wednesday) 1:10–14
> First Friday lesson (Thursday) 2:8–11
> Second Friday lesson (Thursday) 2:12–15
> Third Friday lesson (Thursday) 3:1–9
> First Saturday lesson (Friday) 3:22–30
> Second Saturday lesson (Friday) 4:1–6
> Third Saturday lesson (Friday) 5:1–11

Composers have been interested in Jeremiah's text since the fifteenth century. In the sixteenth century, the golden age of polyphony, numerous *Lamentations* flourished throughout Europe, including those of Claudin de Sermisy (1535), Heinrich Isaac (1535), Cristóbal de Morales (1564), Palestrina (who wrote five books of them from 1564 on), Orlandus de Lassus (1585), Tomás Luis de Victoria (1581), and Thomas Tallis. In 1582, the Council of Trent printed a copy of the "Tonus lamentationum" which served as a basis for most of the compositions, including those of Charpentier. The text of *Lamentations*, deeply expressive and poignant, lent itself ideally to the principle of accompanied monody, a fruit of the Italian melodramatic reforms of the late sixteenth century. Composers of this period were quick to use it in compositions usually for solo voice and continuo, with or without other instruments.

In the second half of the seventeenth century and at the beginning of the eighteenth, Tenebrae lessons gained great popularity in France and developed as a genre. Michel Lambert, the master of the *air de cour*, composed his first set in 1662, with another cycle appearing in 1689. In turn, François Couperin in 1712–1714, Sébastien de Brossard in 1721, and Michel Richard Delalande in 1730 left admirable examples.

Charpentier's *Neuf leçons de ténèbres* (H. 96–110) is the only complete cycle by the composer available today. There are actually twelve lessons in the set, some of them duplicates. The first version (H. 96–106) is written almost exclusively for one voice (*dessus* or *haut-dessus*); only two lessons (H. 98, 103) are for two voices.

Charpentier indicated three possibilities for the third *Leçon du vendredi saint*.[6] With three female singers at his disposal in the Abbaye-aux-Bois ("Mère Sainte Caecile," *haut-dessus;* "Mère Camille," *haut-dessus;* and "Mère Desnots," *haute-contre*), Charpentier added to his original version a new *Seconde leçon du jeudi saint à voix seule* (H. 107), the last three lessons for each day (H. 108–110) in which he utilized three-part writing.[7] The composition of the *Lettres hébraïques de la première leçon de ténèbres du vendredi saint* (H. 99), intended as an alternative to the already existing Tenebrae lesson, also reflects that same alternative for enrichment of the vocal scoring.

Except for the *Première leçon du vendredi saint* (H. 105), which makes mention of one treble viol, the *Leçons* call for no instruments other than the continuo (bass viol and, curiously, harpsichord rather than organ). Some instrumental sections (*Ritournelles pour la première leçon de ténèbres du vendredi saint* and *Prélude devant De lamentatione pour le jeudi et le vendredi saint,* H. 100) were written separately and, consequently, may be used on an optional basis. This might have been a result of the clergy's bans on the use of instruments during Holy Week, as illustrated by the following excerpt from a text published in 1674 by the Archbishops of Paris, condemning certain abuses in church:

> We strictly forbid all Superiors of churches and chapels in our diocese . . . to allow the singing, in chorus or with instruments, of any music during Tenebrae, at a time intended for mourning the death of the Savior of us all . . . on pain of banning entry to places where such misconduct is allowed, and other legal penalties against persons who go against this ordinance.[8]

The *Ritournelles pour la première leçon de ténèbres du vendredi saint* are scored alternately for two violins and two tenor viols. Apparently to facilitate identification of the ritornello to be played after each versicle, Charpentier wrote, alongside each, an amusing onomatopoeia containing a vowel indicating the use of violins ("a") or viols ("i"). We cannot resist mentioning here the way the composer labelled the entire set of ritornellos: "tac, tic, tac, nic, nac, nic, frac, fric, frac."

Charpentier's complete *Leçons de ténèbres* are divided into two main categories: some are written in the style of the concerted motet of the day, while the others develop a vocal style that is extremely florid and specifically French. The cycle of *Neuf leçons de ténèbres* provides the most polished example of this latter style, both by

Charpentier and by other composers of his period.

It was Michel Lambert, one of the great composers of *airs de cour*, who wrote the first French monodic Tenebrae lessons that influenced those lessons by composers of later generations. Consequently, Tenebrae lessons became a typical French genre by dint of the burgeoning use of ornamentation in the style of the *air de cour*.

To understand the extraordinary expressivity of Charpentier's *Leçons*, three elements should be considered. First, the "Tonus lamentationum" on which all lessons by French composers of the period are based and which gives the chant its fascinating and distinctively Gregorian solemnity. Here, in turn, are the melody of the "Tonus" from the beginning of the *First Lesson for Holy Wednesday* and Charpentier's corresponding composition:

Second, the florid recitative style is distinctively French. Charpentier's *Leçons* unfold in the form of a long declamation to which copious ornamentation is added. Here we encounter the "double" technique of the *air de cour*, which consists of decorating an initially simple melody with melismas and extremely subtle, even-mannered ornaments, in keeping with the sensibilities of *préciosité* of the period.

The *port de voix* (an appoggiatura from the lower note, which in a sung text amounts to an anticipation of the syllable to come on the preceding note [see preceding musical example, *Incipit*]) is found abundantly in Charpentier, but so is the *cadence* (or *tremblement*) that the composer indicated by an elaborate system of symbols, some of which curiously are not found in any other music of the time, making their precise execution questionable.[9]

This characteristic texture of the Tenebrae lessons lasted from Lambert to Delalande. In 1680, Charpentier tried his hand at Lambert's ornamented declamation and carried it even further, to the far limits of complexity and vocal virtuosity. Couperin and Delalande reserved that texture, which eventually acquired an archaic tone, for their *lettres hébraïques;* but in the versicles they used another, much less florid style. Delalande exercised greater flexibility in the form by introducing a *rondeau* structure into his *Troisième leçon du vendredi saint*, the "Recordare" serving as a refrain. Such a pattern can be observed in all Charpentier's *Leçons*, including the cycle that concerns us here, in particular, in the second version of the last *Leçons* of each day.

The third distinctive element of Charpentier's *Leçons* is the expressivity of Italian music, which discreetly gives the French style whatever it might be lacking in depth and dramatic sense.

The *Leçons* for solo voice are obviously the ones with the most elaborate ornamentation. Each versicle begins with syllabic declamation, which then gives way to an extremely florid and rhythmically complex vocal line, above which are noted many *tremblements*. Although this abundant ornamentation is essentially decorative in nature and is rather systematically applied, in certain places it clearly is motivated by expressive demands, such as when bringing out the meaning of a word or a passage of the text. At such times it is supported by sophisticated harmonies.

Such is the case in the *Première leçon du mercredi saint* (H. 96), with the falling chromaticism ("plorans ploravit," she weeps), the diminished seventh chord ("inter angustias," into captivity), the change of mode (from F major to the "obscure and plaintive" F minor) and the chromatic bass line that behaves like a chaconne bass but does not repeat itself ("viae Sion lugent," the ways of Zion do mourn).

In the *Seconde leçon du mercredi saint* (H. 97), the mere contours of the vocal line create a sense of great weariness, and over a falling bass line, the melody, at first inert, suddenly comes to life only to sink back slowly ("deposita est vehementer," she fell into extreme dejection). In this passage, there is a cross relation between the C-natural in the bass and the C-sharp in the vocal line.

The *Troisième leçon du mercredi saint* (H. 98), for two voices, offers a fine example of tone-painting (to be found again in H. 108) on the phrase "de excelso" (from the heavenly heights), which launches a rising scale of sixteenth notes. Likewise in *Seconde leçon*

du jeudi saint (H. 103), the daughter of Jerusalem's sorrow is compared with the vastness of the sea (*"mare"*) in a long vocal melisma first rising toward the upper register, staying there (while the bass line quakes in its turn), and rising again before finally subsiding in the following measure. *Seconde leçon du jeudi saint à voix seule* (H. 107) repeats the same descriptive effect, with only a slight variant at the end.

The *Troisième leçon du mercredi saint* (H. 98) contains another beautiful passage ("tota die moerore confectam," he has made me desolate and faint all the day) in which Charpentier inserts a poignant chromatic fall in the soprano line, ending on a moving diminished seventh chord in the penultimate bar. The "Jerusalem convertere," less ornate than its counterparts in the first two Wednesday lessons, owes its dramatic intensity to the manner in which the two voices overlap and answer each other. The "Jerusalem" sections of all three Wednesday lessons are also used in the Thursday and Friday lessons.

One of the greatest examples of Charpentier's individuality is his use of silence, which he always treats with rare subtlety. Several fine examples of this are in the *Leçons de ténèbres*. In the *Seconde leçon du jeudi saint* (H. 103), the singing abruptly stops after each repetition of the word *deficerent* (they swooned). In *Première leçon du vendredi saint* (H. 105), the singing ceases after the word *silentio* on a tritonal suspension. In *Seconde leçon du vendredi saint* (H. 106), the entire phrase ("adheasit lingua lactentis ad palatum ejus in siti," the tongue of the sucking child cleaves to the roof of the mouth for thirst) is strikingly interrupted by numerous pauses in the bass and vocal line.

The second version of the last three lessons for each day (H. 108, 109, 110) is scored for three voices, and the style is different from that of the preceding ones. Melismatic textures no longer prevail, but more often give way to a finely crafted counterpoint favoring imitation among the different voice parts. Charpentier somewhat abandons the improvisational character of the Lambert style in favor of something more meter-oriented, structured, and, in short, more modern. We find ourselves faced with a stylistic juxtaposition of lush, melismatic vocal texture alongside solid contrapuntal developments. Yet this diversity in no way compromises the unity of these pieces; on the contrary, it gives them an even greater expressive impact.

A number of features in the *Troisième leçon du mercredi saint* (H. 98) reappear in the *Troisième leçon du mercredi saint à trois parties*

(H. 108). This is equally the case for both versions of the *Seconde leçon du jeudi saint* (H. 103, 107) and the *Troisième leçon du jeudi saint* (H. 104, 109). Nevertheless, a certain amount of Italian-style workmanship is unique to the second version (H. 108), including, for example, the agitation, indeed the frenzy, of "quoniam vindemiavit me" (my adversary has shorn me of my possessions), or the heightened expression of "posuit me desolatam" (he hath made me desolate).

Once again, the "Jerusalem" penned at the end of *Leçon du mercredi*, in Charpentier's words, "shall serve for the three final lessons of all three days."

The *Troisième leçon du jeudi saint à 3 voix* (H. 109) displays an extraordinary variety of textures. In the opening bars, the Hebraic letter *aleph* enchants us with its elegance and lyricism, as well as with its delicate "echo" effect at the end. For the versicle "Tantum in me vertit et convertit manum suam tota die" (he turns his hand against me all the day), Charpentier turned as far as possible from the florid style by writing a fugue. Thus, while certainly concerned about textural contrasts, he particularly demanded the right expression. Could the inexorable suffering described in the text be more effectively conveyed than by the repetition of the same thematic material?

The three subsequent versicles, each of which begins with the letter *beth*, are also remarkable. Overall unity is assured by the letter itself, sung first by one voice, then by two, and finally by three voices. The melody stays in the soprano line as Charpentier enriches the musical texture of each repetition with another part. The versicles, like the introductory letter, are also written for one, two, and three voices. The first versicle employs the melismatic style. The second versicle's duet, in the minor, features imitative counterpoint between the two voices, employing chromaticism and dissonance, and a very beautiful chain of suspensions on "felle et labore" (gall and travail). The third versicle employs yet another style, a textural device used so frequently by the composer, namely, the use of bass pedal to evoke the calm of night, the darkness of the shadows (see *Canticum in nativitatem Domini*, H. 393; *In nativitatem Domini Nostri Jesu Christi*, H. 414; or the first version of this *Leçon*). On a nine-measure dominant pedal, the voices (also immobile at first) sketch a few imitative figures around the notes of the triad before the latter is clearly established. The mood of suspense is even more effective since Charpentier demands, at the end of the versicle, a "long silence."

The *Troisième leçon du vendredi saint* (H. 110) begins with the traditional "Incipit Oratio" modelled on the Gregorian theme and treated by the composer in a manner that is both austere and intense. In this solo lesson, Charpentier differentiates his style no less tellingly from one versicle to the next. Could there be a more perfect expression of "lassis non dabatur requies" (we labor and have no rest) than the sudden abundance of broken or deceptive cadences? What could be more poignant than the tenderness mixed with restraint, even modesty, that envelops the despair of the final versicle ("Mulieres in Sion humiliaverunt, et virgines in civitatibus Juda" [They ravished the women in Zion, and the maids in the cities of Judah])?

The admirable music that Charpentier left us in his Tenebrae lessons represents one of the finest examples of the fusion of styles, bringing together their respective riches. Despite their unquestionably French character, they contain a dramatic strain that the composer brought with him from Italy, and which he incorporated into the French tradition in the most natural manner imaginable.

Charpentier is often viewed as a fabulous architect of grand choral masses. His ability to compose for solo voice is perhaps not emphasized enough. The latter skill is most evident in *Leçons de ténèbres*, where the voice is treated with such flexibility and subtlety, and at times with such virtuosity, that there can be no doubt about the overwhelming impact this music had on contemporary listeners during the three-day period devoted to the Passion of Christ.

RESPONSORIES

The responsorial text for Holy Week recounts the episodes in the Passion of Christ. The *Neuf répons du mercredi saint* (H. 111–119) comprise short pieces for one, two, and three voices, with alternating recitatives and more melodic sections, often in *rondeau* form.

The *Second répons après la seconde leçon du premier nocturne* ("Tristis est anima mea") features poignant suspensions on "et ego vadam immolari pro vobis" (and I will sacrifice myself for you).

In the *Quatrième répons après la première leçon du second nocturne* ("Unus ex discipulis meis"), the gentle marchlike setting of the phrase "Vae illi per quem tradar ego" (Woe unto them who betray me) serves as a refrain in contrast to the other sections. The tone is tender but firm.

The same concern for contrast appears in the *Cinquième répons après la deuxième leçon du second nocturne* ("Eram quasi agnus innocens") in which both recitatives are followed by the air "Venite."

The *Sixième répons après la troisième leçon du second nocturne* ("Una hora non potuistis") begins in a deeply introspective mood, which then gradually becomes more animated. Just before the end, the three voices imitatively embellish the word *surgite* (arise) with an irresistible ascending thrust.

The workmanship of the *Huitième répons après la seconde leçon du troisième nocturne* ("Revelabunt coeli iniquitatem Judae") is remarkable from beginning to end. After the beautifully striking dissonances of the first part, Charpentier embarks on a vigorous fugue (with "et terra adversus" as subject and "et manifestum erit" as countersubject) that contrasts with the previous calm. Another abrupt change of tone plunges the listener into dramatic depths with effects at times verging on the operatic ("Recede a nobis").

In the *Neuvième répons après la troisième leçon du troisième nocturne du mercredi saint* ("O Juda, qui dereliquisti consilium pacis"), the composer uses a strange harmony in the central section when referring to Judas' betrayal. On the word *dolos* (deceit), a veil seems to pass over the music before it achieves partial stability above a dominant chord.

Charpentier composed the admirable Tenebrae cycle just discussed for the Abbaye-aux-Bois and other smaller pieces as well. The composer noted the names of nuns in two of them dating from 1677–1678: the *Domine salvum pour trois religieuses* (H. 288) and the *Motet de la Vierge pour toutes ses fêtes pour les mêmes religieuses* (H. 322). Two other works written during the same period, *O sacrum à trois* (H. 239) and *O sacrum pour trois religieuses* (H. 240), as well as *Miserere à 2 dessus, une haute-contre et basse continue* (H. 173) of 1680, feature similar scoring and might have been composed for the abbey.

WORKS FOR PORT-ROYAL

The titles of five of Charpentier's manuscripts mention "For Port Royal": *Messe, Pour le Port Royal* (H. 5); *Pange lingua pour des religieuses, Pour le Port Royal* (H. 62); *Magnificat, Pour le Port Royal* (H. 81); *Dixit Dominus, Pour le Port Royal* (H. 226); and *Laudate Dominum omnes gentes, Pour le Port Royal* (H. 227).

Today, the mention of Port-Royal generally conjures up the rigorous doctrines of Jansenism, the *Provinciales* of Pascal, and the austere paintings of Philippe de Champaigne, but nothing related to music. The Jansenist philosophy was indeed quite averse to any form of artistic expression capable of awakening the individual to sensual pleasures or leading him or her to a state of "diversion" (divertissement, in the Pascalian sense). According to Cornelius Jansen, author of the celebrated *Augustinus,* music was considered particularly dangerous for the souls of the daughters of Saint-Bernard:

> And whosoever shall resolve to make any efforts to rise to the peak of perfection, which consists of a denial of one's pleasures according to the immutable law of truth, and to work, or to deprive oneself completely of sensual delights, *like sounds,* smells, delicacies of the table, and other temptations of the flesh, or to temper them with moderation, shall be forced to confess that this maxim is quite true . . . and one's own conscience will oblige one to admit that it is easier not to indulge in any of these pleasures at all, no matter how justifiable they be, than to practice them without committing many sins.[10]

After reading such a text, one wonders how a musician, even one as deeply religious as Charpentier, was allowed to compose in the midst of the Jansenist movement, so hostile to the "art of sounds." Nor should one forget that Charpentier worked for the Jesuits, out-and-out enemies of Port-Royal. By what miracle (with no pun intended in this context) could he have worked on both sides at once? These are indeed baffling questions.

When Charpentier wrote his pieces for Port-Royal, two establishments existed under that name: Port-Royal des Champs and Port-Royal de Paris. The former was built in 1204 in the Chevreuse Valley. La Mère Angélique Arnauld began to exercise her authority there at the start of the seventeenth century and reestablished the doctrine of Cîteaux which had been relaxed during the course of the previous centuries. Because of the unhealthy living conditions of the site and lack of sufficient funds for the abbey's eighty nuns, a second establishment was founded in the Faubourg Saint-Jacques in Paris in 1625. The nuns first settled in the Hôtel de Clagny, and then, in 1645, began constructing a monastery based on plans by the architect Antoine Le Pautre. No longer dependent on Cîteaux, Port-Royal de Paris was incorporated into the archbishopric of the capital. The group adopted the name Daughters of the Blessed Sacrament. The black scapular was replaced by a white one embellished with a scarlet crucifix, as seen in the paintings of Philippe de Champaigne. In 1648, some of the nuns went back to Port-Royal des Champs, and both houses coexisted for twenty years. When some of the nuns refused to sign the Formulary condemning the five propositions taken from Jansen's *Augustinus*, Louis XIV separated the two abbeys. Port-Royal de Paris was henceforth completely unconnected with the Jansenist movement, while Port-Royal des Champs remained its only center until its eradication by the king in 1711.

In January 1685 the sister of François Harlay de Champvallon, archbishop of Paris and one of the staunchest adversaries of Jansenism, was named abbess of Port-Royal de Paris. On 20 July 1687, the Cordeliers held a service to celebrate the archbishop's recovery from an illness and

> begged Madame the Abbess of Port-Royal, worthy sister of the illustrious prelate, to allow it to be held in her church on the 20th of last month, the Feast of Saint Margaret, her namesake. Father Gardien, in the company of his officers and around thirty monks, arrived at the church of Port-Royal on the morning of the feast day. They began by chanting Terce, and then High Mass was sung with all the ceremonies of the great convent, and several accompanied motets to the Blessed Sacrament, Saint Margaret, and for the king, following which Sext was sung. . . . Nones and vespers were sung at the usual time in plainchant and fauxbourdon. . . . A musical salutation ended the feast. It was sung by the same Fathers who performed the entire service of the day in a manner quite befitting their zeal for the archbishop and for the Abbess of Port-Royal.[11]

The placement of *Messe, Pour le Port-Royal* among Charpentier's manuscripts corresponds to the date of the above-mentioned ceremony. In addition to the regular sections of the Ordinary, this mass contains parts referring specifically to Saint Francis and Saint Margaret, in obvious dedication to François Harlay de Champvallon and his sister Marguerite.[12] Moreover, it is possible the two psalms *Dixit Dominus* and *Laudate Dominus omnes gentes,* as well as the *Magnificat,* all contained in an undated notebook, were performed for the "fauxbourdon" vesper service on that day. There can no longer be any doubt: Charpentier could only have written for the Paris convent, or the *"mauvais frère"* in the words of Sainte-Beuve.

The church of Port-Royal of Paris (which can still be visited today at 123, Boulevard de Port-Royal) bears the name of the Blessed Sacrament and is a masterpiece of architecture. The interior of this small edifice of admirable proportions has white walls completely devoid of all decoration (the decoration envisioned by Le Pautre could not be executed due to the great expense). It was described in its day as "the prettiest and most devout [church] in Paris, even though it is among the plainest."[13] It once housed some treasures: an alabaster vase said to be from Canaan; "a ciborium made of agate, embedded in gold, and decorated with diamonds; a crystal sun decorated in gold; a diamond crucifix";[14] and the "Holy Thorn" that miraculously cured Pascal's niece, Marguerite Périer, and Sister Catherine de Sainte-Suzanne, daughter of Philippe de Champaigne. Some of the latter's paintings, including the *Ex-voto* of 1662 executed in an act of thanksgiving for Catherine's recovery, used to adorn the walls of the church.

The names of the singers are noted in four pieces: *Magnificat* (H. 81), *Dixit Dominus* (H. 226), *Laudate Dominum omnes gentes* (H. 227), and *Élévation à 3 dessus* (H. 256) of 1684. These were a young female boarder, or novice, Mlle Du Fresnoy, and two nuns, Mère de Sainte Agathe and Mère de Saint Bernard, all of whom sung in *haut-dessus.* Except for the organ, no instruments are employed.

Examining the works for Port-Royal (especially *Messe, Pange lingua,* and *Stabat Mater*), one is struck by their individual style, in contrast to the extravagant ornamentation of the Tenebrae lessons. The extremely simple texture verges on austerity. It is almost exclusively monodic, with little ornamentation and using the archaic device of fauxbourdon. Is this severity to be interpreted as the still-visible stamp of Jansenism that Port-Royal de Paris had not fully been able to shake off? In spite of this severity, *Magnificat, Dixit Dominus,* and *Laudate Dominum* have verses scored for two and three parts in which imitative devices and ornamentation are not uncommon. Apparently the vespers service was less strict than the mass.

Despite the severe doctrines concerning "sensual delights," the Jansenists' liturgical practices included musical performances which, while limited exclusively to plainchant without any instruments, not even organ, attracted the admiration of listeners. Père Comblat, who happened to be at Port-Royal des Champs in June 1678, reported the following:

> They sing the ordinary Roman plainchant, according to the Paris order, being of the same diocese, but never with any embellishment or anything that indicates superficiality or affectation, or which gives the slightest reason to believe that one is showing off the voice or trying to distract anyone. The singer usually has a wonderful voice. She guides you through the psalms and

antiphons with a plaintive, languishing tone that pierces the heart. . . .

I am told that all the young women who entered the convent with worldly, artificial voices were made to keep silent for three or four months. No one was permitted to sing until they learned to listen to themselves properly and give their voice an intelligent tone and an expression that remained faithful to the pronunciation. This was done to make their song a genuine prayer.[15]

Even if the Paris nuns performed the ecclesiastical chant in a manner that was surely less austere than that of the des Champs nuns, and even though they would insert into their services "modern" compositions like those of Charpentier (indeed, such a practice would have been unthinkable for Port-Royal des Champs), Père Comblat's account seems nevertheless to reflect the individual quality of Charpentier's works.

The hymn *Pange lingua* (which seems to be one of the first compositions—1681—for Port-Royal) is strictly monodic. Only the first two stanzas are set to music (one for the soloist, the other for chorus in unison). The music is supposed to be repeated for the subsequent stanzas in the same alternating fashion. *Stabat mater pour des religieuses* (H. 15) reflects the same compositional technique, and probably belongs to the Port-Royal pieces.

As previously mentioned, *Magnificat, Dixit Dominus,* and *Laudate Dominum* display great similarities in texture, notably in the use of fauxbourdon. This technique goes back to the fifteenth century and consists of a strict parallel motion in all the parts.

In the example given here, the parts proceed chord by chord in root position, while a true fauxbourdon results in parallel sixth chords. This type of polyphony permits utter intelligibility of the text. Every other verse in *Magnificat* and *Dixit Dominus* is written in this manner. Charpentier initially planned to set all the verses in the same fauxbourdon style. Ultimately, perhaps fearing it would be too monotonous, he wrote a fauxbourdon tailored to each verse with rhythmic variations.

A close study of the manuscript reveals that *Dixit Dominus* and *Magnificat* were performed at Port-Royal and elsewhere. Alongside the names of the singers, Charpentier added indications for male voices ("*haute-contre*," "*taille*," and "*basse*") and even the identity of the singers, namely, Dumont the Elder and Dumont the Younger (H. 226) and Dun and Beaupuy (H. 81). While the first two names are unknown today and not found in other scores, the latter two names often appear in the composer's works, especially those written for the Jesuits.

Élévation à 3 dessus ("O clementissime Domine Jesu") (H. 256) stands out from the other pieces through its much more distinctive and expressive writing. This was due, perhaps, to its placement within the liturgy of the mass "at the moment of the elevation of the host," as Charpentier noted at the top of his score.

While maintaining a strictly symmetrical structure (of which the air "Non netu es" occupies the center), the composer adapted his style to the emotions of the text: adoration ("O clementissime Domine Jesu," long chords on the opening utterance, the three vocal parts in imitation); grief ("Heu heu mi Jesu," recitative); rejoicing ("Non netu es," lively with vocal embellishment); grief again ("Heu tristis et subita mutatio," recitative, even more expressive than the first one), and a return to the opening section.

Unlike the poignancy and incandescence of so many of Charpentier's religious pieces, the Port-Royal works limit expressivity. The composer shaped his art to the requirements dictated by the restricted means at his disposal. A melody, usually without any great complexities, and a simple harmonic language combine to keep the musical emotions from overwhelming the sacred content of the text as much as possible. As servant of the word which it discreetly accompanies, the music is and makes no pretense to be anything other than the symbol of the presence of the Holy Spirit.

Chapter 8

The Jesuits: Church and Stage

Even more [musical plays] have been done this year. Besides the tragedy of Saül, *which was performed in Latin verse, there was one in French verse entitled* David et Jonathas. *Since the latter was set to music, it is fitting the work be given the name of opera. It could not have received greater applause.*

Mercure Galant, *March 1688*

Charpentier's appointment by the Jesuits was due to several biographical and musical factors. Not long before she died, Mlle de Guise manifested a concern to permanently establish the composer by recommending him to the most powerful religious order in Europe, the Society of Jesus. Besides a certain amount of prestige that Charpentier could acquire from such an arrangement, Marie de Lorraine was thereby providing him with material security. The composer occupied that post for ten years with a salary reaching as high as 2400 livres per year, a considerable sum, though fees for his musicians were deducted from it.[1]

Charpentier furthermore possessed certain assets that the Jesuits could not help but appreciate. First, he had been a pupil of Carissimi. No French composer could boast of such a heritage. Thus Charpentier provided a link with Rome, the center of the Counter-Reformation. That he had worked with Molière and Thomas Corneille, both former pupils of the Jesuit colleges, could only enhance his eligibility.

Beyond these factors was "the uncommon excellence" of his music that convinced the Society's fathers of the soundness of their choice. As Sébastien de Brossard suggests:

In the opinion of all true connoisseurs he had always been considered the most profound and the most knowledgeable of
modern composers. That is probably what caused the RR.P.P.
Jesuits in the Rue Saint-Antoine to enlist him as music master of
their church, then a most illustrious post.[2]

The grandeur and originality of Charpentier's music is due to a combination of exceptional musical talent and deep faith, each comple-
menting the other. The Jesuits, who in Rome had such composers as
Palestrina, Victoria, or Carissimi in their service, made no mistake in
choosing him.

THE CHURCH

In the middle of the sixteenth century, the Jesuits in France settled in
the Hôtel de Clermont, the future Collège Louis-le-Grand. In 1580,
Cardinal Charles de Bourbon, uncle of the future Henri IV, bought a
house in the Rue Saint-Antoine which he put at the disposal of the
group as a Maison Professe for monks who had taken their vows.
Conflicts with the League chased the Jesuits out of France. They
returned, however, in 1604, and Louis XIII gave them a more
spacious site on which to erect a new church to replace their first
chapel, which had become too small.

On 7 March 1627 Louis XIII laid the cornerstone for the new
church (construction would be completed in 1641). Brother Étienne
Martellange, an architect member of the group, was put in charge of
the construction. He drew much of his inspiration from the Gesù in
Rome, the symbol of Baroque Jesuit art. The floor plans of both
churches are in the shape of a Latin cross and both have one central
nave with connected chapels running parallel, a structure designed
to accommodate processions as well as promote individual prayer.
The Église Saint-Louis (today called Saint-Paul-Saint-Louis) is still
admired for its splendid facade, a felicitous mixture of baroque and
classic style. We also can admire the architecture of the nave with its
monumental pilasters and Corinthian capitals, its entablature with
richly sculpted frieze, its wrought iron balustrade (then gilded), and
the dome and its pendentives in bas-relief representing the four
Evangelists. The same cannot be said of the interior decoration and
accumulation of shapes and colors that gave the church its richness,
none of which survives. Gone are the paintings, the innumerable art
objects, statues, bronze bas-reliefs, gilded wood panels, sumptuous
funeral monuments, the gilded wrought iron pulpit, and the solid

silver tabernacle. The latter, in the shape of a miniature church, had its fore-panel and two back-panels decorated with statues of the Evangelists and scenes from the life of Christ. It was embellished with angels' heads and garlands of flowers, and its dome was topped with a statuette of the triumphant Savior.

Along the same mirrorlike approach, the arrangement of the gigantic high altar's three stories reflected the church's exterior facade. The first two levels were flanked by black-marble columns with gilded bronze capitals against a white-marble background. In the center of the first story was Simon Vouet's *The Presentation to the Temple*, surrounded by statues of Ignatius Loyola and Saint Francis Xavier in niches, and of Charlemagne and Saint Louis on the far sides.

Above these was another canvas by Vouet, *The Apotheosis of Saint-Louis*, (the painting reproduced on the jacket of the present volume), with statues of Mary Magdelen and John on either side. Higher still was *The Dolorous Virgin Raising Her Eyes Toward Christ Suffering on the Cross*, which dominated the entire structure. This work by Père Turmel, the most grandiose retable ever seen in a Paris church, arranged the representation of personages and events along a sweeping ascending movement, like an actual drama stirring up the religious fervor of the congregation. But the Jesuit taste for theatrics went even further. Indeed, the appearance of the high altar was modified according to the liturgical calendar. As if its rich decoration was not enough, the altar was supplemented with other ornaments, reliquaries, silver vases, floral garlands, and incense. Artifice was carried to extremes by decorating that which was already decorative. Just as in the theater, there were, quite literally, scene changes. The central tableau, *The Presentation to the Temple*, was replaced at certain times of the year by two other canvases, *The Deliverance of the Souls from Purgatory* by Philippe de Champaigne and *The Resurrection of Christ* by Claude Vignon. Finally, for funeral services, all external sources of light were obstructed so that the glow of strategically placed candles outlined and highlighted the altar's architectural details.

In this extravagantly lush setting, ceremonies surpassed anything the imagination could conceive. One eyewitness account wondrously revealed the following description:

> After the midday meal, we were at the Jesuits' church. All around the church were seen more than 4000 lighted candles, not counting the candelabra that illuminated the altar, depicting

heaven and filled with figures of angels. The coat-of-arms of the king and queen were displayed on it, supported by the little winged torsos. Through the use of machinery and mechanical devices, the Host was lowered into the hands of the Bishop. . . . There was also a magnificent concert of music made up of the best of the king's singers and reinforced by those of that very church, who are excellent. . . . The king, the queen, the cardinal, and most of the great courtiers attended.[3]

A few years later, Mme de Sévigné described the atmosphere of the canonization ceremony of Francis Borgia on 17 January 1672: "All the musicians of the Opéra are sparing no effort for the occasion, the streets are illuminated as far as the Rue Saint-Antoine: the people are all crazy about it."[4] One wonders whether a religious service or a gala opening night is being described!

One of the numerous attractions of the Jesuit ceremonies was the exceptional quality of the sermons delivered by the finest orators, the most famous of which was Louis Bourdaloue (1632–1704). After having taught rhetoric, philosophy, the physical sciences, and theology, Bourdaloue devoted himself to preaching sermons, which he practiced at court for over twenty years. A less influential personage than Bossuet, the other great preacher of the period, Bourdaloue owed his success to his magnetic personality, high ethical standards, and the austerity of his sermons. Along with Louis XIV's confessor, Père de La Chaise, he was in part responsible for the king's conversion to a more Christian life. Bourdaloue sermonized, La Chaise advised, and their combined efforts produced the desired results. Mme de Maintenon had merely to add the finishing touches to the designs of the two Jesuits.

Bourdaloue's sermons, which Mme de Sévigné never missed unless "the crowds were overwhelming," caused hordes of carriages to block traffic throughout the neighborhood.[5] The crowds were so large that lackeys would reserve seats for their masters as early as five o'clock in the morning for the afternoon service.

This atmosphere of secular piety, an extravagant, permanently staged feast of faith, naturally demanded the addition of music. But if this specifically Jesuit sort of ostentation seems extravagant today, one should remember that others at the time had the same feeling about it:

I must say that in one of the Maisons of Paris inhabited by the most learned men of the most irreproachable moral standing, a fact which even their enemies, whom they are not without, would grant them, and in a church where as fine a sermon can be heard as anywhere in France, vespers is never heard without some part of it being sung by members of the Opéra. The loft is decked with Opéra singers in street dress who sing and act out one or two psalms, as though they were warming up or preparing the characters that these gentlemen play an hour later. This church is so much the church of the Opéra that those who cannot attend the latter console themselves by going to vespers in the former. It does not cost as much. A newly appointed artist would consider his rank and employment only partially fulfilled if he were not invited to sing there.[6]

One of those "gentlemen" who frequently sang at the church but whom Lecerf noticed as having "a different look than his colleagues, a Christian appearance," was bass Jean Dun.[7] A singer with the Académie Royale, Dun created the role of Créon in *Médée* and other major roles for Lully. His name also turns up in twenty sacred works of Charpentier, notably in *Miserere des Jésuites* (H. 193). Were all the works in which Dun participated sung in the Jesuit church? There is no proof, but it would seem quite possible.

The name "M. Dun" first appears in three motets from the early 1670s (*Psalmus 2us 6us supra centesimum à 4 voix* "Nisi Dominus," H. 160; *Laetatus sum*, H. 161; and *Exaudiat à 8 voix, flûtes et violons*, H. 162), but it was added for some performances in the 1690s. But the writing of his name in the *Magnificat à 8 voix et 8 instruments* (H. 74) of 1681–1682 and the *Dixit Dominus* (H. 190) of 1683–1684 seems contemporary with the time of composition. Dun's name appears most frequently between 1688 and 1698 (the date of Charpentier's appointment to the Sainte-Chapelle). Does this mean that Charpentier began working for the Jesuits on a regular basis in the early 1680s? This seems confirmed by the existence of a "Salve regina des Jésuites" (H. 27)[8] from 1680, and especially by the commentary in *Mémoire des ouvrages de musique . . . de M. Charpentier*[9] concerning the two sacred dramas *Mors Saülis et Jonathae* of 1681–1682 (H. 403) "Grand motet ou dialogue, pièce pour les Jésuites en tragédie" and *Josue* also from 1681–1682 (H. 404) "Historia pour les Jésuites." Charpentier began composing exclusively for them in 1688 by becoming the official "music master of the church of the [Jesuit] Collège, then of the [church] of the Maison Professe of those Holy Fathers."[10]

During that period, other singers are mentioned alongside Dun in the manuscripts. First there was Beaupuy, who was in the service of Mlle de Guise. There were also artists who, like Dun, were connected with the Académie Royale: Jean Boutlou (*haute-contre*), Desvoyes (*taille*), Charles Hardouin (bass), and Benoît Hyacinthe Ribon (*haute-contre*). Then there were other, freelance singers like François Cochet (*taille*), who came from the Sainte-Chapelle where he remained from 1684 to 1689; Jacques Molaret (*taille*), who was accepted as a cleric at the same Sainte-Chapelle on 5 February 1695; Lescuyer (bass) whose grandfather [?] Simon was a singer in the Chapelle Royale; Amiot (*haute-contre*); Guenet (bass); and Tonnenche (*taille*).

In one cycle of Tenebrae responsories for Holy Week (H. 126–134), the name of M. Bluquet (*haut-dessus*) appears next to that of Dun's. Bluquet is also mentioned in a Magnificat (H. 77) and an antiphon for the vespers of a confessor not pontiff (H. 33) in which he sang with two other *hauts-dessus*, MM. Favalli and Carli. Was Bluquet actually François Blouquier, singing master of the demoiselles of music of the King's Chamber, and the person who sang *haute-contre* and bass in the Chapelle from 1733 to 1756? Without knowing his date of birth, can it be presumed that Bluquet was singing treble as a boy in the 1690s?

In 1679, Paolo Lorenzani brought back five castratos from Italy to reinforce the children's chorus at the Opéra and at the Chapelle: among them were Antonio Favalli and Tomaso Carli. The French accepted these "unnatural" voices, as long as they came from abroad. Favalli and Carli adapted so well to their French environment that they became naturalized citizens in 1720. Other names found in the works written during 1688–1698 are Boman [?] (perhaps Beaumont, a bass who became a member of the king's music in 1692); Pierre Chopelet (*haute-contre*), a dancer and singer with the Académie Royale; Ducroc (*taille*); Sebret (bass); and Solé (*haute-contre*).

Instrumentalists are indicated only once—in the *Psalmus David 5tus post septuagesimum* "Notus in Judea Deus" (H. 206) in which Dun sang. Also mentioned are M. Converset, who played for the Dauphin, and M. Marchand *père*, who should not be confused with the celebrated Louis Marchand, organist for the Jesuits at the church in the Rue Saint-Jacques, who crossed paths with Charpentier. The musician mentioned in the manuscript is perhaps Pierre Marchand, officer of the Monsieur's music and of the King's Chamber beginning in 1686.

While there is a lack of precise documentation concerning Charpentier's activities at the church of the Jesuit Collège in the Rue Saint-Jacques and at that of the Maison Professe in the Rue Saint-

Antoine, we are hardly any better informed about other choirmasters. The best known among them was Henry Desmarest, Charpentier's successor for a very short time in 1698 at the Église Saint-Louis. Desmarest perhaps replaced Charpentier a few years earlier at the church of the Jesuit Collège. One of the first music masters of the Society, Nicolas Métru, assumed his duties in 1642; Lully was his pupil. Other music masters include "M. Josselin music master in the Rue Saint-Jacques," described in September 1682 by the *Mercure Galant;* Claude Oudot, who in 1687 conducted a Te Deum for the Jesuits when he was associated with the Convent of the Petit Saint-Antoine, opposite the Maison Professe (he was also a singer with the Duc d'Orléans's musical ensemble and a composer of the Académie Française); Charles Masson, "music master of Saint Louis of the Maison Professe of the RR.P. Jesuits," to whom we owe a *Traité des règles pour la composition de la musique;* and finally Edme Foliot, choirmaster for fifteen years beginning in 1710. Although these music masters did not lodge with the Jesuits, in 1692, Charpentier lived in the Rue Dauphine.[11]

The organists' names are more familiar to us: Louis Marchand, organist at the church of the Jesuit Collège, and Delalande, organist at the Église Saint-Louis (the church that since 1643 had possessed a fine instrument with three keyboards and twenty stops) and at Petit Saint-Antoine until 1679.

The *Mercure Galant* published accounts of three important Jesuit ceremonies where Charpentier's music received notice.

In April 1691 Charpentier's music

> sounded admirable and attracted larger and larger audiences into the church of the Collège Louis-le-Grand to hear the Tenebrae sung over the usual three-day period. This music was all the more impressive since it perfectly expressed the meaning of the words being sung and made one appreciate their force.[12]

On 25 August of the following year, the gazette reported the observance of the Feast of Saint Louis at the church of the Maison Professe in the Rue Saint-Antoine as follows:

> [A]n extraordinary throng of people of quality. . . . The music, which was by Charpentier, enchanted the entire audience, particularly a motet expressly written for the Feast Day. We can add nothing more to the reputation he has been making for himself from day to day.[13]

The third occasion on which Charpentier's music was played at an important Jesuit ceremony took place on 21 April 1695 for the funeral of Maréchal Duc de Luxembourg. The ceremony was held

> in the church of the Maison Professe of the Jesuits in the Rue Saint-Antoine, one of the largest and most commodious [churches] for this kind of ceremony. The building is long and spacious, with no separation between the choir and the nave, in the manner of Italian churches. It was all draped in black from the floor to as high as the cornices. . . . After the windows were shut and all daylight blocked out, the interior of the church was illuminated only by candlelight. The Mass commenced at eleven o'clock and was celebrated by M^r l'Évêque, Comte de Noyon, Pair de France, with musical accompaniment provided by a large number of the finest musicians in Paris. The composition was written by Charpentier. . . . Father de La Rue, the famous Jesuit preacher, delivered the funeral oration.[14]

According to the chronology (see the Chronological Table), it is suggested that the 1691 Tenebrae music was that of the responsories H. 126–134, the 1692 motet for Saint Louis *In honorem Sancti Ludovici Regis Galliae* (H. 418), and that the mass for the funeral of the Duc de Luxembourg was *Messe des morts à 4 voix et symphonie* (H. 10).

The Novitiate (located on the site of the present-day Rue Bonaparte, nos. 80–86) constituted one of three great Jesuit establishments in Paris. Youthful candidates wishing to enter the Society of Jesus received special training there for two years. The sobriety and plainness of its architecture was in contrast to the decorative richness of the Église Saint-Louis. The Novitiate had been consecrated in 1640 in the name of Saint Francis Xavier, and it is likely that the motet *In honorem Sancti Xaverii Canticum* (H. 355) as well as the *Canticum de Sancto Xaverio reformatum* (H. 355a) were destined for performance there on 3 December (1690? and 1691?), on the saint's feast day. Contemporary with *In honorem Sancti Xaverii Canticum* (H. 355), the *Motet pour Saint François de Borgia* (H. 354) honors another great Jesuit figure.

If one examines the works belonging to the period 1688–1698, one notices only three Latin oratorios among them: *In nativitatem Domini Canticum* (H. 416), *Dialogus inter Christum et homines* (H. 417), and *In honorem Sancti Ludovici Regis Galliae* (H. 418). None of the great Biblical frescoes composed earlier are among the works of this period.

Nevertheless, these pieces, mostly motets, illustrate the extreme diversity of Jesuit ceremonies in which music obviously played an important role: masses, vespers (psalm and Magnificat settings, hymns, antiphons), feasts of the Virgin and Saints, Benedictions, general rejoicing (Te Deum settings, trumpet tunes), temporal observances (consecration of bishops), and processions (*Litanies*). The two most important periods for the liturgy of that period were centered around Christmas and Easter. It was during Advent and Lent that the sermons of Father Bourdaloue attracted huge crowds to the Rue Saint-Antoine. *Leçons de Ténèbre,* motets for the Passion, *Messe pour le samedi de Pâques, Antiennes 'O' de l'Advent,* instrumental *noël* settings, and the *Midnight Mass* all appear in the right place in Charpentier's manuscripts.

Although we have no definite chronological point of departure for any of these works, we have attempted, by studying contemporary newspaper reports, to determine on what occasions some of them might have been performed.

In August 1695, Louis-Antoine, Cardinal de Noailles, succeeded François Harlay de Champvallon. Various ceremonies in honor of the new archbishop of Paris took place over the next few months. One of them occurred on 9 December at the Jesuit Collège, in the presence of the archbishop "as well as several bishops and persons of quality."[15] Could that have been the occasion when the lavish *Ouverture pour le sacre d'un évêque pour les violons, flûtes et hautbois* (H. 536) was heard?

On 23 January 1695 another archbishop had been consecrated in the Jesuit church of the Novitiate.[16] *Ouverture pour le sacre d'un évêque pour les violons, flûtes et hautbois* (H. 537) may have been performed at that occasion. The composition is located in the manuscripts right after the *Messe de minuit* (H. 9) in the volume preceding the one containing the funeral mass for the Duc de Luxembourg.

The ten years that Charpentier was with the Jesuits fell within the long period of war that Louis XIV was waging with the rest of Europe. The numerous French victories were celebrated by as many Te Deums. Of the four composed by Charpentier, two were written during those years. *Te Deum* (H. 146), with its brilliant orchestration (trumpets, timpani, bass trumpet, flutes, oboes, violins, organ, bassoons) might have celebrated the Maréchal de Luxembourg's victory at Steinkerque on 3 August 1692, and *Te Deum à quatre voix* (H. 147), the surrender of Charleroi on 11 October 1693.

Volume 5 (1693?) of *Mélanges* contains several instrumental preludes for pieces composed earlier. We can assume that Charpentier, in the middle of composing the opera *Médée,* had no

time to write new pieces for the church. He therefore returned to
scores originally written without instruments, dating mainly from the
early years of his Jesuit post. Charpentier enriched these works with
preludes for two treble instruments (probably violins) which doubled
the two upper parts of the chorus throughout.

While the Jesuits made the most of the splendor that music was
likely to add to their ceremonies, Charpentier found the kind of
opportunity that allowed his genius to shine, a "setting" which suited
him perfectly. Indeed, all year long the Église Saint-Louis radiated
incomparable magnificence. The Jesuit "ars persuandi" resorted to
every art and trick to lead the faithful, along the most persuasive
paths, into praising and worshiping God. The beauties of architecture, sculpture, painting, and decorations; the pervasive odors of
incense, glowing candles, and the blazing candelabra; the priests'
rich velvet, silk, and lace finery; the swell of the preacher's voice, now
menacing, now reassuring; and finally the music, filling this
atmosphere of devotion and magnificence with its chords—all combined to turn ceremonies into sophisticated and enchanting spectacles "ad majorem Dei gloriam."

THE COLLÈGE

The main objectives of the fathers of the Society of Jesus included the
necessity of asserting the existence of the Catholic religion in the
face of the strong tide of the Protestant Reformation and of forming
the sort of people within whom

> would be reconciled dogmatic faith and the rational need to
> understand, Christian morality and interest in worldly things
> that represented the new era, the treasury of images charac-
> teristic of the world of Christian thought, and the taste for
> beauty-inspired, esthetic rejoicing awakened by the spirit of
> Humanism and the Renaissance.[17]

Educating the young appeared to be the preferred means of
achieving these goals, a means capable of impressing the elements of
that "devotio moderna" on their minds as early and as indelibly as
possible. In 1551, Ignatius of Loyola, hoping to reorganize
Catholicism in Germany, established the Germanic College of Rome
as a model for other institutions. It was established as a place for
reflecting on methods of instruction and as a meeting place for the
best pupils of all nations. Other such establishments sprang up

rapidly throughout Europe. By the end of the century, in spite of attacks by the Sorbonne and the Parlement, the Jesuit Collège of Clermont had become the most important school in Paris through the quality of its teachers and the size of its student body. Declared a royal foundation by Louis XIV in 1683, it took the name Collegium Ludovici Magni, or Collège Louis-le-Grand.

In 1599 the *Ratio atque Institutio Studiorum Societatis Jesu,* a document that set forth the programs and the principles of teaching in all Jesuit establishments, was circulated. Music is hardly mentioned in it, singing being considered "tedious and of little use." In real life, however, things were quite different.

Soon after these schools were created, theatrical productions began to satisfy the desire for spectacles, which tended to draw people away from the church and stimulate the imagination, a necessary complement in the education of the mind. At first, in accordance with the rules of the *Ratio Studiorum,* academic productions were infrequent, exclusively in Latin, and drawn from "saintly and pious" subjects, with no female roles. Soon, however, these restrictions were ignored. Though only one, and later two, Latin tragedies were given on the average each year (at least in the seventeenth century), it became customary to insert French interludes with song and dance between the acts of the plays. The themes that were chosen also broke the rules, since the authors sometimes drew them from Greek or Roman history and even from secular comic material. Ultimately female characters were introduced, although they were played by schoolboys *en travesti.*

If indeed the Jesuits wanted their theatrical ventures to succeed, they could not overlook those things that made secular drama so popular. Therefore they did not ignore the fact that, particularly in France, dance was considered "one of the most fashionable and honorable exercises in which the most distinguished persons throughout history have tried to excel which they have been proud to master."[18] The king, himself an excellent dancer, declared that the dance was "one of the most respectable and most essential [arts] for the development of the body one of the most useful for our nobility and for others who have the honor of approaching us."[19]

Beginning in 1650 ballets became independent spectacles at the Collège Louis-le-Grand, calling on the finest court choreographers and dancers. Based principally on allegorical themes, Jesuit ballets were linked as much as possible to the Latin tragedies they accompanied, although they also celebrated current events (*Le Mariage du*

Lys et de l'Impériale in 1660 for the marriage of Louis XIV, *La Destinée de Monseigneur le Dauphin* upon the birth of the Dauphin, or the *Ballet de la paix* in 1679, celebrating the Peace Treaty of Nimègue).

The composers of the music for the ballets were rarely mentioned in the programs. Only a few of them are known today, such as André Campra. The musical scores are even less informative. Nevertheless there exists a 1690 score entitled *Les Ballets des Jésuites, composés par MM. Beauchant, Desmatins, et Colasse, recueillis par Philidor Laisné* (The Ballets of the Jesuits, composed by Messieurs Beauchant, Desmatins, and Colasse, compiled by Philidor the Elder), which contains ten ballets, three of which were written for the Collège d'Harcourt.

For the latter school, located not far from the Collège Louis-le-Grand, Charpentier composed *Le Combat de l'amour divin*, a ballet intended to be performed as interludes between the acts of Pierre Corneille's *Polyeucte Martyr*, written in 1640 but performed at Harcourt in 1680. All that remains of Charpentier's ballet is *Ouverture du prologue de Polyeucte* (H. 498) for the Collège at Harcourt. This French-style overture in two sections had originally been composed for Molière's *Le Dépit amoureux*, revived in Paris the year before. Following it are several ballet entries of various shapes and forms: "Profane Loves, Games and Pleasures," "Grace and Virtues," "The Picklocks," "Love the Blacksmith," "Triumphal March" in *rondeau* form and brilliantly scored (trumpets and drums), and "Combatants" with characteristic dotted rhythms. Pantomimes translate the feelings expressed in the spoken passages ("on parle"): "Anxiety," "Attention or Applause," "Sadness," "Marks of Enthusiasm," "Despair," "Noble and Base Feelings," alternating several times more and more rapidly, the first emotion represented by use of the high register of the violins and the second by the low register, and finally "Joy Alone."

Satisfying contemporary public taste also meant staging extravagant productions able to compete with the grandiose scenery, machinery, props, and sumptuous costumes of the Académie Royale. There were no fewer than three performing areas at the Collège Louis-le-Grand. The largest, reserved for summer productions (Latin tragedy and ballet) given during the distribution of diplomas, was installed in the main courtyard. The stage extended from the rhetoric classroom to the chapel's grilled partition and to the refectory building. A huge canvas sheltered spectators seated on risers, while other spectators watched from windows that served as loges. The second theater, not as large, was home to Carnival performances. This theater was installed in another courtyard, that of the "Mans neuf." It was on this stage that *Celse Martyr* and *David et Jonathas* were given. A third area inside the Collège, called the *salle des actions* or "aula," was reserved for winter performances (in the eighteenth century) and for rehearsals of other spectacles.

The very large audiences—in the thousands—were of the highest social standing: the royal family and their guests, the most distinguished courtiers, the highest ecclesiastical and artistic leaders of Paris, as well as students who were not involved in the performance (the student body then numbered 2000) and relatives of those privileged to be in the production. The priests taught their pupils the art of acting, combining the art of pronunciation with that of histrionics, valuable not only for the theater but for making one's way in society. The preparations were lengthy, but the success that was achieved by the productions made up for the patient work of the masters and their students.

It was not until 1683 that the French musical interludes between the acts of Latin tragedies performed during Carnival season developed into genuine tragedies with music and acquired as great an importance as the summer ballets. After having secured a monopoly in the field of dance, the Jesuits were now fixing their sights on the opera, then reigning supreme at the Académie Royale with Lully's tragédies lyriques.

The subjects of these tragedies with music were closely linked to the Latin plays. Compare the following titles: *Eustachius Martyr* and *Eustache* (1684), *Demetrius* and *Démétrius* (1685), *Jephtes* and *Jephté* (1686), *Celsus martyr* and *Celse martyr* (1687), and *Saül* and *David et Jonathas* (1688). The music for all these works has unfortunately disappeared, with the exception of *David et Jonathas*, compiled in 1690 by André Danican Philidor the Elder, the king's librarian.[20]

Besides *Celse martyr* and *David et Jonathas*, Claude Oudot's *Demetrius* is the only other piece whose composer is known to us.

On 10 February 1687, at one o'clock in the afternoon, the fifth-year students performed *Celsus martyr*, a Latin tragedy in three acts by Père Pallu, with *Celse martyr*, a tragedy in music in five acts "serving as interludes to the Latin play." Père Bretonneau wrote the text for the latter and Charpentier the music, but the score, unlike the score of *David et Jonathas,* did not survive.

The story of *Celsus martyr* takes place during the reign of Diocletian. Celsus is a young, newly converted Christian, who despite the opposition of his father Marcien, governor of Antioch, carries his faith to the limit and dies, massacred by his own people. While the Latin tragedy primarily describes the father-and-son relationship, the tragedy in music brings on Marcionille, the mother, who, after Celsus' martyrdom, is converted as well.

A year later, on 28 February, at one o'clock in the afternoon, *Saül,* tragedy in five acts by Father Pierre Chamillart, was performed by fifth-year students (*du seconde*), who were identified as follows (in Latin, of course):

Saul, king of the Israelites: Joannes Baptista Molé de Champlatreux, of Paris

Jonathan, eldest son of Saul: Franciscus Colbert de Maulevrier, of Paris

Seila, wife of David and daughter of Saul: Armandus Le Noir, of Paris

Achish, king of the Philistines: Joannes Dominicus de Montmorency, of Brussels

Abinadab, younger son of Saul: Petrus de Tourmont, of Paris

David, Saul's son-in-law and enemy, having fled to Achish: Carolus de Morangies, of Montpellier

Doeg, the Edomite: Claudius de Condé, of Paris

The story of Saul had already shown up several times in the Jesuit theater beginning in 1635 with *Jonathas,* followed by *Saül* in 1651, *Jonathas liberatus* in 1659, *Justitia Saulis filios immolantis, ou le Théâtre de la justice dans la punition des enfants de Saül* in 1661, and *Jonathas* in 1669. It returned again after the tragedy *Saül* in 1688. To accompany the latter, Père Bretonneau and Charpentier created *David et Jonathas,* a tragedy in music in five acts and a prologue.

The Jesuit Father François Bretonneau (1660–1741) did not enjoy the popularity of some of his colleagues like Bourdaloue, Jouvancy, La Rue, or Porée. His career as a dramatist was short-lived, for he mainly devoted himself to preaching and publishing his colleagues' sermons. His own sermons were published in 1743, two years after his death. The publisher, Père Berruyer, wrote:

Père Bretonneau lacked only polite pronunciation and those external graces of which the fairest discourse cannot be deprived without losing much of its merit in the opinion of the greater number of its listeners. It is not that his actions did not have much soul and fire. They had indeed perhaps too much. But they were not accompanied by that gift of pleasing, which Art cannot supply when Nature has denied it. . . . Skilled theologian, enlightened director, a lover of work and retreat, yet sociable and a pleasant conversationalist . . . but more than all that, a perfect man of religion, upright, zealous, fervent, and a model of all the virtues of his state.[21]

Initially it may seem strange that the Jesuits could have been allowed to perform their tragedies in music while Lully's monopoly banned all nonauthorized musical-dramatic performances. Why is it that the Surintendant took no action against the strong competition that Jesuit drama represented over the course of the years 1685–1688, especially since he exercised that privilege in 1677 after the performance of a tragédie-ballet, *Persée*, given at Louis-le-Grand? Many things had changed since then, however. Louis XIV was beginning to retire from the public life he had thus far enjoyed to lead a more austere existence in which religion gradually began to play a more important role. As a result the king started to lose interest in Lully's operas and, in general, in the great artists who had contributed to the glory of his reign. As for the Jesuits, their widespread influence and power were enormous at that time. The increasing influence of Père de La Chaise on the king, who had entrusted the direction of his soul to him, appeared permanent. Did Lully, who was abandoned by Quinault in 1686, still believe he could challenge the mounting success of the Jesuits' musical theater with his ordinances? Apparently not, since tragedies in music continued to proliferate over the years without the Surintendant trying to do anything to undermine their popularity.

In 1685 Charpentier had produced his final work for the Comédie-Française, which from then on dropped music from its repertoire. Two years later, he composed *Celse martyr*, finally waging his revenge on the person who could no longer thwart him. By 1688, when *David et Jonathas* was performed at Louis-le-Grand, Lully was dead. Sheer coincidence? It is impossible to say for certain.

In any case, the *Mercure Galant* did not shirk from reporting loud and clear the performance of *David*, calling it an "opera" and discussing Charpentier at length and in the most glowing terms:

I must tell you about three operas. One was performed by the Jesuits on the 28th of last month. Since you might be surprised by this, I'll explain. The Collège Louis-le-Grand being full of pensioners of the highest quality, and who leave it only to assume the highest positions of Church and State, the Robe and the Sword, it is required that these youths become accustomed to the boldness and the correct manner necessary for speaking in public. With that end in mind the Jesuits take pains to exercise [that skill] by performing two tragedies every year.... Formerly these tragedies were interspersed only with ballets, because dance is quite essential for good deportment (*bonne grâce*) and corporal agility. Since the rise of music in popularity, however, it has been deemed appropriate to combine it with [the drama], so as to make the entertainment complete. Even more [tragedies] have been done this year. Besides the tragedy of *Saül* which was performed in Latin verse, there was one in French verse entitled *David et Jonathas.* Since the latter was set to music, it is fitting that the work be called an opera. It could not have received greater applause, either in the rehearsals or in the performance. The music was by Charpentier whose works have always enjoyed great success. The comedy of *Circé* and those of *Le Malade imaginaire* and *L'Inconnu,* as well as others for which he has written the music, attest to this. It can be said that since what he has done in his works has created so much approbation, they would have pleased even more if they had had a greater number and quality of voices to execute them.[22]

Even without any knowledge of the scores that preceded *David et Jonathas,* it is certain that Charpentier's tragedy surpassed all the others in length and quality, and that it marked the epitome of the genre. The proof: Philidor's copy (its pricelessness due, moreover, to the fact that it is the only extant example of Jesuit music drama), and the revivals of the work—quite exceptional—at Louis-le-Grand on 10 February 1706, at the Collège d'Harcourt on 12 August 1715 and in other provincial schools (in Amiens and La Flèche on 4 September 1741). After 1690, the interludes to Latin tragedies leaned more toward the pastorale and ballet repertoire, with contributions by Lalouette, La Chapelle, and Campra.

It is regrettable that the music of *Celse martyr* no longer exists. It is very probable that it did not match the music of *David et Jonathas,* since at a revival of the Latin tragedy in 1703, it was accompanied by new music.

In 1695 the Jesuit Collège at Rennes commissioned Charpentier to write another score, which also is lost.

The Père de Longuemare, regent of rhetoric at the Jesuit school in Rennes, continuing to exercise his happy and prolific genius in anything related to the art of his profession, presented on the 16th day of last March a play in three acts. Titled *L'Apothéose de Laodomas*, in memory of the Maréchal Duc de Luxembourg, the interludes suited the subject. The words, as well as the music composed by Charpentier, were most agreeable.[23]

L'Apothéose de Laodomas was an allegorical play depicting the Maréchal Duc de Luxembourg, victor at Neerwinden and Steinkerque, in the guise of Laodomas (conqueror of nations). The first musical interlude consisted of shepherds' lamenting "the tragic death" of Laodomas; the second introduced the "Genius of France" and the "Genius of Flanders"; and the third interlude brought things to a close with a concert of rejoicing.

David et Jonathas

How can it be that no one has imagined or attempted an opera on Christian themes? None has ever been presented to my knowledge, other than the *Jonathas* of Charpentier, played at the Collège de Clermont. A spectacle in which the Jesuits refuse to permit even one woman or the slightest trace of the most harmless *galanterie* only half deserves to be called an opera; aside from that, *Jonathas*, it seems to me, is too dry and wanting in moral and pious sentiments to be called a Christian opera. I would like a subject taken from the Bible or the lives of the saints, with a background of Christianity, lightened by an appropriate blend of unobjectionable *galanterie*. That would probably not be so difficult to arrange.[24]

The above was written by, of course, Lecerf de la Viéville.

If *David et Jonathas* (H. 490) verges on the tragédie lyrique in length and structure (five acts with prologue), the similarity ends there. On the contrary, its divergence from the official model of the court opera (which Charpentier was not able to escape in *Médée*) and the originality of its conception and its language are what makes this tragedy in music a real masterpiece and a major creation in the history of late seventeenth-century musical theater.

The work of Père Bretonneau and Charpentier also occupies a unique position, lying beyond the traditional role of musical interludes in spoken plays, whether within the framework of religious drama or of theater in general. One is reminded of the comédies-ballets of Molière, who was certainly inspired by what he saw and heard at the Jesuit Collège when he was a student there. Although it is inseparable from the Latin play (which is why we shall include the synopsis of *Saül* in our analysis of the work), *David et Jonathas* contains its own unifying thread linking one act to the next. That is the reason why contemporaries gave it the name of opera. Built on the same subject, each tragedy in some way complements the other, the tragedy in music avoiding straight narrative and everything related to the action proper in the Latin tragedy (with the exception of Act V). In the musical composition, this results in an almost total absence of recitative (the essence of Lully's tragédies lyriques). In the staging, it results in an absence of special machine effects which ordinarily accompanied the mighty deeds of heroes.

Instead, *David et Jonathas* emphasizes the psychological, personal side of the characters (each act focusing on one of them at a time) and reveals the humanity behind their official facades. In the music, Charpentier discloses this humanity with an admirable sense of detail and concern for expressivity.

The two tragedies also complement one another in their setting and plot. In *Saül* "the action takes place on the mountain of Gelboë," which is to say in the Israelite camp, while in *David et Jonathas* "the scene is near the mountains of Gelboë between the camp of Saul and that of the Philistines." One more complementary element: the dramatis personae, some of whom appear only in the Latin tragedy (Seila, Abinadab, Doeg) while Joabel only turns up in *David.*

The prologue is common to both tragedies, to the ten acts that follow, and in no way resembles the usual sort of introduction to the traditional tragédie lyrique—a grand portico to the glory of the king with no connection to the tragedy proper. This prologue plunges us immediately into the core of the subject. In fact, what happens in it determines the outcome of the entire work.

When dealing with a work from the Jesuit repertoire, whether ballet or tragedy, it is essential to place it within the context of the Society for whom "divert" not only rhymed with "convert," but where religion was an affair of politics (and vice versa). The religious or mythological subjects nearly always disclosed more or less distinct allusions to noble personages or current events, usually by means of allegory. Sometimes the "keys" were explicitly stated in the programs; other times, their discovery was left to the spectators' discernment and, in particular, to the students for whom that sort of exercise constituted one facet of their regular instruction, falling under the heading of symbol deciphering or enigma solving.

For a look at the "allegorical reading" of *David et Jonathas*, we can do no better than turn to the excellent notes by Jean-Louis

Martinoty, which accompany the recording of the work on the Erato label. Below are a few passages that discuss the ideological significance of the tragedy:

> In *David et Jonathas*, allegory, or the allusion to seventeenth-century events, is naturally very closely linked to the history and personalities of the time. However, unlike the traditions of contemporary theater (especially the Jesuit, and even the Jansenist stage), it was linked less to topical conflicts than to the prevailing ideology that provided their articulation: "royal authority is sacred, paternal, absolute and subject to reason" (Bossuet: *Politique tirée de l'Écriture Sainte* [Policy Derived from Holy Scripture], p. 84, Book III). The work provides such interpretation in the form of parables, with a complete and refined exegesis, with each scene being discussed in a doctrinal commentary of rare subtlety....
>
> *David et Jonathas* ... is a lesson in political conduct and a presentation of the doctrine of obedience to God and to His representatives on earth, the king and the pope. The work aims to teach how, and for whom, to take sides....
>
> Saul is the Lord's anointed and the instrument of His will, up to the moment when he no longer obeys it and loses contact with the Almighty, who seeks and finds another champion in the person of David....
>
> The king, deriving his authority from God, is accountable only to God, who alone could punish him (if Louis were in error, God, not man, could punish him); but God makes use of man (David) to punish the wicked king who does not respect His laws (if Louis is in the right, then he becomes the David sent by God). In each case, the "divine nature of the absolute monarch is asserted, as is the certainty of remaining in the path of the Lord as long as one remains in the path marked out by the king."

To that end, Père Bretonneau and, in particular, Charpentier developed a work of remarkable architectural structure, to which only a bar-by-bar analysis can do full justice. The entire composition, in both senses of the term, is held together by echo effects, repetition, and symmetry within each act as well as between acts. Somewhat self-contained, the tragedy is presented as an immense metaphor of the inevitability of fate personified by Samuel in the prologue, one that brings down characters who get caught up in its web of suffering and death. Even David, crowned king at the end of the work, does not escape the grief of lost love.

One of the touchstones for a deeper understanding of *David et Jonathas* is its use of tonality, something Charpentier always gave particular attention to in his theoretical writings and compositions.

Indeed, each act, except the fifth, not only draws its individuality from its featured character (successively David, Joabel, Saul, and Jonathan), but is at the same time the object of a particular structure. Remarkably emerging from the tonal organization, this structure allows an extremely clear understanding of the psychology of each of the characters and their relationships among themselves and with God. It also takes into account the opposing forces of good and evil (Act II), the public and the private (Acts I and V). Each act is thus given a specific form (binary, ternary, symmetrical, or asymmetrical), as will be seen in the following analysis of the work.

Unlike the tragédie lyrique, *David et Jonathas* employs only an orchestra of four-part strings (*dessus, hautes-contre, tailles,* and basses), to which flutes and oboes are sometimes added. Because Philidor's copy is incomplete, it is possible that other instruments (bassoons, trumpets, drums) were used in certain spots. The choruses are also four-part. All the singing roles were interpreted by male voices, including that of the Witch (*haute-contre*). Jonathan (*dessus*) was performed by a boy.

Prologue. A French overture in two sections opens this prologue. The extent of the fugal section's development is rare for the period, especially in France: subject, countersubject, new expositions of the subject in related keys, free section, recapitulation. The shape of the rhythmically incisive theme and the contrapuntal writing are in no way inferior to a Bach fugue.

Saul appears, alone and lost ("Où suis-je? Qu'ai-je fait?"), encountering, after his desperate appeal to God, only silence. He sings a poignant solo magnificently accompanied by muted strings playing *en louré* (repeated notes played in rapid pairs with an accent on the first). This mood is twice broken: on "Fuyons, fuyons" (Saul's first attempt to escape his dilemma) and after the unbearable silence from God, when Saul decides to turn to the underworld. The restlessness that comes over the orchestra at that point illustrates the character's extreme agitation.

Scene 2 shows Saul before the Witch. The two sing a duet that contrasts with the previous scene, in an utterly charming style. Charpentier the dramatist creates this momentary calm to prepare us for the fateful blow about to sweep down upon Saul.

In the next scene, the Witch, surrounded by a flock of demons, commands the elements to subside and the day to turn to night, the orchestra punctuating her expressive recitative. An incantation ensues ("Ombre, ombre, c'est moi qui vous appelle"), which the Witch must repeat twice before Samuel finally appears.

This scene of black magic could have been the pretext for a considerable amount of operatic scenic effects, or, for example, an infernal chorus, but in this instance the demons simply appear, perform a few pantomimes, then vanish without a word. The scene is treated on the whole with great restraint; by its varied texture, the orchestra alone illustrates the manifestations of the powers of darkness. The drama remains centered on itself, on Saul's sense of expectancy.

The ghost of Samuel emerges from the depths: the very low register of the voice, the four-part bass accompaniment (completely unheard of for its time), the extremely broad tempo, and the wide spacing of the declamation give this apparition an imposing presence. It is through the voice of Samuel that terrible divine punishment swoops down upon Saul. Forsaken by God, condemned to bow before David and to perish along with his children, Saul must prepare to accept the fate weighing not only upon him, but on all the characters of the tragedy up to the final "catastrophe."

After this striking prologue which sets forth the destitution and the suffering of the deposed king of Israel, Act I of *Saül* was performed, followed by Act I of *David et Jonathas,* and so on.

***Saül,* Act I.**[25] When Saul sees himself sorely beset by the Philistines, who as he knows are stationed all around him, and since he knows the Witch's answer, and that the war threatens death for Jonathan, he considers making peace which would bring him closer to the others. Abinadab does his best to persuade him against the plan, arguing that it would be dishonorable for a man of his rank to flee because of lying oracles. Meanwhile Jonathan maintains that peace presents no danger, no shame, and could possibly be obtained from Achish, king of the Philistines, with whom David has taken refuge. At the mere mention of David, Saul, moved by continued resentment, loses his temper. Consequently, Seila, David's wife, having immediately understood from the commotion in the camp that a battle was brewing, goes to Saul's side. She entreats her father to give up the fight and to conclude an alliance that would lead to peace. The obvious dangers that this war implies for her father and her husband torment her. Saul, yielding to the pleading of Seila and Jonathan, seems ready to call on David as mediator for peace. While Saul wanders off in the camp, Jonathan blames his brother Abinadab for wishing to dissuade his father from so necessary a peace and, at the same time, suspecting his brother's designs on the throne, goes to Saul to persuade him to conclude the peace. Shortly thereafter, Abinadab approaches Doeg and openly explains his plot to him: he wishes to use all his forces to bring about the battle that will lead to the death of his father and brother, just as the Witch predicted. Doeg at first opposes Abinadab's plan but, overcome by his pleading, promises his support.

David et Jonathas, **Act I.** Act I opens with a "triumphal march" in the "joyous and very warlike" key of D major (part A). Common folk, shepherds, soldiers, and prisoners all sing the praises of David in a way that almost systematically alternates soloist(s) and chorus. The chorus repeats and expands on the utterances of the soloists; for example, "one of the people" / "Chorus of the People." The over-stated praise is structured in a musically conventional way: this is the official world in which the celebration of the hero, like that of Louis XIV in the prologue of a tragédie lyrique, observes the same rhetorical rules of hyperbole.

In scene 2, written in A major (part B), we witness David's transition from hero to human being. David (*haute-contre*) enters and thanks those who have just sung his praises. The following scene shows him alone. There is a complete shift to the "effeminate, amorous, and plaintive" E minor. This is the core of the act (C) in which the hero is stripped of all pretense and shown to be torn between his duty toward God and his feelings for Jonathan. A mournful prelude introduces his solo accompanied by strings. At the end of this soliloquy, his dilemma remains:

> *Quoi qu'ordonne le sort: vaincu ou victorieux*
> *Moi-même je péris ou je perds ce que j'aime.*

> Whatever fate decrees, vanquished or victorious
> I must perish myself or lose what I love.

The string accompaniment, suspended in the last part of David's solo, returns, this time muted (with *sourdines*), in a new transition section (A major) (B') in which David steps outside his inner monologue to implore God to spare Jonathan's life.

Scene 4 takes us back to the official world of the beginning of the act (return to D major) (A'). While promising to remain at David's side in case of war, Achish (bass), the king of the Philistines, announces to David that Saul is about to ask for peace. The act ends with additional praises. The prisoners sing of "the charms of freedom," and a minuet rounds off the festivities.

Saül, Act II. Jonathan, seeking a delay for his friend, waits for David, summoned by Saul. Saul announces the arrival of Achish and David, who have come to settle the peace. He asks Jonathan to go out to meet them, but already, realizing David would be there, Saul regrets having granted his trust. Seila, seeking David, finds Saul absorbed in thought and very upset, both physically and mentally. She remains motionless before her father's gaze; overwhelmed and divided by many fears, she cannot withhold her complaints. As they talk, the king of the Philistines appears, proposing peace only as long as Saul forgives David. Saul is not happy with this condition, but at last bends to the pleas of his daughter and his officials. When he sees David approaching, the poor man grows uneasy. He appears consumed by an inner fire and finally becomes raving mad at the sight of this enemy, the famous David. David's faith and holy strength guarantee the future. He returns to the camp on the contemptible advice of the Philistine, thanks to the pleas of Jonathan and Seila and even thanks to Saul himself. Achish becomes indignant over Saul's rage, takes up his arms, and desires to go back. Finally, at the entreaties of Jonathan and Seila, he reluctantly consents to negotiate peace with Saul once more. Out of the sight of others, a deeply moved Jonathan embraces David, then tells him of the Witch's revelation and the designs of his brother Abinadab. With this, Abinadab himself enters and states falsely that Saul wishes to see no one but Jonathan before the start of the battle. This time Jonathan truly reproves his brother and immediately returns to his father to please him. Although Abinadab senses that his brother has discovered his plot, he decides to go ahead with it and goes to seek his father to make him suspect his brother.

David et Jonathas, Act II. Act II contrasts the force of evil (Joabel, war) with that of good (David and Jonathan, peace). It opens with a prelude in which oboes double the strings. Joabel (*taille*), one of the chiefs of the Philistine army and a friend of Saul, attempts to persuade David to fight. At the urging of the "Chorus of Jonathan's Escort which is heard but not seen," David leaves to rejoin his friend.

Scene 2 is cleverly constructed on two distinct levels alternating between the malevolent interventions of Joabel and the radiant interventions of the two choruses "of David's escort" (two *dessus*) and "of Jonathan's escort" (two *dessus* and *haute-contre*), celebrating the two friends' happiness. The singing only fires Joabel's anger as he goes back and forth between his furiously syncopated air ("Dépit jaloux, haine cruelle") and recitative, broadly constructed along the lines of the *rondeau*. The air serves as refrain.

This first half of the act (A) (G major), in which the simultaneous presence of the rival realms of war and peace can be read more specifically as a metaphor of war, is followed by scene 3, (B) (C major), consisting almost entirely of an immense chaconne ("Goûtons les charmes"). The chaconne serves as a grand unifying and pacifying movement, which combines soloists and chorus and ends with a beautiful orchestral passage.

Saül, Act III. Abinadab, perhaps spurred on by Jonathan's threats, perhaps touched by his brother's love, regrets that his scheme might lead to the latter's death. The young man's ambition causes him easily to return to his former intentions on the evil advice of Doeg. Together they finally convince Saul, who was still undecided, to fight the enemy. Achish, to keep his promise, comes to Saul to offer peace once more, but in vain. He thus departs in indignation and threatens Saul with never accepting any more offers of compromise. Saul prepares for battle when he perceives Jonathan in the distance. Abinadab wrongly accuses Jonathan of going to join David in the camp of the Philistines. Seila, who had learned of the battle's imminence from Achish, gives up hope for David and hastens to Saul. Saul casts her off without even hearing her. Quite to the contrary and mistrusting feminine wiles, he orders Doeg to keep an eye on her. While Saul returns to camp to launch the attack, Seila sees Jonathan and David and informs them of the outcome of the last meeting between Saul and Achish. In vain David pleads with Jonathan to go back to his father and join the fight rather than to follow his love. Jonathan cannot be persuaded to fight against his friend. Doeg, addressing each of the two friends, manages to separate them and announces that Achish is approaching with a well-armed troop searching for David, against whom he fears Saul will be severe. David joins Achish and the Philistines.

David et Jonathas, Act III. A prelude built on two distinct themes (the first contrapuntal, the second harmonic) opens Act III, in which Saul is the central character. Saul has not appeared in *David et Jonathas* since the prologue. His vacillation and the torment in which he finds himself since Samuel's prophecy have been shown thus far only in the Latin tragedy.

From the moment he enters in scene 1 (A) (F major "furious and quick-tempered"), a very angry Saul dwells on "danger," "treachery," and "swift vengeance." Achish tries to convince him of David's good intentions. The taut rhythm of Saul's recitative contrasts with the calm arioso of the king of the Philistines, in triple meter, accompanied by two treble instruments. But Saul is deaf to it. They both then sing a duet in which each persists in his own manner (Achish: "Malgré tant de rigueurs il est toujours fidèle"; Saul: "Après tant de faveurs il fut toujours rebelle").

The central scene (B) consists of a long monologue for Saul, whose conflicting emotions and inner turmoil are perfectly expressed in music by contrasts in the recitative (ranging from continuo-supported only to accompanied arioso) and in the orchestration (full strings or trio texture, with and without mutes). There are also frequent metrical and key changes (the "obscure and sad" C minor, A-flat major, "cruel and harsh" E-flat major, and "obscure and plaintive" F minor at the mention of Jonathan), expressive orchestral passages (such as the beautifully crafted counterpoint of the prelude), and moments of abrupt silence. Saul finally concludes that the only possible solution is death.

Scene 3 (A') (F major) brings on the tragedy's principal characters: Saul, David, Jonathan, and Joabel. The sight of David rekindles Saul's fury. Once again, in spite of the young hero's affability, Saul accuses David of desiring to overthrow him and Jonathan of siding with him. Realizing that nothing can dissuade Saul, David goes off with a sigh of "Hélas!" The king calls his guards and rushes after David. Joabel is left alone to gloat over his revenge. The chorus sings with him as the act ends with a lively gigue.

Saül, Act IV. As David has failed to bring the Philistines to make peace with Saul, he says farewell to Jonathan for the last time. With what emotion do they part! They truly believe that each of them could fall under the weapon of the other, so uncertain is the outcome of the battle. Achish, again concerned about David, bids him make haste and urges him to send his friend back to the camp, while also encouraging Jonathan to avoid his father's rage. Achish invites Jonathan to flee and rejoin his brother. In fact, David cannot make his friend guilty of such ignominy, and Jonathan himself is incapable of such action. Seila, who fears Saul's overreaction, begs both of them to leave quickly, but it is not so easy to separate the friends. Impatient with these delays, Achish leads David with some difficulty into his camp. They have hardly left when Saul, who has postponed the battle on account of Jonathan (although he was by now certain of the two friends' separation in the Philistines' camp), rejects Seila's advice and prepares for combat. Meanwhile, Jonathan appears. Saul expresses astonishment, not so much at his return, but at his giving in to his father and preparing to fight. Counting on Jonathan's bravery and valor, Saul regains his morale and urges his sons as best he can to avenge the affront to their father. He asks Jonathan, whom he suspects, however, not to wander off too far. Seila attempts to halt the warriors in vain.

David et Jonathas, **Act IV.** After a prelude which, once again, reveals Charpentier's contrapuntal skill in all its glory, we find David in prayer, renewing his devotion to God. Jonathan arrives. David wants to leave. Jonathan holds him back. In a moving duet, they both sing of past happiness in time of peace, then promise to save each other's life on the battlefield. This first part of the act (A) is in the "grave and pious" D minor.

In scene 3 (B), Jonathan is alone and pours out his grief. An introduction for muted strings, with a long ascending chromatic phrase in the upper part, leads to the air in the "tender and plaintive" key of A minor for Jonathan, torn between "too unhappy a friend" and "too harsh a father." Preparing for battle, the "Chorus of Israelites and Philistines [is] heard but not seen," ingeniously handled from a tonal perspective (passing into A major). Jonathan contemplates with horror the dangers that threaten David. Suddenly, however, he remembers Saul, and he repeats the first part of his air ("A-t-on jamais souffert une plus rude peine?"), extended by a little coda. This is a veritable "aria da capo," an essential element of Italian opera rarely encountered in French music of the time. The third part of the act (scenes 4 and 5) (C), in D major, repeats the warrior tune ("Courons, courons") heard during Jonathan's air and now developed with soloists (Saul, Achish, Joabel) and chorus.

The ternary structure of the act highlights the principal character, whose monologue occupies the middle section (likewise for Saul and David in the previous acts), and depicts the deeply divided sentiments of Jonathan: his love for David (A) and his duty toward Saul represented by the Chorus of Warriors (C). The chorus establishes the key of D major (part A was in D minor), foreshadowing the outcome of the dilemma.

Saül, Act V. Achish tells Seila of the outcome of the battle: victory for the Philistines, David unscathed. Seila, rejoicing at her husband's escape, fears deeply for her father and brothers. Achish retires to rally his soldiers after the battle. David appears and declares that he has refrained from fighting so as to avoid any remorse about Saul, his king and master. Seila, still beside herself with grief, after having grossly insulted David, rushes off to confirm the news. Saul, fearing that he has fallen into the hands of his enemies, orders Doeg to slay him. Out of breath and losing self-control, Doeg tells David that Saul wants to kill himself. David dashes off to prevent the rash deed, but he finds him in the arms of a soldier, wounded by a sword on which he himself has fallen. At the sight of David, Saul's pain and fury revive. He calls for Jonathan. One of Saul's sons who has been wounded in battle is brought to him. Saul thinks it is Abinadab, but seeing Jonathan, whom he believed far from the fight, he grows alarmed. Jonathan, between his father and his friend, declares that death is not hard for him and that he dies faithful to both. Saul, feeling his soul departing and his strength ebbing with his blood, asks to be carried away so as not to gratify David with the sight of his death. Jonathan expires in the gentle embrace of his friend. Achish, consoling David as much as possible, leads him away and orders that Jonathan's body be carried off and prepared for funeral.

David et Jonathas, Act V. Breaking the pattern of chronological action which had up to now overlapped from the Latin play into the tragedy in music, Act V of *David et Jonathas* repeats the dramatic events of the last act of *Saül*, like a film flashback that repeats the same ending from a different perspective. Even though Saul and Jonathan are dead by the end of the play, they are alive again at the beginning of Act V of the tragedy in music. Their suffering and David's grief are once more played out for the audience, though what was missing in *Saül* (the victory celebration of the Philistines and the coronation of David) unfolds in *David et Jonathas* in counterpoint to the harsh fate of Israel's heroes. This sort of exercise in contrasts, evident throughout the work, now reaches its climax while furnishing the "moral" of the piece, the edifying message that formed an inherent part of any Jesuit work of art.

The last act of *David et Jonathas* is the only one in which the action makes its point repeatedly in its sequence of victories and deaths. The prelude entitled "Bruit d'armes" in "lively and warlike" C major (A), with its pointed, panting rhythms and incisive sixteenth notes, plunges us into the heart of the battle between the Philistines and the Israelites. Another short movement in triple meter evokes the structure of the French overture. "Jonathan wounded, supported on the arms of a troop of guards," enters over the ostinato dotted rhythm of the prelude and demands help for Saul.

Scene 2 (B) abandons the initial key for G major, then G minor. Saul discovers his dying son. The sight of him fills Saul with intense sadness (the "obscure and plaintive" F minor, a key Charpentier always used for moments of great suffering), and the Chorus of Guards utters brief but plaintive cries of "Hélas!" Jonathan ("obscure and sad" C minor), in an infinitely tender solo with flutes, welcomes death with relief ("Pouvais-je attendre un sort plus doux?"). Losing his mind, Saul takes one of his guards to be David and tries to kill him ("furious and quick-tempered" F major). The chorus reiterates its helpless cries of "Hélas!"

When the unhappy father decides to avenge himself on David (returning to C major, the key in which the act began) (A'), the "Chorus of Philistines heard but not seen" (scene 3) shouts victory.

In scene 4 (B') (G major, G minor, C minor), David finds Jonathan. The two friends' last meeting and the death of Jonathan in the arms of David is one of the most moving passages ever composed. The economy of the dialogue, cut short by death, is supported by music which also gradually sinks into silence. Like the breath of a dying man, the vocal line continues to hang by a thread and gradually dwindles away to nothing.

The death of Jonathan is followed by a long lament (G minor) by David and the chorus. This lament exhibits some of the same features of the final lament in *Dido and Aeneas*, which was composed by Purcell one year later.

In the following scene, Saul appears "wounded, in the arms of soldiers." He dies in front of David after making one last attempt to strike David down.

The final scene begins with a "Triumphal March" in the same key of D major that opened Act I, showing yet another touch of symmetry. Achish tells David that he has been chosen king, but the emotionally shattered hero's only reply before retiring is, "I have lost what I love, my Lord; for me all is lost."

The final pages of *David et Jonathas* (in C major) (A″) are lavishly orchestrated (a double Chorus of Triumphant Warriors, the bass violins that had accompanied Samuel's solo in the prologue, and the probable use of "trumpets and drums") and serve to usher in the reign of David.

As in scene 1 of Act I, David is not present to receive the honors heaped upon him. His real reward is to serve the Lord. The triumphal scenes crowning the beginning and the end of the tragedy also signify that royal authority raises him above all human concerns, including love, even a love as strong and worthy as David and Jonathan's. Hence *David et Jonathas* is as much political tract as human tragedy. In the words of Jean-Louis Martinoty, it is "a lesson in obedience—blind obedience—which also serves as an initiation into suffering."

Various aspects of *David et Jonathas*, including the prevailing arioso style, the importance of monologues, the physical absence of the chorus, and an overall static tone, place the work somewhere between oratorio and opera. It may be useful to remember that Charpentier composed a Latin oratorio on the same theme, *Mors Saülis et Jonathae* (H. 403), for the Jesuit church.

Without taking into consideration Lecerf de la Viéville's customary dislike of Charpentier and the Jesuits, did problems in classifying the work prevent that critic from considering *David et Jonathas* as a "Christian opera"? Not until 1732 did the Académie Royale present for the first time a tragédie lyrique with a subject based on Holy Scripture. They presented *Jephté* by Michel Pignolet de Montéclair, with a libretto by the Abbé Pellegrin.

If a work like *David et Jonathas* has no antecedent in the history of Jesuit religious theater (which incidentally is rather difficult to explain), can one say that Racine's "Tragedies based on Holy Scripture"—*Esther* (1689) and *Athalie* (1691), also didactic in intent—were cast from the same mold? Both these works were commissioned by the Saint-Cyr institute for girls. In his preface to *Esther*,

Racine explained that these tragedies were meant to "polish the mind" and "develop sound judgment" according to the wish "of reputable persons desiring to adhere to the principal philosophy of that house" that he write "a kind of poem on some pious and moral subject combining song and recitative (*récit*), all held together by a spoken play (*une action*) that would make the thing livelier and less apt to lead to boredom." Racine's verse is admirable, but the musical contribution of Jean-Baptiste Moreau is utterly unworthy of comparison in quantity or quality with Charpentier's extraordinary work for the Jesuits in February 1688.

Chapter 9

The Motets

No other French composer of the seventeenth and eighteenth centuries composed as many motets as did Marc-Antoine Charpentier: eighty-three psalm settings, forty-eight elevation motets, thirty-one Tenebrae lessons, forty-two antiphons, and ten Magnificat settings, as well as litanies, Te Deums, sequences, hymns, motets for saints and liturgical feasts, and various other occasional pieces. In all, Charpentier composed almost four hundred separate pieces! These works display such a consistently high level of musical and spiritual inspiration that Charpentier must be considered as one of the major figures of Western sacred music, alongside Heinrich Schütz and Johann Sebastian Bach. Tireless in his work and deeply religious, Charpentier devoted his life to the celebration of the mercy and the glory of God, with humility and splendor, and in a way that was always unabashedly emotional.

Although Charpentier's motets are in the traditional mold of the French motet of the period, they nevertheless transcend that tradition through the intensity of their religious feeling (not felt to the same degree in the motets of Lully or Delalande) and through a style that is often very original and heavily influenced by Italian music.

Moreover, the kaleidoscopic aspect of these compositions, due to the diverse conditions surrounding their creation—each one for a particular need and function—lends an extraordinary dimension to the work of Charpentier.

Today it is rather difficult to understand the importance of religion in the 1600s, with its ordinary services, its great feast days, and the annual liturgical calendar reflected in the rhythm and constraints of everyday life in periods of sadness and of joy. The works of Charpentier, just like those of Bach within the framework of the

Lutheran church, lead us to the heart of the Catholic liturgy of the period, a liturgy with which they were closely and permanently associated.

In the seventeenth century, the mass, vespers, and the rite of the Blessed Sacrament were the three principal services of the Catholic church. During the reign of Louis XIV, masses—even solemn ones— only rarely provided musical settings of the various parts of the service, other than plainchant or by using old compositions or even new ones that were always written in the old polyphonic style. Charpentier was one of the few composers of his time, if not the only one, to devote himself to the writing of masses in the concerted style reserved then for motets.

If French taste seemed reluctant to accept the sung mass, it was nevertheless customary to introduce motets between the different sections of the service. Pierre Perrin explained:

> As to the length of the Canticles, since they were composed for the king's mass, when three of them are ordinarily sung—a long one, a short one for the elevation, and a *Domine salvum fac regem*—I have made the main ones long enough to fill a quarter of an hour, being well written and not overly repetitive, lasting from the start of the mass until the elevation. The pieces after the elevation are shorter and last until the post-communion, which the *Domine* begins.[1]

The first motets, the ones that could "fill a quarter of an hour" (or even longer, depending on the length of the service, such as the grand motets of Lully and Delalande for the mass of the Chapelle Royale), were generally composed on texts from the psalms of David. Indeed, these psalms were particularly popular in France from 1660 on, due no doubt to their publication in French translations and paraphrases. Bossuet repeatedly referred to the psalms in his sermons. David, the king of kings, was made a prototype of Louis XIV after the events of the Fronde, and he remained so in moments of glory.

Charpentier left a considerable number of pieces on these texts, as well as a good many elevation and *Domine salvum* motets, some of which were used in his own masses.

The psalms followed by the doxology ("Gloria Patri et Filio et Spiritui sancto, Sicut erat in principio et nunc et semper et in saecula saeculorum, Amen"), which was the case for the majority of those of Charpentier, were not sung during mass but during vespers. Originally held in the evening (the translation of the Latin word "vesperae"), the service was moved to the afternoon by Saint Benedict. The vesper service included the reciting or chanting of several psalms followed by antiphons, the hymn, the versicle, and the Magnificat. Sunday vespers were different from those held on specific feast days of the liturgical year (such as Charpentier's antiphons for the vespers of a confessor not pontiff, H. 33–35, and for the vespers of the *Assumption of the Virgin,* H. 50–52).

The rite of the Blessed Sacrament is a more recent addition (fourteenth century) to the Roman Catholic liturgy. It acquired such importance after the Council of Trent that it often replaced the vesper service, to which it had originally been appended. In Theatine churches, the rite of the Blessed Sacrament was held by candlelight.

The rite consisted of the presentation and benediction of the Host, preceded by a processional and followed by a benediction of the congregation. Besides the "Tantum ergo" extracted from the "Pange lingua" hymn, the Office might be accompanied by a wide variety of vocal music, including litanies, hymns, and antiphons to the Virgin. In fact, particular texts became associated with various times of the year, like "Stabat mater" (see H. 15, 387) during Lent and the Passion season, or "O filii et filiae" (H. 312, 339, 356) at Easter time. During the presentation of the Blessed Sacrament, little Eucharistic motets similar to those for the elevation in the mass were sung (for example, *Motet du Saint Sacrement,* H. 278, 280).

In his collection of *Motets* published in 1689, Guillaume Gabriel Nivers precisely indicated the order of the vocal pieces:

> Ritual order dictates that the motet of the Blessed Sacrament be sung first, followed by the verse and the prayer; then a motet for the Blessed Virgin, with verse and prayer; and finally a *Domine salvum fac regem.* After the verse and prayer of the latter, the benediction of the Blessed Sacrament is given silently.[2]

Although Charpentier relied on liturgical texts (psalms, hymns, antiphons, Tenebrae lessons, etc.) in most of his motets, it is not uncommon to run across pieces with specially composed texts, neither based on parts of the Scriptures or the liturgy combined with freely written sections (*Motet pour les trépassés à 8,* H. 311; *In circumcisione Domini,* H. 316; *Pour le Saint Sacrement au reposoir,* H. 346) or having no connection at all with liturgical or Biblical sources (certain elevation motets—H. 238, 241, 245; *In purificationem BVM Canticum,* H. 357; *In festo Corporis Christi Canticum,* H. 358). These free texts are the basis of occasional works (for the death of Marie-Thérèse, thanksgiving offerings for the Dauphin and the king, a motet for the Parlement's red mass) and motets inserted into the liturgy, particularly those honoring the Virgin and the Saints (*Pro omnibus festis BVM*, H. 333; *In honorem Sancti Xaverii Canticum*, H. 355; and motets for Saint Louis—H. 320, 323, 332, and 365.

Throughout the second half of the seventeenth century, modern Latin poetry was very much in favor, as illustrated by Perrin's *Cantica pro capella Regis*. Therefore, it is no surprise to find so many paraliturgical texts among Charpentier's works. Unfortunately, we do not know the author(s) of them. It might be that Du Bois, the well-read tutor of Mlle de Guise's nephew, had a hand in the motets Charpentier composed between 1670–1688. Subsequently, when the composer entered into the service of the Jesuits, certain priests of the Society, such as Le Jay and Jouvancy (who won fame via the tragedies given at the Collège), might have written texts, such as those in honor of Saints Francis Borgia (H. 354) and Francis Xavier (H. 355, 355a). Indeed, since Charpentier certainly wrote the text of his musical *Epitaph*, we should not rule out the possibility that he authored some of his own liturgical texts as well.

In the seventeenth and eighteenth centuries, the term *motet* did not refer to any specific genre but instead designated in a general sense any musical composition in Latin, as the following definitions reveal:

> The motet is a piece made up of several vocal numbers or related, but contrasting, musical settings.[3]
>
> Motet. A musical composition, highly embellished and enriched with all the most advanced writing for 1, 2, 3, 4, 5, 6, 7, 8, and even more voices or parts, often with instruments, but ordinarily, and almost always, accompanied at least by a thoroughbass.... The meaning of the term has now been extended to apply to any piece set to Latin words on any subject whatsoever, as in works in praise of Saints, elevations, and so forth. Even entire Psalms are made into motets.[4]
>
> Today the title "motet" is given to any piece of music set to Latin words, as customary in the Roman Catholic church, such as psalms, hymns, antiphons, responses, and so on. All of it in general is called Latin music.[5]

In spite of these very "broad" definitions, the French motet evolved into a genre endowed with its own distinct characteristics in which two main categories can be discerned. The grand "Versailles" motet for chorus and orchestra symbolized royal grandeur, while the "petit motet" for one or more solo voices, sometimes accompanied by a small instrumental ensemble, symbolized the intimate side of seventeenth-century religious devotion. The latter was the preferred territory of Guillaume Gabriel Nivers, François Couperin, and Marc-Antoine Charpentier. The texts of antiphons, Tenebrae lessons, and elevation motets best served this discreet genre in which outward display was replaced by emotion.

It was with Lully's *Miserere* that the French grand motet was truly born. Like the tragédie lyrique, which was the result of a synthesis of many earlier dramatic forms, the *Miserere* marked the epitome of a trend. From Nicholas Formé through Henri Du Mont, this trend introduced ingredients that added to the development of the motet as it existed in France in 1664.

It took a long time for the new concerted style from Italy to be assimilated into French church music. It was only in the second half of the seventeenth century that thoroughbass, monody, instrumental accompaniment, and the contrast between large chorus and soloists (*grand choeur/petit choeur*) replaced the ancient polyphonic legacy of the Renaissance. Formé (1567–1638), who succeeded Eustache Du Caurroy (1549–1609) in the Chapelle Royale, perpetuated the double-choir scoring of his predecessor's motets. At the same time he steered the motet toward the concerted style by means of greater textural contrasts and by replacing the two identical-sized groups of voices with an ensemble of solo voices against the large chorus. Jean Veillot (d. 1662), choirmaster of Notre-Dame and later the Chapelle Royale, introduced the use of orchestra, which doubled the voices in the large chorus, and was used independently in ritornellos. This was a new concept in French music.

Mélanges on Christian Themes, Cantiques, Litanies and Motets set to music for 2, 3, 4 and 5 parts with thoroughbass by Étienne Moulinié (c. 1600–c. 1669) appeared in 1658. In it an entirely new emphasis was placed on the solo voice, as well as on the continuo accompaniment.

The most original composer of that generation was Guillaume Bouzignac [before 1592–after 1641], whom Mersenne considered one of the composers worthy of note "for the excellence of their art." Since Bouzignac lived most of his life in southern France (Narbonne, Grenoble, Carcassonne, Angoulême, and Rodez), his works most clearly reflect the Italian influence. This influence is confirmed by the dramatic vigor of the works, in which musical expression is closely linked to the meaning of the texts. Bouzignac's language belonged more to the Baroque esthetic than did the language of any other French composer. It was comparable, in a way, to the language of Frescobaldi, for example, in whom is discerned the same expressive discontinuity through constantly contrasting elements (dialogue between solo voice and chorus, frequent alternation of counterpoint and vertical harmonies, or ruptures caused by silences). From the Italians, Bouzignac also adopted lively rhythms, bold melodic intervals, and tone-painting. In addition, he was the first composer in France to write sacred dramas (*histoires sacrées*). That is what links him to Charpentier, even though the latter's music sounds more refined and immersed in a French esthetic which the son of Languedoc seems to have completely ignored.

While Bouzignac's innovations probably had no direct influence on French music, the less radical Italianism of Henri Du Mont (1610–1684) was a determining force in the development of the motet. A native of Liège, he acquired an excellent knowledge of the Italian style, which for several decades had been very much in vogue in Flanders. Arriving in France in 1638, he exploited this important facet of his musical training in Maestricht. This characteristic is clearly documented in Du Mont's first collection of two-, three-, and four-part motets—the *Cantica sacra*—published in 1652. In these motets, the composer made use of thoroughbass and recitative, scoring for treble viol in certain pieces, the juxtaposing of contrasting sections. Dissonance is subtly employed, and there is some tone-painting.

From that time, Du Mont's output leaned toward small-scale works (his teacher Hodemont probably having acquainted him with Viadana's *Concerti ecclesiastici*) as well as large-scale ones (*Motets pour la Chapelle du Roy* published in 1686). These provided building blocks for the French motet. In addition, Du Mont's foray into the field of oratorio, with his "dialogues," illustrates the permanent Italian connections of that composer, whose importance lay in his ability to achieve a perfect fusion of modern Italian trends with French tradition.

In 1663, Du Mont was chosen by the king to be one of four assistant directors of the Chapelle Royale, his colleagues being Pierre Robert, Thomas Gobert, and Gabriel Expilly. During the twenty years that he held that appointment, Du Mont composed his grand motets, which were not published until two years after his death. The motets of Lully and Robert were published at the same time. Throughout the first period of the reign of Louis XIV, all three composers produced as many symbols of the glory of their monarch as of their God.

The standard scoring was established as five soloists, five parts in the chorus, and five instrumental parts. The actual make-up of the ensembles varied, however, from one composer to another, and sometimes from one work to the next.[6]

In Charpentier, who was never appointed to the Chapelle Royale, five-part writing is rarely encountered. Other than several works for Mlle de Guise's singers (generally in six parts), there are only six motets for five-part chorus: *In festo Corporis Christi Canticum* (H. 344), *Pour le Saint Sacrement au reposoir* (H. 346), *Litanies de la Vierge* (H. 85), and the three Tenebrae psalms (H. 228–230) for the Sainte-Chapelle. In the funeral works for Marie-Thérèse (*In obitum*, H. 409; *De profundis*, H. 189) only the orchestra is in five parts.

The majority of Charpentier's grand motets are designed for four vocal parts (*haut-dessus, haute-contre, taille,* and bass) and four-part strings (treble, alto, tenor, and bass)—an ensemble the composer had at his disposal in the Jesuit setting and elsewhere as well. The four parts are sometimes subdivided into eight, thus creating a double chorus and a double orchestra. The double chorus employed by Charpentier was not the same as that employed by the Chapelle Royale composers, which was divided into large and small choir. In Charpentier's music, both ensembles are equally important. The composer's perpetuation of a technique that had disappeared in France is one more example of the Italian, and especially Roman, influence on polychoral pieces. Charpentier even composed a motet for triple chorus (*Salve Regina à trois choeurs*, H. 24), not to mention his *Messe à quatre choeurs* (H. 4) directly inspired by Roman models. Charpentier used this double-choral texture, especially in his early works, until around 1685. He later gave it up, with the exceptions of *Laudate Dominum omnes gentes octo vocibus et totidem instrumentis* (H. 223) and *Beatus vir qui timet Dominum 8 vocibus et totidem instrumentis* (H. 224), dating from the mid-1690s.

The number of soloists in Charpentier's motets varies greatly from three to eight. He used soloists in diverse combinations, with a certain preference for trio groups, which appeared just as frequently in the small motets. For the instrumental accompaniment, trio combinations (two treble parts for flutes, violins, or viols plus basso continuo) exist in all pieces (except H. 53 and H. 17 which have only one flute) or sections not scored for full orchestra. In some motets, woodwinds (flutes, oboes, and bassoons) serve to enrich the string orchestra, as do trumpets and drums in ceremonial pieces (*Te Deum*, H. 146).

Structurally, the motets of Lully, Du Mont, and Robert are similar. They open with an instrumental *symphonie,* then alternate solo passages for one voice or groups of soloists, antiphonal interplay between the *petit choeur* and the *grand choeur,* and orchestral ritornellos introducing or concluding the various sections of the text. The classic example is Lully's *Miserere,* which greatly moved Louis XIV when he heard it, as well as Mme de Sévigné for whom there could be "no other music in heaven" than that of the Surintendant. Through its still-Italian sensibility, harmonic progressions, or the expressivity of certain passages, and through its highly contrapuntal character and its pointillistic rhetoric, which were meant to communicate the words of the text as closely as possible, the *Miserere* is, of all Lully's motets, the one that comes closest to the textures in the motets of Du Mont and Charpentier. Later on, the Surintendant would impress upon his great religious works (*Plaude laetare, Te Deum, Dies irae, De profundis*) a more bombastic, extroverted, and official character. Most of the time he would abandon attention to detail and contrapuntal intricacies in favor of vertical clarity and clear contrast between *petit* and *grand choeur* in regular succession. Whatever this simplification and homogeneity of texture lost in emotional feeling was made up for in powerful dramatic effects.

When we listen to Lully's grand motets, they seem less rich, less expressive, less "touching"—to use a contemporary description—than those of Charpentier. The language of Charpentier gives greater heed to the expression of the "soul's passions," in accordance with Sébastien de Brossard's definition of the "Stile Motectico," which must be "a style which is varied, florid and adaptable to any kind of ornamentation, consequently suitable for expressing diverse passions, especially admiration, awe, grief, and so forth."[7]

Lecerf de la Viéville, too, affirmed that

> the music of a motet, which is, so to speak, its body, must be expressive, simple and pleasing. . . . [T]he passions of an opera are cold, in comparison to those depicted by our church music. . . . [T]he art of music—and of church music more than the secular variety—is nothing more than the art of rousing the emotions in an effective and appropriate manner. . . . [It was necessary to] excuse the extreme simplicity of Lully's church music: some claim that it is forced. As to that, I deny it, though I do admit that it sometimes sounds flat, or whatever term one cares to use, in comparison to the works of other composers. Although I feel I have to submit to the common opinion, which tends to make only a mediocre case for his Latin pieces (except

for his totally admirable *Te Deum*, worthy of him throughout for the expressiveness and beauty of the vocal writing), I have great difficulty rejecting those works that are least admired for their excessive simplicity. If he has sinned in that, his mistakes are truly beautiful and help us to understand that he was not only a great composer but also a great man. Deep down he must have had impeccably good taste or judgment enlightened by some unexplainable superior quality. I must add that the sort of music addressed to the gods which he put in his stage works, like sacrifices and invocations, provides us with admirable examples of the strict observance of our doctrines. Whether people observe them in our church motets as appropriately as he does in his operas, whatever the genre, the Christian shall be excellently moved to worship. The listener shall not fall into the error which the severe Saint Augustine declares a sin; *the music of the song must not affect him any more than the words being sung.* The pleasure that the song creates will be associated and combined with the pleasure created by the psalm text. Truly one will not be any more affected by one than by the other; at least, in the pleasant emotion one feels, one will not be able to distinguish whether the psalm or the music is the main cause of that pleasure.[8]

For Lecerf then, the inveterate Lullist, music must never override the sacred text or overpower it with emotions it does not already itself possess. Indeed, he criticized the Italians for using the text for purposes that went beyond the communication of the meaning, and in particular for their preoccupation with "insistently painting each specific word. . . . They ignore the fact that they weaken the overall meaning of the verse and the thought by toying with that specific meaning of the word."[9]

Charpentier stands at the crossroads of these two esthetics of sound and word. Although he avoided some of the excesses for which the Italians were criticized, he never failed (while preserving "the overall meaning of the verse") to highlight words or expressions with music that could raise the text to a higher emotional level. Nonetheless, the chromaticism and the magnificently complex harmonies and effects of contrast and rupture used by him (but never abused) were the result of his apprenticeship in Italy. Hence, as for their instrumentation, the vocal style of Charpentier's motets differed greatly from the official court motet style as imposed by Lully. In fact, it is much closer in spirit to the motets of Du Mont.

In addition to the Italian influence, Charpentier's language derived other aspects of its originality from the polyphonic heritage of old French masters going back to Eustache Du Caurroy. Marpurg, in his *Treatise on the Fugue* (1753–1754), cites Charpentier as one of the most gifted composers in the art of counterpoint. The extremely diverse, well worked-out textures of Charpentier's choruses, their full-bodied polyphony—the inner parts are never simply made up of "filler" as is so often the case in Lully—and their lengthy developments are proof of Marpurg's claim. Charpentier varies his polyphony from strict homophony *à la Lully* (but also learned from Carissimi) to a contrapuntal opulence sometimes containing a highly ambitious fugal texture. Between these two extremes, all possibilities are exploited. On one end is the double-choir texture along the lines of the dialogue technique of the "cori spezzati." Charpentier naturally uses this texture in eight-part motets and also sometimes within a plain chorus, in which parts are subdivided into two or even three in ensembles of more than four voices. On the other end of the spectrum is the imitative texture in which, once all the voices enter, either resolves into a vertical, syllabic style or develops into free counterpoint. A man of contrasts, Charpentier combines all these textural devices to breathe life into his choruses. Ultimately, since they run the gamut of expression from the most unequivocal strength to the greatest tenderness and from explosive jubilation to intense lamentation, it is frequently the choruses that give a work its unique atmosphere.

Although he only rarely used the term "petit choeur," Charpentier scored his works, albeit less systematically than did his contemporaries, by alternating *petit* (generally a trio texture) and *grand* forces. In his orchestral preludes, he also contrasted the *petit choeur* of instruments (violins and/or flutes on treble parts) with the entire orchestra. The vocal *récits* (then meaning anything sung by a solo voice) in Charpentier's motets generally remain within the bounds of arioso, somewhere between declamatory recitative and air.

Depending on the work, Charpentier either adopted the grand motet form of Lully and Du Mont or treated each section as an independent movement in the style of Delalande, Campra, or Bernier. It is difficult, however, to identify any sort of continuous evolution in the style of his structure from the early motets to those of his maturity. (This applies also to the psalm settings which he composed throughout his career.) In the field of the motet, Charpentier's output is variously marked by advanced pieces like the early "Dies irae" (H. 12) of 1670, the *Magnificat à 8 voix et 8 instruments* (H. 74) from 1681–1682, or the "Bonum est confiteri Domino" (H. 195) from

1687. In view of a few of his later works, however, such as *Motet pour une longue offrande* (H. 434), it seems that formal concerns became more predominant over the years.

Charpentier's esthetic ideal remained that of emotional expressivity based on contrast and on fragmentation of the discourse to connect as closely as possible to the affections (Charpentier would have used the word *passions*) suggested by the text. Still, he was not a Bouzignac, who carried the use of rupture and disjunction to extremes. As stated previously, Charpentier never lost sight of the whole in the pursuit of small details. In this respect, he was truly French. His motets are guided by a great unifying principle derived from tonal stability (modulations within a work, whether for dramatic or purely musical reasons, do not challenge the existence of the main key) and balance in the vocal and instrumental arrangement, as well as in the organization of the versets. Although he stood at the cross-roads of two eras represented by two generations of composers (on one hand, Lully, Du Mont, and Robert, and on the other, Delalande, Campra, and Desmarest), and while he developed what the first three composers instituted and foreshadowed the style of the others, Charpentier nevertheless remained deeply rooted in the seven-teenth century. His religious expression in no way yielded to the galant tone of a Campra, or of certain airs of Delalande that smack of opera.

This is probably one of the reasons Charpentier's works fell into oblivion in the eighteenth century. They no longer corresponded to public taste. No other French composer of his day used chromaticism, dissonance, and the art of modulation as boldly as did he. Even though certain characteristics of his harmonic language stem from the old church modes, Charpentier (especially in his last years) leaned toward a more functional conception of harmony which became that of modern tonality. This same kind of dualism can be seen in his English contemporary Purcell, and it persisted in Bach. For these composers, it was one of the richest resources of their language.

THE PSALM SETTINGS

Charpentier's psalm settings can be divided into two categories: those composed in the style of the grand motet (with chorus) and the smaller-scale motets for a trio of soloists. Added to these are *Psalmus*

David centesimus sexdecimus sine organo (H. 182) for four female voices a capella (probably intended for a convent) and two pieces for Port-Royal (*Dixit Dominus*, H. 226, and *Laudate Dominum omnes gentes*, H. 227). The subsequent addition of preludes to certain works (H. 160a, 168a, 171a) indicates that the latter were performed at least one more time when the instrumental pieces were composed.

A few texts seem to have been favorites of the composer, who set "De Profundis" at least seven times, *Dixit Dominus* and *Laudate Dominum omnes gentes* six times, "Beatus vir qui timet Dominus" five times, "Confitebor tibi" and "Miserere mei Dominus secundum" four times, and "Exaudiat" and "Lauda Jerusalem" three times.

The following table is a complete listing of the motets on psalm texts, and the various versions of a number of them:

Psalm texts	Psalm number	Charpentier's work(s)
Beati omnes qui timent Dominum	127	H. 178
Beatus vir qui non abiit	1	H. 175
Beatus vir qui timet Dominum	111	H. 154, 199, 199a, 208, 221, 224
Benedixisti Domine terram tuam	84	H. 181
Bonum est confiteri Domino	91	H. 185, 195
Cantate Domino canticum novum	97	H. 176
Confitebor tibi Domine	110	H. 151, 200, 200a, 220, 225
Conserva me Domine	15	H. 230
Credidi propter quod locutus sum	115	H. 209, 209a
Cum invocarem exaudivit me	4	H. 198
De profundis clamavi	129	H. 156, 189, 205, 211, 212, 213, 213a, 222, 232
Deus Deus meus ad te	62	H. 188
Deus judicium tuum regi da	71	H. 166
Deus noster refugium	45	H. 218
Dixit Dominus Domino meo	109	H. 153, 190, 197, 197a, 202, 202a, 204, 226
Domine Deus salutis meae	87	H. 207
Domine Dominus noster	8	H. 163
Domine in virtute tua	20	H. 164
Domine quid multiplicati sunt	3	H. 172

Psalm texts	Psalm number	Charpentier's work(s)
Dominus illuminatio mea	26	H. 229
Exaudiat te Dominus	19	H. 162, 165, 180, 180a, 180b
Exurgat Deus	67	H. 215
Fundamenta ejus in montibus sanctis	86	H. 187
In convertendo Dominus captivitatem	125	H. 169
In te Domine speravi	70	H. 228
Jubilate Deo omnis terra	99	H. 194
Judica Domine nocentes me	34	H. 201
Laetatus sum in his quae dicta sunt	121	H. 161, 216
Lauda Jerusalem Dominum	147	H. 158, 191, 210
Laudate Dominum de coelis	148	H. 177
Laudate Dominum omnes gentes	116	H. 152, 159, 182, 214, 223, 227
Laudate pueri Dominum	112	H. 149, 203, 203a
Memento Domine	131	H. 155
Miserere mei Deus secundum	50	H. 157, 173, 193, 193a, 219
Nisi Dominus	126	H. 150, 160, 160a, 231
Nisi quia Dominus erat in nobis	123	H. 217
Notus in Judea Deus	75	H. 179, 206
Omnes gentes plaudite manibus	46	H. 192
Paratum cor meum Deus	107	H. 183
Quam dilecta tabernacula tua	83	H. 167, 186
Quare fremuerunt gentes	2	H. 168, 184
Quemadmodum desiderat cervus	41	H. 174
Super flumina Babylonis	136	H. 170, 171, 171a
Usquequo Domine	12	H. 196

The "Petit" Psalm Settings

The psalm settings for small vocal ensemble (twenty-eight of them) are very attractive pieces in which the diversity of the texts treated inspires rich contrasts in texture, both pictorial and dramatic in turn. The different moods called for by the underlying texts are rendered by the opposition of major and minor modes and by textures ranging from sober, vertical harmonies to sometimes richly ornamented imitative counterpoint.

These motets usually begin with a prelude and imitative entries in the two treble instruments (flutes). The same material is repeated and developed by the three voices without instruments, then accompanied by the instruments. This ternary structure is also characteristic of the grand motet of the time (prelude-*récit*-chorus).

The three motets *Prière pour le roi* (H. 164), *Precatio pro rege* (H. 165), and *Precatio pro filio regis* (H. 166) were all composed in the same period. When Louis XIV led his army into Flanders in the spring of 1677 and again in the spring of 1678, "Prayers for the King"—also called "Forty-eight Hour Prayers"—were ordered by the archbishop of Paris "in all the churches in the city and the diocese for the preservation of the king's safety and for the prosperity of his arms."[10]

The motets for the king are psalms of praise ("Domine in virtute mea," "Exaudiat te Dominus"), glorifying the warrior-monarch. Not only their key signatures (C major "lively and warlike" and F major "furious and quick-tempered"), but also the rousing rhythm (♫♩) running throughout these pieces evoke the spirit of the battlefield. Just as warlike is *Psalmus David 5tus (recte 2us)* "Quare fremuerunt gentes" (H. 184) composed at the end of 1682.

The psalm text "Deus judicium tuum regi da" (H. 166) predicts that the son of God's future reign on earth will be just, peaceful, flourishing, and happy. The allusion is clear.

Psalmus David centesimus trigesimus sextus Super flumina Babylonis (H. 170) evokes the suffering of the exiled Israelites on the banks of the Euphrates. The prelude's chromaticism and bold modulations depict that suffering. The reference to Zion in the first verse for solo voices without instruments is accompanied by particularly dissonant chords (augmented octave, augmented fifth). Later, other striking examples of tone painting occur when the voices sing without any continuo support on "Suspendimus organa nostra," or later, when silence breaks the flow of the vocal line on "adhaere at lingua mea faucibus meis." Charpentier used both these devices in his other setting of the same psalm, *Super flumina Psalmus 136 octo vocibus cum instrumentis* (H. 171). In the third and fourth verses, however, while a dialogue is established in H. 170 between the bass voice representing the oppressor and the women's voices representing the exiled Jews, in H. 171 the two levels of discourse are rendered by the alternation of major and minor.

There is no prelude in *Psalmus 3us* "Domine quid multiplicati sunt" (H. 172) proclaiming faith in the Lord in the face of adversity. Instead, it opens immediately with a powerful invocation by the bass ("Domine Domine") against an orchestral accompaniment independent of the vocal line and creating in the very opening measure one of those cross relations (F-natural vs. F-sharp) of which Charpentier was so fond. A shift of mode (from G minor to G major) occurs on the words "Non timebo" in the middle of the piece. The repeated sixteenth notes work toward creating the feeling of power that comes over the psalmist at this point. The next verse returns to the initial minor mode.

"Quemadmodum desiderat cervus" (H. 174), a long plaint of the exiled soul yearning for God, inspired Charpentier to write some passages of poignant lamentation, with chromaticism and suspensions. The composer respected the binary division of the text, with a reprise of the last two verses. The gradual change in mood from desolation to faith in salvation through the Lord is represented by the succession of minor and major modes.

In the margin of folio 3 of the manuscript can be read the name of the performers, "Pieches." The name can be made out between wavy lines, as though someone—the handwriting is not Charpentier's—had stopped to linger dreamily over the page while surrounding the name with fanciful scrawl.

"Beatus vir qui non abiit" (H. 175) begins with a quiet homophonic ensemble in triple meter, which is contrasted by the restlessness of the verse ("Non sic impii") marked "in quick 4" and swept with vocal runs on the word *ventus.*

"Cantate Domino canticum novum" (H. 176) is entirely devoted to the acclamation of the glory of God throughout the earth. To depict this tremendous outpouring of universal joy, Charpentier alternates syllabic passages of clear, consonant harmonies with others in imitation, adding embellishments to words that naturally lend themselves to such treatment ("jubilate," "exultate," "cantate"). This is carried over into the instruments, whose rich melismas rival the bass solo on "Jubilate in conspectu regis Domini."

In "Laudate Dominum de coelis" (H. 177), Charpentier chose the "magnificent and joyous" key of B-flat major for this song of heavenly praise by all creation. Each repetition of "laudate," occurring a great number of times in the first part of the Psalm, gives way to rich ornamentation. When elements of flora and fauna are enumerated during a passage in strict syllabic texture, the composer's pen lingers on the word *pennatae*, an excuse for flowing ornamentation evoking birds in flight. The work ends not without a certain solemnity ("Hymnus omnibus sanctis ejus").

In *Psalmus Davidis centesimus vigesumus septimus* "Beati omnes qui timent Dominum" (H. 178), the first verse evoking humanity's joy in the fear of God is marked by a rather static quality, interrupted by long melismas on "Beati" repeated at the end of the section. In view of the essentially descriptive text, Charpentier's music is decorative and ornamental without being dominated by any one particular expressive feature. The mood does not turn serious until the last words of the psalm ("Pacem super Israel"), which the composer accompanies with beautiful dissonances.

The *Psalmus David septuagesimus quintus* "Notus in Judea Deus" (H. 179) begins with a fanfarelike prelude on a pedal point, first on the tonic, then the dominant, establishing the warlike mood of the text. The sixth verse ("Dormierunt somnum suum") gives us a magnificent illustration of the drowsiness that takes hold of God's enemies: the melody is stationary, with steadily rocking eighth notes in the bass line. A ritornello, in which the continuo instruments are divided into two independent melodic lines, twice serves to prolong the peaceful mood.

Later on we hear a magnificent example of Charpentier's rhetorical skill when he fragments his discourse: "De coelo auditum fecisti judicium" ("Thou didst cause judgment to be heard from heaven"), marked "grave." The melodic lines are practically stationary, with block harmonies in both chorus and orchestra. On "terra tremuit" (the earth trembled), the tempo is marked "quick," the vocal line imitative and melismatic; on "et quievit" (and was still), note values are long, with suspensions, ending on a full bar of silence. Delalande and Campra also set this verse to music, with equally inspired contrasts. About ten years later, Charpentier set this very beautiful motet a second time, in a larger scoring, for chorus and orchestra (H. 206).

Psalmus David octogesimus quartus "Benedixisti Domine terram tuam" (H. 181) and *Psalmus David 107* "Paratum cor meum Deum" (H. 183) both beautifully illustrate the text through ascending vocal lines. The first one is supported by syncopated bass ("Justitia ante eum ambulavit," Righteousness shall go before him), the second in "echo," which is to say *piano,* in steady whole notes on the C-major scale ("et usque ad nubes veritas tua," and thy truth reacheth unto the clouds).

Charpentier treats the Biblical text of *Psalmus David nonagesimus primus* "Bonum est confiteri Domino" (H. 185) freely. He first uses verses 1 and 13 as refrains and, further on, he repeats the first two verses at the end.

Again, in "Omnes gentes plaudite manibus" (H. 192), the first verse is repeated twice, each time more developed, and the music of the seventh and eighth verses is repeated at the end.

Psalmus 86 "Fundamenta ejus in montibus sanctis" (H. 187) has no prelude. It opens directly on the first verse, magnificently illustrated by a double pedal in the vocal bass and continuo. Over the double pedal the two upper voices proceed in layers of ascending phrases solidly supported by conjunct successions of quarter notes.

In the first section of *Psalmus David nonagesimus 9us* "Jubilate Deo omnis terra" (H. 194), Charpentier makes use of a device encountered more frequently in the grand motets. After the bass soloist has sung the first verse, all three voices repeat it using the same musical material, but enriching it with its contrapuntal texture. The last part of this psalm creates some interesting contrasts between the "lively" "Laudate nomen ejus" and the "quoniam suavis est Dominus," marked *slowly*.

Psalmus David 12us "Usquequo Domine" (H. 196) benefits from the larger scoring found in the religious music written for the Dauphin. It includes four voices, one recorder, one flute, one bass flute, and continuo. After a grave prelude, all the voices and instruments present the first verses in which the anxious psalmist questions God. Suspended harmonies and unexpected modulations accompany these distressed interrogations. The mood lightens gradually as doubt is erased, giving way to praise.

"Nisi Dominus" (H. 231) and *De profundis* (H. 232) are in an autograph manuscript not belonging to the *Mélanges*. Both psalms were set several times by Charpentier in the grand motet style. "Nisi Dominus" contains a passage that sounds strikingly modern, with the following magnificent, interrupted cadence on the word "doloris":

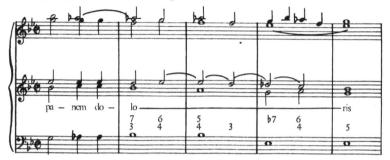

The "Grand" Psalm Settings

Charpentier's very first compositions for chorus (around 1670) were psalm settings intended to be sung during vespers (H. 149–155, *Mélanges* volume XIV, first cahier of the Roman numeral series). The chorus is in four parts and the instrumental accompaniment reduced to two violins (*Confitebor à 4 voix et 2 violons*, H. 151). These are concise works, generally without prelude, presenting each section of the psalm one after the other, with no elaborate development. Each verse receives the same treatment: a solo with or without instrumental accompaniment, duet, trio, and chorus. Here and there, Charpentier varies the fixed vocal distribution within the same verse, alternating the solo ensemble with the chorus as in other motets of the time. The accompaniment of the solos might be through-composed, or, as is characteristic of Charpentier, first in dialogue-form with the voice(s), then coming together in the last part. When the instruments are not used imitatively against the voices in the ensembles and the choruses, they adopt the prevailing rhythm, not yet tracing independent countermelodies. Short ritornellos appear occasionally.

The choral texture is essentially vertical and syllabic; imitations that highlight specific words never last very long. Quite often, Charpentier makes his chorus sound like a double chorus by grouping the parts in pairs (*dessus*/bass and *haute-contre/taille*, *dessus/taille* and *haute-contre*/bass, or *dessus/haute-contre* and *taille*/bass).

While the texture and structure of these first motets later evolved into longer and more complex pieces, they already exhibit all the specific elements of the concerted French motet of the period, as well as the textural devices typical of Charpentier: the *rondeau* form of the "Gloria Patri" (*Confitebor*, H. 151; and "Memento Domine," H. 155), broad modulating chords exchanged between the voices and the instruments on "Quis (Dominus Deus noster)" in "Laudate pueri" (H. 149), and sophisticated harmonies ("qui manducatis panem doloris") in "Nisi Dominus" (H. 150). The latter work, moreover, displays traits typical of Monteverdi ("surgite," the cadence of the "Gloria Patri"). When Charpentier was embarking on the most French of all sacred musical genres, he could not help endowing it with a few Italianisms, discreet ones to be sure, which would nevertheless nourish and enrich all his work to come.

Very quickly (volume XV: H. 158, 160–162) Charpentier introduced new elements that allowed him to develop his discourse. The orchestra of four-part strings and flutes makes its appearance in *Laetatus sum* (H. 161) and *Exaudiat à 8 voix, flûtes et violons* (H. 162). First came preludes, presenting thematic material which would be repeated and developed in the first section of the motet. Like his compatriots, Charpentier divided the orchestra into *petit choeur* (two treble parts for violins and flutes in trio with the thoroughbass) and *grand choeur* combining all the instruments. Both groupings alternated in the preludes and later in the work, with the "little group" accompanying the soloists and the "large group" accompanying all the voices.

While the seventeenth century did not yet boast the type of instrumental colors that Jean-Philippe Rameau would enjoy, Charpentier paid special attention to orchestral timbres which he employed with care, being sensitive to their symbolism, or simply to the variety that they permitted him to introduce into his sacred and secular compositions. In his earliest motets with orchestra, he associated each voice in duets with a separate instrumental part (violins or flutes). *Laetatus sum* contains a short episode in which the bass soloist is accompanied by full strings with mutes. This was probably one of the very first solos with orchestra in the history of the French motet. As early as 1671–1672, Charpentier also indicated dynamics ("fort," "par écho") and tempo ("plus vite," "plus lent," "gai") in his manuscripts.

While the *Laetatus sum* leans toward contrapuntal textures (especially in the "Gloria Patri"), the use of double chorus in the

Exaudiat gives rise to strong antiphony between the two vertically disposed vocal groups. The instrumental *symphonies* in the latter work are more extensive, and the different verses, no longer presented in a straightforward manner, are subjected to considerable development.

Quam dilecta (H. 167), also for double chorus and dating from 1675, has a greater differentiation between choral textures, alternately contrapuntal and vertical, and solo passages; recitative punctuated by ritornellos ("Elegi abjectus"). The tonal range tends toward greater variety, dramatically motivated ("in valle lacrymarum" and "Domine virtutum").

The next works, *Psalmus David 5tus* [recte 2us] *in tempore belli pro rege* (H. 168) and *Psalmus David 125tus* (H. 169) from 1677–1679, reveal the beginning of great structural divisions comprising groups of several verses, beginning with a solo passage and concluding with a large chorus. Charpentier signals the end of the sections with written indications that he would continue to use often, such as "Faites ici une petite pause." This kind of break permitted him to treat the text with more freedom, returning to one verse within the same section after having exposed another in the meantime.

Contrasts between the small and large choruses, strictly practiced in the motets of Du Mont or Lully, were reserved by Charpentier for special purposes, as in *Super flumina Psalmus 136 octo vocibus cum instrumentis* (H. 171) in which the composer very subtly diversifies the vocal density. After the section marked "the entire small chorus divided into two choruses with no instruments except thoroughbass," "the entire small chorus with instruments" enters into dialogue with the "large chorus."

De profundis (H. 189) was composed for the funeral of Marie-Thérèse in 1683. In it, Charpentier uses a five-part string orchestra (*dessus, haute-contre, taille, quinte,* and *basse de violons*), three flutes (two *dessus* and one *taille*), several vocal soloists, and a six-part chorus (*haut-dessus, dessus, haute-contre, taille, basse-taille,* and bass) in an exceptional way. An impressive "prélude" opens the psalm, presenting a very expressive theme in five-part imitation, with a plaintive ascending minor sixth. Delalande would also use that interval in his own *De profundis*. The second part of the prelude uses another thematic element characterized by broad descending phrases that bring to mind the *Messe pour les trépassés à* 8 (H. 2). The soloists (*haut-dessus, haute-contre, taille,* and bass) take up the theme. As each soloist enters, Charpentier ingeniously superimposes the descending lines of the secondary motif in the continuo.

Divided into two groups ("A" and "B") of four parts, the soloists establish a dense dialogue underscoring the mood of supplication toward God ("Domine, exaudi vocem meam"). After a *symphonie* for all the instruments, the first verse is repeated in its entirety, though this time with its polyphonic texture expanded to five, then six parts, accompanied by the orchestra.

This amplification of vocal parts occurs again in the next verses. The "Fiant aures" is first given to the *haut-dessus,* whose solo (with very expressive melismas on "intendentes," a beautiful Neapolitan sixth on "deprecationis"), punctuated by flute ritornellos, is then repeated by two *haut-dessus* voices. Over a continuous eighth-note accompaniment, the bass exposes the "Si iniquitates," this time developed by a trio made up of two *hautes-contre* and bass.

The fourth and fifth verses are given to the large six-part chorus alternating with the small chorus made up of two *haut-dessus,* one *dessus,* and two *hautes-contre* (a total of three real parts). In this work for a truly royal occasion, Charpentier makes the Versailles-style motet his own.

"A custodia" is sung by the bass accompanied by two flutes. When the bass moves on to the "Quia apud Dominum," two *tailles* repeat the last part of the previous verse, superimposing the texts in a completely original manner. After the *petit choeur* in alternating dialogue with the *dessus de violons* and the flutes ("Et ipse redimet Israël"), all the voices attack the "Requiem aeternam" over imposing bass pedals, which provide a solid foundation for the musical structure, symbolizing death and eternity.

Psalm 129 was the psalm most frequently set to music by Charpentier. He wrote six separate versions, to which must be added *De profundis* (H. 213) included in *Messe des morts à 4 voix* (H. 7) and *Gloria patri pour le De profundis en C sol ut bémol à quatre voix, 4 violons et flûtes* (H. 205), the "*De profundis*" apparently lost. The most important setting of Psalm 129 is the one we have just discussed. Chronologically, the first *De profundis* (H. 156) belongs to the series of funeral works from the first volume of the *Mélanges,* though it is completely foreign to them stylistically. Indeed, that motet constitutes an example of the archaic texture that Charpentier sometimes used. In this case, the psalm is treated in unmeasured notation, for one voice or in fauxbourdon.

The *De profundis à 4 voix* (H. 211) begins with a very beautiful bass duet. The two voices first set out in octaves in imitative style. After a rising interval of a fifth in one voice, however, the other answers with a minor sixth, the effect of which has already been noted in the work written for the funeral of Marie-Thérèse. It is indeed interesting to compare the beginnings of both these works, as well as that of the three-part *De profundis* (H. 232). All three are similar:

H. 189

H. 211

H. 232

Returning to the four-part *De profundis*, both bass parts unfold their broad ascending melody and often clash on the interval of a second. In this way extraordinary tension is established in the first verse.

"Requiem aeternam" (strictly speaking, not part of the psalm, but traditionally added to the funeral service) is treated in contrasting modes: "Requiem aeternam dona eis Domine" in *"écho"* over sustained notes, and "Et lux perpetua luceat ei" marked *"plus vite"* (quicker) and *"fort"* (loud) imitatively in fourths.

The same sort of opposing textures and intensities occurs again in the *De profundis* setting of *Psalmus David 129us quatuor vocibus* (H. 212) and in the *Court De profundis à 4 voix* (H. 222). The former touches on keys rarely used at the time, namely, F-sharp minor and C-sharp minor.

With *Psalmus 109us Dixit Dominus 8 vocibus et totidem instrumentis* (H. 190) and *Psalmus 147 "Lauda Jerusalem Dominum"* (H. 191),

Charpentier offers us two works with sumptuous sonorities. A beautiful independent orchestral movement opens the *Dixit Dominus*. While preserving the antiphonal character appropriate for the use of double chorus, Charpentier enriches it with contrapuntal textures much more pronounced here than in the previous works. In "Dominus a dextris tuis," he closely follows the text by differentiating the choral entries with admirable skill; the entries are heard again in the grandiose "Gloria Patri."

The text of "Lauda Jerusalem" is used rather freely by Charpentier, since he repeats the first verse throughout the work. He even repeats it in "Gloria Patri," combining it and sometimes even superimposing it onto the development of other verses. A great fluidity runs throughout the motet, stemming from the omnipresent "Lauda Jerusalem" but also from the tone-painting inspired by expressions and words like "velociter currit sermo ejus" (his word runneth very swiftly), "cinerem" (ashes), "liquefaciet" (melteth), and "flabit" (blow).

Within the verse "Emittet verbum suum" (He sendeth out his word), Charpentier inserts a short descriptive *symphonie* not unlike the *sommeil* in Lully's *Atys*, but which here evokes the melting of ice. An immense "Amen" on the level of the glorious praises lavished upon the entire psalm crowns this sumptuous "Lauda Jerusalem."

Psalmus David 50mus, Miserere des Jésuites (H. 193) was composed in 1685 for Mlle de Guise's singers and later definitely performed again in Saint-Louis in the early 1690s, as indicated by the second version of the prelude (*Miserere à 6 et instruments*, H. 193a). Originally in six parts (*haut-dessus*, two *dessus, haute-contre, taille*, and bass) and two treble instruments, probably viols, the work was adapted by Charpentier for a four-part orchestra of flutes and strings, and the vocal distribution was modified here and there in certain sections. For example, "Amplius lava me," originally for two *dessus*, was later arranged for one *dessus* and one *taille*. In "Quoniam iniquitatem," a quartet (*dessus, haute-contre, taille*, and bass) replaces the three *dessus* and *haute-contre* formation, and so on. In the following analysis of the work, the vocal and instrumental features of the revised version shall be indicated, if necessary, in parentheses.

The first part of *Miserere* is a solidly built, vast triptych of 100 bars, characteristic of the French grand motet in which prelude, solo, and large chorus spring from the same basic material. The prelude presents two motifs (a beautiful arch down the A-minor scale followed by a more rhythmic phrase), which the *basse-taille* soloist takes up, accompanied by two flutes, associating them with each part of the first verse. The exposition of the second verse receives much broader melodic treatment, communicating the idea in the text ("Et in secundum multitudinem miserationum tuarum," According unto the multitude of thy tender mercies). Superimposing the two initial motifs, the chorus repeats and develops the same material in rich polyphony.

The length of the psalm forced Charpentier to be brief in the exposition of certain verses, while other verses are developed at greater length. "Amplius lava me" and "Quoniam iniquitatem" are given to the soloists in duets and later in a quartet, the latter technique rarely used by the composer. The texture is generally imitative, and graceful melismas abound ("iniquitate," "meo"). "Tibi soli peccavi" is sung by the *haut-dessus* concerted with two (violins):

Charpentier here uses the initial "motto" (motif) technique, characterized by a "fragmentary statement that, after a brief rest, is resumed and continued without interruption."[11] Commonly encountered in Italian arias, notably those of Marc Antonio Cesti (1623–1669), this device was frequently used by Charpentier in his religious works (e.g., motets, Latin oratorios).

The next two verses are taken over by the large six-part ensemble and treated as a double chorus with sustained harmonies ("Ecce enim in iniquitatibus conceptus sum"). The passage is characterized by trios marked by stark dissonances ("et in peccatis concepit me mater mea"), pure homophony ("Ecce enim veritatem dilexisti"), and rhythmic incisiveness ("incerta et occulta sapientiae tuae") reminiscent of Carissimi but with the parts grouped in pairs.

"Asperges me," for solo voice and two (flutes) makes use of the initial "motto" technique. "Auditui meo," modulating to A major, is given to a trio (*haute-contre, taille,* and bass). Its dense texture leads the voices into their low register in places. In the choral "Averte faciem," Charpentier returns to the key of A minor and contrasts a first section made up of kaleidoscopic modulations, some luminescent, some dark, with some constantly inventive imitative counterpoint.

After "Ne projicias" and "Redde mihi" for two soloists, "Docebo iniquos" begins with a dialogue between high voices and low voices, sometimes strictly vertical, sometimes embellished with imitative entries. To highlight the second part of the verse ("et impii ad te convertentur"), Charpentier repeats it in a movement marked *"lent"* in which the admirable give-and-take of the voices is made even more expressive through the use of dissonance (e.g., suspensions, augmented chords).

In the following three verses, Charpentier gives the first part to a soloist and the second part to the chorus, each time greatly varying the expression. The final chorus, the longest in the score (91 bars), is launched with "tunc" proclaimed by the three middle voices, and then by full forces. The ensemble shimmers with extraordinary vitality, which includes many fugal entries, forceful chords on "tunc," and a superb peroration on a dominant pedal, completely worthy of Johann Sebastian Bach.

The *Second Miserere 50 à 4 voix et 4 instruments* (H. 219) dates from the mid-1670s. Although quite varied in inspiration, it has neither the emotional fervor nor the dramatic strength of the first *Miserere*. Two other works of Charpentier, *Miserere à 2 dessus, 2 flûtes et basse continue* (H. 157) and *Miserere à 2 dessus, une haute-contre et basse continue* (H. 173), are scored only for small ensembles.

Psalmus David 91us "Bonum est confiteri Domino" (H. 195) was one of the last compositions for Mlle de Guise's singers. Totaling 781 bars, it was the longest motet on a Psalm text set to music by Charpentier. The bi-thematic device noticed in the first section of *Miserere* here asserts itself even more through the dividing of the prelude into two parts, each stating a different motif which the soloists, then the chorus, repeat exactly as in the prelude.

After this extensively developed section, Charpentier's approach to the following verses favors various trio settings: in the high register (*haut-dessus* or *dessus, dessus, haute-contre*), middle register (*dessus, haute-contre, taille*) or low (*haute-contre, taille*, bass). The *haute-contre* remains the pivotal voice throughout.

The composer organizes the last major section of the psalm in *rondeau* form by using the two verses "Justus ut palma florebit" and "Et bene patientes erunt" as refrains. The *rondeau* harks back, in a way, to the binary structure of the opening.

This complex organization of the psalm, which bespeaks a desire on the part of the composer to free himself from a strict linear treatment of the text to satisfy formal requirements, as well as an extraordinarily dense contrapuntal texture, make *Bonum est confiteri Domino* one of Charpentier's most accomplished works.

After 1688, when Charpentier composed for the Jesuits, the psalm settings went back, with a few exceptions, to more modest dimensions. Verses follow each other quickly in the *Dixit Dominus* of *Psalmus David 109us* (H. 197), *Psalmus David 4us* "Cum invocarem" (H. 198), *Psalmus David centesimus undecimus* "Beatus vir" (H. 199), and *Psaume 110ème Confitebor* (H. 200). Nevertheless, textures remain quite rich, diversified, and perpetually changing, as seen in the twenty-two grand psalm settings composed through 1698, most of them for use in the vesper service.

Each of these pieces displays certain peculiarities or traits with which the composer became associated. Some examples are the large independent orchestral section in three parts in *Dixit Dominus* (H. 202) and *Psaume 109*, and the fugal prelude in another *Dixit Dominus* (H. 204)—just like the prelude in *In honorem Sancti Xaverii Canticum* (H. 355), a piece contemporary with the psalm setting.

We have already described the superb *Psalmus David 15tus post septuagesimum* "Notus in Judea Deus" (H. 206). The motet immediately following it in the manuscript, *Psalmus Davidis post octogesimum septimum* "Domine Deus salutis meae" (H. 207), also for Holy Week, is no less prodigious, with its minor modes and chiaroscuro effects.

Although Charpentier often grouped several verses into one single movement in the latter work, he went to extremes in *Psalmus undecimus Davidis post centesimum "Beatus vir qui timet Dominum" 4 vocibus cum simphonia* (H. 208) to vary his texture within the same verse. This diversity was accomplished in one of two ways: by establishing a specific type of structural pattern or by pitting one style against another. The former technique is seen in the fourth verse, "Exortum est in tenebris lumen rectis," and consists of a prelude with mutes, the bass solo, still with muted strings, whose two very calm parts are separated by a short ritornello with quick note values and "loud" dynamics symbolizing daylight. The latter technique is seen in the ninth verse, which is a good example of Charpentier's mastery of the art of contrast. The first part, "Peccator videbit et irascetur" (The wicked shall see it, and be grieved), is stated by the bass solo in florid style. Then on "dentibus suis fremet" (he shall gnash his teeth), the voice repeats the same note C surrounded by a muted-string accompaniment of quarter notes in groups of fours sometimes creating "gnashing" dissonances against the bass. The word *fremet* is repeated, now with elaborate coloraturas descending into the low register, while the characteristic string accompaniment continues. In the last section, "Desiderium peccatorum peribit" (The desire of the wicked shall perish), calm is restored as the steady alternation between the first and fifth degrees of the scale is heard in ostinato fashion in the bass.

The last psalm settings for the Jesuits (H. 209–225) include two other pieces on the text "Beatus vir": *Psalmus David 111 à 4 voix* (H. 221) and *Beatus vir qui timet Dominum 8 vocibus et totidem instrumentis* (H. 224), both beautifully crafted; and *Psalmus David 45* "Deus noster refugium" (H. 218) with lush and powerful choruses. Like the previous psalm settings, the other works, some of which have already been mentioned above, display the same harmonic, contrapuntal, and expressive qualities that Charpentier always used with perfect mastery.

The last three motets on psalm texts date from 1699: *Psalmus David LXX, 3ᵉ psaume du 1ᵉʳ nocturne du mercredi saint* "In te Domine speravi" (H. 228); *Psalmus David 26us, 3ᵉ psaume du 1ᵉʳ nocturne du jeudi saint* "Dominus illuminatio mea" (H. 229); and *Psalmus David 15us, 3ᵉ psaume du 1ᵉʳ nocturne du vendredi saint* "Conserva me Domine" (H. 230). They were scored for a six-part vocal ensemble for the singers of the Sainte-Chapelle and a four-part orchestra. Each motet is divided into two or three large sections. Invariably the first section is given to the soloists, then to all the voices. These mature pieces display great restraint and an unusually dense texture. The perpetually inventive discourse—each verse inspiring a new musical idea—features only rare moments of expansiveness, such as the conclusion of the third psalm, when a graceful melody ("delectationes in dextera tua") soars with an ineffable sense of peace.

MOTETS FOR THE ELEVATION
AND THE BLESSED SACRAMENT

Intended for either mass or Benediction, these works are characterized by their small dimensions (except for *Élévation à 5 sans dessus de violon*, H. 251, which is 312 bars in length), by their scoring (one, two, or three soloists accompanied by an instrumental trio, which, in addition to continuo, uses either two violins and/or two flutes, or two oboes as in *O salutaris*, H. 262), and especially by their individual tone.

There are forty-eight of them (H. 233–280), to which can be added *Salut pour la veille des O* "O salutaris hostia" (H. 36), *Pie Jesu* (H. 427), and *Élévation* "Famem meam quis replebit" (H. 408), which, with its cast of characters, belongs just as much to the domain of the Latin oratorio. *Pie Jesu* harks back, in part, to the last verse of the sequence of the Requiem Mass, found in Charpentier's masses for the dead (H. 234, 263, 269).

Elevation motets were sung during mass between the Sanctus and the Benedictus, "at the moment of the elevation of the Host" as Charpentier noted in one of his scores. Some of these motets are even part of concerted masses, such as "Pie Jesu" and "O salutaris hostia" in *Messe à 8 voix et 8 violons et flûtes* (H. 3). The rest are independent pieces meant to be inserted into the low mass.

During the rite of the Blessed Sacrament, at the moment in which the presentation and benediction of the Host occurred, short motets were sung, just as they were sung during the mass: *Élévation au Saint Sacrement* (H. 264), *Pour le Saint Sacrement à 3 voix pareilles* (H. 270, 271), *Panis quem ego dabo à 5 voix et 2 flûtes—pour le Saint Sacrement* (H. 275), *Adoramus te Christe à 3 voix et 2 flûtes—pour le Saint Sacrement* (H. 276), *Cantemus Domino à 2 voix—pour le Saint Sacrement* (H. 277), and *Motet du Saint Sacrement* (H. 278, 280).

From the order in which the works fall in the manuscripts, it can be seen that certain motets for the elevation or the Blessed Sacrament were probably performed after other ones during the course of the same service. Hence *Élévation pour la paix* (H. 237) came after *Canticum pro pace* (H. 392), *Elevatio* "Venite fideles" (H. 241) after *Prose du Saint Sacrement* (H. 14), "Ave verum corpus" (H. 266) after *Canticum de Sancto Xaverio reformatum* (H. 355a), and so forth.

In addition to motets with liturgical sources (e.g., "Pie Jesu," "O salutaris hostia" set six times, "O sacrum convivium" set four times, "Ave verum corpus," and "Ecce panis angelorum"), the majority of motets for the elevation or the Blessed Sacrament make use of original texts reflecting the provocative sensuality of Baroque religious art. Such texts are full of tender devotion, transports of sweetness and delight in the soul of one who swoons at the sight of the "gentle spouse":

O précieux, ô salutaire, ô merveilleux banquet!
Qui pourra décrire la suavité de ce sacrement
Par lequel toute douceur céleste est savourée dans sa source.
Ah! personne ne le peut!
Soutenez-moi avec des fleurs,
Approvisionnez-moi de pommes!
Voici que tant de douceur me fait défaillir
Que mon âme se met à languir d'amour
Et de désir pour Jésus.

Élévation (H. 245)

O precious, salutary, marvelous banquet!
Who can describe the sweetness of this sacrament
Causing every heavenly delicacy to be savored at its source.
Ah! no one can!
Support me with flowers,
Provide me with apples!
How such sweetness makes me faint,
How my soul begins to languish with love
And desire for Jesus.

The exclamatory *O* with which most of these motets open imme-diately establishes an atmosphere of adoration, effusiveness, compassion, and ecstatic awe. Charpentier breathes all these moods into his *O*s, either through a chordal texture broken by silences (*O sacrum pour trois religieuses,* H. 240), through exchanging between voices ("O pretiosum et admirandum convivium," H. 255), or through long notes sometimes causing the parts to overlap in languorous dissonances (*O sacrum convivium à 3 dessus, Elevatio,* H. 235; *O sacrum à trois,* H. 239; *O amor, Élévation à 2 dessus et une basse chantante,* H. 253; "O pretiosum et admirabile convivium," H. 254; and *Motet du Saint Sacrement à 4,* H. 278).

H. 239

The very beautiful *O amor, o bonitas* (H. 279) ends with an endless melisma on the final "O charitas."

If the prevailing tone in these pieces is one of introspection and tenderness, other feelings, such as jubilation (e.g., "Gaudete dilectissimi," H. 238, or "O coelestis Jerusalem," H. 252), are not excluded. In *O sacrum convivium à 3 dessus, Elevatio* (H. 235), fervent adoration (suspensions, chromatic slides) gives way to the soul's fulfillment (gently swaying triple meter), then to cheerfulness in a brisk, florid "Alleluia." Bathed throughout in infinite tenderness, *Élévation pour la paix* "O bone Jesu dulcis" (H. 237) for three male voices ends in a short instrumental postlude, independent of the preceding vocal section; this is quite uncommon.

Élévation à 2 dessus et une basse chantante "O bone Jesu" (H. 244) opens like a genuine fugue whose theme is composed of two perfectly contrasting elements (long descending notes in the one, short ascending notes in the other). The second element later serves as counter subject.

In *O salutaris à 3 dessus* (H. 261), Charpentier embellishes the word *premunt* with long vocal shakes over an ostinato rhythm in the continuo.

O amor, Élévation à 2 dessus et une basse chantante (H. 253) and the *Élévation à voix seule pour une taille* "Lauda Sion salvatorem" (H. 268) observe *rondeau* form, as do a large number of these motets. In the former, "O amor" is set to a very expressive interval of a descending seventh. In the latter, the reprise of the first section is expanded with long coloraturas on "laudare."

Pie Jesu (H. 427) uses the last verse of the sequence from the Requiem Mass, "Pie Jesu Domine, dona eis requiem," and a text of unknown origin, "Qui pro peccatis hominum." With its descending melodic arches, sequence of sevenths, and falling chromaticism, the prelude for two treble instruments establishes the tone of sweet suffering, which characterizes the prayer that those who are no more may rest in peace.

H. 427

The voices (*haut-dessus, dessus,* and bass) take up the material of the prelude, which is repeated at the end of the motet, attesting to the composer's concern for symmetry already apparent in the arrangement of the text:

> Prelude
> "Pie Jesu"
> Postlude
>
> "Qui pro peccatis hominum"
>
> "Pie Jesu"
> Prelude

THE *DOMINE SALVUM* SETTINGS

Since the reign of Louis XIII, it had been traditional to conclude both High and Low Mass with a *Domine salvum*. The text is taken from Psalm 20:9:

> *Domine salvum fac regem:*
> *Et exaudi nos in die, qua invocaverimus te.*
>
> Lord, save the king:
> And hear our prayer when we call upon you.

Of the twenty-five settings of the *Domine salvum* composed by Charpentier, five were used to conclude masses (H. 281, 283, 285, 299, 303). Like the elevation motets, the *Domine salvum* settings were tailored (except for those in the masses with chorus) to a small group of singers, most often a trio, never for solo voice. The *Domine salvum sine organo en C sol ut* (H. 290) was originally composed for five women's voices without continuo. Charpentier then adapted it to a mixed ensemble and noted at the beginning of the bass part: "*voix et orgue si l'on veut.*" One "Domine salvum" is unfinished (H. 289) and another is a fragment (H. 298).

As official works, Charpentier's *Domine salvum* settings are confined to a style without embellishments or extravagant features of any kind, a style very French (in particular the dotted rhythms of H. 291 and H. 297). They also mix imitation with vertical textures.

THE SEQUENCES

Of the five sequences recognized by the Council of Trent, Charpentier set four in their entirety:[12] the *Prose des Morts* "Dies irae, dies illa" (H. 12), the *Prose pour le jour de Pâques* "Victimae paschali laudes" (H. 13), the *Prose du Saint Sacrement* "Lauda Sion salvatorem" (H. 14), and the *Stabat mater* (H. 15). The latter, which is part of the mass for the Feast of the Seven Sorrows of the Virgin Mary, was written for nuns, perhaps those of Port-Royal (see Chapter 7).

The first of these sequences commands our attention. It is a youth work, yet masterful. It is inventive, powerful, and modern. Charpentier treated the beautiful text by Thomas de Celano (thirteenth century) with particularly convincing expression, and the result is one of his masterpieces. The text consists of eighteen stanzas of three verses each. It is divided musically into five main sections which gradually increase in length over the course of the work. Each section opens with solos for one or more voices and concludes with double chorus and orchestra, plus, in some cases, a short instrumental postlude. Within each section, each verse is treated individually, bearing witness to a great concern for variety and obvious attention to the text.

Charpentier borrows the first notes from Gregorian chant.[13] They are strikingly stated in whole notes and canonic imitation by three male voices (*haute-contre, taille,* and bass). After a pause that is more expressive than functional, the double chorus doubled by the strings attacks the next stanza. Silences between each statement of the first verse ("Quantus tremor est futurus," How great a trembling there will be!) dramatize the meaning of the text. Then the chorus divides and a dense dialogue is established between the two halves. Another silence prepares a superb stroke: a broad cadence with "Quantus" repeated several times, enhancing the word in a highly original manner.

In the second section, Charpentier moves from C minor to C major, a change of mode typical of Italian music upon which the composer frequently drew for dramatic purposes. The key of C major ("lively and warlike") establishes a mood in direct contrast to the previous section. The sound of the last trumpet rousing the dead ("Tuba mirum spargens sonum") inspired the composer to write a passage of extraordinary vitality. This passage is immediately established by the fanfare-like instrumental introduction (repeated notes in a bass pedal under the notes of the triad) that is rounded out with little phrases that are more melodic in shape.

The two vocal *hauts-dessus* take up the thematic material of the little prelude, slightly transforming it through imitation. They then proceed with their duet, which is broken up by brief ritornellos. When the dominant is reached, the instruments followed by two basses render the same stanza.

Although the last ritornello brings back the initial key of C major, the double chorus states the next stanza in minor (yet another use of contrast), beginning with an exchange of poignant chords on the first word ("Mors"). A change of meter (from 3/2 to 2) leads all the voices to an F-minor cadence followed by a pause. On "Cum resurget," Charpentier abandons the homophonic texture and displays all his contrapuntal genius with evocative ascending phrases in eight-part imitation.

Six stanzas make up the third section of the "Dies irae." The first four are given to solo voices: "Liber scriptus" and "Judex ergo" to the *taille* with short ritornellos for two violins; "Quid sum miser" this time to the *haute-contre,* also with violin ritornellos; and finally, "Rex tremendae majestatis" for bass, accompanied by violins throughout. All three voices join in the "Recordare," treated in constant imitation among the parts. The last stanza is brought forth through a clever overlapping device which we shall encounter again in the "Pie Jesu." Before the soloists arrive at a perfect cadence at the end of their trio, the *hautes-contre* of the second chorus enter on "Quaerens me," followed by the other parts of the double chorus without orchestra.

The second part of this stanza calls for a new trio of soloists in the high register (two *hauts-dessus* and *haute-contre*), then full chorus now doubled by the orchestra. A change in meter (from C to 2) permits a broader-paced and more lyrical recapitulation of the text. Throughout this section one must admire Charpentier's love of contrast. His formal concern for the gradual expansion of the discourse is no less impressive.

The fourth section also consists of six stanzas. Although the first three are given to the *haut-dessus* alone, the variety here stems from meter, accompaniment, and key: "Juste judex" (C, ritornellos alternating with solos, C minor/G minor), "Ingemisco tamquam reus" (₵ and 3/2, through-composed accompaniment, modulating by fifths F–G–C), and "Qui Mariam absolvisti" (C, alternating ritornellos with solos, then through-accompanied in C minor). "Preces meae" contains a duet for the *hauts-dessus* and ends with a little *symphonie* for two violins. Next comes one of the most remarkable passages in the entire work. The solo *haute-contre* establishes a dialogue with the chorus, which in turn reiterates the start of the theme of the "Dies irae," like a death knell, before moving on to the dense "Confutatis."

The last section opens with the "Oro supplex" (*taille*, then *haute-contre* and *taille* duet). The shape of the delicately chromatic melody illustrates the text perfectly: "I pray, suppliant and kneeling." No less expressive is the "Lacrymosa" for bass, then trio (*haute-contre, taille,* and bass), accompanied by two violins in a very slow 3/1, with subtle shifts between major and minor. And then, cutting in one bar before the end of the preceding section, comes the sublime "Pie Jesu," crowning the work with infinite tenderness, gentle melodic curves rising terrace-fashion in all the parts, dense polyphony, and shimmering modulations. After one measure of silence, Charpentier's final stroke is the "Amen" on a long, radiant plagal cadence, which at last affirms the key of C major.

THE HYMNS

Charpentier composed settings of a certain number of hymn texts, some of them several times ("Veni creator Spiritus," "Pange lingua," and "Ave maris stella"). The most frequently adopted format was, traditionally, strophic or in verses alternating with organ or with plainchant, not excluding the more diversified style of the concerted motet. The most amazing piece in the entire group is *In Sanctum Nicasium Rothomagensem Archiepiscopum et Martyrem* (H. 55–57), which consists of three hymns written in square notation. Charpentier could not have carried archaism any further. The occasion for which these hymns were written, composed in honor of the first bishop of Rouen, a martyr under Diocletian in 284 A.D., remains to be determined, though it must have been an austere one.

Jesu corona Virginum, Hymne au commun des Vierges à deux dessus et une flûte (H. 53) is one of the composer's very first works using only one flute to accompany the voices instead of the usual pair.

In this case it must have been a matter of necessity (Charpentier having no second flute at his disposal) rather than a matter of choice. An antiphon to the Virgin, "Veni sponsa Christi" (H. 17), is from the same period and also has only one flute. In *Jesu corona Virginum*, the strict homophony of the odd-numbered stanzas contrasts with the concerted style of the even-numbered couplets.

"Veni creator Spiritus" is a Pentecost Sunday hymn that can also be sung before mass to invoke the Holy Spirit. It seems to have been for that type of setting, or for the "catechism" (H. 69, 70), that Charpentier's pieces on this text were conceived.

Hymne du Saint Esprit à 3 voix pareilles avec symphonie et choeur si l'on veut (H. 54) displays the same kind of structure and contrasting effects as *Jesu corona Virginum*.

Veni creator pour un dessus seul au catéchisme (for solo *dessus* at catechism) (H. 69), *Veni creator Spiritus pour un dessus seul pour le catéchisme* (H. 70),[14] and *Pour le Saint Esprit* (H. 362) are settings of the first couplet only. It is possible to sing the others to the same music as the composer prescribes (in H. 69): "Go to the second couplet and to all the others if necessary."

It is a pity that the end of "Veni creator Spiritus" in the *Hymne du Saint Esprit* (H. 66) is lost (due to the missing *Cahier* LVI). The style of that beautifully proportioned score for five soloists, chorus, flutes, strings, and continuo with bassoon is much freer and multi-faceted than are previous pieces. Furthermore, it has a very interesting contrast in the fifth verse between "Hostem repellas longius" (Chase the enemy from us) in quick, repeated notes, and the calm "Pacemque dones protinus" (Hasten to give us peace).

Charpentier left five works on the Thomas Aquinas text "Pange lingua," for the Feast of the Blessed Sacrament or the procession of Maundy Thursday vespers (*Pange lingua à 4 pour le jeudi saint*, H. 68). One of them was composed for Port-Royal (H. 62; see Chapter 7).

In his *Pange lingua* settings, the composer uses not only the same key signature (A minor), but also the same melodic opening. Three of them (H. 58, 61, 62) open with C–A–E, and the other two (H. 64, 68) open with E–E–F. All are echoes rather than genuine quotations of Gregorian melodies. Strophic treatment is used exclusively in H. 62 and partially in H. 58, 61, and 64. In *Pange lingua à 4* (H. 68), the couplets are alternately scored for organ and for voices. Finally, note the rhythmic unity prevailing throughout H. 61 (each verse begins with ♪♩. ♪ ♪♪ , slightly modified for the second ♪♪ ♪♪ , and notice also the two beautiful preludes (H. 61, 64).

"Ave maris stella" is part of the Marian vespers. Charpentier composed four versions of the text. Three of them (H. 63, 65, 67) alternately score the couplets for voices and for organ, or for orchestra (H. 65, third and seventh couplets). In H. 67 the composer employs a very unusual ensemble of three bass voices, but in H. 63 he opts for the high register of two *dessus* in very florid style.

Hymne pour toutes les fêtes de la Vierge (H. 60), the fourth "Ave maris stella" setting, ranges from imitative counterpoint to block harmonies. The third verse is cast as a dialogue between the bass solo and two instruments on one hand, and the solo *haut-dessus* and *dessus* on the other. The two soloists share the text, with brilliant runs in the former group on "Solve vincla reis" (Break the chains of the guilty), and homophony in the other on "Profer lumen caecis" (Give light to the blind). The following verse ("Monstra te esse matrem"), in an altogether different vein ("tenderly"), expresses the request that Mary intercede with her Son on behalf of all sinners.

Iste Confessor (H. 71), a prayer mixed with praise, is addressed to the saints. Charpentier scored it for two vocal *dessus* without continuo.

TENEBRAE LESSONS AND RESPONSORIES

We already touched on the music for Holy Week when discussing the cycle of *Les Neuf leçons de ténèbres* (H. 96–110) and *Les Neuf répons du mercredi saint* (H. 111–119) in Chapter 7. The composer, however, wrote other lessons and responsories before and after those composed for the Abbaye-aux-Bois. An overall look at his significant output (thirty-one *Leçons* and nineteen *Répons*) allow one to trace his development of the genre, from 1670 to the mid-1690s.

Tenebrae Lessons

Charpentier's very first compositions were Tenebrae lessons (volume I, fol. 1–5v of the *Mélanges*). First are three pieces: *Première leçon du vendredi saint* (H. 91); *Troisième leçon du mercredi saint* (H. 92); and *Troisième leçon du jeudi saint* (H. 93), followed a few pages later by an *Autre Jerusalem pour les leçons de ténèbres à 2 voix* (H. 94) and a fourth Tenebrae lesson, *Troisième leçon du vendredi saint* (H. 95).

The latter contains a very beautiful chromatic passage on the last verse ("Mulieres in Sion"). In these lessons, Charpentier made use of a florid style that he would develop further in his works of 1680. It is also interesting to note that in his great cycle ten years later, the composer went back to his Tenebrae lesson, *Troisième leçon du mercredi saint* (H. 92), practically note-for-note.

In the 1690s, Charpentier took up the tenebrae genre for the Jesuits, after having ignored it for some time. No complete cycle is extant, however.[15] Only groupings from three lessons exist: *Première leçon de ténèbres* for Wednesday, Thursday, and Good Friday (H. 120–122), *Seconde leçon de ténèbres* for Wednesday, Thursday, and Good Friday (H. 138–140), and *Troisième leçon de ténèbres* for Wednesday, Thursday, and Good Friday (H. 123–125, 135–137, and 141–143).

In these works, Charpentier abandoned the ornamental profusion of his earlier lessons, even if a few traces of melismatic texture subsist in some sections of the Hebraic letters or within certain verses. Yet the prevailing style is that of the concerted in one or more motet parts with instruments. Despite a certain fidelity to the *tonus lamentationum*, the chant, so shorn of embellishment, has lost a great deal of its expressive power. Other elements, however, serve to enrich the composition, such as the primary role accorded the instruments in spite of the very strict clerical ordinances banning their use. In the *Première leçon de ténèbres* for Wednesday (H. 120) and Thursday (H. 121), muted strings and flutes play in alternate verses. In the Good Friday lesson (H. 122), flutes accompany the vocal line, while the ritornellos make use of the entire orchestra (flutes, oboes, bassoon, strings, organ). Lessons H. 123–125 follow the same alternating pattern, between oboe (or flute) and transverse flute on one hand, and the two violins on the other. Flutes and violins are also present in lessons H. 135–137.

The Hebraic letters, sometimes reduced to one or two notes, are stated in the heart of the instrumental ritornellos which therefore take on the role formerly assigned to the chant. The letters, however, are still often vocalized, just like certain key words of the text. The expressive force derives essentially from the harmonic language Charpentier borrows from his first *Leçons*, thus remaining faithful to certain aspects of his musical rhetoric and even repeating devices used before. Examples included the modulation to F minor on "Viae Sion lugent" in H. 120, the dominant pedal suspension on "In tenebrosis" in H. 124 and 136, the mournful chromaticism on

"Mulieres in Sion humiliaverunt" in H. 125 and 137, or the provocative deceptive cadences on "lassis non dabatur requies" in H. 137.

Responsories

Although not constituting a complete cycle, the nine responsories (H. 126–134) were written for the Jesuits for the same Holy Week. With various forces at his disposal, Charpentier judiciously chose a different scoring for each *Répons* (ranging from solo voice to full chorus, from two flutes to full orchestra), so that each piece comes across as a little independent *scena.*

The *Second répons après la seconde leçon du premier nocturne du mercredi saint* "Tristis est anima mea" (H. 112) is written for two *tailles.* It is a simple transposition of a responsory included in the cycle of *Neuf répons du mercredi saint* of 1680.

The *Second répons après la seconde leçon du premier nocturne du jeudi saint* "Velum templi" (H. 128) is one of the most beautiful examples of pictorial music Charpentier ever composed. It contains sixteenth-note runs for the tearing of the temple veil, muted quarter notes *en louré* by the strings for the earthquake, the cry of the thief, agitated eighth notes ("loud") in the orchestra when the rocks crack and the graves open, and thrilling, climbing phrases in the chorus at the moment of the resurrection of the saints.

Pure emotion prevails in the *Second répons après la seconde leçon du second nocturne du jeudi saint* "Tenebrae factae sunt" (H. 129). It pictures the moment just before his death when Jesus on the cross calls to God. Charpentier closely follows every word and every breath of the suffering Christ, while the orchestra weaves an impressive lament around the vocal line with mournful dissonances and pregnant silences. Everything here is eloquent, describing actions and sights: the voice in the low register ("Tenebrae factae sunt"), the leaps of consecutive fourths ("exclamavit"), the tenderness of the modulation when Christ addresses His Father ("Deus meus"), the descending series of sevenths ("Et inclinato capite"), the fall of a diminished fifth followed by a minor third at the moment of death ("emisit spiritum"), and the astounding harmonies of the final measures.

The *Second répons après la seconde leçon du second nocturne du vendredi saint* "O vos omnes" (H. 134) is written in the unusual time signature of 3/1. Charpentier focused all his attention on the word *dolor.* This word is the object of expressive vocal elaboration ("dolorem meum") and of striking harmonic progression with a passing C-sharp that is bold, to say the least ("si est dolor").

The *Répons après la première leçon de ténèbres du jeudi saint pour une haute taille et 2 flûtes* "Omnes amici mei" (H. 144) is one of Charpentier's last works for the Jesuits.

THE ANTIPHONS

Charpentier's forty-two antiphons can be divided into the following categories: those in honor of the Virgin (the most numerous); the O-antiphons of Advent (H. 37–43); the antiphons for the vespers of a confessor not pontiff (H. 33–35), the first of which was written for castrato voices (MM. Favalli and Carli); the cheerful "Veni sponsa Christi" (H. 17) for *haut-dessus, dessus,* flute, and continuo; the *Antiphona in honorem beate Genovefae voce sola* (H. 29), notable for its beautiful coloratura ending; and finally the instrumental antiphons (H. 516, 517, 525, 526, 532).

According to a tradition going back to the eighth century in France, the cycle of antiphons for Advent, the seven Os, was sung with the greatest solemnity before and after the Magnificat was sung during the vesper service on the seven days prior to the Christmas vigil of December 17–23. Their text embraces "the mystery of the first coming of Christ, from its most distant beginnings to its complete realization."[16] The initial letters of each of these antiphons, from the first to the last, spell out Christ's response to his Church's anticipation: ERO CRAS (I will be tomorrow).

Charpentier noted on his manuscript: *Les 7 O suivant le Romain* (The 7 Os following the Roman), a reference to the Roman breviary, which was different from the Parisian, which was reformed in 1680. In fact, the work dates from the early 1690s.

An instrumental *noël* was performed before each antiphon. Opening the cycle was a *Salut de la veille des O* "O salutaris hostia" (H. 36) which could be replaced by *Antienne à 3 voix pareilles pour la veille des O* "O admirabile commercium" (H. 49), composed later.[17]

This is how Charpentier conceived the work as a whole:

> *Laissez paître* [vos bêtes] (see H. 531)
> *Salut de la veille des O* "O salutaris hostia"
> *O créateur* (see H. 531)
> *First O,* "O sapientia"
> *O nuit*

Second *O*, "O Adonaï"
Vous qui désirez [sans fin] (see H. 531)
Third *O*, "O radix Jesse"
Les bourgeois de Châtre (see H. 534)
Fourth *O*, "O clavis David"
Où s'en vont ces gais bergers (see H. 534)
Fifth *O*, "O Oriens"
Joseph s'est bien marié (see H. 534)
Sixth *O*, "O rex gentium"
Or nous dites Marie (see H. 534)
Seventh *O*, "O Emmanüel Rex"

Each antiphon is structured in the same way. First comes the invocation ("O sapientia," "O Adonaï," etc.), which Charpentier treats in long suspended notes, creating as if by magic the anticipatory atmosphere so suited to the Advent season. The voices present the rest of the text in imitation; on "Veni," the vigorous call to the coming of Christ, the tempo becomes more animated ("lively") and shifts from duple to triple meter. The final bars return to the peaceful, solemn mood of the opening. The overall tone of these antiphons is serious, with concern, nevertheless, for illustrating certain words with melismas (e.g., "flammae," "aeternae," "desideratus"), expressive silences (*Third O*), contrasts between soloist and chorus (*Fourth O*), and dissonant harmonies ("sedentes in tenebris et umbra mortis"). Only the *Sixth O* ("O rex gentium") stands apart from the rest in its more secular tone of the *haute-contre* in dialogue with two violins.

The antiphons to the Virgin bear witness to the era's, and the composer's, preoccupation with the Marian cult. Alongside isolated pieces, the manuscripts contain two cycles. Three *Antiennes pour les vêpres de l'Assomption de la Vierge* (H. 50–52) are part of the Office of Lauds. Charpentier indicated which psalm each one was follow: "Assumpta est Maria" was to be sung after "Dixit Dominus," "In odorem unguentorum" after "Laetatus sum," and "Pulchra es et decora" after "Lauda Jerusalem Dominum." The two obbligato violins in the first antiphon are notated in the G clef on the second line, rarely used in French music of the period.

The other cycle (H. 44–47) includes the four most popular antiphons to the Virgin. They were sung one by one at the end of Complines, according to liturgical custom. Hence, as Charpentier specified, *Alma redemptoris* occurred "between the Saturday vespers before the first Sunday of Advent and the Complines on the Day of Purification;" *Ave Regina coelorum* "between vespers on the day after Purification and the Thursday vespers"; *Regina coeli* "between Saturday Complines and None on the first Saturday after Pentecost"; and *Salve Regina* "between vespers on the eve of Trinity Sunday and None on the Saturday before the first Sunday of Advent."

Instead of the customary minimal scoring for these antiphons, Charpentier used chorus accompanied by two violins. The four pieces together make a very beautiful, unified set, while preserving the individual atmosphere of each text. Contemporary with the seven Os of Advent, they display the same method of emphasizing the opening words by repeating and extending them with long notes or embellishments. After *Alma redemptoris mater* with its Gregorian melismas and intensified in its second part by a few dissonances, and after *Ave Regina coelorum* also displaying medieval chant in its first bars, *Regina coeli* overflows with joyous, light-hearted coloratura on all the words that call for it: "laetare," "resurrexit," and, of course, the "Alleluia" which serves as a refrain at the end of each phrase. The only moment of repose comes in the magnificent "Ora pro nobis," after which the Easter rejoicing returns to the fore in the stunning final "Alleluia."

This was not the first time that Charpentier treated these texts. He had already set to music "Alma redemptoris mater" (H. 21) and written two versions of *Ave Regina coelorum* (H. 19, 22) as well as four other settings of "Regina coeli" (H. 16, 30, 31, 32).[18]

One of the notable features of Charpentier's religious output is that it offers several different settings of the same text. It therefore seems necessary and interesting to provide at least one detailed comparison of the different versions inspired by the same literary source. We have chosen to do this with the five *Salve Regina* settings because of the beauty of the text and the works themselves, and because of the relationship between the text and the music, a basic component of the composer's art. This relationship is particularly instructive in view of the many similarities and variants from one piece to the next. The comparison will help us understand the composer's position vis-à-vis the text—sometimes by aggravating it, so to speak, with a musical stroke designed to emphasize each word by drawing upon the most expressive resources of his palette of sounds, and sometimes by using a simpler, less sophisticated style. Between these two approaches the diversity so characteristic of Charpentier's music is seen, as well as the two sides of the esthetics of the time—Italian expressivity versus French "naturalness"—from which the composer alternately drew his inspiration.

The *Salve Regina* text is believed to be the work of Adhémar de Monteil, bishop of Puy-en-Velay from 1087 to 1098, who preached in support of the First Crusade with Pope Urban II. It is certainly the most beautiful and the most poignant supplication to the Virgin Mary in the liturgy, combining tenderness, despair, and ardent prayer.

> *Salve, Regina, mater misericordiae;*
> *Vita, dulcedo et spes nostra, salve.*
> *Ad te clamamus, exsules, filii Hevae.*
> *Ad te suspiramus gementes et flentes*
> *In hac lacrimarum valle. Eia ergo,*
> *Advocata nostra, illos tuos misericordes*
> *Oculos ad nos converte. Et Jesum,*
> *Benedictum fructum ventris tui,*
> *Nobis post hoc exilium ostende.*
> *O clemens, o pia, o dulcis virgo Maria!*

> Hail, Holy Queen, mother of mercy;
> Hail, our life, our sweetness, and our hope.
> To thee we cry, poor banished children of Eve.
> To thee we send up our sighs mourning and weeping
> In this vale of tears. Turn then,
> O our Advocate, thine eyes of mercy toward us
> And after this our exile, show us
> The blessed fruit of thy womb, Jesus.
> O clement, o loving, o sweet Virgin Mary!

These are the *Salve Regina* settings of Charpentier:

1. *Salve Regina* (H. 18): 104 measures for *haut-dessus, dessus, bas-dessus,* and continuo (1671–1673).
2. *Salve Regina à trois voix pareilles* (for three identical voices) (H. 23): 147 measures for *haute-contre, taille,* bass, and continuo (1677).
3. *Salve Regina à trois choeurs* (for triple chorus) (H. 24): 143 measures (1677–1678).
4. "Salve Regina des Jésuites" (H. 27): 72 measures, for *taille* and continuo (1680).
5. *Salve Regina à 4 voix et 2 violons* (for 4 voices and 2 violins) (H. 47): 108 measures (1694–1695).

All five works are of average proportions, in keeping with the length of the text. Apart from the last antiphon requiring two concerted violins, and the third antiphon's instrumental prelude (H. 23a),[19] composed later, these *Salve Regina* settings employ only basso continuo. The vocal distribution, however, reveals a great concern for variety on the part of the composer.

For the first three pieces, Charpentier adopted the "grave and pious" key of D minor, perfectly suited to the mood of the *Salve Regina*.[20] That choice also stems from an adherence to Gregorian tradition, from which Charpentier borrowed not only its D minor mode, but also the exact intonation (H. 24). In this way the composer preserved the modal character, although it was transposed and slightly altered by the use of the leading tone (H. 23), but still recognizable in H. 18.

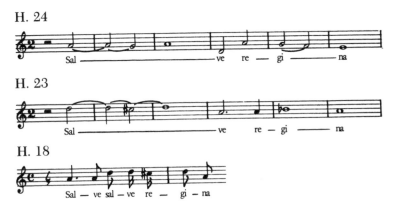

H. 24

Sal —————————————— ve   re — gi ———— na

H. 23

Sal ———————————— ve   re – gi ———— na

H. 18

Sal — ve sal – ve   re —   gi – na

The fourth antiphon is in a "tender and plaintive" A minor, feelings still appropriate to the text. No such correspondence, however, is to be found for the last piece in C major. What is more, the initial melodies of these last two *Salve Regina* settings are unrelated to plainchant. After having stayed as close as possible to liturgical tradition in his first three compositions, Charpentier then detached himself from it completely.

On the first words, "Ad te clamamus exsules filii Hevae," Charpentier develops the same musical idea from one work to another, namely, an ascending melody more or less dramatic in expression. Three types of intervals are used: whole tone (H. 47); the direct and energetic leap of a fifth (H. 18, 27) followed immediately by a much more expressive minor sixth (occurring in H. 27 in the basso continuo in imitation of the vocal line); and half-tone, which creates chromaticism and the inevitable tension that it brings (H. 23, 24). The latter two antiphons, which are contemporary with each other or composed a year apart at the most, appear to be quite similar in places. Charpentier repeated certain passages note-for-note from the piece for three voices in the piece for three choirs.

With the exception of H. 47, the suffering of exile is communicated throughout by harmonies under the sway of dissonances. These dissonances are created by suspensions (H. 18, 23, 27) and chords altered by an augmented fifth (H. 23, 24), with the addition of poignant chromaticism in the bass line (H. 23, 27).

The phrase "Ad te suspiramus gementes et flentes in hac lacrimarum valle" communicates sighing. It is an expression of the longing that carries those who suffer toward the Mother of Mercy. These words find their most convincing counterpart in the musical sigh, with silences adding a gentle breathlessness to the text as the vocal line embarks on its upward climb (H. 23, 24). These silences are also present in H. 18. In H. 27, Charpentier underscores "Ad te suspiramus" with a fall of a diminished fifth.

The words "In hac lacrimarum valle" evoke a theme dear to Baroque composers, namely, that of tears one loved to shed, in church as well as at the opera. The word *valle,* which occurs in everyone of these works, imposes an inescapable downward pull on the entire phrase.

In the first antiphon (H. 18), this descent is achieved in imitation among the three voices in conjunct steps. Then, while the first voice is immobilized on a long note, the other two voices pursue their downward motion. In the following two pieces Charpentier slackens these downward progressions to an extreme by having the voices all sink chromatically in parallel motion. In this way he creates particularly dissonant harmonic clusters: tritones (H. 24), fifths (H. 24), and augmented sixths and sevenths.

This autonomous steering of melody and outright freedom with regard to musical syntax for expressive needs inevitably bring to mind the old Italian masters. A century earlier, Gesualdo, for example, wanted to arouse emotion with maximum intensity, so he turned the musical language of his time inside out. Through his outrageous treatment of the rules of "nature" and French taste, Charpentier no doubt offended more than one ear.

The last two antiphons return to a greater simplicity of texture. Notice, however, the reprise of the vocal line in the bass (H. 27) and some very beautiful entries in imitation (H. 47).

The phrase "O clemens, o pia, o dulcis Virgo Maria," occurs after the confident "Eia ergo, advocata nostra" (marked "affectionate" in H. 27). This final section returns to the mood of pious adoration of the opening of the antiphon, and reverts permanently to a smooth texture. All these pieces display the same gentle, rocking triple meter— generally triadic harmonies modulating in even steps (H. 18, 27)— and supple, conjunct melody favoring the interval of a descending third in which is heard all the humility filling the hearts of those before the Virgin Mary.

Salve Regina à trois voix pareilles (H. 23) concludes with an impressive nine-bar tonic pedal over which the major mode radiantly emerges. *Salve Regina à trois choeurs* (H. 24) reveals all Charpentier's skill as a colorist and harmonist; the choirs answer each other in broad modulating chords with shimmering repetitions of the vowel "O," pursuing their dialogue in echo fashion until the end of the work.

On hearing this piece, one cannot help but be struck by its Italian pedigree. Its similarity to Gesualdo—as already mentioned—for its bold harmonies, to Monteverdi, or to Cavalli's *Salve Regina* composed for Saint Mark is amazing. Like the Venetian composer, Charpentier treats his work in terms of space and of light. A mixture of archaism (the Gregorian opening), bold expression, and sumptuous polyphony, *Salve Regina à trois choeurs* takes its inspiration from an art claiming to be the bearer of emotion.

This large group of antiphons to the Virgin also includes *Sub tuum praesidium* (H. 20) and *Antiphona sine organum ad Virginem* (H. 28) on the same text[21] but with basso continuo; two very similar versions of "Inviolata integra et casta"—H. 26 and H. 48 (*Antienne à la Vierge pour toutes les saisons de l'année*, "Inviolata" *reformé*); and *Antiphona in honorem beatae Virginis a redemptione captivorum* (H. 25) on a nonliturgical text.

THE LITANIES TO THE VIRGIN

Another contribution to the Marian cult are the *Litanies de la Vierge* whose text was set by Charpentier nine times. One of these works (H. 83) was composed for Mlle de Guise's singers. Most of the other settings were apparently destined for the Jesuit church. Three of them (H. 87, 88, 90) are paired with *De profundis* psalm settings (H. 211, 212, 222). The scoring varies from small trio to large chorus.

Although certain elements recur in all these litanies, there are several notable differences, particularly between the works written almost exclusively in a syllabic, vertical style (H. 87–90) and those using very free counterpoint (H. 82–86). In the latter works especially one senses an atmosphere of great tenderness, vocal expansiveness, lyrical expression, and richness of harmony.

Of the nine versions, the one entitled *Litanies de la Vierge à 6 voix et 2 dessus de violes* (H. 83) is not only the most expansive, but also one of the most remarkable. The prayer to the Virgin, alternately assigned to trios (*haut-dessus* / two *dessus* or *haute-contre* / *taille* / bass) and to a six-part ensemble, is by turns humble, ardent, joyous, and ultimately imploring, never losing its fervent tone and unflagging inspiration. Since the *Litanies de la Vierge* belonged to the evening service, it is in the context of that devotion that the beautiful and soothing descending phrases of the "ora pro nobis" in H. 83 should be heard.

Within the work's main tonality of D minor, "grave and pious," Charpentier manages to include passages in other keys, in keeping with the text (just as he does in his other *Litanies*). Particularly expressive is the modulation that plunges one from D major into G minor when the prayer becomes most intense:

> *Salus infirmorum*
> *Refugium peccatorum*
> *Consolatrix afflictorum*
> *Auxilium christianorum*
> *Ora pro nobis.*
>
> Health of the sick,
> Refuge of the sinners,
> Comforter of the afflicted,
> Help of Christians,
> Pray for us.

In such a passage, Charpentier becomes astonishingly attentive to detail, assigning a melodic motif almost systematically to every word. "Refugium" is subjected to slight chromatic tension which is dispelled by long, gentle curves on "peccatorum," and, like a sob, by the little sixteenth-note motif followed by a drop of a fourth on "consolatrix."

THE MAGNIFICAT SETTINGS

It seems absolutely astonishing for one composer to have written ten Magnificat settings, yet that is the number of times Charpentier set the celebrated text of the canticle of the Virgin for the Sunday vespers. One Magnificat (H. 81) was written for the nuns of Port-Royal de Paris (see Chapter 7), another for the singers of the Hôtel de Guise (H. 75). *Magnificat à 3 voix sur la même basse avec symphonie* (H. 73), as its title indicates, is written entirely over an ostinato bass; it is one of the most interesting works of the lot. Six Magnificat settings use full chorus, and one uses double chorus. The latter, *Magnificat à 8 voix et 8 instruments* (H. 74), makes use of the Gregorian introit for the first psalm tone, while the Magnificat settings H. 73, 75, and 76 use the fifth psalm tone.

In spite of the different stylistic traits of each work, some features recur from one piece to the next. These features include the introduction "Magnificat anima mea" usually sung by the *haute-contre*, the systematic use of the chorus for "Fecit potentiam" and of the soloists for "Et misericordia ejus" and "Suscepit Israel," and the silence after "et divites dimisit inanes." Intended by Charpentier as a rupture, this silence is further reinforced by various devices, such as a cadence on a weak beat with the instruments in "echo" (H. 72), vocal coloraturas that fade away one after the other on the final syllable of "inanes" (H. 77), or a reprise of the chorus's last "inanes" by the soloists (H. 80). In one Magnificat setting (H. 78), each group of words is associated with a specific register of the organ; the *cornet* accompanies "et divites" and the *jeux doux* "divisit inanes."

Although as different as can be, *Magnificat à 3 voix* (H. 73) and *Magnificat à 8 voix et 8 instruments* (H. 74) display the same strict attention to structural detail and illustrate Charpentier's utter mastery in that domain. The former uses an uninterrupted obbligato bass, whose descending tetrachord (G–F–E-flat–D) is repeated eighty-nine times. This device was commonly observed by Italian composers since the early seventeenth century, and Monteverdi left some famous examples of it in his *Lamento della ninfa* and *Zefiro torna*. Charpentier adopted it himself several times, most success- fully in the *Magnificat à 3 voix*. Using all his technical skill and imagination, the composer guides his voices with the greatest freedom over the very constraining bass line, in a constant flow of inspiration in which melodic pliancy and harmonic richness are marvelously balanced.

Magnificat à 8 voix et 8 instruments is almost perfectly sym- metrical in structure. It is built around the big central double chorus "Fecit potentiam":

Prelude	32 bars
"Magnificat anima mea Dominum"	52 bars
(*haute-contre*, double choir, double orchestra)	
"Quia fecit mihi magna"	26 bars
(*haut-dessus*, 2 flutes, continuo)	
"Et misericordia ejus"	29 bars
(*haute-contre*, *taille*, bass, continuo)	
"Fecit potentiam"	100 bars
(double choir, double orchestra)	
"Suscepit Israel"	38 bars
(*haut-dessus*, 2 violins, continuo)	
"Sicut locutus est"	26 bars
(*haute-contre*, *taille*, bass, continuo)	
"Gloria Patri"	72 bars
(bass, double choir, double orchestra)	

As in *Miserere* (H. 193) and "Bonum est confiteri Domino" (H. 195), the opening bars present two motifs repeated by the solo *haute- contre* ("Magnificat") and the chorus "Et exultavit." Into his dense and brilliant choral texture, Charpentier interjects a few snatches of ostinato bass and multiplies the canonic imitations at the octave. This procedure, which gives the impression of recycling, as though the music was turning inside-out, reaches its climax in the "Gloria Patri."

THE TE DEUM SETTINGS

No military victory, no event affecting the lives of the royal family went by without being celebrated throughout France by some sort of Te Deum performance. All composers of the day composed at least one Te Deum to be played as soon as the occasion presented itself.

Only four of Charpentier's Te Deum settings survive. He seems to have written at least six of them. His notes at the top of the scores of both four-part Te Deum settings (H. 147, 148) show that the he considered them to be numbers "5" and "6" respectively. The very first setting, a large-scale work, is the *Te Deum à 8 voix avec flûtes et violons* (H. 145). Composed in 1672, it received several performances, including a thanksgiving celebration for Louis XIV's return to health in February 1687. *Te Deum* (H. 146), which has made Charpentier famous today, and *Te Deum à quatre voix* (H. 147) were written for the Jesuits in the 1690s (see Chapter 7). Finally, *Te Deum à 4 voix* (H. 148) dates from 1699, when Charpentier was at the Sainte-Chapelle.

Te Deum à 8 voix avec flûtes et violons (and also oboes[22]) is one of Charpentier's first works with such a large scoring. Its richness is fully exploited by the composer in a style that is brilliant and full of contrasts between the vast choral sections and the solos, quite diverse themselves, between the powerful vertical textures of the double choir in dialogue and the great fugal expansions, and between the vocal exuberance of some of the verses and the reliance on strict syllabic style of others. The originality and effectiveness of the passage in which the vocal scoring gradually increases through successive entries of pairs of soloists of the same tessitura (*tailles, hauts-dessus, hautes-contre,* and finally basses) is to be admired. The two verses, "Tibi cherubim et seraphim incessabili voce proclamant" and "Sanctus" are stated simultaneously, one joyfully vocalized and the other held on one note for several bars until the voices, finally all together, vigorously intone the "Domine Deus Sabbaoth." Although this Te Deum predates Lully's by five years, a difference between the two works is felt, with Mlle de Guise's composer displaying greater sophistication in the formal conception and arrangement of the different sequences than his contemporary.

Te Deum (H. 146) in D major, the only one calling for trumpets and drums as used in other great Te Deum settings of the period (e.g., by

Lully, Delalande, Campra), is the work that marked Charpentier's debut on records in 1953 and the end of his long neglect, at least for the general public. Since then, this Te Deum has enjoyed numerous recordings, not counting those of the prelude alone, as well as the imitations it has inspired in the field of "popular music." Even though it only reflects a tiny facet of Charpentier's vast output, the Te Deum is worthy of the reputation it has acquired over the past four decades.

The "Prélude" in *rondeau* form alternates between the celebrated fanfare and two couplets without trumpets and drums. It achieves utterly classical symmetry in the eight-bar groups (themselves subdivided into two sections, one suspensive, the other conclusive) and in the keys touched upon in each couplet (the dominant A major, the relative B minor, and the dominant of the dominant, E major). The theme is solidly established in the "joyous and very warlike" key of D major imposed by the use of trumpets. Its initial leap of a fourth—characteristic of trumpet calls—creates such a lofty, ceremonial atmosphere that it is no wonder its impact remains just as brilliant three centuries later. In fact, its hymnlike character bears a striking resemblance to the *Marseillaise* even though Rouget de Lisle certainly never heard the Prelude in D.

Charpentier does not restrict the trumpets and drums to the prelude. They reappear during the course of the work, always with the same brilliance, either to accompany choruses or in independent *symphonies*.

After the prelude, the bass intones the "Te Deum laudamus" in a beautiful ascending phrase covering the entire D major scale in leaps of thirds and fifths, or by steps, which lends a great deal of vigor to the movement. The chorus, modulating abruptly into B minor, directly attacks the next verse, emphasizing the word *Patrem* with a beautiful melodic flourish. It is answered by a long conjunctly descending phrase in the orchestra that illustrates "veneratur." The chorus returns without basses ("Tibi omnes angeli") and is followed by the soloists in dialogue with flutes and oboes. Each one continues the same mood of celestial weightlessness and abandons the clear, vertical texture only for a few lovely imitative flourishes on "Sanctus."

The next section opens with a rousing fanfare which then interacts antiphonally with the choir before joining it in a jubilant ensemble ("Te martyrum"). Another vigorous fanfare depicting the trumpets of the Last Judgment frames the bass solo ("Judex crederis"). As before, a brusque modulation into E minor plunges the listener into a sphere totally unlike the previous one; it is the supplicating prayer of sinners sung by the *haut-dessus* accompanied by two flutes in a solo bathed by an outpour of tender lyricism. Then another contrast occurs in the chorus "Aeterna fac," which is composed in a style Charpentier favored throughout this Te Deum: the part writing is homophonic (the use of imitation being infrequent, never lasting more than a few bars) and in dialogue with the orchestra (this time without trumpets and drums) in double-choral style. Spanning several verses, this large chorus concludes with a magnificent coda on "et in saeculum saeculi."

The incisive theme of the introduction to the last part "In te Domine speravi" resembles the prelude and serves as the subject for the grandiose fugue concluding the Te Deum.

Throughout the work, Charpentier combines splendor and introspection in the most natural manner. The introspective side is consistently sustained through the composer's extremely conscientious treatment of the text and through his "gift of knowing how to set words to the most appropriate tones." That is what makes this Te Deum one of the most attractive of all those created during the reign of Louis XIV.

Te Deum à quatre voix (H. 147) oddly states the "Te Deum laudamus" after the second phrase "te Dominum confitemur," while *Te Deum à 4 voix* (H. 148) omits the first part of the verse. Presumably it was sung in plainchant instead, as was the custom in the concerted mass. Of smaller dimensions than the two preceding pieces, these two Te Deum settings—the first one with string orchestra doubling the voices, the second without instruments—are beautifully crafted, but without the pomp and circumstance usually associated with this type of piece.

MOTETS IN HONOR OF THE VIRGIN

Charpentier's devotion to the Virgin, which is quite evident in his liturgical pieces (antiphons, litanies, Magnificat settings), is also expressed in his motets devoted to various feast days of the Virgin Mary: *Nativité de la Vierge* (H. 309) on 8 September and *Pour la conception de la Vierge* (H. 313) on 8 December.

The Feast of the Purification of Mary, 2 February, also commemorates the presentation of Jesus in the temple. The words *Lumen ad revelationem* from the canticle of Simeon (Luke 2:29–32) inspired this feast's candlelight procession (Candlemas) symbolizing Jesus, the enlightener of souls. *In festo purificationis* (H. 318) uses in its middle section the text of the Canticle of Simeon ("Nunc dimitis"). The last part, "O res miranda," is very beautiful. The sense of wonder at the marvelous event is expressed in a mood of utter calm and meditation. *In purificationem BVM Canticum* (H. 357) contains this same sense of adoration in its last measures ("O ineffabile mysterium, o admirabile commercium"), after the joyous tone of the rest of the piece.

The *In Assumptione beatae Mariae Virginis* (H. 353), for 15 August, displays all the characteristics of the Latin oratorio in the narrative quality of the first trio ("Suspirabat Maria"), the Virgin's solo ("Hei mihi quia incolatus meus") answered by the choir in "Noli flere," Christ's solo ("Surge propera, dilecta mea"), and the final choral commentary ("Et introducet matrem").

Several motets are destined for "all the feasts of the Virgin." The text of the *Motet de la Vierge pour toutes ses fêtes pour les mêmes religieuses* (H. 322[23]), the nuns (*les mêmes religieuses*) being those of the Abbaye-aux-Bois, is a free adaptation of four verses of the Song of Solomon (4:1, 8, 11; 1:9). The musical treatment is sober; not until the melismas rise higher and higher on the last word, *coronaberis*, does the texture suddenly become freer.

In the first part of the *Motet pour toutes les fêtes de la Vierge* (H. 327), Charpentier makes use of an antiphon for the nativity of the Virgin. He profusely embellishes the word *cantamus* (let us sing) with the same repetitive effect noted in *Magnificat à 8 voix et 8 instruments* (H. 74).

"Nigra es sed formosa" comes directly from the Song of Solomon (1:4). It is not unusual to encounter such Biblical references in several other motets to the Virgin (see above). The work contains an interesting direction for the singer (*dessus*), who is instructed to hold a long note "without embellishment" (*sans trembler*).[24]

Pro omnibus festis BVM (H. 333) opens with an independent prelude in three sections (ABA').[25] The first section is full of dissonance, in contrast to the second section's fugue. This fugue is built on a plainly tonal subject that Charpentier uses throughout the entire section, in its initial format and also inverted.

The motif's opening interval of a third is repeated later in the motet ("splendor" and "ex mille millibus") during the most intense outbursts of emotion and jubilation.

The anonymous text of this motet had already been used with a few slight changes in *Canticum in honorem beatae Virginis Mariae inter homines et angelos* (H. 400) a few years before. *Pro omnibus festis BVM* (H. 333), an antiphonal motet, could also be placed among the Latin oratorios.

In *Supplicatio pro defunctis ad beatam Virginem* (H. 328) for *haut-dessus, dessus,* bass, two recorders, one bass flute, and continuo (harpsichord, viol), Charpentier makes use of the first three stanzas of the prayer to Mary for the souls in purgatory ("Languentibus in purgatorio"), which was used on Sundays in November. The rest of the text is from an unknown source. It is one of the most beautiful pieces to the Virgin. Grave and meditative, evoking the souls' torments, it is the loveliest, most tender invocation of Mary's compassion. Here and there one is reminded of the *Litanies* or the *Salve Regina* settings. On top of all the tension resulting from harmonic clashes, striking modulations, and melodic turns like the descending diminished seventh on the first "O Maria," this prayer is remarkable for the sophistication of some of the musical effects specifically called for by Charpentier. Among these effects are the solo bass flute accompaniment when the voices sing "Manum tuam extende mortuis, qui sub poenis languent continuis" (Extend your hand to the dead who groan in torment without end), or the holding of a note by the first recorder and the bass flute, on the last "O Maria," while the other voices are instructed to observe "a little silence."

The motet *Ad beatam Virginem Canticum* (H. 340) contains a very curious passage in which the long notes (half notes and whole notes) have dots over them, each dot carrying the value of a quarter note:

Us —— que — in —— se —— nec – tam et se – ni – um   et   se —— ni - um

The dots in this example indicate the accents to be made to express the shakiness of old age suggested by the text. Did Charpentier know the celebrated "Shivering Scene" from Lully's *Isis* composed eight years earlier, which probably inspired Purcell in *King Arthur*? In any case, the technique has a surprising effect in such a composition.

Charpentier dedicated still other motets to the Virgin: *Gaudia Virginis Mariae* (H. 59) and *Gaudia beatae Virginis Mariae* (H. 330), both hymns of praise on the text "Gaudia Virgo mater Christi"; *Motet pour la Vierge à 2 voix* (H. 359) and *Motet de la Vierge à 4* (H. 390), also on the same text of a hymn by Saint Casimir, "Omni die dic Maria"; *Motet pour la Vierge* (H. 334); *Pour la Vierge* (H. 360); *A la Vierge à 4 voix pareilles* (H. 371); and *La Prière à la Vierge du Père Bernard* (H. 367) with a very elaborately vocalized "Amen" for the choir.

MOTETS IN HONOR OF SAINTS

Saint Louis

The saint Charpentier honored most frequently in his works was Saint Louis (1215–1270), canonized in 1297. Four motets are dedicated to this saint: *Motet de Saint Louis* (H. 320), of which only the first fourteen measures remain; *In honorem Sancti Ludovici Regis Galliae Canticum tribus vocibus cum simphonia* (H. 323); *In honorem Sancti Ludovici Regis Galliae* (H. 332); and *In honorem Sancti Ludovici Regis Galliae Canticum* (H. 365). There is, in addition, a Latin oratorio titled *In honorem Sancti Ludovici Regis Galliae* (H. 418).

On 25 August of each year, the great churches of Paris honored Saint Louis. In the Chapel of the Louvre this feast was solemnly observed by the Académie Française, where motets by Claude Oudot could be heard. There is nothing surprising about Charpentier's output if one recalls that the Jesuit church bore the name of the king-saint, or that the Sainte-Chapelle was established by Saint Louis on his return from the Crusades. Yet, no work dedicated to the saint exists from that latter part of the composer's career (unless it is lost), though it is not impossible that Charpentier revived motets composed earlier. Besides the motets for the Jesuits (H. 365, 418, perhaps 332), it is possible that H. 323 was intended for the service given by Le Brun in the Église Saint-Hyppolite on 25 August 1679 (see Chapter 11).

The motets H. 320, 323, and 332 use the same laudatory text ("In tympanis et organis laudate regem regum") set in the triumphant keys of C major (H. 323, 332) and D major (H. 320).

The joyous, warlike atmosphere associated with the key of D major also opens the fourth motet (H. 365), which is larger-scaled than the previous ones (soloists, choir, and an orchestra of flutes, oboes, strings, and continuo), but set to a different text ("Dies tubae et clangoris"). The three-part prelude (ABA') with contrasting sections is a characteristic for the genre, though it is in no way indebted to the French overture. After a fanfare on an emphatic, sustained rhythm with harmonies based on the tonic chord, the second part, which is more introspective, highlights the timbre of flutes in combination with oboes, then violins. The overture is a preview of the entire work, which is based on the two themes of war and Saint Louis's faith in the Lord. A solo trio (*haute-contre, taille,* and bass) repeats the material of the fanfare, whose opening rhythm ♩ ♫ ♩ ♩ , in a virtually continuous ostinato figure in the bass, is heard again in the chorus "Et praeliare."

This work displays some similarities to the Latin oratorio. It has two *récits.* In the first *récit* ("Effundam indignationem meam") for bass accompanied by muted strings, God speaks (the same vocal and instrumental scoring is used in God's solo in *Judicium Salomonis*). In the second *récit* ("Certamen forte") for *taille* with two violins and two flutes, Saint Louis addresses the Lord in the key of D minor. Between the two solos is a robust chorus ("Accingere gladio tuo"), followed by a solo for the *haut-dessus* featuring descriptive melismas ("sagittae," "potentis," "cadent"), after which the chorus is repeated "da capo." The rest of the work (trios and choruses) permanently abandons the warlike mood to praise the king-saint.

Saints Borgia and Xavier

The titles of *Motet pour Saint François de Borgia* (H. 354), *In honorem Sancti Xaverii Canticum* (H. 355), and *Canticum de Sancto Xaverio reformatum* (H. 355a) leave no doubt about their destination. These works evoke the figures of two famous Jesuits associated with the founding of the Society.

In 1565, Francis Borgia (1510–1572), whose feast is 10 October, became the third Superior General of the order. Eighteen years earlier he had founded the first Jesuit college in Gandia, his native town in the Spanish kingdom of Valencia. Francis Xavier (1506–1552) was one of the seven companions of Ignatius of Loyola. He devoted his life to the evangelization of distant lands (Japan, the Indies, China) and died during one of his missions on the Isle of Sancian. His feast falls on 3 December. The three motets, all in the key of B-flat major ("magnificent and joyous"), sing the praise of the two saints.

Motet for Saint Francis Borgia appears in the form of a little piece for solo *haute-contre* and two treble instruments.

In honorem Sancti Xaverii Canticum is a larger work, glorifying the missionary and the miracles that the saint achieved in the world. After a busy fugal prelude, the *haut-dessus* depicts Francis Xavier as an angel in a stunning garland of sixteenth notes, which represent the ascent of God's missionary, complete with dynamic markings (alternately "soft" and "loud" to emphasize the spatial effect).

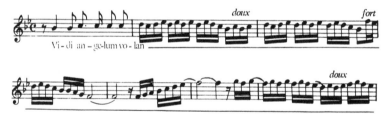

The sweet sonorities of the flutes interact in dialogue with the voice, and the description continues: haloed in light, the angelic Francis Xavier is ubiquitous, over land and sea. An interlude for strings rises higher gradually and the voice, now accompanied by violins, traces the rising path of the sun, to which the saint is now compared. After a duet for the *hauts-dessus* inviting "people immersed in the shadows" to come to this source of light, the choir celebrates the work of the Lord. On five separate occasions, a silence serves to represent, better than any song, everyone's stunned admiration before such great marvels, prior to their joyous outburst ("Cantabimus canticum").

At the center of the work is the solo for "Xaverius," accompanied in turns by muted strings, full orchestra, and solo flutes. Moving imperceptibly from accompanied recitative into arioso, then to an air with repeat, the evangelist addresses God and affirms, confident in the love that sustains him, that no torment can stop him in his mission.

This solo needs to be analyzed word-by-word and note-by-note to realize the extent of the rhetorical effects: repetitions; a superb high-lighting of "ego autem" through a quickening of the tempo, and later of "charitatem" through augmentation; and a series of melodic progressions building on the words "tribulatio an angustia an fames an nuditas an periculum an persecutio an gladius an mors?" (Is my torment poverty, hunger, nakedness, danger, persecution, the sword, or death?) which culminates on the last word sung on the suspended third of the chord. Each phrase of the solo invariably begins in G minor ("serious and magnificent") and ends in B-flat major ("mag-nificent and joyous"). "Serious" and "joyous," but in both cases "magnificent"!

In the last part of the motet, the chorus praises the "preacher," the "apostle," and the "master of pagans" who throughout the world—here a sublime passage for the *haute-contre* and flutes ("Stetit et mensus est terra," He stood up and encircled the globe)—accomplished miracles and brought the dead back to life. Charpentier achieves a fine contrast between the word *mortuis* suddenly sung at "half-voice" (*à demie voix*) and suspended, and the word *resurgent*, which bursts into imitation in all the parts. After another richly descriptive passage ("Contriti sunt montes saeculi, incurvati sunt colles mundi," The centuries-old mountains are worn, the hills of the world are rounded), the final chorus ("Et adduxit"), in a sort of grand sacred dance, glorifies Francis Xavier's missionary work.

This motet appears to be a typical example of Jesuit art as it com-monly flourished in sermons or tragedies. The deep rhetorical eloquence of the text (the anonymous author was certainly a priest of the Society of Jesus) is amplified and magnified even more by Charpentier's music. If there is such a thing as "Jesuit" music, this must surely be it.

Canticum de Sancto Xaverio reformatum (H. 355a), as its title indicates, is a reworked version of the previous motet. It is distin-guished from the previous work by its length (150 bars shorter), its instrumentation (additions of oboe and bassoon), and a different arrangement of the text. Certain passages are gone (one section of the solo for "Xaverius," the last chorus); others are subjected to an expanded development, notably the chorus "Cantabimus canticum," which is repeated at some length to conclude the work.

Miscellaneous Saints

It was principally at the beginning of his career that Charpentier
wrote his little motets honoring various saints. Among the motets are
"Gaudete fideles" (H. 306) for Saint Bernard (20 August); "O doctor
optime" (H. 307) for Saint Augustine (28 August)—it may be recalled
that Du Bois, the tutor of Mlle de Guise's nephew, translated the
Sermons of Saint Augustine; "Jubilate Deo fideles" (H. 310) for Saint
Francis (17 September or 4 October); *Pour Sainte Anne* (H. 315) (26
July); *Pour le jour de Sainte Geneviève* (H. 317) (3 January); and *Motet
de Saint Laurent* (H. 321) (10 August). *In honorem Sancti Benedicti*
(H. 347) (21 March) and *Motet de Saint Joseph* (H. 368) (19 March)
are later works.

    Canticum Annae (H. 325) uses an Old Testament text from 1
Kings 2:1–10. In this work Anne is Samuel's mother, while in the
motet *Pour Sainte Anne* (H. 315) she is the Virgin's mother. A striking
similarity will be noted, however, between the very Italian allure of
the opening measures of these two pieces, both written in the key of
B-flat major. In *Canticum Annae,* this rhythmic vitality persists
throughout, although occasionally it allows for sequences that are
more linear ("Dominus judicabit fines terrae") or more turbulent
("infirmata est, Dominus mortificat").

    In honor of Saint Mary Magdalen, penitent, whose feast is 22 July,
Charpentier composed three pieces, with slight variations, on the
same text: *Magdalena lugens voce sola cum simphonia* "Sola vivebat in
antris" (H. 343), *Sola vivebat in antris à 2 voix et deux flûtes pour la
Magdeleine* (H. 373), and *Magdalena lugens* "Sola vivebat in antris"
for three male voices, as part of the *Méditation pour le Carême* (H.
388).

    These three motets, in somber minor keys, all display the same
mood of adoration mixed with grief that carries the "perfect lover"
(*parfaite amante*) toward Christ. The words "O amor meus, cor et
delitium" are repeated at length, with tenderness, in gentle ternary
symmetry.

    Also on similar texts, with a few minor variants between them, are
Charpentier's two motets for the Feast of Saint Theresa (15
October): *Pour Sainte Thérèse* (H. 342) for three voices and *Flores,
flores, o Gallia à 2 voix et 2 flûtes pour Sainte Thérèse* (H. 374). The
two scores are very similar: an abundantly embellished first section
precedes a brisk gigue rhythm, which is followed by a passage that is
intensified by chromaticism and suspensions, and finally by a song

glorifying Theresa and Christ. The first two sections are repeated in the second piece, while only the second section is repeated in the first piece.

Charpentier also composed various little motets for the Common of Saints: *Pour plusieurs martyrs, motet à voix seule sans accompagnement* (H. 361); *Pro Virgine non martyre* (H. 369); *Pour un confesseur non pontife* (H. 375); *Motet pour un confesseur* "Beatus vir" (H. 376); and *Pour tous les saints* (H. 377).

MOTETS FOR OTHER FEASTS AND TIMES OF THE YEAR

Nativity

The little *In nativitatem Domini Canticum* (H. 314) is full of freshness and foreshadows the later sacred dramas on the nativity theme.

The name "Jesus," which was officially given to him at the time of circumcision, is honored on 1 January. *In circumcisione Domini* (H. 316) refers to the baptism of that name. In this motet the vocal trio, in dialogue with the instruments, uses worshiping terms in a tone of tender adoration: "O nomen amabile, o nomen laudabile, o nomen admirabile."

Lent

During Lent, the faithful would flock to the churches to hear the great preachers of the time, such as the famous Jesuit Bourdaloue. Between the different parts of the sermon, the orator would insert "pauses" during which little motets could be performed. Such was probably the purpose of the Lenten motet "Peccavi Domine" (H. 378) for three voices and especially of the *Méditation pour le Carême* (H. 380–389), a work considered "excellent" by Sébastien de Brossard. The ten brief pieces that make up this work form a sort of scenic backdrop for the Passion of Christ. They contain a mixture of liturgical texts ("Tristis est anima mea," "Tenebrae factae sunt," "Stabat mater"), Biblical passages (in the fifth and tenth pieces), and free-composed texts like "Sola vivebat in antris." Each *Méditation* is presented as a tableau, or a little dramatic scene involving the principal protagonists of the Passion:

First Meditation: The desolation of the world
Second Meditation: The prayer of the sinner
Third Meditation: Jesus announces his imminent death to his
    disciples
Fourth Meditation: Judas's betrayal
Fifth Meditation: Peter's denial
Sixth Meditation: Jesus before Pilate
Seventh Meditation: Death of Jesus on the cross
Eighth Meditation: Lament of the Virgin Mary
Ninth Meditation: Lament of Mary Magdalen
Tenth Meditation: The sacrifice of Abraham

This last piece seems to lie outside the Passion story; as the conclusion of the cycle, it should be regarded as a parable of the sacrifice of an innocent lamb.

Characters ("Jesus," "Petrus," "Pilatus") appear in the piece just like characters appear in the Latin oratorio, a genre that the *Méditations* closely resemble. Some of the pieces can even be considered as oratorios, such as the fifth piece, which is an abridged version of *Le Reniement de Saint Pierre* (H. 424). As is appropriate for such a period of penitence, the texture is strikingly austere. Only three men's voices and continuo are used, and each piece is short and mainly declamatory. The final bars of the second, fifth, and seventh *Méditations*, however, are so heartrending, and contain such turbulent harmonies, that they make the listener burn with emotion. Music for the eye as well as the ear, Charpentier's *Meditations for Lent* remind us of miniature scenes in stained-glass windows—there to help worshipers focus their thoughts inward in meditation.

The three short motets for Holy Week—*Pour la Passion de Notre Seigneur, Première pause* (H. 349), *Pour la Passion, Seconde partie* (H. 350), and *Pour le jour de la Passion de Notre Seigneur Jésus-Christ* (H. 351)—were inserted, like the Lenten *Méditation*, into the various pauses of the sermon. The mighty effect of the opening "O crux" in H. 349 and 351 is remarkable.

Easter and Pentecost

After the penitent season of Lent and Holy Week comes Easter Sunday when desolation is replaced by joy in the mystery of the resurrection. With *Chant joyeux du temps de Pâques* (H. 339) to commemorate the redemption, Charpentier offers a work that is thoroughly imbued with the spirit of Easter rejoicing, translated into a sumptuous apotheosis of vocal coloratura. As in his other two works on the same text (*O filii à 3 voix pareilles*, H. 312, and *O filii pour les voix, violons, flûtes et orgue*, H. 356), the composer uses the simple, moving Gregorian melody that Liszt would recall two centuries later in his oratorio *Christus*. In the first and second verses, Charpentier subjects the Gregorian theme to the ornamental technique of the *air de cour*, a technique he had already used to such sublime effect in the Tenebrae lessons:

While adhering to the strict strophic form of the liturgical text, the composer at times gives his work a theatrical allure by dramatizing his discourse. For example, in the second stanza, the names of the three Marys ("Et Maria Magdalene, et Jacobi, et Salome") are each uttered by a different voice, or a distinction is made between the narrator and the characters (Jesus, Thomas).

In the "Alleluia" punctuating each stanza, Charpentier displays a luxurious, extroverted style that feeds on the intense feeling of joy in view of the miracle of the resurrection. This vocal exuberance is again manifested in the duet of the penultimate stanza, which is crafted totally in the Italian style ("In hoc sanctissimo, sit laus et jubilatio").

Although based on the same text, *O filii à 3 voix pareilles* (H. 312) is written in a much more sober style.

O filii pour les voix, violons, flûtes et orgue (H. 356) contains only one seven-bar "Alleluia" for four voices and a "Couplet des violons" on the traditional melody. In general, the work is arranged strophically, alternating vocal and instrumental textures.

Another little motet ("Haec dies," H. 308) also celebrates Easter Sunday.

The little *Motet pour la Trinité* (H. 319) is for the Sunday after Pentecost. In the first part of the work, the texture proceeds in waves of descending phrases illustrating the meaning of the text ("O altitudo divitiarum sapientiae et scientiae Dei," How vast the treasures of God's wisdom and knowledge).

Feast of the Blessed Sacrament

The Feast of the Blessed Sacrament, also called Corpus Christi, is celebrated on the Thursday following Trinity Sunday. The occasion for solemn processions, it was celebrated with incomparable lavishness in the seventeenth century. Music was added to specific parts of the service, as Charpentier indicates in his manuscripts: Prelude when the king has arrived at the reposoir (H. 344), Prelude during the procession and which must reach an end when the Blessed Sacrament is placed on the altar [Charpentier wrote *sur l'hôtel* instead of *sur l'autel*] (H. 348), and [prelude] when the Blessed Sacrament is near the reposoir (H. 358).

Magnificently decorated altars (*reposoirs*) with flowers and candles were installed along the processional route. Each stop of the Blessed Sacrament was marked by a prayer from the liturgy or by a musical motet, such as *Pour le Saint Sacrement au reposoir* (H. 346) and *Pour la seconde fois que le Saint Sacrement vient au même reposoir* (H. 372).

Besides *Prose du Saint Sacrement* "Lauda Sion salvatorem" (H. 14) and the "Pange lingua" hymns, Charpentier wrote several motets for this feast on liturgical texts, including *Pour un reposoir* "Ave verum corpus" (H. 329) and *Motet du Saint Sacrement pour un reposoir* "Ecce panis angelorum" (H. 348). He also wrote motets on other freely inspired texts.

In festo Corporis Christi Canticum (H. 344) dates from 1686 and seems to have been performed in the presence of Louis XIV in the Versailles chapel.[26] It is scored for five vocal parts and two treble instruments. A singer by the name of M. Sebret (bass) took the part of Christ in a tripartite solo (air-recitative-reprise of the air) using Matthew 11:28 ("Venite ad me omnes"). A beautiful fugue with very tender inflections ("Vere tu Domine suavis es") concludes the work.

The jubilant *In festo Corporis Christi Canticum* (H. 358) contrasts with the emotional poignancy of *Pour un reposoir* ("O pie, o dulcis, o Jesu fili Mariae," H. 329), *Pour le Saint Sacrement au reposoir* (H. 346), and *Pour la seconde fois que le Saint Sacrement vient au même reposoir* (H. 372). *Pour le Saint Sacrement au reposoir* (H. 346) is bathed in an atmosphere of deep introspection which is established by the opening phrase sung by the *taille* ("Oculi omnium in te sperant Domine"). The melody, which is restrained yet veering into the high register, translates the movement and the expectancy of glances turned toward God. It culminates in the semi-motionless glow of "O nos felices filii, o nos beati."

In the first part of *Pour la seconde fois que le Saint Sacrement vient au même reposoir*, the text, which is built entirely on a series of adoring adjectives ("Quam dulcis, quam clemens, quam mitis, quam bonus, quam patiens, humilis et mansuetus!"), is treated with infinite tenderness in a syllabic, vertical style. This technique is repeated three times after the invocation "O Deus, o salvator noster" to prevent the listener from being distracted from the emotional force contained in the words themselves.

Canticum Zachariae "Benedictus Dominus" (H. 345) could have been performed not only for the Feast of the Blessed Sacrament, but also for the Office of Lauds. This text by the father of Saint John the Baptist is from the Gospel According to Saint Luke (1:68–79). There are two distinct parts: the giving of thanks to the Messiah, who is the Redeemer of the world, and the proclaiming of the prophetic mission of Saint John the Baptist. Charpentier set the canticle in the "sweetly joyous" key of G major. To underline the word *salutem* in the fourth verse, Charpentier calls for *tremblements* (single, then double trills). The magnificent, brilliantly contrapuntal six-part choruses ("Et erixit cornu salutis nobis," "Ut sine timore," and "Illuminare his") dominate the work.

Miscellaneous Feasts

A certain number of motets can only be connected tentatively to a particular feast or special occasion. These include one *Pour plusieurs fêtes* (H. 379), the cycle *Quatuor anni tempestates* (H. 335–338), "Quae est ista" (H. 426), "Eamus, volamus" (H. 429), *Domine non secundum pour une basse taille avec 2 violons* (H. 433), "O coelestis Jerusalem" (H. 435), "Dilecte mi" (H. 436), "Ferte, ferte coronas coelites" (H. 437), "Venite et audite omnes" (H. 438), and *Bone pastor* (H. 439).

Quatuor anni tempestates (H. 335–338) constitutes what might be called Charpentier's "Four Seasons." This extremely original work is adapted from the Song of Solomon and divided into four parts: *Ver* (Spring), *Aestas* (Summer), *Autumnus* (Autumn), and *Hyems* (Winter). It is written for two *hauts-dessus* without instruments; only a prelude, *Prélude pour l'été à 3 flûtes* (H. 336a), was composed at a later date.

To communicate the restless sensuality of the text, Charpentier adopts a distinctly Italian style, borrowing the typical technique of the *caccia* (i.e., canonic imitations between two voice parts in close pursuit of one another), its wide melodic intervals, and its florid embellishments. The entire work overflows with high spirits and tremendous energy which occasionally turns into a mystical intoxication ("inebriamini" in the *Autumnus*). In the area of vocal virtuosity, *Quatuor anni tempestates* represents the Italian counterpart of the ornamental French tenebrae style. As he does elsewhere on occasion, Charpentier uses Italian terminology "da capo," "primo soprano," and "allegro," the latter used interchangeably with its French equivalent, "gai."

In the same vein, although in a less florid style, is the very short motet "Quae est ista" (H. 426). Languorous throughout, the first part of "Dilecte mi" (H. 436) abounds with all the chromaticism, suspensions, unresolved cadences, and augmented chords of which Charpentier's harmony was capable.

OCCASIONAL MOTETS

For the House of Guise

Motet pour les trépassés à 8 (H. 311) belongs to the series of works written during the years of mourning (1671–1672) that struck the House of Guise. Just like *Messe pour les trépassés à* 8 (H. 2) and *Prose des Morts* (H. 12), which were also composed under those tragic circumstances, *Motet pour les trépassés* is a wonderful work. Mournful throughout, in the "effeminate, amorous, and plaintive" key of E minor, it opens with a grave prelude with frequent modulations. Based on the same thematic material is the "Lamentations of the Souls in Purgatory" ("Miseremini mei"), with both choirs blocked vertically in hieratic fashion. After a passage for three voices, without basses ("Quia manus Domini"), the double choir repeats "Miseremini mei," this time with the parts entering in imitation before returning to the impressive block harmonies.

The entire first part offers a number of bold harmonic strokes. Then the "Heu mihi Domine" that follows strikes the listener in the very first bar with a chord containing an interval of a second. It is an attack with no preparation. Assigned successively to *haute-contre, taille,* and bass, and then to all three, this section unfolds in an extremely tense, even turbulent vein. The plaintive interjection "heu" (which, according to Charpentier, should be pronounced "hey") returns incessantly, often accompanied by the most dissonant of harmonies.

After a partial reprise of "Miseremini mei," "Ah! Penis crucior" for two *haut-dessus* voices, although less mournful in tone, is still not without a certain tension. The tension is due this time to the chromatic harmonies and the repetition of the exclamatory "Ah!"

Conforming to a perfectly symmetrical pattern, "Miseremini mei" is repeated in its entirety.

For the Royal Family

Gratiarum actiones ex sacris codicibus excerptae pro restituta serenissimi Galliarum Delphini salute (H. 326) is arguably the most beautiful piece that Charpentier composed for the Dauphin, to whom it is dedicated. The fragile health of Louis XIV's son made him highly susceptible to fevers. It was in celebration of the young prince's recovery at the end of 1680 that Charpentier, then in the Dauphin's service, composed this motet.

The work is divided into two main parts: first, the pain and suffering of the invalid in the face of death and the cry for the Lord's mercy in the "obscure and sad" key of C minor; then, as he is fond of doing, Charpentier switches to the major mode to celebrate the return to health and to give thanks to God for his blessings.

Initially gently chromatic, the prelude then lightens the texture by periodically dispensing with the continuo, leaving only the sound of the flute trio (two treble and one bass). The sad tone created by this instrumental introduction is succeeded by a much more poignant feeling of suffering in face of the terrible vision of death ("Circumderunt me dolores et terrores mortis"). There is a beautiful chromatic line in the bass, answered later in contrary motion by the line containing the words "efferbuerunt interiora mea," with a most expressive series of chord progressions (diminished third, tritone, major and minor sixths, diminished fifth, and seventh).

The second section is full of joy and gratitude. It is primarily given to the full vocal and instrumental ensemble, treated antiphonally (opening) or all together (end). At the center are placed a duet for the two *dessus* that unleashes some lively melismatic passages ("laetitia") and a bass solo that ends on a long note ("in aeternum"), which is enveloped by the flutes' calm descending lines.

For the recovery of Louis XIV six years later, Charpentier lifted a portion of the text from his own thanksgiving motet for the Dauphin and composed a new piece for two *hauts-dessus,* two flutes, two violins, and continuo:[27] *Gratiarum actiones pro restituta regis christianissimi sanitate anno 1686* (H. 341). Once again there are two sections with plaintive C-minor harmonies in the opening one and a cheerful C-major atmosphere in the second.

Also for the king's recovery, Charpentier penned *Gratitudinis erga Deum Canticum* (H. 431). The very diverse texture of this motet communicates that combination of grief and joy which runs throughout these thanksgiving offerings.

Luctus de morte augustissimae Mariae Theresiae reginae Galliae (H. 331) is one of the works that the death of Queen Marie-Thérèse inspired the composer to write in 1683. Alongside the great fresco of *In obitum* (H. 409) and the *De profundis* (H. 189), *Luctus* represents the intimist side of the funeral lament, a genre in which Charpentier emphatically excelled.

The first part of the work is an invitation to all to lament, to weep, and to sigh over the harsh death that has just devastated the kingdom. The text is built entirely on an accumulation of terms related to tears and sighs ("luctum," "dum planctu et dolore, dum fletu et moerare," "plange," "luge," and "plorate"). It also requires silence and the cessation of all singing or any other sound that does not constitute lamentation. Nowhere else does silence play such an important role in the works of Charpentier, who used it so masterfully. The silences mainly account for the dark mood, one of deepest affliction. It is as though to demonstrate the truth of the statement that grief is never more genuine than when it is silent.

After a passage extolling the virtues of Marie-Thérèse, the work concludes with an ardent prayer ("O Jesu clementissime") and with the glorious ascension of the queen hailed with "Amens" that shower the ear with densely imitative part-writing.

For Religious and Political Institutions

Certain events affecting the country and religious or political institutions are echoed in pieces like the *Motet pendant la guerre* (H. 363) with its characteristic texture of repeated notes and arpeggios, *Offertoire pour le sacre d'un évêque à 4 parties de voix et d'instruments* (H. 432), or the sumptuous *Motet pour une longue offrande* (H. 434) which was written to commemorate the annual reopening of Parlement.

The latter is one of Charpentier's last works, or in any case his final large motet. Like *Judicium Salomonis* in the field of the Latin oratorio and like *Assumpta est Maria* in the field of the mass, this motet reveals the composer at his full artistic maturity.

Nearly 800 measures long, *Motet pour une longue offrande* was originally called *Motet pour l'offertoire de la Messe Rouge.*[28] It is constructed in four large parts, each one longer than the preceding one. Each part is independent, possesses its own tonal atmosphere, and is focused on one particular idea in the text. Each is naturally related to the Parlement's ceremonial "Red Mass." Except for the first section which has no chorus, Charpentier fashioned the other three sections along the same line—prelude, solos, chorus—but each time varying the order of the sections. The orchestra is in the foreground throughout the motet, as much in the "preludes" and "symphonies" (which are unusually long and greatly varied in their instrumentation) as elsewhere when it accompanies the chorus. The composer doubles the chorus and also enriches its polyphonic texture with independent contrapuntal lines.

The overture-prelude is scored for all the instruments (i.e., flutes, oboes, and strings) entering in densely written imitation. From the home key of D major Charpentier modulates in the course of the development to the relative B minor, dominant A major, and subdominant G major, a classic tonal progression. Accompanied by flutes and oboes, the bass solo appears as the Lord in his role of Judge ("Paravit Dominus") and only distantly recalls the first notes of the prelude (descending arpeggio on the D major chord).

The second section abruptly modulates to C major (a fine dramatic effect) and begins with a "prelude" of sweeping sixteenth-note runs that foreshadow certain orchestral pages of Rameau. The chorus, in turn, voices its own quick runs, illustrating the shower of flames and sulphur that descends upon sinners as a form of punishment; it then continues in a homophonic texture ("Bibet omnes peccatores terrae"). A separate trio of male voices follows ("Vidi impium") in the key of G major, after which the chorus is repeated.

The following part takes refuge in the "tender and plaintive" atmosphere of A minor to offer its appeal for divine mercy. The "Symphonie" abandons the full orchestra to highlight passages scored alternately for flutes and violins in an atmosphere of great tenderness. The mood is prolonged in the duet ("Deus justus et patiens"), and then in the chorus ("Speravi"). The chorus affirms with vigorous accents on "non" its determination not to be confounded in eternity.

The last and longest section ("Justus es Domine") returns to the initial key of D major for a tremendous hymn of praise to God, his justice, goodness, power, honor, patience, and mercy. Its "Symphonie" this time sets flutes antiphonally against all the strings and unfolds in a large-scale format. All elements (soloists, small chorus, large chorus, and instrumental ritornellos) contribute to the sumptuous edifice.

Having reached the end of our journey through the immense corpus of Charpentier's motets—masterpieces but certainly also more modest works—one cannot help but be genuinely dazzled. The composer, who was just as comfortable with small formats as with large, draws on greatly varying sources of inspiration. Finding the perfect expression for each text, he generates uncommon emotion and presents it freshly. This essential branch of the works of Charpentier and of seventeenth-century French sacred music in general is still little known and has only partially been explored. It deserves great attention from performers. In these motets, they will find a prodigiously rich repertoire that is marvelously adaptable to the most diverse conditions, just as they existed for Charpentier, from the modest forces of the convents or private chapels to the sumptuous ensembles of the greatest churches in Paris.

Chapter 10

The Latin Oratorios

*It is his youthful experience in Italy that a few extreme French
purists, or those jealous of the excellence of his music, have seized
upon quite inappropriately when criticizing his Italian taste. It
can be said without flattering him that he extracted only the good.
His works display it well enough.*

Sébastien de Brossard, 1724

The Latin oratorios make up the most genuinely original branch of
Charpentier's entire output. Here more clearly than anywhere else
the composer demonstrates his affinity with Italian music, above all
with Carissimi. What might have amounted only to a souvenir of the
young Marc-Antoine's stay with the greatest composer of oratorios of
the seventeenth century, a sort of homage by the pupil to his master,
in fact generated an entirely separate body of works forming an
essential part of his catalog. Even more extraordinarily, Charpentier's
Latin oratorios were created in a country that displayed no interest at
the time in a kind of music that was both dramatic and religious. The
composer introduced the genre to France, but he nevertheless failed
to establish it firmly. His thirty-five or so Latin oratorios remain an isolated phenomenon in French music of the time and bore no progeny.

Even Sébastien de Brossard, the great connoisseur and defender
of Charpentier's works, curiously ignored the sacred Latin dramas in
his definition of *oratorio:*

> *Oratorio:* A sort of spiritual opera, or a weaving-together (*tissu*)
> of dialogues, solos, duets, trios, ritornelli, grand choruses, and so
> forth, whose subject is drawn either from the scriptures or from

265

the life of a saint. Or else it is an allegory on one of the religious mysteries, or on some moral question. Its music should be enriched with the most sophisticated and learned techniques of the art. The words are almost always in Latin and generally taken from the Holy Writ. Many of them have Italian texts, but such works could also be written in French. In Rome there is nothing more common than this sort of oratorio, especially during Lent. A quite lovely one by Sieur Lochon has just been presented to the public; it is for four voices and two violins.[1]

Although the term *oratorio* was used as early as 1640 by Pietro della Valle, it did not enter into common usage until the eighteenth century.[2] Neither Charpentier nor Carissimi ever used it. The Italian composer entitled his pieces *motetto, dialogo,* or *historia;* the Frenchman used the terms *dialogus, canticum,* and *historia,* though he also referred to these works simply as motets.[3] Indeed, the boundary between motet and Latin oratorio is not always easy to determine, and the respective identities of the two genres were difficult to establish, even by the end of the seventeenth century.

The oratorio as it existed in the mid-seventeenth century was the outgrowth of musical forms and traditions whose origins in some cases dated back to the Middle Ages. A distinction was made between two main categories: the *volgare*, or vernacular oratorio, and the oratorio *latino.* Both types of oratorios developed conjointly in Italy, with no basically musical differences.

The vernacular oratorio was created under the impetus of Philip Neri, founder of the Congregazione dell'Oratorio in Rome in the 1550s. During pious gatherings organized at the church of San Girolamo della Carità, and later at Santa Maria in Vallicella, Neri's musician friends would compose and sing *Laudi Spirituali.* These strophic and polyphonic songs would occur before and after the sermon. Little by little, the *lauda* began to take on a dialogue format and, under the influence of the melodramatic reform which gave birth to opera toward the end of the sixteenth century, it adopted the use of monody and thorough bass. In 1600, the year of Jacopo Peri's *Euridice,* Emilio de'Cavalieri's *Rappresentazione di anima e di corpo* was given in the Oratory of Santa Maria in Vallicella. Mid-way between oratorio (the religious subject) and opera (the scenic performance and ballet), Cavalieri's work constitutes the near-ideal artistic meeting point between the sacred and the secular. In the first half of the seventeenth century, the *volgare* type of oratorio retained the musical elements of the *Rappresentazione di anima e di corpo* (recitatives, arioso-style airs, instrumental ritornellos, and choruses), but abandoned the scenic element. In his *Teatro armonico spirituale* (1619), Francesco Anerio assigned the narrative role, until then given to the chorus, to a soloist (*il testo* or *il storico*). In his oratorios *Il Trionfo* and *La Fede* composed between 1630 and 1642, Francesco Balducci gave increasing importance to the narrative part (i.e., the *historia*) and divided the oratorio into two parts, following the division of acts in opera.

As for the Latin oratorio, it has its different origins. Its antecedents are to be found in the liturgical dramas of the Middle Ages, in the Passions whose solos were given to three characters (the narrator or evangelist, Christ, and the crowd, or *turba,* represented by one person and later by a group of the faithful), and finally in the Latin motet. The latter was influenced in the beginning of the seventeenth century by the new concerted style (*mottetto concertato*), while detaching itself from the liturgy. Set to narrative and dramatic texts, these motets were sung during ceremonies similar to the ones organized by Philip Neri, though the faithful who attended them were from a higher social class. Performances took place in the Oratory of the Arciconfraternità del San Crocifisso in the San Marcello church in Rome. The oratorios of Carissimi also were performed in that church on Fridays during Lent.

It is difficult to know exactly how many sacred oratorios Carissimi composed. All his manuscripts were destroyed in the eighteenth century, and his works have come down to us mainly in copies, mostly French. Only about fifteen pieces can be identified, more than half of which (of large or average dimensions) generally make extensive use of the chorus: *Baltazar, Ezechia, Diluvium universale, Dives malus, Abraham et Isaac, Jephte, Jonas, Judicium extremum,* and *Judicium Salomonis.*

The majority of the texts are in prose (unlike the versified texts of the *volgare* oratorio), and are drawn from the Old Testament. The others come from the New Testament, from a combination of the New and Old Testaments, or from non-biblical sources. In biblical oratorios, the libretto is a mixture of exact quotes and freely adapted passages from the Bible. Freely adapting texts provided greater dramatic flexibility and more appropriate musical expression.

While other composers conformed to a bi-partite division, Carissimi's oratorios consist of only one part. This idiosyncrasy can be explained thus: in the Oratory of San Marcello the sermon was framed not by two parts of the same work, but by two different pieces, one inspired by the Old Testament, the other by the New.[4]

Narrative passages are assigned to an *historicus,* who, depending on the work and even within a single work, may be one or several different soloists in turn, a small group of singers, or even the chorus. The latter plays a prime role: besides its narrative or descriptive function (*Jonas*), it bears the dramatic and emotional force of the entire work inasmuch as it participates in the action in the same way as the *turbae* in Passions, provides moral commentary, or gives vent to great grief, as in *Jephte.* Carissimi's choral style is generally homophonic, rhythmically conforming to the accents of the text, and harmonically simple. The composer does not hesitate to make use of double and triple choruses (e.g., *Dives malus, Jonas, Judicium extremum,* and *Diluvium universale*), treated in the antiphonal style that Rome had inherited from Venetian polychoral music.

In the solo passages, Carissimi alternates recitatives with very expressive ariosos and airs (binary or strophic). Instrumental accompaniment is reduced to two violins over continuo, and to short preludes and ritornellos. Formal unity and balance are ensured by tonal stability and by the structural arrangement of solos, choruses, and symphonies.

Alongside the *historiae,* Carissimi left more intimate works without dramatic action in the form of dialogues between two singers or two groups of singers (e.g., *Martyres, Duo ex discipulis Jesu,* and *Job*).

A composer for the Jesuits, Carissimi, like Philip Neri and the Oratorians, epitomized the spirit of the Counter-Reformation by advocating an art that was closely linked to religion and its rites. In this light, the oratorios of Carissimi can be considered veritable sermons in music created to sway and edify the faithful and to exalt Christian virtues by expressive means that were both austere and profoundly moving. From these oratorios Charpentier acquired the emotional depth that shows forth in such an individual manner in his Latin oratorios. This emotional depth is the very essence of Charpentier's art.

To consider Charpentier the only French composer of seventeenth-century oratorios is not entirely justified, even though none of the composers mentioned below left any body of work in this domain that measures up, either in size or degree of achievement, to that of Charpentier.

The first of these composers was Guillaume Bouzignac, originally from southern France, directly in contact with Italian music, and Carissimi's contemporary. His *histoires sacrées* on Nativity and Passion themes are in the form of short dialogues. They are full of contrast and punctuated by exclamations and interrogations. In short, they are singularly animated.

While there was little chance for Charpentier to have been acquainted with Bouzignac's compositions and hence to be influenced by them in any way, he was certainly familiar with the sacred dramas of René Ouvrard, through the intermediary Loulié. Impressed by Carissimi's music which he had heard during his sojourns in Rome, Ouvrard in the 1660s set out to compose works imitating the Italian's oratorios. We can form no opinion of these works today, since they are lost.

Henri Du Mont, the court composer who received his youthful training in the Italian style, also tried his hand at the dramatic oratorio genre in dialogue motets that are clearly Italian in inspiration. The most remarkable of these pieces, *Dialogus de anima*, involves God, a sinner, and an angel. It concludes with a large five-part chorus. Sébastien de Brossard, who made a copy of this work, called it a "very excellent species of oratorio." After 1668, however, Du Mont abandoned that vein to adopt a more French esthetic.

Like Carissimi, Charpentier approached the oratorio genre in several ways. His output ranged from short dialogues for two soloists and basso continuo to well-developed pieces calling for large vocal and instrumental forces. Using the same stylistic elements as those of his teacher, Charpentier enriched them with traits characteristic of French music. The result was the more flexible and florid quality of his recitative, and the dance rhythms on which he based some of his airs. Above all else, he developed choral texture by varying it much more than did the Roman composer, and he assigned a much greater role to instrumental music by inserting in his oratorios dramatic or descriptive symphonies of the type found in Lully's operas. As a result, Charpentier perfectly reconciled the genre's Italian origins with the language of his own time and native country. Finally, the composer's deep religious faith and dramatic genius worked together to fill these works with a rare intensity.

Charpentier's oratorios fall into three main categories according to their dimensions, content, and atmosphere:[5] the *historiae*, the *cantica*, and the *dialogi*.

Charpentier used the term *historia* only once—in *Historia Esther* (H. 396). The text of this long piece (643 measures) for soloists, chorus, and concerted instruments is drawn from the Bible. Fourteen other compositions displaying identical or similar characteristics can be classified under this label: *Judith sive Bethulia liberata* (H. 391), *Caecilia Virgo et Martyr octo vocibus* (H. 397), *Filius prodigus* (H. 399), *Extremum Dei judicium* (H. 401), *Sacrificium Abrahae* (H. 402), *Mors Saülis et Jonathae* (H. 403), *Josue* (H. 404), *In obitum augustissimae nec non piissimae Gallorum reginae Lamentum* (H. 409), *Praelium Michaelis archangeli factum in coelo cum dracone* (H. 410), *Caedes sanctorum innocentium* (H. 411), *Caecilia Virgo et Martyr* (H. 413), *Caecilia Virgo et Martyr* (H. 415), *Judicium Salomonis* (H. 422), and *Le Reniement de Saint Pierre* (H. 424).[6]

The texts, all Latin, come from the Old Testament (e.g., *Judith, Historia Esther, Sacrificium Abrahae, Mors Saülis et Jonathae, Josue,* and *Judicium Salomonis*), the New Testament (e.g., *Filius prodigus, Praelium Michaelis archangeli, Caedes sanctorum innocentium,* and *Le Reniement de Saint Pierre*), or from both (e.g., *Extremum Dei judicium*). As in the texts of Carissimi's oratorios, Charpentier's anonymous librettist(s) combined borrowings from the Holy Scriptures with free interpolations that are dramatic and poetic in nature.

The three works evoking the character and story of Saint Cecilia are hagiographic. Their text of unknown origin only twice uses antiphons from the vespers for Saint Cecilia's feast day. *In obitum,* an occasional work for the funeral of Marie-Thérèse, is on an entirely original text and can be considered a pure motet. Nevertheless, the presence of characters, its narrative aspect, and its strong theatricality tend to link this work to the world of the Latin oratorio.[7]

These pieces employ a large chorus, sometimes even a double chorus, and most of them call for orchestra. They exceed 300 bars in length, and the longest, *Judith,* has 1200 bars. The pieces tell a story (hence the generic label) necessitating an *"historicus"* who can be a soloist, a small solo ensemble, or a chorus, as is found in Carissimi's works. Unlike Carissimi, however, but in imitation of other Italian composers, Charpentier divides several of his *historiae* into two parts. With the exception of *Le Reniement de Saint Pierre,* all the *historiae* end with a large chorus underscoring the moral significance of the story.

The term *canticum* (canticle) is found in the titles of some of the pieces and denotes three different types of works. The first type is liturgical (*Canticum BVM,* H. 76; *Canticum Zachariae,* H. 345). The second type is synonymous with motet[8] (e.g., *Canticum Annae,* H. 325; *In festo Corporis Christi Canticum,* H. 344, 358; *In honorem*

Sancti Xaverii Canticum, H. 355; *Canticum de Sancto Xaverio,* H. 355a; *In honorem Sancti Ludovici Regis Galliae Canticum,* H. 365; and *Gratitudinis erga Deum Canticum,* H. 431). The third type denotes those works belonging to the oratorio genre (*Canticum pro pace,* H. 392; *Canticum in nativitatem Domini,* H. 393; *In honorem Caeciliae, Valeriani et Tiburtii Canticum,* H. 394; *In nativitatem Domini Nostri Jesu Christi Canticum,* H. 414; *In nativitatem Domini Canticum,* H. 416; *In nativitatem Domini Nostri Jesu Christi Canticum,* H. 421). *Canticum in honorem beatae Virginis Mariae inter homines et angelos* (H. 400), considered by some to belong to the oratorio genre, is nonetheless related to the *dialogi* category, which will be discussed below. Among the pieces classified as motets, some contain oratorio-like features: the presence of characters ("Christus" in H. 344 and H. 353, or "Xaverius" in H. 355 and H. 355a), or the emergence of a dialogue (H. 365).

Compared to the *historia,* the *canticum* is of more modest proportions and is not always scored for full forces. Most of the *cantica* only call for three soloists and two treble instruments. The three Nativity pieces (H. 393, 414, 421) and the one in honor of Saint Cecilia (H. 394) appear in the form of an abbreviated *historia.* Although *Pour la fête de l'Épiphanie* (H. 395) does not contain the term *canticum* in its title, it is constructed along the same lines. Despite their extreme brevity, some of the Lenten *Méditations* (H. 383, 384, 385, 386, 388, 389) could also be considered *cantica* (see Chapter 9).

Hitchcock has identified a second type of *canticum* as more meditative and lyrical. Action in this second type of *canticum* is less important, and a narrator is not always required. *In resurrectione Domini Nostri Jesu Christi* (H. 405), *In honorem Sancti Ludovici Regis Galliae* (H. 418), *Pestis Mediolanensis* (H. 398), and *Nuptiae sacrae* (H. 412) belong to this group. The last two examples are quite similar to the Carissimi *mottetto concertato,* a cross between the Latin motet and the oratorio.

The *dialogi* make up the last group of works belonging to the oratorio. Except for *Élévation* (H. 408) and *Pour Saint Augustin mourant* (H. 419), the titles of the pieces are self-explanatory: *In circumcisione Domini, Dialogus inter angelum et pastores* (H. 406); *Dialogus inter esurientem, sitientem et Christum* (H. 407); *Dialogus inter Christum et homines* (H. 417); *Dialogus inter angelos et pastores Judae, In nativitatem Domini* (H. 420); *Dialogus inter Magdalenam et Jesum, 2 vocibus* (H. 423); and *Dialogus inter Christum et peccatores* (H. 425).

On the whole, many of the characteristics of the *cantica* (e.g., light scoring, conciseness) can be found in the *dialogi*. The difference is that the latter, as the name indicates, focus essentially on the dialogue between two characters, between one character and a group, or between two groups who come together at the end of the work. The texts of the *dialogi* are for the most part entirely composed of or adapted very freely from biblical sources.

The *historiae* and most of the other pieces were composed between mid-1670 and 1686. Some of the pieces mention the names of Mlle de Guise's singers: *Nuptiae sacrae* (H. 412), *Caecilia Virgo et Martyr* (H. 413, 415), and *In nativitatem Domini Nostri Jesu Christi Canticum* (H. 414). Other important works such as *Judith, Historia Esther,* or *Filius prodigus* give us no clue where they were first performed.

When one examines the chronology of the Latin oratorios, one notices that very few—indeed not one major *historia*—were composed during the composer's Jesuit period (1688–1698). This cannot fail to astonish us, since the Jesuit setting ostensibly would seem, more than any other, to have been destined to inspire and present such works. Nevertheless, we do know (see Chapter 8) that *Mors Saülis et Jonathae* (H. 403) and *Josue* (H. 404) were intended for the Jesuits in the early 1680s. *Pestis Mediolanensis* (H. 398) from late 1679 celebrates Saint Charles Borromeo, who was associated with Francis Borgia; it probably was commissioned by the Society of Jesus. How can it be that Charpentier did not pursue this type of composition between 1688 and 1698? If the composer abandoned the oratorio genre during that ten-year period, he was given the opportunity to take it up again magnificently in *Judicium Salomonis* at the end of his career when he was music master at the Sainte-Chapelle.

Like the Italian oratorios, Charpentier's Latin oratorios were inserted in the middle of religious services, in the same way motets were inserted in the services. Most of his oratorios make reference to liturgical feast days (e.g, *In resurrectione Domini Nostri Jesu Christi, In circumcisione Domini,* the five Christmas oratorios, and *Le Reniement de Saint Pierre*), to feasts of individual saints (e.g., *Caecilia, Pour Saint Augustin*), or to other specific occasions (*Canticum pro pace, In obitum*). It is not impossible that other oratorios outside the liturgical calendar could have been performed as part of the Lenten *musicales* at the Hôtel de Guise or in other settings, foreshadowing performances totally detached from their religious context, such as the performances of Mondonville's oratorios by the Concert Spirituel or of Handel's oratorios in the eighteenth century.

THE *HISTORIAE*

Judith sive Bethulia liberata

Judith sive Bethulia liberata (H. 391) is Charpentier's first *historia*, as well as his longest, exceeding 1000 measures. It is divided into two parts, the first concluding with an instrumental interlude, "Nuit" ("Night" music).

The text is adapted from the Apocrypha (Judith 7–13). The final benediction is inspired by a lesson of the Feast of the Assumption, in which Judith appears as a substitute for the Virgin Mary. It is therefore very possible this work was performed on 15 August.

The first setting of part one is at the foot of the mountains in the city of Bethulia, which Holofernes (bass) and the Assyrians are holding under siege by depriving its citizens of water. We are then transported to the camp of the thirst-ridden Israelites, who command their chief, Ozias (*taille*), to surrender to Holofernes. Judith (*haut-dessus*), a widow of great beauty, appears and promises to deliver them. In the second part Judith goes to Holofernes' camp with her servant. Seduced by the young woman's beauty, the Assyrian chief receives her in his tent. While Holofernes sleeps, Judith beheads him, then returns to her people and tells them they have been liberated.

The opening bars ("Chorus Assyriorum," Chorus of the Assyrians: "Stabat Holofernes") sound very much like Carissimi, with dactylic meters (one long and two short syllables), pure homophony sustained by transparent harmonies, and, between the two phrases, a modulation characteristic of the Roman master (fifth degree of A minor to first degree of the relative key of C major), as found, for instance, in *Jephte* (chorus "Plorate filii Israel").

Judith consists largely of narration and exchanges between characters. It is essentially dominated by recitative that is heavily influenced by the Italian style, with its repeated notes, narrow vocal range, and strict syllabic writing.

The use of the Phrygian cadence also proves characteristic:

Sometimes this cadence alternates with an augmented sixth (as in the first example). In *Rules of Composition* (p. 407), Charpentier explained that these two types of cadences serve perfectly to punctuate the narrator's discourse when introducing the speech of a character:

> The cadence of a seventh resolved to a sixth occurs when the bass descends one degree. This one is employed in a conclusive sense, but nevertheless demands something after it. This cadence is employed in the middle of a song, and in music it is the equivalent of the [punctuation marks] : or ; or ? in discourse.

Charpentier diversified his recitative by alternating the role of *historicus* between soloists, trio ensembles, and choruses, the latter two fluctuating between homophonic texture and imitative counterpoint. Like Carissimi, the French composer varied his texture within sections of recitative by moving from pure declamation to a more lyric arioso that blossoms into a beautiful florid passage (Judith's "Quod est hoc verbum Ozias"). The long dialogue between Holofernes and Judith follows this pattern.

The airs in *Judith* are all in *rondeau* form (Ozias's "Aequo animo" ABA, Judith's prayer "Domine Deus" ABA, her "Aperite portas" ABA, and "Laudate Dominum Deum" ABACA). They belong to the category of "affective airs," as defined by Hitchcock:

> The basic structural principle of the affective airs is that of a *rondeau*. The appropriateness of this principle is apparent only through an investigation of the relationship between the texts of the affective airs and their music. Such an investigation shows the composer makes a very nice reconciliation between the largely unsymmetrical and formless prose on which the airs are based and the formalized, balanced structure of a *rondeau*.
>
> The affective airs are settings of speeches that are based on a single affection. Usually the first sentence of the text embodies the affection in terse, even understated terms. This "key-sentence" opens the door to further elaboration of the main

thought. Thus, for example, when Ozias, chief of the Israelites, attempts to reassure his people who are dying of thirst, he begins: "Brethren, be of good courage." This sums up the affection that underlines the rest of his speech: "Let us yet endure five days, in which space the Lord our God may turn his mercy toward us; for he will not forsake us utterly. And if these days pass, and there come no help unto us, I will do according to your word." Charpentier's manner of forming an air from such a text is to set the key-sentence as the principal section of a *rondeau;* the remainder of the text is used for the episode(s). Such episodes are set off from the principal sections by different meters, keys, thematic content, and textures; not infrequently declamatory recitative style is employed, especially if the text is lengthy.[9]

The choruses in *Judith* act as narrator and are also active participants in the drama ("Filii Israel"). They are not very elaborately crafted and remain essentially homophonic, as in Carissimi's works. Twice, however, Charpentier introduces the French practice of alternating small and large choruses ("Vade in pace" and "Hymnum cantemus"), adding some very personal touches like the syncopated rising phrase ("et ascendens illa") or the absolutely superb pedal writing ("in laqueo oculorum suorum eam").

In the middle of the work, Charpentier placed a little instrumental piece "Nuit," after Judith has left the city of Bethulia in the dark to reach Holofernes' camp by dawn. The three-part writing for flutes and violins does not equal the beauty of *Cantiques de Noël* or of *Judicium Salomonis,* but it perfectly captures the mood of the *sommeil* with its long note values, ternary rhythm, and modulating harmonies.

Judith begins in A minor and ends in A major. The change in mode occurs after the murder of Holofernes, when Judith returns triumphant to Bethulia. On the whole, the harmonic texture of the work is rather simple, with some Italian strokes here and there: the Neapolitan sixth (in Judith's Prayer "et humilitatem filiorum Israël") and a major-minor contrast that achieves its full effect in the dialogue between Ozias and Judith.

Historia Esther

Historia Esther (H. 396) is taken from the Old Testament (Esther 1–8). Charpentier had the same forces at his disposal for this work as he did for *Judith:* soloists, four-part chorus, flutes, violins, and organ. The texture of the two works is similar, especially in the predominance of recitative.

King Ahasuerus (*taille*), whose kingdom extends from India to Ethiopia, is giving a great feast in the palace of Shushan. After Queen Vashti's disobedient behavior, he consults Memucan (bass), prince of Persia, who advises him to choose a new wife. Young women are commanded to appear before him. Among them, a young Jewess named Esther (*haut-dessus*) instantly pleases Ahasuerus, who makes her his new queen. Esther, whose parents are dead, has a tutor named Mordecai (*taille*), one of the Jewish captives brought from Jerusalem by Nebuchadnezzar. After his marriage, Ahasuerus promotes Haman (bass), son of Hammedatha, above all princes in the kingdom. That position earns Haman respect from everyone except Mordecai, which enrages Haman. At Haman's request, Ahasuerus commands the extermination of all Jews in the kingdom. Mordecai asks Esther to beg her husband to spare the lives of her people. Trembling, she appears before Ahasuerus, who assures her she will not be harmed. But Haman can no longer tolerate Mordecai's disrespect and wants him hanged. At that moment, Esther's tutor reveals the plot against Ahasuerus. In appreciation, Ahasuerus raises Mordecai to a position of honor. During the feast she gives for Ahasuerus, Esther asks the king to have mercy on her people and to denounce Haman. Ahasuerus orders Haman to be hanged and gives the Jews their freedom.

The recitative treatment and the absence of any structured airs or instrumental movements (other than a few brief ritornellos) give the work a certain austerity. Only a few passages, like the chorus "Quod cum audivit Mardochaeus" describing the suffering of the Jews, the tone-painting of magnificence ("jactantiam"), jubilation ("hilarior"), and rage ("iratus" and "ardentibus"); Ahasuerus' arioso ("Quid habes Esther?"); and the final chorus serve to spark musical interest. Ahasuerus' solo, smacking of both recitative and air with its recurring motifs, is in two parts built around a pause expressing Esther's silent response to the king's questions. In the last section, the thematic material (a sixteenth-note motif depicting cheerfulness) is exposed by Esther, then taken up by the chorus alternating with solo passages for the heroine.

Saint Cecilia *Historiae*

Charpentier composed four different settings of the story of Saint Cecilia, whose feast day is 22 November. His great contemporary, Henry Purcell, also honored the saint in the two *Odes* of 1683 and

1692. While the English composer celebrates Cecilia as the patron saint of music, however, Charpentier's oratorios are concerned with the saint's life, conversion, and martyrdom. At the French court, the feast of Saint Cecilia was not regularly observed until 1687, and Charpentier's last work on the theme (H. 415a) dates from a year before that. At the beginning of the eighteenth century, Italy in turn paid homage to the saint in oratorios, and in the *Saint Cecilia Mass* by Alessandro Scarlatti.

The presence of singers from the Hôtel de Guise in two of the four pieces (H. 413, 415) leads to the conjecture that all the *historiae* in honor of Saint Cecilia were composed under the impetus of Charpentier's benefactresses. The text, freely inspired for the most part, is the same in all four works. Used only partially in H. 394 and 415, it otherwise is subjected to only slight modifications from one piece to the next. It influences the overall structure, tone, and stylistic similarities. The theme of conversion through flowers is strikingly baroque in its sensuality, and weaves a provocative link between the body and the soul.

Chronologically, *In honorem Caeciliae, Valeriani et Tiburtii Canticum* (H. 394) is the earliest of the four versions (1676). In order follow *Caecilia Virgo et Martyr octo vocibus* (H. 397) (1677–1678), *Caecilia Virgo et Martyr* (H. 413) (1684), and *Caecilia Virgo et Martyr* (H. 415) (1685).

Caecilia Virgo et Martyr octo vocibus (H. 397) is the longest of the four (908 measures). It demands the greatest number of performers (soloists, double chorus, double orchestra, and continuo). It is also the only *historia* written in a minor key (G minor). Like H. 413, it has two parts, the first focusing on the conversion of Tiburtius by Cecilia and Valerianus, the second on the saint's martyrdom under the tyrant Almachius. The characters ("Interlocutores") are Cecilia, a noble Roman woman ("Caecilia nobilis Romana") (*haut-dessus*); Valerianus, husband of Cecilia ("Valerianus maritus Caeciliae") (*taille*); Tiburtius, brother of Valerianus ("Tiburtius frater Valeriani") (*haute-contre*); Almachius, the tyrant ("Almachius Tyrannus") (bass); Chorus of the Faithful ("Chorus fidelium"); Chorus of the Angels ("Chorus angelorum"); and a narrator ("Historicus").

In both H. 397 and H. 413, one notices a greater diversity in the writing than in *Judith* and *Esther*. The subject and especially the text, written specifically to be set to music, played no small part in this development. The libretto of *Caecilia* opens with an antiphon for the vespers of the saint: "Est secretum Valeriane, quod tibi volo dicere:

Angelum Dei habeo amatorem, qui nimio zelo custodit corpus meum" (There is a secret, Valerianus, that I wish to convey to you: I have an Angel of God for a lover, who guards my person with great zeal). The librettist, however, inserted some foreign elements between the two phrases to create a form of dialogue between Cecilia and Valerianus. Later, another antiphon is used by the narrator.[10]

Scored for double orchestra, the prelude for H. 397 is majestically conceived. The opening subject is in dotted notes, followed by a subject that Charpentier would reuse in the "Nuit" in *In nativitatem Domini Canticum* (H. 416).

These motifs are treated imitatively, mainly between the *dessus* and the basses, amid very dense counterpoint in all the orchestral parts. The prelude of H. 413 also displays this bi-thematicism, though in a much more clear-cut manner, by alternating measures of duple and triple meter. This device, also seen in the prelude to *Josue,* is typical of Carissimi.

After the dialogue between Cecilia and Valerianus, an angel offers flowers to the couple, which he in turn presents to Tiburtius. The emotion felt by the brother of Valerianus is expressed in H. 397 through the use of a quarter tone (marked X in the example). Though known to contemporary theoreticians, this technique is exceptional.[11]

Tiburtius is skeptical until Cecilia and Valerianus convince him that the flowers are a sign from God. In this arioso-like trio, which is as lovely as the scent of flowers, form and content become one. In the first section, which takes places prior to the conversion of Tiburtius, Valerianus's part and the part for the two spouses are based on different thematic material. In the second section, the three characters are united in a similar spirit of divine adoration and join in the same song. The chorus, in turn, expresses its enchantment with adoring "O's" ("O, o Christi fidem profitentium coelestis harmonia"). While a postlude in H. 413 serves as bridge to the second part, H. 397 has a more imposing prelude on a sarabande rhythm, with the two parts of the orchestra in dialogue with each other.

The second section of *Caecilia Virgo et Martyr* proves much more dramatic. Cecilia first appears before Almachius, her executioner, who has just executed Valerianus and Tiburtius. In contrast to the furious and menacing discourse of Almachius, the saint exhibits the tranquility and glory of those whose faith cannot be shaken by even the most terrible death. The tension of the dialogue culminates in Cecilia's vigorous solo "Abscinde, combure, crudelis avare." Hitchcock classifies this solo as an example of the "poetic air," which he defines as follows:

> By definition the poetic air is a setting of a text which already has a formal organization of its own. The composer's purpose is not, then, to organize his setting so that a text is reconciled with the formal principles of music, but the reverse. The poetic airs are thus more obviously dependent on textual structure than are the affective airs. And since the poetry which occurs in the texts is most frequently in a regular metrical structure, the poetic airs are more songlike than the affective airs. . . . Indeed, most of the poetic airs are reminiscent of the light seventeenth-century *chansons* (as opposed to the more serious *airs de cour*), or of the spirited *canzonetti* of the Italians. Quick triple meters and a homophonic style of accompaniment, well suited to the usually light-hearted poetry, are typical.[12]

To Almachius's increasingly explicit threats, Cecilia replies with tenderness. Then, herself calling for death, she repeats her air. In exasperation Almachius pronounces her death sentence.

There is a rupture and change of tone: Cecilia is about to die. Hence the minor mode, sublime harmonies, silences, and a melodic line abruptly interrupted in the middle of a cadence that resolves only in the bass. In H. 413, Charpentier uses the Neapolitan sixth (B flat), so well-liked by the Italians, whose use and effect he described in his treatise (see p. 392) as "for the purpose of expressing sorrow or the feeble last words of a dying man."

The chorus breaks into a sad plaint, filling the air with heart-rending sighs ("Heu, heu"). In H. 413 an angel exhorts the Chorus of the Faithful to rejoice over the happy death of Cecilia, who is now with God. Then a second angel joins the first in song glorifying the saint, whom the Chorus celebrates in turn. This episode, which is considerably expanded in H. 397 because of the exceptionally rich forces at Charpentier's disposal, takes the form of a monumental apotheosis in which the breathtaking virtuosity of a quartet of angels and the rich, impressive polyphony of double chorus and double orchestra are joined by the full sonority of the *grands jeux* of the organ, an instrument traditionally associated with Cecilia, the patron saint of music. In both works, Charpentier admirably succeeds in shifting imperceptibly from extreme sadness to cheerful rejoicing, the desolate lamentation of the Chorus of the Faithful gradually transforming, on the angels' initiative, into a song of jubilation. There is no doubt that in *Caecilia Virgo et Martyr octo vocibus* (H. 397), composed three or four years after *Judith* and only a few months after *Esther* (works still very similar to Carissimi's oratorios), one can measure the heights to which Charpentier's genius would lift him.

Caecilia Virgo et Martyr (H. 415) presents only the first half of the story. Charpentier had planned a second section as in H. 413 and H. 397.[13] A prologue, which was supposed to be performed "after the overture," was added to the work. Entitled "Harmonia coelestis" and composed for *haut-dessus* and two treble instruments, the *Prologue* (H. 415a) is an invitation to listen to the story of Saint Cecilia who, having rejected the pleasures of the flesh and conquered her tempter, now reigns in heaven. Addressed specifically to a female audience, this version with prologue must have been performed, according to Hitchcock, in a convent.[14]

Written two years after H. 413, *Caecilia Virgo et Martyr* (H. 415) is nearly an exact duplicate of the former, with only three differences. First, the prelude, which is longer and in a single movement, is constructed on a reversible three-part counterpoint.[15] Second, the conversion of Tiburtius is not achieved through the influence of Cecilia and Valerianus, but through the intervention of an angel. In contrast to Tiburtius's recitative, the angel's appearance gives rise to a light, quick strophic air in gavotte rhythm which at the end of each of its two stanzas blossoms into an airy melismatic section extended by the instrumental accompaniment as the voice is immobilized on a long note. Third, the closing chorus is subjected to a few alterations so that its texture is more contrapuntal than the texture of H. 413.

Filius prodigus

Filius prodigus (H. 399) narrates the parable of the prodigal son taken from Luke 15:11–32. Besides the autograph, two extant copies indicate how highly regarded and influential the work was. One copy was made by Sébastien de Brossard (H. 399b); the other (H. 399c), dating from the beginning of the eighteenth century, comes from an anthology containing three oratorios by Carissimi (*Jephte, Jonas,* and *Vir frugi et pater familias*), which is currently in the Bibliothèque de Versailles. Charpentier's oratorio was written in 1680. Originally conceived for soloists, chorus, and two treble instruments, Charpentier added a prelude (H. 399a) for four-part string ensemble, which also doubled the voices in the first chorus.

Filius prodigus is divided into two sections and displays highly sophisticated textures on every level of composition. The recitative is frequently relieved by arioso passages highlighting the words of the text, like the one in which the distraught son (*haute-contre*) decides to return home ("Surgam ergo," I shall rise) or, further on, when the son faces his father in contrition and admits his error ("Erravi sicut ovis quae periit," I have wandered like a lost sheep). Overflowing emotion and joy are expressed in the tone-painting accompanying the words *amplexus* (duet for father and son) and *laetentes* (father's solo "Cito, cito").

To thank his father for having pardoned him, the son sings the only air in the score ("Gratias ergo"). It is an affective air whose refrain is repeated a fourth higher. Charpentier had already used this type of sequentially transposed repetition in the recitative "non, non sum dignus vocari filius tuus" (no, I am not worthy to be called your son).

Filius prodigus is also notable for its choruses, three in all, each one serving a different purpose. The first ("Accepta ergo a patre") is unlike the usual type of narrative chorus in that it not only tells the story, but truly "lives" each situation (the departure of the son to a distant land, the famine threatening him, the dissipation of his wealth, and the growing awareness of his misfortune). It emphasizes each key-word with a different texture: broad melismas on "regionem," chromaticism on "fames," suspended notes on "substantiam suam," and long lamentation on "at que gravi pressus egestate," tinged with dissonance. The second chorus ("Sumite tympana") represents the crowd rejoicing at the son's return: vigorous rhythm, vertical part-writing alternating with exciting ritornellos. Finally, the

Chorus of the Faithful ("Gratias tibi Deus clemens") exposes the moral of the work: the virtue of forgiveness.

Extremum Dei judicium

Although drawn from a few passages in the Old Testament (Deuteronomy 32:1, 5–6, 22) and the New Testament (Matthew 25:35–36, 41–43), the greater portion of the text of *Extremum Dei judicium* (H. 401), notably the choruses, is freely invented, allowing the composer greater freedom in the organization of his work. It is a grand fresco whose different levels of sound (e.g., "Deus," "Angeli," "Trumpet sounds," "Chorus hominum," "Chorus damnatorum," and "Chorus electorum") almost permit the audience to visualize the terror of the Last Judgment in the way Michelangelo or Rubens depicted it. Indeed, the work's power derives from its pyramid-like arrangement and from the contrast between solo elements and choruses, all brought to life by the composer's powerful, dramatic, and tenderly lyric inspiration.

After an instrumental prelude *en trio,* God's first solo (bass), "Audite coeli," addressed to the entire universe from earth to the heavens, distinguishes between the image of the God of goodness (short binary air accompanied by the instruments, "Generatio prava") and the God of wrath (menacing sixteenth-note runs). The terror-stricken chorus ("O, o pavor! O, o tremor! O portentum!") utters a series of chords falling gradually into the lower tessitura. Then the small chorus and large chorus alternately describe the apocalyptic spectacle unfolding before them.

After the sound of trumpets (*bruit de trompettes*), two angels (*hautes-contre*) in canon-style summon the living and the dead to submit to God's judgment. The two trumpets repeat their call before the chorus which, in long chordal phrases punctuated by fermatas, describes the great movement of the dead being brought back to life.

God first addresses the elect, then the damned. His two solos mirror each other and exhibit the same *rondeau* structure; the middle part ("Esurivi enim") is the same in both solos, except that the text is negated in the second version. The two airs are differentiated by their atmosphere in accordance with the affective nature of each key: the "magnificent and joyous" B-flat major and the "cruel and harsh" subdominant E-flat major. While the first solo ends with a very long note symbolizing the eternal life promised to the elect, the second one contains God's curse ("Maledicti, maledicti peccatores") repeated each time in a higher register.

God's two-part solo is followed by the Chorus of the Damned ("Chorus Damnatorum") and the Chorus of the Elect ("Chorus Electorum"), separated by another angel duet. In the "obscure and awful" key of B-flat minor, the Chorus of the Damned launches its cries of suffering. The impetuous rhythm and furiously sweeping melodic contours ("Cadite montes") depict the terrifying descent to Hell of the unfortunate souls. Their laments reach a peak on "Ah," with each part entering variously on a different note of the tonic chord.

Light returns with the Chorus of the Elect accompanied by instruments in calm ternary symmetry, cleverly constructed through repetitions, varied each time (e.g., by use of small or large choir, different key, melodic variations). Then the rhythm broadens, and final bliss emerges out of celestial weightlessness.

Sacrificium Abrahae

Along with *Extremum Dei judicium* and *Judicium Salomonis*, *Sacrificium Abrahae* (H. 402) is one of three oratorios whose subjects were also treated by Carissimi. Charpentier dealt with the subject a second time in the last of his Lenten *Méditations* (H. 389). The text is directly inspired by Genesis 21:1–8, 22:1–19. The many narrative passages are alternately scored in an exceptionally diverse manner for solo voice, duet, trio, and chorus (whose texture is usually homophonic).

Charpentier begins his *historia* with the birth of Isaac. The joy of Abraham (*taille*) and Sarah (*dessus*) is expressed in a duet in *rondeau* form; at the refrain's reprise, the two characters' melodic lines are inverted. This joyful scene provides the composer with a contrast to the episode in which Abraham is commanded by God to sacrifice his beloved son. On the way to the place designated by God for the sacrifice, Isaac (*haute-contre*) reiterates his questions ("Pater mi") to the unfortunate Abraham, who cannot bring himself to reveal the truth. The preparations for the sacrifice are described by the chorus with mounting tension, climaxed by the great melodic ascent on "desuperque ligno composito alligavit Isaac" (he arranged the wood whereupon he placed the bound Isaac). Dramatic tension mounts, the chorus is temporarily reduced to only two parts, then resumes using very frequently modulating harmonies. Abraham clutches his knife to kill Isaac: there is a perfect cadence, then silence. In an unexpected key, the angel stops Abraham and addresses him in a joyful air, promising him a long line of descendants (illustrated by melismas on the words "stellas" and "arenam"). The father and his son then rejoice in a duet dominated by imitative texture.

The last part of the work, expressing the moral of the story (i.e., the fear of God and obedience to Him), is built on two utterly contrasting themes, first exposed by Abraham and Isaac, then repeated and varied by the chorus. The first theme ("Beati qui timent Dominum") is a tender melody in triple meter and parallel notes. The second theme is composed of two elements ("Quoniam augebit Deus" and "et multiplicabit") treated imitatively. The drama concludes with a new melodic phrase ("et reges populorum") emphatically stated in dactylic meter.

Mors Saülis et Jonathae (H. 403) was composed some six or seven years before *David et Jonathas*, the opera written for the Jesuit Collège. It is the most theatrical of all Charpentier's *historiae*. Action plays a very important part in it, and a large portion of the work is given to dialogues between the various characters, some of them drawn directly from biblical text (1 Kings 28 and 2 Kings 1). Paradoxically, there is even more action in the oratorio *Mors Saülis et Jonathae* than in the opera *David et Jonathas*. (For an analysis of the latter and its relationship to the Latin tragedy *Saül*, see Chapter 8).

Mors Saülis et Jonathae

Despite differences between the two works which stem respectively from their genre and their functions, the two have some things in common, such as the sorceress' invocation scene ("Maga" in *Mors Saülis et Jonathae*, "La Pythonisse" in *David et Jonathas*), the dialogue between Saul and Samuel—occurring in the first part of the oratorio and in the opera's prologue—and choruses of battle and of lamentation.

The *historia* opens with a fanfare-prelude ("Rumor bellicus"), followed by the narrative four-part chorus "Cum essent congregati." The composer alternates among the first half of the choir (marked "A," depicting the Philistines), the other half (marked "B," depicting the Israelites), and the combined choruses ("everyone") accompanied by instruments. This procedure is continued in the other choruses, whether they function as narrators or as actors. Assuming his singers were placed some distance apart from each other, the composer may have wished to create contrasting spatial sonorities.

The sorceress' air ("Aether umbrosus"), which summons the powers of darkness to reveal the ghost of Samuel to Saul, displays a highly individual texture. Using the *haute-contre*'s dark, low register in unison with the basso continuo, the extremely slow air in 3/1 meter builds on both *rondeau* (ABA) and strophic forms (reprise of the first A part on a different text). The first part of the sorceress' air is sung after a "Symphonie" *en trio* (probably two violins and organ) in the same 3/1 meter; the air also borrows its first notes from the "Symphonie," though it soon departs greatly from the melody. The second section ensues, still in triple meter, but quick (the time signature is marked 3). Everything shifts from the "obscure and plaintive" key of F minor to the "furious and quick-tempered" F major. After a recitative (part B) marked "whispered" (*murmuré*) and remaining in the extreme low register of the voice, the entire "Symphonie" (slow air–quick air) is repeated.

The second part of the *historia* is divided into two episodes. The first, focused on Saul's pleas for a soldier to slay him, conforms to a symmetrical structure. At either extreme are placed two little airs in *rondeau* form for Saul, each with the same refrain ("Tolle, quaeso"). The battle between the Philistines and the Israelites occurs at midpoint, with Saul's anguished cries cutting through the chorus' call to arms ("Ad arma, ad arma!"). Charpentier reproduced the effect of this aural perspective in Act IV of *David et Jonathas*.

The last part of the work brings on David (*taille*). The unfortunate soldier who ultimately obeyed Saul's wish appears before David to confess the deed. David's anxious interrogation of the soldier and the latter's confused responses are rendered in very expressive recitative, frequently punctuated by silence. Their dialogue is interrupted by the strains of the chorus' sad plaint, "O sors, sors infelix et acerba! O mors, mors crudelis et amara!" The final words of each phrase are emphasized by harmonies appropriate to such sentiments:

In his treatise (see p. 399), Charpentier calls the penultimate chord of the above cadence "very plaintive." The chorus is composed in short sections, some reprised note-for-note, others slightly varied.

Still under David's interrogation, the soldier describes Saul's last moments, which we have already witnessed. The existence of such a solo violates all dramatic sense and can only be due to blind fidelity to the biblical text. The soldier even goes so far as to report Saul's words to practically the same music that had accompanied them when first pronounced, a musical device which, nevertheless, is not without a certain originality.

Alone, David gives vent to his grief. He mourns the death of Jonathan, his beloved friend, in an air in *rondeau* form with two couplets (ABACA) plaintively inflected ("Doleo, doleo").

The final chorus ("Montes Gelboë") poignantly stresses the names "Saül" and "Jonathas." It derives its unity chiefly from the *rondeau* form used one last time by Charpentier in this composition.

Josue

Josue (H. 404) depicts the biblical episode of Moses' successor, Joshua (Joshua 10:1–14), warring against Adonizedec and the Amorite kings. Joshua asks the Lord to stop the orbit of the sun and the moon.

The "prelude for 8 instruments" lies within the purest Italian antiphonal tradition and presents the type of texture that dominates virtually all the choruses. They play a major role and represent, in turn, the Amorites, the Israelites, and the faithful.

The first chorus ("Congregati igitur"), for only four voices, is introduced by a warlike fanfare *en trio* which also serves as ritornello. This is a declamatory chorus with a solid chordal texture, successively assigned to each part of the double chorus.

The next chorus, for eight voices, is extremely original in many ways. Beginning as narrator of the action ("the noise of the battle echoing throughout nature"), it changes into an active participant in the drama ("the defeated Amorites, the triumphant Israelites"). Throughout this passage, different texts sung by each part of the chorus, as well as the antiphonal style, work together to create an incredibly rich texture. Above all the tumult, the sun ("Sol") and the moon ("Luna"), which God has immobilized, are represented by long notes in the soprano lines of each chorus. The "Chorus filii Israël," in dialogue with the instruments, ends *a capella*, proclaiming victory.

The last chorus ("Chorus fidelium") borrows the first part of its text from Psalm 116: "Laudate Dominum omnes gentes." Very brilliant, it contains florid melismas in parallel thirds for the two high solo voices, while the densely antiphonal choral writing also echoes the soloist's joyous melismas ("laudamus," "glorificamus," and "magnificamus").

In obitum

In obitum augustissimae nec non piissimae Gallorum reginae, Lamentum (H. 409) is one of Charpentier's most extraordinary oratorios and is unique in the history of funeral music of the period. It was written to commemorate the death on 31 July 1683 of Queen Marie-Thérèse, but the precise circumstances of its performance remain shrouded in mystery to this day (see "The Queen's Funeral" in Chapter 5). How could such a large-scale, deeply individual score have escaped the notice of contemporary reporters, which were otherwise so meticulous about describing the most insignificant ceremony in honor of the deceased queen?

In obitum has 825 bars and calls for a particularly sumptuous scoring, which Charpentier penned quite carefully. The five-part orchestra (a rare occurrence in Charpentier's religious works) includes string quintet (*dessus, hautes-contre, tailles, quintes,* and *basses de violons*), recorder, transverse flute, and tenor or bass flute doubling the strings in the *tutti*. The vocal writing has seven parts, namely, *haut-dessus, dessus, bas-dessus, haute-contre, taille, basse-taille,* and bass.

As described earlier (see Chapter 5), *In obitum* is the finest musical representation of the funeral ceremony as it was celebrated in the second half of the seventeenth century. Surely it is no coincidence that this one-of-a-kind work is by a composer who was so in touch with the Church and its theatricality.

Like other funeral settings, *In obitum* springs essentially from the contrast between the feelings of grief caused by death and jubilation because of the prospect of eternal life. The work is built entirely upon this opposition, reflected in the two-part structure and, within the second part itself, in the dialogue between the grieving populace and the joyous song of the angel.

After a prelude that is at once very majestic and very sad, a messenger ("Nuncius," *taille*) announces with great lamentation the death of Marie-Thérèse to the people. His solo (ABA) continues the same syncopated rhythm of the prelude. The melodic line descends inexorably, then resorts to intervals as expressive as the diminished third or minor sixth, and to chromaticism.

The dreadful revelation is made over the course of several phases, creating a certain dramatic "suspense," reinforced by the anxious questions of three characters representing the people (*haute-contre, taille,* and bass). On the word *expiravit* the flutes sadly conclude the messenger's solo; then the chorus expresses its shock ("O sors infelix et acerba!") as it pours out its grief, weeping, sighing, and constantly reiterating the same words, the same expressions of despair ("O mors crudelis et amara!"; "Heu! Dolentes!"; and "Ah! Periit!"). Next, the three allegorical graces ("Fides," Faith, *haut-dessus*; "Spes," Hope, *haut-dessus*; and "Charitas," Charity, *dessus*) mourn the queen in long descending phrases, featuring glorious suspensions on the words "in carmine doloris lugeamus." The chorus takes up its plaint again, invoking all nature to mourn and concluding the immense lamentation with a return of "O sors infelix et acerba!"

The second part opens with a prelude marked "lively." An angel (*haute-contre*) appears and urges the faithful to sing joyous hymns. As at the beginning of the first section, a dialogue is established, this time between the angel (whose song in C major leads to lengthy melismas) and the three soloists, still weeping ("Heu! Dolentes!") in the initial key of C minor.

After the symphony's reprise, a spirit of rejoicing is permanently established. The three graces followed by the other soloists (duets) restate the angel's words. Finally, all the voices join in praising Marie-Thérèse's eternal reign in heaven and Louis XIV's reign on earth.

Praelium Michaelis

Unfortunately, we have only the first part and the beginning of the second part of *Praelium Michaelis archangeli factum in coelo cum dracone* (H. 410).[16] The high quality of what remains makes us regret all the more its current fragmentary state.

The work is inspired by Revelation 12, which recounts the celestial combat between Michael and the dragon. The first part centers completely around the fight, reflected in the powerful, warlike style that abounds in the prelude's repeated notes, arpeggios, and bass pedals. This style is also evident in the solos (for "Historicus" *taille*, then *haute-contre*, and "Draco" and "Michael" basses) swept with tempestuous melismas, and in the choruses' constantly hammering rhythms. In the double choruses, in which Michael's good angels confront the dragon's bad angels, the part-writing becomes strikingly dense and furious.

With its ternary rhythm and parallel thirds, the prelude to the second part reestablishes calm. The "Historicus" announces Michael's victory over the dragon. At that point, the score breaks off.

Caedes sanctorum innocentium

Caedes sanctorum innocentium (H. 411) relates Herod's command to massacre the children of Bethlehem. The beginning of the text is taken from Matthew 2:13, 17–18, where Joseph is instructed by the angel to flee into Egypt with Mary and the Child Jesus.

Charpentier turned this cruel episode into a magnificently inspired work full of contrasting emotions, both plaintive and powerful, going from the deepest suffering to the expression of the sweetest beatitude. Along with the Angel ("Angelus") (*haute-contre*), the narrator ("Historicus") (*taille*), and Herod ("Herodes") (bass), three groups figure in this *historia:* Chorus of Mothers ("Chorus matrem") (*haut-dessus, dessus, bas-dessus*), Chorus of Guards ("Chorus satellitum") (*haute-contre, taille,* bass), and Chorus of the Faithful ("Chorus fidelium") (combining all six voices).

The first two groups are pitted against each other in a vigorous passage ("Ad arma! Pereat Herodes!"), partially repeated after the mothers' lamentation ("O crudel martyrium"). Alarmed by the wailing of the unhappy women ("Heu! Nos miseras"), three of the faithful ask the mothers why they are weeping, then tell them to be of good cheer since their dead children will be evermore in heaven at

God's side. The work ends with a radiant chorus praising the kingdom of Christ where the innocent reign amid the joys of eternal life.

Le Reniement de Saint Pierre

Le Reniement de Saint Pierre (H. 424) has come down to us thanks to a copy by Sébastien de Brossard, who described the work as "a story or oratorio in the Italian style about Saint Peter's denial and repentance for 5 voices CCATB *cum organo.*"

Unlike Italy and Germany, France in Charpentier's time was hardly interested in Passion works. *Le Reniement de Saint Pierre*, an important portion of the Passion drama, is therefore an exception. The text is largely drawn from Matthew 26, with a few passages from the other Gospels (Mark 14, Luke 22, and John 18). No freely interpolated sections provide the material for structured airs and choruses that dramatize the story, as in other oratorios. None of these embellishments are found in *Le Reniement de Saint Pierre*, where fidelity to the biblical text goes hand in hand with extreme economy of means: only five voices (*haut-dessus, dessus, haute-contre, taille,* and bass) and continuo, without concerted instruments.

More than in any other oratorio, Charpentier drew his inspiration from the emotional and theological essence of the text, resulting in a score that genuinely serves the word, and is extremely faithful to it. In this sense, Charpentier came close to the style of the Passions of Heinrich Schütz, whose music never overpowers the text. Never losing sight of the divine message, Charpentier's music achieves its purpose and its expressiveness only inasmuch as it obeys the exigencies of that message.

While *Le Reniement de Saint Pierre* must be considered in its Catholic context and, in that light, cannot rival the stark austerity of the Passions of Schütz, Charpentier's musical setting is just as intimately tied to the sacred word. The syllabic and chordal style of all the narrative ensembles except the last one permits the meaning of the text to come across perfectly. The solos for Jesus (*taille?*, Petrus (*haute-contre,*) and the Historicus (bass) are respectful of the Latin prosody. They employ sequential repetitions or tone-painting on certain groups of words ("dispergentur," "irruerunt," "fugerunt") while never altering the purity of the declamation. Only Jesus' last intervention ("Converte Petre") tends toward a more melodic vein, approaching the air, with its second phrase highlighted through repetition ("Calicem quem dedit mihi pater non vis ut bibam illum?"

This cup that my Father gave me, do you not want me to drink it?).

When the chorus abandons its narrative function to become an active participant in the drama, the part-writing becomes more animated ("Non te negabimus") and more complex in the admirable quartet ("Nonne tu Galileus es") in which the doorkeeper (Ostiaria, *haut-dessus*), the servant girl (Ancilla, *dessus*), and a relative of Malchus (Cognatus Malchi, *taille*), the soldier whose ear Peter cut off, accuse the disciple in densely imitative music. Peter defends himself with vehement "no's" until the crowing of the cock ("Et continuo gallus cantavit"), at which point the key changes abruptly and his blindness ends.

Christ then looks upon Peter with a glance that is both terrible and gentle; in the music this is depicted in the word *tunc* sung by all the voices on a chord of the dominant and followed by silence. The chorus comments on the encounter between Peter and Jesus, with melismas on their names. Peter remembers, and this time Christ's word ("verbi Jesu") is underlined by a hemiola (a binary division of a bar in triple meter), a device Charpentier inherited from Carissimi and employed rather frequently.

The final section of *Le Reniement* contains only the words "flevit amare" (he wept bitterly), which are repeated inexorably, like the tears shed by Peter, for thirty-three measures. Each voice unfolds in broad, sweeping melismas whose counterpoint increases the number of suspensions. Poignant dissonances depict the inconsolable grief of the repentant Peter.

Judicium Salomonis

While *Le Reniement de Saint Pierre* is an introspective masterpiece of inward prayer, *Judicium Salomonis* (H. 422) is another masterpiece, revealing the other side of religious sensibility of the epoch, a side centered on more sumptuous celebrations. It is obvious that the liturgical or social context of each work (the former intended for the austere Lenten season, the latter for the ceremonies accompanying the convening of Parlement) determined its musical conception. What is remarkable is that Charpentier was able to adapt to such exigencies in composing two works so stylistically unlike one another and yet both so successful.

From the manuscripts, it appears Charpentier probably composed another work on the same subject some twenty years before he wrote this great *Judicium Salomonis*.[17] Though non-extant and probably a smaller-scale work, it would have been interesting to compare it to the 1702 work.

The text of *Judicium Salomonis* is mainly drawn from 3 Kings 3[1 Chronicles 3, in Protestant Bibles] and Psalm 117:1–3, "Confitemini Domino." The rest is freely inspired.

For this great *historia* Charpentier benefitted from the support of the "extraordinary musical forces" that on important occasions "fortified" the regular ensemble of the Sainte-Chapelle (see Chapter 15). Thanks to the preservation of separate parts (H. 422a), we know the exact scoring. The chorus was made up of six *dessus*, five *hautes-contre*, five *tailles,* and ten basses, while the orchestra consisted of two flutes and oboes, four string parts (three *dessus*, two *hautes-contre*, two *tailles,* and two bass violins), and organ continuo.

Judicium Salomonis was apparently the very last composition Charpentier wrote. It can be considered his musical testament because of the prodigious diversity of its textures (that essential trait of all his works, and one which the composer himself considered the musical ideal), the perfect synthesis of French and Italian styles, as well as the sumptuous architecture supporting the entire composition. Indeed, everything in this remarkable work deserves our attention, especially the large, brilliant, and varied choruses of unusual vocal and instrumental density. Full of rhythmic excitement, these choruses directly foreshadowed those in Handel's oratorios.

The first of the two sections that make up *Judicium Salomonis*, essentially narrative and descriptive, is devoted to the glory of Solomon and to the happiness and piety of his people; it is set throughout in C major. The prelude's majestic dotted rhythms sound not unlike the first page of a French overture. The narration is assigned in turn to one soloist, to the chorus, to a trio of men's voices (*haute-contre, taille,* and bass), and back to the chorus.

Linked to the preceding *récit* for the *Historicus* (bass), the first chorus is like a vast diptych whose dividing point is a change in meter (from C to 6/4). It begins with two powerful chords on the word *tunc,* which the orchestra "embroiders" with sixteenth-notes. After a quick imitative episode ("Tunc laetata est") lending extraordinary rhythmic impetus to this chorus of rejoicing, the texture becomes chordal and remains so, except for rare moments, until the end of the chorus. Sometimes the vocal and instrumental parts interweave in rich, polyphonic textures; sometimes they blend together. Ritornellos punctuate the exposition of the verses, which employ new thematic material each time, though the rhythm remains constant throughout (opening on the upbeat, hemiolas at cadences).

The ensuing trio perpetuates the 6/4 meter. The joyful tone, however, gives way to more intimacy and lyricism, expressed by melismas ("adoravit Deum") and by the very beautiful ascending melodic line ("et expansis in coelum palmis") that depicts Solomon's offering to God.

The air for Solomon (*taille*), "Benedictus es," which gives thanks to the Lord, is interspersed with graceful flute ritornellos. Charpentier enlarges its *rondeau* form into a veritable da capo aria, whose Italian workmanship is accentuated by the long melisma on "laudabilis."

The chorus "Ideo cunctis" renews the pace and brio of the first chorus. Notable are the dynamic effects ("Longe lateque sonor audiebatur" repeated in echo-fashion by voices and instruments, then "more softly" in the orchestra only) that translate the sound picture described by the text ("with cymbals and instruments of music sounding, with voices dropping from the heights to the depths and rising from the depths to the heights"). This first section concludes with a reprise of the "Confitemini" from the preceding chorus.

Strictly speaking, the judgment of Solomon takes place only in the second part. In striking contrast to what has just been heard, Charpentier plunges us into the dreamy realm of night with one of the most beautiful "Nuit" symphonies he ever wrote. In their low register, muted strings trace slowly ascending chromatic lines over a bass pedal. After a cadence, the *hautes-contre* and *taille* violin parts and the organ ("*jeux doux*") in unison are joined by the two flutes and trace a gently undulating motif of slurred pairs of notes. The last part, which brings all the instruments together, rises conjunctly (and even chromatically in the *haute-contre* part) over a progression of sevenths in the bass. Once again Charpentier achieves a perfect combination of French and Italian elements. While the instrumentation and the vocal part-leading in the central episode are directly influenced by Lully *sommeils*, the exquisite harmonies of the opening and closing measures could only have been conceived by the Italianist Charpentier.

Unlike the first section of the work set in C major throughout, the second section unfolds amid a changing tonal scheme, in accordance with its highly dramatic and emotional content. Unity arises from the harmonic logic that guides the composer in his choice of keys. The main key of C, at first in the minor mode, shifts at the end to the major, thus returning to the opening tonality. Gravitating around C minor are the relative E-flat major (Solomon's solo) and the dominant G major (second part of God's solo and the chorus "Et facto mane"). The judgment episode is given its own distinctive main key (G minor), causing in its turn a modulation to the neighboring key of B-flat major (in Solomon's lines). In this score which clearly ushers in the eighteenth century, Charpentier uses tonality not only for its expressive possibilities, but also for cohesiveness and building musical discourse.

God appears to Solomon in a dream, so Solomon, in a recitative accompanied by two violins and punctuated by flute ritornellos, prays for wisdom and the ability to distinguish good from evil ("Domine Deus meus"). In a magnificent arioso ("Quia non petisti"), God (bass) grants Solomon not only that which he desired, but also wealth, glory, and long life. This solo consists of a first section in C minor in which the majestic vocal line is accompanied by muted full strings and a second section in G major, more declamatory, with the instruments merely punctuating the text. At the conclusion of the divine intervention, the accompaniment gradually dissolves: the vision evaporates and the last shadows of night dissipate.

The narrating chorus, first grave ("Et facto mane"), then lively ("Comedentibus autem illis"), introduces the appearance of the two mothers. The real mother (Vera madre, *dessus*, a role sung at the work's premiere by Bruslard, a choirboy in the Sainte-Chapelle) explains her dispute with the false mother (Falsa madre, *haute-contre*) to Solomon in a heart-rending recitative ("Obsecro mi Domine"): both women live in the same house and gave birth within a few days of each other; one night, the false mother's child died of suffocation; the false mother exchanged her dead child for her neighbor's living child. Each sentence is sung on a note lower than the one before, allowing Charpentier to vary the articulation of this long recitative and communicate the real mother's anguish.

The quarrel between the two women erupts in an extremely agitated duet ("Non est ita") recalling the duet on the same text in Carissimi's oratorio. After a brief solo intervention by Solomon, the duet is repeated. Solomon proposes that the living child be divided in two and that one-half be given to each woman. The real mother begs Solomon to allow the child to live and to give him to the false mother, who prefers that the child be divided. There is a new duet for the two women, each trying to put forth her own speech, which Charpentier magnificently differentiates in the music. On the syllabic style of one woman the other's furious melismas on the word *dividatur* are superimposed.

In the key of C major which now returns limpid and radiant, Solomon renders his judgment by restoring the child to its real mother. The chorus solemnly expresses its admiration ("Audivit omnis Israel") and directly addresses (small, then large chorus) the magistrates of the Palais de Justice, inviting them to rejoice ("Gaudete") and to follow the luminous paths of justice paved by God.

THE CANTICLES

Canticum pro pace was doubtless intended for the celebration of a victory by the French army, then at war with Holland. It is therefore an occasional work, half motet and half oratorio, comparable to *In obitum* (H. 409), though more modestly proportioned. Like *In obitum*, this work also features the intervention of an angel (*haute-contre*), who in this instance calls an end to combat. There also are two allegorical figures appropriate for the subject, Pax and Justitia (*hauts-dessus*).

The score is particularly outstanding for its splendid double chorus writing. Essentially antiphonal, it moves from a warlike tone ("Ad arma clamate") to an expression of joy ("Jubilemus") and to a calmer atmosphere in the rapturous passages hailing the angel's appearance ("Quoenam lux") or celebrating peace ("O pax optata").

Pestis Mediolanensis (H. 398) is an evocation of the plague that ravaged the city of Milan in 1576–1577 and the zealous intervention of its archbishop Carlo Borromeo. The work dates from 1679 and was probably performed on the saint's feast day, 4 November. It is in two parts (not explicitly indicated by Charpentier) in contrasting modes (C minor and C major) and atmospheres.

After a prelude (H. 398a) for four-part strings, the horrors of the plague and the devastation of those stricken by it are narrated without any particular character intervening. The *récit* is first assigned to solo voices (*taille, haute-contre*, then bass) who sing together in the poignant "Clamabant," repeated after a new appearance by each soloist. Then Charpentier gradually increases his forces to a double quartet of soloists followed by a double chorus with instruments. On a versified text, a *cantilena* for two voices simultaneously uses strophic and *rondeau* form. The last line of each couplet is taken up by a trio (*dessus, haute-contre,* and *taille*), with rich melismas on the word *fervens.*

The second part consists of a large chorus that rejoices in honor of Saint Carlo Borromeo. It alternates with solo passages and serves as a long, then a short reprise.

In *Nuptiae sacrae* (H. 412), Charpentier draws on the Song of Solomon for inspiration. There is also a quote from Psalm 44:11–12. The work is organized around the dialogue between the Husband (Sponsus) (*basse-taille*) and the Wife (Sponsa) (*haut-dessus*), and their subsequent duet in a style that breaks into evocative melismas. Ample space is afforded the six-part chorus which, from the very first measures, invites the celebration of the mystical wedding in brilliant counterpoint ("Incipite Domino"). It returns on several later occasions, alternating rich imitative textures with chordal progressions distributed among the upper parts (*haut-dessus* and two *dessus*) and the low voices (*haute-contre, taille,* and bass) in double-choral fashion. It never loses that aura of freshness which runs through the entire work.

Chronologically, *In honorem Caeciliae, Valeriani et Tiburtii Canticum* (H. 394) is the first of the four *historiae* about Saint Cecilia. The limits imposed by the light scoring (*haut-dessus, dessus,* bass, two treble instruments, and basso continuo) surely influenced Charpentier's decision to retain only the first half of the story (the conversion of Tiburtius). Hence, the work unfolds in an atmosphere of utter happiness, unclouded by Cecilia's martyrdom and death.

The first appearance by Cecilia comes after the prelude and is remarkable for the way Charpentier treats the text. It is a recitative in ABA form. The recapitulation is used to emphasize Cecilia's words, "Est secretum Valerianus quo tibi volo dicere" (It is a secret, Valerianus, that I wish to tell thee), and thus to establish the tone of intimacy running throughout the work. Within the recitative, Charpentier inserts a brief arioso (B) that emphasizes the privileged relationship between the saint and the angel: "Angelum Dei habeo amatorem *qui nimio zelo custodit corpus meum,*" I have an angel of God for a lover *who very zealously guards my body* (the words in italics correspond to the five bars of arioso).

The beginning of the dialogue between Cecilia and Valerianus is addressed to Tiburtius. It juxtaposes the major and minor modes of G to depict the physical and spiritual agitation of Cecilia's brother caused by the exquisite scent of the flowers offered by the angel. After Tiburtius's conversion, all three characters sing in sweet, celestial harmony.

Pour la fête de l'épiphanie (H. 395) employs the same forces as the preceding piece. The text of this little *canticum* is largely taken from Matthew 2:1–12. Charpentier chose the "grave and pious" key of D minor (though the work concludes in D major) to recount the journey of the Magi to Bethlehem. Recitative style predominates in the solo passages as well as in the trio ensembles. The only character who appears is Herod, assigned to a bass. In the last part, the music follows the text very closely. Just before the entrance of the Magi in the house sheltering Mary and the Infant Jesus, Charpentier provides a "little pause." He expresses the adoration of Jesus on a dominant pedal and represents the gift-offering by having three different voices utter, one after the other, "aurum" (*haut-dessus*), "thus" (*dessus*), and "myrrham" (bass).

Were it not for its opening phrases, given separately to Mary Magdalen (*haut-dessus*) and Mary Salome (*dessus*), as well as the narrative episode "Et ecce terrae motus," *In resurrectione Domini Nostri Jesu Christi* (H. 405) could be classified among the *dialogi*, since the rest of the work consists of dialogue between the two Marys and the angel (bass). The various exchanges in the text are clearly articulated by metrical changes (3 for the angel, a slower 3/2 for the two women). This rhythmic differentiation also occurs in the three-voice *récit* describing the earthquake, in the angel's appearance, and in the terror of the guards at the sepulchre, with, moreover, a marked tonal instability particularly affecting the passage "et facti sunt velut mortui" (and became as dead men).

The text of *In resurrectione Domini Nostri Jesu Christi* is taken from Matthew 28:2–7. It is enriched by direct interventions of Mary Magdalen and Mary Salome and, in the last ensemble, by Psalm 117:24, which is followed by a joyous "Alleluia."

In honorem Sancti Ludovici Regis Galliae (H. 418) constitutes one of the five works celebrating the French saint-king, Louis IX (see Chapter 9). The instrumental prelude for two flutes, two violins, and continuo (harpsichord and viol) is, without doubt, the most beautiful part of the score. For forty measures, the musical tension is consistently sustained by a harmonic skill that attests to Charpentier's mastery in that domain. All the intervals and chords that ensure the expressivity of its message occur here: ninths, sevenths, augmented octave, seconds, augmented fourths, diminished fifths, and a chromatic bass. The grief-stricken mood continues in the narrator's solo (*haute-contre*), which describes the agony of Saint Louis (*taille*) among his dead friends, and in the king's flute-accompanied supplication to God. Imperceptibly the mood becomes less and less mournful ("Accedite et erudimini" for the three-voice ensemble with all the instruments). After God summons Saint Louis in a solo (bass), "Rex terrae serve meus" (accompanied by violins and shifting to the major mode), the finale ("Plaudite populi") sings the glory of the king and of Christ.

In this work there is an obvious allusion to Louis XIV when God addresses Saint Louis: "Nascetur tibi filius secundum cor meum, ipse destruet inimicos meos, et pugnabit solus pro gloria nominis mei" (A son shall be born to you from my heart, who shall destroy my enemies and fight single-handedly for the glory of my name). These words inevitably ring with the echo of the wars which the king of France embarked on during the 1690s.

Besides the little *In nativitatem Domini Canticum* (H. 314), Charpentier composed five Christmas oratorios on two texts. The first text ("Frigidae noctis umbra"), adapted from Luke 2:8–16, is used for *Canticum in nativitatem Domini* (H. 393), *In nativitatem Domini Nostri Jesu Christi Canticum* (H. 414), and *In nativitate Domini Nostri Jesu Christi Canticum* (H. 421), with a few variations from one work to the next. The second text ("Usquequo avertis faciem tuam Domine") is also taken from Luke (2:10–15), but with the addition of an introduction arranged from Psalm 12, as well as a quotation from Isaiah (45:8, "Rorate coeli de super"). This text serves *In nativitatem Domini Canticum* (H. 416) and *Dialogus inter angelos et pastores Judae, In nativitatem Domini* (H. 420).[18] Curiously, there is also a setting of it by André Campra entitled *Nativitas Domini Nostri Jesu Christi*. Campra's work, which was composed in the last years of the seventeenth century, is contemporary with Charpentier's oratorios. The musical layout of the solos and choruses in Campra's work is virtually identical to Charpentier's, and there is even a shepherds' march. How is it that this same text was used by both composers?

Nearly twenty-five years separate H. 393 and 421, both of which require a small ensemble: *haut-dessus, dessus,* bass, two treble instruments, and thorough bass in the former, and two *hauts-dessus*, one *dessus*, and continuo in the latter. A third work, H. 414, falls chronologically between the two (1684) and calls for a larger formation: *haut-dessus*, two *dessus*, *basse-taille*, five-part choir, two treble instruments, and basso continuo. The length of these works is also variable: 117 bars in H. 393, 330 bars in H. 414, and 220 bars in H. 421. Nevertheless, the three works have several points in common.

The nocturnal calm and the shepherds' watch are suggested by a stationary bass and melodic parts made up of notes that are repeated or that descend conjunctly. The angel's appearance breaks this peaceful mood. After reassuring the frightened shepherds ("Nolite timere"), God's messenger announces the coming of the Savior and invites the shepherds to journey to Bethlehem. They prepare to leave ("Surgamus") in a lively ensemble. Only H. 414 contains an orchestral march in *rondeau* form. Arriving at the manger, the shepherds hail the Infant Jesus in a light, graceful air ("Salve puerule"). The air is poetic with its clear-cut phrases and minuet rhythm.[19]

In addition to the strophic technique, there occurs another kind of repetition often encountered in the *chansons* of the first half of the century: the solo melody is restated, harmonized by the vocal ensemble (H. 414, 421). An instrumental ritornello is placed between each couplet.

In nativitatem Domini Canticum (H. 416) and *Dialogus inter angelos et pastores Judae, In nativitatem Domini* (H. 420) are developed at greater length than the preceding pieces: 821 bars in the first, 577 bars in the other. Their scoring is also more imposing: soloists, four-part chorus, flutes, string orchestra, and basso continuo, with organ mentioned in certain places.

The first part is a grand introduction to the Nativity, which prepares the mood of hope for salvation and the mystery of the Immaculate Conception. This section (in C minor in H. 416, in A minor in H. 420) is introduced in H. 416 by a magnificent prelude; its final bars demonstrate how freely Charpentier used counterpoint.

After the *tailles*'s somber recitative ("Usquequo"), the Chorus of the Righteous ("Chorus Justorum") continues in the same dark vein until the quicker "Veni de excelso." Great tenderness surrounds the bass solo, "Consolare filia Sion," which is accompanied by two flutes and two violins and is constructed like a *rondeau*. Between the elegant descending contours of two choruses ("Utinam dirumperes coelos" and "Rorate coeli de super") occurs another bass solo ("Prope est ut veniat Dominus") in dialogue with the orchestra, joyful and full of hope. On the whole, H. 420 is similar to H. 416, with the same concern for the text and the musical effects it inspires.

After "a bit of silence" in H. 416 comes the "Nuit," a portion of which had been composed, with slight differences, some fifteen years earlier for *Pastorale sur la Naissance de Notre Seigneur Jésus Christ* (H. 483). Here, Charpentier constructs a symphonic move-ment in three tonally coherent parts (A, C minor; B, to the dominant G minor; C, returning to C minor). This passage, perhaps the com-poser's most beautiful piece of "Nuit" music, breathes calm and serenity through and through. It is scored for muted strings that hold long notes, while the other parts in counterpoint proceed in regular conjunct notes that end on an impressive dominant pedal fourteen bars long.

Another work, H. 420, also contains a "Nuit" enriched with "soft flutes" (*flûtes adoucies*). This time, Charpentier opts for a network of fugal textures in which the theme, after its imitative exposition in each part, continues to makes its rounds until the final cadence.

In both oratorios, the composer effects a striking contrast by following the "Nuit" with a "Shepherds' Awakening" (Réveil des bergers) in the major, played loudly in well-marked rhythm. The angel then appears in a blinding light and addresses the shepherds in the "Nolite temere" so familiar to us from other Christmas oratorios. The Chorus of Angels sings glory to God and peace toward mankind. After another dancelike orchestral piece, all fall adoringly before the newborn infant ("O infans, o Deus, o salvator noster"). This poignant moment is followed by a *chanson* ("Pastores undique") that displays the same features as the "Salve puerule" (see above). The piece, H. 416, concludes with a chorus celebrating the salvation sent by God, justice, and peace.

THE *DIALOGI*

These pieces always feature a dialogue between heaven and earth, with Christ or his representative angel on one side and human beings (men, shepherds, sinners, allegorical figures of Hunger and Thirst) on the other. In most cases the character of Christ is assigned to the traditional bass range, and the Angel to high voices (*dessus, haute-contre*).

Two of the *dialogi* contain only two characters: *Pour Saint Augustin mourant* (H. 419) and *Dialogus inter Magdalenam et Jesum 2 vocibus* (H. 423). Christ is sung in these pieces by *haut-dessus* (H. 419) and *haute-contre* (H. 423).

Canticum in honorem beatae Virginis Mariae inter homines et angelos (H. 400) is a fabulous hymn of praise to the Virgin (see also *Pro omnibus festis BVM*, H. 333).[20] It takes on a dramatic aspect through the questions addressed to the angels (two *dessus*) by the men (*haute-contre, taille*, bass), who extol Mary with highest praise. Then all together address the Holy Mother before inviting the people and the heavens to join in their songs.

In circumcisione Domini, Dialogus inter angelum et pastores (H. 406) seems more suited to the Feast of the Nativity (1 January is also, in the liturgy, the octave of Christmas) than to the celebration of the name bestowed on Jesus at the time of his circumcision (see *In circumcisione Domini,* H. 316). We meet the same characters of the Christmas oratorios here, and certain textural elements, like the prelude in the style of the "Nuit" symphonies or the strophic air "Linquite oves."

Dialogus inter esurientem, sitientem et Christum (H. 407) and *Élévation* (H. 408) were composed within a short time of each other (end of 1682 and 1683) and use identical vocal forces (Esuriens, *haut-dessus/dessus;* Sitiens, *dessus;* Christus, bass) as well as the same text ("Famem meam quis replebit") of unknown origin. The subject is "a dramatic version of the dogma of transubstantiation, which is derived ultimately from the scene of the Last Supper."[21] The title of the latter score indicates its liturgical destination, which was probably the same as the destination of H. 407. It exhibits ("O panis angelorum") the tone of emotional effusion and adoration characteristic of elevation motets. The other piece, H. 408, adds instruments to the singers: two nonspecified treble parts, two *tailles de violes,* and thoroughbass (bass violin and harpsichord). Its partwriting is also richer and more developed.

Because of its precise reference to the Last Supper, *Dialogus inter Christum et homines* (H. 417) seems to have been written for Holy Week. *Dialogus inter Christum et peccatores* (H. 425) was published in 1725 by Ballard in *Mélanges de musique.* Ballard attributed its text to the Reverend Jesuit Father Commire.

Chapter 11

The Masses

The sung mass in France during the seventeenth and much of the eighteenth centuries poses a particular problem in that it remained outside the stylistic developments that affected other forms of music, both sacred and secular. While the concerted style had a great impact on the motet, the mass remained virtually unchanged for almost two centuries.

Most of the masses heard in Paris and in the provinces during the reign of Louis XIV were written decades earlier and occasionally adapted to current taste by additional instrumentation (a technique practiced by Sébastien de Brossard in works of François Cosset or Charles d'Helfer), or they were new masses composed in the old style: *a capella* as in the style of Giovanni Palestrina, polychoral on occasion, or even in plainchant.

How can such conservatism in the composition of the mass be explained? Unlike the motet, whose ties to the liturgy remained rather loose, the mass was the very heart and principal means of expression. Therefore it was natural that the strict prescriptions of Roman Catholic reform in France were felt most strongly in that domain. Moreover, there was considerable resistance by composers of religious music to the concerted style coming from Italy. Most of these choirmasters lived in the closed world of their own church or cathedral and continued to compose music subjected to tradition. If the provincial choirs proved particularly conservative, certain Paris chapels were no less so. Thus Jean Mignon (1640–1710), Charpentier's contemporary and music master at Notre-Dame, composed six masses which remained for many years in the choir's repertory. These were works for four to six voices, in the old Franco-Flemish contrapuntal style and *a cappella*.[1] Charpentier's successor,

André Campra, struggled to introduce violins into the choir loft.

Another factor contributing to the situation was the king, who left his mark on French music with the stamp of his own taste. Indeed, Louis XIV did not like sung masses, preferring the low masses celebrated in his chapel at Versailles, during which motets were sung. Thus developed the great Versailles motet which favored the sumptuous textures of the concerted style, admittedly more attractive than the austere counterpoint of the mass.

The lack of royal interest in masses set to music affected the attitude of court composers who, from 1670 onward, stopped composing them completely. Only Henri Du Mont, music master of the Chapelle Royale from 1663 to 1683, wrote five plainchant masses intended for use not in the Chapelle Royale but in convents. These five masses were used for a long time thereafter in French parishes.

During this long period of stagnation, a few attempts were made to modernize the mass. Still, these were rare and in no way diminished the prevailing apathy. In 1638, Nicolas Formé composed a mass for double choir. Instead of setting two equally balanced vocal ensembles in dialogue, however, he pitted a small four-part chorus of soloists against a large five-part chorus, in the new concerted style. Around the same period, Antoine Boesset (or his son Jean-Baptiste?) wrote three masses with thoroughbass accompaniment.

Against that rather bleak background, Charpentier's masses stand out and even take on exceptional brilliance. Charpentier was, in fact, the only composer who dared approach the mass using the same musical language that other French composers reserved exclusively for the motet. In his approach to the mass, he went against the tide of his compatriots.

Charpentier's twelve masses are spread out over his entire career, from the *Messe pour les trépassés à 8* (H. 2) written in the early 1670s to *Assumpta est Maria* (H. 11) composed for the Sainte-Chapelle at the end of his life. The Jesuits seem to have looked favorably upon Charpentier's masses: five of them, in fact, were composed during 1691–1695: *Messe à 4 voix, 4 violons, 2 flûtes et 2 hautbois pour M. Mauroy* (H. 6), *Messe pour le samedi de Pâques* (H. 8), *Messe de minuit à 4 voix, flûtes et violons pour Noël* (H. 9), *Messe des morts à 4 voix* (H. 7), and *Messe des morts à 4 voix et symphonie* (H. 10).

Mauroy, to whom one of the masses is dedicated, belonged to an important family from Champagne Province. Some of its members occupied high administrative and diplomatic positions. Séraphin de

Mauroy, for example, was secretary at the Roman embassy from 1650 to 1652. The Abbé Testu de Mauroy was Madame's chaplain and, later, director of the Académie Française where he appointed M. Du Bois, one of the regular visitors to the Hôtel de Guise, in 1693. Which member of this great dynasty was referred to in the dedication of the mass has not been determined.

In 1679, the *Mercure Galant* reported that on the occasion of the Feast of Saint Louis,

> Le Brun, chief painter of His Majesty, who celebrates [the feast] every year with particular enthusiasm, had a mass sung that day in the parish of Saint Hyppolite. The symphony was composed by M. Charpentier. The church was completely draped in the richest Gobelin tapestries. They represented the life of the king and were admired as much as the music, by all those who were there.... Trumpets and oboes were part of the festivities and made the accomplishments of the Gobelins known far and wide.[2]

Nonetheless, no mass seems to have been composed at that time. Instead, the manuscripts contain a motet for Saint Louis (*In honorem Sancti Ludovici Regis Galliae Canticum tribus vocibus cum simphonia*, H. 323) which could have been performed for the aforementioned ceremony.

Besides their sheer number, it is the diversity of Charpentier's masses as well as their great originality that today inspires our surprise and admiration. Indeed, each of these twelve compositions possesses its own individuality with regard to scoring (e.g., four voices, six voices, double chorus) as well as liturgical function (e.g., mass for the dead, for Easter, Christmas, Assumption), or style, which ranges from monodic to polychoral, from parody mass to mass with instruments, from fauxbourdon austerity to the flamboyant concerted style. Some scores even appear to be one-of-a-kind, such as the *Messe pour plusieurs instruments au lieu des orgues* (H. 513) and *Messe de minuit à 4 voix, flûtes et violons pour Noël* (H. 9), while others were without antecedent in France, such as *Messe à quatre choeurs* (H. 4).

In some cases, motets are added to the sections of the Ordinary, such as the Kyrie, Gloria, Credo, Sanctus ... Benedictus, and Agnus Dei. This was the case for the "Elevation" (H. 2, 3, 7, and 10) or "Domine salvum" (H. 1, 3, 4, 6, and 11), as was done in the low masses heard by the king in his Chapelle (see Chapter 8).

During the celebration of mass, it was common for the organist to interpolate short pieces at certain points. Reference is made to these in all Charpentier's masses except those for the dead (H. 7, 10) and the one for instruments. These short pieces are generally placed before and/or after the Kyrie, Christus, Sanctus, and Agnus Dei. The organ piece sometimes replaces whole sections of the mass (e.g., the Benedictus in H. 11, the first and third Sanctus in H. 8). Elsewhere, Charpentier allows a choice between the organ and an instrumental movement (H. 3, 6) or the elevation motet (H. 5, 8).

Like motet settings of identical texts, masses provided the sort of material that suited a composer like Charpentier while still conforming to the expressive codes of an entire musico-liturgical tradition. It was up to the composer to transcend those codes and to revitalize them through his talent or genius, emotion, and persuasive force.

While the Kyrie is invariably written for the chorus, the more meditative Christe is assigned to the soloists, generally a trio of male voices. At the beginning of the Gloria, "Et in terra pax" is characterized by textural nuances (e.g., echo effects, mutes, and dynamic indications such as "sweet" [*doux*] or "in a low voice" [*à voix basse*]) or by a slowing of the tempo (*lentement*). The subsequent "Laudamus te, benedicimus te" tends to be "loud" or "loud and lively."

The text of the Credo was unquestionably the part of the mass that most inspired Charpentier as a baroque composer. The Credo permitted him to introduce all possible effects of contrast and shifting moods. For example, there is the contrast between the dark "Crucifixus" which Charpentier sets for low voices in a minor key, with special treatment of the word *passus* (suffered), and the "et resurrexit" in the major, joyously melismatic. There is another contrast between the homophonic "et incarnatus est" and the richly contrapuntal treatment of "cujus regni non erit finis" or of "et vitam venturi saeculi." The text of the Credo focuses on the image of the Lord's descent among humanity and his return, after his sacrifice, to the Father. The composer never failed to associate the words *descendit* and *ascendit* with corresponding melodic motion. In the Sanctus, vocal lyricism contrasts with the dense, energetic part-writing of the "Hosanna in excelsis." The mass concludes with the calm, introspective Agnus Dei.

THE SUNG MASSES

Untitled, H. 1 is probably Charpentier's first mass. It is simply and skillfully crafted and rarely ventures beyond vocal block writing, while saving some interesting surprises for certain moments. Examples of these surprises include chromatic motion in all parts on the word *passus* in the Gloria, or the stupendous harmonic progression of the "Miserere nobis" in the Agnus Dei. In the Sanctus, Charpentier enriches his chorus with two extra parts, one of which is a *concordant* (signifying, in the seventeenth century, a male voice lying between baritone and bass), while the "Hosanna" is scored for double chorus.

Composed not long after the previous mass, *Messe à 8 voix et 8 violons et flûtes* (H. 3) is much more richly scored and more than twice as long. It is contemporary with the other double-choir mass *pour les trépassés*, though not on the same level of inspiration. This piece is an example of the large form with its extra movements and expansive working out of material, the utter mastery of which Charpentier seems to have acquired very early. This mass demonstrates the extent to which Charpentier was able to make use of all the possibilities offered to him by the double chorus: homophony in all the parts, more or less densely written dialogue between the two ensembles, and rich contrapuntal texture in imitation.

The *Messe à quatre choeurs* (H. 4) is a unique example of French sacred music. During his sojourn in Rome, Charpentier became familiar with the large Italian polychoral masses. He had even copied down one of them, namely, *Missa mirabiles elationes Maris sexdecimus vocibus del Beretta*. The transcription also contained annotations and additional *Remarks*. All that remained for him was to compose a polychoral mass of his own, something he did a few years after his return to France.

Using the same forces as those used by Beretta, Charpentier's *Messe à quatre choeurs* falls within the purest Roman polychoral tradition, a tradition inspired by the late sixteenth-century Venetian art of the *cori spezzati* perfected by Giovanni Gabrieli. Abstaining from the monolithic texture of Roman masses, whose massive and weighty effects often hinder the expression of the text, Charpentier never ignored the word underlying the structure as a whole. His desire to diversify musical language and to adapt it to every phase of the liturgical text is clearly evident throughout this mass.

To vary the reprise of the Kyrie for quadruple chorus, which was sung after the Christe, Charpentier wrote out the choral parts in two ways: the second time, choirs 2 and 4 sing what choirs 1 and 3 sang the first time, and vice-versa.

The Gloria opens with a quartet of *dessus* singing the incipit "Gloria in excelsis Deo" usually chanted by the celebrant. Then all sixteen voices sing together "Ex in terra pax," not dividing into separate parts until the word *pax* is exchanged among the choirs. The whole passage is conceived in simple yet luminous harmonies. Alternating between all four choirs, part of the voices (double choir), and solo sections (a double trio of male voices in the "Domine Deus"), the Gloria continues up to the melismatic writing of the "amen," which sounds like wings flapping or the lapping of water along the shore. The Credo that follows is just as interesting with its contrasting effects and great expressivity.

If the texture is generally of the harmonic type, a concern for melody is nonetheless present, as illustrated by this irresistibly melodious phrase from the Sanctus, one of the most beautiful Charpentier ever composed.

In the *Messe à quatre choeurs*, Charpentier emerges as a fabulous architect who possessed the greatest sense of balance and proportion, two commendable qualities for a French composer, judging from what Jean-Jacques Rousseau wrote nearly a century later:

> There are some pieces of music for two or more choruses, which answer each other, and sometimes are all sung together. . . . But this plurality of choruses, which is very often practiced in Italy, is seldom used in France. They find that it does not produce a very pleasing effect, that its composition is not very easy, and that too great a number of musicians are needed for performing it.[3]

In contrast to the *Messe à quatre choeurs*, the *Messe, Pour le Port Royal* (H. 5) is almost entirely in monodic style. Again one must turn to Italy for an antecedent in the *Missa Dominicalis* written by Lodovico Grossi da Viadana in 1607. The originality of Charpentier's mass stems from the style in which it was composed and its construction, which was unique in the field of the sung mass. Indeed, in addition to the sections of the Ordinary (e.g., Kyrie, Gloria), it includes sections from the Proper of Saint Margaret and Saint Francis (see Chapter 7). For each of these two saints, Charpentier composed an Introit, a Gradual, an Offertory, and a Communion.

To avoid the monotony of a one-part texture, especially in a work that is nearly 1000 measures long, Charpentier attempted to vary his composition by alternating timbres of the women's voices or by varying the vocal density, as in this excerpt from the Credo.

The composer also managed a few passages lying outside the monodic treatment: four bars for two voices in the Gloria, more in the Credo, as well as a section for three voices in the "Et incarnatus est." The two Offertories are cast in a less austere, more diversified style. "Offertory for Saint Margaret" is for two voices in imitation. In "Offering for Saint Francis," Charpentier introduces a *rondeau* air-recitative-air. During the air the two voices that were first treated individually join in thirds and embellish the word *celebrate* with a long melisma. The Sanctus also contains some beautiful florid lines.

Messe à 4 voix, 4 violons, 2 flûtes et 2 hautbois pour M. Mauroy (H. 6) is the longest of all the masses. Richly orchestrated, it contains numerous "symphonies" alternately scored for large and small instrumental choirs. Here we also find large, extremely well-developed fugal movements.

Barely more than 200 measures in length, *Messe pour le samedi de Pâques* (H. 8) includes neither a Credo nor an Agnus Dei, as is correct for the Saturday before Easter. The Gloria does not undergo the long development that it does in the other masses, and its texture is essentially vertical. Ample space, however, is given to interpolated passages on the organ, with the following registrations specified by the composer: *"plein-jeu," "jeux agréables," "petits jeux,"* or *"sur les jeux doux."*

The Charpentier mass best known to today is *Messe de minuit à 4 voix, flûtes et violons pour Noël* (Midnight Mass) (H. 9). This work has been recorded a number of times, and its special charm has insured it a well-deserved popularity. The composer revived the tradition of the parody mass in this work, although the parody mass was almost completely out-of-fashion by the end of the seventeenth century. Charpentier based the mass on popular carols adapted to the liturgical text, though never deprived of their original simplicity:

1. *Joseph est bien marié*

2. *Or nous dites Marie*

3. *Une jeune pucelle*

Of the ten *noëls* used (to which is added an eleventh without text: "For the offertory, the violins play *Laissez paître vos bêtes*"), seven were also arranged by Charpentier in the form of short instrumental pieces (H. 531, 534). The *Messe de minuit* does not depart from the spirit of the themes which inspired it. The independent parts are invested with the same melodic and harmonic clarity characteristic of the *noël*. In this mass, Charpentier achieved a perfect synthesis between the secular and the liturgical, between popular art and learned writing. From beginning to end, his mass consistently maintains a spirit of freshness and joy. One can easily imagine the enchantment felt by listeners of the day when first hearing this work, so full of charming simplicity, cast in the joyful spirit of Advent, and in which everyone could recognize familiar melodies.

If there is no known antecedent to *Messe de minuit*, it served as a model for a few eighteenth-century works like *Missa quinti toni pro nocte ad die festi natalis Domini* written in 1700 by Sébastien de Brossard. Perhaps also inspired by Charpentier's composition were Bodin de Boismortier's motet titled *Fugit nox*, which was full of popular tunes, and Jean-François Lesueur's *Messe oratorio de Noël* of 1786.

THE ORGAN MASS

The organ mass, begun very early by the Italians, became a typically French genre at the end of the seventeenth century. Nivers, Lebègue, Boyvin, Grigny, and Couperin contributed several works to this genre, including a few masterpieces of the organ literature.

Charpentier's *Messe pour plusieurs instruments au lieu des orgues* (H. 513) displays all the characteristics of the organ mass. Therefore we can easily conjecture that it was written for a church that did not have a large organ, a situation which the composer remedied by choosing instruments capable of reproducing some of the many registers of French organs of the time. Hence we hear *flûtes douces*, transverse flutes, oboes, crumhorn, and four-part strings.

The organ mass was an extremely well-defined genre whose features were precisely, even rigidly, observed. The constraints grew mainly out of the liturgy which meticulously regulated the number and length of organ solos during the service, and even the manner in which certain verses were to be treated, including a prescription against ornamenting the plainchant in any way. There were also musical rules concerning the character of each solo (*plein-jeu*, fugue, dialogue) and its registration.

Like the organists, Charpentier adapted to all these prescriptions. Hence, like Couperin and Grigny, he used the Gregorian theme from Mass IV, *Cunctipotens genitor Deus*, as a cantus-firmus bass in long notes:

The organ mass included twenty-one pieces alternating with choral plainchant. The pieces were arranged as follows: five verses for the Kyrie, nine for the Gloria, three for the Sanctus, and two for the Agnus Dei. These sequences were supposed to be very short. Only the Offertory and the *Deo gratias* allowed longer pieces. Charpentier's mass is incomplete. We only have the first of three verses of the Sanctus and the end of the second Agnus Dei. The *Deo gratias* does not seem to have been planned.

Guided by the need to reproduce the sonorities of the various registers of the organ with other instruments (an imaginative notion by itself), Charpentier demonstrated a knowledge of orchestral colors that was quite extraordinary for his time. Moreover, he managed to adopt the specific textures of the organ; although he had never written for the instrument, his mass displays the great knowledge he had of it. The Kyrie contains successively a *plein-jeu* in "all the instruments," a fugue "for the oboes," a duo "for the violins of the small choir," a trio for "*flûtes douces*" and "transverse flutes," and it ends with the *plein-jeu.*

The other two inseparable forms of the organ mass are the solo *récit* and the dialogue. We find them both in the Gloria. The seventh couplet, "Quoniam," is treated as a solo for the crumhorn (which is also an organ register that was then quite popular) accompanied by low flutes. The "Tu solus altissimus" makes further use of the crumhorn, though this time in dialogue with the oboe.

"Offering for two choirs" is presented in the form of a vast triptych-dialogue between the "woodwind choir" and the "violin choir," in the style of Giovanni Gabrieli's Venetian *canzone.*

A kaleidoscope of contrasts, colors, and concision, the *Mass for several instruments instead of organ*, as we hear it today detached from its liturgical context, proves a pure delight for the ear.

MASSES FOR THE DEAD

No better proof of the conservatism of kings can be found than in their choice of funeral masses written to accompany them to their final resting place. Sébastien de Brossard stated that *Missa pro defunctis* of Eustache Du Caurroy, written in 1606 and first performed for the funeral of Henri IV four years later, continued to be played "at the obsequies and funeral services of kings and princes in Saint-Denis" until 1725.[4] *Missa pro defunctis* composed in 1656 by Charles d'Helfer would be sung on 27 July 1774 on the occasion of Louis XV's funeral service.

Except for the *Messe des morts* composed by Jean Gilles around 1697 in Toulouse and not heard in Paris until a Concert Spirituel in 1760, the only known Requiem Masses composed in the late seventeenth century were Charpentier's three works: *Messe pour les trépassés à 8* (H. 2), *Messe des morts à 4 voix* (H. 7), and *Messe des morts à 4 voix et symphonie* (H. 10). The text of the Requiem Mass is not set in its entirety, however; the only sections composed are the Kyrie, the Sanctus, the Pie Jesu, and the Agnus Dei. In addition, H. 7 has the psalm *De profundis* (even though it is not part of the liturgy of the mass for the dead) and H. 10 has the "Dies irae" sequence.

Messe pour les trépassés à 8 (H. 2) is almost completely dominated by long melodic contours, either sweeping downward or rising toward heaven; hence its overall unity. All these contours are arranged in full counterpoint, effected through imitation or contrary motion (e.g., Kyrie, Sanctus). This is not to ignore other powerful antiphonal sections for the double chorus (e.g., second part of the Kyrie and "Hosanna").

The very beautiful instrumental symphonies preceding each section, with dialogues between flutes and strings (e.g., Kyrie, Agnus Dei), establish a mood of intense fervor that continues throughout the vocal sections.

In the Pie Jesu, suspensions that give the prayer an almost mournful tone are added to the wide descending intervals, a sort of grand genuflection, in the vocal parts. Also contributing to the mournful tone is the melodic interval of a descending diminished fourth on the "qui tollis" of the second Agnus Dei, written for a trio of male voices.

Besides the infinitely delicate modulations on the words *dona eis requiem* (in the Pie Jesu and Agnus Dei), it is the final "Sempiternam" that truly transports the listener to an incredibly celestial sphere. Over a long dominant pedal point, the vocal parts move along an amazing harmonic sequence in which every chord creates a surprise—are we in E or in A, in major or minor?—finally illuminating the entire work with a breathtaking, totally unexpected, major chord:

1st choir

2nd choir

Messe des morts à 4 voix (H. 7) is scored only for soloists and four-part chorus, without concerted instruments. Unlike what we find in other masses, the second Kyrie is not a repeat of the first. Here, Charpentier bases his triptych (Kyrie-Christe-Kyrie) on a dramatic progression different from the usual *rondeau* form. After the restrained opening, Kyrie in D minor, the Christe is a poignant dialogue between a double trio of men's voices. Abruptly changing key to B-flat major, the second Kyrie is attacked by the chorus as though affirming something that has been held back until now.

The Pie Jesu is for two *hauts-dessus*. The first voice makes its last entry directly on a diminished seventh with the continuo, making the tone of this prayer for the dead even more fervent.

The *De profundis* constitutes the last section of the mass. Beginning somberly and nearly stationary, with the voices in the low register and on long notes, the psalm then passes from the gently rocking motion of the double-chorus writing (*dessus–hautes-contre/tailles*–basses) of "Speret Israël" to the harsh dissonances of "iniquatibus ejus" and of "Requiem aeternam." The "Et lux perpetua" finally emerges in the outer parts in evocative contrary motion and asserts itself in solid imitative counterpoint.

In *Messe des morts à 4 voix et symphonie* (H. 10), the third mass for the dead, the orchestra occupies an all-important position, whether introducing or accompanying the vocal parts. There are interesting reminiscences of earlier works, such as the expressive ascending minor sixth in the prelude of the Kyrie, a characteristic of the *De profundis* (H. 189) of 1683, or, at the start of the Christe, the first measures of the *Magnificat à 3 voix* (H. 73), even though the imitation is on the fourth, not on the octave, and on a different beat. The Pie Jesu for two *dessus*, a marvel of religious fervor and vocal grace, recalls the opening of the mass by repeating the ascending minor sixth.

In the "Dies irae," the principal section of the mass, the full orchestra (strings, flutes, and oboes) acquires a truly dramatic role when introducing the powerful chorus "Tuba mirum" with a sumptuous fanfare. If this "Dies irae" lacks the opulence and expressive force of *Prose des morts* (H. 12), it nevertheless deserves our attention for the diversity of its textures, for its imaginative word-painting ("cum resurget," "quidquid latet," "voca me," and "lacrymosa"), as well as for certain harmonic strokes, like the bold anticipation of B-flat on "tantus labor" or the highly expressive chromatic line in the first flute during the orchestral introduction to "Oro supplex."

Dedicated to the Virgin, *Assumpta est Maria, Missa six vocibus cum simphonia* (H. 11) is Charpentier's last mass. It is perhaps his most perfect one as well, displaying the serene mastery of a composer at the peak of his powers. Two versions of this mass exist, one for four-part string orchestra, found in the *Mélanges*, and the other in separate parts (H. 11a, Bibliothèque Nationale, catalog no. Vm¹ 942) scored for small trio ensemble (two violin *dessus* parts and basso continuo). Nevertheless, outside of the reduced accompaniment in the work as a whole, only the "symphonies" preceding the Kyrie, the Sanctus, and the Agnus Dei differ from those of the first version.[5]

For the first time in a mass, the composer employs a six-part choir (two *dessus*, *haute-contre*, *taille*, *basse-taille*, and bass), which provides a richly polyphonic texture. Still, we should note that the two *dessus* usually sing the same part, which reduces the actual number of parts to five. The soloists are almost exclusively used in groups of three, a pattern favored by the composer throughout the work. By combining different timbres, by matching or contrasting high and low registers, Charpentier gives each of his ensembles a different character: two *dessus* and *haute-contre;* two *dessus* and *basse-taille;* or *haute-contre*, *taille*, and *basse-taille*.

The work opens with an instrumental "symphonie" (H. 11), which initially is for two parts without harmonic support, then for full strings. Similarly, the Kyrie is first stated by a trio of soloists before the chorus takes over.

In the Gloria and the Credo, Charpentier embarks on an absolutely remarkable musical setting of the text, highlighting every possible nuance of expression and symbolic significance ("et unam sanctam catholicam et apostolicam Ecclesiam"). The composer employs uncommonly effective means without excessive development; sometimes a few bars suffice to depict the essential. This concentration on detail, however, is never carried so far as to mar the work's marvelous overall balance. Although every phrase or group of phrases has its own atmosphere, Charpentier links them together with extraordinary naturalness and ease.

Just listen to the Gloria: the richness of the chorus descending slowly into the low register on "Et in terra pax hominibus," the double-chorus effects on "Laudamus te," the fast melismas on "glorificamus te" and the slow ones on "gratias," and the concise proportions of the solos ("Domine Deus").

Not one word of the Credo escapes the composer's attention. Again, there is a richness in the first chorus ("Patrem omnipotentem"), with a magnificent melodic line in the upper voices and subtle, light harmonies on "visibilium omnium et invisibilium." The "Deum de Deo" calls for a dialogue between two solo groups, one of low voices, the other of high voices. Charpentier makes extremely original use of the *haute-contre* part which, alternating between two different ensembles, serves as a kind of pivot for both groups. The composer later repeats this technique on the words "cujus regni."

Another admirable page is the "Et incarnatus est," in which the chorus, without the baritones and basses, achieves a sound of utter transparency in which every word becomes clear. A total contrast is then created between the minor-mode "Crucifixus" in the low voices and the major-mode "Et resurrexit" with radiant melismas in the high voices.

We then arrive at "et unam sanctam catholicam et apostolicam Ecclesiam," a grandiose structure in block harmonies modulating by fifths and, at the same time, incredibly introspective. The fugue that concludes the Credo, "et vitam venturi saeculi," rivals the contrapuntal sumptuousness of the end of the Gloria.

The last three movements of the mass are for chorus, with orchestral symphonies preceding the Sanctus and the Agnus Dei.

According to Charpentier's annotations after the Sanctus ("Here a short elevation is to be sung if time permits" and "Benedictus for the organ if time permits"), the *Assumpta est Maria* mass seems to have been written for a very precisely timed service, almost to the minute. The composer intended to follow the *Domine salvum* chorus with a motet ("Go to the exit motet"), but the page on which he wrote this direction remained blank.

Chapter 12

Airs and Cantatas

"Brillantes fleurs naissez." The words are by the illustrious M. de La Fontaine, and the air by the famous M. Charpentier, who has such a great knowledge of all the beauties of music.
Mercure Galant, October 1689

These two branches of Charpentier's secular music, the airs and the cantatas, represent only a minor part of his output. They fully deserve our attention for several reasons: the pure beauty or emotional impact of certain airs; the importance of the composer's role as a precursor in the field of the cantata; the influence of Italy (the pieces written in the language of Carissimi hold special interest); and finally the creative originality of a work like the *Epitaphium Carpentarii*.

THE AIRS

Unlike most of his other works, most of Charpentier's airs were published. Some of them appeared during his lifetime in the *Mercure Galant* between 1678 and 1695, the others in the eighteenth century by the celebrated Ballard in his *Recueils d'airs sérieux et à boire* or in the *Mélanges de musique* in the company of the greatest composers of both centuries, including Lully, Campra, Couperin, Pignolet de Montéclair, Bodin de Boismortier, and Rameau.

As we have seen, Donneau de Visé, Charpentier's friend and collaborator, never missed an opportunity to praise the composer in the columns of his gazette. The publication of an air would also be accompanied by short eulogistic remarks by the editor to his imaginary provincial female reader:

> I believe that you shall be enormously grateful for this air ["Quoi! rien ne peut vous arrêter," H. 462], since it is by M. Charpentier, famous for a thousand works which have enchanted all of France.[1]

> You will have good reason to be happy with me for the couplets by Mlle Castille which so pleased you and which you have already seen set to music at the beginning of this letter. I give them to you again with other notes, so that you may sing them in a different manner. M. Charpentier, who has just set them as an air ["Ah! qu'ils sont courts les beaux jours," H. 442] has made a kind of *rondeau* out of them. In it you will find that special gracefulness that makes you love these works.[2]

> M. Charpentier, with whose talent and merits you are acquainted, is working on stanzas from *Le Cid* [H. 457–459]; each month he will offer a couplet from them.[3]

Charpentier's airs (thirty-two in all) have their origin in the *air de cour*, a genre that enjoyed great success in France from the end of the sixteenth century.[4] Until around 1630, the term *air de cour* was applied as much to dance tunes, drinking songs, bawdy tunes, and *airs de ballet* as it was to *airs galants*. The latter gradually eclipsed the others, and the *air de cour* became a specific literary and musical genre that was tender and *précieux* in character. Composers like Pierre Guédron, Antoine Boesset, and Étienne Moulinié developed the *air de cour* to a highly refined state of melodic expressivity.

In the second half of the seventeenth century, the *air de cour*, as it had been written down until then (in lute tablature), gradually adopted the continuo accompaniment of the *air sérieux*. A disciple of Pierre de Nyert, who had brought the Italian manner of expression and melodic virtuosity to France, Michel Lambert became the greatest composer of the *air de cour* of his time. He introduced the characteristically French practice of the *double,* a richly ornamented reprise. In the naturalness of his declamation and in the dramatic tone of some of his airs, Lambert paved the way for the recitative of the future operas of Lully.

Charpentier's airs fall naturally into that French vocal tradition in which conciseness and simplicity do not preclude expressivity and florid embellishments. Apart from the latter—there are no *doubles* in his airs—we find all these traits in Charpentier's pieces. While the majority of his airs are of the serious, *galant* variety, there are also some lighter pastoral airs, *airs à boire*, a parody of the air from Molière's *Le Médecin malgré lui* ("Qu'il est doux charmante Climène," H. 460), an air for the king ("A ta haute valeur," H. 440), and some very original settings of stanzas from Corneille's *Le Cid* (H. 457–459).

Usually for solo voice (*dessus* or *haute-contre*) and basso continuo, some of the airs call for two voices: two *dessus* ("Allons sous ce vert feuillage," H. 444; "Fenchon, la gentille Fenchon," H. 454; and "Tout renaît, tout fleurit," H. 468), *dessus* and bass ("Ayant bu du vin clairet," H. 447). Others call for three voices: *haut-dessus, dessus*, and bass ("Beaux petits yeux d'écarlate," H. 448) or *haute-contre, taille*, and bass ("Veux-tu, compère Grégoire," H. 470).

Unaccompanied airs are rare; only seven exist. Among these is "Brillantes fleurs" (H. 449), which exists in four versions, two of which (H. 449b, H. 449c) also have a continuo part. It is possible that the drinking tunes, "Consolez-vous, chers enfants de Bacchus" (H. 451), "Beaux petits yeux d'écarlate" (H. 448), and "Veux-tu, compère Grégoire" (H. 470) adhere to the "double continuo" practice so popular at the time, in which the sung bass line is identical to the bass in the accompaniment.

The structure of Charpentier's airs is of two types. The standard air was used by all composers of the day. Most frequent is the binary structure of the *air de cour* with or without reprise. Examples include AB ("Brillantes fleurs, naissez," H. 449), AAB ("Amour, vous avez beau redoubler mes alarmes," H. 445), or AABB ("Consolez-vous, chers enfants de Bacchus," H. 451). Sometimes a strophic arrangement appears, each couplet repeating the melody of the first verse ("Celle qui fait tout mon tourment," H. 450). The second type of air is in *rondeau* form and includes ABA' ("Oiseaux de ces bocages," H. 456) or ABACA ("Allons sous ce vert feuillage," H. 444).

Like Michel Lambert, Charpentier sometimes employed an "obbligato bass" ("Sans frayeur dans ce bois," H. 467; "Que je sens de rudes combats," H. 459). "Ruisseau qui nourris dans ce bois" (H. 466) is also generally built on an ostinato bass, though the originality of its accompaniment stems mainly from the perpetual eighth-note figure depicting the flowing brook.

Drinking Songs

The *air à boire* remained popular throughout the seventeenth century. It is often for a bass voice, perfectly suiting the comic nature of the drinking song. The texts contain words chosen above all for their sonority—onomatopoeia is common—enabling the music to flow delightfully in a truly intoxicating series of alliterative clashes. Hence, in "Consolez-vous chers enfants de Bacchus," the catalog-like "si fin, si divin, si puissant, si bon, si charmant, si brillant, si pétillant" is swept along by the momentum of a great ascending melody; or in "Veux-tu compère Grégoire," the "glou-glou" and "plin plan plin plan" are repeated.

Recueil d'airs à boire en duo et en trio (Bibliothèque Nationale, Ms Y 296[1]) contains "Veux-tu compère Grégoire" and two other airs exploiting the same musical and literary wit. One of these airs is the burlesque "Fenchon, la gentille Fenchon" (H. 454), and the other is the bitingly satirical "Beaux petits yeux d'écarlate" (H. 448).

Serious Airs

Charpentier's serious airs are tender and *galant*. Generally they are written in a clear-cut style, using simple melodies moving in conjunct intervals, of which the French were so fond. What could be simpler to hum, for example, than the *chansonnette* "Auprès du feu l'on fait l'amour" (H. 446) or the *musette* "Faites trêve à vos chansonnettes" (H. 453)?

If Charpentier explored the "chanson" category of the French air, his theatrical instincts could not be genuinely satisfied by it. Therefore, whenever the subject turns to the heartbreak of love's infidelity or the death of a beloved, the musical expression darkens, tending toward chromaticism and dissonance. Furthermore, the melody abandons its facile manner to follow more closely the inflections of the text, sometimes turning into a genuinely operatic recitative with rhetorical effects and sudden changes of meter.

In "Retirons-nous, fuyons" (H. 465), the light, carefree first section in a brisk tempo is followed by a much more expressive second section. The vocal line ("Vous mourrez de dépit et je mourrai d'amour") is drawn out in languorous suspensions, not coming to rest until the final cadence.

The last bars of "Rendez-moi mes plaisirs" (H. 463) attain the heights of pathos. Charpentier first states "ou me donnez la mort" (or give me death) simply, over a slow melody descending one step at a time and ending on a beautiful deceptive cadence. Then the same phrase is repeated with greatest fervor. After only four measures, the vocal line falls a minor seventh, then stabilizes—while the bass embarks on a no-less-bold interval of a diminished third—before the last fall of a minor third, cushioned by the appoggiatura D-C.

"Tristes déserts" (H. 469) sounds straight out of a tragédie lyrique. Besides carrying the descriptive title of *Récit*, and justifiably so, it is no less expressive or moving than the death of Créuse in *Médée*. Sustained by an inspired dramatic intensity, this heartrending lament of an abandoned lover rises to the heavens, subsides, breaks into silence, and touches on the darkest colors of the composer's palette (C minor "obscure and sad," and F minor "obscure and plaintive"). In the final bars, the harmonic progressions are absolutely astounding (submediant minor–subdominant mixed, as in "Rendez-moi mes plaisirs," and which Charpentier uses as a signature for "death," the last word in both airs). Just listen to the end of Créuse's solo in Act V of *Médée:* D-flat/B-natural; Charpentier is being consistent.

"Non, non, je ne l'aime plus" (H. 455) is the longest (143 bars) of all the airs. It alternates sections in the form of little airs brimming with imitation between the vocal line (*haute-contre*) and the continuo, and with recitative passages. The dramatic tension reaches its peak in the last recitative ("Chercher ce que l'on fuit, fuir ce que l'on désire") on a long rising chromatic phrase.

Airs from *Le Cid*

At the beginning of 1681, the *Mercure Galant* published three airs based on Rodrigue's first three stanzas in Act I, scene 6 of *Le Cid*, written some forty-five years before. This unique work for *haute-contre* and continuo was perhaps performed by Charpentier. His music is closely wedded to the already highly musical rhythm of the text's irregular meter, which according to Corneille was appropriate for expressing "irresolution and anxiety." The music passes from recitative to air as in an opera or a cantata and manages to suggest Rodrigue's struggle with his deep dilemma.

Although published separately, the three pieces are meant to follow one another. All are written in the key of G minor and are linked by ritornellos. In the first stanza, "Percé jusques au fond du coeur" (H. 457), Charpentier exclusively uses the strictest recitative (repeated notes supported by sustained harmonies in the bass). The recitative does not lack expressive qualities, which are created by the careful shaping of the declamation, by the repetition of certain words, by numerous key-changes, and by the gradually increasing movement in the accompaniment.

"Que je sens de rudes combats" (H. 459) is constructed entirely on an ostinato bass repeated every five bars; over it, the vocal line unfolds in the utmost freedom. Ascending phrases prevail, followed by abrupt falls into the low register, suggesting the lack of solution to Rodrigue's dilemma. To show that the hero's indecisiveness remains complete, Charpentier states the last two verses (*"Faut-il laisser un affront impuni? / Faut-il punir le père de Chimène?"* Should an affront go unavenged? / Should Chimène's father be punished?) in the high and middle registers of the voice respectively; he then repeats them, inverting the registers.

"Père, maîtresse, honneur, amour" (H. 458) is in two sections. The first section returns to recitative, melodically much freer than that of the first stanza and with bolder harmonies, especially in the cross relation between F-sharp and F-natural on the antithetical "aimable tyrannie." The second part, in triple meter, takes up a flowing chaconne-like melody. The ritornello ends in an "obscure and sad" C minor.

Did Corneille ever hear his Rodrigue set to music? One year after these stanzas appeared in the *Mercure Galant*, Charpentier began his work on *Andromède* for the Comédie-Française revival.

THE CANTATAS

For Sébastien de Brossard in 1703, the cantata was

> a large composition with words in Italian, varied by recitative, by ariettas and different movements; usually for solo voice and basso continuo, often with two violins or several instruments. . . . Recently French cantatas have been done with great success; the subject of the singing is a drama [*histoire*] whose different actions are delineated by different movements.[5]

The first French compositions titled cantata date from the beginning of the eighteenth century. Jean-Baptiste Morin, who published three books of *Cantates françaises de une à trois voix avec ou sans symphonie*, a few of which were composed after 1701, is considered the father of the genre. From that time on, composers of the day wrote cantata after cantata (twelve hundred between 1703 and 1730). Among the composers were Nicolas Bernier, Jean-Baptiste Stuck (Batistin), Elisabeth Jacquet de La Guerre, André Campra, and Louis-Nicolas Clérambault. These French musicians belonged to the circle of Philippe d'Orléans (who wrote a few cantata texts himself) and pledged allegiance to a genre that had been flourishing in Italy since the beginning of the seventeenth century and in which Luigi Rossi and Carissimi in Rome, and later Stradella and Alessandro Scarlatti in Naples, had distinguished themselves.

Although the cantata did not become French in name until the eighteenth century, it had found one of its masters twenty years earlier in Charpentier. It is hardly surprising that Carissimi's student wanted to compose oratorios and that he also put his Italian studies to practical use by trying his hand at these dramatic yet small-scale compositions.

Cantatas with Italian Texts

Of the works by Charpentier belonging to the cantata genre, several have Italian texts, obviously not by accident. Three of them are duos consisting of only one section. "Superbo amore" (H. 476) and "Il mondo così va" (H. 477) are contained in an anthology of *Cantates et airs italiens de différents auteurs*. The third duo "Beate mie pene" (H. 475), found in a *Recueil d'airs italiens anciens de différents auteurs* and just as impossible to date as the other two compositions, seems more Italianate, with its densely imitative writing and long strings of vocalises.

The *Serenata a tre voci e simphonia* (H. 472) is found in the *Mélanges* and dates from 1685. After an instrumental introduction, the three-part vocal ensemble (*dessus, haute-contre,* and bass) alternates with solo sections. The texture is Italian from beginning to end, in the assertive character of the melody, the rhythmic vitality, the employment of the opening "motto" technique in the solo parts (see Chapter 9), and the prevalence of imitation in the ensembles.

Epithalamio

From the same year as the *Serenata*, the *Epithalamio In lode dell'Altezza Serenissima Elettorale di Massimiliano Emanuel Duca di Baviera* (H. 473) is a solemn cantata written in honor of the Dauphine's brother. It is scored for five voices ("due soprani," "contralto," "tenore," and "basso") and a lavish assortment of instruments ("Prima tromba," "Seconda tromba," "Taballi" [*sic*], "Primo violino, piva⁶ e flauto," "Secundo violino, piva e flauto," and "Cembalo, violone e fagotto"). Charpentier took advantage of the various colors of all these timbres, alone or in combination, particularly in the prelude.

Epithalamio, a truly "international" work, unites the two major stylistic trends of the day. The French style is represented by the prelude in D major (the key required for the trumpets) in *rondeau* form; its fanfarelike *tutti* refrain is in the manner of Te Deum settings of the period, notably the one with trumpets (H. 146). Also French in character is the very official first section for the chorus, which is repeated at the end of the work.

The middle parts ("Allegro" for two sopranos and two flutes, bass solo accompanied by two violins, and "Allegro" for the three voices) exploit typically Italian traits in the flowing vocalises of the soprano duet, in the bass solo ("Accorete"), and in the Monteverdian treatment of the voices in the trio.

Orphée descendant aux enfers

Orphée descendant aux enfers (H. 471) is the work that comes closest to the ideal of the eighteenth-century French cantata. Nonetheless, it contains certain operatic elements that would no longer appear in future cantatas, including an instrumental overture, the presence of several different characters, and a division into recitative and air segments that was not yet systematized. Charpentier later used this episode from the Orpheus myth in his little opera *La Descente d'Orphée aux enfers* (H. 488), an expanded version of the cantata setting.

Charpentier clearly indicated the instruments that accompany Orpheus in Hades: two violins (one of which is the "violin of Orpheus"), recorder, transverse flute, and bass viol. The instrumentation is quite interesting and original, not only because of the varying combinations of timbres, but also because of the important, though still tentative, role that Charpentier assigns to the first violin in the "Récit d'Orphée." It is clearly an Italian influence, since at that time in France the violin only took a secondary role, generally in connection with dance music, while in Italy it was the king of instruments. This is, moreover, the only time in all his works that the composer made use of it as a solo instrument and not in duo-formation. The graceful "Récit for Orpheus on the violin" comes immediately after the overture. The latter, melodically and harmonically much more intense, passes from a vocal style (the first phrase in the violin) to an instrumental style (arpeggios).

After the violin solo, the great monologue for Orpheus (*haute-contre*) returns to the expressive intensity of the introduction. The voice naturally develops it, the music meticulously following the text. At first it is dark and mournful ("Effroyables enfers"), declaimed in eloquent intervals of sevenths, the music is soon followed by a rising chromatic phrase: "aucun de vos tourments." It then becomes plaintive (with "hélas" reiterated in the falling minor thirds that Charpentier was so fond of in this sort of context), and finally expresses exhaustion (a long sinking phrase in the Italian manner, with its string of suspensions on "ou laissez-moi descendre aux ombres du trépas").

Orpheus' singing reaches the ears of Ixion and Tantalus, who suddenly feel delivered from their torments. Accompanied by flutes and violins, Orpheus repeats his lament and then joins the two denizens of Hades in singing the "lover's moral," a device frequently used in the tragédie lyrique which later became a feature peculiar to the French cantata:

> *Hélas, rien n'est égal au bonheur des amants*
> *Pour peu que l'amour touche une âme*
> *Elle ne ressent plus tous les autres tourments.*

> Alas, nothing equals the happiness of lovers,
> For although love may touch a soul but lightly
> [That soul] no longer feels any other pain.

In this early cantata, Charpentier gladly combined the demands of French declamation with rich Italian harmonies. One might expect more virtuosity, but the composer, while filling his score with unusually rich part-writing, never oversteps the limits of French good taste. The whole piece seems immersed in a languor that soothes the cruel torments of love and Hades.

In the eighteenth century, the Orpheus theme also inspired some beautiful cantatas from composers like Louis-Nicolas Clérambault and Jean Philippe Rameau.

Cantate française de M. Charpentier

The authenticity of *Cantate française de M. Charpentier* ("Coulez, coulez charmants ruisseaux," H. 478) for solo *taille* and two violins has not been proven. In three parts (air-recitative-air), it nevertheless displays perfect ease in the handling of constantly flowing, graceful melody.

Epitaphium Carpentarii

Epitaphium Carpentarii (H. 474) smacks of a miniature opera, though it borrows its musical syntax from the Latin oratorio and the motet. A sort of semi-secular, semi-religious Latin cantata, if indeed it must be assigned to one genre, this amazing parody of the *tombeau* remains unique in its category. It is clear the composer was more concerned with words than with music, the latter used essentially as a vehicle for the text. This explains the lack of grand expressive gestures. Apart from a bit of obligatory word-painting (e.g., "fugiamus," "melos," "volabis," "gaudium") and the angels' limpid melismas, textures remain clear and simple from beginning to end, for maximum comprehension of the text (see Appendix 1).

In this half-serious and half-humorous epitaph, Charpentier allows himself a certain compassion toward François Chaperon, his predecessor at the Sainte-Chapelle (see Chapter 1). Nonetheless, the gibes made at the poor man are far from innocuous; the composer manifestly refuses to forgive him for having landed the position before him. The text states, in fact, that the "tedious and discordant" music and "dissonances of that ass of a Chaperon" shall be inflicted upon the living as "punishment" and "purgatory" so that, after death, they may better appreciate the "sweet anti-Capronic" music of the angels. Charpentier also makes a reference to his teacher Carissimi, who, at the time the *Epitaphium* was composed, was no longer alive.

Chapter 13

The Instrumental Music

In comparison to the rest of his work, Charpentier's output in the instrumental domain seems rather thin. This observation must be qualified, however, according to whether one considers only the independent pieces or includes those connected to motets, oratorios (e.g., preludes, symphonies) and incidental music (e.g., overtures, dances), which are quite numerous in themselves and bespeak the composer's genuine talent.[1]

Charpentier was a singer and, even though he was probably capable of accompanying on the harpsichord or the organ, and perhaps even somewhat of a flutist, he was primarily a composer of vocal music. Nevertheless, he was required to compose instrumental works to honor commissions, especially in the field of religious music, while his individual curiosity caused him to take an interest in new forms, like the sonata. He seems, however, to have written no pieces for solo instrument.

Not all the isolated instrumental pieces can actually be called independent works.[2] Some preludes were originally for works that have apparently been lost (e.g., *Prélude pour Sub tuum praesidium à trois violons*, H. 527; *Prélude pour le second Magnificat à 4 voix sans instruments*, H. 533; *Prélude pour le Domine Salvum*, H. 535; *Prélude*, H. 538; and *Prélude pour le second Dixit Dominus à 4 voix sans instruments*, H. 539), or that were perhaps sung in plainchant (e.g., *Symphonie devant Regina*, H. 509; *Pour O filii*, H. 511). A whole series of compositions could be described as "quick-serve," including *Prélude pour ce qu'on voudra non encore employé* (Prelude for any occasion not yet used) (H. 521); *Offerte non encore executée* (Offering not yet performed) (H. 522); *Ouverture pour quelque belle entreprise à cinq* (Five-part Overture for any major undertaking) (H.

540). Other compositions are unfinished, such as *Commencement d'ouverture pour ce que l'on voudra en la rectifiant un peu* (H. 546).

Unlike most scores of the period, Charpentier's manuscripts usually indicate the precise nature of the instruments employed, and sometimes even their number (see below, *Pour un reposoir,* H. 508, and *Symphonies pour un reposoir,* H. 515). In his works Charpentier used the entire palette of instrumental colors that any seventeenth-century composer would have had at his disposal: violins, viols, flutes both end-blown and transverse, oboes, bassoons, trumpets, drums, harpsichord, organ, theorbo, serpents, and crumhorn. Frequently the composer proved his ability as an orchestral colorist, an unusual ability for the period. The most striking example of this ability is the *Messe pour plusieurs instruments au lieu des orgues* (H. 513) (see Chapter 11).

The Feast of the Blessed Sacrament (Corpus Christi) and its processions is represented by three scores: *Pour un reposoir* (H. 508), *Symphonies pour un reposoir* (H. 515), and *Pour un reposoir* (H. 523). As in the vocal pieces (see Chapter 9), the entire staging of the meticulously arranged ceremony transpires in the manuscripts, and the music occurs at precise moments.

Pour un reposoir (H. 508) is orchestrated for five-part strings. After a French-style overture in two sections, the versets for the instruments alternate with the priest's plainchant versets. The instrumental sections are based on the Gregorian "Tantum ergo" melody in one of two ways. In some it is given to the treble part, which is harmonized by the other three:

a)

In other sections it constitutes the theme of a fugue:

b)

In the first verset Charpentier alternates between the large choir (*tous*) and the small choir ("three *dessus,* one *haute-contre,* one *taille,* and two *quintes*"). A dance movement (*allemande grave*) in AABB form was to be played "when the procession returns." In that piece, the small choir of instruments is formed by a trio consisting of "two *dessus,* one *dessus,* and two basses."

Symphonies pour un reposoir (H. 515) is structured on the same model as the preceding work, combining the modernity of the outer movements with the archaic style of the middle versets. The "overture as soon as the banner comes into view" is also in two sections; in the second, there is a change of meter (from 3/2 to 6/4) and of texture. The *Pange lingua* "for four violin parts" was to be played "when the Holy Sacrament is placed on the altar." The Gregorian melody is here treated in an even more traditional manner than in *Pour un reposoir* (H. 508). It appears as a cantus firmus in the bass, in whole notes, over which the three other parts develop in well-balanced, richly harmonized counterpoint.

Between the "Nobis datus for the priests" and the "Verbum caro for the priests," "In supremae for the small choir," made up of two parts of "two *dessus*" and "three basses and harpsichord," treats the theme in imitation. In the "Tantum ergo for the violins," the cantus firmus is played by the treble part, solidly accompanied by a steady bass in the lower parts, first in quarter notes, then in eighth notes. "After the benediction, when the priests are far enough away for them not to be heard, the strings are to play an allemande," a piece that is now lost.

Pour un reposoir (H. 523) consists only of an "overture as soon as the procession appears." All four parts very clearly indicated: "violins and transverse flute," "*haute-contre* and transverse flute," "*taille* and *basse de flûte,*" and "harpsichord and *[basses de] violons.*" At the end of the piece, Charpentier specifies: "Things must be arranged so that the Holy Sacrament is placed [on the altar] before the conclusion of the preceding overture, which will then serve as a prelude to the motet that follows" ("Ave verum corpus") (H. 329).

French-style overtures like this one, alternating the small choir and the large choir of instruments, and orchestrated in accordance with the lavishness of the ceremonies they accompanied, were composed for various solemn occasions. Three of them were intended for consecrations of bishops—*Pour le sacre d'un évêque, ouverture pendant qu'il s'habille* (H. 518), *Ouverture pour le sacre d'un évêque pour les violons, flûtes et hautbois* (H. 536), *Ouverture pour les violon, flûtes et hautbois* (H. 537)—and one more with no other specification than *Ouverture pour l'église* (H. 524).

The first work (H. 518) dates from 1679. It is scored for five-part strings and followed by an *Offrande pour un sacre,* also instrumental. The other two works (H. 536, 537), written in 1695 (?), are large, beautifully crafted orchestral pieces (132 bars and 161 bars, respectively). The first was to be "repeated until the bishop goes to the altar."

Offerte pour l'orgue et pour les violons, flûtes et hautbois (H. 514) and *Offerte non encore executée* (H. 522) were destined for insertion into the Office of the Mass (Offertory), like the double-choir *Offerte* from *Messe pour plusieurs instruments au lieu des orgues* (H. 513) to which the bi-choral writing (woodwinds and strings) and long bass pedal points of H. 514 bear resemblance. The continuo in H. 514 is colored by the presence of "serpents, crumhorn, bassoon, and organ."

Offerte non encore exécutée is less archaic in style. The various instruments including flutes, oboes, four-part strings, and bassoon are employed with great concern for contrasts. An example is in the extremely dense dialogue between flutes and oboes. The instruments are also employed with a remarkable autonomy of the parts (notably in the seven different entries at the beginning of the piece, in which the bassoon is treated independently from the rest of the continuo). Consequently, this enriches the polyphonic texture and gives special emphasis to the contrasts in timbre.

Charpentier composed five instrumental antiphons (*Après Confitebor, Antienne [in] D minor,* H. 516; *Après Beati omnes, Antienne en G,* H. 517; *Antienne,* H. 525; *Antienne,* H. 526; and *Antienne pour les violons, flûtes et hautbois à quatre parties,* H. 532). As the titles of the first two pieces indicate, these instrumental antiphons filled the same role in the liturgical service as did the vocal antiphons. All five are orchestral pieces of modest dimensions, sober in style.

Among the numerous works that celebrate Christmas (e.g., oratorios, pastorales, and masses), the instrumental *noël* settings (H. 531, 534) are certainly not the least attractive. Six (H. 534) of the nine were destined to be played between the 'O' Antiphons for Advent (H. 36–43) (see Chapter 9). Charpentier made use of these *noël* settings in the *Messe de minuit* (H. 9). He also preserved the original flavor of the individual orchestral timbres known to all, unlike organists of the following century (e.g., Jean-François Dandrieu, Louis-Claude

Daquin, or Claude Balbastre) whose *noël* settings were a pretext for showing off their keyboard virtuosity. Even Delalande, in his *Symphonies des Noëls* for flutes, oboes, and strings, dressed up the traditional *noël* character with introductory ritornellos, melodic variations, or *doubles*. Charpentier, on the other hand, adds only a minimum of personal touches. Among these are trills and contrasts in instrumental color—violins and flutes (in, for example, *Vous qui désirez sans fin, Une jeune pucelle,* and the second version of *Les Bourgeois de Châtre*). The same applies to dynamic touches: the first violin marked *"fort"* or *"cornet d'orgue"* accompanied by the rest of the strings, muted (*Or nous dites Marie*). We also note two different harmonizations of the same melodic phrase (*Or nous dites Marie*), use of the *double* (slightly altered in *Vous qui désirez sans fin* and *Or nous dites Marie,* but more obvious in *A la venue de Noël*), of triple-meter variation (e.g., in the first version of *Les Bourgeois de Châtre* and in *Où s'en vont ces gais bergers*), a sketchy fugal treatment (e.g., *Une jeune pucelle*), the addition of a little coda (e.g., *Joseph est bien marié, Or nous dites Marie*), strophic form (e.g., *O créateur, Vous qui désirez sans fin*), and *rondeau* form (e.g., *O créateur,* second version of *Les Bourgeois de Châtre*). All these effects are used so sparingly, however, that they never compromise the popular character of the melodies.

The manuscripts contain various pieces with unspecified titles: H. 510 and 512 for a trio combination, a four-part *Prélude [in G minor] pour les violons et flûtes* (H. 528), *Prélude [in C] à quatre parties de violons avec flûtes* (H. 530), and a *Symphonie [in G minor] à 3 flûtes ou violons* (H. 529) on an ostinato bass.

Besides two major works, namely, the *Concert* (H. 545) and the *Sonate* (H. 548), Charpentier's secular instrumental music includes many dances. Among them are the minuet and passepied preceded by a *Prélude pour les flûtes et les hautbois devant l'ouverture* (H. 520), *Menuet pour les flûtes allemandes* and *Autre menuet pour les mêmes flûtes* (H. 541), a *Capriccio* (Caprice) for three violins (H. 542), and a *Marche de triomphe* for strings, trumpets, drums, flutes, and oboes followed by a *Second air de trompettes* (H. 547) for the same scoring. These last two grandiose *rondeaux* are brilliant, richly orchestrated ceremonial movements, the former in duple time, the latter in triple time. In both works, the refrain features a splendid fanfare for instru-mental tutti. The couplets in the March are scored for small trio-choirs (oboes, flutes, and treble strings); in the *Air,* oboes and flutes answer each other in the first couplet, while the treble strings join them in the second couplet.

The Bibliothèque Municipale in Versailles contains a manuscript dating from roughly 1720 in which there is a *Trio de M. Charpantier* [*sic*] not listed in Hitchcock's *Catalogue.* It was copied by the Elder Philidor, the royal librarian to whom we are indebted for the copy of *David et Jonathas.*[3]

Concert pour quatre parties de violes (H. 545) in D minor is from the end of 1680 or early 1681. Its instrumentation (two *dessus*, one *taille*, and two *basses de violes*) reflects the French taste in chamber music for viols, which would gradually be supplanted by the violin. This *Concert* falls within the tradition of the *Fantaisies* of Eustache Du Caurroy and the more recent fantasias of Étienne Moulinié. Such instrumentation and four-part texture had gone out of fashion by the end of the century, when Italian-style three-part style was preferred over it. This is evident in the prelude's highly contrapuntal texture, with imitative treatment and melodic lines in contrary motion. The other movements are arranged in a dance suite, including another untitled prelude in a style resembling the allemande, a sarabande, a triple-meter "gigue anglaise," a duple-meter "gigue française," and a passacaglia. The structure of these dances alternates between *rondeau* (sarabande and passacaglia) and binary AABB (allemande) or AAB (gigues). They reflect the usual tonal relationships observed in dance suites of the period, including tonic-dominant (A) and dominant-tonic (B), the only exception being the "gigue anglaise" whose intermediate cadence occurs in the relative major.

François Couperin's claim that he was the first French composer to have written a sonata should not be accepted at face value. Several years prior to the composition of "La Pucelle," Charpentier had written (around 1685[4]) the very first French sonata which he entitled *Sonate for 2[transverse] flutes, 2 violins, bass viol, a 5-stringed bass violin, harpsichord, and theorbo.* Like everything that came from Italy, the sonata was regarded suspiciously by advocates of French music. That is why Couperin italianized his name when he decided to present it to the public. Charpentier apparently had no need for such subterfuge, for his listeners were probably limited to the sophisticated musical circle of the Hôtel de Guise.

Charpentier's *Sonate* (H. 548) is related to the Italian *sonata da camera* form, being a freely arranged suite of dances, and to the *sonata da chiesa* in the opening "Grave" movement (despite its French title *récit*). It consists of nine movements, some of which are linked to others, as in Couperin's sonatas. The two outer movements only are in the key of C major. The second movement, a *récit* for solo viol, is in D minor, and Charpentier remains in that key in the sarabande, the *récit* for bass violin, the bourrée, and the gavotte. The gigue is in G minor and the passacaglia in C minor.

The first movement ("Grave") employs all the instruments (flutes and violins *en trio*, bass viol, and continuo consisting of bass violin, theorbo, and harpsichord, though the bass violin occasionally breaks away from the other two continuo instruments for some imitative interplay with the bass viol). This highly expressive movement combines French melodic grace with Italianate harmonies and their numerous sevenths.

Not until the following movements does Charpentier pit the two styles of the day against one another, and he does so with humor. In the manuscript he writes, "The viol has some fun" and "The bass violin has some fun, too." The solo viol *récit*, followed by a sarabande, spotlights this French instrument *par excellence* in some very idiomatic chordal writing.

In his *Sonate*, Charpentier calls for a "five-string bass violin" possessing a greater range than a four-string one, particularly in the high register (fifth string).[5] Here its range extends from D^1 to A^3. If the instrument is truly French (the bass violin must be distinguished from the Italian violoncello), its similarity to the violin family, and especially the solo virtuosic writing (tremolos and runs) that Charpentier gives it in the "Récit de la basse de violon," provide an eloquent sample of ultramontane style.

In the bourrée, the bass viol detaches itself from the rest of the continuo to play in counterpoint with the bass violin.

The gavotte alternates textures of tutti, flutes alone, and violins alone. The continuo regroups all the other instruments, though the bass viol is silent when the violins play alone, and the bass violin is silent in the flute passages.

Linked to the lively gigue for violin and continuo (bass violin, harpsichord, and theorbo) is a graceful and tender passacaglia, given in turn to the first flute, the first violin, and both instruments together. All the instruments are once again used in the chaconne marked "lively," bringing the *Sonate* to a brilliant conclusion.

This very beautiful work surely makes one regret that Charpentier did not leave more instrumental pieces. It proves that he was well acquainted with the various possibilities of instrumental techniques and colors in a way that was amazing for that period. He was also familiar with the art of combining vocal styles (the beautiful melody of the air "Rendez-moi mes plaisirs," H. 463, may be recognized in the passacaglia) with specifically instrumental textures. Even in an unfamiliar domain, Charpentier became a precursor by turning once again to Italy. His *Sonate* is an absolutely perfect introduction to Couperin's *Goûts réunis.*

Chapter 14

Tutor to the Duc de Chartres and Composer of *Médée*

It is this opera, more than any other without exception, from which may be learned the essentials of good composition.
Sébastien de Brossard, 1724

TUTOR TO THE DUC DE CHARTRES

In the early 1690s, Charpentier was asked to give lessons in composition to the Duc de Chartres, the king's nephew, and Mlle de Guise's cousin and godchild. A few years earlier, Étienne Loulié had taught the future regent the rudiments of music and had given him lessons on the flute and the viol.[1] Philippe of Orléans also learned to play the harpsichord.

After his marriage on 18 February 1692 to Mlle de Blois, daughter of Louis XIV and Mme de Montespan, the eighteen-year-old duke spent the spring and summer at the front with the Maréchal de Luxembourg. In October he returned to Paris, remaining there until June 1693. It seems to have been during that nine-month period[2] that he became the "disciple" of Charpentier, who had been chosen "to show him the basics of composition."[3] During the creation of *Médée* which preoccupied the composer until the autumn of 1693, Charpentier tutored the duke and gave him a short treatise he had written sometime before to which he added some "augmentations" destined for his royal pupil (see Appendix 2).[4]

According to his mother, the Princess Palatine, Philippe had a passionate love of music:

> I often tell my son that it will drive him mad, when I hear him talking endlessly about major and minor, flats and sharps, and other things of the sort that I know nothing about; but the Dauphin, my son, and the Princesse de Conti go on talking about these things for hours at a time.[5]

The duke's love of music, along with his undisputed talent, resulted in the composition of several motets, including a five-part *Laudate Jerusalem Dominum*. He also composed operas. The first of them, *Philomèle*, written with the help of Charpentier, was performed three times at the Palais-Royal. Since the duke objected to publishing the work, the music is now lost. Later, Philippe of Orléans composed a tragédie lyrique, *Penthée* (1705), to a libretto by the Marquis de La Fare, his captain of the guard. The duke also composed *Suite d'Armide ou la Jérusalem délivrée*, which was performed at Fontainebleau in 1712.

Although instructed by Loulié in the French style, the Duc de Chartres proved an ardent advocate of Italian music. It was within his circle that the new genres of the cantata and the sonata blossomed in the eighteenth century. Did his association with Charpentier have something to do with this taste for the ultramontane esthetic? Whatever the case, the sharp tongue of Lecerf de la Viéville had the following to say about the composer's influence on his pupils:

> Bad teachers ruin your voice . . . and I noticed last year how they also ruin your taste. I saw a woman of high rank and great intelligence who had learned the art of composition from the late Charpentier. Charpentier had so filled that woman with Italian maxims that she, an authority on hundreds of subjects, had reached a point where her admiration for our new operas extended only to the *fourth act of Alcide*, and she could not stand *L'Europe Galante*. Therefore it is easy to imagine . . . how a teacher with wretched taste corrupts that of his students. Good taste is only natural inclination guided by principles. Far from giving them principles which are true, well-founded, and which refine the light of natural inclination, a bad teacher gives [pupils] false principles which further cloud and misdirect that inclination. I believe that, although Charpentier has had students of the highest quality, he has ruined others.[6]

Even though he had other teachers in subsequent years (e.g., Charles-Hubert Gervais, André Campra, Nicolas Bernier, Henry Desmarest), the Duc de Chartres did not forget Charpentier. In 1698 he made the composer "music master of the Sainte-Chapelle of Paris."[7] In appreciation for "the special protection" that the duke "had the kindness to bestow on Monsieur Charpentier, our uncle," Jacques Édouard dedicated in 1709 his edition of the anthology of *Motets mêlés de symphonie* to "His Royal Highness, Monseigneur le Duc d'Orléans."

Médée

In 1693, the year of *Médée*'s premiere, Lully had been dead for six years, but his reign had not yet ended. Indeed, the privilege for the Académie Royale granted to him on 13 March 1672 extended posthumously to his children. After nearly a fifteen-year period during which only the tragédies lyriques of the powerful Surintendant were performed (at the rate of one per year, from *Cadmus et Hermione* in 1673 to *Armide* in 1686), Lully's final work, the pastoral *Achille et Polixène*, was completed by his pupil and secretary Pascal Colasse and performed in November 1687. The years that followed saw a succession of works by his sons Louis and Jean Lully (*Zéphyre et Flore, Orphée*) and by Colasse (*Thétis et Pélée, Énée et Lavinie, Astrée*), most of them without much success. Other composers began to try their hand in the field which until then had been monopolized by Lully and his offspring. Among them were Theobaldo di Gatti (*Coronis*) in 1691, Marin Marais in collaboration with Louis Lully (*Alcide*) and Henry Desmarest (*Didon*) in 1693, and finally, in December 1693, Charpentier (*Médée*).

Ever since *David et Jonathas* (1688), the composer had stayed away from the operatic genre. Would he have wanted to renew his theatrical ties, after all the difficulties encountered when Lully was alive? He knew that he would have to deal with the reactions of the "envious and ignorant," and hostile, Lully faction. It is quite possible the Duc de Chartres, then his pupil, may have personally encouraged Charpentier to tackle the stage of the Académie Royale. Philippe displayed his support and admiration by personally attending several performances of *Médée*.

> A new opera entitled *Médée* is now being given. It is a time-honored classical subject admired throughout history. Hence there is nothing further to be said about its plot or characters that the Ancients have not already told us. Even though it is very difficult to treat in an opera the same amount of material as in an ordinary [spoken] tragedy, because an opera contains less verse

than would be necessary for two acts of a non-musical tragedy, it can be said that the operas *Médée* and *Bellérophon* by the same [librettist], are filled with as much plot as any of our plays. The emotions in them are so vivid, and especially in *Médée*, that if that role were but spoken, it would not fail to make a great impression on the audience. Judge for yourselves how, given the opportunity to make beautiful music, Mlle Rochois, one of the finest actresses in the world, who acts with warmth, subtlety, and intelligence, shines in this role and brings out its beauties so well. All Paris is enchanted with the manner in which this excellent actress performs it, and one cannot admire her enough. This opera was set to music by Charpentier, whose multi-faceted stage music has delighted us in various plays over the past twenty years. *Le Mariage forcé, Le Malade imaginaire, Circé*, and *L'Inconnu* are proof of that. In those earlier works are two Italian airs, as charming as the one in the opera *Médée*. This should not surprise us, since Charpentier studied music in Italy under Charissimi [*sic*].... True connoisseurs find a great deal to admire in the opera *Médée*. Charpentier, who has had it printed, had the honor of presenting it to the king a few days ago, and His Majesty told him that he was convinced he was an able man, and that he knew that there were very lovely things in his opera. Although it has only been given nine or ten performances thus far, Monseigneur le Dauphin has already twice attended, and His Royal Highness Monsieur has seen it four times. It has had the fate of beautiful works, which are first opposed by the envious, only to shine all the more afterwards. This is what happened to several works by Lully, which later were admired by all Paris. Envy is never associated with mediocre works, which have their day without it occurring to anyone to speak well or ill of them. The decorations and costumes for the opera *Médée* are by Berin [*sic*]. His reputation and ability are so well-established in these two areas, I can say no more about them without doing him injustice.[8]

Like Rameau, though for different reasons, Charpentier was fifty years old when his first tragédie lyrique was performed on 4 December 1693. He turned to his former stage collaborator Thomas Corneille for the libretto. Known mainly for his rather superficial comedies and his stage plays, Corneille nevertheless had already worked for the Académie Royale after Quinault, Lully's official librettist, fell from grace. In 1678, Corneille re-worked the comédie-ballet *Psyché* and, the following year, collaborated with Fontenelle on the text of *Bellérophon*. At the age of sixty-eight, Corneille wrote his last work for the lyric stage, *Médée*.

Jean Berain, who was responsible for the "decorations and

costumes for the opera *Médée*," had been appointed artist of the King's Chamber and Cabinet in 1674. His principal duties consisted of executing "all sorts of drawings, perspectives, illustrations and costumes . . . for comedies, ballets, *courses de bagues,* and carrousels" at court.[9] A few years later, he replaced the machinist Carlo Vigarani at the Académie Royale. The brilliant designer of Lully's spectacles, Berain continued to place his prodigious talent in the service of the successors of the Surintendant.

In Act I of *Médée*, Berain imagined a majestic public square framed on either side by rows of double columns alternating with statues and trophies. In the middle of the stage, he erected a triumphal arch whose central opening revealed a second arch in fine perspective. In Act III, Medea invoking the "Black Maidens of the Styx" appeared as a sorceress, with a magic wand, in a vaulted cave whose galleries extended far into the distance. Through an opening in the vault winged demons descended, while downstage ugly animals crawled about.[10]

The role of Medea was played by Marthe Le Rochois.

> [I]n the opinion of the famous actor Baron, [Marthe Le Rochois] was the greatest actress and the finest exponent of the declamatory style to appear on any stage. . . . With eyes full of fire, capable of expressing all emotions, her ability to communicate the most varied attitudes, with an aura of a goddess and admirable gestures, she combined all this with the most beautiful voice in the world.[11]

First attracting notice in *Proserpine* in 1680, Le Rochois subsequently created all the leading female roles in Lully's tragédies lyriques. She caused a sensation as Armide.

Jason was played by the countertenor Duménil, who owed his fame as much to his voice and acting as to his debauchery. Originally a cook, his exceptional vocal gifts caused Lully to notice him. Despite the musical instruction given to him by Lully, Duménil was never able to read a score; he learned his roles by imitating other singers. He appeared for the first time at the Académie Royale as a Triton in the prologue to *Isis* in 1677. With Le Rochois, he created the great Lully roles of Atys, Thésée, Persée, and Renaud. "Nothing was greater than hearing the scenes that he played with the illustrious Demoiselle Rochois."[12]

Françoise Moreau (Créuse) debuted at age fifteen in the prologue to *Phaéton* in 1683. Her loose behavior earned her the mockery of the *chansonniers* of the day.

We have already encountered the baritone Jean Dun, who created the role of Créon. Dun was one of the singers of the Académie Royale that the Jesuits hired for their church music. Like the other soloists in *Médée,* he became famous through the works of Lully and his successors.

All performances of *Médée* took place at the Palais-Royal theater. In fact, no tragédies lyriques were given at court between 1691 and 1697, but this did not prevent the royal family from going to hear *Médée.* The king went first, followed by the Dauphin who, on Friday, 11 December "came to Paris to see the new opera *Médée*"[13] and the Duc de Chartres who, according to the *Mercure Galant,* saw it no less than "four times."

The public reception of *Médée* was quite mixed and certainly did not live up to the expectations of the composer who, after a twenty-three year career, only enjoyed partial revenge on his rival. The Lullists, led by Lecerf de la Viéville, who referred to the "wretched opera *Médée,*" tried to outdo each other in sarcastic remarks:

De Charpentier et de Thomas Corneille
Venez tous voir l'opéra merveilleux;
N'y portez point ni d'esprit ni d'oreille,
Il suffira que vous ayez des yeux.[14]

Of Charpentier and of Thomas Corneille
Come one and all to see the marvelous opera;
Bring with you neither intelligence nor ear,
For eyes alone will suffice.

Autrefois je chantais l'Achille
De l'Opéra de Campistron:
Médée échauffe aussi ma bile:
Chantons-la sur le même ton.[15]

In the past I used to carry on about *Achille [et Polyxène]*
The opera by Campistron:
Médée also stirs my bile:
Let us carry on about it on the same note.

A l'Opéra, Dieux! la belle machine
Qu'a fait faire Francine
Pour y prendre un rat, pauvre Jason,

Qu'as-tu fait à Corneille?
Pour te faire affront,
Point de chanson,
La musique à l'oreille
Ne vaut pas Didon.
Jamais pour un Opéra si mauvais
On ne fit plus d'apprêt;
Croit-on nous amuser
Et nous charmer
Avec si peu d'attraits?
Aussi l'on est bientôt désabusé
De ces colifichets.[16]

At the Opéra, heavens! the beautiful machinery
Created by Francine
To catch a rat. Poor Jason,
What have you done to Corneille?
To add insult to injury,
There are no tunes;
The music to our ear
Is worse than that of *Didon.*
Never has an opera this bad
Been afforded such lavish preparations.
Are we to be entertained
And delighted
With such meager attractions?
One is soon disillusioned
By these cheap baubles.

Charpentier was criticized particularly for voluntarily dissociating himself from the Lullian esthetic through stylistic complexities that departed from the *style naturel* of his rival, and through overly sophisticated harmonies:

En vain d'autres auteurs sur la scène tragique
Hasardèrent l'essai de leur veine harmonique,
Leurs opéras bientôt, et leurs noms détestés
Dans le gouffre d'oubli furent précipités.
C'est ainsi, qu'éprouvant le triste sort d'Icare,
Tombèrent et Bouvard et La Coste, et La Barre,
Théobalde, Rebel, et même Charpentier,

Qui du temple sacré, profanant le sentier,
Répandit dans Médée avec trop d'abondance
Les charmes déplacés d'une haute science.[17]

In vain other authors of the tragic stage
Tried their hand at musical inspiration;
Their operas and their hated titles
Soon fell into the depths of oblivion.
Suffering the same fate as Icarus,
Thus fell Bouvard, La Coste, La Barre,
Théobalde, Rebel, and even Charpentier
Who, desecrating the path to the sacred temple,
Lavished excessively on *Médée*
The misplaced charms of a noble art.

Some critics considered the music of *Médée* "very difficult," and went so far as to dub Charpentier the "barbarian composer."[18] One of the reasons contributing to the work's being dropped seems to have been the unwillingness of the musicians in the orchestra to perform it:

> This work which foreigners have regarded as a masterpiece had no success in France. It was due, we add, to the negligence of the musicians of the orchestra; and in punishment for either their incapacity or their malice, for the next ten years fifty francs per year were deducted from their salaries.[19]

Fortunately, *Médée* also had its supporters, including Donneau de Visé (see *Mercure Galant* quoted above) and Sébastien de Brossard. The latter felt that it was

> unquestionably the most learned and the most elaborate of all those [works] which have been published, at least since the death of Lully. Although due to the cabals of the envious and the ignorant, it was not received as well by the public as it deserved, or even as well as many others, it is this opera, more than any other without exception, from which may be learned the essentials of good composition. Because of this I have long felt that I ought to place it in the ranks of the theoreticians, which is to say the teachers of the art of music, rather than that of ordinary operas.[20]

The public's response was presumably the same as that of the critics. Most of the audience rejected many of the score's novelties and were irritated by a small group of Charpentier's supporters who applauded those very features.

Although such heated controversy gives the impression that Charpentier launched a challenge to the genre that Lully had invented and nurtured, it must be acknowledged that *Médée* in all respects falls into the mold of the Lully tragédie lyrique. Indeed, how could the similarity have been avoided? All opera composers until Rameau (and including Rameau) conformed to it.

Although long skeptical about the validity of opera in French, Lully, in *Cadmus et Hermione,* had shown his new compatriots a genre which until that time had belonged exclusively to the Italians. Over the twenty-seven years that he had lived in France, nearly twenty of which were spent composing court entertainments, Lully had gradually freed himself of his Italian origins and had assimilated in a phenomenal way the elements of the French esthetic. He thus became its most persuasive defender and representative. In the tragedy in music that the Surintendant launched in collaboration with Philippe Quinault, author of his librettos, he synthesized the elements of the genres that he had practiced, such as the court ballet, the comédie-ballet, and the pastoral, while retaining the general components of air, small ensemble, chorus, and divertissements mixed with dances. In addition he adopted the grand machinery and sumptuous sets and costumes of the "stage plays," themselves derived from Italian opera. From the latter source he also took the allegorical aspect of its prologues and the famous slumber scenes (*sommeils*) that appear in Cavalli in particular. His experience as conductor of the musicians of the King's Chamber and the Écurie also led him to furnish his operas with rich orchestral textures and with symphonic effects as yet unheard of, even in Italy.

It was in the French classical tragedy of Corneille and of Racine that Lully and Quinault found the most striking features of tragedy in music, the ones that gave it its great unity and special flavor. Among them are subjects drawn mainly from classical mythology, a five-act structure springing from a well-knit plot as opposed to the complicated intrigues of Italian operas, and above all else, textual clarity and declamation. Indeed, the keystone of tragedy in music lies in the recitative that Lully fashioned after the sort of declamation that could be heard in spoken theater. Referring to the great Racinian tragedienne La Champmeslé, the Florentine declared to his singers, "If you want to sing my music well, go listen to La Champmeslé." The sound of the word, of the verse, and the utter intelligibility of the discourse are essential in Lullian tragedy, where music remains the servant of the word.

Rousseau, in his definition of recitative, later emphasized the close similarity between singing and declamation:

> *Recitative:* Manner of singing which greatly resembles speech, a declamation in music, in which the composer must imitate as much as possible the inflections of the voice of the declaimer.
>
> Meter is not at all observed when singing recitative; the metrical patterns governing airs would spoil recitative-declamation. The rhythmic accent of the word, whether grammatical or rhetorical, alone must determine the slowness or the speed of the sounds, as well as their pitch.[21]

This concern with adapting the melodic line and rhythm of the musical phrase to the changing pattern of the discourse, and hence with obeying only the literary text, gives Lully's recitative that "naturalness" so admired by contemporary audiences:

> Expressivity is the universal aim of painting, and of poetry enhanced by music. In this respect, whenever a composer applies inappropriate tones to a line of verse or a thought, whether or not those tones are new and learned is of no interest to me.... Poorly linked poetry and music go in separate directions. My attention wavers when thus divided, and the pleasure that my ears may take in the harmonies has nothing to do with my heart, and is consequently very cold. It no longer paints, because it paints differently. Hence it is bad.... But as soon as my thought pleases, strikes, moves me on its own, I no longer need to look for an elegant [musical] phrase; it is enough that the words effectively render the meaning.... Effective expression, effective painting, that is the *chef-d'oeuvre*, that is the supreme goal, everything. Whatever it might cost the composer to achieve it, be it accusations of sterility or careless workmanship, he will always gain considerably by it.[22]

In contrast to the obvious distinction between recitative and aria in Italian opera, there is no clearly perceptible difference between the two forms in French tragedy in music. One passes imperceptibly from one to the other, and the smaller-scale air, which is developed from the *air de cour*, never contains the type of lyrical expansion of which the Italians were so fond.

In *Médée*, the French style of recitative naturally prevailed, even though Charpentier made something more "musical" out of it, particularly through the use of richer harmonies. Lully's harmonies indeed always remain extremely simple (with a few exceptions, such as the falling asleep of Atys over a chromatic bass worthy of Charpentier), for he did not want to overpower the discourse with a kind of expression that would have "polluted" the ideal clarity sought by the composer.

In the use of harmonies, Lully was primarily concerned with their tonal functions which were becoming established by the second half of the seventeenth century, and which allowed him to structure his discourse very effectively.[23] Alongside this tonal organization, the architecture of his large-scale works stems from a general framework consisting of a prologue and five acts. Each act is divided into an appropriately dramatic part (whose pace is established by a series of recitatives, airs, and duos connected by short orchestral ritornellos) and a divertissement combining choruses, descriptive *symphonies*, and dances. Although linked to the tragedy, the divertissement employs characters lying outside the plot (e.g., divinities, allegorical figures) and provides an opportunity for spectacular battle scenes, funeral processions, and celebrations of all kinds. The composer is freer here than in the rest of the tragedy to expand his musical material through extensive development and repetition, since the dramatic action is temporarily suspended.

Charpentier, who was well-acquainted with his rival's works, adopted all their features in *Médée* with the aid of Thomas Corneille, himself no novice in the field. Appointed in 1685 to the Académie Française after his brother's death, Corneille assumed a far more difficult responsibility by taking up the subject treated by Pierre in his first tragedy of 1635.

Turning from spoken tragedy to tragédie lyrique and from an esthetic of the early decades of the seventeenth century to a later one, Thomas Corneille found himself obliged to adapt the situations, the characters, and the prosody to the constraints of sung drama. Even though he sometimes drew directly from his brother's text, he tightened the plot and gave *Médée* more tonal variety, more pathos, and a more subtle psychological treatment of the title character in particular. He included ingredients befitting the lyric genre, such as the conventional prologue and divertissements, each focusing on one character (e.g., Jason in Act I, Créuse in Act II, Médée in Act III, and Créon in Act IV). Finally, the strict alexandrine prosody of *Le Cid* is replaced, in Thomas Corneille's works, by much more flexible and diversified meters, and not infrequently by free verse.

The score of *Médée* was published in 1694 by Christophe Ballard, "the king's sole printer of music." Charpentier dedicated his work quite naturally to Louis XIV, in conventional terms of modesty and courtesy:

Sire,

The particular patronage that Your Majesty has always given the Fine Arts obliges everyone involved in them to dedicate the fruit of their labors to you. And as Music is one of your most frequent pleasures, it would be little deserving of that patronage if when providing a spectacle for your subjects it did not appear in public under the glorious auspices of Your Majesty. You know, Sire, better than anyone in your kingdom, all the touching and subtle powers [of Music], and if *Médée*, which I make so bold as to present to you, has the good fortune to please you in any one of its aspects, I can desire no more of what I set out to achieve. Please accept, Sire, this humble mark of my zeal, and by offering you this work, permit me to show everyone that my sole ambition is to be able to contribute something to the pleasurable diversion so necessary for Your Majesty in the tedious and continual efforts [you] make for the glory of the State, and for the benefit of his People. I am with the deepest respect,

Your Majesty's

very humble, very obedient
and very faithful servant and subject,
Charpentier

Prologue. The prologue of *Médée* naturally adheres to the rules of the genre observed by the operas of Lully. Unrelated to the tragedy, it consists of an eloquent homage to the king by conventional type-figures. The people and shepherds appear alongside the allegorical figures of Victory, Fame, and Bellone, goddess of war. Musically, similarities to Lully's prologues are noticeable: airs generally repeated by the chorus, dances, and, of course, the overture with its first section in dotted-notes and duple meter, a second triple-meter fugal section, and a concluding section returning to the mood of the opening. The large, five-part orchestra of the Académie Royale is employed, composed of *dessus, hautes-contre, tailles, quintes,* and *basses de violons.* The main key of the prologue is the "lively and warlike" C major, as befitting the evocation of the powerful and victorious King Louis XIV.

"The stage represents a rustic setting, embellished by Nature with rocks and waterfalls."

The Leader of the people (bass) intones a robust air, "Louis is triumphant, all yields to his power." Binary in form (AAB), the air is repeated and developed in block harmonies by the four-part chorus (*dessus, hautes-contre, tailles,* and basses) and by the five-part orchestra. Trio passages for *hauts-dessus, bas-dessus,* and *hautes-contre* twice serve to lighten the texture of this section.

An instrumental "Air" introduces a trio of shepherds, again amplified by the chorus, inviting Victory, Fame, and Bellone to appear. The triple meter, the contrapuntal interweaving of phrases, the repetition of words ("paraissez," "descendez") as well as the melody of continuously rising and falling scales lend this passage an extremely graceful incantatory mood.

The scenery then changes to "a whirl of descending clouds which soon reveal the Palace of Victory advancing until it occupies the whole stage. In the middle of the palace are Fame, Victory, and Bellone." They take turns singing alone, in pairs, and in a trio. Short ritornellos for three-part violins and/or flutes punctuate their lines. The Chorus of Shepherds repeats the last words of Victory, "He will conquer ever so often, on land and on sea." It is then time for the ballet—a *loure* followed by quick-tempo *canaries*, and a repeat of the *loure*.

A shepherd (*haute-contre*) sings a short air "In youth if one is not flighty" in minuet form which passes to the instruments who treat it in *rondeau* fashion, with the couplets in the oboes. Then follows a song for one, then two shepherdesses, still in minuet rhythm. In the same manner that he linked the *loure* to the *canaries*, Charpentier extends his minuets with a passepied, the dance that Sébastien de Brossard considered "a minuet whose tempo is very quick."

Imitating the first notes of the passepied, the chorus accompanied by the entire orchestra (strings, flutes, oboes, and bassoons) embarks on the war song "The noise of drums and trumpets," then twice repeats the much earlier "He will conquer."

The prologue concludes with a reprise of the overture, during which "the palace returns to where it had come from; the whirl of clouds closes again and rises back into the sky."

Despite its official framework, the textures of the prologue to *Médée* are remarkable in all respects. Charpentier combines a wide variety of airs, choruses, instrumentation, and contrasting dance types with a formal concern for tonal stability (C major, A minor, C major) and structural amplification (air-chorus, reprises), giving this section a great sense of unity.

Act I. The first pages of the published score are curiously headed *Jason, tragédie,* as though the authors had hesitated between that title and *Médée*. The action takes place in Corinth where Medea and Jason with their children have taken refuge from the Thessalian army. With the exception of Créuse, all the characters in the tragedy are presented in Act I: Medea, princess of Colchis (soprano) and her maid Nérine (soprano); Jason, prince of Thessalia (*haute-contre*) and his confidant Arcas (taille); Créon, king of Corinth (bass); and Oronte, prince of Argos (baritone).

"The scene represents a public square, ornamented with a triumphal arch, statues and trophies mounted on pedestals."[24]

A ritornello in a "furious and quick-tempered" F major introduces scene 1. Borrowing the ritornello's motif, Medea's solo ("To beguile my woes") soon develops into recitative. While recitative is completely absent in the prologue, it is firmly established in the opening bars of the tragedy. As in Lully's works, the recitative of Charpentier, with its frequent metrical changes and anapestic rhythm closely wedded to the text, hovers constantly between strict musical declamation and more melodic passages, like fragments of airs.

Medea tells Nérine her suspicions about Jason's infidelity. The confidante tries to explain Jason's position to her, namely, that Jason is trying to obtain the favor of Créuse so that Créon will protect Medea and her family from the rage of Arcaste, who wishes to avenge Pelias, one of the enchantress' victims. Nérine does not succeed in reassuring Medea, whose grief only increases during their dialogue and suddenly erupts into fury on the words "Let him fear me." The strings, silent until this point, burst into a rush of sixteenth notes introducing Medea's majestic but menacing solo ("A docile dragon"), which rises above the five-part accompaniment in the orchestra in repeated, hammered notes. The string symphony very effectively concludes this very brief passage, which stands out from the rest of the scene because of its special character and its key of B-flat major, subdominant of F. The enchantress has revealed the range of her powers, which she will not hesitate to use if need be.

This scene ends with an air for Nérine, repeated in duet form with Medea. Nérine advises her mistress to dissemble ("Constrain your woes to silence"). The calm triple meter of the air is in contrast to the preceding outburst of violence.

Scene 2 brings Medea and Jason face to face. The mood is "grave" (D minor). The scene is built around the very beautiful duet, "Nothing but woeful cares," in which the lovers, in canonic imitation, seem to recapture their former happiness. Medea's doubts give way to Jason's professions of fidelity. In the A-major air that follows ("Stop these unnecessary evasions"), Jason, confident of having convinced Medea of his sincerity, declares he will see Créuse no more. The enchantress, reassured, talks him out of it.

In scene 3, Jason remains in private with his confidant, Arcas. Accompanied by two recorders, he sings a little air in *rondeau* form ("How happy I would be if I were less loved") with a middle section in recitative. Although the part A melody remains the same in the opening section and in the reprise, Charpentier varies its harmonization.

Does the gradually descending bass line in the first exposition refer to Medea and the more assertive one to Créuse's victory over the heart of Jason, as suggested by the structure of the text?

A   *Que je serais heureux, si j'étais moins aimé!*

B   *Médée avec ardeur dans mon sort s'intéresse,*
    Je lui dois toute ma tendresse
    D'une autre cependant je me trouve charmé
    Et malgré moi j'adore la Princesse.

A   *Que je serais heureux si j'étais moins aimé!*

A   How happy I would be if I were less loved!

B   Medea is passionately concerned about my fate,
    I owe her all my affection;
    However, I find myself charmed by another,
    And in spite of myself I adore the Princess

A   How happy I would be if I were less loved!

After Arcas warns him about Medea's wrath and he recognizes his own betrayal, Jason, in a long air in *rondeau* form (ABA'CA) supported by five-part muted strings, expresses his wish to be united with Créuse. As in scene 2 which evolved from D minor to D major, the initial tonality of G minor gives way to G major. The move from minor to major in both cases depicts the thoughts of the protagonists, whose doubts and hesitations are transformed into certainty, even if that certainty is based on a lie.

Suddenly, from backstage, the Chorus of Corinthians is heard welcoming Oronte, the hero who has come to offer Créon his strong support. It comes as an absolute surprise, as the action of the play was far from the problems of politics and war. Charpentier, however, deploys his usual skill in such offstage numbers, whose dramatic impact (remember Act IV of *David et Jonathas*) is always powerful.

Scene 4 brings on Créon and his court. A fanfare with trumpets and drums in D major (the key of the rest of the act) introduces Oronte and his entourage. The prince of Argos first expresses himself in recitative ("My Lord, as Thessaly attacks your state"), but the thought of Créuse draws him into a spirited air ("I dare hope for everything from the ardor that drives me") accompanied by a trio of violins. After an exchange of formalities between the two pretenders to the hand of Créon's daughter, the fanfare is repeated while "the Corinthians enter singing and dancing."

Scene 6 consists of the Act I divertissement. A short tenor air for a Corinthian ("Run to the Field of Mars"), in three sections, is repeated verbatim by the four-part Chorus of Corinthians. Then it is the turn of the three-part Chorus of Argians, following Oronte's air ("Let us run, let us fly with fearless courage") in binary form; in this case, the chorus only takes up the second half.

Both choruses and all the instruments (including oboes, trumpets, and drums) unite in a grand and sumptuous passage ("Let the serried battalions") alternating large and small choirs, full orchestra and a trio of oboes and violins, and also homophonic texture and imitative treatment ("la gloire et l'amour"). "[T]he Corinthians give a display of wrestling" and "the Argians execute a gallant dance."

Following two instrumental pieces, a fanfare "*rondeau* for the Corinthians" and a gentler "air for the Argians," there is a song-duet ("What happiness accompanies tenderness") on a sarabande rhythm, an instrumental sarabande, and the second couplet of the song for the Corinthian and the Argian. The grand chorus "Let the serried

battalions" is repeated, and the act, after this brilliant divertissement, concludes with an orchestral entr'acte.

Act II. "The stage represents a vestibule with a large portico."
In scene 1, Créon (recitative-accompanied air) assures Medea of
his protection, but asks her to leave the Corinthian court. Medea
accepts ("Without surprise I hear my sentence"), thinking that Jason
will accompany her. But Créon insists that she leave alone before the
day is out. To the heartrending cries of the offended wife ("I am
driven away, exiled, and torn from my own self"), Créon responds
with indifference in a light air ("Let us silence the malcontents").

Créuse enters. Medea turns to her and makes an emotional plea,
alternately accompanied by transverse flutes and five-part strings.
The princess remains silent, and Medea leaves the stage while the
instruments continue their dialogue.

With Medea gone, the tonal atmosphere brightens from G minor
to C major. Créon rejoices. In a short recitative followed by a graceful air with continuo accompaniment, Créuse appears as an obedient
girl for whom love cannot exist without glory.

In scene 5, Jason and Créuse find themselves alone. It is time for
tender vows and promises of fidelity. The lovers' happiness is
expressed in two duets ("Let us savor the happy joy" and "Ah let us
say it a hundred times").

Oronte appears and declares his love to Créuse. She feigns to
accept it, a pretense whose somewhat mechanical nature is felt in the
accompaniment of her air, with an ostinato eighth-note motif. Oronte
then pays "tribute" to Créuse, which provides the divertissement for
this act. In play-within-the-play fashion, the characters temporarily
cease being actors to become spectators.

"A small Argian boy representing Cupid appears in a chariot
drawn by slaves of different nations and sexes."

After a prelude scored for strings, the Chorus of Love's Slaves
and an Argian (*haute-contre*) take turns celebrating the beauty of
Créuse. Then Cupid (*dessus*), sweetly accompanied by three flutes
(two trebles, one bass), addresses Créuse. His solo is interspersed
with ritornellos during which the entertainments are readied:
"Cupid gives his bow to Créuse," "Cupid invites Créuse to step into
his chariot," and "Jason and Oronte place themselves on either side of
her." Thus another divertissement is made possible, within the main
one: Cupid "places himself at Créuse's feet" to watch the spectacle.

The second part of the divertissement is built around two dances, a chaconne and a passacaglia of approximately equal length. These are dances based on the variation principle over a bass line which, without duplicating itself exactly each time, adheres to four- or eight-bar units throughout. Such grand orchestral pages first became a feature of French music when Lully introduced them into his tragédies lyriques (*Amadis* and *Armide*). To extend their range and to reinforce their structure, he inserted vocal episodes alternating with passages for orchestra alone. Charpentier had already used the passacaglia (instrumental only) in *Circé* (H. 496), *Le Rendez-vous des Tuileries* (H. 505), and *Vénus et Adonis* (H. 507) and the chaconne in *Les Arts florissants* (H. 487) and *David et Jonathas* (H. 490). In *Médée* he employs both dances consecutively, something Lully had never attempted. Charpentier, on the other hand, had already placed a chaconne after a passacaglia in his *Sonate* (H. 548).

The chaconne in *Médée*, in A major, is first heard in the orchestra. It is then heard in an air for an "Italian maiden" ("Chi teme d'amore") and is repeated by three-part chorus (*hauts-dessus, dessus,* and *hautes-contre*).

The passacaglia, more serious in tone than the chaconne and in the more "tender" key of A minor, is scored first for orchestra, then for "three slaves" (French this time), then for five-part chorus (*hauts-dessus, dessus, hautes-contre, tailles,* and basses). The orchestra concludes the dance on its own.

The introduction of an episode in Italian into *Médée* must have annoyed the Lullists. This was thanks not only to Thomas Corneille, but even more to Charpentier, who was not content merely with its linguistic application. Indeed, in comparing the respective textures of the chaconne and the passacaglia, it is apparent the composer also extended this Franco-Italian confrontation to musical treatment. The florid, virtuosic vocal line on the Italian *non ha* is in clear contrast to the much more conventional one on the French word *gloire*. Above all, it was in his choice of instrumentation that Charpentier meant to show the differences of each style most clearly. After the Italian-style trio formation of flutes during the chaconne's solo, to which two violins are added for the three-part chorus, the passacaglia features an utterly French dialogue between the small choir and the large five-part choir (incidentally, the only occasion that this vocal scoring is used in *Médée*).

The major attraction of this divertissement is not simply the historical curiosity of the confrontation of French and Italian musical textures. Much more interesting is the way Charpentier uses it to expand the structure of his discourse, beginning with the solo, to the small three-part chorus, and ending with the large five-part chorus. Moreover, passing from four-bar units in the chaconne to eight-bar units in the passacaglia also contributes to an amplification of musical space.

Cupid, Oronte, and Jason ask Créuse to choose the one she loves, which she refrains from doing. Hence, no hopes are extinguished, and a triumphal chorus celebrates the victory of love. As in the preceding act, an instrumental entr'acte concludes Act II.

Act III. "The stage represents a place destined for Medea's incantations."

Act III revolves around Medea, who remains on stage throughout. The intense inner turmoil of the humiliated woman last seen in Act II, scene 2, develops into vengeful fury.

Scene 1 opens with a ritornello that is both descriptive (the "storm" Oronte refers to upon entering) and prophetic. It is prophetic in that it foreshadows the sorcery scene of the divertissement. Oronte offers his protection to Medea, who informs him of Jason's love for Créuse. For the first time, the Argian prince loses his proud assurance; the broken phrases of his recitative bespeak his distress. The two rejected lovers decide to join forces (in a duet), but Jason approaches, and Medea, suddenly abandoning her resentment, is overcome with emotion.

The "tender and plaintive" A minor flute ritornello that introduces scene 2 speaks volumes about Medea's love for Jason. This scene between the former lovers is set almost entirely in recitative. There is a great difference between Jason's light, hypocritical distress and Medea's serious, sometimes heartrending tone, as in her long, sobbing phrase "I feel my tears flowing":

or in the harmonization of Jason's "but I am leaving, and you remain behind":

The harmonization with chromaticism in the bass line and the interval of a diminished third between the F-natural and the D-sharp was used by Charpentier in moments of extreme distress, generally in connection with death (see below, the final moments of Créuse). In this instance, Jason's departure is worse than death for Medea. This long recitative is interrupted only by two little airs evoking the state of mind of each character, namely, Jason's "If with all my blood I must save your life" (fast, C major) and Medea's "Nothing is sweeter to me than to believe" (slow, A minor). Showing how far she is willing to go in her love for Jason, Medea now declares that she is ready to sacrifice herself for the glory of her weak hero.

Placed at the very core of the tragedy, scene 3 contains the most beautiful air in the score. Medea, alone, ponders the indifference and weakness of Jason, in whose behalf she has become guilty of the most heinous crimes. In structure and content, Medea's air is strongly reminiscent of Cybèle's ("Espoir si cher et si doux") at the end of Act III of Lully's *Atys*, when the goddess discovers that Atys loves Sangaride. In *Médée*, the *rondeau* refrain is "What a price for my love, what fruit of my crimes!" Charpentier alters the melody in its final statement, extending the line and the tessitura for heightened emphasis. Besides the dramatic string accompaniment, written in the lower ranges and with highly expressive counterpoint, the composer once again makes use of his rich harmonic palette to give this air extraordinary intensity and emotional impact. The string accompaniment anticipates the vocal line (the echo effect continuing throughout), and the use of the subdominant in the second measure, the rising chromaticism—B-flat, B-natural, C—and the ninth and augmented fifth chords in measure 5 all combine to create a dramatic tension missing in Lully's operas.

The first couplet, though more lyrical, perpetuates the lamenting tone of the refrain, the changes in meter and tone with every phrase of the second couplet reflect Medea's inner turmoil. At the line, "[a]nd the oblivion of the hundredfold vows he swore to me," the orchestra is suddenly silent, leaving the voice supported only by an expressive chromatic line in the continuo.

In scene 4, Nérine informs Medea of the imminent wedding of Jason and Créuse and of the reason for the enchantress' exile. This is too much to bear; Medea is finally roused. A powerfully rhythmic prelude in repeated notes introduces her air, "It is done, I am forced to do it." This is in total contrast to the preceding: wide melodic intervals and strongly accented rhythm over a busy thoroughbass, in which the orchestra merely serves to punctuate (but with what force!) every one of her phrases.

Nérine tries to calm Medea. The enchantress is pacified for a moment, but the rushing instrumental bass line expresses her continuing fury, which is released in the ascending vocalise of "volez" (fly). Evil spirits appear "in the air and immediately disappear," bringing her the gown intended for Créuse.

In scene 5, Medea invokes the spirits of Hades ("Black maidens of the Styx"). The scene is essentially dominated by an orchestral texture (prelude) in the low strings (with bassoons doubling the bass violins), with long dissonant pedal points broken by silences.

The Act III divertissement, much more closely linked dramatically to the tragedy than the first two, commences with scene 6. It is a scene of black magic orchestrated by Medea. This kind of scene was enjoyed by audiences of the day and accompanied by numerous stage effects.

The spirits of Hades respond to Medea's call in the form of "a troop of demons" who suddenly appear. Medea commands them to add their flames to the poisons with which she has coated Créuse's gown, to cause the princess to suffer as much as possible. Jealousy (*taille*) and Vengeance (bass), followed by a chorus for three parts (i.e., *hautes-contre, tailles,* and basses), punctuate Medea's orders with their powerful "Hell obeys your command."

In the last scene, Medea calls on the infernal powers a second time ("God of Hades and the dark realms") in the "cruel and harsh" key of E-flat major and over an accompaniment of muted strings. She orders them to cause an earthquake. Then there is a "loud noise from beneath the ground" as the orchestra alternates long notes and repeated notes. Again the allegorical figures and chorus respond to Medea's invocation, interspersed with instrumental airs for the demons, as the stage becomes more and more animated. "Flying demons" bring Créuse's gown and "an infernal cauldron into which they throw the herbs that make up the poison Medea needs to apply to the gown." Then "monsters rise up and, after spreading poison from the cauldron on themselves, they languish and die." In turn, "Medea takes poison from the cauldron and spreads it on the gown."

After these horrible sights, the act ends with a brief line for Medea ("You have served my wrath; it is enough, let us retire"). She then "takes away the gown and the demons disappear," while a whirling orchestral interlude concludes this impressive scene with all requisite fury.

Act IV. In accordance with the baroque law of contrast, the grim spectacle of Medea's lair and her hellish orgies is followed by a return to an atmosphere of peace and light. The decor ("[t]he scene represents the fore-court of a palace and a magnificent garden in the background") and the prelude, marked "tenderly" and scored delicately for flutes alternating with violins, creates a complete mood change.

In scene 1, Cléone sings of the beauty of Créuse dressed in the gown given to her by Medea. In scene 2, the princess enters and dazzles Jason with her charms. It is an utterly *galant* scene, made up of a series of short solos, until the duet ("May love in its just anger").

After a "courtly" encounter between Jason and Oronte (scene 3), the Argian prince finds himself alone with Medea. The enchantress' determination frightens him ("Will the joy of avenging yourself bring the princess back to me?"). Medea, who pretends not to hear, reaffirms her decision in a short, quick air based on an ostinato bass in eighth-note triplets on the C major scale.

The following scene is in two parts. The first part, in the dark key of C minor, shows Medea hesitating one last time, horrified by her destructive plans and remembering that she is "a mother and a wife." A short recitative for Nérine describing the physical appearance of her mistress ("Her eyes wander, her steps are unsteady") leads to the second part, in C major, in which Medea represses her human feelings and gives in freely to her fury. The orchestra, silent since the end of Act III, accompanies the enchantress' gradual changes of mood in a remarkably effective manner.

Enter Créon (scene 6), unaware of Medea's cruel plans. The king of Corinth commands the enchantress to depart, but she agrees to leave only on the condition that Créuse marry Oronte. Surprised by this demand, Créon reminds her of his kingly authority. The enchantress replies: "When you boast of being king, remember that I am

Medea!" Their roles have been reversed since Act II, for it is now Medea who commands and threatens. Créon is infuriated by such audacity and summons his guards. To the sound of a "Charge" followed by an air for "the combatants" in dotted rhythms, "the guards try to seize Medea; she touches them with her wand, whereupon they turn their weapons on each other." Medea continues to challenge the king with more magic spells. As the "Charge" is replayed and Créon tries to approach Medea, "the guards encircle him to prevent it."

In the Act IV divertissement, we suddenly enter a magical fairy kingdom. Medea "makes a circle in the air with her wand, and soon afterwards phantoms appear with the faces of beautiful women." A "tender prelude" for flutes introduces the "gentle phantoms" summoned by the enchantress. A solo, a duet, and three-part chorus for high voices intone rocking, triple-meter airs accompanied by flutes and oboes, while the characters dance gracefully ("First air for the phantoms" and another air for the "phantoms and guards").

This divertissement, ostensibly quite artificial and lacking the tragic tone of the previous acts, gives the grim catastrophe of the last act even greater impact. To the strains of a ritornello evoking the flight of the actors in the divertissement, "the phantoms disappear, and the guards, charmed by their beauty, abandon the king and follow [the phantoms]." Unlike the previous divertissements, this one does not close the act. The magical spells have not succeeded in intimidating Créon, who insists on exercising his authority, so Medea decides to drive the king mad. During a brief orchestral interlude, "Madness appears with her torch and passes before Créon."

The last scene where Créon is confronted with Madness ("Black divinities, what do you want of me?") is particularly impressive for its low-string orchestration (*hautes-contre, tailles, quintes,* and basses), not unlike that accompanying Samuel's ghost in the prologue of *David et Jonathas.* Créon's incoherent speech undergoes constant changes of meter and is broken by silences and stretched over wide, evocative intervals.

A furious interlude closes the act.

Act V. "The stage represents Medea's palace."

This is the only act without a divertissement, which renders its brutally tragic outcome only more horrible. In scene 1, Nérine (after the instrumental prelude) describes Créon's demented condition. Medea, still haunted by Jason's betrayal, is far from moved to pity by the news. Instead, it only rekindles her desire for vengeance, which she decides to take out on her children. No sooner has she blindly uttered the murderous words, "Let us not spare them," than she realizes the atrocity of what she has said. After a long silence, she repeats the same words in an altogether different tone: the note-values lengthen and become regular, the melody is immobilized, the orchestra supports the voice on the same rhythm, and there is a move to the subdominant, with a suspended cadence in place of the perfect cadence of her first utterance.

Then, still accompanied by full five-part string sonorities, Medea continues, torn between her desire for vengeance and maternal love. The former gets the better of her.

Mirroring scene 2 of Act II, Medea confronts Créuse in scene 2 of Act V. This time, however, it is Créuse who comes to plead with Medea to save her father. The gulf between the two characters is widened through the use of contrasting modes (C minor for Créuse, C major for Medea). The enchantress repeats the same conditions she proposed to Créon: Créuse must renounce Jason and marry Oronte. Before the princess can give her answer, the orchestra and the "invisible" Chorus of Corinthians interrupt the two women's dialogue with a poignant lament ("Fatal misfortune, pitiless fate!").

In the following scene, Cléone enters and explains what Créon's madness led him to do: he killed Oronte before ending his own life. The chorus, now on stage, repeats the doleful lament before striking out at the gods' injustice ("Let us refuse our incense") in a quicker tempo and in the major mode.

With Oronte dead, Créuse expresses her revulsion over the crimes of Medea. Her vain protests only serve to precipitate the inevitable outcome of the tragedy. "Medea touches Créuse with her wand and exits." The orchestra seethes beneath her gesture, which takes effect almost immediately. Créuse writhes in pain as her vocal line becomes almost a cry ("I burn"). She then begins to succumb, overcome by the pain that ravages her (descending sevenths).

Jason (scene 6) discovers Créuse in agony. Time suddenly seems to be suspended as the two lovers sing their final duet ("Alas, alas, about to be united by the sweetest chains"). Bathed in calm serenity, the atmosphere is in surprising contrast to the intense suffering of the preceding scenes. The sad, tender voices of Jason and Créuse blend and interlace as if to ward off the inevitability of the death about to separate them.

While the composer and librettist spare us the sight of Oronte and Créon dying, the final moments of Créuse unfold before our eyes in a passage of overwhelming, indeed, nearly unbearable poignancy. The orchestra, silent since the exit of Medea, reenters in the "dark and plaintive" key of F minor, anticipating Créuse's vocal line. Her melody, supported by long, suspended chords, unfolds in stepwise motion, sparing of itself, in three descending waves, each time a step lower. The discourse is broken by numerous silences. After one last ascent ("It is over"), the last notes fade away in an unexpected, impressive broken cadence. The orchestra alone brings the scene to a close with the pathos of the diminished third in the bass line (D-flat–B-natural) which, in Charpentier's works, is invariably associated with death.

Alone and distraught, Jason cries vengeance. Medea appears in the air on a dragon. The heartless woman informs her lover of the last crime she has committed in achieving her revenge: she has stabbed his children to death. Leaving Jason overcome by such horrors,

> Medea rushes through the air on her dragon, and at the same time the statues and other ornaments of the palace disintegrate. Demons appear from all sides carrying fire in their hands and

setting the palace ablaze. These demons vanish, night falls and the edifice remains no more than ruins and monsters, after which a hail of fire descends.

To the sounds of a rushing symphony, the work concludes abruptly with the triumph of Medea and the desolation of Corinth.

With *Médée*, Charpentier once again produces evidence that his genius, far from being only that of an outstanding composer for the church, achieves its most complete expression in the field of dramatic music, even when working under difficult constraints. *Médée* is, in fact, one of the most beautiful and one of the most interesting musical tragedies composed during the entire period when the genre existed and flourished, from Lully to Rameau. Charpentier, on the Surintendant's ground, demonstrates ample ability to match his rival on all levels: in overall structure, a feeling for stage effects and dance combined with powerful drama, a gift for instrumentation and a brilliant use of the orchestra in the service of the drama, and a careful proportioning of recitatives, airs, duets, and small and large choruses. Moreover, Charpentier stamped his work with several personal touches: the Italian episode, invisible choruses, orchestral effects (Créon's mad scene), and harmonic subtleties whose effects have been repeatedly pointed out.

If the work did not hold the stage for long, it was not because the score was lacking in quality, as was the case of certain contemporary tragedies in music.[25] Indeed, Charpentier was not the only composer of the period to suffer criticism for having indulged in an overly individual style. Desmarest, in connection with his tragedies *Circé* (1694) and especially *Théagène et Cariclée* (1695), also endured the bitter reproach of having preferred to "work on his own" instead of having "copied M. Lully."[26] Those failures did not discourage Desmarest, however, since he went on to present other new works at the Académie Royale. As a former pupil of Lully, he was much in favor at court, and such setbacks could not have had much effect on his career in general. For Charpentier it was another story. *Médée* was his first and last tragedy in music performed at the Académie Royale. How did he take this failure? Did he abandon stage music for good, being upset by the unjust criticism of his work? Or was he not affected by it at all, having experimented with a genre in which he did not find the same freedom of expression that had blossomed in *David et Jonathas*? We will most likely never know the whole truth.

Chapter 15

The Sainte-Chapelle

*Today, the treasurer, being well informed concerning the good life,
conduct, and ability of master Marc-Antoine Charpentier, native
of the diocese of Paris, told the [Society of Jesus] that he had
chosen and appointed him to fill the post of music master of the
choirboys.*

Register of the Sainte-Chapelle, 28 June 1698

Founded by Saint Louis as a sanctuary for the crown of thorns and
other holy relics of the Passion of Christ, the Sainte-Chapelle thereafter enjoyed the special attention of the kings of France, who
throughout history donated other priceless treasures to it. A marvel of
Gothic style, the perfection of the church's architecture and the airy
splendor of its stained glass have always been greatly admired. But
the Chapelle of the kings of France was not only "one of the most
beautiful abodes in paradise" (in the words of a fourteenth-century
theologian); from the Middle Ages to the French Revolution it also
served as an important center of musical activity. In addition to
Charpentier, composers such as Claudin de Sermisy, Pierre Certon,
René Ouvrard, and Nicolas Bernier were associated with the
Chapelle.

The music master's position of the Sainte-Chapelle was one of the
most prestigious posts a musician could aspire to, second only to that
of the Chapelle Royale. Did Charpentier ever aspire to it well before
his appointment in 1698? The allusions to his predecessor Chaperon
in the *Epitaphium Carpentarii* lead one to presume he did. The composer, having reached the age of fifty-five, had been in the service of

the Jesuits for ten years. *Médée* was his only venture beyond his duties for the Society. In spite of the prestige of the Maison Professe, the range of activities in his present post was considerably narrower than the range of activities in the post left vacant by the death of François Chaperon on 20 May 1698.

The Sainte-Chapelle register entry for Saturday, 28 June 1698 reads as follows:

> Today, the treasurer, being well informed concerning the good life, conduct, and ability of master Marc-Antoine Charpentier, native of the diocese of Paris, told the [Society of Jesus] that he had chosen and appointed him to fill the post of music master of the choirboys left vacant by the death of François Chaperon; further that, Monsieur l'Abbé de Neuchelles being about to propose a regular cleric to serve the church under its prebend, [the treasurer] had proposed the aforementioned Charpentier to him. That although he was quite convinced that he composed and knew music to perfection, he nevertheless had sent him to the Cantor to be examined in accordance with the rules and custom of the Sainte-Chapelle. [The Cantor] having found him capable, [the treasurer said] he would be appointed before the next high mass, that he will put him in charge of the regular sermon in the sacristy in the presence of Monsieur l'Abbé de Neuchelles and others who will be in attendance, and that he will assign him the place in the choir formerly occupied by the deceased, which is the last high stall on the right side. Which was done and executed as stated above.[1]

Three days later,

> Master Marc-Antoine Charpentier . . . requested that the [Society of Jesus] place him on the roster to be paid in future for his attendance at religious services, like the other clerics. He was granted this, beginning last Saturday when the Treasurer received him, the day he began attending services.[2]

Though Charpentier was chosen to fill this post, he had not been the only candidate. There had been at least one other, namely, Sébastien de Brossard, who wanted to leave Strasbourg where he was master of the chapel at the cathedral. For once, however, luck was on the side of Charpentier, who enjoyed the protection of Philippe of Orléans, his former pupil. Brossard explained:

> Fleuriau, then treasurer, had one of his relatives write me in Strasbourg where I was at the time. It took a week to receive the letter and to travel by mail coach to Paris; during that week, Sieur Charpentier had Monseigneur le Duc de Chartres, his disciple,

act so efficiently, that the Abbé Fleuriau was obliged to give him
the post. I found [the post] filled upon my arrival, but I got over
my disappointment swiftly.[3]

Though not an ecclesiastic (which Brossard was), Charpentier
was appointed a cleric, a requisite imposed by his new position. This
practice, however, though apparently quite common, was not to
everyone's liking.

> I confess that music masters who are appointed in Paris are all
> too frequently laymen: Charpentier and Bernier at the Sainte-
> Chapelle, Campra and Lalouette at Notre-Dame, and so forth.
> But those and a few others were people who received special
> consideration, due to their distinguished ability.[4]

When Charpentier arrived at the Sainte-Chapelle, the institution's administration had remained essentially unchanged since
1248. Under the supervision of a treasurer (Louis Gaston Fleuriau
until 1699, followed by Antoine Bochard de Champigny) was a large
assemblage of canons, chaplains, clerics, churchwardens, bailiffs, and
officers. In the late seventeenth century, the choir school numbered
five to eight ordinary chaplains, six to twelve ordinary clerics, and
eight choirboys. It was one of the two largest choir schools in Paris,
along with that of Notre-Dame. It was under the supervision of the
cantor (Michel Gobert between 1683 and 1708). A substitute
treasurer, the cantor specifically was in charge of religious services
and choir discipline. It was the music master, however, who directed
musical performances.

As head of the choir, Charpentier had to participate in all
ceremonies at the Sainte-Chapelle. His duties also included composing music and instructing the choirboys in solfeggio, plainchant,
counterpoint, and vocal technique. Did he also teach them composition, as sometimes occurred at the Sainte-Chapelle of Dijon or at
Notre-Dame?[5] René Ouvrard, one of Charpentier's predecessors at
the Sainte-Chapelle, taught the art of composition to the young
Étienne Loulié, then a choirboy.[6]

The following event reveals something about the qualities
expected in a music master. Seeking a music master in 1702, the
diocese of Toul in Lorraine turned to the "three most celebrated
masters in Paris—Lalouette at Notre-Dame, Charpentier at the
Sainte-Chapelle, and Garnier at Saint Germain l'Auxerrois."
Charpentier and his colleagues replied to Father du Mureau that a
good master must know how "to compose two sorts of music, one over

plain-chant for making counterpoint, which is the touchstone for knowing whether a man knows the rules of composition, the other on . . . psalms, canticles, or the like, for making descriptive music."[7]

Choirboys in the Sainte-Chapelle were selected on the basis of their seriousness and the quality of their voice. Poor candidates, those "having neither voice nor ear," were rejected. Recruited around the age of seven or eight, some of them remained in the Society's service for ten years. During the services, they were attired in "albs [white linen robes] and black woolen copes" and stood "on the cobblestone floor of the choir."

A grammar teacher (e.g., André Convers from 1696 to 1726) instructed them in literature and Latin. He and the music master received wages (3000–4000 livres for the latter) and were boarded and lodged with the choirboys at the royal treasury's expense. They lived in the choir school house on Rue de Jérusalem. The building included bedrooms for the masters and the choirboys, a kitchen, a refectory, an infirmary, and a library containing dictionaries and Latin books. It was the grammar teacher's responsibility to escort the choirboys from the house to the church for the services in the most orderly manner, then to bring them back along with the music master.

The Sainte-Chapelle had an organist, also lodged on the Palais grounds. For more than a century, the post was occupied by members of the La Guerre dynasty: Michel (the composer of *Le Triomphe de l'Amour*, the first French pastorale in music) from 1633 to 1678; Jérôme, his son, from 1678 to 20 September 1698, when he was replaced by his brother, Marin. The latter died 16 July 1704, so Jérôme resumed the organist's duties until 1738. Marin de La Guerre was at the Sainte-Chapelle almost exactly the same period of time that Charpentier held the post of music master. The two men presumably knew each other earlier, since the husband of Élisabeth Jacquet was first organist at the Jesuit Église Saint-Louis in 1679 before being appointed to Saint-Séverin in 1690, and ultimately to the Sainte-Chapelle. The organ was built several times and restored again in 1671 and in 1697 (new stops were added) before its complete transformation in 1771 by the famous Clicquot. A small portable organ was also employed.

Life at the Sainte-Chapelle was hardly as calm and contemplative as one might imagine. Disagreements and quarrels occurred almost constantly. Everyday concerns of individuals, matters of rank and seniority, anything at all might lead to petty, sometimes violent, disputes. Legal proceedings that members of the Society and those in the choir school brought against each other sometimes continued for decades, like the one between the canons and the perpetual chaplains, who wished to be exempted from having to sing at services like ordinary chaplains. After thirty-eight years of litigation, the chaplains finally won their case and were exempted from that obligation in 1681 by royal decree.

In addition to the misbehavior of some or the unwillingness of others to cooperate, there were disturbances brought on by the frequent turnover in the choir school personnel, illnesses and requests for time off, temporary employment, and constant rivalry with neighboring parishes. All this gives a more precise, complete picture of the church's truly "high strung" climate.[8]

At the "general assembly of Monday, 1 October 1703" attended by "the six perpetual chaplains, the ordinary chaplains, and clerics of the treasurers and canons, the assistant church wardens and the music master and grammar instructor," the treasurer was forced to call certain members of the Society to order. First was "Master Alexandre Charpentier, one of the ordinary clerics," for the "injurious and impertinent speeches" that he "continues to make" and "his defiance of the reminders he is given concerning his duty." Another time

> [t]he treasurer made a speech strongly condemning the negligence of several persons who make a habit of not arriving at church until after the service has begun, or, when in attendance, sing very nonchalantly and even excuse themselves from doing so altogether for very slight indispositions. He then expressed his indignation over the long-reigning abuse among almost all the chaplains and clerics, who take off at least two mornings per week, even feast days and Sundays, and warned them that, in accordance with the proceedings of the twenty-sixth of last month, those who take off more than one morning for their repose or who are absent from service on Sundays and feast days shall be deprived of their allowance for the services they do not attend.[9]

The music masters sometimes gave the Society great cause for concern. Arthus Aux Cousteaux, initially a cleric *haute-contre*, and after 1642 a master, was almost dismissed several times for the "insolent and irreverent conduct" that he "commits daily," like beginning the service "most of the time seated in his pulpit without standing up, rushing into the psalmody without waiting for the versicle to finish and without observing any pause for meditation, speaking and scolding in church often as loudly as those who are singing."[10]

In 1687, legal proceedings were initiated against François Chaperon, who had violated Society rules. In reply to the *Mémoire* (now lost) he wrote in his defense, the chaplains and clerics printed a text that spelled out the rights and duties of the music master. The tone is harsh, perhaps excessively so, in proportion to Chaperon's errors. The administrative body of the Sainte-Chapelle in this case exhibited a total lack of consideration for its music master, whom it treated as "an inferior," and showed its desire to keep him occupied with clearly defined duties that must not be overstepped:

> For indeed, Chaperon possesses no office or benefice in the Sainte-Chapelle, and renders service to the Church only in consideration of the wages he receives, just like the master organist who performs and composes as well as he . . . and the one has no more connection to service of the Church than the other.
>
> The ties keeping them being wages and financial gain, it should not be surprising that they often change jobs, either by being dismissed or by leaving voluntarily for a more lucrative position. It seems that their choirs pass on to them the inconstant, fickle qualities of sound and wind which are their lot, transporting them abruptly from one diocese to another, and from church to church within the same diocese. This is the common condition of all restless, wandering mercenaries until the hammer of necessity stops them and nails them down.
>
> . . . .
>
> It is true that the choirmaster's role must always carry with it a certain amount of stature and privileges; but it is only over those whom said Chaperon has the right to teach, like the choirboys, that his [music] master's authority extends, and not at all over the chaplains and clerics who learn nothing from him and who are all capable of teaching *him* something of the art of singing and composing, in which they are just as qualified as he.
>
> . . . .
>
> [I]n whatever way one regards his duties, he seems to be merely a mercenary paid for all the work that he must do, and if by virtue of the treasurer's commission, which he improperly describes as a fee, he is placed among the officers, it still cannot be said that he is a member of the administrative corps. He is with the corps of the Sainte-Chapelle, of which his alleged fee does not make him a member, since he may be separated from it without injuring the body [*corps*]. He is with the choirboys, like hair, nails, and other superfluous parts of the body that can be cut off when desired, for music is not the essence of the service which occurs in church; it is merely a commodity and a formality.[11]

Unlike Arthus Aux Cousteaux and Chaperon, Charpentier was not discussed very much. The reasons for that probably stem from his natural discretion and the lack of scandal in his life, conduct such as was expected of a music master who was disciplined and mindful of the Society's imposed hierarchy. The registers' sometimes long-winded accounts mention Charpentier's name only to mark his appointment and to announce his death, a smooth five and one-half years, with no record of misconduct, no reprimands.

Like his colleagues, the music master was present at the general assemblies of 1 July 1700 and 1 October 1703, but not at the one on Wednesday, 2 January 1704, a little less than two months before his death. Was he ill? Unfortunately we will never know.

The Sainte-Chapelle was a stronghold of tradition. The canonical hours (e.g., the Little Hours, including matins, lauds, vespers) were celebrated by the entire ecclesiastical college, and Gregorian chant and psalmody were used in it. On special occasions, the music took on archaic forms, such as the "very grave and very pious" fauxbourdons sung at the Dauphin's funeral service in 1711 and at the king's service in 1715. Besides the organist, the only instrumentalists connected with the choir school were those who played serpents, bassoons, and cornets—the traditional church instruments.

To enrich certain musical performances, Chaperon in 1680 introduced the custom of *musiques extraordinaires* calling on "outside musicians to fortify the music of the Sainte-Chapelle."[12] This practice continued for the rest of the century and into the eighteenth century. Not only were singers and instrumentalists not belonging to the choir school engaged, but sometimes composers outside the Sainte-Chapelle were called on, such as Delalande and Lalouette for the Tenebrae of 1680.[13]

We do not know the exact number of musicians who were added to the approximately twenty-five permanent singers (the scoring itself being approximate and variable). For the two funeral services mentioned above, the registers indicate the use of "a dozen musicians" for one and only "six extra musicians" for the other.[14] These fluctuations probably depended on the music master's requirements, on the importance of the occasion, and on the Society's willingness to pay additional fees. From what we have been able to find out about the performance conditions of some of Charpentier's works, there would seem to have been as many as forty performers in a piece like *Judicium Salomonis* (H. 422).[15]

The two-story structure of the Sainte-Chapelle originally allowed the king and members of his family living in the Palais direct access to the upper chapel from their apartments. The lower chapel, dedicated to the Virgin, was reserved for the Palais servants. Enshrining the holy relics of Christ's Passion, the upper chapel had a single nave illuminated by an immense multicolored stained glass window. Until the French Revolution, a loft of fine Renaissance-style woodwork separated the choir from the nave, with two adjacent lateral altars used for worship. Two large recesses level with the jube (still extant today) served as seats of honor for the treasurer and the cantor, and on ceremonial days for the king and the queen or their guests.

Wooden stalls enhanced the appearance of the choir. The high altar, placed at the front of the apse, consisted of a long flagstone table surrounded by decorative sculptures, notably by bronze angels, the work of Germain Pilon. Behind the altar stood a bronze-gilt reliquary roughly one meter in height. It contained the holy relics and was therefore locked with ten different keys. Dating from 1631, it was a scale-model reproduction of the Sainte-Chapelle decorated with pearls, precious stones, and fifteen figures of angels bearing different musical instruments. At the west end of the chapel was the organ loft (it still exists) covered by a baldaquin. Two little spiral stairways on either side provided access to the loft. There, on Good Fridays, the holy relics were exposed for the devotion of the congregation, invalids being allowed to touch them.

Ceremonies took place in the upper chapel. On solemn feast days, "when responsories and antiphons would be sung from the book," the musicians were grouped on two opposite sides. Sometimes, however, one side would sound "weaker than the other either due to the inequality of the voices or to an imbalance in the number of singers, which greatly diminished the majesty and beauty of the service and the music." It was therefore arranged to have "both sides sing together."[16] For large performances with *musiques extraordinaires,* platforms were erected in the choir for the musicians.

Processions were invested with a great deal of pomp, especially for the Feast of Saint Louis, which would be attended by

> the religious of certain orders. . . . On the day of the Feast of Saint Louis, the Cordeliers officiate, while the Jacobins only watch, though it is a Jacobin who delivers the panegyric in honor of Saint Louis. The next year the Jacobins officiate and the Cordeliers attend, and it is a Cordelier who delivers the panegyric. The religious of those two orders come in procession

and in vast numbers on the eve of Saint Louis, to say the first vespers; the following day, they say high mass after the procession in which they carry Saint Louis's crown of thorns. The treasurer, the canons, and the singers of the Sainte-Chapelle and all the lower choir participate in this procession and chant alternately with the religious, each officiating according to custom. Upon the return of the procession, the treasurer who officiates pontifically in the Sainte-Chapelle delivers the orations and gives the benediction, after which he retires along with all the canons and the entire lower choir.[17]

In his five and one-half years at the Sainte-Chapelle, Charpentier seems to have composed relatively little.[18] We count only nine works, though, generally speaking, they are all masterpieces. These last compositions are identifiable by their placement in the manuscripts and by their titles (e.g., *Motet pour une longue offrande*, H. 434) but also, in the case of five of them (i.e., *Psalmus David LXX, 3ᵉ psaume du premier nocturne du mercredi saint*, H. 228; *Psalmus David 26tus, 3ᵉ psaume du premier nocturne du jeudi saint*, H. 229; *Psalmus David 15tus, 3ᵉ psaume du premier nocturne du vendredi saint*, H. 230; *Assumpta est Maria Missa six vocibus cum simphonia*, H. 11; and *Judicium Salomonis*, H. 422), by the names of singers connected with the Society of Jesus: choirboys Simon Beaulieu, Charles Bersan, and Denis Bruslard; the *gagiste* Jacques Cousin (*haute-contre*); ordinary clerics Eloy-Augustin Antheaume (*basse-taille*), Jacques Molaret[19] (*taille*), François Royer (*basse-taille*), and Claude Terrier (*haute-contre*); and ordinary chaplains Jacques Dangoulesme (*haute-contre*), Claude Touzelin (*basse-taille*), and Pierre-Philippe Warnier (*taille*). In *Judicium Salomonis* the role of God was given to a singer who was not a member of the Sainte-Chapelle, M. Vignon, certainly Michel Vignon, husband of Marie-Jeanne Danican Philidor and singer in the Chapelle Royale and the King's Chamber.

Only *Judicium Salomonis* is precisely dated: 1702.[20] *Assumpta est Maria*, which directly precedes it in the manuscripts, is probably from 15 August of the same year.[21] In the Arabic-numeral series of the *Mélanges*, the Tenebrae psalm settings (H. 228–230) indicate the presence of M. Antheaume, who left the Sainte-Chapelle to enter the service of the royal music on 29 August 1699. Since Charpentier did not arrive until June 1698, the psalm settings were therefore composed for Holy Week of 1699. Consequently, *Motet pour une longue offrande* (H. 434), *Élévation* (H. 273), and *In nativitate Domini Nostri Jesu Christi Canticum* (H. 421) can be dated 1698, and (the sixth) *Te Deum à 4 voix* (H. 148) in the first months of 1699.

On 20 August 1699, a little less than two months following Charpentier's appointment,

> Monsieur the Treasurer told the [Society of Jesus] that the king of England had sent one of his chaplains to inform him that he and the queen had vowed to visit the Sainte-Chapelle on the Feast of Saint Louis between four and five o'clock to attend *Salut* [evening service] there, whereupon it was announced that the vespers bells be rung at one-thirty for [vespers] to begin at two o'clock sharp. Inasmuch as there is [normally] no Salut on that day, the music master [should] be alerted to prepare a motet and a few other prayers with a *Domine Salvum fac Regem* set to music.[22]

On Monday, 25 August, the Feast of Saint Louis,

> Monsieur the Treasurer assembled the [Society of Jesus] in the sacristy immediately after the procession, since the king and the queen of England had informed him they would be leaving Saint-Germain-en-Laye before two o'clock to arrive at the Sainte-Chapelle at around four o'clock.... that the *tapissier* would be instructed to bring a carpet to be laid between the high altar and the door to the choir; that at the foot of the high altar a prie-dieu covered in crimson velvet embellished all around with gold fringe would be set in place ... with two armchairs of the same pattern for the king and queen and several stools to be behind the ladies in their retinue; that the little organ in the middle of the choir would be moved toward the left-side stalls of Messieurs the Canons where the musical ensemble will be placed; that since Saint Louis's crown of thorns is displayed on the altar from the procession until the end of vespers, the true cross given to kings for worship would [also] be displayed there.[23]

The last manuscripts contain no motets in honor of Saint Louis and no *Domine salvum* settings. Are the compositions lost, or did Charpentier, alerted only five days before the ceremony and hence lacking the time to write any new pieces, turn to earlier scores? For example, there is the motet *In honorem Sancti Ludovici Regis Galliae Canticum* (H. 365) which was recopied (H. 365a), though incompletely, into the "problematic" cahier [b] also containing the variant copies of two little motets (*Pour le Saint Esprit*, H. 364a, and *Élévation à 3 voix pareilles*, H. 264a), and the end of the *Messe des morts à 4 voix* (H. 7a). Was the mass then used for the funeral service of Nicolas Dantard? The register entry for 10 July 1698 tells us that the perpetual chaplain will be interred this evening around five o'clock at the foot of the altar of his chapel of Saint Blaise in the lower Sainte-Chapelle; that after vespers, the service for the dead with nine lessons with lauds will be sung, and tomorrow around eight o'clock a *high Requiem Mass* [author's italics] for the repose of his soul, and that there will be a performance in the nave, with Monsieur the Chantre officiating.[24]

Although *Te Deum à 4 voix* (H. 148) seems to have been composed at the beginning of 1699, it was not until 1702 that the Sainte-Chapelle registers began referring to several Te Deum performances commemorating Louis XIV's latest victories: on 9 September 1702 for "the victory that the king's army won in Italy over the emperor's"; on 25 October for "the advantage achieved by His Majesty's armies over the imperial army in Germany"; on 21 March 1703 for "the capture of Fort du Kell by His Majesty's troops commanded by the Maréchal de Vilars"; on 11 July for "the victory won in Flanders"; on 22 September "for the capture of Brisac by the king's army commanded by Monseigneur le Duc de Bourgogne"; on 28 November "for the capture of Landau and the victory won in Germany over the emperor's troops by those of the king commanded by the Maréchal de Tallard"; and finally on 5 January 1704 "for the capture of Augsburg by the elector of Bavaria united with the king against the emperor in support of Monseigneur le Duc d'Anjou in the unbroken succession of the king of Spain." Was the last of Charpentier's Te Deum settings performed on every single one of these occasions?

The Sainte-Chapelle is situated in the heart of the walled enclosure of what was formerly the palace of the king, and later of Parlement, and which after the French Revolution became the Palais de Justice. The reopening of Parlement, which took place annually on 12 November, "the day after [the Feast of] Saint-Martin," was commemorated by the celebration of a mass, called *Messe rouge* because of the magistrates' scarlet robes. It was sung in the chapel of the great hall of the Palais (today the Salle des Pas-Perdus) by "the entire corps of the Sainte-Chapelle, ordinary chaplains and clerics and the music master with his choirboys."[25] As in the Sainte-Chapelle, the musicians were placed on risers (*"échafault"*).

For these ceremonies, Charpentier composed *Motet pour une longue offrande* or *Motet pour l'offertoire de la messe rouge*[26] (H. 434) in 1698, and *Judicium Salomonis* (H. 422) in 1702. Both works are of large dimensions and sumptuously scored (for soloists, choir, string

orchestra, flutes, and oboes) and directly inspired by the circumstances of their premieres, the justice of humanity being transposed
to the realm of God.

Were any other compositions, which are lost today, destined for
these ceremonies? It is possible, although it is just as likely that the
same work was performed several times.

The *Mercure Galant,* which every year reported on Parlement's
opening ceremony, mentions the existence of Charpentier's music
only three times:

> The convening of the Parlement occurred on Wednesday the
> 12th of this month, and commenced with a solemn mass cele-
> brated by Berthier, first bishop of Blois, in the chapel of the great
> hall of the Palais. Messieurs of the Parlement attended it in the
> usual fashion, the presidents in red robes and ermine fur, and the
> council members and secretaries of the court in red robes. The
> music, which was composed by Charpentier, music master of the
> Sainte-Chapelle, was deemed most excellent.[27]

Charpentier died in February 1704 at the Sainte-Chapelle. He
was sixty years old. Nothing is known about his final days or the cause
of death.

> Sunday, 24 February 1704. This day, the Treasurer called a spe-
> cial assembly of the [Society of Jesus] in his quarters after
> vespers concerning the death of Marc-Antoine Charpentier,
> music master of the Sainte-Chapelle, who died this morning
> around seven o'clock. [The Society of Jesus] has decided to inter
> him tomorrow after vespers, to sing the vespers for the dead and
> matins with nine lessons in the presence of the corpse, and the
> day after tomorrow, after the daily matins and lauds, the lauds for
> the dead, and, before the daily mass, a high mass for the dead at
> which M. Gobert, cantor, will officiate.[28]

Was the "high mass for the dead" written by the defunct music
master, who had composed such beautiful masses? Charpentier was
interred in the Sainte-Chapelle, but the registers do not specify the
exact location.[29] Certain members of the personnel, mainly
treasurers and canons, had a sepulchre in the lower chapel (one can
still see a rather large number of flagstone memorials there) and in
the little church of Saint-Michel, on the grounds of the Sainte-
Chapelle. Although the music master was not entitled to such consideration, even after his death, the minutest details concerning
Charpentier's burial fees are described at great length:

Saturday, 8 March 1704. This day . . . master Denis Ragot *sous-chefcier*, appeared before the [Society of Jesus] to say that he was still in possession of seventeen pounds of wax candles from the burial of the late Marc-Antoine Charpentier, of which he is ready to make such use as [the Society] wishes. The [Society] decided that it will give one-half pound of candles to each of the Messieurs [of the Sainte-Chapelle] and that [Ragot] will take the rest.

This same day, the [Society] examined the memorandum of the allotments which must be made to those who attended the vigils and nine lessons at the mass and interment of the defunct Marc-Antoine Charpentier, music master. Noticing that the expense for this was excessive, [the Society] decided to reduce it. The example made of it will serve in future upon the deaths of perpetual chaplains, ordinary chaplains and clerics of Messieurs and other officials.

A record of the sums to be distributed to all who took part in the composer's obsequies follows:

[T]he treasurer, to each of the canons, to the perpetual chaplains, to the ordinary chaplains and clerics, to the officiating priest, to the deacon and assistant-deacon, to the choristers, for the celebrant, to the choirboys, to the grammar master, to the assistant church wardens, to the *sous-chefcier*, to the vicar of the lower Sainte-Chapelle, to the *habitués*, to each usher, to the embroiderer, for the bier and the grave, for the borrowed candelabra, for four Augustinians who carried the corpse, for those who prayed to God next to the corpse until it was carried away, to the *distributeur*, to the cross-bearer, to the bell ringer for the ringing of the bell.[30]

For more than a month, the post left vacant by the death of Charpentier remained unfilled. On 5 April, Nicolas Bernier, music master of the Église Saint-Germain-l'Auxerrois, was chosen by the treasurer to occupy it.

Et lux perpetua luceat ei[1]

To anyone who wanted to become a composer, Marc-Antoine Charpentier would have said, "Go to Italy, that is the real source. I have not given up hope, however, that one day the Italians will come to learn from us, but I will no longer be here."[2] Charpentier would have advised thus in anticipation of that mingling of styles that French composers at the start of the eighteenth century would not be long in achieving. The author of *Médée* died just as Italian music was becoming fashionable in France. Within the space of a few years, an extraordinary amount of Italian airs, cantatas, and sonatas burst on the scene, though apparently without anyone remembering that Charpentier was the first French composer to have led the way to these different genres in his own country.

The future of the oratorio was to be quite different, however. Very few works of that genre were composed before 1750. As for the concerted mass, it still proved of very little interest for French composers in an era when the motets of Delalande and Campra were flourishing at Versailles, and when sacred music was beginning to leave the chapel for the concert hall thanks to the popularity of the Concert Spirituel.

Charpentier was as solitary a figure in public as he was in his private life. A bachelor, his relationships with others seem to have been kept primarily on a professional level. His teaching activities, however, reveal that he had a need to share and communicate his knowledge. He appears today to have possessed a curious combination of modesty and ambition, contradictory feelings that are difficult to sort out. We are left with a two-sided picture. On one side, we see a conscientious composer who took pride in his craft and left his neatly penned manuscripts in good order. On the other side we see an artist struggling for legitimate recognition. Although he was gifted with originality and an avid curiosity, those qualities seem to have had difficulty asserting themselves during the course of the various patronages Charpentier enjoyed. Considering the lack of recognition he received, that capacity for opening doors must have gradually turned inward. Charpentier ended his career most unobtrusively, in the highly conservative setting of the Sainte-Chapelle. He left no will; his only personal effects seem to have been the manuscripts that his nephew inherited.

Charpentier is the most paradoxical of all composers. A marginal figure in comparison to some of his contemporaries covered by glory and honors, he is now beginning to be studied and appreciated with the kind of interest that none of those same contemporaries inspire, at least for the moment.

Backward-looking and innovative at the same time, Charpentier, like Monteverdi, had no problem working in both the old and the new styles. At the turning point between two eras, he cultivated the polyphonic tradition of the old masters, composed *a cappella* or in fauxbourdon, but also marvelously exploited all the contrasting effects of the concerted style. His concept of harmony, the keystone of his entire work, was based—with its dissonances and cross relations—just as much on purely expressive notions as on formal principles of tonality then being established.

His music is French, but with a strain of pathos and sensuality that the Italian baroque possessed in abundance and that French classicism was trying to repress. He was also Italianate, though he never completely rejected the moderation and restraint of the French esthetic. Charpentier's works consistently display that concern for diversity which the present volume has tried to emphasize.

Charpentier is one of the few composers who equally excelled in music for the church and in music for the theater, even if in the latter he was unable to realize its full potential. Essentially a composer of vocal music, he was constantly aware of the expressive possibilities of the text. His most beautiful pages are those in which word and music unite and lift one another into a higher emotional plane. Like all baroque artists—and Charpentier was more baroque than any other French composer of his period—he had a taste for the magnificence and the splendors of the theater and the church, although that taste was always tempered by deep, genuine emotion. Not at all ostentatious in manner, the art of Charpentier belongs to the domain of poignant introspection, which probably explains why it moves us so deeply today. Serious in tone most of the time, Charpentier also knew how to be light and comic. His music, however, only rarely explodes and never lets out all the stops. It is guided by a self-restraint or modesty that probably reflects the composer's temperament.

While there are still many gray areas concerning Charpentier's life and personality, our knowledge about him has nevertheless increased considerably over the past few years, and it will certainly continue to be enriched by new discoveries in the future. His music, for the most part still unknown either on disc or in concert, is waiting for performers to continue to reveal all its facets, and for an ever-growing public finally to discover Charpentier as "one of the most excellent composers France ever had."

Appendix 1

Epitaphium Carpentarii

The humorous aspect of *Epitaphium Carpentarii* (Funeral Oration of Charpentier) has been described earlier (see Chapters 1 and 12). The passage for the three angels ("Profitentes unitatem") is a shameless parody of the liturgy. The humor of the text derives largely from the puns on the names Carissimi (which in Latin means "very dear") and especially Chaperon (*Capronus* can be associated with the Latin *caprinus*, meaning "goat"). Each reference to Chaperon and his music (e.g., *caproni musicam, asininos capronini tritus*) must therefore be interpreted in this satirical and pejorative sense.

Interlocutores: Ignatius, Marcellus, Umbra Carpentarii, tres angeli

Speakers: Ignatius, Marcellus, Ghost of Charpentier, Three Angels

IGNATIUS: Quid audio? Quod murmur horrisonum simul es harmonicum aures meas pepulis?

IGNATIUS: What do I hear? What terrible roar, yet similar to harmony, strikes my ears?

MARCELLUS: Quid video? Terra tremit. Hic lapis inhiat. Hic tumulus evomit umbram. O portentum, fugiamus!

MARCELLUS: What do I see? The earth trembles. The rock gapes open. The tomb disgorges a ghost. O horror, let us flee!

UMBRA: Amici, viatores, nolite timere! Sistite gradum et audite verba oris mei! Hic terminus viae et vitae vestrae ac meae. Ille ego qui natus pridem ac notus eram saeculo; en denatus hoc late o nudus nullusque sepulchro pulvis, finis et esca vermium. Satis vixi, sed parum si spectetur aeternitas.

GHOST: Friends, travelers, have no fear. Stop and listen to my words. This is the end of life's path—yours and mine. I am he who was born long ago and was widely known in this century, but now I am naked and nothing, dust in a tomb, at an end, and food of worms. I have lived enough, though too briefly in comparison to eternity.

UMBRA, IGNATIUS, MARCELLUS: O aeternitas quam longa, o vita quam brevis es!

UMBRA: Musicus eram, inter bonos a bonis, et inter ignaros ab ignaris nuncupatus. Et cum multo major numerus esset eorum qui me spernebant quam qui laudabant, musica mihi parvus honos sed magnum onus fuit; et, sicut ego nihil nascens intuli in hunc mundum, ita moriens nihil abstuli.

IGNATIUS, MARCELLUS: Dic nobis, umbra chara, multumme differt caelestis a terrena musica.

UMBRA: Ah, socii! Qui Carissimi nomen habebat in terris Capronus, Chapronus vocatur in coelis. Domine, Deus meus, quem amo, quem possideo: sana, purifica, sanctifica aures istorum ut possint audire sacros angelorum concentus! Audivit Deus deprecationem meam. Tacete socii! Silete! Tacete!

TROIS ANGES QU'ON ENTEND ET QU'ON NE VOIT POINT:
Profitentes unitatem,
veneremur trinitatem
pari reverentia,
tres personas asserentes
personali differentes
a se differentia!
Patri natus est aequalis,
nec id tollit personalis
amborum distinctio;
patri compar filioque
spiritalis ab utroque
procedit connexio.
Pater, verbum sanctum flamen,
Deus unus sed hi tamen
habent quaedam propria.
Una virtus, unum numen,
unus splendor, unum lumen,
una tribus gloria!

UMBRA, IGNATIUS, MARCELLUS: O suave melos, o dulcis anticapronica musica!

GHOST, IGNATIUS, MARCELLUS: O eternity, how long you are; o life, how brief you are!

GHOST: I was a musician, considered good by the good musicians, and ignorant by the ignorant ones. And since those who scorned me were more numerous than those who praised me, music brought me small honor and great burdens. And just as I at birth brought nothing into this world, thus when I died I took nothing away.

IGNATIUS, MARCELLUS: Tell us, dear ghost, whether heavenly music differs from that on earth.

GHOST: Ah, comrades, he who held the name of Carissimi on earth is called Chaperon in heaven. Lord, my God, whom I love and cherish: make healthy, purify and sanctify the ears of these men so they may hear the sacred concert of the angels. God has heard my prayer. Be silent comrades! Be still! Be silent!

THREE ANGELS WHO ARE HEARD BUT NOT SEEN:
While proclaiming it unity,
let us worship the Trinity
with equal reverence,
affirming three persons,
differing among themselves
with different personalities!
The Son is the Father's equal
which does not deny their
distinct identities;
the Holy Spirit is the equal
of the Father and the Son
and arises as one with them.
The Father, Word, sacred flame,
one God, but all three
having their own qualities.
One virtue, one power,
one splendor, one light,
one glory in three persons!

GHOST, IGNATIUS, MARCELLUS: O lovely song, o sweet non-Chaperonian music!

IGNATIUS, MARCELLUS: Taedet me vitae meae. Ah quando, anima mea, ad coelestem patriam volabis, ut mellito hujus ce melodiae nectare replearis?

UMBRA: O amici, vivite laeti, at non immemores lethi! Quis enim vestrum scit an cras an hodie an hac ipsa forsitan hora sit moriendum. Poenitentiam agite, ad caproni musicam currite. Hanc in supplicium vobis et purgatorium eligite, et post morten aeternae gaudia vitae gustabitis.

UMBRA, IGNATIUS, MARCELLUS: Beatus ille, qui pro delendis culpis suis, fastidiosa et discordi caproni musica, aures suas fatigabit, castigabit capronabit, quoniam post mortem auditui ejus dabitur gaudium et laetitia in aeternum! Beatus ille, qui pro delendis culpis suis asininos capronini tritus patienter audiet, quia post mortem aeternae gaudia vitae gustabit, et nectareos angelorum concentus in fonte voluptatis potabit!

IGNATIUS, MARCELLUS: My life wearies me. Ah, my soul, when will you fly to the celestial homeland, so that you may quench your thirst for the honeyed nectar of this song?

GHOST: O friends, live joyously, but not unmindful of death. For who among you knows whether tomorrow, today, or this very hour he will die. Repent and embrace the music of Chaperon. Choose it as your own punishment and purgatory, and after death you shall taste the joys of eternal life.

GHOST, IGNATIUS, MARCELLUS: Blessed is he who, to purge his sins, will tire, castigate, and Chaperonize his ears with sickening and discordant, goatish music; after death, joy and happiness will be given as an eternal reward for listening to it. Blessed is he who, to purge his sins, will listen patiently to that asinine hack-work of Chaperon; after death, he shall taste the joys of eternal life and drink the nectarlike harmony of the angels in the fountain of delight.

Theoretical Writings

The theoretical writings of Charpentier include *Remarques sur les Messes à 16 parties d'Italie* (Remarks on the Roman Polychoral Masses) (H. 549), *Règles de composition par Mr Charpentier* (Rules of Composition by Mr. Charpentier) (H. 550), and *Abrégé des règles de l'accompagnement de Mr Charpentier* (Summary of Mr. Charpentier's Principles of Accompaniment) (H. 551).

Remarks on the Roman Polychoral Masses consists of three autograph leaves at the end of a copy of *Missa mirabiles elationes Maris sexdecimus vocibus del Beretta,* Beretta being the name of the Roman composer.[1] The copy was made by Charpentier. The mass itself is annotated. While the French composer admired the textures of certain passages (e.g., "unorthodox, but beautiful" in the Credo, "beautiful passage" for the amen of the Credo, "remarkable passage" for the amen of the Sanctus), he did not hesitate to criticize other passages he considered controversial in the area of harmony (e.g., "3 unisons that could be avoided," "7th neither prepared nor resolved," "this passage is unorthodox, seventh resolved upward").

Both *Rules of Composition* and *Summary of the Principles of Accompaniment* exist in two manuscript copies, neither of them autographs. The copy reproduced in the present volume was originally made by Étienne Loulié, inventor of the sonometer.[2] It appears alongside other manuscripts by Charpentier that were added to the Brossard Collection in 1702. The second copy also belongs to that collection.[3]

It is generally affirmed that Charpentier's theoretical writings were intended for use by his pupil, the Duc de Chartres.[4] According to recent research, it appears that *Rules of Composition* (or at least a major portion of them) were not originally destined for the future regent but were written a few years before Charpentier taught the prince composition.[5] On two occasions Étienne Loulié worked with this copy of the treatise as it has come down to us. The bulk of the manuscript was copied around 1690, when Loulié entertained "the hope of being engaged to teach composition to that gifted prince."[6] Then, after May 1693, Loulié

> had the opportunity to consult the original manuscript of Charpentier's treatise, which is to say an autograph copy given by the composer to the Duc de Chartres. Noticing that the prince's manuscript was more complete than his, made several years before, Loulié copied "augmentations" into the margins and at the end of the cahier and numbered each page of his own transcription to correspond with the new version. The Duc de Chartres therefore granted him permission to enter his apartment and to work there with pen and ink. That session with the duke was not an isolated event, however. Loulié consulted Charpentier's manuscript, noticed the existence of its additional material, went back home to get his own copy, and then came back to the Palais-Royal to correct the manuscript in his possession.[7]

Indeed, the beginning of folio 13 (p. 406 below) of *Rules of Composition* contains the remark "Additions taken from the original of the Duc de Chartres," as well as diverse notes added in the margins of the preceding leaves.[8] Hence in folio 6, (p. 395 below), one reads, "In the original of the Duc de Chartres, it says that this 4th rule allows no exception." What Charpentier wrote specifically for his pupil at the Palais-Royal was only the material reflected by those "augmentations" and marginal notes.

The second manuscript of *Rules of Composition* and *Summary of the Principles of Accompaniment* is a copy that Loulié presumably made for Sébastien de Brossard around 1699. The two manuscripts differ in only a few details.[9]

"This treatise, excellent as it is, has never been printed. That is what makes it so unique and valuable," wrote Brossard in his *Catalogue* (p. 365). In fact, Charpentier had not written *Rules of Composition* for publication but as a teaching guide for private use. It must therefore be considered from that standpoint and be excused if it sometimes seems too brief or incomplete. On the other hand, certain redundancies and the apparent lack of order are due to Loulié's copy which, in the "augmentations," repeats points already made in the first version of the treatise.

On three occasions, Charpentier alludes to Italian music (pp.

392, 400, and 410) to illustrate certain traits that he practiced in his works. The composer's fondness for dissonance, as expressed in *Rules of Composition,* stems from his attraction to the ultramontane style. It bespeaks a singular boldness in comparison to Charpentier's French compatriots, who were much more conservative in that domain. Furthermore, the composer's concept of polyphony derives from the masters of previous generations whose music could produce the most unexpected clashes through freedom of the melodic lines and through an absence of any distinction between "real tones" and "accidentals." Traces of these kinds of archaisms are found in examples of consecutive fifths (p. 393) or augmented and diminished octaves (pp. 400 and 402), which result from the simultaneous use of the ascending and descending melodic minor mode. Similarly, the composer was still thinking in terms of intervals, not chords, and in terms of modes, not tonalities. Nevertheless, his table of key-feelings established a psychological or affective association for each of eighteen keys and appears surprisingly modern. Indeed, thirty years later, Rameau (who probably had no knowledge of his predecessor's theoretical writings) reproduced in his *Treatise on Harmony* the same sort of characterization of keys, though on a more general level:

> The major mode taken in the octave of the notes C, D, or A is suitable for songs of gaiety and rejoicing; in the octave of the notes F or B-flat, it is suitable for tempests, furies, and similar matters. In the octave of the notes G or E, it is suitable for both tender and lively songs; the grand and the magnificent can also be expressed in the octave of the notes D, A, or E.
>
> The minor mode taken in the octave of the notes D, G, B, or E is suitable for sweetness and tenderness; in the octave of the notes C or F, it is suitable for tenderness and plaints; in the octave of the notes F or B-flat, it is suitable for songs of lamentation.[10]

Charpentier's treatise, like his work, falls into that crucial transition period in the evolution of musical language, in which ancient modality and the burgeoning use of tonality coexisted and mutually enriched each other.

Another very interesting passage in *Rules of Composition* occurs when Charpentier borrows the punctuation signs of oratory to illustrate the effect of different cadences (p. 407). Conversely, Grimarest later wrote on the subject of tragic declamation that "creating meaningful silences and sighs within longer speeches, like one is accustomed to doing in music, makes a great effect."[11] The Abbé Du

Bos dreamed of a "tragedy whose declamation would be written in [musical] notation."[12]

We can only regret that Charpentier's treatise makes no mention of the many ornaments used by the composer in his works, including those signs used only by him. Nor does he discuss, in the section devoted to meter, the time signature ₵ 3/2 which he used frequently and which no theoreticians of the period mention.

Summary of the Principles of Accompaniment occupies the last page of the *Rules of Composition* and contains only a few clearly stated recommendations, ruled this time by the totally French ideals of "discretion" and "good taste."

N.B. In the following transcriptions, musical examples originally written in the C clef have been transcribed to G clef.

REMARKS ON THE ROMAN POLYCHORAL MASSES

The whole process merely consists of finding four different basses, only two of which may descend a fifth or ascend a fourth to the cadence. The third [bass] imitates the first treble line (that is, descends one step to the octave of the final note), and the other [bass] ascends one step to it in imitating the second treble line.

Example

For the best effect, the cadence should last for two measures to give time for the parts to finish differently and one after another, which produces an admirable effect.

I do not feel the Italians are correct in writing several unisons and octaves among the parts as often as they do; nevertheless I would prefer consecutive unisons to octaves.

For example,
all the choruses start with all their parts entering on a hurried fugue. Two parts beginning with several unisons at the same time and within the same choir would create a very fine effect, though it must be done sparingly.

Care should be taken to see that the upper and lower syncopated parts allow enough room for the other voices to enter, especially when the beat is slow. This must be done almost always.

Two consecutive unisons or octaves can be avoided without much trouble.

The Italians are not correct in believing they are avoiding two octaves by arranging the parts in notes of different length, which they do quite often.

Example

In the Amen of the Credo of
the above mass
there is a beautiful passage,
namely:

the fugue[13] says

and the counterfugue[14]
says

here is the beautiful
passage

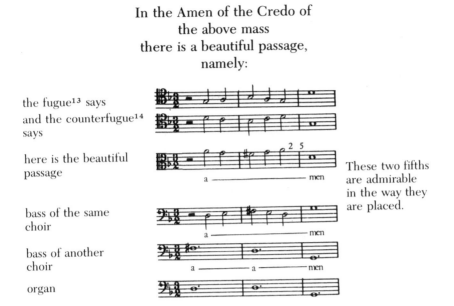

These two fifths
are admirable
in the way they
are placed.

bass of the same
choir

bass of another
choir

organ

The number of rests the Italians practice so often prevents the 2 octaves. They [the Italians] even believe they are resolving them when they make two parts end at the same time and start back up again at the same time, provided they put a breath between them.

Example

permissible

I would write
as follows

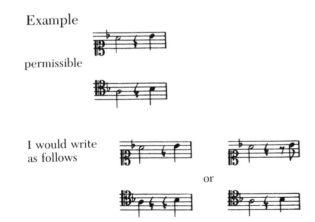

or

The most beautiful thing about Roman polychoral masses is the entry of all four basses embark on a double fugue almost simultaneously.

Example

I find it is easier to compose in
16 parts than in 8 because the
liberties taken in 16 would not
make as bad an effect as in 8.

Example of the liberties
the Italians take.

They tie a dissonance in one part only.[15] The other [voices] can
attack it without preparation and resolve it when they wish.

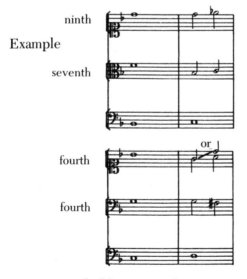

I approve of this because it is
impossible to hear in sixteen
parts if the dissonance is
prepared and resolved as it
ought to be, but in eight one
can hear it.

Forbidden intervals are acceptable in 16 [parts],
in 8 they are pardonable,
in 6, 4, 3, 2, and 1, intolerable.

RULES OF COMPOSITION BY MONSIEUR CHARPENTIER

Four couplets which one should know by heart

Do not pass from O to O except by contrary motion;
There is nothing wrong in moving from O to A.

Avoid passing from A to O by the same motion,
But do not be afraid to move from A to A.[16]

O signifies the perfect consonances, namely,
The octave, the fifth, the fourth, and their doublings.

A signifies imperfect consonances, namely,
The minor and major third and sixth, and their doublings.

Perfect Consonances

Octave, Fifth, Fourth
Called perfect because one may neither add to them nor
diminish them without creating a dissonance.

Example

Imperfect Consonances

Major and Minor Thirds and Sixths
Called imperfect because one may remove or add a semitone to
them without creating a dissonance.

Example[17]

There is no harmony at all without the third; if there is none
against the bass, it must be between the parts.

The fifth alone determines the chord; that is why one must never
make two consecutive fifths unless they are of different species, so as
not to harm that diversity which is the whole essence of music.

I call two consecutive fifths those which are placed over the bass
and ascend or descend one step at a time, and not otherwise.

Example

Bad fifths because they are
of the same species.

Two consecutive fifths,
good because they are of different species.

There is nothing wrong with several consecutive octaves between the parts because they do not determine the chords.

The plainchant of the church sung by children and adults on the octave prove this, since they are not at all harsh to the ear. I plan to talk about several consecutive fourths in the section dealing specifically with the fourth.

On Cross Relations

A cross relation occurs when a note sounded in an upper part creates a tritone against a note heard immediately afterwards in a lower part or in the bass.

Very bad if it does not move directly away from the F.

Very good because it only lingers on the E.

This relation is of the fifth and not of the tritone.

By putting a flat to the B or a sharp to the F, the cross relation would be avoided.

Very good because there is a relation of a perfect fourth and not of a tritone.

The cross relation caused by the leading note or the supertonic of the mode or the cadence which one wants to make is not only permitted but its avoidance is forbidden.

The Supertonic and the Leading Tone
Of the Mode and of the Cadence

All modes and all cadences in which one plans to close should have a semitone leading-note and a whole-tone supertonic above their finals [i.e., key-notes].

After these leading tones, one must always ascend a semitone. After the supertonics, one must always descend a whole tone.

It is commonly said that after all sharps, one must always ascend a semitone, but that is too general a statement. This applies only when the sharp is a leading tone of a mode or of a cadence with which one is dealing.

The rule which also states that after all flats one must always descend a semitone or a tone is not general enough. One must also descend a tone after sharps when they are a tone above the key-note of the mode or of the cadence being formed.

On Permissible Cross Relations

A cross relation caused by the leading note or the supertonic of a mode or of a cadence is not only permissible, but its avoidance is forbidden.

For example, the mode or the cadence dealt with here is in D; E is the supertonic of D; C-sharp is the leading note of D.

The cross relation caused by the leading tone of D is so agreeable that it is forbidden to avoid it.

The cross relation caused by the supertonic of D is so agreeable that it must not be avoided.

The Italians avoid the cross relation by flattening the super-tonic.[18] They do this for the purpose of expressing sorrow or the feeble last words of a dying man.

Recapitulation

Place a third against the bass or between the parts and the harmony will be correct.

Avoid two consecutive fifths of the same species, which is to say, only when the bass ascends or descends by conjunct degrees, so that diversity will be maintained.

Avoid cross relations except those caused by semitone leading tones or supertonics of modes or cadences with which you will be dealing, so that the ear will be satisfied.

On Motion

Similar motion occurs when the parts ascend or descend simultaneously. It impedes the diversity that music demands.

Contrary motion occurs when one part ascends while the other descends. It contributes marvelously to diversity.

The Treatment of Perfect and Imperfect Consonances

The perfect consonances—octave, fifth, and fourth—are signified by O.

The imperfect consonances—major and minor third and sixth—are signified by A.

First Rule
Do not pass from O to O except by contrary motion.

That is to say, two consecutive perfect chords in similar motion harm diversity. They should occur only by contrary motion.

Exception
One may go from the octave to the fifth by similar motion, provided the upper part ascends only a tone or the bass descends only a tone.

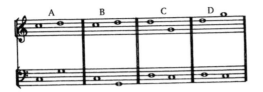

A. Good because one part ascends by a wide interval while the other ascends only a tone.

B. Better because the rule [of contrary motion] is observed.

C. Good because one part descends by a wide interval while the other descends only a tone.

D. Better because the rule [of contrary motion] is observed.[19]

One may go from the fifth to the octave by similar motion provided the upper part descends only a tone.

Example[20]

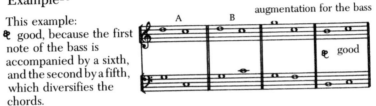

augmentation for the bass

This example:
€ good, because the first note of the bass is accompanied by a sixth, and the second by a fifth, which diversifies the chords.

€ good

A. Good because one part descends by a wide interval and the other by a single step.

B. Better because the rule [of contrary motion] is followed.

Several consecutive fourths or fifths in similar motion are still permitted between the upper parts provided they are of different species and move conjunctly.

Example

C. These are good because they move by degrees conjunctly and because the first and the last, which are more incisive than the others, are of a different species.

D. Good for the same reason.

You will notice, incidentally, that the fourth is a fifth inverted, and that the fifth is a fourth inverted. That is what gives them something in common in this particular case.

Second Rule
There is nothing wrong in moving from O to A.

That is to say, [there is nothing wrong] when one passes directly from a perfect chord to an imperfect chord by any kind of motion. Whether one ascends, the other descends, or both simultaneously ascend or descend, diversity is always maintained because one is perfect and the other imperfect.

Only exception

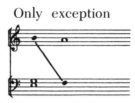

If the eleventh [=B] does not move directly above the F, it will create a cross relation.

Third Rule
Avoid passing from A to O by the same motion.

That is to say, from an imperfect chord one may pass to a perfect concord only by contrary motion.

The reason that allows one to pass from a perfect to an imperfect chord by all types of motions would seem to allow the same thing when one wishes to pass from an imperfect to a perfect chord. The third rule, however, must be faithfully observed. The treatment of the sixth to be given later will demonstrate its result.

Exception

One is permitted to pass from the third to the fifth and the octave by similar motion, provided the upper part ascends or descends by only one degree.

Example
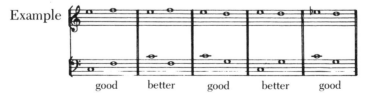

good   better   good   better   good

These three examples are good because the upper parts move only by one degree when the bass moves a fourth, and this creates diversity.

Fourth Rule
Do not be afraid to move from A to A.

That is to say, one may write several consecutive thirds and sixths in all types of motion, without going against diversity, because they are almost always of different species.

In the original of the Duc de Chartres, it says that this 4th rule allows no exception.

Exception

One may not write two consecutive major thirds when the bass descends a tone and does not move directly to the next note because it creates a cross relation.

Example

E. False relation if the eleventh lingers too long on F.

F. Relation of the fifth and, consequently, good.

I have marked the third note of the above in black to show three consecutive major thirds. One may write as many as three consecutive [major thirds], but no more.

I will speak about the fourth only among the dissonances.

Treatment of the Sixth

One should never write a sixth unless there is a danger of writing two consecutive fifths. That is to say, [do not write a sixth] if the bass does not ascend or descend by conjunct degrees.

All sixths must be resolved.

When the bass ascends a tone to linger on the second note, a major sixth is written over the first note.

When the bass ascends a semitone and lingers on the second note, a minor sixth is written on the first note.

But when the bass ascends a tone and goes upwards, major or minor sixths are written according to the figuration as long as the bass continues to ascend, because there is always danger of writing two consecutive fifths.

When the bass ascends a semitone and goes upwards, one continues writing major or minor sixths as long as the bass continues to ascend, because of the same danger.

When the bass descends a semitone and lingers on the second note, a major sixth is written on the first note.

When the bass descends a semitone and goes downward, a fifth or a sixth is written on the first note and a minor sixth on the second [note]. One continues to write a major or minor sixth as long as [the bass] continues descending, because there is always danger of writing two consecutive fifths.

When the bass descends a tone and lingers on the second note, a major sixth is written on the first note.

If the bass descends a tone and continues to move downward, a natural sixth [*sixte naturelle*] is written on the first and second notes, a natural sixth on the third, and major or minor sixths for as long as the bass continues to descend, because one is always afraid of two consecutive fifths.

Treatment of the Major Sixth

The major sixth resolves to the octave a semitone higher, to the fifth with one part remaining stationary [while the other ascends or descends a tone], or to the third, one or two degrees lower.

Example[21]

Major Sixth

Minor Sixth

The minor sixth resolves in the same ways as the major sixth, except to the octave.[22]

Exception

The minor sixth resolves to the octave with good effect when it ascends a tone afterwards.

Minor sixth resolved to the 8th.

This is the only way to resolve it satisfactorily to the octave.

Bad because one never ascends to an octave except by its leading tone.

If one were to pass from either the major or the minor sixth to the octave in other ways than those I have just indicated, the sixth would not be properly resolved, and one would be breaking the Third Rule which teaches never to pass from an imperfect chord to a perfect one by similar motion.

A. Badly resolved and breaks the Third Rule because it resembles two consecutive fifths.

B. Badly resolved, because it violates the Third Rule and both chords proceed disjunctively.

C. Badly resolved, for the minor sixth is never resolved on the octave.

D. Badly resolved, because it violates the Third Rule and resembles two consecutive fifths.

E. Badly resolved, for the major sixth is never resolved to the fifth unless one part remains stationary or moves a tone lower.

F. Badly resolved; it also violates the Third Rule.

G. Very bad, for it is not resolved at all. The two parts jump and violate the Third Rule and the diversity (= contrary motion).

H. Frightful, because of the tritone; moreover, it is badly resolved and violates the Third Rule.

Dissonances

There are thirteen dissonances:
1. The major ninth
2. The minor ninth
3. The augmented octave
4. The diminished octave
5. The major seventh
6. The minor seventh   and very small, that is, diminished
7. The augmented fifth
8. The diminished fifth   or false
9. The tritone
10. The perfect fourth
11. The diminished fourth
12. The major second   Note that he does not mention the
13. The minor second   augmented, or very large second.
And their doubles or octaves.

Strong and Weak Beats

Note that there are strong and weak beats in music.

In a measure with four beats, the first and third beats are strong, the second and fourth are weak.

In a measure with two beats, the first is strong and the second is weak.

In a measure with three beats, all the beats are equal; if desired, the second and third [beats] can be weak, but the first is always long [i.e., stressed].

All the beats [in triple time] are strong and equal. When there are several notes of equal value in the same measure, if the number is even, the first [note] will be strong, the second weak, the third strong, and the fourth weak; and if the number is odd, the first will be weak.[23]

Measure

6/4 and 6/8 have two equal beats, so beat two in a bar.
9/4 and 9/8 time have three equal beats, so beat three in a bar.
12/8 time has four equal beats, so beat four in a bar.
4/8 time has two equal beats, so beat two in a bar.

Treatment of the Dissonances

The ninth is prepared on a weak beat, suspended on a strong beat, and resolved by descending one degree on the next ∿ weak beat.

∿ which is its nearest consonance

Example

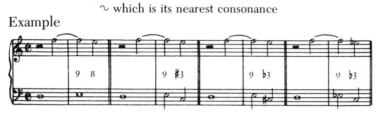

The seventh is prepared on the weak beat, suspended on a strong beat, and resolved by descending one degree on the next weak beat.

Example

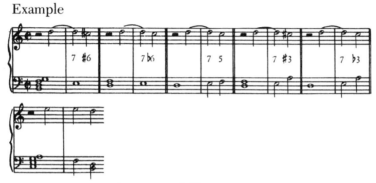

Augmented Dissonances

Augmented dissonances, like the augmented octave, the augmented fifth, and the augmented fourth, are taken with or without a preparation, as desired, on any beat of the measure. They resolve by ascending one degree.

The augmented octave is treated as the following examples illustrate.

This chord is very plaintive.[24]

The augmented octave may be treated only in the manner illustrated in A and B, and it is accompanied by an augmented sixth in example C.

The augmented fifth may or may not be prepared. It may be taken on any beat of the measure and it resolves by ascending one degree or by remaining stationary.

Example[25]

The augmented fourth or tritone may or may not be prepared on any beat of the measure and resolves by ascending one degree higher.

Example

A. Prepared, and resolved a semitone higher on the octave, sixth, or third.

B. Not prepared, and resolved a tone higher.

C. When it is followed by a fourth.

D. Good Italian treatment. The major third is implied.

You will notice in the above example that the second is prepared only mentally on G as the bass descends. It then becomes the unison or the octave. This is called preparation by supposition.

Treatment of the Fourth

The fourth is considered sometimes a consonance and other times a dissonance.

The fourth, although a perfect consonance, is nevertheless treated like a dissonance. It is much harsher than the fifth even though it is a fifth inverted.

When the fourth is considered a dissonance, it is prepared by itself on a weak beat, suspended on a strong beat, and resolved on a weak beat by descending one degree.

Example of the fourth as a dissonance

When one considers the fourth as a perfect chord, it is taken without being prepared on any beat, accompanied by the sixth, and resolved to a sixth one degree higher.

Example

A. The fourth is resolved to the sixth and taken on the strong beat.

B. The fourth is accompanied by the sixth, taken and resolved on the strong beat.

C. The fourth is taken on the weak beat and properly resolved on the sixth.

You will notice in passing that when the fourth is considered as a perfect consonance, it always moves conjunctly.

Two consecutive fourths of the same species or of different species are allowed against the bass, but no more [than two].

Example

Diminished Dissonances

Diminished dissonances, like the [diminished] octave, fifth, and false fourth, are prepared on any beat of the measure, and resolved by descending a semitone lower.

Example

The diminished fourth always requires the minor third.

A. False octave on a weak beat, not prepared.
B. False octave on a strong beat, without preparation.
C. Prepared by the bass.

False or Diminished Fifth

D. False fifth, not prepared, on a strong beat and resolved properly.

E. Taken on a weak beat and resolved satisfactorily.

F. Prepared and resolved satisfactorily.

Notice that all the diminished dissonances always move conjunctly.

False or Diminished Fourth

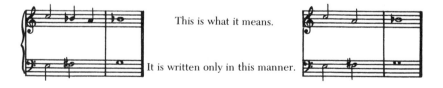

This is what it means.

It is written only in this manner.

Treatment of the Second

Difference between the ninth and the second. The difference between the ninth and the second is that the ninth is suspended or resolved by itself descending one degree, but the second is only suspended and resolved in the bass by descending one degree.

The second is always prepared in the bass on a weak beat, taken on a strong beat, resolved by *remaining stationary* while the bass descends one degree on a weak beat.

Example

On the Held Note

The ninth and the seventh above a note held in the bass are written on weak beats moving by conjunct degrees. They are resolved by descending one degree to their nearest consonances.

None of the augmented dissonances may be taken over a note held in the bass.

Diminished dissonances may be taken over a note held in the bass. They resolve by descending a semitone to the nearest consonance.

The fourth over a note held in the bass is taken on any beat of the measure. It moves by conjunct degrees and resolves by ascending or descending one degree to its nearest consonances.

The second may be taken over a note held in the bass on weak beats or weak notes. It resolves by ascending or descending one degree to its nearest [consonances].

Over a note held in the treble part or in some other upper part, the bass is allowed all the dissonances, except the augmented and diminished ones, on weak beats or notes. They are resolved by ascending or descending one degree to the nearest consonances.

Recapitulation

The ninth, seventh, and fourth are prepared on a weak beat. They are suspended on a strong beat and resolved by falling one degree.

Augmented dissonances may or may not be prepared on any beat of the measure. They resolve by ascending one degree.

Diminished dissonances may or may not be prepared on any beat of the measure. They resolve by descending one degree.

End of the Rules

Routines

When the treble part descends a minor third, have the bass form a major third with the second note of the treble part. When the treble part descends a major third, have the bass form a minor third with the second note of the treble part.

Example[26]

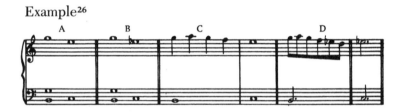

A. The treble part descends a minor third; the bass forms a major third with it.

B. The treble part descends a major third; the bass proceeds to form a minor third with it.

When the treble part is prepared and subsequently descends one degree, the bass must always form the ninth, seventh, or fourth against the prepared note. When the bass is prepared and subsequently descends one degree, the treble part must always form the fourth, second, or tritone against the prepared notes.

On the Mode

The mode is the range of an octave from, for example, low C to high C.

There are as many modes as there are notes.

~ as there are notes in the scale.

All the modes can be related to the mode of C or D.

The mode of C has a major third. ·

The mode of D has a minor third.

All modes with a major third resemble the mode of C.

All modes with a minor third resemble the mode of D.

The modes have three essential degrees, namely, the final which is the tonic of the mode, the third above the final which is called the mediant, and the fifth above the final which is called the dominant.

Modes with a major third have only two essential degrees, namely, the final and the dominant.

Modes with a minor third have three essential degrees, namely, the final, the mediant, and the dominant.

The semitone leading note serves to ascend agreeably to the chord of the mode, and the supertonic serves to descend agreeably to it.

The dominants of the modes with a minor third have a semitone above them which serves to descend agreeably to them.[27]

When the bass does what the treble part has done, that is to say, when it has the same notes that the treble had, give to the treble part [the same notes] the bass had.

The above example is called inversion.

The sixth is a third inverted.

The third is a sixth inverted.

That is how fugues with two, three, and four inventions or subjects harmonize to create all the beauty of music.

By practice we become skilled workers.

Fabricando fabri fimus.

ADDITIONS TAKEN FROM THE ORIGINAL
OF THE DUC DE CHARTRES

Sixths and thirds, augmented, major, minor, and diminished.

aug. 6th   maj. 6th   min. 6th   dim. 6th   maj. 3rd   min. 3rd   dim. 3rd

Definition of Music

Music is a harmonious combination of high, middle, and low sounds.

The third, either against the bass or between the parts, creates all the harmony.

Diversity alone makes for all that is perfect in it, just as uniformity makes for all that is dull and unpleasant. Changes in tempo and mode are very good and contribute marvelously to the diversity that music demands.

Properly prepared and resolved dissonances, combined with perfect and imperfect consonances, produce not the least of this diversity.

Music composed only of consonances would be dull, and if too filled with dissonances, would be harsh, because these two extremes transgress against diversity. Diligently avoid cross relations as well as the omission of the third between the parts or against the bass.

Why the Modes Are Transposed

The first and least important reason for this is to make the same piece of music singable by all sorts of voices.

The second and principal reason is the expression of different emotions, for which the different key-feelings are very appropriate.

The Key-Feelings[28]

C major	Gay and warlike
C minor	Dark and sad
D minor	Grave and pious
D major	Joyous and very warlike
E minor	Effeminate, amorous, and plaintive
E major	Quarrelsome and clamorous

E-flat major	Cruel and Harsh
E-flat minor	Horrible, frightful
F major	Furious and quick-tempered
F minor	Dark and plaintive
G major	Sweetly joyous
G minor	Serious and magnificent
A minor	Tender and plaintive
A major	Joyous and pastoral
B-flat major	Magnificent and joyous
B-flat minor	Dark and frightening
B minor	Solitary and melancholy
B major	Harsh and plaintive

Cadences

Cadence in music has two meanings. The first is the precise and exact observance of time values, and the second is a fall or a rest which occurs from time to time. The cadences in which the bass ascends a fourth or descends a fifth are the periods of music and should be used only by way of conclusion. That is why all musical compositions end with this kind of cadence. It is called a final cadence when it falls on the tonic of the mode.

The cadence of a seventh resolved to a sixth occurs when the bass descends one degree.[29] This cadence is employed in a conclusive sense, but nevertheless demands something after it. It is employed in the middle of a song. In music it is the equivalent of the [punctuation marks] : or ; or ? in discourse.

A half cadence occurs when the bass ascends a fifth or one degree, or when it descends a fourth to one of the chords of the mode. It is employed only to divide as much of the phrase as necessary to make sense, just as commas in discourse separate the subordinate clauses of a sentence.

Imagine that G is a chord of the mode C.

Of the Essential Chords of the Modes

The minor modes have three essential chords on which one should make cadences, namely, the final, its third, and its upper fifth.

The major modes have only two essential chords on which one should make cadences, namely, its final and its fifth.

Minor Mode		Major Mode
A Dominant	Any other		G Dominant	Any other
F Mediant	cadence which		C Final	cadence
D Final	is used will be			which is used
	called outside			will be called
	the mode.			outside the
				mode.

Of the Supertonics and Leading Tones of the Modes or Cadences Which One Plans to Use

All the cadences in which there is a descending fifth or an ascending fourth have a whole-tone [supertonic] above their final and a half-tone [leading tone] below their final.

Example

Cadence of C	Cadence of D
D Supertonic	E Supertonic
C Final	D Final
B Leading tone	C-sharp Leading tone

The dominant of the minor modes has, besides the supertonic and leading tone, another semitone above it falling most agreeably.

Dominant of the Minor Mode

The mode of D
Za:[30] Leading tone
A: Dominant

One commonly says that it is always necessary to ascend a semitone after a sharp, and to descend a semitone after a flat, but this rule is too general. It is only after the sharp leading tone below a cadence that one should deem it necessary to ascend a semitone. And it is only after a flat or the semitone leading tone above the dominant in a minor mode where one should fall, and always by descending a semitone.

These tones and leading tones are so privileged and lead so naturally to the cadences that one makes, that the cross relation which might result should not be avoided but should be used as much as possible.

On the Cross Relation

The cross relation is the interval of the tritone formed by a note in an upper part against a note in the lower parts or in the bass itself. It occurs immediately afterwards and comes to a pause.

Example

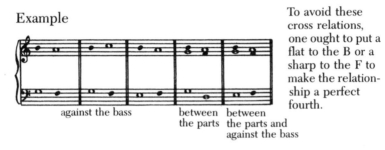

against the bass   between between
the parts the parts and
against the bass

To avoid these cross relations, one ought to put a flat to the B or a sharp to the F to make the relationship a perfect fourth.

False relations excellent to treat and bad ones to avoid:

Excellent because it is caused by the leading tone of C. | Bad because the leading tone of C is altered. | Bad because the supertonic of C is altered.

Recapitulation

Great diversity in music; the third between the voices or against the bass; dissonances skillfully blended with perfect and imperfect consonances; no cross relations unless they are caused by supertonics and leading tones of the cadences being made; natural expression of the subject; good choice of tempos and modes which are appropriate to the emotion one wishes to depict; the music cannot fail to be just as beautiful as it is good [if you abide by these rules].

The ninth and seventh over a note held in the bass occur on a weak note and are resolved one degree lower on their nearest consonance.

Example

On the Beauties of Music

Regular modulation, that is to say, the chords so well linked together that they pass inevitably from one to the other make it flow as smoothly as possible.

The avoidance of forbidden intervals greatly contributes to beautiful modulation.

Enumeration of the forbidden intervals which must be avoided:

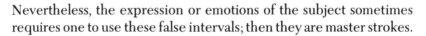

Nevertheless, the expression or emotions of the subject sometimes requires one to use these false intervals; then they are master strokes.

Imitation at the fifth or the fourth, ascending as well as descending, is not one of the least beauties [of music].

Imitation must be short and light.

Fugue is the imitation of the melody at the fourth or the fifth, ascending as well as descending.

Fugue should be longer and more serious than imitation.

The Italians never compose just one fugue, but two, three, and four simultaneously, which makes their music so admirable.

The most beautiful kind of fugue is one that is spirited and pressing.

That is why one should never place a rest in a part when composing a fugue for a vocal piece.

Experience teaches more than all the rules.

SUMMARY OF THE PRINCIPLES OF ACCOMPANIMENT
OF MR. CHARPENTIER

Avoid forbidden cross relations.

Avoid two consecutive fifths.

On the organ, avoid playing with one hand that which you are playing with the other.

Place the third between the parts if you do not put it against the bass.

Over all the dominants of the modes, place a major third unless it is marked differently, and you will be accompanying correctly.

Never be ambitious to display the quickness of the hands.

Listen to the voice of the singer; raise it if it goes flat; if it goes sharp, lower it by repeating the note two or three times. Such is tasteful and discreet accompaniment.

Those who make such commotion and who lift up their hands to thump the keyboard are incapable of accompanying well.

That which is said about one instrument can and must be applied to all the others.

When the voice rests, the brilliance of the hand [of the accompanist] may be displayed without offending good taste.

Chronological Table of Works

Virtually all the works of Marc-Antoine Charpentier are found in the twenty-eight autograph manuscript volumes bearing the title *Mélanges*. This collection of over 4000 pages was sold in 1727 by Jacques Édouard, the composer's nephew and heir, to the king's library. Today this collection is in the Paris Bibliothèque Nationale (BN), in the card catalogue under Rés. Vm1 259. They are bulky volumes (395 mm × 270 mm) bound in leather.

Existing alongside the *Mélanges* are other manuscripts (some autograph, some not) and printed sources. Certain pieces were copied by Sébastien de Brossard (1655–1730), an important figure of the period whom we have referred to on many occasions. He was an ecclesiastic (receiving minor orders in 1675), a theoretician (devoting himself to the problems of musical notation), a lexicographer (his *Dictionnaire de musique* published in 1703 was the first of its kind in France), and a bibliophile (he bequeathed his sizeable library to Louis XV in exchange for a modest pension), as well as a composer of motets, Tenebrae lessons, cantatas, violin sonatas, and *airs sérieux et à boire*. He did not disguise his love of Italian music, which shows through his own compositions, and he always defended Charpentier in face of "extreme French purists." Brossard wrote thus about Charpentier: "Charpentier composed . . . a quantity of other works, both sacred and profane, which are of uncommon excellence, and one will find the catalogue [mentioned] below among the manuscripts, for there are very few things of his in print."[1]

In 1900, Michel Brenet established for the first time a *"liste sommaire* of the works of Marc-Antoine Charpentier."[2] This attempt at classification was considerably enriched in 1910 by Jules

412

Écorcheville.[3] But it is H. Wiley Hitchcock's *Catalogue raisonné des oeuvres de Marc-Antoine Charpentier*, published in 1982, which gives an exhaustive list of Charpentier's entire output and which today serves as an indispensable reference. In it, pieces are cataloged by genre (i.e., masses, other liturgical works, psalm settings, motets, airs, cantatas, pastorales, divertissements, operas, incidental music, instrumental music, theoretical writings) and each carries an identification number (e.g., H. 1, H. 2, up to H. 551) (see "Catalog of Works").

The chronological table presented below lists Charpentier's works in the order they occur in the manuscripts. Although the *Mélanges* indicate no dates, it nevertheless seems the composer copied his pieces in a certain order, as they were composed, into two series of parallel cahiers (see below). This chronological system was explained lucidly by Hitchcock in the introduction to his *Catalogue*.[4]

CONTENTS OF THE *MÉLANGES*

Each of the twenty-eight volumes contains groups of manuscripts or fascicles—the *cahiers*—with their own numbered pages.[5] It was not until after the cahiers were bound, which seems to have occurred sometime after their acquisition by the royal library, that the volumes were folioed.[6] Sometimes pages are also numbered, somewhat systematically, at the end of cahiers. In volume XVII (cahiers XXIII–XXIV) a double numbering system appears (the numbering in parentheses refers to cahiers, antedating the numbering of the volume).

When dealing with the *Mélanges* from a chronological point of view, one must be careful not to consider the volumes as consecutive. In fact, Charpentier used two series of cahiers simultaneously, one numbered in arabic, the other in roman numerals. Why two series? Initially, it seems the composer wanted to classify his works according to genre. At the beginning of cahier 1, he noted "Pièces différentes" and at the beginning of cahier I "Messes, psaumes et hymnes." He adhered to this arrangement in the first few pages but ceased to make any distinction thereafter. We find all genres combined in both series. Patricia M. Ranum claimed that the music contained in the cahiers of the arabic-numeral series was written exclusively for the Guises between 1670 and 1688.[7] After that date, Charpentier continued to copy his works into one or the other series for a reason which remains unknown.

Each series contains seventy-five cahiers, some of which are missing (eleven in the first series, twelve in the second). The music in the missing cahiers is unfortunately lost.

The arabic-numeral cahier series combines volumes I through XII, and the roman-numeral cahier series combines volumes XIV through XXVIII. In neither case do the volumes adhere to any logical order, if one examines the numerical ordering of the cahiers, which do follow a chronological pattern. This is why, in the chronological table, we give the volume number for each piece, followed by the number of the cahier or cahiers (the same work sometimes overlapping from one cahier to one or two others).

The order of the volumes is as follows:

1. Arabic-numeral series: I, II, III, IV, XI, VI, VII, VIII, IX, X, V, XII.
2. Roman-numeral series: XIV, XV, XVI, XVII, XIX, XVIII, XXVIII (fol. 37–68), XX, XXI, XXII, XXIII, XXV (fol. 1–19), XXIV (fol. 1–45), XXV (fol. 20–80), XXVI, XXVII (fol. 1–36).

While H. W. Hitchcock was justified in assigning to certain cahiers whose numbers have disappeared places in the two main series (these are indicated in brackets in the following table), six problematic cahiers remain. The first two are numbered "I" and "II" (volume XIII). The other four carry no number, so Hitchcock has identified them by letter ("a," "b," "c," and "d"). We have placed these six cahiers after the two main series.

CHRONOLOGY

To establish when the works of Charpentier were written, we have proceeded one step at a time. Like Hitchcock, we started by using certain pieces as touchstones. First, the performance dates of the stage music (1672–1685) are indicated by the account books in the archives of the Comédie-Française. Other works linked to specific events also serve as points of reference, such as the changes made in the breviary of Paris churches in 1680 (H. 96–110 and H. 111–119; see Chapter 7); the recovery of the Dauphin at the end of 1680 (H. 326); the death of Queen Marie-Thérèse on 30 July 1683 (H. 189, 331, 409); the marriage of Maximilian-Emanuel II, Elector of

Bavaria, in 1685 (H. 473); the recovery of the king in January–February 1687 (H. 489); and the *Messe, Pour le Port-Royal* (H. 5) on 20 July 1687 (see Chapter 7).

Finally, certain pieces containing the names of performers also serve as points of reference, such as the Pièche sisters, who sang for the Dauphin, for whom Charpentier worked beginning in 1679 (see Chapter 5). In both series of the *Mélanges,* the names of the sisters appear for the first time in H. 170 and H. 174, which allows both of these motets to be dated 1679. Likewise, date of composition of the three Tenebrae psalms (H. 228–230) for the Sainte-Chapelle can be deduced as follows: since the singer Antheaume left the Sainte-Chapelle in September 1699, and Charpentier was appointed music director there in June 1698, these psalm settings must date from Holy Week of the year 1699.

The last work that can be dated with certainty is *Judicium Salomonis,* whose manuscript of separate parts (H. 422a) carries the date of its first performance: 1702.

All these dates are printed in bold type in the following table.

The second step in dating the *Mélanges* consisted of adding to the established data other less precise or less definite elements, which still allowed the general outlines of the works as a whole to be kept in perspective.

The names of performers in the manuscripts help us to place groups of works into the corresponding time periods of the various positions held by Charpentier: at the Hôtel de Guise from 1684 to 1687 (even though Charpentier was there at the beginning of the 1670s, he then had only a much smaller group of singers at his disposal) and at the Sainte-Chapelle between 1698 and 1704. Between those two periods fall the works for the Jesuits (see Chapter 8).[8] It is interesting to note that the majority of the missing cahiers mark the turning points between these three periods—cahiers 51, 52, 53, 67, 68, 69, 71, 72, and 73 in the arabic-numeral series, and cahiers LII, LIII, LXXI, LXXII, and LXXIII in the roman-numeral series. It is difficult to precisely date the middle period because it cannot be linked to any absolutely certain points of reference.

Whenever possible, we have linked the sacred works to the liturgical feasts for which they were intended. This allows us to reconstruct annual cycles created by Holy Week, Christmas, saints' days, and so forth, and hence to reduce the margin of doubt.

Finally, my last step was to focus on the recent research of Patricia M. Ranum and on my own investigations which shall be discussed presently. Based on her meticulous study of the paper and ink of the manuscripts, and by comparing the chronology of Charpentier's cahiers with the activities of the Guises as recorded in the gazettes and other period documents, Patricia M. Ranum has proposed the following possibilities:[9]

> H. 91–93 (vol. I, cahier 1): Holy Week 1670 at the Abbaye de Monmartre in the presence of Madame, wife of the Duc d'Orléans (S.S. p. 357; G.d.F. April 1670).
> H. 2, 311, 156, and 12 (I, 3–5): pieces for the funerals of the Duc de Guise (who died 30 July 1671) and of Marguerite de Lorraine (April 1672) (S.S. p. 358).
> H. 94 (I, 2): Holy Week 1672 at the Abbaye de Monmartre (S.S. p. 358).
> H. 95 and 157 (I, 6): Holy Week 1673 (S.S. p. 358).
> H. 508 (I, 7): octave of the Holy Sacrament (E.L.; G.d.F. June 1673).
> H. 509–512 (I, 7): between June 1673 and March 1674 (E.L.).
> H. 393 (II, 12): Christmas 1676 (E.L.).
> H. 479 (II, 13): 5 October 1676, *"opéra"* given by Mme de Guise for the baptism of the Duc de Chartres and of Mlle de Chartres at Saint-Cloud (S.S. p. 358; G.d.F. October 1676).
> H. 395 (II, 14): January 1677 (E.L.).
> H. 480 (XI, 37): November 1682 (S.S. p. 358; M.G. December 1682).
> H. 489 (VIII, [49]–50): 31 January 1687 (S.S. pp. 356, 360; M.G. February 1687; G.d.F. January 1687).
> H. 431 (VIII, 50): 20 January 1687 (S.S. p. 356; M.G. January 1687; G.d.F. January 1687).

I have opted to begin both the arabic-numeral series and the roman-numeral series in 1670. The first works that can be dated with certainty are the *Ouverture de la Comtesse d'Escarbagnas* and the *Intermèdes nouveaux du Mariage forcé* (8 July 1672) in volume XV, cahier XVI.

The period of 1688–1698 (arabic- and roman-numeral series) is the one that posed the most problems for reasons indicated above.

Nevertheless, I have attempted to establish the most precise chronology possible by using the cycle of the liturgical calendar and clues furnished by the two main chronicles of the time (the *Mercure Galant* and the *Gazette de France*) concerning the ceremonies of Jesuit institutions in Paris. Charpentier is mentioned only three times in these accounts. The absence of his name on other occasions does not mean that his music was not used, since reporters of the day did not always take the trouble to mention the music performed in the services.

Since the details of ceremonies and historical events, as well as conjecture about those details, which allow us to establish a chronology for this period have already been presented during the course of this book (particularly in Chapter 8), we shall reproduce here only a list of the works concerned and dates proposed. Because this chronology nevertheless remains conjectural, a question mark has been placed after all dates in this period.

Arabic-numeral series
 H. 126–134 (X, 59): Holy Week 1691 (?) (see M.G. April 1691, quoted in Chapter 8, p. 173).
 H. 146 (X, 62): August (?) 1692 (?) (see Chapter 8, p. 175).
 H. 418 (X, 63): 25 August 1692 (?) (see M.G. August 1692, quoted in Chapter 8, p. 173).
 H. 180a, 180b, 197a, 199a, 200a, 76a, 203a, and 209a (V, 63): 1693 (?) (preludes added to previously composed works) (see Chapter 8, p. 175–176).
 H. 147 (V, 64): October (?) 1693 (?) (see Chapter 8, p. 175).
 H. 536 and 432 (V, 66): 9 (?) December 1695 (?) (see Chapter 8, pp. 175).
 H. 90 and 222 (V, 66): March–April (?) 1696 (?) (see Chapter 4, p. 110).

Roman-numeral series
 H. 537 (XXV, LXVI): 23 (?) January 1695 (?) (see Chapter 8, p. 175).
 H. 10 (XXVI, LXVIII): 21 (?) April 1695 (?) (see M.G. May 1695, quoted in Chapter 8, p. 173–174).
 H. 372 (XII, 70): originally placed just before H. 432 (V, 66).[10]

THE PROBLEM OF THE PRELUDES

Most of the preludes whose dates of composition differ from those of the works to which they are linked were, logically, composed some time after those works. The composer enriched pieces that had already been performed with an instrumental introduction in view of a new performance. Four of these preludes (or, in the case of the fourth work, symphonies), however, are found in cahiers that precede the cahiers of the works to which they belong. These are the preludes H. 398a, 399a, 404a, and 402a. For the first two, the gap is only a few months; H. 404a is obviously a rejected first version; but H. 402a poses a real problem. The latter, *Symphonies ajustées au Sacrifice d'Abraham,* are found in cahier XVII (1673–1674), while H. 402 (cahier XXX) was written several years later (1681). Furthermore, Charpentier indicated the existence of a prelude (lost) in cahier XI (1672), while the *Mémoire des ouvrages . . . de M. Charpentier* refers to a *Prélude pour le Sacrifice d'Abraham* (also lost) which was originally in cahier IX (1671).[11] Therefore, as a precaution, I have added a question mark to the date for H. 404.

THE PROBLEMATIC CAHIERS

The problem cahiers include "I," "II," "a" (vol. XIII), "b" (vol. XVII), "c" (vol. XXIV), and "d" (vol. XXVIII).

If "I" can be dated definitely and "II" with near certainty (see Chapter 4), it is more difficult to date the remaining cahiers. Cahier "b" contains copies of works (with a few variants) composed around 1693. Cahier "d" contains pieces for Port-Royal that were perhaps performed on 20 July 1687 (see Chapter 7). It is impossible to date the others.

Certain works contained in the *Mélanges* are incomplete. In the case of five of them—H. 324, 544, 428, 430, and 543—only a very short fragment remains. Hitchcock has cataloged them, but they are not included in the table below.

LOST WORKS

Not every one of Charpentier's works has survived. Among the lost works are those in the missing cahiers. The lost works can be reconstructed, at least partially.

48: the continuation of H. 415 and perhaps the *Sonata* (H. 548) written at the time of *Les Arts florissants* (H. 487) and contained in the preceding cahiers.

XX, XXI, XXII: *L'Inconnu* (17 November 1675), *Le Triomphe des dames* (7 August 1676), *Les Amours d'Acis et de Galathée* (February 1678)?

XL: continuation of H. 410 and perhaps the piece for the death of Marie-Thérèse performed at the Carmelite convent in the Rue du Bouloir in the month of December 1683.

LII: works for Port-Royal (H. 226–227, 81), today in cahier "d"?

LVI: continuation of H. 66 and perhaps the *Leçons de ténèbres* (the second lesson for each day) which would complete the cycle (first lessons in cahier LV and third lessons in cahier LVII).

LIX: continuation of H. 298.

LXVII: *Apothéose de Laodomas* in memory of M. le Maréchal, Duc de Luxembourg, given on 16 March 1695 at the Collège des Jésuites in Rennes? The following cahier contains the *Messe des morts* (H. 10), which we believe was intended for the funeral of the Maréchal.

In addition to the contents of the *Mélanges*, *Mémoire des ouvrages ... de M. Charpentier*, which was given to the king's library when the manuscripts were sold, mentions other pieces, most of which are no longer extant. Among these lost pieces are the following:

Cahier IX of the *Mélanges*, besides the works which have come down to us, also included *Allemande grave pour un reposoir* (probably the one mentioned in H. 515; see Chapter 13); *Branles* [i.e., dance tunes] *pour des violons à 4 parties;* several *courantes* as well as *sarabande espagnole, bourrée, menuet, passepied, Prélude pour le Sacrifice d'Abraham* [see above], and *Symphonie pour trois violons, Élévation, Dilecte mi,* H. 436(?).[12]

Préludes pour le Magnificat, H. 80; *pour le Dixit (Dominus) du Port-Royal,* H. 226; *pour le Magnificat du Port-Royal,* H. 81; *pour Laudate Dominum omnes gentes,* H. 227.[13]

Motet pour les plaies de Saint François, Domine salvum pour haute-contre et taille, Motet pour la Vierge pour haute-contre et taille, H. 359(?); a continuation of the *Motet de Sainte Cécile* (continuation of H. 415?); *Élévation pour le jour de la Toussaint, Hymne de Sainte Ursule, Salve regina à trois voix pareilles, Motet pour un confesseur,* H. 375; *Motet pour un confesseur non pontife,* H. 376; *Lauda Sion à voix seule,* H. 268; *Motet pour tous les saints,* H. 377; *Ave regina coelorum,* H. 22; *Élévation: O amor, o bonitas, à voix seule,* H. 279; *Motet pour le Carême,* H. 378; *Motet pour le Saint-Sacrement. Egredimini Filiae Sion, avec flûtes,* H. 280; *Élévation: Panis angelicus à voix seule,* H. 243; *Symphonie pour le motet de Saint Louis;* several other pieces; *Motet pour Sainte Anne.*[14]

Nisi Dominus and *De profundis,* H. 231 and 232(?).

All parts of the grand motet *Judicium Salomonis,* H. 422a.

An Italian mass for quadruple choir and instruments containing a very magnificent fugue. M. Charpentier composed this mass in Rome for the *mariniers.* This music is very learned [see Chapter 2, p. 34].

All parts of the *Fête de Rueil* with symphony, H. 485a.

All parts of the opera *Les Arts florissants,* H. 487a.

All parts of the *Messe de l'Assomption,* H. 11a.

Packet no. 3, Italian music by the same composer:

The parts to a mass with symphony.

Another Italian work, 60 pages in 4º, another piece in 4º for solo voice for good weather, *récit* from *Marcello in Siracusa,* six cahiers of a mass, *Serenata,* parts of a psalm setting *Laudate pueri, Beatus vir* del Signor Francesco Alessi, two other masses, introit to a mass of the Holy Spirit, motet of Carissimi, several curious pieces.

Dixit Dominus, Confitebor, Beatus vir which has only the continuo, *Laudate Dominum omnes gentes, Magnificat, Domine ad adjuvandum.*

Several motets.

Eight books of Italian music containing airs notated with the words. These must be examined to be appreciated.[15]

Three works are not mentioned in the *Catalogue raisonné.* Anticipating future additions to his work, Hitchcock suggested that they be classified by a number with the suffix *bis,* which we have done: H. 454*bis,* H. 495*bis,* and H. 548*bis* (see p. 477).

HOW TO READ THE CHRONOLOGICAL TABLE

The chronological table is divided into three main parts:

1. *Mélanges*
   Arabic-numeral series
   Roman-numeral series
   Problematic cahiers
2. Other manuscripts.
3. Published works: 1676–1737.
   Airs sérieux et à boire published in the *Mercure Galant.*
   Motets mêlés de symphonie published by Jacques Édouard
   in 1709.
   Pieces published by Ballard in the seventeenth and
   eighteenth centuries.

The first column in the table assigns a number to the work which will be referred to in "Classification of Works by Scoring," a study that follows the chronological table.

The second column indicates the "H" number from Hitchcock's *Catalogue raisonné* (see also "Catalog of Works").

The third column gives the original French title of the work, and the first words of the text (if there is no other title, to differentiate between pieces bearing identical titles, or for easier identification of the many psalm settings and responsories).

The fourth column identifies the scoring (see discussion below for further details).

The fifth column mentions the genre (with the liturgical text in some cases) or the author (in the stage music).

Where appropriate, the sixth, seventh, and eighth columns list the source of the manuscript and its date. The criteria for classification of the published works differ from those of the manuscript compositions, which explains the change in format [between the *Mélanges* and the other sections of the table].

The last column gives other identifying traits, including, for example, the names—sometimes abbreviated, as in the manuscripts—of the musicians who first performed the works. This information is helpful in establishing the date of a work.

Scoring

As done elsewhere in the present volume, this table uses period terminology [in the fourth column].

Instruments
    b = bass   org = organ
    bc = basso continuo   str = strings
    bs = bassoon(s)   t = *taille*
    d = *dessus*   tp = trumpet(s)
    dr = drums   trans = transverse flute
    fl = flute(s)   vl = viol(s)
    hps = harpsichord   vn = violin(s)
    ob = oboe(s)

When tessitura is not specified, it is understood to be *dessus*
(treble), meaning flute, oboe, trumpet, or violin. Instrumentation is
not always indicated by Charpentier. In such cases, treb./2 treb.
refers to treble instrument(s).

The basso continuo instruments are those mentioned in the
manuscripts.

The four-part string ensemble, marked str (4), is composed of
dessus (G treble clef, first line), *haute-contre* (C soprano clef), *taille*
(C clef, second line), and bass (bass clef)

In five-part string textures, marked str (5), the *quinte* (C alto clef,
today's viola clef) is added.

Voices
    b = bass (bass clef)
    bt = *basse-taille* or baritone (F clef, 3rd line)
    bd = *bas-dessus* or mezzo-soprano (C clef, 2nd line)
    d = *dessus* or soprano (C soprano clef)
    hc = *haute-contre* or alto/countertenor (C alto clef)
    hd = *haut-dessus* or high soprano (G treble clef)
    t = *taille* or tenor (C tenor clef)

Small letters are used to indicate vocal soloists, and capital letters
for chorus.

In works in which Charpentier requires several soloists of the
same tessitura (e.g., first and second bass), their number may be
reduced to one singer when the parts do not occur simultaneously.

This solution has been adopted in the masses and motets, but in secular and sacred pieces of a theatrical nature (e.g., Latin oratorios), the number of singers corresponds to the number of vocally differentiated characters.

In the pieces involving chorus, it is sometimes difficult to specify their true scoring. For example, does the piece call for a group of soloists (one or two to a part) or a larger ensemble? The first instance (i.e, a group of soloists) applies to the works destined for the singers of the Hôtel de Guise (and their names are duly noted in the last column). Other pieces also seem to call for a small group of soloists (e..g., *Messe pour les trépassés à 8*, H. 2). The table, however, usually designates scorings of this type as chorus, in the way Charpentier himself understood the word. Thus the table uses the word *chorus* to indicate soloists singing together as well as refer to a larger ensemble of voices, the meaning we usually give to the word today.

The problem of sound density also applies to the orchestra. Rare are the works in which Charpentier clearly specifies the number of instruments used. It is left to the performer to decide on the number of string players to a part, to determine whether, for example, two flutes or two stands of flutes are needed. When the instruments are only called on to double the voices (their parts not being written out separately), it must also be determined whether all voices should be doubled, or merely the *dessus.*

To answer these questions, the performer must closely examine the manuscript, place the work within its cultural and chronological context, study its textures (is it better suited to a small or a large scoring?), and compare it to neighboring works.

The limitations of this book do not allow us to deal with this subject in any more detail. The subject requires a separate study, with no assurance of definitive answers, at least for the time being.

MÉLANGES

1. Arabic-numeral Series

No.	H.	Title	Scoring	Genre/Text	Volume/Cahier	Folio/Page	Date	Special comments
1	91	*Leçons de ténèbres*	hd, d, hc; 2 fl, bc	Motet	I, 1	1–5	1670 Holy Week	
2	92	*Autre Leçon de ténèbres Troisième du mercredi saint*	hd, d; bc	Motet	I, 1	5–6v	1670 Holy Week	
3	93	*Autre Leçon de ténèbres Troisième du jeudi saint*	hd, d; bc	Motet	I, 1	6v–8	1670 Holy Week	
4	306	"Gaudete fideles"	hd, d; 2 fl, bc	Motet for St. Bernard	I, 1–2	8–9	1670 20 August	
5	53	*Jesu corona Virginum, Hymne au commun des Vierges à 2 dessus et 1 flûte*	2 d; fl, bc	Motet (hymn)	I, 2	9–10	1670	
6	307	"O doctor optime"	hd, d; bc	Motet for St. Augustine	I, 2	10–10v	1670 28 August	
7	426	"Quae est ista"	hd, d; bc	Motet	I, 2	11–11v	1670–71	
8	308	"Haec dies quam fecit Dominus"	hd, d; 2 fl, bc	Motet (Easter)	I, 2	11v–12	1671 Easter	
9	16	"Regina coeli"	hd, d; bc	Motet (antiphon to the Virgin)	I, 2	12v	1671	
10	17	"Veni sponsa Christi"	hd, d; fl, bc	Motet (antiphon to the Virgin)	I, 2	12v–13	1671	
11	282	"Domine salvum"	hd, d; bc	Motet	I, 2	13v	1671	
12	233	"Ave verum corpus"	hd, d; 2 treb., bc	Motet	I, 2	13v–14	1671	

#	No.	Title	Instrumentation	Type	Vol.	Folios	Date/Occasion	Notes
13	309	*Nativité de la Vierge*	hd, d; bc	Motet	I, 2	14v–15	1671 8 September	
14	310	*Saint François*	hd, d; 2 treb., bc	Motet	I, 2	15–16	1671 17 September or 4 October	
15	234	*Autre Jerusalem pour les Leçons de ténèbres à 2 voix pour la seconde du jeudi saint*	hd, d; bc	Motet (excerpt)	I, 2	16–17	1672 Holy Week	
16	2	*Messe pour les trépassés à 8*	2 hd, hc, t, b, hd, hc, t, b/2 hd, 2 hc, 2 t, 2 b; 2 fl, str (4/4), bc (b, vn, org)	Mass	I, 3	18–26	1671 August–September 1672 April–May	
17	234	"Pie Jesu"	hc, t, b, hd, hc, t, b/2 hd, 2 hc, 2 t, 2 b; bc (org)	Motet	I, 3	22v–23v	1671 August–September 1672 April–May	Part of the preceding mass
18	311	*Motet pour les trépassés à 8* "Miseremini mei"	2 hd, hc, t, b, HD, HC, T, B/HD, HC, T, B; str (4/4), bc	Motet	I, 4	27–32v	1671 August–September 1672 April–May	
19	156	*De profundis*	hd, hc, t, b; bc	Motet (Psalm 129)	I, 4	32v–33	1671 August–September 1672 April–May	
20	12	*Prose des Morts* "Dies irae"	2 hd, hc, t, 2 b, HD, HC, T, B/HD, HC, T, B; str (4/4), bc (org)	Motet (sequence of the *Messe des morts*)	I, 5	35–48v	1671 August–September 1672 April–May	
21	18	*Salve Regina*	hd, d, bd; bc (org) (transposable: hc, t, b)	Motet (antiphon to the Virgin)	I, 5	49–50v	1671–73	

No.	H.	Title	Scoring	Genre/Text	Volume/Cahier	Folio/Page	Date	Special comments
22	19	*Ave Regina coelorum*	hd, d, bd; bc	Motet (antiphon to the Virgin)	I, 5	50v–52	1671–73	"Melles B. et T."
23	235	*O sacrum convivium à 3 dessus, Elevatio*	hd, d, bd; bc	Motet	I, 5	52–53	1671–73	
24	157	*Miserere à 2 dessus, 2 flûtes et basse continue*	hd, d; 2 fl, bc	Motet (Psalm 50)	I, 6	54–59v	1673 Holy Week	"Melle Magdelon," "Melle Margot"
25	95	"Incipit oratio Jeremiae"	hd, d; 2 treb, bc	Motet	I, 6	59v–62	1673 Holy Week	"Melle Mag.," "Melle Marg."
26	508	*Pour un reposoir*	str (5)	Instrumental	I, 7	63–66	1673 Feast of Holy Sacrament	
27	509	*Symphonie devant Regina*	2 treb, b	Instrumental	I, 7	66v	1673–74	
28	510	"Prélude"?	2 treb, b	Instrumental	I, 7	66v	1673–74	
29	511	*Pour O filii*	2 treb, b	Instrumental	I, 7	67	1674 Easter	
30	512	"Prélude"?	2 treb, b	Instrumental	I, 7	67	1674	
31	513	*Messe pour plusieurs instruments au lieu des orgues*	fl à bec (2 d, 2 alto, 3 t, 4 b), fl trav (2 d, 1 t), 2 ob, cromorne (b), str (4)	Instrumental mass	I, 7–8	67v–78	1674–76	Incomplete
32	159	"Laudate Dominum omnes"	hc, t, b; 2 treb, bc	Motet (Psalm 116)	I, 8	78v–80	1674–76	
33	20	*Sub tuum praesidium*	hc, t, b; bc	Motet (antiphon to the Virgin)	I, 8	80–81	1674–76	
34	315	*Pour Sainte Anne* "Gaude felix Anna"	2 hd, bc	Motet	II, [9]	2	1674–76 26 July	

No.	H.	Title	Scoring	Genre	Vol.	Folios	Date	Remarks
35	391	*Judith sive Bethulia liberata*	2 hd, hc, 2 t, 2 b HD, HC, T, B; 2 fl, 2 vns, bc (org)	Latin oratorio	II, [9] 10–11	4–19	1674–76 15 August?	
36	392	*Canticum pro pace*	2 hd, hc, t, b HD, HC, T, B/HD, HC, T, B; str (4/4), bc	Latin oratorio	II, 11	19v–33	1674–76	
37	237	*Élévation pour la paix*	hc, t, b; 2 treb., bc	Motet	II, 11–12	33v–35v	1674–76	cf. No. 76 (H. 237a)
38	163	*Psalmus David VIII* "Domine Dominus noster"	hd, d, b; 2 treb., bc	Motet (Psalm 8)	II, 12	35v–40	1674–76	
39	427	*Pie Jesu*	hd, d, b; 2 treb., bc	Motet	II, 12	40v–42	1674–76	
40	393	*Canticum in nativitatem Domini*	hd, d, b; 2 treb., bc	Latin oratorio	II, 12	42–44v	1676 Christmas	
41	238	*Élévation* "Gaudete dilectissimi"	b; 2 treb., bc	Motet	II, 12–13	45–47	1676	
42	286	*Domine salvum*	hd, d, b; 2 treb., bc	Motet	II, 13	47–48	1676	
43	394	*In honorem Caeciliae, Valeriani et Tiburtij canticum*	hd, d, b; 2 treb., bc	Latin oratorio	II, 13	48v–52	1676 22 November	
44	479	*Petite Pastorale*	hc, t, b; 2 fl, bc	Pastorale	II, 13	52v–57	1676 5 October	Incomplete; also called *Le jugement de Pan* (*Mémoire des ouvrages . . . de M. Charpentier*)
45	316	*In circumcisione Domini*	hd, d, b; 2 treb., bc	Motet	II, 13	57v–59v	1677 1 January	
46	317	*Pour le jour de Sainte Geneviève*	hd, d, b; 2 treb., bc	Motet	II, 13–14	59v–63v	1677 3 January	
47	395	*Pour la fête de l'Épiphanie*	hd, d, b; 2 treb., bc	Latin oratorio	II, 14	64–67	1677 6 January	
48	318	*In festo purificationis*	hd, d, b; 2 treb., bc	Motet	II, 14	67v–70v	1677 2 February	
49	164	*Prière pour le roi* "Domine in virtute tua"	hd, d, b; 2 treb., bc	Motet (Psalm 20)	II, 14–15	71–76	1677	

No.	H.	Title	Scoring	Genre/Text	Volume/Cahier	Folio/Page	Date	Special comments
50	165	Precatio pro rege "Exaudiat te Dominus"	hd, d, b; 2 treb., bc	Motet (Psalm 19)	II, 15	76v–83	1677	
51	166	Precatio pro filio regis "Deus judicium tuum regi da"	hd, d, b; 2 treb., bc	Motet (Psalm 71: 1–17)	II, 15–16	83–89	1677	
52	58	Pange lingua	hc, t, b; 2 treb., bc	Motet (hymn of the Holy Sacrament)	II, 16	89–90v	1677 ?Feast of the Holy Sacrament	
53	21	"Alma redemptoris mater"	2 hd; bc (transposable: 2 hc)	Motet (antiphon to the Virgin)	II, 16	90v–92	1677	
54	22	Ave Regina	2 hd; bc	Motet (antiphon to the Virgin)	II, 16	93–95	1677	Pub: Motets mêlés de symphonie, 1709
55	23	Salve Regina à trois voix pareilles	hc, t, b; bc	Motet (antiphon to the Virgin)	II, 16	95–98v	1677	
56	319	Motet pour la Trinité	d, hc, b; bc	Motet	II, 16	98v–100v	1677 Feast of the Trinity	
57	59	Gaudia Virginis Mariae	3d; bc	Motet (hymn to the Virgin)	II, 16	100v–102v	1677–78	
58	24	Salve Regina à trois choeurs	HD, HC, T, B/HD, HC, T, B/hc, t, b; bc	Motet (antiphon to the Virgin)	III, 17	1–7	1677–78	cf. No. 75 (H. 23a)
59	320	Motet de Saint Louis	hc; 2 treb., bc	Motet	III, 17	7v	1677–78 25 August	Incomplete
60	321	Motet de Saint Laurent	hc; 2 treb., bc	Motet	III, 17	9–10v	1677–78 10 August	

No.	H.	Title	Scoring	Genre	Vol.	Folio	Date	Notes
61	239	*O sacrum à trois*	2 hd, hc; bc	Motet	**III**, 17	10v–12	1677–78	cf. H. 239a *O sacrum convivium de Charpentier pars [?]* 1670, BN, Vm¹ 1693, partial copy of H. 239
62	396	*Historia Esther*	2 hd, hc, 2 t, 2 b; HD, HC, T, B; 2 vns, fl, bc (org)	Latin oratorio	**III**, 17–18	12v–31	1677–78	
63	287	*Domine salvum*	hc, t, b; 2 treb., bc (org)	Motet	**III**, 18–19	31–32v	1677–78	
64	288	*Domine salvum pour trois religieuses*	2 hd, hc; bc	Motet	**III**, [19]	33–33v	1677–78	"Mère Camille," "Mère Sainte Caecile," "Mère Desnots"
65	322	*Motet de la Vierge pour toutes ses fêtes pour les mêmes religieuses*	2 hd, hc; bc (org)	Motet	**III**, [19]	33v–35	1677–78	"Mère Camille," "Mère Sainte Caecile," "Mère Dhénaut"
66	397	*Caecilia Virgo et Martyr octo vocibus*	5 hd, 2 hc, 2 t, b; HD, HC, T, B/HD, HC, T, B; str (4/4), bc (b. vls, org)	Latin oratorio	**III** [19]–20	35v–57	1677–78 22 November	
67	240	*O sacrum pour trois religieuses*	2 hd, hc; bc	Motet	**III**, 20	57v–58	1677–79	
68	168	*Psalmus David 5tus in tempore belli pro rege* "Quare fremuerunt gentes"	2 hd, 2 hc, 2 t, 2 b; HD, HC, T, B/HD, HC, T, B; str (4/4), bc (b. vl, org)	Motet (Psalm 2) (Charpentier's error)	**III**, 20	58–68	1677–79	cf. No. 10 (H. 168a)
69	60	*Hymne pour toutes les fêtes de la Vierge* "Ave maris stella"	hd, d, b; 2 treb., bc	Motet (hymn to the Virgin)	**III**, 20–21	68v–73	1677–79	
70	14	*Prose du Saint Sacrement* "Lauda Sion salvatorem"	hd, d, b; 2 treb., bc	Motet (sequence of the Holy Sacrament)	**III**, 21	73–79	1678–79 Feast of the Holy Sacrament	
71	241	*Elevatio* "Venite fideles"	b; 2 treb., bc	Motet	**III**, 21	79v–80v	1678–79	

No.	H.	Title	Scoring	Genre/Text	Volume/Cahier	Folio/Page	Date	Special comments
72	169	*Psalmus David 125tus* "In convertendo Dominus"	2 hd, 2 hc, 2 t, b/HD, HCT, B/HD, HC, T, B; str (4/4), bc (b. vn, org)	Motet (Psalm 125)	**III**, 21–22	80v–92	1678–79	
73	170	*Psalmus David centesimus trigesimus sextus Super flumina Babylonis*	hd, d, b; 2 fl, bc	Motet (Psalm 136)	**III**, 22	92v–97	**1679**	"Demoiselles Pieches"
74	25	*Antiphona in honorem beatae Virginis a redemptione captivorum*	hc, t; 2 treb, bc	Motet	**III**, 22	97v–99	1679	
75	23a	*Prélude pour Salve Regina à 3*	2 treb, bc	Instrumental	**III**, 22	100	1679	This prelude seems more suited to No. 58 (H. 24) than to No. 55 (H. 23)
76	237a	*Prélude en A mi la ré pour O bone Jesu à 3 voix pareilles pour la paix*	2 treb, bc	Instrumental	**III**, 22	101	1679	cf. No. 37 (H. 237)
77	242	*Ecce panis voce sola, Élévation*	d; bc	Motet (sequence of the Holy Sacrament, excerpt)	**III**, 22	102	1679	
78	243	*Panis angelicus voce sola, Élévation*	hd; bc	Motet (hymn for the Holy Sacrament)	**III**, 22	103	1679	Pub: *Motets 1709*
79	323	*In honorem Sancti Ludovici Regis Galliae Canticum tribus vocibus cum simphonia*	hd, d, b; 2 treb, bc	Motet	**III**, 22	104–107	1679 25 August	
80	171	*Super flumina Psalmus 136 octo vocibus cum instrumentis*	2 hd, 2 hc, 2 t, 2 b, HD, HC, T, B/HD, HC, T, B; str (4/4), bc	Motet (Psalm 136)	**III**, 22–23	108–115	1679	cf. No. 321 (H. 171a)

	H.	Title	Scoring	Genre	Vol.	Fol./pp.	Date	Notes
81	518	*Pour le sacre d'un évêque*	str (5)	Instrumental	III, 23	115v–120	1679	
82	398	*Pestis Mediolanensis*	2 hd, 2 hc, 2 t, 2 b HD, HC, T, B/HD, HC, T, B, 2 fl, str (4/4), bc (org)	Latin oratorio	III, 23–24	120–130	1679 4 November	cf. No. 311 (H. 398a)
83	172	*Psalmus 3us* "Domine quid multiplicati sunt"	hd, d, b; 2 treb., bc	Motet (Psalm 3)	III, 24	130v–135v	1679–80	
84	244	*Élévation à 2 dessus et 1 basse chantante*	hd, d, b; bc (transposable: hd, d, bd)	Motet	III, 24	135v–137v	1679–80	
85	245	*Élévation pour 1 dessus, 2 violons et l'orgue*	hd; 2 vns, bc (org)	Motet	III, 24	138–139	1679–80	
86	246	*Élévation* "Caro mea"	hd, d, b; bc	Motet	III, 24	139v–141	1679–80	
87	247	"O pretiosum et admirabile convivium"	hd; bc (transposable: t)	Motet	III, 24	142	1679–80	
88	173	*Miserere à 2 dessus, 1 haute-contre et basse continue*	2 hd, hc; bc (org)	Motet (Psalm 50)	IV, 25	1–7v	1680 Holy Week	
89	26	"Inviolata integra et casta es Maria"	2d, b; bc	Motet (antiphon to the Virgin)	IV, 25	8–11	1680	
	H. 96–110	The Nine Leçons de Ténèbres						
90	96	*Première leçon du mercredi saint*	d; bc	Motet	IV, 26	13–16v	**1680 Holy Week**	
91	97	*Seconde leçon du mercredi*	d; bc	Motet	IV, 26	16v–19v	**1680 Holy Week**	
92	98	*Troisième leçon du mercredi*	hd, d; bc (b. vl, hps)	Motet	IV, 26	19v–22	**1680 Holy Week**	
93	99	*Lettres hébraïques de la première leçon de ténèbres du vendredi saint*	2d, hc; bc	Motet	IV, 26	22	**1680 Holy Week**	

No.	H.	Title	Scoring	Genre/Text	Volume/Cahier	Folio/Page	Date	Special comments
94	100	*Ritornelles pour la première leçon de ténèbres du vendredi saint; Prélude devant De lamentatione pour le jeudi et le vendredi saint*	2 vns, 2 t. vls, bc	Instrumental	IV, 26	22v–23v	1680 **Holy Week**	
95	101	*Prélude pour la première leçon de ténèbres du mercredi saint*	2 treb., bc	Instrumental	IV, 26	23v	1680 **Holy Week**	
96	102	*Première leçon de ténèbres du jeudi saint*	d; bc	Motet	IV, 26	23v–27	1680 **Holy Week**	
97	103	*Seconde leçon du jeudi*	hd, d; bc	Motet	IV, 26	28–33	1680 **Holy Week**	
98	104	*Troisième leçon du jeudi*	d; bc	Motet	IV, 26	34–39	1680 **Holy Week**	
99	27	"Salve Regina"	t; bc	Motet (antiphon to the Virgin)	IV, 26	40	1680	*Salve Regina des jésuites* (added by an unknown hand)
100	105	*Première leçon du vendredi saint*	d; treb. vl, bc	Motet	IV, 27	41–44	1680 **Holy Week**	
101	106	*Seconde leçon du vendredi saint*	hd; bc	Motet	IV, 27	44–46	1680 **Holy Week**	
102	107	*Seconde leçon du jeudi saint à voix seule*	d; bc	Motet	IV, 27	46v–48	1680 **Holy Week**	
103	108	*Troisième leçon du mercredi à 3 parties*	2 hd, hc; bc	Motet	IV, 27	48v–51v	1680 **Holy Week**	
104	109	*Troisième leçon du jeudi saint à 3 voix*	2 hd, hc; bc	Motet	IV 27–28	51v–55v	1680 **Holy Week**	"Mère Sainte Caecile," "Mère Camille," "Mère Desnots"
105	110	*Troisième leçon du vendredi saint*	2 hd, hc; bc	Motet	IV, 28	55v–58v	1680 **Holy Week**	"Mère Sainte Caecille," "Camille"

106	111	*Premier répons après la première leçon du premier nocturne* "In monte Oliveti"	2 hd, hc; bc	Motet	**IV, 28**	58v–59	**1680 Holy Week**
107	112	*Second répons après la seconde leçon du premier nocturne* "Tristis est anima mea"	2 hd; bc	Motet	**IV, 28**	60–60v	**1680 Holy Week**
108	113	*Troisième répons après la troisième leçon du premier nocturne* "Amicus meus"	hc; bc	Motet	**IV, 28**	60v–61	**1680 Holy Week**
109	114	*Quatrième répons après la première leçon du second nocturne* "Unus ex discipulis meis"	hd, hc; bc	Motet	**IV, 28**	61–62	**1680 Holy Week**
110	115	*Cinquième répons après la deuxième leçon du second nocturne* "Eram quasi agnus"	hd; bc	Motet	**IV, 28**	62–62v	**1680 Holy Week**
111	116	*Sixième répons après la troisième leçon du second nocturne* "Una hora non potuistis"	2 hd, hc; bc	Motet	**IV, 28**	62v–64	**1680 Holy Week**
112	117	*Septième répons après la première leçon du troisième nocturne* "Seniores populi"	hc; bc	Motet	**IV, 28**	64–64v	**1680 Holy Week**
113	118	*Huitième répons après la seconde leçon du troisième nocturne* "Revelabunt coeli"	2 hd, hc; bc	Motet	**IV 28–29**	64v–68v	**1680 Holy Week**
114	119	*Neuvième répons après la troisième leçon du troisième nocturne du mercredi saint* "O Juda, o Juda"	2hd; bc	Motet	**IV, 29**	68v–69	**1680 Holy Week**

No.	H.	Title	Scoring	Genre/Text	Volume/Cahier	Folio/Page	Date	Special comments
115	399	*Filius prodigus*	hd, 2 hc, 2 t, 2b HD, HC, T, B; 2 vns, bc (org)	Latin oratorio	IV, 29	70–80	1680	cf. No. 309 (H. 399a), H. 399b, Brossard collection, BN, VM¹ 1480, & H. 399c, Bibliothèque de Versailles, Ms. 58 (copy with variants)
116	400	*Canticum in honorem beatae Virginis Mariae inter homines et angelos*	2 d, hc, t, b; bc	Latin oratorio	IV, 29–30	80v–88v	1680	
117	325	*Canticum Annae*	hd, d, b; 2 treb, bc	Motet	IV, 30	89–95v	1680 26 July	
118	401	*Extremum Dei judicium*	hd, 2 hc, t, 2 b HD, HC, T, B; 2 treb, 2 tps (optional), bc	Latin oratorio	IV 30–31	96–109	1680	
119	326	*Gratiarum actiones ex sacris codicibus excerptae pro restituta serenissimi Galliarum Delphini salute*	hd, d, b; 2 fl, fl, bc (b. vn, b. vl, hps)	Motet	IV 31–32	109v–119	**end 1680**	"Magd.", "Marg.", "Friz."
120	403	*Mors Saülis et Jonathae*	2 hd, 2 hc, 2 t, 2 b HD, HC, T, B; 2 vns, bc (org)	Latin oratorio	IV, 32	119v–134v	1681–82	
121	250	*Elevatio* "Ascendat ad te Domine"	bt; 2 treb, bc	Motet	IV, 32	134v–136	1681–82	
122	63	"Ave maris stella"	2d; bc (org)	Motet (hymn to the Virgin)	IV, 32	136v–138	1681–82	
123	82	*Litanies de la Vierge à 3 voix pareilles*	hc, t, b; bc	Motet	XI, 33	1–4	1681–82	

		Title	Instrumentation	Genre	Vol.	Fol.	Date	Notes
124	74	*Magnificat à 8 voix et 8 instruments*	hd, hc, t, b, HD, HC, T, B, HD, HC, T, B; 2 fl, ob, str (4/4), bc (b. vns, bs, org)	Motet (canticle of the Virgin)	XI, 33	4v–15	1681–82	"Mr. Dun"
125	180	*Exaudiat pour le roi à 4*	2 hd, hc, t, b, HD, HC, T, B; 2 vns (optional), bc (org)	Motet (Psalm 19)	XI, 33	15v–20	1681–82	cf. No. 222 (H. 180a)
126	404	*Josue*	2 hd, hc, t, 2 b, HD, HC, T, B/HD, HC, T, B, str (4/4), bc	Latin oratorio	XI, 34	23–36v	1681–82	
127	183	*Psalmus David 107* "Paratum cor meum Deum"	hc, t, b; bc	Motet (Psalm 107)	XI, 34	37–40	1681–82	
128	185	*Psalmus David nonagesimus primus* "Bonum est confiteri Domino"	hd, d, b; 2 treb., bc (hps)	Motet (Psalm 91)	XI, 35	42–48v	1681–82	
129	186	*Psalmus David octogesimus tertius* "Quam dilecta"	hd, d, b; 2 treb., bc (org)	Motet (Psalm 83)	XI, 35	49–56	1681–82	
130	291	"Domine salvum"	2 hd, 2 hc, HD, HC, T, B/HD, HC, T, B; str (4/4), bc	Motet	XI, [36]	58v bis–61	1681–82	
131	330	*Gaudia beatae Virginis Mariae*	hd, d, b; 2 treb., bc	Motet	XI [36]–37	61–69	1681–82	
132	480	*Les Plaisirs de Versailles*	hd, d, hc, b; 2 treb., (fl?), b. fl, bc (b. vl)	Divertissement	XI, 37	69–84	End of 1682	
133	187	*Psalmus 86* "Fundamenta ejus"	2d, b; bc	Motet (Psalm 86)	XI, 37	84v–86v	1682–83	
134	407	*Dialogus inter esurientem, sitientem et Christum*	2d, b; bc (org)	Latin oratorio	XI, 37	86v–88	1682–83	
135	331	*Luctus de morte augustissimae Mariae Theresiae reginae Galliae*	hc, t, b; 2 treb., bc	Motet	VI, 38	1–6v	**1683** (after 30 July)	

No.	H.	Title	Scoring	Genre/Text	Volume/Cahier	Folio/Page	Date	Special comments
136	332	*In honorem Sancti Ludovici Regis Galliae*	hc, t, b; 2 treb, bc (org)	Motet	VI, 38	7–11	1683 25 August	
137	471	*Orphée descendant aux enfers*	hc, t, b; 2 vns, fl à bec, fl trav, bc (b. vl)	Cantata	VI, 38	11–16	1683–84	
138	252	*Élévation* "O coelestis Jerusalem"	hc, t, b; bc	Motet	VI 38–39	16v–20v	1683–84	
139	190	*Psalmus 109us, Dixit Dominus, 8 vocibus et totidem instrumentis*	2 hd, hc, t, 2 b, HD, HC, T, B/HD, HC, T, B; 2 fl, ob, str (4/4), bc (b. vns, bs, org)	Motet (Psalm 109)	VI, 39	21–34	1683–84	"Mr. Dun," "Mr. Beaupuy"
140	253	*O amor, Élévation à 2 dessus et 1 basse chantante*	hd, d, b; bc or hc, t, b; bc	Motet	VI, 39	34v–36	1683–84	cf. No. 413 (H. 253a)
141	191	*Psalmus 147* "Lauda Jerusalem"	2 hd, hc, t, b, HD, HC, T, B/HD, HC, T, B; str (4/4), bc (b. vn, org)	Motet (Psalm 147)	VI, 40	37–46v	1683–84	
142	192	"Omnes gentes plaudite manibus"	hd, d, b; 2 treb, bc	Motet (Psalm 46)	VI, 40	47–52	1683–84	
143	293	"Domine salvum"	hd, d, b; 2 treb, bc	Motet	VI, 40	52v–53v	1683–84	
144	294	*Autre Domine* "Domine salvum"	hd, d, b; 2 treb, bc	Motet	VI, 40	53v–54	1683–84	
145	254	"O pretiosum et admirabile convivium"	2 d; bc	Motet	VI, 40	55	1683–84	
146	333	*Pro omnibus festis BVM*	hd, d, bd, hc, t, b, HD, D, BD, HC, T, B; 2 treb. vls, bc (b. vl, theorbo, org) (certain solo parts transposable)	Motet	VI, 41	56–62	1683–84	

No.	H.	Title	Scoring	Genre	Vol.	Folio	Date	Performers / Notes
147	75	*Magnificat à 3 dessus*	hd, d, bd; bc	Motet (canticle of the Virgin)	VI, 41	62–65v	1683–84	"Melle Brion," "Melle Thorin," "Melle G.M…on"
148	255	"O pretiosum et admirandum convivium"	hd, d, b; 2 treb, bc (org) (transposable: hc instead of b)	Motet	VI, 41	66–67	1683–84	
149	83	*Litanies de la Vierge à 6 voix et 2 dessus de violes*	hd, 2 d, hc, t, 2 b, HD, 2 D, HC, T, B; 2 treb, vls, bc (org) (certain solo parts transposable)	Motet	VI 41–42	67–76v	1683–84	"Br.," "Tal.," "Melle Thorin," "Isab.," "Gr. M.," "Charp.," "Boss.," "Beaup.," "Carl."
150	413	*Caecilia Virgo et Martyr*	hd, 2 d, hc, t, b, HD, 2 D, HC, T, B; 2 treb. vls, bc (b. vl, org)	Latin oratorio	VI, 42	77–89	1684 22 November	"Mlle Brion," "Melle Isab.," "Grand M.," "Charp.," "Mr. Joly," "Boss.," "Carlie"
151	414	*In nativitatem Domini Nostri Jesu Christi Canticum*	hd, 2 d, bt, HD, 2 D, HC, T, B; 2 treb, bc	Latin oratorio	VI 42–43 [a]	89–96	1684 Christmas	"Melle Isab.," "Brion," "Talon," "Gr. M.," "Joly"
152	193	*Psalmus David 50mus, Miserere des Jésuites*	First version: hd, 2 d, hc, t, bt or b, HD, 2 D, HC, T, B; 2 treb, bc (hps)	Motet (Psalm 50)	VII [43b]	1–18	1685	"Brion," "Talon," "Isabelle," "Grand Maison," "Charp.," "Bossan," "Joly, "Carlie," "Beaupuy," "Dun"; cf. No. 412 (H. 193a); other ms source (orchestra version): cf. No. 535
153	472	*Serenata a tre voci e simphonia*	d, hc, b; 2 treb, bc	Cantata	VII [43b–44]	18–24v	1685	
154	339	*Chant joyeux du temps de Pâques*	2 hd, d, hc, t, bt or b, HD, D, HC, T, B; 2 treb. vls, bc	Motet	VII, 44	25–34v	1685 Easter	"Bri.," "Tal.," "Isab.," "G. M.," "Charp.," "Bos.," "Joly," "Carl."
155 (1)	495b	*Le Malade imaginaire rajusté autrement pour la 3ᵉ fois*	Str (4)	Instrumenal	VII, 44	34v–35v	**1685** 15 September **1686** 11 January	

No.	H.	Title	Scoring	Genre/Text	Volume/Cahier	Folio/Page	Date	Special comments
156	486	*La Couronne de fleurs, Pastorale*	2 hd, 2 d, hc, t, 2 b, HD, D, HC, T, B; 2 treb. vls, bc	Pastorale	**VII** 44–45	35v–50v	1685	"Mlle Isabelle," "Brion," "Gr. Maison," "Charp.," "Bossan," "Carlié," "Beaupuy"
155 (2)	495b	*Satyres pour la fin du prologue du Malade imaginaire rajusté pour la 3e fois*	Str (4)	Instrumental	**VII**, 45	51–51v	**1685** 15 September **1686** 11 January	
155 (3)	495b	*Suite du Malade imaginaire, Nouvelle ouverture de l'entrée des Mores du Malade imaginaire*	Str (4)	Instrumental	**VII**, 45	51v–52	**1685** 15 September **1686** 11 January	
157	506	*Dialogue d'Angélique et de Médor*	d, t; bc	Dancourt	**VII**, 45	52v–[53v]	1685 1 August	
158	29	*Antiphona in honorem beatae Genovefae voce sola*	d; bc	Motet	**VII**, 45	53v–54	1686? 3 January	
159	473	*Epithalamio In lode dell'Altezza Serenissima Elettorale di Massimiliano Emanuel Duca di Baviera*	2 d, b, 2 D, HC, T, B; 2 tp, 2 fl, 2 ob, 2 vns, dr, bc (b. vn, bs, hps)	Cantata	**VII** 45–46	54v–63	**1685**	
160	487	*Les Arts Florissants, Opéra*	3 hd, d, hc, t, b, HD, D, HC, T, 2 B; 2 fl, 2 treb. vls, bc (b. vl, org)	Divertissement	**VII** 46–47	63v–86v	1685	"Brion," "Talon," "Gr. M.," "Charp.," "Isab.," "Beaupuy," cf. H. 487a (separate parts, in BN, Ms. Vm⁶ 18), "Mlle Brion," "Mlle Thorin," "Mlle Talon," "Mlle Grand Maison," "Mr. Charp.," "Mr. Beaupuy," "Mr. Bossan," "Mr. Carlié"
161	340	*Ad beatam Virginem Canticum*	hc, t, b; 2 fl, 2 vns, bc	Motet	**VII**, 47	86v–90	1685	

No.	H	Title	Instrumentation	Genre	Vol.	Folio	Date	Other ms source
162	415	Caecilia Virgo et Martyr	2 hd, d, hc, t, HD, 2 D, HC, T, B; 2 treb. vls, bc	Latin oratorio	VII, 47	92–100	1685 22 November	Brion, Talon, "Isabelle," "Gr. Maison," "Charp.," "Bossan," "Beaupuy," "Carlié"; cf. No. 384 (H. 415a)
		Cahier 48 Missing					1685–86	
163	342	Pour Sainte Thérèse "Flores, o Gallia"	2 hd, d; bc	Motet	VIII [49]	2–4	1686 15 October	
164	343	Magdalena lugens voce sola cum simphonia "Solat vivebat in antris"	hd; 2 vns, bc	Motet	VIII [49]	4–6	1686 22 July	Other ms source in Brossard collection, BN, Vm¹ 1739, no.II, pp. 17–22); cf. also H. 343a (separate parts), BN, Vm¹ 1266, no. 8
165	489	Idylle sur le retour de la santé du roi	hd, hd or d, hc, t, b, HD, D, HC, T, B, 2 treb., bc	Divertissement	VIII [49]–50	6v–15	1687 31 January?	"Mlle Isab.," "Brion," "Melle Guyot," "Tal.," "Gr. M.," "Anth.," "Boss.," "Beaup.," "Carl."
166	431	Gratitudinis erga Deum Canticum	hd, d, b; 2 treb., bc	Motet	VIII, 50	15v–20	1687 20 January?	"Magd.," "Marg.," "Friz."
167	345	Canticum Zachariae	hd, d, hc, t, b, HD, 2 D, HC, T, B; 2 treb., bc	Motet	VIII, 50	20v–30	1687	"Guy.," "Br.," "Tal.," "Isab.," "Gr. M.," "Anth.," "Boss.," "Beaup.," "Carl."
168	258	Elevatio "Nonne Deo"	d; bc (transposable: hc)	Motet	VIII, 50	31	1687	
		Cahiers 51, 52, 53 Missing					1687–90?	
169	197	Psalmus David 109us "Dixit Dominus"	hc, t, b/HD, HC, T, B; bc	Motet (Psalm 109)	VIII, 54	32–33v	1688–90?	cf. No. 227 (H. 197a)
170	76	Canticum BVM "Magnificat"	hc, t, b/HD, HC, T, B; bc (org)	Motet (canticle of the Virgin)	VIII, 54	34–36	1688–90?	cf. No. 230 (H. 76a)
171	198	Psalmus David 4us "Cum invocarem"	hd, hc, 2 t, b, HD, HC, T, B; fl, str (4), bc (org)	Motet (Psalm 4)	VIII, 54	36–39	1688–90?	

No.	H.	Title	Scoring	Genre/Text	Volume/Cahier	Folio/Page	Date	Special comments
172	30	"Regina coeli"	hc, t, b; bc	Motet (antiphon to the Virgin)	VIII, 54	39v–40	1688–90?	
173	199	*Psalmus David centesimus undecimus* "Beatus vir"	hd, hc, t, b/HD, HC, T, B, bc (org)	Motet (Psalm 111)	VIII, 54	40–43v	1688–90?	"Dun," "Mr. l'Écuyer"; cf. No. 228 (H. 199a)
174	200	*Psalmus 110ème, Confitebor*	hd, 2 hc, t, b, HD, HC, T, B; bc (org)	Motet (Psalm 110)	VIII, 54	43v–46v	1688–90?	"L'Escuyer"; cf. No. 229 (H.200a)
175	31	*Regina coeli, voce sola cum flauti*	hc; 2 fl, bc	Motet (antiphon to the Virgin)	VIII, 54	47–78	1688–90?	
176	296	"Domine salvum"	2 t, b; bc	Motet	VIII, 54	48	1688–90?	
177	201	*Psalmus David 34us* "Judica Domine nocentes me"	hd, d, 2 b; 2 treb., bc	Motet (Psalm 34: 1–8)	IX, 55	1–3	1688–90?	"Mlle Magd," "Mlle Marg," "Mr. Bastaron," "Mr. Frison"
178	202	*Dixit Dominus, Psalmus David 109us*	hd, hc, t, b/HD, HC, T, B, 2 fl, ob, str (4) bc (b. vn, bs, org)	Motet (Psalm 109)	IX, 55	4–9v	1688–90?	
179	77	*Magnificat*	2 hd, hc, t, b/HD, HC, T, B; 2 fl, str (4), bc	Motet (canticle of the Virgin)	IX, 55r	9v–17	1688–90?	"Bluquet"
180	297	*Domine salvum pour un haut et un bas dessus*	hd, d; bc	Motet	IX, 55	17	1688–90?	
181	353	*In Assumptione beatae Mariae Virginis*	hd, 2 t (or hc & t), b, HD, 2 T (or HC & T); B; 2 fl, str (4), bc (b. vn, org)	Motet	IX, 56	18–23	1690? 15 August	"Ducroc," "Joly," "Bowman"
182	260	*Elevatio* "O sacramentum pietatis"	2 t, b; 2 fl, 2 vns, bc	Motet	IX, 56	23v–25	1690?	"Mr. L'escuyer"

183	203	*Psalmus supra centesimum duodecimus* "Laudate pueri"	2 hd (or hd & t), hc, t, b/HD, HC, T, B; bc	Motet (Psalm 112)	**IX**, 56	25–28	1690?	cf. No. 231 (H. 203a)
184	67	*Ave maris stella*	hd, hc, t, 3b; bc (org)	Motet (hymn to the Virgin)	**IX**, 56	28–29	1690?	"Amiot," "Cochet," "L'Ecuyer," "Guenet," "Dhun"
185	354	*Motet pour Saint François de Borgia*	hc; 2 treb, bc	Motet	**IX**, 56	30	1690? 10 October	
186	525	*Antienne*	2 fl, str (4), bc, org	Instrumental	**IX**, 57	31–31v	1690?	
187	204	*Psalm 109* "Dixit Dominus"	2 t (or hc &/or hd & t), b/HD, HC, T, B; fl, str (4), bc (org)	Motet (Psalm 109)	**IX**, 57	31v–36v	1690?	
188	526	*Antienne*	2 fl, str (4), bc, org	Instrumental	**IX**, 57	36v–37	1690?	
189	78	*Magnificat*	hc, 2 t (or hd & t), b, HD, HC, T, B; 2 fl, str (4), bc (org)	Motet (canticle of the Virgin)	**IX**, 57	37v–42	1690?	
190	205	*Gloria Patri pour le De profundis en C sol ut b mol à 4 voix, 4 violons et flûtes*	2 t, b/HD, HC, T, B; fl, str (4), bc	Motet (excerpt)	**IX**, 57	43	1690?	
191	355	*In honorem Sancti Xaverij Canticum*	2 hd, hc, t, b, HD, HC, T, B; 2 fl, str (4), bc (org)	Motet	**IX**, 58	44–51	1690? 3 December	
192	416	*In nativitatem Domini Canticum*	hc, t, b/HD, HC, T, B; 2 fl, str (4), bc (b. vn, org)	Latin oratorio	**IX**, 58	51v–61	1690? Christmas	
193	531	*Noël, O créateur* / *Autre Noël* "Laissez paître vos bêtes," / *Autre Noël* "Vous qui désirez sans fin"	2 fl, str (4), bc	Instrumental	**IX**, 58	61–63	1690? Christmas	
194	206	*Psalmus David 5tus post septuagesimum* "Notus in Judea Deus"	hc, t, b/HD, HC, T, B; 2 fl, str (4), bc (b. vns, org) (certain solo parts transposable)	Motet (Psalm 75)	**X**, 59	1–7	1691?	"Mr. Dun," "Mr. Marchand père," "Mr. Convercet"

No.	H.	Title	Scoring	Genre/Text	Volume/Cahier	Folio/Page	Date	Special comments
195	207	*Psalmus Davidis post octogesimus septimus* "Domine Deus salutis"	hc, t, b/HD, HC, T, B; 2 fl, str (4), bc (org)	Motet (Psalm 87)	X, 59	7v–12v	1691?	"Mr. Dun"
196	126	*Second répons après la seconde leçon du premier nocturne du mercredi saint* "Tristis est anima mea"	2 t; bc	Motet	X, 59	13	1691? Holy Week	
197	127	*Premier répons après la première leçon du second nocturne du mercredi saint* "Amicus meus"	t; 2 fl, bc	Motet	X, 59	13v–14	1691? Holy Week	
198	128	*Second répons après la seconde leçon du premier nocturne du jeudi saint* "Velum templi"	hc, t, b/HD, HC, T, B; fl, str (4), bc	Motet	X, 59	14–15	1691? Holy Week	
199	129	*Second répons après la seconde leçon du second nocturne du jeudi saint* "Tenebrae factae sunt"	b; str (4), bc	Motet	X, 59	15v–16	1691? Holy Week	"Mr. Dun"
200	130	*Second répons après la seconde leçon du premier nocturne de vendredi saint* "Jerusalem surge"	2 t; 2 treb., bc	Motet	X, 59	16–17	1691? Holy Week	
201	131	*Troisième répons après la troisième leçon du second nocturne du vendredi saint* "Ecce quomodo"	hc; str (4), bc	Motet	X, 59	17–17v	1691? Holy Week	"Ribon"
202	132	*Troisième répons après la troisième leçon du second nocturne du mercredi saint* "Unus ex discipulis meis"	b; 2 vns, bc	Motet	X, 59	18	1691? Holy Week	"Mr. Dun"

203	133	*Premier répons après la première leçon du second nocturne du jeudi saint* "Tanquam ad latronem"	b; 2 fl, 2 vns, bc	Motet	X, 59	18v–19	1691? Holy Week	"Mr. Beaupuy"
204	134	*Second répons après la seconde leçon du second nocturne du vendredi saint* "O vos omnes"	hd; 2 fl, bc	Motet	X, 59	19v–20v	1691? Holy Week	"Mr. Bluquet"
205	546	*Commencement d'ouverture pour ce que l'on voudra en la rectifiant un peu*	str (4)	Instrumental	X, 59	20v	1691?	Incomplete
206	359	*Motet pour la Vierge à 2 voix*	hc, t; bc	Motet	X, 59	21	1691?	
207	360	*Pour la Vierge*	t, b; bc	Motet	X, 59	22	1691?	
208	6	*Messe à 4 voix, 4 violons, 2 flûtes et 2 hautbois pour Mr. Mauroy*	2 hd, hc, t, 2 b, HD, HC, T, B; 2 fl, 2 ob, str (4), bc (b. vns, bs, org)	Mass	X, 60–61	23–51	1691?	
209	299	*Domine salvum*	2 hd, HD, HC, T, B; 2 fl, str (4), bc	Motet	X, 61	49–51	1691?	Part of the preceding mass
210	547	*Marche de triomphe pour les violons, trompettes, timbales, flûtes et hautbois; Second air de trompettes, violons, flûtes, hautbois et timbales*	tp, 2 fl, 2 ob, str (4), b. tp, dr, (bc b. vns, bs, org)	Instrumental	X, 61	51v–53	1691?	
211	208	*Psalmus undecimus Davidis post centesimum, Beatus vir qui timet Dominum 4 vocibus cum simphonia*	2 hd, hc, t, b, HD, HC, T, B; 2 fl, ob, str (4), bc (bs, org)	Motet (Psalm 111)	X, 61	53–62v	1691?	"Beaupuy"
212	361	*Pour plusieurs martyrs, Motet à voix seule sans accompagnement*	b	Motet	X, 61	62v–63	1691?	
213	532	*Antienne pour les violons, flûtes et hautbois à 4 parties*	2 fl, ob, str (4), bc (org)	Instrumental	X, 61	63–64	1691?	

No.	H.	Title	Scoring	Genre/Text	Volume/Cahier	Folio/Page	Date	Special comments
214	355a	*Canticum de Sancto Xaverio reformatum*	2 hd, hc, t, b, HD, HC, T, B; 2 fl, ob, str (4), bc (bs, org)	Motet	X, 62	65–72v	1691? 3 December	Reworked version of H. 355 *In honorem Sancti Xaverij Canticum* (vol. IX, cah. 58, 4–51)
215	266	"Ave verum corpus"	hc; 2 fl. trav, bc	Motet	X, 62	72v–73	1691–92?	
216	146	*Te Deum*	2 hd, hc, t, b, HD, HC, T, B; 2 fl, 2 ob, tp, str (4), b. tp, dr, bc (b. vns, bs, org)	Motet	X, 62	73v–85	1692? August?	"Mr. Beaupuy"
217	300	*Domine salvum à 3 dessus*	2 hd, d; bc	Motet	X, 62	86	1692?	
218	418	*In honorem Sancti Ludovici Regis Galliae*	hc, t, b; 2 fl, 2 vns, bc (b. vl, hps)	Latin oratorio	V, 63	1–5	1692? 25 August	
219	366	*Pour le Saint Esprit* "Veni Sancte Spiritus"	hc, t, b; bc	Motet	V, 63	5–5v	1692?	
220	267	*Élévation* "Verbum caro panem verum"	hc, t, b; bc	Motet	V, 63	5v–6	1692?	
221	8	*Messe pour le samedi de Pâques à 4 voix*	2 hd, hc, t, b, HD, HC, T, B; bc (org)	Mass	V, 63	6v–8v	1693? Easter	
222	180a	*Premier prélude pour l'Exaudiat à 4 violons sans instruments à la ré sol dièse à 2 violons*	2 vns, bc	Instrumental	V, 63	8v	1693?	cf. No. 125 (H. 180)
223	180b	*Second prélude à 4 violons pour le même Exaudiat*	str (4), bc	Instrumental	V, 63	9	1693?	cf. No. 125 (H. 180)
224	138	*Seconde leçon de ténèbres du mercredi saint*	hc; bc	Motet	V, 63	11–12	1693? Holy Week	
225	139	*Seconde leçon de ténèbres du jeudi saint*	hc; bc	Motet	V, 63	12v–13v	1693? Holy Week	

226	140	*Seconde leçon de ténèbres du vendredi saint*	hc; bc	Motet	V, 63	13v–14	1693? Holy Week	
227	197a	*Prélude pour le premier Dixit Dominus en petit en ré sol bémol*	2 treb., bc	Instrumental	V, 63	15	1693?	cf. No. 169 (H. 197)
228	199a	*Prélude pour le premier Beatus vir à 4 voix sans instruments*	2 treb., bc (org)	Instrumental	V, 63	15	1693?	cf. No. 173 (H. 199)
229	200a	*Prélude pour le premier Confitebor à 4 voix sans instruments*	2 treb., bc (org)	Instrumental	V, 63	15v	1693?	cf. No. 174 (H. 200)
230	76a	*Prélude pour le premier Magnificat à 4 voix sans instruments C sol ut*	2 treb., bc (org)	Instrumental	V, 63	15v	1693?	cf. No. 170 (H. 76)
231	203a	*Prélude pour Laudate pueri Dominum à 4 voix sans instruments en g ré sol naturel*	2 treb., bc	Instrumental	V, 63	16	1693?	cf. No. 183 (H. 203)
232	533	*Prélude pour le second Magnificat à 4 voix sans instruments d la ré bécarre*	2 treb., bc (org)	Instrumental	V, 63	16	1693?	
233	160a	*Prélude pour Nisi Dominus Dominus à 4 voix sans instruments C sol ut*	2 treb., bc (org)	Instrumental	V, 63	17	1693?	cf. No. 286 (H. 160)
234	209a	*Prélude pour Credidi à 4 voix sans instruments C sol ut*	2 treb., bc	Instrumental	V, 63	17	1693?	cf. No. 431 (H. 209)
235	147	*(5ª) Te Deum à 4 voix*	2 hd, hc, t, b, HD, HC, T, B; str (4), bc (org)	Motet	V, 64	18–21v	1693? October?	
236	534 (1)	*Noëls sur les instruments: Les Bourgeois de Châtre / Où s'en vont ces gais bergers / Joseph est bien marié / Or nous dites Marie*	2 fl, str (4), bc	Instrumental	V, 64	21v–24v	1693? Advent– Christmas	

No.	H.	Title	Scoring	Genre/Text	Volume/Cahier	Folio/Page	Date	Special comments
		H. 36–43 Salut de la veille des O et les 7 O suivant le Romain						
237	36	*Salut pour la veille des O* "O salutaris hostia"	hc, t, b; bc	Motet	V, 64	24v–25	1693? Advent	
238	37	*Premier O* "O sapienta"	hc, t, b; bc	Motet (antiphon for Advent)	V, 64	25v–26	1693? Advent	
239	38	*Second O* "O Adonaï"	hc, t, b; bc	Motet (antiphon for Advent)	V, 64	26–27	1693? Advent	
240	39	*Troisième O* "O radix jesse"	hc, t, b; bc	Motet (antiphon for Advent)	V, 64	27–27v	1693? Advent	
241	40	*Quatrième O* "O clavis David"	hc, t, b/HD, HC, T, B; str (4), bc	Motet (antiphon for Advent)	V, 64	27v–28v	1693? Advent	
242	41	*Cinquième O* "O Oriens"	hc, t, b/HD, HC, T, B; str (4), bc	Motet (antiphon for Advent)	V, 64	28v–29	1693? Advent	
243	42	*Sixième O* "O rex gentium"	hc; 2 vns, bc	Motet (antiphon for Advent)	V, 64	29–29v	1693? Advent	"Mr. Chopelet"
244	43	*Septième O* "O Emmanuel rex"	hc, t, b; bc	Motet (antiphon for Advent)	V, 64	30–30v	1693? Advent	
245	534 (2)	*A la venue de Noël Une jeune pucelle* "Les Bourgeois de Châtre"	2 fl, str (4), bc	Instrumental	V, 64	30v–33	1693? Advent–Christmas	
		Cahier 65 missing					1694–95?	
246	44	*Antienne à la Vierge Alma redemptoris à 4 voix et 2 violons*	hc, t, b/HD, HC, T, B; 2 vns, bc	Motet	V, 66	36–37v	1694–95?	

247	45	Antienne à la Vierge Ave Regina coelorum à 4 voix et 2 dessus de violon	hc, t, b/HD, HC, T, B; 2 vns, bc	Motet	V, 66	38–40	1694–95?
248	46	Antienne à la Vierge Regina coeli à 4 voix et 2 dessus de violon	hc, t, b/HD, HC, T, B; 2 vns, bc	Motet	V, 66	40–42	1694–95?
249	47	Antienne à la Vierge Salve Regina à 4 voix et 2 violons	hc, t, b/HD, HC, T, B; 2 vns, bc	Motet	V, 66	42–44	1694–95?
250	220	Psalmus David 110 à 4 voix "Confitebor"	hc, t, b/HD, HC, T, B; bc	Motet (Psalm 110)	V, 66	44–48	1694–95?	"Dun," "Hardouin"
251	221	Psalmus David 111 à 4 voix "Beatus vir"	hc, t, b/HD, HC, T, B; bc (org)	Motet (Psalm 111)	V, 66	47–52	1694–95?	"Dun," "Hardouin"
252	536	Ouverture pour le sacre d'un évêque pour les violons, flûtes et hautbois	2 fl ("if there are any"), ob?, str (4), bc (org)	Instrumental	V, 66	52v–53v	1695? 9 December?
253	432	Offertoire pour le sacre d'un évêque à 4 parties de voix et d'instruments	hc, t, 2b/HD, HC, T, B; strings (4), bc	Motet	V, 66	54–59	1696?	"Mr Dun," "Hard."
254	90	Courtes Litanies de la Vierge à 4 voix	hd, hc, t, b, HD, HC, T, B, bc	Motet	V, 66	59–60	1696? March–April?
255	222	Court De profundis à 4 voix	hc, t, b/HD, HC, T; bc	Motet (Psalm 129)	V, 66	60v–61	1696? March–April?
256	48	Antienne à la Vierge pour toutes les saisons de l'année "Inviolata, integra"	hc, t, b; bc	Motet	V, 66	61v–63	1696?
257	371	A la Vierge à 4 voix pareilles	hc, 2 t, b; bc	Motet	V, 66	63v–65	1696?
		Cahiers 67, 68, 69 missing					1696–98?
258	372	Pour la seconde fois que le Saint Sacrement vient au même reposoir "O Deus, o salvator"	hc, t, b/HD, HC, T, B; str (4), bc	Motet	XII, 70	1–6	1696? Feast of the Holy Sacrament	"Mr. Des Voyes," "Mr. Tonnenche," "Mr. Dun," "Mr. Hardouin"
		Cahiers 71, 72, 73 missing					1696–98?

No.	H.	Title	Scoring	Genre/Text	Volume/Cahier	Folio/Page	Date	Special comments
259	434	*Motet pour une longue offrande*	2 hd, hc, t, b, HD, HC, T, B; 2 fl, 2 ob, str (4), bc (b. vns, bs, org)	Motet	XII, 74	7–19v	1698 12 November	
260	273	*Élévation* "O vere, o bone"	hc; bc	Motet	XII, 74	20	1698	
261	421	*In nativitate Domini Nostri Jesu Christi Canticum*	2 hd, d; bc	Latin oratorio	XII, 74	20v–22v	1698 Christmas	
262	148	(6th) *Te Deum à 4 voix*	2 hd, hc, t, b, HD, HC, T, B; bc (org)	Motet	XII, 74	23–28	1699	
263	228	*Psalmus David LXX, 3ᵉ psaume du premier nocturne du mercredi saint* "In te Domine speravi"	2 hd, hc, t, bt, HD, HC, T, BT, B; str (4), bc (b. vns, org)	Motet (Psalm 70)	XII, 75	35–41	1699 Holy Week	"Mr. D'angoulesme," "Mr. Molaret," "Mr. Royer," "Mr. Terrier," "Mr. Antheaume," "Bersan," "Beaulieu"
264	229	*Psalmus David 26tus, 3ᵉ psaume du premier nocturne du jeudi saint* "Dominus illuminatio"	2 hd, hc, t, bt, HD, HC, T, BT, B; str (4), bc (org)	Motet (Psalm 26)	XII, 75	41v–47	1699 Holy Week	"Bersan," "Bruslard," "Mr. Antheaume," "Mr. Dangoulesme," "Mr. Molaret," "Mr. Royer," "Mr. Terrier"
265	230	*Psalmus David 15tus, 3ᵉ psaume du premier nocturne du vendredi saint* "Conserva me Domine"	hd, hc, t, bt, HD, HC, T, BT, B; str (4), bc	Motet (Psalm 15)	XII, 75	47v–55	1699 Holy Week	"Mr Dangoulesme," "Mr. Molaret," "Mr. Antheaume," "Mr. Royer," "Terrier," "Bersan"

2. Roman-numeral Series

No.	H.	Title	Scoring	Genre/Text	Volume/Cahier	Folio/Page	Date	Special comments
266	149	"Laudate pueri"	2 d, hc, t, b D,HC,T,B; 2 treb., bc	Motet (Psalm 112)	XIV, I	1–4	1670–71	
267	150	"Nisi Dominus"	d, hc, t, b, D,HC,T,B; 2 treb., bc	Motet (Psalm 126)	XIV, I	4v–6	1670–71	
268	151	*Confitebor à 4 voix et 2 violons*	2 hd, hc, t, b, HD, HC, T, B; 2 vns, bc	Motet (Psalm 110)	XIV, I–II	6v–11	1670–71	
269	72	"Magnificat"	d, hc, t, b, D,HC,T,B; 2 treb., bc	Motet (canticle of the Virgin)	XIV, II	11–14v	1670–71	
270	152	"Laudate Dominum omnes gentes"	2 d, hc, t, b, D,HC,T,B; 2 treb., bc	Motet (Psalm 116)	XIV, II	14v–16v	1670–71	
271	153	"Dixit Dominus"	2 hd, hc, t, b/HD, HC,T,B; 2 treb.,bc	Motet (Psalm 109)	XIV, II–III	17–23	1670–71	
272	154	"Beatus vir"	2 hd, hc, t, b/HD, HC,T,B; 2 treb.,bc (org)	Motet (Psalm 111)	XIV III–IV	23–29	1670–71	
273	155	"Memento Domine"	2 hd, hc, t, b/HD, HC,T,B; 2 treb.,bc	Motet (Psalm 131)	XIV, IV	29–33	1670–71	
274	1	"Kyrie eleison"	2 d, hc, t, b/D, HC, T, B; 2 treb., bc (org) Sanctus: 2 d, 2 hc, t, b Hossana: D, HC, T, B/D, HC, T, B	Mass	XIV IV–V	34–47	1670–71	

No.	H.	Title	Scoring	Genre/Text	Volume/Cahier	Folio/Page	Date	Special comments
275	281	*Domine salvum*	2 hd, hc, t/HD, HC, T, B; 2 treb., bc	Motet	XIV, V	45–47	1670–71	Part of the preceding mass
276	158	*Psalmus David 147* "Lauda Jerusalem"	2 hd, hc, t, b, HD, HC, T, B; 2 vns, bc	Motet (Psalm 147)	XV, VI	1–4	1670–71	
277	54	*Hymne du Saint Esprit à 3 voix pareilles* "Veni creator Spiritus"	hc, t, b; 2 vns, bc & choir (HD, HC, T, B) (optional)	Motet (Pentecost hymn)	XV, VI	4v–5v	1670–71	
278	3	*Messe à 8 voix et 8 violons et flûtes*	2 hd, 2 hc, 2 t, 2 b, HD, HC, T, B/HD, HC, T, B; 2 fl, str (4/4), bc (b. vns, bs, org)	Mass	XV, VI–VII–VIII	6–40	1670–71	
279	236	*Élévation, O salutaris*	b; 2 fl, bc	Motet	XV, VII	31v–32	1670–71	Part of the preceding mass
280	283	*Domine salvum*	2 hd, hc, t, b/HD, HC, T, B/HD, HC, T, B; 2 fl, str (4/4), bc	Motet	XV VIII	36–40	1670–71	Part of the preceding mass
281	514	*Offerte pour l'orgue et pour les violons, flûtes et hautbois*	2 fl, 2 ob, str (4), bc (serpents, cromorne, bs, org)	Instrumental	XV VIII	40v–42	1670–71	
282	73	*Magnificat à 3 voix sur la même basse avec symphonie*	hc, t, b; 2 treb., bc	Motet (canticle of the Virgin)	XV VIII	42–46	1670–71	
283	13	*Prose pour le jour de Pâques*	2 hc, b; bc	Motet (sequence)	XV VIII	47–48	1671 Easter	
284	312	*O filii à 3 voix pareilles*	2 hc, b; bc (org)	Motet	XV VIII	48v–50v	1671 Easter	
285	284	*Domine salvum à 3 voix pareilles avec orgue*	2 hc, b; bc (org)	Motet	XV VIII	51–51v	1671	

		Title	Scoring	Genre	Vol.	Folio	Date	Notes
286	160	*Psalmus 2us 6us supra centesimum à 4 voix* "Nisi Dominus"	hd, hc, t, b, HD, HC, T, B; bc	Motet (Psalm 126)	XV, IX	53–55	1671	"Mr. Beaupuy," "Mr. Dun"; cf. No. 233 (H. 160a)
287	55	*In Sanctum Nicasium Rothomagensem Archiepiscopum et Martyrem Hymnus ad vesperas*	t	Hymn to Saint Nicaise of Rouen	XV, IX	55v	1671	
288	56	*Hymnus in eundem ad matutinum*	b	Hymn to Saint Nicaise of Rouen	XV, IX	55v–56	1671	
289	57	*In eundem ad laudes*	t	Hymn to Saint Nicaise of Rouen	XV, IX	56	1671	
290	313	*Pour la conception de la Vierge*	hd, hc; bc	Motet	XV, IX	56v–57	1671 8 December	
291	161	*Laetatus sum Psalmus David vigesimus primus post centesimum*	hd, hc, t, 2 b, HD, HC, T, B; 2 fl, str (4), bc (b. vns, org)	Motet (Psalm 121)	XV, IX	57–62v	1671	"Mr. Beaupuy," "Mr. Dun"
292	314	*In nativitatem Domini Canticum* "Quem vidistis pastores"	d, hc, t; b; 2 fl, 2 vns, bc	Motet	XV, IX	63–65	1671 Christmas	
293	145	*Te Deum à 8 voix avec flûtes et violons*	2 hd, 2 hc, 2 t, 2 b, HD, HC, T, B/HD, HC, T, B, fl, ob, str (4/4), bc (b. vns, org)	Motet	XV, X	66–86	1672	cf. No. 319 (H. 145a)
294	162	*Exaudiat à 8 voix, flûtes et violons*	2 hd, hc, t, b, HD, HC, T, B/HD, HC, T, B, 2 fl, str (4/4), bc (b. vns, org)	Motet (Psalm 19)	XV, XI	87–102	1672	cf. No. 320 (H. 521)
295	515	*Symphonies pour un reposoir*	str (4), bc	Instrumental	XV, XI	102v–105	1672 Feast of the Holy Sacrament	

No.	H.	Title	Scoring	Genre/Text	Volume/Cahier	Folio/Page	Date	Special comments
296	4	*Messe à 4 choeurs*	4 hd, 2 hc, 2 t, 4 b, HD, HC, T, B/HD, HC, T, B/HD, HC, HC, T, B/HD, HC, T, B, str (16), bc (4 org)	Mass	XVI XII–XIII–XIV	1–35	1672	
297	285	"Domine salvum"	hd, hc, t, b/HD, HC, T, B, HD, HC, T, B, HD, HC, T, B; str, (16), bc (4 org)	Motet	XVI XIV	32–35	1672	Part of the preceding mass
298	494	*Ouverture de la Comtesse d'Escarbagnas Intermèdes nouveaux du Mariage forcé*	hc, t, b; str (4), bc	Molière	XVI XV	38–48	**1672 8 July**	
299 (1)	495	*Ouverture du prologue du Malade imaginaire (dans sa splendeur)*	str (4)	Molière (1st version)	XVI XVI	49–50	**1673 10 February**	
300	495a	*Le Malade imaginaire (avec les défenses). Ouverture, Prologue, Premier intermède, Second intermède*	hd, d, hc; str (4), bc	Molière (2nd version)	XVI XVI	52–56	**1674 4 May**	"Mr. Poussin," "Melle Babet"
299 (2)	495	*Le Malade imaginaire, Second intermède*	3 hd, hc; str (4), bc	Molière (1st version)	XVI XVII	57–67	**1673 10 February**	"Mouvant," "Marion," "Hardy," "Poussin," "Duvivier," "Nivelon," "Dumont"
299 (3)	495	*Le Malade imaginaire Cérémonie des Médecins, Ouverture*	str (4)	Molière (1st version)	XVI XVII	69–70	**1673 10 February**	
301	402a	*Symphonies ajustées au Sacrifice d'Abraham*	2 treb, bc	Instrumental	XVI XVII	90 (recto 70v)	1673–74	cf. No. 332 (H. 402)
299 (4)	495	*Le Malade imaginaire Cérémonie des médecins*	hd, d, hc, t, b, HD, D, HC, T, B; str (4), mortars, bc	Molière (1st version)	XVI XVII	71–88	**1673 10 February**	"Mouvant," "Hardy," "Marion," "Poussin," "Forestier, "Frison"

No.	H.	Title	Genre/Attribution	Scoring	Cahier	Folio	Date	Notes
302	496	Circé	T. Corneille & Donneau de Visé	3 hd, 3 hc, t, 2 b, HD, 2 HC, T, B; str (4), bc (b, vls, b. vn, hps)	XVII XVIII–XIX	1–17	1675 17 March	"Bast.," "Pouss.," Des Trich., "La Grang.," "Mr. Guérin," "Mr. de Verneuil," "Hub.," "De Gaye," "Mr. Marchand"
303	167	Quam dilecta Psalmus David octogesimus tertius	Motet (Psalm 83)	2 hd, hc, t, b, HD, HC, T, B/HD, HC, T, B, 2 fl, str (4/4), bc (b. vns, b. vl, org)	XVII XIX	17v–27	1675	cf. No. 533 (H. 425)
304	516	Après Confitebor Antienne D la ré sol bquarre	Instrumental	2 fl, str (4), bc (org)	XVII XIX	27–28	1675	
305	517	Après Beati omnes Antienne en G ré sol bquarre	Instrumental	str (4), bc	XVII XIX	28–29	1675	
306	425a	Prélude pour Mementote peccatores	Instrumental	2 treb, bc (org)	XVII XIX	29	1675	
		Cahiers XX, XXI, XXII missing					1675–79	
307	497	Sérénade pour le Sicilien	Molière	hc, b; str (4), bc	XVII XXIII	30–32v ([1]–6)	1679 9 June	
308	498	Ouverture du prologue de Polyeucte pour le collège d'Harcourt‡	P. Corneille instrumental	tp, b. tp, dr, str (4)	XVII XXIII	33–40 (7–21)	1679 11 July	Original title was *Ouverture du Dépit amoureux* (Molière), for the revival of 1679. Pierre Corneille's *Polyeucte Martyr* was staged at the Collège d'Harcourt in 1680.
309	399a	*Prélude* for Filius prodigus	*Instrumental*	*str (4)*	XVII XXIII	40–40v (21–22)	1679	cf. No. 115 (H.399) and H. 399b, H. 399c
310	168a	*Prélude pour Quare fremuerunt gentes à 8 voix*	Instrumental	str (4)	XVII XXIII	41–41v (23–24)	1679	cf. No. 68 (H. 168)
311	398a	*Prélude pour Horrenda pestis*	Instrumental	str (4)	XVII XXIII	41v–42 (24–25)	1679	cf. No. 82 (H. 398)
312	404a	*Prélude pour Josue*	Instrumental	str (4/4)	XVII XXIII	42–43 (25–27)	1679	cf. No. 126 (H. 404)

No.	H.	Title	Scoring	Genre/Text	Volume/Cahier	Folio/Page	Date	Special comments
313	519	Symphonies pour le Jugement de Salomon	str (4)	Instrumental	XVII XXIII	43–43v (27–28)	1679	
314	540	Ouverture pour quelque belle entreprise à cinq	str (5)	Instrumental	XVII XXIV	44–45 (1–3)	1679	
315	541	Menuet pour les flûtes allemandes/Autre menuet pour les mêmes flûtes	2 fl. trav, b	Instrumental	XVII XXIV	45v (4)	1679	
316	520	Prélude, menuet, passepied pour les flûtes et hautbois devant l'ouverture	2 fl, 2 ob, bs	Instrumental	XVII XXIV	46–46v (5–6)	1679	
317	542	Caprice pour trois violins	2 vns, b	Instrumental	XVII	46v (6)	1679	
318	499	Ouverture du prologue de l'Inconnu	2 fl, 2 ob, 2 tp, str (4), bs	T. Corneille & Donneau de Visé; instrumental	XVII XXIV	47–51v (7–16)	**1679** **17 October**	Original title was *Ouverture du prologue d'Acis et de Galathée* (November 1678)
319	145a	Prélude pour le Te Deum à 8 copié dans le cahier où est le Te Deum	str (4)	Instrumental	XVII XXIV	52–52v (17–18)	1679	cf. No. 293 (H. 145)
320	521	Prélude pour ce qu'on voudra non encore employée	str (4)	Instrumental	XVII XXIV	53 (19)	1679	Original title was *Prélude pour l'Exaudiat à 8 éprouvé*; cf. No. 294 (H. 162)
321	171a	Prélude pour Super flumina	str (4)	Instrumental	XVII XXIV	53v (20)	1679	cf. No. 80 (H. 171)
322	522	Offerte non encore exécutée	2 fl, 2 ob, str (4), bs	Instrumental	XVII XXIV	54–55v (21–24)	1679	
323	174	"Quemadmodum desiderat cervus"	hd, d, b; 2 treb, bc	Motet (Psalm 41)	XIX XXV	1–9	**1679**	"Piesches"
324	175	"Beatus vir qui non abiit"	hd, d, b; 2 treb, bc	Motet (Psalm 1)	XIX XXVI	10–16	1679–80	
325	248	Élévation "O salutaris hostia"	b; 2 treb, bc	Motet	XIX XXVI	16–17v	1679–80	

No.	H.	Title	Genre / Text	Scoring	Vol.	Page	Date	Remarks
326	176	"Cantate Domino canticum novum"	Motet (Psalm 97)	hd, d, b; 2 treb, bc	XIX XXVII	18–30	1679–80	
327	289	"Domine salvum"	Motet	hd, d, b; 2 treb, bc	XIX XXVII	30v	1679–80	Incomplete (9 bars)
328	177	"Laudate Dominum de coelis"	Motet (Psalm 148)	hd, d, b; 2 treb, bc (hps)	XIX XXVIII	32–40	1679–80	
329	500	*Les fous divertissants*, Comédie	R. Poisson	d, 2 hc, t, b; str (4), bc	XVIII XXIX	1–13	**1680 14 November**	"Mr. de Villiers," "Mr. Guérin," "Mr. de Lagrange," "Mr. Verneuil," "Du V.," "Bapt."
330	545	*Concert pour 4 parties de violes*	Instrumental	2 treb. vls, t. vl, b. vl	XVIII XXIX	13v–17	1680–81	
331	501	*La Pierre philosophale*	T. Corneille & Donneau de Visé	2 hd, hc, b, HD, HC, T, B; str (4), bc (b, vn, hps)	XVIII XXIX–XXX	17v–20	**1681 23 February**	"Mr. Hub.," "Mr. de Vern."
332	402	*Sacrificium Abrahae*	Latin oratorio	4 d, 2 hc, 2 t, 2 b, D, HC, T, B; str (4), bc	XVIII XXX	21–29	1681?	cf. No. 301 (H. 402a) & H. 402b *Le sacrifice d'Abraham*, in Brossard collection, Vm^1 1479, vol. IV, (copy with variants)
333	178	*Psalmus Davidis centesimus vigesimus septimus* "Beati omnes"	Motet (Psalm 127)	hd, d, b; 2 treb., bc	XVIII XXX	29v–33v	1681	
334	61	*Pange lingua*	Motet (hymn of the Holy Sacrament)	hd, d, b; 2 treb., bc	XVIII XX–XXXI	34–36	1681 Feast of the Holy Sacrament	
335	62	*Pange lingua pour des religieuses, Pour le Port Royal*	Motet (hymn of the Holy Sacrament)	hd/HD; bc	XVIII XXXI	36	1681 Feast of the Holy Sacrament	

No.	H.	Title	Scoring	Genre/Text	Volume/ Cahier	Folio/ Page	Date	Special comments
336	502	*Endimion, Tragédie mêlée de musique*	hc, t, b/HD, HC, T, B; str (4), bc (b. vn, hps)	Anonymous	XVIII XXXI	36v–45v	**1681** 22 July	"Mr. Guérin"
337	503	*Air pour des paysans dans la Noce de village au lieu de l'air du marié*	str (4)	Brécourt; instrumental	XVIII XXXI	46	1681–82	
338	179	*Psalmus David septuagesimus quintus* "Notus in Judea Deus"	hd, d, b; 2 treb., t. or b. vl, bc	Motet (Psalm 75)	XVIII XXXI	46v–52v	1681–82	
339	249	"O salutaris hostia"	hd; bc	Motet	XVIII XXXI	52v	1681–82	
340	327	*Motet pour toutes les fêtes de la Vierge*	hd, d, b; 2 treb., bc	Motet	XVIII XXXII	53–59	1681–82	
341	328	*Supplicatio pro defunctis ad beatam Virginem*	hd, d, b; 2 fl, b, fl, bc (b. vl, hps)	Motet	XVIII XXXII	59v–67	1681–82	
342	405	*In resurrectione Domini Nostri Jesu Christi*	hd, d, b; 2 treb., bc	Latin oratorio	XXVIII XXXIII	37–44	1682 Easter	
343	181	*Psalmus David octogesimus quartus* "Benedixisti Domine terram tuam"	hd, d, b; 2 treb., bc	Motet (Psalm 84)	XXVIII XXXIII	44–49	1682	
344	182	*Psalmus David centesimus sexdecimus sine organo* "Laudate dominum omnes gentes"	2 hd, d, bd	Motet (Psalm 116)	XXVIII XXXIII	49v–50v	1682	
345	28	*Antiphona sine organo ad Virginem* "Sub tuum praesidium"	2 hd, bd	Motet (antiphon to the Virgin)	XXVIII XXXIII	50v–51	1682	
346	290	*Domine salvum sine organo en C sol ut*	2 hd, d, bd	Motet	XXVIII XXXIII	51–51v	1682	

		Title	Instrumentation	Genre	Vol.	Pages	Date	Notes
347	504	*Andromède, Tragédie*	hd or d, hc, t, b, HD, HC, T, B; 2 fl, str (4), bc (b. vn, b. vl, hps)	P. Corneille	XXVIII XXXIV	52–68	**1682** 19 July	"Mlle. Dyot," "Mr. de Villiers," "Mr. Guérin," "De la Grange," "Messrs. de Verneuil et Hubert"
348	292	"Domine salvum"	hc, t, b/HD, HC, T, B/HD, HC, T, B; bc	Motet	XX XXXV	1–2	1682	
349	429	"Eamus volamus"	hd, d, b; 2 treb., bc	Motet	XX XXXV	2v–4	1682	
350	184	*Psalmus David 5tus* "Quare fremuerunt gentes"	hd, d, b; 2 treb., bc	Motet (Psalm 2) (Charpentier's error)	XX XXXV	4–10v	1682	
351	406	*In circumcisione Domini* Dialogus inter angelum et pastores	hc, t, b; 2 treb., bc	Latin oratorio	XX XXXV	11–14	1683 1 January	
352	523	*Pour un reposoir*	2 fl. trav, b. fl, str (4), bc (b. vn, hps)	Instrumental	XX XXXV	14–14v	1683 Feast of the Holy Sacrament	
353	329	"Ave verum corpus"	hd, d, b; 2 fl, str (4), bc (b. vn, hps, org)	Motet	XX XXXV–XXXVI	14v–17v	1683 Feast of the Holy Sacrament	
354	188	*Psalmus 62* "Deus Deus meus ad te"	hd, d, b; 2 treb., bc	Motet (Psalm 62)	XX XXXVI	18–23	1683	
355	524	*Ouverture pour l'église*	str (4), bc	Instrumental	XX XXXVI	23v–24	1683	
356	408	*Élévation* "Famen meam quis replebit"	hd, d, b; 2 treb., 2 t. vls, bc (b. vn, hps)	Latin oratorio	XX XXXVI	24–28v	1683	
357	409	*In obitum augustissimae nec non piissimae Gallorum reginae Lamentum*	2 hd, d, hc, t, 2 b, 2 HD, D, HC, T, BT, B; fl, fl. trav, t. fl, str (5), bc (b. vn, org)	Latin oratorio	XX XXXVI–XXXVII–XXXVIII	28v–48	**1683** after 30 July	

No.	H.	Title	Scoring	Genre/Text	Volume/Cahier	Folio/Page	Date	Special comments
358	189	*De profundis*	2 hd, d, 2 hc, 2 t, b, HD, D, HC, T, BT, B; 2 fl, t, fl, str (5), bc (b. vn, org)	Motet (Psalm 129)	XX XXXVIII–XXXIX	48v–63	**1683** after 30 July	
359	251	*Élévation à 5 sans dessus de violon* "Transfige dulcissime Jesu"	2 d, hc, t, b; bc	Motet	XX XXXIX	63v–67v	1683	
360	410	*Praelium Michaelis archangeli factum in coelo cum dracone*	(hd), hc, (2 t), 2 b, HD, HC, T, B/HD, HC, T, B, 2 vns, bc (org) (Voices in parenthesis are used in the uncompleted second part.)	Latin oratorio	XX XXXIX	68–76v	1683 29 September	Incomplete
		Cahier XL missing					1683	
361	411	*Caedes sanctorum innocentium*	hd, d, bd, hc, t, b, HD, D, BD, HC, T, B; 2 treb. vls, bc	Latin oratorio	XXI XLI	1–10	1683 28 December	"Mlle. Brion"
362	481	*Actéon, Pastorale en musique*	hd, 2 d, 2 bd, hc, t, b, HD, BD, HC, T, B; 2 fl, 2 treb., bc (b. vl, hps)	Pastorale	XXI XLI–XLII	10v–29	1684	
363	256	*Élévation à 3 dessus* "O clementissime Domine"	3 hd; bc	Motet	XXI XLII	29v–30	1684	"Mlle. du Fresnoy," "Mère Saint Bernard," "Mère Sainte Agathe"
364	481a	*Actéon changé en biche*	hd, d/HD, 2 D, HC, T; 2 treb., bc	Pastorale	XXI XLII	30v–34	1684	Reworked version of *Actéon* (H. 481)
365	412	*Nuptiae sacrae*	hd, 2 d, hc, bt, b, HD, 2 D, HC, T, B; 2 treb. vls, bc	Latin oratorio	XXI XLII–XLIII	34v–47v	1684	"Br.," "Tal.," "Isab.," "C, M.," ("Thor.,") "Charp.," "Bossan," "Joly," "Carlie"
366	334	*Motet pour la Vierge*	d; bc	Motet	XXI XLIII	48	1684	

367	257	*Elevatio* "Gustate et videte quam suavis sum"	hd; bc	Motet	XXI XLIII	48–48v	1684	
368	482	*Sur la naissance de Notre Seigneur Jésus Christ Pastorale*	hd, 2 d, hc, t, b, HD, D, HC, T, B; 2 treb. vls, bc (org)	Pastorale	XXI XLIV	49–57	1684 Christmas	"Brion," "Isabelle," "Gr. M.," "Charp.," "Bos.," "Carl," "Joly"
369	483	*Pastorale sur la naissance de Notre Seigneur Jésus Christ*	hd, d, bt, b, HD, D, HC, T, B; 2 fl, 2 treb. vls, bc (org)	Pastorale	XXI XLIV–XLV	57–74v	1684 Christmas	"Brion," "Talon," "Isabelle," "Gr. Maison," "Charp.," "Boss.," "Joly," "Beaup."
370	484	*Il faut rire et chanter, Dispute de bergers*	hd, d, hc, bt or b, HD, D, HC, T, B; 2 treb., bc	Pastorale	XXI XLV–XLVI	74v–85v	1685	"Brion," "Talon," "Isabelle," "Gr. M.," "Charp.," "Bos.," "Joly," "Carlie"
371	505	*Chaconne du Rendez-vous des Tuileries; Ouverture du Rendez-vous des Tuileries*	str (4)	Baron (instrumental)	XXI XLVI	86–87v	**1685 3 March**	
	335–338	*Quatuor anni tempestates*						
372	335	*Ver*	2 hd; bc	Motet	XXI XLVI	88–90	1685	
373	336	*Aestas*	2 hd; bc	Motet	XXI XLVI	90–92	1685	cf. No. 414 (H. 336a)
374	337	*Autumnus*	2 hd; bc	Motet	XXI XLVI	92v–95	1685	
375	338	*Hyems*	2 hd; bc	Motet	XXI XLVI	95–97v	1685	
376	194	*Psalmus David nonagesimus 9 nus* "Jubilate Deo"	hd, d, b; 2 treb., bc (b. vl, org)	Motet (Psalm 99)	XXI XLVI	97v–103	1685	
377	485	*La fête de Rueil*	3 hd, hc, t, bt or b, HD, HC, T, B; 2 fl. trav, 2 "petites flûtes," 2 "flûtes douces," 2 ob, str (5), bc (b. vns, bs, hps)	Pastorale	XXII XLVII–XLVIII	1–22	1685	cf. H. 485a (separate parts), BN Ms. Vm^6 17

No.	H.	Title	Scoring	Genre/Text	Volume/Cahier	Folio/Page	Date	Special comments
378	440	Air pour le roi "A ta haute valeur"	hd; bc	Air	XXII XLVIII	17–17v	1685	
379	507	Vénus et Adonis	hd, hc; str (4), bc	Donneau de Visé	XXII XLVIII	22v–31v	**1685 23 September**	
380	495b	Second air pour les tapissiers du Malade imaginaire reformé pour la 3ᵉ fois	str (4)	Instrumental	XXII XLVIII	31v	**1685** 15 September **1686** 11 January	
381	483a	Seconde partie du Noël français qui commence par "Que nos soupirs"	2 hd, d, hc, t, bt or b, HD, D, HC, T, B; 2 fl, 2 treb. vls, bc (org)	Pastorale	XXII XLVIII–XLIX	32–42	1685 Christmas	"Br.," "Talon," "Isab," "Gr. M.," "Charp.," "Beaussan," "Beaupuy," "Carl."
382	344	In festo Corporis Christi Canticum "Venite ad me"	hd, d, hc, t, b, HD, D, HC, T, B; 2 treb., bc (Passage for hd & d transposable for 2b)	Motet	XXII XLIX	42v–47	1686 Feast of the Holy Sacrament	"Mr. Sebret"
383	295	"Domine salvum"	hd, d, b; 2 treb., bc	Motet	XXII XLIX	47–48	1686	
384	415a	Prologue de Sainte la Caecile [sic] à 6 et instruments, Harmonia coelestis	d; 2 treb, bc	Latin oratorio (excerpt)	XXII XLIX	48v–49v	1686 22 November	cf. No. 162 (H. 415)
385	483b	Seconde partie du Noël français qui commence par "Que nos soupirs Seigneur"	hd, hd or d, hc, t, b, HD, D, HC, T, B; 2 treb., bc	Pastorale	XXII XLIX–L	50–54v	1686 Christmas	"Guy," "Br.," "Tal.," "Gr. M.," "Anth.," "Boss.," "Beaup."
386	195	Bonum est confiteri Domino Psalmus David 91us	2 hd or 2 d, hc, t, b, HD, 2 D, HC, T, B; 2 treb. vls, bc	Motet (Psalm 91)	XXII, L	55–69	1687	"Br.," "Guy," "Isab," "Tal.," "Gr. M.," "Anth.," "Boss.," "Carl.," "Beaup."
387	259	Élévation "Transfige amabilis Jesu"	hd, d, b; bc (org)	Motet	XXII, L	69–69v	1687	

No.	No.	Title	Instrumentation	Genre	Vol.	Folios	Date	Notes
388	346	Pour le Saint Sacrement au reposoir	hd, d, hc, t, b, HD,D,HC, T,B; fl, fl. trav, bc	Motet	XXIII, LI	70–71v	1687 Feast of the Holy Sacrament	
389	196	Psalmus David 12us, "Usquequo Domine"	hd,d,bt,b;fl.àbec, fl. trav, b. fl, bc (org)	Motet (Psalm 12)	XXIII, LI	72–76v	1687	"Magd.," "Marg.," "Frizon"
390	347	In honorem Sancti Benedicti	hd, d; bc	Motet	XXIII, LI	77–78	1687 21 March	
391	5	Messe, Pour le Port Royal	3 d/D; bc (org)	Mass	XXIII, LI	78–83v	**1687 20 July**	
		Cahiers LII–LIII missing					1687–89?	
392	64	Hymne du Saint Sacrement "Pange lingua"	hd, hc, t, b, HD, HC, T, B; 2 fl, str (4), bc	Motet	XXII LIV	84–86v	1688–89? Feast of the Holy Sacrament	"Mr. Dun," "Mr. Lecuyer"
393	348	Motet du Saint Sacrement, Pour un reposoir "Ecce panis"	hd, d, b; 2 treb., bc	Motet (sequence of the Holy Sacrament, excerpt)	XXII LIV	86v–88	1688–89? Feast of the Holy Sacrament	
394	84	Litanies de la Vierge à 3 voix pareilles avec instruments	hc, t, b; 2 treb., bc (org)	Motet	XXII LIV	88v–91	1688–89?	
395	65	Ave maris stella	2 hd, hc, b, HD, HC, T, B; str (4), bc (org)	Motet (hymn to the Virgin)	XXII LIV	91v–94	1688–89?	
396	120	Première leçon de ténèbres du mercredi saint pour une basse	b; 2 fl, 2 ob, str (4), bc (bs, b. vns, org)	Motet	XXIII LV	1–4	1690? Holy Week	
397	121	Première leçon de ténèbres du jeudi saint pour une basse	b; 2 fl, 2 ob, str (4), bc (bs, b. vns, org)	Motet	XXIII LV	4v–6v	1690? Holy Week	
398	122	Première leçon de ténèbres du vendredi saint pour une basse	b; 2 fl, 2 ob, str (4), bc (bs, b. vns, org)	Motet	XXIII LV	6v–8v	1690? Holy Week	
399	349	Pour la Passion de Notre Seigneur, Première partie	hc, t; bc	Motet	XXIII LV	8v–9	1690? Holy Week	

No.	H.	Title	Scoring	Genre/Text	Volume/Cahier	Folio/Page	Date	Special comments
400	350	Pour la Passion, Seconde partie	hc; t; bc	Motet	XXIII LV	9	1690? Holy Week	
401	66	Hymne du Saint Esprit "Veni creator Spiritus"	2 hd, hc, t, b, HD, HC, T, B, 2 fl, str (4), bc (b. vns, bs, org)	Motet (Pentecost hymn)	XXIII LV	9v–13v	1690?	Incomplete
		Cahier LVI missing					1690?	
402	123	Troisième leçon de ténèbres du mercredi saint pour une basse taille avec 2 flûtes et deux violons	bt; ob. or fl. fl. trav, 2 vns, bc (org)	Motet	XXIII [LVII]	14–19	1690? Holy Week	"Mr. Beaupuy"
403	124	Troisième leçon de ténèbres du jeudi saint pour une basse taille avec 2 flûtes et 2 violons	bt; ob. or fl. fl. trav, 2 vns, bc (org)	Motet	XXIII [LVII]	19v–22	1690? Holy Week	
404	125	Troisième leçon de ténèbres du vendredi saint pour une basse taille avec 2 flûtes et deux violons	bt; ob. or fl. fl. trav, 2 vns, bc (org)	Motet	XXIII [LVII]	22–25	1690? Holy Week	
405	351	Pour le jour de la Passion de Notre Seigneur Jésus Christ	hc, t; b; bc	Motet	XXIII [LVII]	25v–26	1690? Holy Week	
406	68	Pange lingua à 4 pour le jeudi saint	hd, hc, t, b; org, bc	Motet (hymn of the Holy Sacrament)	XXIII [LVII]	26	1690? Holy Week	
407	69	Veni creator pour un dessus seul au catéchisme	hd; bc	Motet (Pentecost hymn)	XXIII [LVII]	26v	1690?	Pub: Mélanges de musique, Paris, J.-B.-C. Ballard, 1731
408	352	Second Motet pour le catéchisme à la pause du milieu, A la Vierge "Sub tuum praesidium"	hd; bc (transposable: hc or t)	Motet (antiphon to the Virgin)	XXIII [LVII]	26v	1690?	
409	70	Veni creator Spiritus pour un dessus seul pour le catéchisme	hd; bc	Motet (Pentecost	XXIII [LVII]	26v	1690?	

No.	Cat.	Title	Instrumentation	Genre	Vol.	Fol.	Date	Notes
410	356	*O filii pour les voix, violons, flûtes et orgue*	1 soloist, HD, HC, T, B; fl, str (4), bc (org)	Motet (for Easter)	XXIII LVIII	27	1690? Easter	
411	527	*Prélude pour Sub tuum praesidium à trois violons*	2 vns, bc (b. vn)	Instrumental	XXIII LVIII	27v	1690–91?	
412	193a	*Prélude pour le Miserere à 6 et instruments*	str (4), bc	Instrumental	XXIII LVIII	27v	1690–91?	cf. No. 152 (H. 193)
413	253a	*Prélude pour O amor à 3 violons*	2 vns, bc (b. vn)	Instrumental	XXIII LVIII	28	1690–91?	cf. No. 140 (H. 253)
414	336a	*Prélude pour l'Été à 3 flûtes*	2 fl, bc (b. fl)	Instrumental	XXIII LVIII	28	1690–91?	cf. No. 373 (H. 336)
415	528	*Prélude en g ré sol b à 4 pour les violons et flûtes*	fl, str (4), bc	Instrumental	XXIII LVIII	29	1690–91?	
416	529	*Symphonie en g ré sol bmol à 3 flûtes ou violons*	2 fl or 2 vns, bc	Instrumental	XXIII LVIII	29v	1690–91?	
417	530	*Prélude en C sol ut b quarre à 4 parties de violons avec flûtes*	fl, str(4)	Instrumental	XXIII LVIII	29v	1690–91?	
418	85	*Litanies de la Vierge*	2 hd, hc, t, b, 2 HD, HC, T, B; 2 fl, 2 vns, bc (b. vl, hps)	Motet	XXIII LVIII	30–34v	1690–91?	
419	357	*In purificationem BVM Canticum*	2 hd; 2 fl, 2 vns, bc	Motet	XXIII LVIII	35–35v	1691? 2 February	
420	32	*Antienne à la Vierge à 2 dessus "Regina coeli"*	2 hd; bc	Motet	XXIII LVIII	36–36v	1691?	cf. H. 32a & H. 32b, *Troisième Regina coeli* (separate parts), Archives des Augustines in the monastery of the Hôtel-Dieu, T 11 C 295, Quebec, Canada
421	358	*In festo Corporis Christi Canticum, Pour le reposoir "Pandite portas populi"*	2 hd, b; 2 treb., bc	Motet	XXIII LVIII	36v–40	1691? Feast of the Holy Sacrament	

No.	H.	Title	Scoring	Genre/Text	Volume/Cahier	Folio/Page	Date	Special comments
422	298	"Domine salvum"	hc, t, b; bc	Motet	XXIII / LVIII	40	1691–92?	Incomplete; cf. No. 427 (H. 298a)
		Cahier LIX missing					1691–92?	
423	135	Troisième leçon de ténèbres du mercredi saint	hc, t, b/hc, t, b; 4 fl, 4 vns, bc (org)	Motet	XXIII / LX	41–45	1692? Holy Week	
424	136	Troisième leçon de ténèbres du jeudi saint	hc, t, b/hc, t, b; 2 fl, 2 vns, bc (org)	Motet	XXIII / LX	45v–49	1692? Holy Week	
425	137	Troisième leçon de ténèbres du vendredi saint	hc, t, b/hc, t, b; 2 fl, 2 vns, bc (org)	Motet	XXIII / LX	49–52v	1692? Holy Week	
426	417	Dialogus inter Christum et homines	hc, t, bt, b; 2 fl, 2 vns, bc	Latin oratorio	XXIII / LX	53–55v	1692? Holy Week	"Mr. Molaré," "Mr. Beaupuy," "Mr. Ribon," "Mr. Dun"
427	298a	Prélude pour Domine salvum à 3 voix pareilles	2 treb, bc (b. vl, org)	Instrumental	XXIII / LX	56	1692?	cf. No. 422 (H. 298)
428	261	O salutaris à 3 dessus	2 hd, d; bc (org)	Motet	XXIII / LX	56–57	1692?	
429	362	Pour le Saint Esprit "Veni creator Spiritus"	hc, t, b; bc	Motet (Pentecost hymn)	XXV / LXI	1–1v	1692? Pentecost	
430	86	Litanies de la Vierge à 2 dessus et une basse chantante	2 hd, b; bc	Motet	XXV / LXI	2–3v	1692–93?	
431	209	Credidi propter quod Psalmus David 115us	hd, hc, t, b, HD, HC, T, B; bc	Motet (Psalm 115)	XXV / LXI	4–7	1692–93?	"Beaupuy," "Dun"; cf. No. 234 (H. 209a)
432	210	Lauda Jerusalem Psalmus David 147us	hd, hc, t, b, HD, HC, T, B; str (4), bc	Motet (Psalm 147)	XXV / LXI	7–10	1692–93?	
433	33	Première antienne pour les vêpres d'un confesseur non pontife	2 hd, d; bc	Motet	XXV / LXI	10–11	1692–93?	"Mr. Favalli," "Mr. Tomasso," "Mr. Bluquet"

434	34	*Troisième antienne pour les vêpres d'un confesseur non pontife*	hc, t, 2 vns, bc	Motet	XXV LXI	11–12v	1692–93?	
435	35	*Cinquième antienne pour les vêpres d'un confesseur non pontife*	2 hd; bc	Motet	XXV LXI	12v–13v	1692–93?	
436	262	*O salutaris*	hd; 2 ob, bc (bs)	Motet	XXV LXI	13v–14	1692–93?	
437	363	*Motet pendant la guerre* "Quarre fremuerunt gentes"	hd, hc, t, b, HD, HC, T, B; 2 vns, bc	Motet (Psalm 2:1–2)	XXV LXI	14–17v	1692–93?	
438	87	*Litanies de la Vierge à 4 voix*	2 hd, hc, 2 t, b, HD, HC, T, B; bc	Motet	XXIV LXII	1–3v	1692–93?	
439	211	*Psalmus Davidis vigesimus nonus supra centesimum, De profundis à 4 voix*	2 hd, hc, 2 t, 2 b, HD, HC, T, B; bc	Motet (Psalm 129)	XXIV LXII	3v–6v	1692–93?	"Mr. Hard."
440	88	*Litanies de la Vierge à 4 voix*	2 hd, hc, t, b, HD, HC, T, B; bc	Motet	XXIV LXII	7–10	1692–93?	
441	212	*Psalmus David 129us quatuor vocibus* "De profundis"	2 hd, hc, t, 2 b, HD, HC, T, B; bc	Motet (Psalm 129)	XXIV LXII	10–13v	1692–93?	
442	79	*Troisième Magnificat à 4 voix avec instruments*	hc, t, b/HD, HC, T, B; 2 fl, str, bc (b. vns)	Motet (canticle of the Virgin)	XXIV LXII	14–23	1692–93?	"Mr. Boutlou," "Mr. Hard," "Mr. Desvoyes," "Solé"
443	71	*Iste Confessor*	2 d	Motet (hymn)	XXIV LXII	23v–24	1692–93?	
444	7	*Messe des morts à 4 voix*	2 hd, 2 hc, 2 t, 2 b, HD, HC, T, B; bc	Mass	XXIV LXIII	26–32	1692–93?	
445	263	*Élévation* "Pie Jesu"	2 hd; bc	Motet	XXIV LXIII	28v	1692–93?	Part of the preceding mass
446	213	*De profundis*	2 hd, hc, t, b	Motet (Psalm 129)	XXIV LXIII	29v–32	1692–93?	Part of the preceding mass

No.	H.	Title	Scoring	Genre/Text	Volume/Cahier	Folio/Page	Date	Special comments
447	364	*Pour le Saint Esprit* "Veni Sancte Spiritus"	hc, t, b; bc	Motet (Pentecost sequence, opening)	XXIV LXIII	32v–33	1692–93?	
448	264	*Élévation au Saint Sacrement* "O amantissime salvator"	hc, t, b; bc	Motet	XXIV LXIII	33–34	1692–93?	
449	365	*In honorem Sancti Ludovici Regis Galliae Canticum*	2 hd, 2 hc, t, b, HD, HC, T, B; 2 fl, 2 ob, str (4), bc (b. vns, bs, org)	Motet	XXIV LXIII	34v–41v	1693? 25 August	
450	214	*Psalmus Davidis decimus sextus post centesimum* "Laudate Dominum"	hc, t, b/HD, HC, T, B; bc	Motet (Psalm 116)	XXIV LXIII	41v–43	1693–94?	
451	265	*Élévation* "Bone pastor"	hc, t, b; bc	Motet (sequence of the Holy Sacrament, excerpt)	XXIV LXIII	43	1693–94?	
452	301	*Domine salvum à 3 voix pareilles*	hc, t, b; bc	Motet	XXIV LXIII	44	1693–94?	
453	302	*Domine salvum à 3 voix pareilles*	hc, t, b; bc	Motet	XXIV LXIII	45	1693–94?	
454	215	*Psalmus David 67us* "Exurgat Deus"	hc, t, b/HD, HC, T, B; 2 treb., bc	Motet (Psalm 67)	XXV LXIV	20–23v	1693–94?	
455	367	*La prière à la Vierge du Père Bernard*	hc, t, b/HD, HC, T, B; 2 treb., bc	Motet	XXV LXIV	23v–25v	1693–94?	
456	216	*Psalmus Davidis CXXIus* "Laetatus sum"	hc, t, b/HD, HC, T, B; 2 treb., bc	Motet (Psalm 121)	XXV LXIV	26–30v	1693–94?	
457	217	*Psalmus 123us* "Nisi quia Dominus"	hc, t, b/HD, HC, T, B; 2 treb., bc	Motet (Psalm 123)	XXV LXIV	30v–34	1693–94?	
458	218	*Psalmus David 45us*	hc, t, b/HD, HC, T,	Motet	XXV LXIV	34–38	1693–94?	

459	141	*Troisième leçon de ténèbres du mercredi saint pour 1 basse*	b; 2 treb., bc	Motet	XXV LXV	39–41	1694? Holy Week
460	142	*Troisième leçon de ténèbres jeudi saint pour une basse*	b; 2 treb., bc	Motet	XXV LXV	41–42v	1694? Holy Week
461	143	*Troisième leçon de ténèbres du vendredi saint pour 1 basse*	b; 2 treb., bc	Motet	XXV LXV	42v–44v	1694? Holy Week
462	89	*Litanies de la Vierge*	2 hd, hc, t, b, HD, HC, T, B; bc	Motet	XXV LXV	45–47	1694?
463	368	*Motet de Saint Joseph*	hd, hc, t, b, HD, HC, T, B; bc	Motet	XXV LXV	47–47v	1694? 19 March
464	219	*Second Miserere 50 à 4 voix et 4 instruments*	2 hd, hc, t, b, HD, HC, T, B; 2 fl, str (4), bc	Motet (Psalm 50)	XXV LXV	47v–59	1694?
465	369	*Pro Virgine non martyre*	hc, t, b; bc	Motet	XXV LXV	59–61	1694?
466	535	*Prélude pour le Domine salvum en f ut fa à 4 voix*	2 treb., bc	Instrumental	XXV LXV	61	1694?
467	9	*Messe de minuit à 4 voix, flûtes et violons pour Noël*	2 hd, hc, t, b, HD, HC, T, B; 2 fl, bc (org)	Mass	XXV LXVI	62–77	1694? Christmas
468	537	*Ouverture pour le sacre d'un évêque pour les violons, flûtes et hautbois*	2 fl, ob, str (4), bc	Instrumental	XXV LXVI	77v–79	1695? 23 January?
469	268	*Élévation à voix seule pour une taille* "Lauda Sion salvatorem"	t; bc	Motet (sequence of the Holy Sacrament, 1–4)	XXV LXVI	79–80	1695?	Pub: *Motets mêlés de symphonie*, 1709
470	370	*Pour le catéchisme*	hd; bc	Motet	XXV LXVI	80	1695?
		Cahier LXVII missing					1695?
471	10	*Messe des morts à 4 voix et symphonie*	2 hd, hc, t, b, HD, HC, T, B; 2 fl, ob, str (4), bc	Mass	XXVI LXVIII	1–24	1695? 21 April?	"Mr. Dun"

No.	H.	Title	Scoring	Genre/Text	Volume/Cahier	Folio/Page	Date	Special comments
472	269	*A l'élévation de la sainte hostie* "Pie Jesu"	2 hd; bc	Motet	XXVI LXVIII	22	1695? 21 April?	Part of the preceding mass
473	223	*Laudate Dominum omnes gentes octo vocibus et totidem instrumentis*	hd, hc, t, b, HD, HC, T, B/HD, HC, T, B; 2 fl, str (4/4), bc	Motet (Psalm 116)	XXVI LXIX	25–32v	1695?	
474	224	*Beatus vir qui timet Dominum 8 vocibus et totidem instrumentis*	2 hd, hc, t, b, HD, HC, T, B/HD, HC, T, B; 2 fl, str (4/4), bc	Motet (Psalm 111)	XXVI LXIX	33–46v	1695?	
475	270	*Pour le Saint Sacrement à 3 voix pareilles* "O dulce, o ineffabile"	hc, t, b; bc	Motet	XXVI LXX	47–48	1695?	
476	271	*Pour le Saint Sacrement à 3 voix pareilles* "Amate Jesum omnes"	hc, t, b; bc	Motet	XXVI LXX	48–49	1695?	
477	272	*Élévation à 2 dessus et une basse* "Quare tristis est anima mea"	2 hd, b; bc	Motet	XXVI LXX	49v–50	1695?	
478	49	*Antienne à 3 voix pareilles pour la veille des O*	hc, t, b; bc	Motet	XXVI LXX	50v–51	1695? Advent	
479	433	*Domine non secundum pour 1 basse taille avec 2 violons*	bt; 2 vns, bc	Motet	XXVI LXX	51–52v	1696?	
480	225	*Confitebor à 4 voix et instruments*	hc, t, b/HD, HC, T, B; 2 fl, str (4), bc (b. vn)	Motet (Psalm 110)	XXVI LXX	53–60v	1696?	"Boutlou," "Des voyes," "Mr. Hard.," "Mr. Dun"
481	144	*Répons après la première leçon de ténèbres du jeudi saint pour 1 haute taille et 2 flûtes* "Omnes amici mei"	t; 2 fl, bc	Motet	XXVI LXX	61–62	1696? Holy Week	
		Cahiers LXXI, LXXII, LXXIII missing					1696–1702	

No.	H.	Title	Scoring	Genre/Text	Volume/Cahier	Folio/Page	Date	Special comments
482	11	*Assumpta est Maria Missa six vocibus cum simphonia*	2 hd, 2 hc, t, bt, 2 HD, HC, T, BT, B; +str (4), bc (org) H. 11 +2 fl, 2 vns, bc (b. vls, b. vn, org) H. 11a	Mass	XXVII LXXIV	1–15v	1702 15 August	"Mr. Dangoul . . . ," "Mr. Molaret," "Mr. Royer" cf. H. 11a (separate parts, BN, Vm^1 942) "Bruslart," "Mr. Touzelin"
483	303	*Domine salvum*	2 HD, HC, T, BT, B; str (4), bc (org)	Motet	XXVII LXXIV	14v–15v	1702 15 August	
484	422	*Judicium Salomonis*	d, 2 hc, 2 t, 2 b, HD, HC, T, B; 2 fl, 2 ob, str (4), bc (b. vns, bs, org)	Latin oratorio	XXVII LXXIV	19–36	**1702 12 November**	"Mr. Royer," "Mr. Cousin," "Mr. Molaret," "Mr. Ouarnier," "Bruslart" cf. H. 422a (separate parts BN, Vm^1 1481) "Mr. Vignon"

3. Problematic Cahiers

No.	H.	Title	Scoring	Genre/Text	Volume/Cahier	Folio/Page	Date	Special comments
485	495	*Après l'ouverture* "Quittez vos troupeaux"	2 hd, d, hc, t, b (B), 2 fl, str (4), bc	Molière (Prologue to *Le Malade imaginaire*)	XIII "I"	1–40	**1673 10 February**	
486	488	*La descente d'Orphée aux enfers*	2 hd, 2 d, 2 hc, t, bt, b; HD, HD, D (2D), HC, T, B; 2 fl, 2 t, vls, bc (b. vl, hps)	Opera	XIII "II"	41–59	1686?	Incomplete? "Guy," "Tal.," "Isab.," "Bri.," "Gd. M.," "Anth.," "Charp.," "Boss.," "Beaup.," "Carl.," "Anth.," "Pierot," "Loullié" [sic]

No.	H.	Title	Scoring	Genre/Text	Volume/Cahier	Folio/Page	Date	Special comments
487	474	*Epitaphium Carpentarii*	hd, d, 2 hc, t, b; bc	Cantata	XIII "a"	60v–65	?	
488	15	*Stabat mater pour des religieuses*	d/D; bc	Motet (sequence)	XIII "a"	65	?	
489	7a	". . . tollis peccata mundi"	hc, t, b/HD, HC, T, B; bc	Mass for the dead	XXVII "b"	41–41v	After 1693?	Copy with variants of the end of No. 444 (H. 7)
490	213a	"De profundis"	2 hd, hc, t, b, HD, HC, T, B; bc	Motet	XXVII "b"	41v–44	After 1693?	Copy with variants of No. 446 (H. 213); 30 bars shorter
491	364a	*Pour le Saint Esprit* "Veni Sancte Spiritus"	hc, t, b; bc	Motet (Pentecostal sequence, opening)	XXVII "b"	44v–45	After 1693?	Copy with a few minor variants of No. 447 (H. 364)
492	264a	*Élévation à 3 voix pareilles* "O amantissime salvator"	hc, t, b; bc	Motet	XXVII "b"	45–47	After 1693?	Copy (2 bars shorter) of No. 448 (H. 264)
493	365a	*In honorem Sancti Ludovici Regis Galliae Canticum*	2 hc, b/HD, HC, T, B; 2 fl, ob, str (4), bc (b. vns, bs)	Motet	XXVII "b"	47–51	After 1693? 25 August	Copy of the opening of No. 449 (H. 365)
494	538	*Prélude pour [. . .]*	2 treb., bc (org)	Instrumental	XXIV "c"	46	?	
495	539	*Prélude pour le second Dixit Dominus à 4 voix sans instruments f ut fa*	2 treb., bc	Instrumental	XXIV "c"	46	?	
496	80	"Magnificat"	hd, hc, t, b, HD, HC, T, B; bc (org)	Motet (canticle of the Virgin)	XXIV "c"	47–51	?	
497	419	*Pour Saint Augustin mourant* "Bonum certamen"	2 hd; bc	Latin oratorio	XXVIII "d"	1–3	? 28 August	Pub: *Motets mêlés de symphonie,* 1709
498	50	*Antienne pour les vêpres de l'Assomption de la Vierge*	bd; 2 vns, bc	Motet	XXVIII "d"	3–4	? 15 August	

		Title	Instrumentation	Genre	Vol./pp.	Date	Notes
499	51	*Pour les mêmes vêpres, Antienne*	hd; 2 fl, bc	Motet	XXVIII "d" 4–5	?/15 August	
500	52	*Antienne pour les mêmes vêpres*	2 hd, bd; bc	Motet	XXVIII "d" 6–7	?/15 August	
501	274	*Élévation* "O sacramentum pietatis"	bd; 2 fl, 2 vns, bc	Motet	XXVIII "d" 7–9	?	
502	226	*Dixit Dominus, Pour le P. Royal*	3 hd/2 HD; bc (org) (transposable for hc, t, b & HD, HC, T, B)	Motet (Psalm 109)	XXVIII "d" 10–12, 18, 19–20	1687?	"Mlle du Fr.," "Mère de Sainte Ag.," "Mère de Saint Bern.," "Dumont l'aîné," "Dumont cadet"
503	227	*Laudate Dominum omnes gentes, Pour le P.R.*	3 hd/2 HD; bc (org)	Motet (Psalm 116)	XXVIII "d" 13–15	1687?	"Mlle du Fr.," "Mère de Sainte Ag.," "Mère de Saint Bern."
504	81	*Magnificat, Pour le P.R.*	3 hd/2 HD; bc (org) (transposable for hc, t, b & HD, HC, T, B)	Motet (canticle of the Virgin)	XXVIII "d" 15–18, 20–22	1687?	"Mlle du Fre.," "Mère de Sainte Ag.," "Mère de Saint Bern."
505	420	*Dialogus inter angelos et pastores Judae, In nativitatem Domini*	hd, hc, t, b, HD, HC, T, B; 2 fl, str (4), bc (b. vns, org)	Latin oratorio	XXVIII "d" 23–36	?/Christmas	

OTHER MANUSCRIPTS

No.	H.	Title	Scoring	Genre	Source	Date	Special comments
506	231	"Nisi Dominus"	hd, d, b; 2 treb., bc	Motet (Psalm 126)	Autograph, BN, Rés. Vmc. Ms. 28, pp. 1–26	?	
507	232	*De profundis*	hd, d, b; 2 treb., bc	Motet (Psalm 129)	Idem, pp. 27–50	?	
508	275	*Panis quem ego dabo à 5 voix et deux flûtes pour le Saint Sacrement*	hd, d, hc, t, b; 2 fl, bc	Motet	Autograph, BN, Rés. Vmc. Ms. 27, fols. 1–8v	Early 1680s?	"Pieche" (for the entire manuscript). "Mr. Anthoine", "Mr. Joseph"
509	373	*Sola vivebat in antris à 2 voix et deux flûtes pour la Magdeleine*	hd, d; 2 fl, bc	Motet	Idem, fols. 9–13v	Early 1680s?	
510	374	*Flores, flores, o Gallia à 2 voix et 2 flûtes pour Sainte Thérèse*	hd, d; 2 fl, bc	Motet	Idem, fols. 14–18v	Early 1680s?	Pub: *Motet à deux dessus, avec accompagnement de violons, et basse continue par M. Charpentier, Mélanges de musique,* Paris: J.-C. Ballard, 1729
511	276	*Adoramus te Christe à 3 voix et 2 flûtes pour le Saint Sacrement*	hd, d, b; 2 fl, bc	Motet	Idem, fols. 19–27	Early 1680s?	
512	277	*Cantemus Domino à 2 voix pour le Saint Sacrement*	hd, d; bc	Motet	Idem, fols. 27v–31	Early 1680s?	
513	304	*Domine salvum fac regem à 2 voix C sol ut pour le roi*	hd, d; bc	Motet	Idem, fols. 31v–32	Early 1680s?	Pub: *Motet à deux dessus, avec la basse-continue, de Monsieur Charpentier, Mélanges de musique,* Paris: J.-B.-C. Ballard, 1730

514	445	"Amour vous avez beau redoubler mes alarmes"	hc; bc	Air	Idem, fols. 32v–33	?

H. 380–389   Méditations pour le Carême

515	380	Première méditation "Desolatione desolata est terra"	hc, t, b; bc	Motet	Brossard Collection BN, Vm¹ 1175bis, vol. I, fols. 108v–110	?
516	381	Deuxième méditation "Sicut pullus hirundinis"	hc, t, b; bc	Motet	Idem, fols. 110v–112	?
517	382	Troisième méditation "Tristis est anima mea"	hc, t, b; bc	Motet	Idem, fols. 112v–113	?
518	383	Quatrième méditation "Ecce Judas"	hc, t, b; bc	Motet (responsory, excerpt)	Idem, fols. 113v–115	?
519	384	Cinquième méditation "Cum cenasset Jesus"	hc, t, b; bc	Motet	Idem, fols. 115–118	?
520	385	Sixième méditation "Quarebat Pilatus"	hc, t, b; bc	Motet	Idem, fols. 118–119v	?
521	386	Septième méditation "Tenebrae factae sunt"	hc, t, b; bc	Motet	Idem, fols. 120–121	?
522	387	Huitième "Stabat mater"	hc, t, b; bc	Motet (sequence, excerpt)	Idem, fols. 121v–122v	?
523	388	Neuvième, Magdalena lugens "Sola vivebat in antris"	hc, t, b; bc	Motet	Idem, fols. 122v–124	?
524	389	Dixième "Tentavit Deus Abraham"	hc, t, b; bc	Motet	Idem, fols. 124–126	?
525	278	Motet du Saint Sacrement à 4 "O sacrum convivium"	hd, hc, t, b, HD, HC, T, B; bc	Motet	Brossard Collection BN, Vm¹ 1175bis, vol. I, fols. 126–127	?
526	390	Motet de la Vierge	hd, hc, t, b, HD, HC, T, B; bc	Motet	Idem, fols. 127v–128v	?

No.	H.	Title	Scoring	Genre	Source	Date	Special comments
527	423	*Dialogus inter Magdalenam et Jesum 2 vocibus Canto e Alto cum organo*	d, hc; bc (org)	Latin oratorio	Brossard Collection BN, Vm¹ 1478, vol. IV	?	
528	424	*Le reniement de Saint Pierre* "Cum cenasset Jesus"	hd, d, hc, t, b, HD, D, HC, T, B; bc	Latin oratorio	Brossard Collection BN, Vm¹ 1269, vol. II, pp. 1–23	?	
529	436	"Dilecte mi"	hc, t, b; bc (org)	Motet	Idem, pp. 25–31	?	
530	437	"Ferte, ferte corona coelites"	2 hd, b; bc (org)	Motet	Idem, pp. 32–40	?	
531	438	"Venite et audite omnes"	2 hd, b; bc (org)	Motet	Idem, pp. 41–54	?	
532	341	*Gratiarum actiones pro restituta regis christianissimi sanitate anno 1686*	2 hd; 2 fl, 2 vns, bc	Motet	Idem, pp. 57–68	?	Other source: Brossard Collection BN, Vm¹ 1264 (1–5) Cantio IIIa (separate parts). Two violins only.
533	425	*Dialogus inter Christum et peccatores* "Mementote peccatores"	2 hd, bt; bc	Latin oratorio	Idem, pp. 69–75	?	cf. No. 306 (H. 425a)
534	378	*Pour le Carême*	2 d, b; bc	Motet	Idem, pp. 76–89	?	Pub: *Motets mêlés de symphonie,* 1709
163	342	*Pour Sainte Thérèse*	2 hd, d; bc	Motet	Idem, pp. 90–96	?	cf. *Mélanges,* vol. III, fols. 2–4
535	193	*Psalmus David 50mus Miserere*	hd or d, 2 hc, 2 t, b, HD, 2 D, HC, T, B; 2 fl, str (4), bc	Motet	Idem, pp. 97–189	1690–91?	cf. No. 152 (first version)
536	435	"O coelestis Jerusalem"	hd, d, b; bc	Motet	Brossard Collection BN, Vm¹ 1175 ter, vol. I, fols. 14–20	?	
537	439	*Bone pastor*	hd, d, b; bc (b.vl)	Motet	BN, Vm¹ 1272, Cantio XII, pp. 30–46	?	

				1688 28 February	Copy made in 1690 by Philidor the Elder
538 490 *David et Jonathas*	5 hd, 3 hc, 2 t, 4 b, HD, HC, T B; 2 fl, 2 ob, str (4), bc (b. vns, hps)	Tragedy in music P. Bretonneau	BN, Ms. Cons. Rés. F. 924	1688 28 February	Copy made in 1690 by Philidor the Elder
539 492 *Amor vince ogni cosa, Pastoraletta IIa. del Sigr. Charpentier*	hd, d, hc, t, b; 2 treb., bc	Pastorale	Brossard Collection BN, Ms. Vm^7 71, pp. 1–79	?	
540 493 *Pastoraletta italiana IIa del Sigr. Charpentier* "Cupido perfido"	hd, d, hc, b; 2 treb.	Pastorale	Idem, pp. 81–111	?	
541 475 "Beate mie pene"	2 d; bc	Duet	BN, Vm^7 53, pp. 74–77	?	
542 476 "Superbo amore"	hd, d; bc	Duet	BN, Vm^7 18, pp. 70–72	?	
543 477 "Il mondo così va"	hd; bc	Duet	BN, Vm^7 18, pp. 70–72	?	
544 478 "Coulez, coulez charmants ruisseaux"	t; 2 vns, bc	Cantata	Avignon, Bibliothèque du Musée Calvet, Ms. 1182, pp. 25–32	?	*Cantate française de M. Charpentier.* Attribution doubtful.
545 454 "Fenchon, la gentille Fenchon"	2 d; bc	Air	BN, Ms. Y 296 (1) pp. 271–274	?	
546 470 "Veux-tu, compère Grégoire"	hc, t, b	Air	Idem, pp. 284 bis–288	?	Other sources: BN, Ms. Y 292, pp. 32–38, *Recueil d'airs sérieux et à boire ... pour l'année 1702.* Paris: C. Ballard, pp. 225–229, *Airs choisis ...* Paris: Prault fils, Boivin, Le Clerc, 1738, pp. 24–28

No.	H.	Title	Scoring	Genre	Source	Date	Special comments
547	448	"Beaux petits yeux d'écarlate"	hc, t, b	Air	Idem, pp. 316–321	?	Other sources: BN, Ms. Fol. Y 183, pp. 58–60, Ms. Y 292, pp. 51–58, *Mélanges de musique* Paris: J.-B.-C. Ballard, 1726, pp. 11–15, *Airs choisis*, Paris: Prault fils, Boivin, Le Clerc, 1738, pp. 31–36
548	461	*Air à voix seule* "Quoi! je ne verrai plus"	hc; bc	Air	BN, Thibault, Rec. H.P. No. X, pp. 14–16	?	
549	464	*Air à voix seule* "Rentrez trop indiscrets soupirs"	d; bc	Air	Idem, pp. 20–22	?	Other source: Paris Bibliothèque Sainte-Geneviève, Ms. 2368, fols. 15–16
550	455	*Air à voix seule* "Non, non, je ne l'aime plus"	hc; bc	Air	Idem, pp. 26–37	?	
551	466	*Air à voix seule* "Ruisseau qui nourris"	d; bc	Air	Idem, pp. 38–42	?	Other source: Paris Bibliothèque Sainte-Geneviève, Ms. 3175, fols. 89v–91v, *Air sérieux*
552	441	*Air tendre* "Ah! laissez-moi rêver"	d; bc	Air	Idem, pp. 91–93	?	Other source: Paris Bibliothèque Sainte-Geneviève, Ms. 3175, fols. 57v–59v, *Air à voix seule*
553	495c	*Profitez du printemps*	hd; bc	Air	BN, Vm^7 4822, fol. 98v	?	Arrangement for solo voice (*haut-dessus*) of part of the second intermède of *Le Malade imaginaire*

554	548	*Sonate pour 2 flûtes allemandes, 2 dessus de violon, une basse de viole, une basse de violon à 5 cordes, un clavecin et un théorbe*	2 fl. trav, 2 vns, b. vl, b. vn, hps, theorbo	Instrumental	Autograph (separate parts), BN, Ms. Vm7 4813	ca. 1685?	Manuscript deposited in BN with the separate parts of *Les Arts florissants* (H. 487a). Hence the two works seem to have been composed around the same time.
555	454 bis	"Il faut aimer, c'est un mal nécessaire"	d	Air	*Recueil des airs d'Atys 1676 de J. B. Lully et airs sérieux et à boire de différents auteurs, à 1 voix*, BN, Rés. Vmf. ms. 11, fols. 63v–64	1676?	
556	495 bis	*Le Malade imaginaire* 1673 Prologue—Premier intermède—Second intermède—Troisième intermède	2 hd, 2 d, 2 hc, 2 t, b, HD, HC, T, B; str (4), bc	Molière	Bibliothèque de la Comédie-Française, *Théâtre français*, vol. II, pp. 132–182	1673 1674 1685	
557	548 bis	*Trio de M. Charpentier*	2 treb, b	Instrumental	Bibliothèque municipale de Versailles, André Danican Philidor, *Suites d'orchestre*, ca. 1720, Ms. Musicaux 139/143, p. 65	?	Bass part only in *Simphonies de M. de Lully*, Ms. Musicaux 119/121, p. 16 (Bibliothèque de Versailles)

ÉDITIONS

The works printed between 1676 and 1737 fall into three categories.

1. *Airs sérieux et à boire* published in the *Mercure Galant*

No.	H.	Title	Scoring	Date published	Other sources
558	462	*Air nouveau* "Quoi! rien ne peut vous arrêter"	d; bc	January 1678	
559	452	*Air* "En vain rivaux assidus"	d; bc	February 1678	
560	443	*Air nouveau* "Ah! qu'on est malheureux"	d; bc	November 1678	
561	467	*Chaconne* "Sans frayeur dans ce bois"	d; bc	March 1680	
562	442	"Ah! qu'ils sont courts les beaux jours"	d; bc	June 1680	
563	499a	*Le Bavolet*	d; bc	October 1680	Cf. *Recueil complet de vaudevilles . . . qui ont été chantés à la Comédie Française*, Paris, 1753, pp. 40–41 (*dessus* without continuo) and *Airs de la Comédie Française*, Paris: P. Ribon, n.d., p. 12 (bass voice without continuo).
564	451	*Air nouveau* "Consolez-vous chers enfants de Bacchus"	bt	October 1680	
565	457	"Percé jusques au fond du coeur"	hc; bc	January 1681	
566	459	"Que je sens de rudes combats"	hc; bc	February 1681	
567	458	"Père, maîtresse, honneur, amour"	hc; bc	March 1681	

| 568 | 449 | *Air* "Brillantes fleurs, naissez" | d | October 1689 | Cf. H. 449a, "Feuillages verts, naissez," Paris: Bibliothèque de l'Arsenal, Ms. 3235, vol. 1, pp. 70–71, *Les duos à la mode, petits et grands, anciens et nouveaux,* Amsterdam: Michel Charles Le Cène, ca. 1750, pp. 5–6; H. 449b, "Charmantes fleurs, naissez," BN, Ms. Vm^7 4822, fol. 12v, *Airs choisis,* Paris: Prault fils, Boivin, Le Clerc, 1738, pp. 29–30; H. 449c, "Printemps, vous renaissez," *Nouvelles poésies spirituelles et morales sur les plus beaux airs de la musique française et italienne avec une basse continue,* IInd anthology, Paris: G. Desprez, Ph. N. Lottin, Guichard, 1731, p. 65. H. 449a: 2 d. H. 449b, 2 d; bc. H. 449c: hd; bc. |
| 569 | 450 | "Celle qui fait mon tourment" | d; bc | July 1695 | Cf. also *Recueil d'airs sérieux et à boire,* Paris: C. Ballard, 1695, pp. 156–157. |

ADVERTISEMENTS FOR THE AIRS PUBLISHED IN THE *MERCURE GALANT*

H. 462   *Air nouveau* (New Air)   pp. 230–231

"I believe that you shall be enormously grateful for this air, since it is by M. Charpentier, famous for a thousand works which have enchanted all France, and among others, for the Moorish Air from *Le Malade imaginaire* and for all those from *Circé* and *L'Inconnu*. He was in Italy for a long time, where he often encountered Charissimi [*sic*], the greatest composer we have had in a great while. You have read the words of M. Charpentier's air; here they are set to music."

H. 452   *Air*   pp. 18–19

"The air is by M. Charpentier, whose works you tell me are so highly regarded in the provinces."

H. 443   *Air nouveau*   p. 347

"You shall not be displeased to see for the second time a madrigal that you have already read with delight, for I offer it to you this time set to music by M. Charpentier."

H. 467   *Chaconne*   p. 287

"I have been given a very pleasant chaconne which I share with you. It is by M. Charpentier. His name shall cause you to receive it with delight."

H. 442   "Ah! qu'ils sont courts les beaux jours"   pp. 209–210

"You will have good reason to be happy with me for the couplets by Mademoiselle Castille, which so pleased you, and which you have already seen set to music at the beginning of this letter. I give them to you again with other notes, so that you may sing them in a different manner. M. Charpentier, who has just set them as an air, has made a kind of *rondeau* out of them. In it you will find that special gracefulness that makes you love these works. Examine this one; but when singing "Ah! qu'ils sont courts les beaux jours," etc., do not forget that you should take heed of the moral of these verses."

H. 499a   *Le Bavolet*   p. 333

"Here is the *Bavolet* of M. Charpentier, which you were so eager to see set to music, and which the Guénégaud troupe added last season to the gallant play *L'Inconnu*. Since a few performances of it are supposed to be given presently, after All Saints' Day, those from your province who attend will be able to tell you how much this charming song is loved."

H. 451 *Air nouveau* p. 189
"The music to the new song that I send you is by M. Charpentier."

H. 457 "Percé jusques au fond du coeur" pp. 246–247
"I give you something very old and yet quite new. It is old because of the verses and new because of the music. M. Charpentier, with whose talent and merits you are acquainted, is working on stanzas from *Le Cid;* each month he will offer a couplet from them. Here is the first one set to music."

H. 459 Second couplet taken from stanzas from *Le Cid*, set to music pp. 249–250
"M. Charpentier, who was in Rome for three years, derived great benefits from it. All his works bear witness to it. I give you the continuation of what he began."

H. 458 Third couplet taken from stanzas from *Le Cid*, set to music p. 306
"Here is another in the series of what M. Charpentier began."

H. 449 *Air* pp. 297–298
"Although the song that I give you is not new, it is currently being performed so much in Paris that it can only be received with favor in the provinces. The words are by the illustrious M. de la Fontaine, and the music by the famous M. Charpentier, who has a great knowledge of all the beauties of music."

H. 450 *Gavotte* p. 193
"Here are some words that were added to a gavotte by M. Charpentier, so well-known for his compositions. Since it is very popular now, you will have no trouble getting all the couplets for it."

2. *Motets mêlés de symphonie* published by Jacques Édouard in 1709: short pieces for one, two or three voices and thorough bass. The first one (H. 268) is a variant of the autograph manuscript; originally for tenor and continuo; the published version is for soprano, two flutes, and continuo.

No.	H.	Title	Scoring	Pages	Manuscript sources
570	268	*Lauda Sion*	hd; 2 fl, bc	1–7	*Mélanges*, vol. XXV, fols. 79–80
571	375	*Pour un confesseur non pontife*	hc, t; bc	8–10	None
572	376	*Pour un confesseur*	hc, t; bc	11–12	None
573	377	*Pour tous les saints*	t; bc	12–14	None
574	279	*Pour une élévation* "O amor, o bonitas"	hd; bc	15–18	None
575	280	*Motet du Saint Sacrement* "Egredimini filiae Sion"	hd; 2 vns, bc	19–26	None
54	22	*Ave Regina*	2 hd; bc	27–29	*Mélanges*, vol. II, fols. 93–95
534	378	*Pour le carême*	2 d, b; bc	30–38	Brossard Collection, BN, Vm¹ 1269, pp. 69–75
497	419	*Pour Saint Augustin*	2 hd; bc	39–43	*Mélanges*, vol. XXVIII, fols. 1–3
78	243	*Panis angelicus, Élévation*	hd; bc	44	*Mélanges*, vol. III, fol. 103
576	379	*Pour plusieurs fêtes*	hc, t; b; bc	45–60	None
577	305	*Domine salvum*	hc, t, b/HD, HC, T,B; fl, ob, str (4), bc	60–64	None

3. Pieces published by Ballard in the seventeenth and eighteenth centuries.

No.	H.	Title	Scoring	Genre	References
578	496	*Airs de la Comédie de Circé excerpt avec la basse continue*	hd; bc/hc; bc/b; bc/2 hd; bc/hd, hc; bc/2 hd, hc; bc	Airs	Paris: C. Ballard, 1676
579	496a	Parodies of two airs from *Circé*		Airs	*Parodies bachiques, sur les airs et symphonies des Opéra, recueillies et mises en ordre par Monsieur Ribon*, Paris: C. Ballard, 1695, pp. 242–244
580	496b	Parodies of eight airs from *Circé*		Airs	Idem H. 496a, *Seconde édition*, Paris: C. Ballard, 1696, pp. 282–290
581	496c	Parodies of eight airs from *Circé*		Airs	*Nouvelles parodies bachiques, mêlées de vaudevilles ou rondes de table*, Paris: C. Ballard, vol. III, 1702, pp. 101–108
582	491	*Médée*	5 hd, 4 d, 2 hc, 2 t, bt, 2 t, HD, D, HC, B; 2 fl, b, fl, 2 ob, tp, dr, str (5), bc (b. vns, bs)	Tragedy in music T. Corneille	Paris: C. Ballard, 1694
569	450	*Chanson à danser* "Celle qui fait mon tourment"	d; bc	Air	*Recueil d'airs sérieux et à boire*, Paris: C. Ballard, 1695, pp. 156–157
583	491a	Parodies of two airs from *Médée*		Airs	*Parodies bachiques, sur les airs et symphonies des Opéra, recueillies et mises en ordre par Monsieur Ribon*, Paris: C. Ballard, 1695, pp. 240–241
584	491b	Parodies of two airs from *Médée*		Airs	Idem H. 491a, *Seconde édition*, Paris: C. Ballard, 1696, pp. 280–281
585	491c	Parodies of two airs from *Médée*		Airs	*Nouvelles parodies bachiques, mêlées de vaudevilles et rondes de table*, Paris: C. Ballard, vol. III, 1702, pp. 96–100

No.	H.	Title	Scoring	Genre	References
546	470	*Trio, Air à boire* "Veux-tu, compère Grégoire"	hc, t, b	Air	*Recueil d'airs sérieux et à boire . . . pour l'année 1702*, Paris: C. Ballard, pp. 225–229
586	499a	"Si Claudine ma voisine"	b	Air (excerpt from *L'Inconnu*)	*Recueil d'airs sérieux et à boire . . . pour l'année 1703*, Paris: C. Ballard, pp. 194–201. Cf. also *Airs de la Comédie-Française*, Paris: chez Pierre Ribon, n.d., p. 12, and *Recueil complet de vaudevilles . . .qui ont été chantés à la Comédie-Française*, Paris: 1753, pp. 40–41
587	447	*Air à boire* "Ayant bu du vin clairet"	d, b; bc	Air	*Recueil d'airs sérieux et à boire . . . pour l'année 1704*, Paris: C. Ballard, pp. 172–173
588	460	"Qu'il est doux, charmante Climène"	d	Air (based on "Qu'ils sont doux, bouteille mamie" from *Le Médecin malgré lui* by Molière [I, 5])	*La clef des chansonniers*, Paris: J.-B.-C. Ballard, 1717, vol. I, pp. 74–75. Cf. also H. 460a "Deux beaux yeux, un teint de jaunisse," BN, Fonds Weckerlin 189 C, vol. III, fols. 103–104; H. 460b "Le beau jour dit une bergère," BN, Rés. Vmc. ms. 201 (2), vol. II, p. 150; and H. 460c "Un flambeau, Jeannette, Isabelle!" ed. J. Tiersot, *Noëls français*, Paris: Heugel, 1901, p. 24
589	425	*Dialogue en trio* "Mementote peccatores"	2 hd, bt; bc	Latin oratorio	*Mélanges de musique*, Paris: J.-B.-C. Ballard, 1725, pp. 126–139
547	448	*La Vieille* "Beaux petits yeux d'écarlate"	hd, d, b (bc?)	Air	*Mélanges de musique*, Paris: J.-B.-C. Ballard, 1726, pp. 11–15
590	446	*Chansonnette* "Auprès du feu l'on fait l'amour"	d; bc	Air	*Mélanges de musique*, Paris: J.-B.-C. Ballard, 1728, p. 211
591	469	*Récit* "Tristes déserts, sombre retraite"	d; bc	Air	*Mélanges de musique*, Paris: J.-B.-C. Ballard, 1728, pp. 71–73
592	468	*Printemps, duo* "Tout renaît, tout fleurit"	2 d; bc	Air	*Mélanges de musique*, Paris: J.-B.-C. Ballard, 1728, pp. 78–79
593	465	*Récit* "Retirons-nous, fuyons"	d; bc	Air	*Mélanges de musique*, Paris: J.-B.-C. Ballard, 1728, pp. 84–86

594	444	*Pastorelle, duo* "Allons sous ce vert feuillage"	2 d; bc	Air	Mélanges de musique, Paris: J.-B.-C. Ballard, 1728, p. 180
595	374	*Motet à deux dessus, avec accompagnement de violons et basse continue* "Flores, flores, o Gallia"	hd, d; 2 vns, bc	Motet	Mélanges de musique, Paris: J.-B.-C. Ballard, 1729, pp. 2–9. Manuscript source: BN, Rés. Vmc. Ms. 17, fols. 14–18v
596	463	*Air sérieux* "Rendez-moi mes plaisirs"	hc; bc	Air	Mélanges de musique, Paris: J.-B.-C. Ballard, 1729, pp. 42–43
513	304	*Motet, à deux dessus, avec la basse continue* "Domine salvum"	hd, d; bc	Motet	Mélanges de musique, Paris: J.-B.-C. Ballard, 1730, pp. 2–3. Manuscript source: BN, Rés. Vmc. Ms. 27, fols. 31v–32
407	69	*Motet à voix seule* "Veni creator Spiritus"	hd; bc	Motet	Mélanges de musique, Paris: J.-B.-C. Ballard, 1731, p. 2. Manuscript source: *Mélanges*, vol. XXIII, fol. 26v
597	456	*Air sérieux* "Oiseaux de ces bocages"	d; bc	Air	Concerts parodiques, 4th book, Paris: J.-B.-C. Ballard, 1732, pp. 37–38
598	453	*Musette* "Faites trêve à vos chansonettes"	hd	Air	Les parodies nouvelles et les vaudevilles inconnus, 7th book, Paris: J.-B.-C. Ballard, 1737, pp. 62–63

Classification of Works by Scoring

The numbers following the scoring abbreviations (explained on p. 422) correspond to the numbers in the first column of "Chronological Table of Works." Also, the precise instrumentation of the continuo is not given in this section; refer to the table.

1. VOCAL WORKS WITHOUT THOROUGHBASS

Solo voice
    d: 555, 563, 568, 588, 598 (**hd**).
    t: 287, 289.
    b: 212, 288, 563, 564 (**bt**), 586.

Two voices
    2 d: 443, 568.

Three voices
    2 hd, bd: 345.
    hc, t, b: 546, 547.

Four voices
    2 hd, d, bd: 344, 346.

2. VOCAL WORKS WITH THOROUGHBASS

Solo voice
    hd or **d:** 77, 78, 87, 90 (and 95[**2 treb.**]), 91, 96, 98, 101, 102, 110, 158, 168, 339, 366, 367, 378, 407, 408, 409, 470, 543, 549, 551, 552, 553, 558, 559, 560, 561, 562, 563, 568, 569, 574, 578, 590, 591, 593, 597.

hc: 108, 112, 168, 224, 225, 226, 260, 408, 514, 548, 550, 565, 566, 567, 578, 596.

t: 87, 99, 468, 469, 573.

b: 578.

Two voices

2 hd, or hd and d, or 2 d: 2, 3, 6, 7, 9, 11, 13, 15, 34, 53, 54, 92, 97, 107, 114, 122, 145, 180, 372, 373 (and 414[2 fl and b. fl]), 374, 375, 390, 420, 435, 445, 472, 497, 512, 513, 541, 542, 545, 568, 578, 592, 594.

hd or d, hc: 109, 290, 527, 578.

d, t: 157.

d, b: 587.

2 hc: 53.

hc, t: 206, 399, 400, 571, 572.

2 t: 196.

t, b: 207.

Three voices

3 hd, or 2 hd, d, or 3d: 57, 163, 217, 261, 363, 428, 433.

hd, d, bd, or 2 hd, bd: 21, 22, 23, 84, 147, 500.

2 hd, hc: 61, 64, 65, 67, 88, 103, 104, 105, 106, 111, 113, 578.

hd, d, b, or 2 hd, b, or 2 d, b: 84, 86, 89, 133, 134, 140, 387, 477, 530, 531, 533 (bt and 306[2 treb. inst.]), 534, 536, 537, 589 (bt).

d, hc, b: 56.

2 hc, b: 283, 284, 285.

hc, t, b: 33, 55, 123, 127, 138, 140 (and 413[2 vns]), 172, 219, 220, 237, 238, 239, 240, 244, 256, 405, 429, 447, 448, 451, 452, 453, 465, 475, 476, 478, 491, 492, 515, 516, 517, 518, 519, 520, 521, 522, 523, 524, 529, 576.

2 t, b: 176.

Four voices

hd, hc, t, b: 19, 406.

hc, 2 t, b: 257.

Five voices

2 d, hc, t, b: 116, 359.

Six voices

hd, hc, t, 3 b: 184.

hd, d, 2 hc, t, b: 487.

Solo voice and one instrument
    d; treb. vl: 100 (and 94[**2 vns, 2 t. vls**].

Solo voice and two instruments
    hd; 2 vns: 85, 164, 575.
    hd; 2 fl: 204, 499, 570.
    hd; 2 ob: 436.
    bd; 2 vns: 498.
    hc; 2 vns: 243.
    hc; 2 fl: 175, 215 (**fl. trav**).
    hc; 2 treb. inst: 60, 185.
    t; 2 vns: 544.
    t; 2 fl: 197, 481.
    b; 2 vns: 202, 479 (**bt**).
    b; 2 fl: 279.
    b; 2 treb. inst: 41, 71, 121 (**bt**), 325, 459, 460, 461.

Solo voice and more than two instruments
    bd; 2 fl, 2 vns: 501.
    hc; strings (4): 201.
    b; 2 fl, 2 vns: 203.
    b; ob or **fl, fl. trav, 2 vns**: 402 (**bt**), 403, 404.
    b; strings (4): 199.
    b; 2 fl, 2 ob, strings (4): 396, 397, 398.

Two voices and one instrument
    hd, d, or **2 d; fl**: 5, 10.

Two voices and two instruments
    hd, d; 2 fl: 4, 8, 24, 509, 510.
    hd, d; 2 vns: 532 (**2 hd**), 595.
    hd, d; 2 treb. inst: 12, 14, 25.
    hc, t; 2 vns: 434.
    hc, t; 2 treb. inst: 74.
    2 t; 2 treb. inst: 200.

Two voices and more than two instruments
    2 hd; 2 fl, 2 vns: 419, 532.
    hd, hc; strings (4): 379.
    hc, b; strings (4): 307.

Three voices and two instruments
    hd, d, hc; 2 fl: 1.
    hd, d, hc; 2 treb. inst: 148.

hd, d, b; 2 fl: 73, 119 (+ b. fl), 341 (+ b. fl), 511.

hd, d, b or 2 hd, b; 2 treb. inst: 38, 39, 40, 42, 43, 45, 46, 47, 48, 49, 50, 51, 69, 70, 79, 83, 117, 128, 129, 131, 142, 143, 144, 148, 166, 323, 324, 326, 327, 328, 333, 334, 338 (+ t. vl), 340, 342, 343, 349, 350, 354, 376, 383, 393, 421, 430, 506, 507.

d, hc, b; 2 treb. inst: 153.

hc, t, b; 2 fl: 44.

hc, t, b; 2 vns: 277.

hc, t, b; 2 treb. inst: 32, 37 (and 76[2 treb. inst]), 52, 63, 135, 136, 282, 351, 394.

Three voices and more than two instruments

hd, d, b; 2 treb. inst, 2 tenor vls: 356.

hc, t, b; 2 fl, 2 vns: 137 (fl. à bec, fl. trav), 161, 218.

2 t, b; 2 fl, 2 vns: 182.

hd, d, hc; strings (4): 300.

hc, t, b; strings (4): 298.

hd, d, b; 2 fl, strings (4): 353.

Four voices and two instruments

hd, d, hc, b; 2 treb. inst: 540.

hd, d, 2b; 2 treb. inst: 177.

Four voices and more than two instruments

hd, d, hc, b; 2 treb. inst (fl?), b. fl: 132.

hd, d, bt, b; fl à bec, fl. trav, b. fl: 389.

d, hc, t, b; 2 fl, 2 vns: 292.

hc, t, bt, b; 2 fl, 2 vns: 426.

Five voices and two instruments

hd, d, hc, t, b; 2 fl: 508.

hd, d, hc, t, b; 2 treb. inst: 539.

Five voices and more than two instruments

d, 2 hc, t, b; strings (4): 329.

Six voices and instruments

2 hc, 2 t, 2 b; 4 fl, 4 vns: 423, 424, 425.

Soloists, chorus (one-part)

hd or d; HD or D: 335, 488.

3 hd; D: 391.

Soloists, chorus (two-part):
   3 hd; 2 HD: 502, 503, 504.

Soloists, chorus (4): 169 (and 227[**2 treb. inst**]), 170 (and 230[**2 treb. inst**]), 173 (and 228[**2 treb. inst**]), 174 (and 229[**2 treb. inst**]), 183 (and 231[**2 treb. inst**]), 221, 235, 250, 251, 254, 255, 262, 286 (and 233[**2 treb. inst**]), 431 (and 234[**2 treb. inst**]), 438, 439, 440, 441, 444, 446, 450, 462, 463, 490, 496, 502, 504, 525, 526.

Soloists, chorus (4), two violins: 155 (and 309[**strings (4)**]), 118 (+ **2 optional trumpets**), 120, 125 (and 222[**2 vns**] or 223[**strings (4)**]), 246, 247, 248, 249, 268, 276, 277, 437.

Soloists, chorus (4), two instruments: 266, 267, 269, 270, 271, 272, 273, 274, 275, 454, 455, 456, 457, 458.

Soloists, chorus (4), flute(s), two violins: 35 (**2 fl**), 62.

Soloists, chorus (4), strings (4): 241, 242, 253, 258, 331, 332, 336, 395, 432, 556.

Soloists, chorus (4), flutes, strings (4): 171, 179 (**2 fl**), 181 (**2 fl**), 187, 189 (**2 fl**), 190, 191 (**2 fl**), 192, 194 (**2 fl**), 195 (**2 fl**), 198, 291 (**2 fl**), 347 (**2 fl**), 392 (**2 fl**), 401 (**2 fl**), 410, 442 (**2 fl**), 464 (**2 fl**), 467 (**2 fl**), 480 (**2 fl**), 505 (**2 fl**).

Soloists, chorus (4), two flutes, oboe, strings (4): 178, 208 (**2 ob**), 211, 214, 259 (**2 ob**), 449 (**2 ob**), 468, 471, 484 (**2 ob**), 493, 538 (**2 ob**), 577 (**fl**).

Soloists, chorus (4), two flutes, two oboes, trumpets, bass trumpet, timpani, strings (4): 216.

Soloists, chorus (4), two transverse flutes, recorders, two oboes, strings (5): 377.

Soloists, chorus (5): 528.

Soloists, chorus (5), two instruments: 151, 152, 154 (**2 treb. vls**), 156 (**2 treb. vls**), 165, 167, 364, 368 (**2 treb. vls**), 370, 382, 385, 388 (**fl. and transv. fl**).

Soloists, chorus (5), four instruments: 362 (**2 fl, 2 treb. inst**), 369 (**2 fl, 2 treb. vls**), 381 (**2 fl, 2 treb. vls**), 418 (**2 fl, 2 vns**).

Soloists, chorus (5), and more than four instruments: 159 (**2 fl, 2 ob, 2 vns, tp, timp**), 299 (**strings [4]** and 485[+ **2 fl**]), 302 (**strings [4]**), 582 (**2 fl, b. fl, 2 ob, 2 tp, timp, strings [5]**).

Soloists, chorus (6), two instruments (two treble viols): 146, 149, 150, 162 (and 384), 361, 365, 386.

Soloists, chorus (6), four instruments: 160 (**2 fl, 2 treb. vls**), 482 (**2 fl, 2 vns**), 486 (**2 fl, 2 tenor vls**).

Soloists, chorus (6), and more than four instruments:
strings (4): 263, 264, 265, 482, 483.
2 fl, strings (4): 535 (and 412).
2 fl, tenor fl, strings (5): 358.

Soloists, chorus (7), flute, transverse flute, tenor flute, strings (5): 357.

Soloists, double chorus (4/4): 58 (and 75[**2 treb. inst**]), 348.

Soloists, double chorus (4/4), two violins: 360.

Soloists, double chorus (4/4), strings (4/4): 17, 18, 20, 36, 66, 68 (and 310), 72, 80 (and 321), 126, 130, 141.

Soloists, double chorus (4/4), two flutes, strings (4/4): 16, 82 (and 311), 124 (+ **ob**), 278, 280, 293 (**fl, + ob**), 294, 303, 473, 474.

Soloists, quadruple chorus, strings (16): 296, 297.

3. INSTRUMENTAL WORKS

Two instruments: 27, 28, 29, 30, 75, 76, 232, 315 (**2 transv. fl**), 317 (**2 vns**), 411 (**2 vns**), 416 (**2 fl** or **2 vns**), 427, 466, 494, 495, 557.

Four viols (**2 treble, tenor, bass**): 330.

Two flutes, two oboes, and bassoons: 316.

Two transverse flutes, two violins, bass viol, bass violin, harpsichord, theorbo: 554.

Strings (4): 295, 305, 313, 320, 337, 355, 371, 155 (and 380).

Strings (5): 26, 81, 314.

Two flutes, strings (4): 186, 188, 193, 236, 245, 304, 352 (**2 transv. fl** and **b. fl**), 415 (**fl**), 417 (**fl**).

Two flutes, oboes, strings (4): 213, 252, 322 (**2 ob** and **bassoon**), 468.

Flutes, oboes, crumhorn, strings (4): 31, 281 (+ **serpents**).

Two trumpets, two flutes, two oboes, bassoons, strings (4): 318.

Trumpets, bass trumpet, timpani, strings (4): 210 (+ **2 fl** and **2 ob**), 308.

Catalog of Works

The following list is based on H. Wiley Hitchcock's catalog, *Catalogue raisonné des oeuvres de Marc-Antoine Charpentier* (1982), in which Charpentier's musical works are arranged and numbered by genre. A second numbering system, listing the composer's works in the order in which they were composed, is referred to in "Chronological Table of Works" and "Classification of Works by Scoring."

H. 1	[Untitled mass] "Kyrie eleison"	H. 13	*Prose pour le jour de Pâques* "Victimae paschali laudes"
H. 2	*Messe pour les trépassés à 8*	H. 14	"Lauda Sion salvatorem"
H. 3	*Messe à 8 voix et 8 violons et flûtes*	H. 15	*Stabat mater pour des religieuses*
H. 4	*Messe à quatre choeurs*	H. 16	"Regina coeli"
H. 5	*Messe, Pour le Port Royal*	H. 17	"Veni sponsa Christi"
H. 6	*Messe à 4 voix, 4 violons, 2 flûtes et 2 hautbois pour M. Mauroy*	H. 18	*Salve Regina*
		H. 19	*Ave Regina coelorum*
		H. 20	*Sub tuum praesidium*
		H. 21	"Alma redemptoris mater"
H. 7, 7a	*Messe des morts à 4 voix*	H. 22	*Ave Regina*
H. 8	*Messe pour le samedi de Pâques*	H. 23	*Salve Regina à trois voix pareilles*
H. 9	*Messe de minuit à 4 voix, flûtes et violins pour Noël*	H. 23a	*Prélude* (for H. 24)
		H. 24	*Salve Regina à trois choeurs*
H. 10	*Messe des morts à 4 voix et symphonie*	H. 25	*Antiphona in honorem beatae Virginis*
H. 11, 11a	*Assumpta est Maria, Missa six vocibus cum simphonia*	H. 26	"Inviolata, integra et casta"
		H. 27	"Salve Regina"
H. 12	"Dies irae"	H. 28	"Sub tuum praesidium"

H. 148	*Te Deum à 4 voix*	H. 178	"Beati omnes"
H. 149	"Laudate pueri"	H. 179	"Notus in Judea Deus"
H. 150	"Nisi Dominus"	H. 180	*Exaudiat pour le roi à 4*
H. 151	*Confitebor à 4 voix et 2 violons*		"Exaudiat pour Versailles"
H. 152	"Laudate Dominum omnes gentes"	H. 180a	*Prélude*
		H. 180b	*Prélude*
H. 153	"Dixit Dominus"	H. 181	"Benedixisti Domine terram tuam"
H. 154	"Beatus vir qui timet Dominum"	H. 182	"Laudate Dominum omnes gentes"
H. 155	"Memento Domine"	H. 183	"Paratum cor meum Deum"
H. 156	*De profundis*		
H. 157	*Miserere à 2 dessus, 2 flûtes et basse continue*	H. 184	"Quare fremuerunt gentes"
H. 158	"Lauda Jerusalem"	H. 185	"Bonum est confiteri Domino"
H. 159	"Laudate Dominum omnes gentes"	H. 186	"Quam dilecta"
H. 160	"Nisi Dominus"	H. 187	"Fundamenta ejus in montibus sanctis"
H. 160a	*Prélude*		
H. 161	*Laetatus sum*	H. 188	"Deus, Deus meus ad te"
H. 162	*Exaudiat à 8 voix, flûtes et violons*	H. 189	*De profundis*
		H. 190	*Dixit Dominus*
H. 163	"Domine Dominus noster"	H. 191	"Lauda Jerusalem"
H. 164	"Domine in virtute tua"	H. 192	"Omnes gentes plaudite manibus"
H. 165	"Exaudiat te Dominus" (*Precatio pro rege*)	H. 193	*Miserere des Jésuites*
		H. 193a	*Prélude*
H. 166	"Deus judicium tuum" (*Precatio pro filio regis*)	H. 194	"Jubilate Deo omnis terra"
H. 167	*Quam dilecta*	H. 195	*Bonum est confiteri Domino*
H. 168	"Quare fremuerunt gentes"	H. 196	"Usquequo Domine"
H. 168a	*Prélude*	H. 197	"Dixit Dominus"
H. 169	"In convertendo Dominus"	H. 197a	*Prélude*
		H. 198	"Cum invocarem exaudivit me"
H. 170	*Super flumina Babylonis*	H. 199	"Beatus vir qui timet Dominum"
H. 171	*Super flumina*		
H. 171a	*Prélude*	H. 199a	*Prélude*
H. 172	"Domine quid multi-plicati sunt"	H. 200	*Confitebor*
		H. 200a	*Prélude*
H. 173	*Miserere à 2 dessus, une haute-contre et basse continue*	H. 201	"Judica Domine nocentes me"
		H. 202	*Dixit Dominus*
H. 174	"Quemadmodum desiderat cervus"	H. 203	"Laudate pueri"
		H. 203a	*Prélude*
H. 175	"Beatus vir qui non abiit"	H. 204	"Dixit Dominus"
H. 176	"Cantate Domino canticum novum"	H. 205	*Gloria patri pour le De profundis*
H. 177	"Laudate Dominum de coelis"	H. 206	"Notus in Judea Deus"
		H. 207	"Domine Deus salutis meae"

H. 208	*Beatus vir qui timet Dominum*
H. 209	*Credidi propter quod*
H. 209a	*Prélude*
H. 210	*Lauda Jerusalem*
H. 211	*De profundis à 4 voix*
H. 212	*De profundis*
H. 213	*De profundis*
H. 213a	*De profundis*
H. 214	"Laudate Dominum omnes gentes"
H. 215	"Exurgat Deus"
H. 216	"Laetatus sum"
H. 217	"Nisi quia Dominus"
H. 218	"Deus noster refugium"
H. 219	*Second Miserere 50 à 4 voix et 4 instruments*
H. 220	"Confitebor tibi Domine"
H. 221	"Beatus vir qui timet Dominum"
H. 222	*Court De profundis à 4 voix*
H. 223	*Laudate Dominum omnes gentes*
H. 224	*Beatus vir qui timet Dominum*
H. 225	*Confitebor à 4 voix et instruments*
H. 226	*Dixit Dominus, Pour le Port Royal*
H. 227	*Laudate Dominum omnes gentes, Pour le Port Royal*
H. 228	"In te Domine speravi"
H. 229	"Dominus illuminatio mea"
H. 230	"Conserva me Domine"
H. 231	"Nisi Dominus"
H. 232	*De profundis*
H. 233	"Ave verum corpus"
H. 234	"Pie Jesu"
H. 235	*O sacrum convivium à 3 dessus*
H. 236	"O salutaris"
H. 237	*Élévation pour la paix* "O bone Jesu dulcis"
H. 237a	*Prélude*
H. 238	"Gaudete dilectissimi"
H. 239	*O sacrum à trois*
H. 240	*O sacrum pour trois religieuses*
H. 241	"Venite fideles"
H. 242	*Ecce panis voce sola, Élévation*
H. 243	*Panis angelicus, Élévation*
H. 244	*Élévation à 2 dessus et une basse chantante* "O bone Jesu"
H. 245	*Élévation pour un dessus, deux violons et l'orgue*
H. 246	"Caro mea vere"
H. 247	"O pretiosum et admirabile convivium"
H. 248	"O salutaris hostia"
H. 249	"O salutaris hostia"
H. 250	"Ascendat ad te Domine"
H. 251	*Élévation à 5 sans dessus de violon*
H. 252	"O coelestis Jerusalem"
H. 253	*O amor, Élévation à 2 dessus et une basse chantante*
H. 253a	*Prélude*
H. 254	"O pretiosum et admirabile convivium"
H. 255	"O pretiosum et admirabile convivium"
H. 256	*Élévation à 3 dessus* "O clementissime Domine Jesu"
H. 257	"Gustate et videte"
H. 258	"Nonne Deo"
H. 259	"Transfige amabilis Jesu"
H. 260	"O sacramentum pietatis"
H. 261	*O salutaris à 3 dessus*
H. 262	*O salutaris*
H. 263	"Pie Jesu"
H. 264	*Élévation au Saint Sacrement*
H. 264a	*Élévation à 3 voix pareilles*
H. 265	"Bone pastor"
H. 266	"Ave verum corpus"
H. 267	"Verbum caro, panem verum"
H. 268	"Lauda Sion salvatorem"

H. 269	"Pie Jesu"	H. 305	*Domine salvum*
H. 270	*Pour le Saint Sacrement à 3 voix pareilles,* "O dulce, o ineffabile convivium"	H. 306	"Gaudete fideles"
		H. 307	"O doctor optime"
		H. 308	"Haec dies"
		H. 309	*Nativité de la Vierge*
H. 271	*Pour le Saint Sacrement à 3 voix pareilles,* "Amate Jesum omnes gentes"	H. 310	*Pour Saint François*
		H. 311	*Motet pour les trépassés à 8*
		H. 312	*O filii à 3 voix pareilles*
H. 272	*Élévation à 2 dessus et une basse*	H. 313	*Pour la conception de la Vierge*
H. 273	"O vere, o bone"	H. 314	*In nativitatem Domini*
H. 274	"O sacramentum pietatis"	H. 315	*Pour Sainte Anne*
		H. 316	*In circumcisione Domini*
H. 275	*Panis quem ego dabo*	H. 317	*Pour le jour de Sainte Geneviève*
H. 276	*Adoramus te Christe*	
H. 277	*Cantemus Domino*	H. 318	*In festo purificationis*
H. 278	"O sacrum convivium"	H. 319	*Motet pour la Trinité*
H. 279	"O amor, o bonitas"	H. 320	*Motet de Saint Louis*
H. 280	"Egredimini filiae Sion"	H. 321	*Motet de Saint Laurent*
		H. 322	*Motet de la Vierge pour toutes ses fêtes*
H. 281	*Domine salvum*	
H. 282	"Domine salvum"	H. 323	*In honorem Sancti Ludovici*
H. 283	*Domine salvum*	
H. 284	*Domine salvum à 3 voix pareilles avec orgue*	H. 325	*Canticum Annae*
		H. 326	*Gratiarum actiones ex sacris codicibus excerptae pro restituta serenissimi Galliarum Delphini salute*
H. 285	"Domine salvum"	
H. 286	*Domine salvum*	
H. 287	*Domine salvum*	
H. 288	*Domine salvum pour trois religieuses*	
H. 289	"Domine salvum"	H. 327	*Motet pour toutes les fêtes de la Vierge*
H. 290	*Domine salvum sine organo*	
		H. 328	*Supplicatio pro defunctis*
H. 291	"Domine salvum"	
H. 292	"Domine salvum"	H. 329	"Ave verum corpus"
H. 293	"Domine salvum"	H. 330	*Gaudia beatae Virginis Mariae*
H. 294	"Domine salvum"	
H. 295	"Domine salvum"	H. 331	*Luctus de morte augustissimae Mariae Theresiae reginae Galliae*
H. 296	"Domine salvum"	
H. 297	*Domine salvum pour un haut et un bas dessus*	
		H. 332	*In honorem Sancti Ludovici*
H. 298	"Domine salvum"	
H. 298a	*Prélude*	H. 333	*Pro omnibus festis BVM*
H. 299	*Domine salvum*	
H. 300	*Domine salvum à 3 dessus*	H. 334	*Motet pour la Vierge*
		H. 335–338	*Quatuor anni tempestates*
H. 301	*Domine salvum à 3 voix pareilles*	
		H. 335	*Ver*
H. 302	*Domine salvum à 3 voix pareilles*	H. 336	*Aestas*
		H. 336a	*Prélude pour l'été à 3 flûtes*
H. 303	*Domine salvum*	
H. 304	*Domine salvum*	

H. 490	*David et Jonathas*		*Tuileries, Chaconne,*
H. 491	*Médée*		*Ouverture du*
H. 491a	Parody	H. 506	*Dialogue d'Angélique*
H. 491b	Parody		*et de Médor*
H. 491c	Parody	H. 507	*Vénus et Adonis*
H. 492	"Amor vince ogni cosa"	H. 508	*Pour un reposoir*
H. 493	"Cupido perfido"	H. 509	*Symphonie devant*
H. 494	*Ouverture de la*		*Regina*
	Comtesse	H. 510	"Prélude"
	d'Escarbagnas	H. 511	*Pour O filii*
H. 495	*Le Malade imaginaire*	H. 512	"Prélude"
	(Ouverture, Prologue,	H. 513	*Messe pour plusieurs*
	Second intermède,		*instruments au lieu des*
	Cérémonie des		*orgues*
	médecins)	H. 514	*Offerte pour l'orgue et*
H. 495a	[Revision] *Ouverture,*		*pour les violons, flûtes*
	Prologue, Premier		*et hautbois*
	intermède, Second	H. 515	*Symphonies pour un*
	intermède		*reposoir*
H. 495b	[Revision] *Rajusté*	H. 516	*Après Confitebor,*
	autrement pour la 3ème		*Antienne [in D minor]*
	fois, Satyres pour la fin	H. 517	*Après Beati omnes,*
	du prologue, Nouvelle		*Antienne en G*
	ouverture de l'entrée	H. 518	*Pour le sacre d'un*
	des Mores, Second air		*évêque*
	pour les tapissiers	H. 519	*Symphonies [for] le*
H. 495bis	*Prologue, Premier*		*Jugement de Salomon*
	intermède, Second	H. 520	*Prélude, menuet,*
	intermède, Troisième		*passepied pour les*
	intermède		*flûtes et hautbois*
H. 495c	*Profitez du printemps*	H. 521	*Prélude pour ce qu'on*
H. 496	*Circé*		*voudra*
H. 496	Parodies	H. 522	*Offerte*
H. 497	*Sérénade pour le*	H. 523	*Pour un reposoir*
	Sicilien	H. 524	*Ouverture pour l'église*
H. 498	*Ouverture du prologue*	H. 525	*Antienne*
	de Polyeucte/Ouver-	H. 526	*Antienne*
	ture du dépit amoureux	H. 527	*Prélude pour Sub tuum*
H. 499	*Ouverture du prologue*		*praesidium à trois*
	de l'Inconnu/Ouver-		*violons*
	ture du prologue d'Acis	H. 528	*Prélude [in G minor]*
	et Galathée		*pour les violons et flûtes*
H. 499a	*Le Bavolet,* "Si	H. 529	*Symphonie [in G*
	Claudine ma voisine"		*minor] à 3 flûtes ou*
H. 500	*Les Fous divertissants*		*violons*
H. 501	*La Pierre philosophale*	H. 530	*Prélude [in C] à quatre*
H. 502	*Endimion*		*parties de violons avec*
H. 503	"Air pour des paysans		*flûtes*
	dans la Noce de	H. 531	Noël settings for
	village"		instruments: "Laissez
H. 504	*Andromède*		paître vos bêtes," *O*
H. 505	*Rendez-vous des*		*créateur, Vous qui*
			désirez sans fin

Notes

CHAPTER 1

1. See Appendix 1, where the complete text of the *Epitaphium Carpentarii* is reproduced with English translation, as well as Chapter 12.

2. [Since the original publication of this volume in French in 1988, Patricia Ranum (1991) has suggested that one likeness of the composer does exist. See Plate 1. Trans]

3. *Le Malade imaginaire* by Molière and Charpentier had already been performed in 1860 thanks to Édouard Thierry, who published *Documents sur le Malade imaginaire.*

4. *Le Malade imaginaire*, comédie-ballet in three acts by Molière, in a restoration by Saint-Saëns (Paris: Durand, 1894).

5. Norbert Dufourcq devoted an article to these recordings: "Le disque et l'histoire de la musique. Un exemple: Marc-Antoine Charpentier," *Recherches sur la musique française classique* 3 (1963), pp. 207–220.

6. Lecerf de la Viéville, *Comparaison*, part 3, p. 138.

7. Trévoux, *Mémoires*, August 1709, p. 1488.

8. *Journal historique de Verdun* (July 1712), quoted in Lowe, *Marc-Antoine Charpentier et l'opéra de collège*, p. 133.

9. In that same year Titon du Tillet wrote in *Description du Parnasse Français* (1727, p. 146): "Most of these pieces of music have not yet been printed, although they have been performed with great success: they are in the hands of Sieur Édouard, his nephew, a Paris bookseller who is looking for the opportunity to offer them to the public, with help in handling the cost of printing or engraving."

10. Omont, "La bibliothèque du roi," pp. 228–229. The catalog mentioned in the bill of sale was located in 1982 by François Lesure, head librarian of the Music Department at the Bibliothèque Nationale in Paris. Hitchcock gives a detailed description of it in "Marc-Antoine Charpentier, Mémoire et Index," pp. 5–34.

11. Written by an anonymous hand on the back of the flyleaf of the first volume, the term *mélanges* refers to the inclusion of compositions on French and Latin texts in a single work.

CHAPTER 2

1. In hope of finding a birth or baptismal certificate, I searched various card catalogs, indexes, publications, and collections of civil deeds in the National Archives, the Bibliothèque Nationale, and parish registers of the City of Paris that survived the great fire of 1871. Unfortunately, my search was unsuccessful.

2. Lacombe, *Dictionnaire portatif;* Laborde, *Essai sur la musique ancienne et moderne,* vol. 3; Choron and Fayolle, *Dictionnaire historique des musiciens,* vol. 1; Fétis, *Biographie universelle des musiciens.*

3. Brenet, *Les musiciens de la Sainte-Chapelle,* p. 268. Also, National Archives, Registres de la Sainte-Chapelle, LL 610, fol. 41.

4. Titon du Tillet revised his dating in *Description du Parnasse Français* (1760), p. 27.

5. Brenet, "Marc-Antoine Charpentier," p. 65.

6. Dassoucy, *Les rimes redoublées de Monsieur Dassoucy.*

7. This opinion, "in his youth," from Sébastien de Brossard, *Catalogue des livres de musique,* p. 226, and from Titon du Tillet, *Description du Parnasse Français* (1727), p. 144.

8. Hitchcock, *Catalogue raisonné,* p. 48; and Cessac, "Éléments pour une biographie," p. 6.

9. For further information on the history of Charpentier's family, see P. M. Ranum, "A Sweet Servitude," pp. 346–360, and "Étienne Loulié."

10. Mersenne, *Harmonie Universelle,* part 2 of *L'Art d'embellir la voix,* pp. 356–357.

11. With the foundation of the Académie de France in Rome in 1666, the king assured travel and living expenses to deserving young artists.

12. Titon du Tillet, Supplement to *Description du Parnasse Français,* p. 755, quoted in Antoine, *Henry Desmarest,* p. 34.

13. Ibid.

14. Maugars, *Réponse faite à un curieux.*

15. *Mercure Galant,* February 1681, p. 249 and February 1687, p. 301. Also January 1678, p. 231: "He was in Italy a long time, where he often encountered Charissimi [*sic*], the greatest composer we have had in a great while"; March 1688, p. 321: "Thus he acquired his musical training in Rome under Charissimi, the most highly respected composer in Italy"; December 1693, pp. 333–334: "M. Charpentier having learned music in Italy, under Charissimi"; and December 1693, p. 224, where Sébastien de Brossard also mentions the composer's Roman sojourn: "M. Charpentier, whom I believe to be Paris-born, remained for a few years in Rome where he was a disciple and devoted champion of the celebrated Carissimi."

16. On the occasion of a revival of the play in 1682, Charpentier was commissioned to compose a new score.

17. Dassoucy noted in *Rimes redoublées,* published in 1671, "I have been back from Rome for more than a year and a half." Further in that source is the text, "In Rome, 25 July 1665." The second edition, however, titled *Les Rimes redoublées de Monsieur Dassoucy* is undated but conceivably

written in 1672 since the author specifies that "it has been nearly three years since I returned from Rome." This edition contains the note, "In Rome, in the year 1662." Dassoucy elsewhere recorded the events of his life and travels, with his usual verve, in *Les Aventures de M. Dassoucy* (2 vols., 1677) and *Les Aventures d'Italie* (1677).

18. When Dassoucy speaks of *pièce de machines* (stage play), he is alluding to *Le Malade imaginaire* even though it is a comédie-ballet.

19. Although Charpentier is not explicitly named, the circumstances alluded to leave no doubt as to the person's identity.

20. [A hospital for the insane. According to Pierre Richelet (*Dictionnarie Français*, 2 vols., Geneva: Slatkine Reprints, 1970), *Incurables* was the name of an institution for poor invalids who were not expected to recover. Trans.]

21. Dassoucy, *Les Rimes redoublées de Monsieur Dassoucy,* pp. 121–122.

22. The notion of Marc-Antoine as painter actually comes from an older source, *Histoire de l'Académie Royale de musique* by the Parfaict brothers, pp. 79–80, where one reads that Charpentier "became interested in painting in early youth. At the age of fifteen, he left his native land for Rome to improve his knowledge of that art. But he had hardly arrived when, instead of continuing to practice what he had come for, he gave it up to devote himself to music, fascinated by Carissimi. That composer, finding Charpentier had a great deal of natural aptitude, devoted himself to teaching Marc-Antoine all he knew, until Charpentier became the equal of his master and earned the title Phoenix of France."

23. There was also Ciray Charpentier, "player of instruments"; Jean Charpentier, "dancing master"; and Nicolas Charpentier, "organ maker."

24. Memoirs of Mlle de Montpensier and Lecerf de la Viéville, *Comparaison,* part 2, p. 184.

25. Maugars, *Réponse faite à un curieux.*

26. Lecerf de la Viéville, *Comparaison,* part 3, pp. 129–130.

27. Charpentier's copy is located in the Bibliothèque Nationale, Vm¹ 1477.

28. Sébastien de Brossard, *Catalogue des livres de musique,* pp. 224–225.

29. Quoted in Hitchcock, "Marc-Antoine Charpentier, Mémoire et Index," p. 33.

30. Nicaise, *Correspondance.*

31. Ibid.

32. Serré de Rieux, *Les Dons des enfants de Latone:* 4th canto, pp. 112–113.

33. Ibid., p. 112.

34. Le Moël, "Un foyer d'italianisme," pp. 43–48.

35. Quoted in Picard, "Liturgie et musique," pp. 249–254.

36. Mersenne, *Harmonie Universelle, Livre second des chants,* p. 94, and part 2 of *L'Art d'embellir la voix,* pp. 357, 362.

37. Raguenet, *Parallèle des Italiens et des Français,* pp. 30–31, 33–34, 46–48. [See also J. E. Galliard's translation, pp. 417, 418, 420. Trans.]

38. Raguenet wrote *Défense du Parallèle des Italiens et des Français* in response to the attacks of Lecerf de la Viéville.

39. Lecerf de la Viéville, *Comparaison,* part 3, pp. 163–164.

40. Ibid., part 2, p. 347.
41. Pascal Colasse (1649–1709), Lully's pupil and secretary, was one of the four assistant directors of the Chapelle Royale who won the competition of 1683. He never shook off the Florentine influence. Nicolas Bernier (1664–1734), after serving as choirmaster at Chartres, became music director at Saint-Germain-l'Auxerrois, and in 1704 succeeded Charpentier at the Sainte-Chapelle.
42. Lecerf de la Viéville, *Comparaison,* part 3, p. 138. Lecerf de la Viéville was not immune to contradiction, since he also wrote: "Furthermore M. l'Abbé [Raguenet] is a dangerous connoisseur, if Colasse, Charpentier, Marais, M. des Touches, and Campra do not appear worthy of his esteem, and if he does not consider them great geniuses, even though they have not always been fortunate" (part 1, p. 94).
43. *Mercure Galant,* February 1681, p. 249.
44. Sébastien de Brossard, *Catalogue des livres de musique,* pp. 225–226.
45. Trévoux, *Mémoires,* November 1704, p. 1896.
46. C. and F. Parfaict, *Histoire du théâtre français.*
47. Serré de Rieux, *Les Dons des enfants de Latone:* 4th canto, p. 121.

CHAPTER 3

1. Perrault, *Mémoires de ma vie,* quoted in Benoit, *Versailles et les musiciens du roi,* p. 389.
2. Quoted in Nuitter and Thoinan, *Les Origines de l'opéra français,* pp. 237–240.
3. Ibid., p. 235.
4. See "Lettre de Clément Marot à M. de S . . . touchant ce qui s'est passé à l'arrivée de Jean-Baptiste de Lulli aux Champs-Élysées (Letter from Clément Marot to M. de S . . . concerning what happened upon the arrival of Jean-Baptiste de Lully at the Champs-Élysées)," (Cologne: Pierre Marteau, 1688), quoted in Nuitter and Thoinan, *Les Origines de l'opéra français,* pp. 229–230.
5. Monval, "Documents inédits," pp. 168–169.
6. In August 1672, Mlle de Guise generously paid off part of Perrin's debt, making it possible for him to leave prison the following month (see Nuitter and Thoinan, *Les Origines de l'opéra français,* pp. 279–280).
7. See P. M. Ranum, "A Sweet Servitude," p. 360.
8. "Registre de La Grange," quoted in Despois and Mesnard, *Oeuvres de Molière,* vol. 8, p. 539.
9. La Serre, "Mémoire sur la vie et les ouvrages de Molière," vol. 1, pp. lix–lx.
10. Quoted in Nuitter and Thoinan, *Les Origines de l'opéra français,* pp. 274–275.
11. Ibid., p. 281.
12. For the original French text, see Despois and Mesnard, *Oeuvres de Molière,* vol. 9, pp. 259–260.
13. See Grimarest, *Vie de Molière,* pp. 284–285.
14. Chappuzeau, *Le théâtre français,* p. 60.
15. From the preface to the 1682 edition of Molière's plays, quoted in

Despois and Mesnard, *Oeuvres de Molière*, vol. 9, p. 218.

16. "Registre de La Grange," quoted in Bonnassies, *La musique à la Comédie-Française*, p. 14.

17 The author of the text indicates 19 July, while La Grange's register gives 21 August.

18. The description is by André Félibien, *Divertissements de Versailles.*

19. It could also be Beauchamps, who directed the orchestra on occasion.

20. The burlesque spirit of the interlude of the "musicians," however, clashes with the pastorale interlude of the comedy. For further information, see Charles Mazouer's study, "Molière et Charpentier," in *Cahiers de l'association internationale des études françaises,* Belles Lettres 41 (May 1989). Mazouer analyzes the relationship between text and music in the Molière comédies-ballets that used Charpentier's music.

21. Germain Brice, *Description de Paris* (1684), quoted in Chevalley, "Le vieux Corneille," p. 184.

22. Comédie-Française Archives.

23. For the original French text, see Despois and Mesnard, *Oeuvres de Molière*, vol. 3, pp. 29–31.

24. An anonymous hand noted at the top of one page of the manuscript "Intermèdes nouveaux du Mariage forcé (de Molière)." The allusions in the vocal text have a clear connection with that comedy.

25. Synopsis from the ballet program of *Le Mariage forcé* (1664).

26. The text, "Les rossignols dans leurs tendres ramages / Du doux printemps savourent le retour" (The nightingales in their tender warblings / Are savoring the return of spring), bears some resemblance to the fifth entry of the "Ballet des nations" in *Le Bourgeois gentilhomme:* "Le rossignol sous ces tendres feuillages / Chante aux échos son doux retour" (The nightingale amid the pleasant leaves / Sings his sweet return to the echoes).

27. [So as not to mislead any potential performers of Charpentier's music with approximate translations of seventeenth-century vocal categories, virtually all such references will remain in the original French. They range, from high to low: *haut-dessus* (high soprano or treble); *dessus* (soprano); *bas-dessus* (mezzo-soprano); *haute-contre* (alto or counter-tenor); *taille* (tenor); *basse-taille* (low tenor or baritone); *basse* (bass). Trans.]

28. For more on this, consult the excellent work of H. Wiley Hitchcock, in "Problèmes d'édition de la musique de Marc-Antoine Charpentier" and in *Prologue et intermèdes du Malade imaginaire.* Also see the work of John S. Powell (see note 29).

29. This missing part of *Le Malade imaginaire*, as well as the musical dialogue between Cléante and Angélique (Act II, scene 5), were found by John S. Powell in an eighteenth-century manuscript preserved by the Comédie-Française (H. 495bis). See Powell, "Charpentier's Music for Molière's *Le Malade imaginaire*" and *Marc-Antoine Charpentier: Music for Molière's Comedies.*

30. For more on this, see the conjectures of Despois and Mesnard, *Oeuvres de Molière*, vol. 9, pp. 260, 270–271; and Hitchcock, "Problèmes d'édi-

tion de la musique de Marc-Antoine Charpentier," p. 5.

31. The description of this key comes from Charpentier's own *Règles de Composition* (see Appendix 2) in which the composer, in a table entitled "The Key-Feelings," assigns a specific character to each key.

32. This is the overture included in the autograph manuscript. The copy preserved by the Comédie-Française contains a different overture, also in the French style, but in two sections.

33. "Entretiens galants," Sixth interview in *La Musique*, vol. 2 (Paris: Jean Ribou, 1681), p. 91.

34. "Present were Jean Converset, Jacques Duvivier, and Pierre Marchand, all three violinists of Monsieur, only brother of the king, and being currently employed for plays and comedies of Sieur de Molière.... [They] have collectively agreed to the following, namely, they promise never to separate from one another to perform for plays of the aforementioned Sieur Molière and other comedies being played and produced by the French troupe on the stage of the Palais-Royal except by mutual consent.

"And, if the actors ever want to dismiss one or two of them for whatever reason or pretext, the other two or one shall be required in that case to leave the aforesaid troupe and no longer perform their plays unless all three return together. And, if the aforesaid troupe wishes to call back one or two of the three, none of the parties may return without the consent of all three, or each of the said parties shall be obliged to pay the other two or one a fine of five hundred fifty livres each before being allowed to return, the aforesaid fine of five hundred fifty livres being not comminatory, but mandatory. And it was agreed that if the aforesaid troupe wishes to rehire all three and one or two of the three do not desire to return, in that case the one or two who return will not be required to pay any portion of the aforesaid penalty, just as each of the aforesaid parties shall be at liberty to resign voluntarily and cease performing in the aforementioned plays without having to pay any portion of said penalty. And it was also agreed among the aforesaid parties that if the aforementioned troupe arranges their soft music for only two violins in the treble parts, one harpsichord, one theorbo and one bass violin, in that case the one or two of the three who play will share their fee equally along with the one or two who do not play; and whenever there is no harpsichord or theorbo, the aforementioned Converset shall not be required to forfeit anything."

Original document in the National Archives, Minutier Central 34, p. 199; quoted in Jurgens and Maxfield-Miller, *Cent ans de recherches sur Molière*, pp. 549–550.

35. Quoted in Despois and Mesnard, *Oeuvres de Molière*, vol. 9, p. 219.

36. *Mercure Galant*, July 1682, pp. 358–359.

37. Pierre Corneille, "Argument d'*Andromède*," in Delmas, *Andromède*, pp. 11–12.

38. C. and F. Parfaict, *Histoire du théâtre français*, vol. 10, p. 179.

39. *Gazette d'Amsterdam*, 14 February 1675, quoted in Pierre Mélèse, *Le théâtre et le public*, p. 239.

40. *Gazette de France*, 4 October 1675.

41. *Mercure Galant,* January 1710, pp. 284–286.
42. "Strings are ordinarily six in number and chosen from among the most capable players. They used to be placed either behind the stage, in the wings, or in a pit between the stage and the parterre, on a kind of wooden floor. Lately they have been placed in one of the *loges du fond,* where they can be heard better than anywhere else. They should know the last two lines of each act, so they can begin the *symphonie* promptly, without giving anyone time to yell 'Play!' which often occurs." In Chappuzeau, *Le théâtre français,* p. 119.
43. Quoted in Benoit, *Musiques de cour,* p. 47.
44. Mélèse, *Répertoire analytique des documents contemporains,* p. 161.
45. C. and F. Parfaict, *Histoire du théâtre français,* vol. 11, p. 412.
46. See Boquet, "Naissance d'une troupe," p. 119.
47. *Circé* (Paris: Pierre Bessin, 1675), pp. iii–iv.
48. This air is not copied into the manuscript, but Charpentier indicated: "in Act IV is sung *Viens ô mère d'amour* in book D." (Book D is lost).
49. *Parodies bachiques, sur les airs et symphonies des Opera, recueillies et mises en ordre par Monsieur Ribon* (Paris: C. Ballard, 1695), pp. 242–244; 2nd ed. (Paris: C. Ballard, 1696), pp. 282–290; and *Nouvelles parodies bachiques, mêlées de vaudevilles ou rondes de table* (Paris: C. Ballard, 1702), pp. 101–118 (H. 496a, 496b, 496c).
50. "Avis au Lecteur" (preface) from the comedy of *L'Inconnu,* quoted in C. and F. Parfaict, *Histoire du théâtre français,* vol. 11, p. 424.
51. The registers of the Comédie-Française mention the same instrumentalists as for *Circé.* (We also learn the names of the harpsichordist—La Porte—and the theorbist—Carle André.) Other names appearing again are Mlle Bastonnet; M. Poussin; M. de Baraillon "for the costumes of the ballet"; and M. La Montagne "for having staged the pantomimes." (See Bonnassies, *La musique à la Comédie-Française,* p. 19.)
52. *Mercure Galant,* January 1678, p. 330.
53. *Mercure Galant,* October 1680, p. 333. Another air has come down, "Si Claudine ma voisine," published as an excerpt from *L'Inconnu.*
54. *Mercure Galant,* February 1678, pp. 215–218.
55. Comédie-Française Archives, 8, Registre des comédiens du Roi, 30 April 1680–29 March 1681, fol. 77v.
56. Comédie-Française Archives, 1, Registre pour les seuls comédiens du Roi, 14 April 1681–17 March 1682, fol. 26v.
57. C. and F. Parfaict, *Histoire du théâtre français,* vol. 12, pp. 211–212.
58. Ibid., p. 253.
59. Ibid., pp. 321–322.
60. Comédie-Française Archives, 2, Registre, fol. 107v.
61. *Mercure Galant,* August 1682, p. 187.
62. According to Jolly, "Avertissement," *Le théâtre de Pierre Corneille* (1738 and 1747), p. L: "[T]he king's actors, with His Majesty's support, revived in 1682 the tragedy of *Andromède* in their theatre in the Rue de Guénégaud. . . . M. Corneille expanded some of the verses sung by the actors and actresses." In "Les Musiciens de Corneille 1650–1699," Lila Maurice-Amour compared Corneille's new version and its variants in

Charpentier's score (pp. 62–63). See also Launay, "Les deux versions musicales d'*Andromède*."

63. Pierre Corneille, "Argument d'*Andromède*," *Oeuvres complètes*, ed. Charles Mary-Laveaux, 12 vols. (Paris: Hachette, 1862–1868), vol. 5, pp. 297–298; also in Delmas, *Andromède*, pp. 11–13.

64. All the descriptions of Français Dufort's scenery for *Andromède* come from the 1682 program text, reprinted in Christian Delmas's edition of *Andromède*.

65. Thanks to the *livret*, we know the name of the actress who sang this role: Mlle d'Hennebaut, daughter of Montfleury and an actress at the Hôtel de Bourgogne.

66. In comparing the published version of the comedy with Charpentier's score, Hitchcock ("Marc-Antoine Charpentier and the Comédie-Française," p. 275) noted that the text is not quite the same. He believed the music was composed in 1686, shortly after the first performances of *Angélique et Médor*.

67. *Mercure Galant*, October 1685, pp. 353–354.

CHAPTER 4

1. Saint-Simon, *Mémoires*, vol. 1, pp. 156, 284; vol 2., p. 730.
2. Pierre Corneille, *Oeuvres complètes*, ed. Charles Mary-Laveaux, 12 vols. (Paris: Hachette, 1862–1868), vol. 10, pp. 182–184.
3. From a letter written by the foreign diplomat Bonsi, dated 16 February 1657, quoted in Prunières, *L'Opéra italien*, p. 205.
4. Sévigné, *Correspondance*, vol. 1, pp. 153–154. See also *La Gazette de France*, 7 February 1671.
5. P. M. Ranum, "Mademoiselle de Guise," pp. 223–224, and "Étienne Loulié."
6. See P. M. Ranum, "A Sweet Servitude," p. 358.
7. National Archives, series O1 3262, Argenterie 1672, "Pompe funèbre de Madame douairière d'Orléans."
8. *Gazette de France*, 30 July 1672.
9. Titon du Tillet, *Description du Parnasse Français* (1727), pp. 144–145.
10. P. M. Ranum, "Étienne Loulié."
11. "Épitre" to Mlle de Guise by Philippe Goibault Du Bois in his translation of the letters of Saint Augustine (Paris, 1684), quoted in P. M. Ranum, "Mademoiselle de Guise."
12. P. M. Ranum, "A Sweet Servitude," p. 358.
13. Hitchcock, "Marc-Antoine Charpentier, Mémoire et Index," p. 16.
14. [A *reposoir* is a temporary altar erected in the street for Corpus Christi ceremonies. As the procession approached the alter, an ouverture was played, during which the Holy Sacrament was placed on the alter. After a motet or the singing of a hymn, the benediction was pronounced and the procession moved on. Trans.]
15. Ibid., p. 28.
16. Saint-Simon, *Mémoires*, vol. 1, p. 285.

17. P. M. Ranum, "Mademoiselle de Guise," pp. 225–226, and "Étienne Loulié."
18. P. M. Ranum, "Étienne Loulié."
19. Quoted by P. M. Ranum, "Mademoiselle de Guise," p. 226.
20. Ibid., p. 224.
21. P. M. Ranum, "A Sweet Servitude," pp. 351, 358.
22. Ibid., pp. 348, 351, 358.
23. For the identity and title of each singer, see P. M. Ranum, "A Sweet Servitude," p. 351.
24. Froberville, "*L'Actéon* de Marc-Antoine Charpentier," pp. 75–76.
25. La Laurencie, "Un opéra inédit," pp. 184–193.
26. In addition to the composer's alleged predilection for the countertenor range, the note "me, here" (*moi ici*) above the part indicated for "Charp" can be seen in the manuscript of the *Psalmus David 50 mus, Miserere des Jésuites* (H. 193).
27. This work is found in volume 13, which lies outside the chronology of the other volumes. The work can therefore be dated 1686, just before Charpentier stopped singing and just before the arrival of Anthoine.
28. P. M. Ranum, "A Sweet Servitude," p. 351.
29. Yolande de Brossard, *Musiciens de Paris.*
30. P. M. Ranum, "Étienne Loulié," and "Mademoiselle de Guise," p. 226.
31. P. M. Ranum, "A Sweet Servitude," p. 350.
32. *Mercure Galant*, March 1688, p. 306.
33. P. M. Ranum, "A Sweet Servitude," pp. 349, 352.
34. See the important monograph on him by P. M. Ranum (note 5 above).
35. Joseph Sauveur (1653–1716), mathematician and physicist, was partially deaf, and therefore needed musicians with good ears to conduct his experiments in sound. Loulié was probably one of them, as well as a consultant on certain theoretical questions. In 1686 Sauveur became professor of mathematics for the Duc de Chartres and was the first person to establish acoustics as an independent science.
36. Denis Dodart was a founding member of the Royal Academy of Science.
37. Sébastien de Brossard, *Catalogue des livres de musique*, p. 273.
38. *Mercure Galant*, February 1688, p. 98.
39. P. M. Ranum, "A Sweet Servitude," pp. 353–355.
40. Reprinted in Guiffrey, "Testament et inventaire de Mademoiselle de Guise," pp. 200–233.
41. P. M. Ranum, "A Sweet Servitude," pp. 350, 359.
42. *Mercure Galant*, January 1687, pp. 266–274.
43. *Gazette de France*, 20 January 1687.
44. P. M. Ranum, "A Sweet Servitude," pp. 356, 360.
45. Ibid., p. 357; and *Gazette de France*, 2 April 1670.
46. P. M. Ranum, "A Sweet Servitude," p. 358; and *Gazette de France*, 13 April 1672.
47. P. M. Ranum, "Étienne Loulié."
48. *Gazette de France*, 8 June 1673.
49. P. M. Ranum, "A Sweet Servitude," pp. 355, 360.
50. Ms. Clairambault 1205; and Guiffrey, "Testament et inventaire de

Mademoiselle de Guise."

51. The codicil, dated 28 February 1688, mentions a Charpentier, but it is not the composer. It was Guillaume Charpentier, one of the many domestics working in the kitchens (P. M. Ranum, "A Sweet Servitude," p. 359).

52. P. M. Ranum, "A Sweet Servitude," p. 359.

53. Ms. Clairambault 1205, fol. 704.

CHAPTER 5

1. Spannheim, *Relation de la Cour de France*, p. 59.

2. Bossuet, "De l'Instruction de Monseigneur le Dauphin," p. 5.

3. *Mercure Galant*, March 1688, p. 320.

4. Ibid., January 1681, p. 284.

5. Ibid., April 1681, pp. 340–341.

6. Ibid., January 1682, pp. 100, 114–115.

7. Ibid., May 1682, pp. 183–184.

8. Benoit, *Versailles et les musiciens du roi* and *Musiques de Cour.*

9. In the first volume of *Mélanges,* two works contain these indications: "Mlle Magdelon" and "Mlle Margot" in the *Miserere à 2 dessus, 2 flutes et basse continue* (H. 157); and "Mlle Mag ..." and "Mlle Marg ..." in the motet (H. 95) that follows. Despite the singular coincidence, these cannot be the Pièche sisters, who were too young at the time the pieces were written. (See P. M. Ranum, "A Sweet Servitude," p. 358.)

10. Brenet, *Les musiciens de la Sainte-Chapelle*, p. 221.

11. The chorus (actually an ensemble of solo voices) in the first two scenes is written in three parts. Later the composer wrote the separate *haute-contre* part for these two scenes. The rest of the divertissement consists of four-part ensembles.

12. *Mercure Galant*, December 1682, pp. 46–60.

13. See Hitchcock, "Marc-Antoine Charpentier, Mémoire et Index," p. 17.

14. *Mercure Galant*, April 1683, pp. 310–313.

15. Lecerf de la Viéville, *Comparaison*, part 3, pp. 139–142.

16. Ibid., p. 141.

17. *Discours sur la vie et les ouvrages de M. De La Lande*, preface to the publication of the 40 grand motets of M. R. Delalande, by his widow and François Collin de Blamont (Paris, 1729).

18. Lecerf de la Viéville, *Comparaison*, p. 146.

19. *Mercure Galant*, June 1683, p. 267.

20. *Mercure Galant*, December 1683, pp. 314–316.

21. It might have been contained in the missing Cahier 40 (see the Chronological Table of Works).

22. Bossuet, *Sermon sur la mort*, p. 1073.

23. *Gazette de France*, "Les funérailles de la Reyne faites au Collège de Louis le Grand," 16 August 1683.

24. *Mercure Galant*, October 1683, vol. 1, pp. 56–62.

25. Ibid., January 1687, p. 248.

26. *Gazette de France*, 15 February 1687.

CHAPTER 6

1. Quittard, "Un prologue inédit," supplément.
2. Hitchcock, "Marc-Antoine Charpentier and the Comédie-Française," pp. 280–281.
3. Pierre Soccane's text, "Marc-Antoine Charpentier et *La Couronne de fleurs* à l'hôtel de Guise (1680)," which appeared in *Le Guide du concert* 17/10 (12 December 1930) and is cited in some articles on Charpentier, is definitely spurious.
4. Only the first two words were changed: "Laissez, laissez bergers" was replaced by "Quittez, quittez bergers." In the manuscript of *Le Malade imaginaire*, above Pan's air is written, "This solo digests better (*est mieux digéré*) in *La Couronne des fleurs*." (*Digérer* in seventeenth-century usage also meant "to arrange" or "to combine with.")
5. Hitchcock, *Catalogue raisonné*, p. 353.
6. Judging that this instrumental piece was too long (101 bars), Charpentier replaced it with another only 41 bars long (see *Actéon changé en biche*, H. 481a).
7. Hitchcock, *Catalogue raisonné*, p. 356.
8. Indeed, in the margin of the first version is written: "Instead of this second part, another one I wrote may be sung. See Cahier 48[2nd version] or Cahier 49[3rd version]." Note that the recording by William Christie and the "Arts florissants" ensemble (on Harmonia Mundi) use the lengthiest of the three versions (H. 483a).
9. "Joignons nos flûtes et nos voix " plus minuet (H. 483, scene 6, bars 1–45) and "C'est de l'homme aujourd'hui" (H. 483, scene 6, bars 189–224).
10. The nonautograph manuscripts come from the Brossard Collection (see Chronological Table of Works).
11. The *Mercure Galant* was of the opinion that Charpentier "composes perfectly well in Italian" (March 1688, p. 321).

CHAPTER 7

1. Lecerf de la Viéville, *Comparaison*, part 3, pp. 187–188.
2. Quoted in Biver and Biver, *Abbayes, monastères, couvents de femmes à Paris*, p. 404.
3. Ibid., p. 408.
4. *Mercure Galant*, April 1680, pp. 323–324.
5. Hitchcock, *Catalogue raisonné*, p. 151.
6. "The Recordare for three *dessus* and ritornelle is in one of my large calfskin books" (lost), "The Recordare for 2 *dessus* and ritornelle is in book 2 of the Demoiselles Pièches" (also lost), and "The Recordare for 2 *dessus* and one *haute-contre* is in the cahier" (see H. 110).
7. Perhaps initially composed for another occasion, as, for example, the Tenebrae for the Dauphin sung by the "demoiselles Pièches" (see preceding note).
8. Quoted in its entirety in Launay, "A propos d'une messe de Charles d'Helfer," p. 189.
9. For more on this, consult Käser, "Die Leçons de Ténèbres," pp. 51–58.

10. Quoted in Launay, "A propos d'une messe de Charles d'Helfer," p. 187.
11. *Mercure Galant,* August 1687, pp. 96–99.
12. The author hereby thanks P. M. Ranum for setting her on the right track.
13. Letter from Mother Angélique Arnauld, quoted in Biver and Biver, *Abbayes, monastères, couvents de femmes à Paris,* p. 339.
14. Quoted in Biver and Biver, *Abbayes, monastères, couvents de femmes à Paris,* p. 339.
15. Quoted in Sainte-Beuve, *Port-Royal,* vol. 3, pp. 144–145.

CHAPTER 8

1. Antoine, *Henry Desmarest,* p. 73.
2. Sébastien de Brossard, *Catalogue des livres de musique,* p. 226.
3. Les frères de Villiers, *Journal d'un voyage à Paris en 1657,* (Faugère, 1862), quoted in Lowe, *Marc-Antoine Charpentier et l'opéra de collège,* p. 25.
4. Sévigné, *Correspondance,* vol. 1, p. 419.
5. Ibid., p. 202.
6. Lecerf de la Viéville, *Comparaison,* part 3, pp. 188–189.
7. Ibid., p. 184.
8. The title, added later by an anonymous hand, offers no certainty about the work's destination.
9. See Hitchcock, "Marc-Antoine Charpentier, Mémoire et Index," p. 16.
10. Titon du Tillet, *Description du Parnasse Français* (1727), p. 145.
11. See du Pradel, *Le livre commode des adresses de Paris,* p. 24, which cites Charpentier as one of the masters "who work most excellently on the composition of music."
12. *Mercure Galant,* April 1691, pp. 148–149.
13. *Mercure Galant,* August 1692, pp. 219–220.
14. *Mercure Galant,* May 1695, pp. 245, 251–252.
15. *Gazette de France,* 9 December 1695.
16. "On the 23rd of this month, the Abbé de Gesvres was consecrated Archbishop of Bourges in the Jesuit Church of the Novitiate by Cardinal d'Estrées, assisted by the Bishops of Évreux and Clermont," *Gazette de France,* January 1695.
17. Fülop-Miller, *Les Jésuites,* vol. 2, pp. 167–168.
18. Abbé de Pure, *Idée des spectacles anciens et nouveaux,* p. 280.
19. *Lettres patentes pour la fondation de l'Académie de danse en 1661* (Letters patent for the foundation of the Academy of Dance in 1661).
20. The French, and sometimes the Italian, musical manuscript scores collected by Philidor the Elder constitute an inestimable source of material. Thirty-seven volumes are located in the Bibliothèque Nationale [of Paris], thirty-five in the Bibliothèque Municipale of Versailles, and two hundred ninety-five in the library of Saint Michael's College in Tenbury, England. The score of *David et Jonathas,* which displays numerous lacunae, has been restored and edited by Jean Duron (Paris: CNRS, 1981).
21. Quoted in the text booklet accompanying the LP recording of *David et Jonathas,* Erato STU 71435.

22. *Mercure Galant,* March 1688, pp. 317–320.
23. Ibid., May 1695, pp. 225–226.
24. Lecerf de la Viéville, *Comparaison,* part 3, p. 5.
25. This is a translation of the Latin play's synopsis which was included in contemporary programs (reproduced in the Jean Duron edition of the score; see note 20 above).

CHAPTER 9

1. Perrin, Preface to *Cantica pro capella Regis.*
2. Beechey, "Guillaume Gabriel Nivers."
3. Perrin, Preface to *Cantica pro capella Regis.*
4. Sébastien de Brossard, *Dictionnaire de musique,* p. 59.
5. Rousseau, *Dictionnaire de musique.* [See Waring's English translation, p. 254.]
6. In Lully's compositions, the voices of the *petit choeur* are grouped into first and second *dessus, haute-contre, taille,* and bass; in Du Mont's works, the same voices are grouped into *dessus, haute-contre, haute-taille, basse-taille,* and bass. Robert enriches the five-part ensemble with three additional voices: first and second *dessus,* first and second *hautes-contre, haute-taille, basse-taille, haut-concordant,* and *bas-concordant.* For Lully and Robert, the *grand choeur* consists of *dessus, haute-contre, taille, basse-taille,* and bass; for Du Mont, it consists of *dessus, haute-contre, haute-taille, basse-taille,* and bass. Lully's string orchestra consists of treble, alto, tenor, *quinte,* and bass. The orchestras of Du Mont and Robert differ from it by the presence of two treble parts and by the absence, in Du Mont, of the *quinte,* and, in Robert, of the tenor.
7. Sébastien de Brossard, *Dictionnaire de musique,* p. 117.
8. Lecerf de la Viéville, *Comparaison,* part 3, pp. 66–68, 78–79.
9. Ibid., p. 129.
10. *Gazette de France,* March 1677 and March 1678.
11. Bukofzer, *Music in the Baroque Era,* p. 132.
12. The two short motets *Pour le Saint-Esprit* (H. 364, 366) only use the beginning of the sequence for Pentecost. The latter motet uses the first three stanzas and the former only the opening words "Veni sancte spiritus." Also note the *Élévation* (H. 268) set to the first four stanzas of "Lauda Sion salvatorem."
13. A prelude was intended ("its prelude is in Cahier XVII" is written at the top of the score). This prelude appears to be lost, however, since the Cahier indicated by Charpentier shows no trace of it.
14. Another little motet, *Pour le catéchisme* (H. 370), uses the first verse of the Gloria from the Ordinary of the Mass.
15. It is possible the missing Cahier LVI (volume 23) contained the second *Leçon* for each day, since Cahier LV includes the first lessons for each day and Cahier LVII, the third lessons. It is possible another complete cycle existed.
16. Flicoteaux, *Fêtes de gloire,* p. 64.
17. Charpentier noted in his manuscript, " 'O admirabile commercium' can be sung in place of the preceding 'O Salutaris'."

18. An autograph manuscript of a *Regina coeli* in separate parts (H. 32a and b) was discovered in the archives of the Augustine Monastery of the Hôtel-Dieu in Québec, with the note: "M. Charpantier [*sic*] music director in our college at Paris 1689" (see Desautels, "Un manuscrit autographe.")

19. The *Prélude pour Salve Regina à 3* that Hitchcock attached to the *Salve Regina* (H. 23) seems to be more suitable for H. 24 (compare the opening of each piece).

20. A note at the beginning of H. 23 specifies, however, "It must be transposed in *E mi* to accommodate the voices."

21. Charpentier also used the text "Sub tuum praesidium" in the *Second Motet pour le catéchisme à la pause du milieu, à la Vierge* (Second Motet for Catechism with the pause in the middle, to the Virgin) (H. 352).

22. An annotation in the score, "All the violins of the two choirs without flutes or oboes," presumably indicates that oboes were used in other places.

23. There is some question about the instrumentation of this motet. Besides the basso continuo, the motet calls for two instrumental parts that could be assigned to two flutes (Charpentier wrote "fl." next to each). Hitchcock (*Catalogue raisonné*, p. 257) thought this probably indicated an organ register. In fact, every time these parts appear, Charpentier specified "pedal" in the bass (that line then being only for the *pédalier*), and when these parts are silent, the composer specified "hand." Moreover, the parts were written in the G treble clef—which is unusual for treble instruments—written with the G clef on the first line. This same instrumentation is found in *O filii à 3 voix pareilles* (H. 312) and in *Domine Salvum à 3 voix pareilles avec orgue* (H. 284).

24. A similar indication (*point de tremblement* [no trill]) is found in *Psalmus David octogesimus tertius* ("Quam dilecta") (H. 186).

25. Why did Charpentier write underneath the opening bars of this very fine piece: "On ne joue point ce prélude" (This prelude is not played)?

26. "Grand motet pour le reposoir de Versailles en présence du roi," (Grand motet for the altar of Versailles in the king's presence). See Hitchcock, "Marc-Antoine Charpentier, Mémoire et Index," p. 28.

27. This motet is not contained in the *Mélanges*. Two copies of it by Brossard exist (Bibliothèque Nationale, Paris, Vm¹ 1269, pp. 57–68, and Vm¹ 1264[1–5], Cantio IIIa). The second motet has no flute parts.

28. [*Messe Rouge* (Red Mass) was the ceremonial mass held annually in the Sainte-Chapelle to mark the opening of the French *Parlement*. It was named after the scarlet robes of state worn by the members of the *Parlement*. Trans.]

CHAPTER 10

1. Sébastien de Brossard, *Dictionnaire de musique*. The work of Jacques-François Lochon to which Brossard referred is *Oratorio pour la Naissance de l'Enfant Jésus* published in 1701.

2. The term *oratorio* originally referred to the place reserved for prayer adjoining large chapels. By extension, the word was applied to the

musical genre born there, most notably in the Congregazione dell'Oratorio, the religious congregation founded by Filippo Neri. Although the Italian word has continued to prevail until the present day, there were attempts to Frenchify it in eighteenth-century France. Hence the term *oratoire* is found in the title of two works by Nicolas Bernier (*Motet ou oratoire pour la Sainte Vierge, Motet en manière d'oratoire pour Saint Benoît*) and in Jean-Jacques Rousseau's *Dictionnaire de musique.*

3. Charpentier uses the term *motet* in certain annotations having to do with the following works: *Prélude pour Horrenda pestis* (H. 398a), *Extremum Dei judicium* (H. 401), *Nuptiae sacrae* (H. 412), and *Judicium Salomonis* (H. 422).

4. See Maugars's account in *Réponse faite à un curieux* as cited in Chapter 2 of the present volume.

5. These divisions were established by Hitchcock in his dissertation *The Latin Oratorios of Marc-Antoine Charpentier,* which was condensed into an article bearing the same title. Throughout the present chapter on Charpentier's oratorios I am indebted to the U.S. musicologist's extensive and excellent research. I have also adopted his numbering of the works as given in *Catalogue raisonné.*

6. In *Filius prodigus* and *Mors Saülis et Jonathae* the French term *histoire* is noted in the manuscript.

7. Although Hitchcock classified it as a Latin oratorio in *Catalogue raisonné,* he did not consider *In obitum* as such in his earlier research of 1954 and 1955.

8. In *Dictionnaire de musique,* Sébastien de Brossard stated that the word *canticum* refers to "Motetto, plural Motetti. Some [people] write motteto, others moteto, and so forth. In Latin, the word is motettus, mottetus, motectum, moteta, canticum, or modulus. In French, it is motet."

9. Hitchcock, "The Latin Oratorios," pp. 49–50.

10. "Valerianus in cubiculo Caeciliam cum Angelo orantem invenit" (Valerianus found Cecilia praying in her room with an angel).

11. In his *Dictionnaire de musique,* Sébastien de Brossard mentioned an "enharmonic minor sharp, or simple sharp, indicated by a plain cross X, which raises a note by two commas or about a quarter of a tone." (See Hitchcock, *The Latin Oratorios of Marc-Antoine Charpentier,* p. 212.)

12. Hitchcock, *The Latin Oratorios of Marc-Antoine Charpentier,* p. 239.

13. Included in the list of characters that Charpentier noted on the first page of *Caecilia* (H. 415) are "Almachus Tyrannus" and a "*Chorus angelorum*," who do not appear in the first part. Moreover, "*Prima pars*" is indicated, which logically implies "*Secunda pars*." Finally, as Hitchcock observed in *Catalogue raisonné,* the work fills the last pages of Cahier 47, while Cahier 48 is missing. The second part was very probably in the lost cahier.

14. Hitchcock, *The Latin Oratorios of Marc-Antoine Charpentier,* pp. 90–91.

15. Counterpoint is invertible when the different melodic parts can be inverted (in their respective positions) without causing any problems in the texture, especially in harmony.

16. The oratorio is contained in Cahier XXXIX of the Roman-numeral series of the *Mélanges*. The rest of the work was probably in the next cahier, which is missing.

17. Volume 17 of the *Mélanges* contains some *Symphonies pour le Jugement de Salomon* (Symphonies for the Judgment of Solomon), for insertion into a work that has been lost.

18. Despite the use of the same text, Charpentier indiscriminately titled one *Canticum* and the other *Dialogus*.

19. Hitchcock, *The Latin Oratorios of Marc-Antoine Charpentier*, pp. 239–253; and "The Latin Oratorios," p. 51.

20. The whole title is *Canticum in honorem beatae Virginis Mariae inter homines et angelos in quo ab angelis eximiae dotes ejus narrantur hominibus quod quidem in quocumque festo sive nativitatis conceptionis purificationis visitationis aut assumptionis decantari potest ad libitum* (Canticle in honor of the Blessed Virgin Mary, between men and angels, in which the angels tell mankind of her rare virtues, and which can be sung freely on any of her feast days: Nativity, Conception, Purification, Visitation, or Assumption).

21. Hitchcock, *The Latin Oratorios of Marc-Antoine Charpentier*, vol. 2, p. 138.

CHAPTER 11

1. In the Franco-Flemish contrapuntal style, all the parts are treated equally, the meter is regular and full, and harmonies are simple.

2. *Mercure Galant*, September 1679, pp. 55–56, 63.

3. Rousseau, *Dictionnaire de musique*. [See Waring's English translation, p. 61.]

4. Sébastien de Brossard, *Catalogue des livres de musique*, p. 81, quoted in Launay, "A propos d'une messe de Charles d'Helfer," p. 177.

5. See Jean Duron, "Les deux versions de la Messe *Assumpta est Maria*."

CHAPTER 12

1. *Mercure Galant*, January 1678, pp. 230–231.

2. Ibid., June 1680, p. 209.

3. Ibid., February 1681, p. 246.

4. We have discovered an air ("Il faut aimer, c'est un mal nécessaire") not listed in H. W. Hitchcock's *Catalogue raisonné*. It is found in *Recueil des airs d'Atys 1676 de J.-B. Lully et airs sérieux et à boire de différents auteurs, à une voix* (Collection of Airs from Atys 1676 by Lully and Serious Airs and Drinking Airs by Different Authors, for One Voice) in the Bibliothèque Nationale in Paris (Rés. Vm f. ms. 11, fols. 63–64). Sixteen measures long, this air (H. 454bis) is for solo *dessus* without basso continuo.

   In *Comparaison de la musique italienne et de la musique française* (part 2, pp. 33, 35), Lecerf de La Viéville gives the words from two airs by

Charpentier, "Quand je vous dis que je me meurs d'amour" and "Et comment se garder des ruses de l'amour," for which we have no music. We have not counted these among the thirty-two airs.
5. Sébastien de Brossard, *Dictionnaire de musique*.
6. *Piva* is the Italian term for bagpipe, which could also mean "chalumeau" or reed instrument, and by extension, the seventeenth-century oboe.

CHAPTER 13

1. H. W. Hitchcock has compiled more than 200 instrumental pieces from Charpentier's works in an article titled, "The Instrumental Music of Marc-Antoine Charpentier."
2. These pieces make up the last part of Hitchcock's *Catalogue raisonné* of Charpentier's works (H. 508–548).
3. Philidor (André Danican), *Suites d'orchestre*, Ms. Musicaux 139/143. Another manuscript (Ms. Musicaux 119/121), also in the Elder Philidor's hand, contains only the second treble part (p. 16, *Trio de M. Charpentier*). We have numbered this trio H. 548bis.
4. The autograph manuscript of the separate parts to the *Sonate* were discovered along with the separate parts of the divertissement *Les Arts florissants* (H. 487a), which may be dated 1685. Both works, copied on leaves of the same dimension and with the same watermark, thus appear to be contemporary (see Sadie, "Early French Ensemble Sonata").
5. See Lemaître, "L'orchestre dans le théâtre lyrique français."

CHAPTER 14

1. P. M. Ranum, "Étienne Loulié."
2. Ibid.
3. Sébastien de Brossard, *Catalogue des livres de musique*, pp. 226–227.
4. P. M. Ranum, "Étienne Loulié."
5. Princess of the Palatinate, Letter of 24 March 1695, *Lettres*, p. 117.
6. Lecerf de la Viéville, *Comparaison*, part 2, pp. 296–297.
7. Sébastien de Brossard, *Catalogue des livres de musique*, p. 365.
8. *Mercure Galant*, December 1693, pp. 331–335.
9. Quoted by La Gorce in his remarkable book, *Berain, Dessinateur du Roi Soleil*, p. 16.
10. Ibid., pp. 91–93.
11. P. O. d'Aquin, *Siècle littéraire de Louis XV* (Amsterdam, 1754), p. 165.
12. Durey de Noinville, *Histoire*.
13. *Journal du Marquis de Dangeau*, vol. 4, quoted in Masson, "Journal du marquis de Dangeau," p. 205.
14. *Chansonnier Maurepas*, vol. 7, p. 525, quoted in Mélèse, *Le théâtre et le public*, p. 266.
15. *Recueil de chansons anecdotes, satyriques et historiques*, vol. 5, p. 106, quoted in Mélèse, *Le théâtre et le public*, p. 266.
16. *Chansonnier Maurepas*, vol. 27 (1693), p. 32, quoted in Mélèse, *Le théâtre et le public*, pp. 266–267. [*Didon* is a tragédie lyrique by

Desmarest. It was first produced at the Palais-Royal in September 1693. Trans.]
17. Serré de Rieux, *La Musique,* p. 15.
18. C. and F. Parfaict, *Histoire de l'Académie Royale de Musique,* p. 256.
19. Ibid., p. 258.
20. Sébastien de Brossard, *Catalogue des livres de musique,* pp. 227–228. It is amusing to note that Brossard made a slip of the pen (a meaningful one?) by referring to Charpentier's work as *Circé* in the sentence just quoted which introduces the passage. *Circé* is the title of a tragedy in music by Henry Desmarest, performed in October 1694, which also received bad criticism because of excessive originality.
21. Rousseau, *Dictionnaire de musique.*
22. Lecerf de La Viéville, *Comparaison,* part 1, pp. 169–171.
23. This was brought to light by Jean Duron in his musical and literary commentary on Lully's *Atys* in *L'Avant-Scène Opéra* no. 94 (January 1987), particularly in the article "Réflexion sur Lully, architecte de la tonalité," p. 81. Also recommended is the same author's excellent analysis of *Médée* in *L'Avant-Scène Opéra* no. 68 (October 1984).
24. See page 340 for a more detailed description of this setting.
25. On 17 November 1700 *Médée* was remounted in Lille, but the work suffered the same fate as Corinth. One night, flames enveloped the stage and destroyed the scenery. The incident caused the cancellation of all further performances. In 1704, the year of the composer's death, Campra adapted fragments of other composers' operas into his tragedy *Télémaque. Médée* was used along with other works by Campra, Colasse, Desmarest, and Rebel.
26. See Antoine, *Henry Desmarest,* p. 50.

CHAPTER 15

1. Brenet, *Les musiciens de la Sainte-Chapelle,* pp. 260–261. Also, National Archives, Registres de la Sainte-Chapelle, LL 609, fol. 59v.
2. National Archives, Registres de la Sainte-Chapelle, LL 609, fol. 60.
3. Sébastien de Brossard, *Catalogue des livres de musique,* p. 227.
4. Lecerf de la Viéville, *Comparaison,* part 3, p. 118.
5. See Launay, "L'enseignement de la composition."
6. P. M. Ranum, "Étienne Loulié."
7. Quoted in Douchain, "Les organistes laïques," pp. 173–174.
8. The chapter registers often make very provocative reading.
9. National Archives, Registres de la Sainte-Chapelle, LL 610, fol. 31.
10. Reboud, "Messire Arthus Aux Cousteaux."
11. *Mémoire pour les chapelains et clercs de la Sainte-Chapelle, servant de réponse au mémoire de maître François Chaperon, maître de Musique des enfants du choeur* (Memorandum for the chaplains and clerics of the Sainte-Chapelle serving as reply to the memorandum of director François Chaperon, music director of the choirboys), quoted in Brenet, *Les musiciens de la Sainte-Chapelle,* pp. 243–246.
12. Brenet, *Les musiciens de la Sainte-Chapelle,* pp. 236, 239.

13. See *Mercure Galant,* April 1680, pp. 324, quoted in Chapter 7 above.

14. Brenet, *Les musiciens de la Sainte-Chapelle,* p. 284.

15. The separate parts of two works by Charpentier for the Sainte-Chapelle still exist: *Assumpta est Maria* (H. 11a, though an incomplete set) and *Judicium Salomonis* (H. 422a).

16. Brenet, *Les musiciens de la Sainte-Chapelle,* p. 231.

17. *Mémoires du duc de Luynes,* excerpt quoted in Brenet, *Les musiciens de la Sainte-Chapelle,* p. 300.

18. The works written for the Sainte-Chapelle are naturally found in the last cahiers of both the Arabic-numbered and Roman-numeral series. Missing cahiers (71, 72, and 73, and LXXI, LXXII, and LXXIII) which might have belonged to this period perhaps contained other pieces, now lost.

19. The name Molaret (then written "M. Molaré") also figures alongside "M. Beaupuy," "M. Ribon," and "M. Dun" in *Dialogus inter Christum et homines* (H. 417), a piece dating from the early 1690s, when Charpentier was with the Jesuits. Nothing is known about Jacques Molaret prior to his entry in the Sainte-Chapelle in 1695.

20. A note pinned to one of the separate parts (H. 422a) states: "Motet composed by M. Charpentier for the *Messe rouge* of the Palais in 1702."

21. The mass could not have been performed in 1701, since François Royer, who sang the baritone part, was on leave of absence (see National Archives, Registres de la Sainte-Chapelle, LL 609, fol. 160v). It is impossible to determine whether the version for instrumental trio accompaniment (H. 11a, see Chapter 11) predates or postdates the larger scoring.

22. National Archives, Registres de la Sainte-Chapelle, LL 609, fol. 66.

23. Ibid., fol. 66v–67.

24. Ibid., fol. 61v.

25. Brenet, *Les musiciens de la Sainte-Chapelle,* p. 273.

26. The original title was *Motet pour l'offertoire de la messe rouge.* Charpentier later glued a piece of paper over it, with the new name *Motet pour une longue offrande,* probably on the occasion of another performance.

27. *Mercure Galant,* November 1698, pp. 233–234. Also see November 1699, pp. 184–185; and November 1700, p. 40.

28. Brenet, *Les musiciens de la Sainte-Chapelle,* p. 268. Also, Registres de la Sainte-Chapelle, LL 610, fol. 41.

29. See Titon du Tillet, *Description du Parnasse Français* (1727), p. 144.

30. Brenet, *Les musiciens de la Sainte-Chapelle,* pp. 268–269. Also, Registres de la Sainte-Chapelle, LL 610, fol. 43v.

ET LUX PERPETUA LUCEAT EI

1. May perpetual light shine upon him.

2. J.-M.-B. Clément and Abbé J.-B. de la Porte, *Anecdotes dramatiques,* 1775.

APPENDIX 2

1. This copy is located in the Bibliothèque Nationale, Paris, Ms. Res. Vm^1 260. The *Remarks* are contained in folios 55–56.
2. The manuscript is located in the Bibliothèque Nationale, Ms. n.a. fr. 6355. A facsimile reproduction is found in Ruff, "Marc-Antoine Charpentier's *Règles de composition.*"
3. The copy is located in the Bibliothèque Nationale, Ms. n.a. fr. 6356.
4. Sébastien de Brossard introduced *Rules of Composition* in *Catalogue des livres de musique* (p. 365) as follows: "He wrote this little treatise for Monseigneur le Duc de Chartres, now Duc d'Orléans and Regent of France, whom he was tutoring in composition."
5. P. M. Ranum, "Étienne Loulié."
6. Ibid.
7. Ibid.
8. These notes are printed in small type in the following pages.
9. These differences will be identified in the transcription that follows.
10. Rameau, *Traité de l'harmonie,* p. 157. [See Gossett's translation.]
11. Grimarest, *Traité du récitatif,* p. 174.
12. Du Bos, *Réflexions critiques,* vol. 3, p. 334.
13. Charpentier means the "subject" of the fugue.
14. Presented in contrary motion.
15. [The French verb *lier,* here translated "tie," means "to prepare." Trans.]
16. In *Gradus ad Parnassum,* Johann Joseph Fux gave four rules almost identical to the ones given by Charpentier: "First Rule: One must proceed in contrary or oblique motion from one perfect consonance to another perfect consonance. Second Rule: From a perfect consonance to an imperfect consonance one may proceed in any one of the three motions. Third Rule: From an imperfect consonance to a perfect consonance one must proceed in contrary or oblique motion. Fourth Rule: From one imperfect consonance to another imperfect consonance one may proceed in any one of the three motions."
17. In the second measure of the musical example, there is an error in the manuscript: G-sharp and B equal a minor third, not a major.
18. This is what is now called the Neapolitan sixth.
19. Modern harmonic theory would prohibit examples C and D because the upper parts do not proceed by conjunct motion.
20. "Augmentation for the bass": additional examples. Modern harmonic theory would forbid the third example. The fourth example is incomprehensible.
21. In the fourth bar of the example, there is an error in the manuscript (B-flat/D = 3) and in the added commentary (see following note).
22. Added commentary (Ms. n.a. fr. 6356, fol. 28v).
    Major Sixths
    A. On the octave a semitone higher.
    B. On the fifth on the same note [i.e., one part remaining stationary].
    C. On the fifth a tone higher.
    D. On the minor third one degree lower [ms. error: this is a major third].

E. On the major third two degrees lower.

F. On the minor third two degrees lower.

G. On the major third one degree higher.

Minor Sixths

A. On the fifth on the same note.

B. On the fifth a tone lower [ms. error: should be "a semitone lower"].

C. On the third one degree lower.

D. On the major third two degrees lower.

E. On the minor third two degrees lower [this refers to the last example, the previous one being overlooked here].

23. The last assertion is incomprehensible. (It probably should be the "second" instead of the "first.")

24. The marginal note (i.e., "This chord is very plaintive") is not in Ms. n.a. fr. 6356.

25. The sixth example is copied twice, by mistake, in the manuscript.

26. Example D: error (A-flat instead of A-natural).

27. Referring in this case to the sixth degree.

28. [Charpentier's term is *Énergie des Modes*. I have adhered to H. Wiley Hitchcock's translations of the key-feelings. Trans.]

29. The cadence of a seventh resolved to a sixth is a Phrygian cadence giving the impression of a half-cadence (second example) or an imperfect cadence (third example).

30. *Za* (?) stands for C-sharp.

CHRONOLOGICAL TABLE OF WORKS

1. Sébastien de Brossard, *Catalogue des livres de musique*, p. 225.

2. Brenet, "Marc-Antoine Charpentier."

3. Écorcheville, *Catalogue*, pp. 2–74.

4. Hitchcock, *Catalogue raisonné*, pp. 23–36.

5. Hitchcock uses the word *volume*, although the manuscripts use the word *tome*. I have retained Hitchcock's Roman numerals.

6. See Hitchcock, "Marc-Antoine Charpentier, Mémoire et Index," p. 7.

7. P. M. Ranum, "A Sweet Servitude," p. 357.

8. Ibid., p. 360: "By mid-1688, Charpentier's manuscripts are written exclusively on paper with the Jesuit watermark."

9. Abbreviations used: S.S. = P. M. Ranum, "A Sweet Servitude"; E.L. = P. M. Ranum, "Étienne Loulié"; G.d.F. = *Gazette de France;* M.G. = *Mercure Galant.*

10. Hitchcock, "Mémoire et Index," p. 21.

11. Ibid., p. 23.

12. Ibid.

13. Ibid., p. 32.

14. Ibid., pp. 32–33. Among these pieces, we have been able to identify nine of the motets published by Jacques Édouard.

15. Ibid., pp. 33–34.

Bibliography

WORKS WRITTEN BEFORE 1800

Anselme, Père. *Histoire généalogique et chronologique de la Maison Royale de France.* Paris, 1728.

Bollioud de Mermet, Louis de. *De la corruption du goût dans la musique française.* Lyon, 1746.

Bossuet, Jacques-Bénigne. "De l'Instruction de Monseigneur le Dauphin," March 1679, in *Lettres.* Paris, 1927.

_____ . "Sermon sur la mort," in *Oeuvres.* Paris: La Pléiade, 1961.

Brossard, Sébastien de. *Catalogue des livres de musique théorique et pratique, vocale et instrumentale, tant imprimée que manuscrite, qui sont dans le cabinet du Sr Sébastien de Brossard Chanoine de Meaux* (Catalogue of books on music theory and practice, vocal and instrumental, both printed and in manuscript, which are in the collection of Lord Sébastien de Brossard, Canon of Meaux), ms. 1724, Bibliothèque Nationale, Rés. Vm^8 21.

_____ . *Dictionnaire de musique.* Paris, 1703. Trans. and ed. Albion Gruber, under the title, *Dictionary of Music.* Henryville: Institute of Mediaeval Music, Ltd., 1982.

Chappuzeau, Samuel. *Le théâtre français.* Lyon, 1674. Éditions d'aujourd'hui, Les Introuvables, 1985.

Comédie-Française Archives, 1672–1686.

Dassoucy, Charles Coypeau. *Rimes redoublées.* Paris, 1671.

_____ . *Les rimes redoublées de Monsieur Dassoucy.* Paris, [1672?].

Du Bos, Jean-Baptiste. *Réflexions critiques sur la poésie et sur la peinture.* Paris, 1760. Trans. by Thomas Nugent, under the title *Critical Reflections on Poetry, Painting and Music.* 3 vols. New York: AMS Press, 1978.

Du Pradel, Abraham. *Le livre commode des adresses de Paris.* 2nd. ed. Paris, 1692.

Durey de Noinville, Jacques-Bernard. *Histoire du théâtre de l'Académie Royale de Musique.* Paris, 1757. Geneva: Minkoff, 1972.

Félibien, André. *Divertissements de Versailles donnés par le Roi à toute sa cour, au retour de la conquête de la Franche-Comté en l'année 1674.* Paris: Imprimerie royale, 1676.

Fux, Johann Joseph. *Gradus ad Parnassum.* 1725.

Gazette de France, 1670–1704.

Grimarest, Jean-Léonard le Gallois de. *Traité du récitatif.* Paris, 1707.

———. *Vie de Molière.* Paris, 1705.

Laborde, Jean-Benjamin de. *Essai sur la musique ancienne et moderne.* Paris, 1780.

Lacombe, Jacques. *Dictionnaire portatif des Beaux-Arts.* Paris, 1753.

L'Affilard, Michel. *Principes très faciles pour bien apprendre la musique.* Paris, 1694. Geneva: Minkoff, 1971.

La Serre. "Mémoires sur la vie et les ouvrages de Molière." *Oeuvres de Molière.* Paris, 1734.

Lecerf de la Viéville, Jean-Laurent. *Comparaison de la musique italienne et de la musique française, 1704–1706.* Brussels, 1705–1706. Geneva: Minkoff, 1972.

Loulié, Étienne. *Éléments ou principes de musique mis dans un nouvel ordre.* Paris, 1696. Geneva: Minkoff, 1971. Trans. and ed. Albert Cohen, under the title *Elements or Principles of Music.* Brooklyn: Institute of Mediaeval Music, 1965.

Masson, Charles. *Nouveau traité des règles pour la composition de la musique.* Paris, 1694. Geneva: Minkoff, 1971.

Maugars, André. *Réponse faite à un curieux sur le sentiment de la musique d'Italie, écrite à Rome le premier octobre 1639.*

Mercure Galant. 1678–1704.

Mersenne, Marin. *Harmonie Universelle.* Paris, 1636. 3 vols. Paris: CNRS, 1963.

National Archives. Registres des délibérations et registres mémoriaux de la Sainte-Chapelle. LL 609–610.

Nicaise, Abbé. *Correspondance.* Bibliothèque Nationale, ms. fr. 9360.

Omont, H., ed. "La bibliothèque du roi au début du règne de Louis XV (1718–1736): journal de l'abbé Jourdain, secrétaire de la bibliothèque." *Mémoires de la société de l'histoire de Paris* 20 (1893): 207–294.

Parfaict, François and Claude. *Histoire de l'Académie Royale de musique.* Bibliothèque Nationale, ms. n.a. fr. 6532.

———. *Histoire du théâtre français depuis son origine jusqu'à présent.* Paris, 1734–1749.

Perrin, Pierre. *Cantica pro capella Regis.* Paris, 1665.

Perrault, Charles. *Mémoires de ma vie.*

Princess of the Palatinate. *Lettres (1672–1722).* Mercure de France, 1985.

———. *A Woman's Life in the Court of the Sun King: Letters of Liselotte von der Pfalz, 1652–1722, Élisabeth Charlotte, Duchesse d'Orléans.* Trans. and intro. Elborg Forster. Baltimore: John Hopkins, 1984.

Pure, Michel de. *Idée des spectacles anciens et nouveaux.* Paris, 1668. Geneva: Minkoff, 1972.

Racine, Jean. *Abrégé de l'histoire de Port-Royal.* Paris, 1767. Éditions d'aujourd'hui, Les Introuvables, 1981.

Raguenet, François. *Parallèle des Italiens et des Français en ce qui regarde la*

Musique et les Opéra. Paris, 1702. Geneva: Minkoff, 1976. Trans. by J. E. Galliard (attrib.), under the title "A Comparison Between French and Italian Music." *The Musical Quarterly* 32 (1946): 411–436.

_____ . *Défense du Parallèle des Italiens et des Français.* Paris, 1705. Geneva: Minkoff, 1976.

Rameau, Jean-Philippe. *Traité de l'harmonie réduite à ses principes naturels.* Paris, 1722. Paris: Méridiens Klincksieck, 1986. Trans. by Philip Gossett, under the title *Treatise on Harmony.* New York: Dover Publications, 1971.

Rousseau, Jean-Jacques. *Dictionnaire de musique.* Paris, 1768. Trans. by William Waring, under the title *A Complete Dictionary of Music.* London, 1779. New York: AMS Reprint, 1975.

Sainte-Beuve. *Port-Royal.* La Pléiade, 1953–1955.

Saint-Simon. *Mémoires.* La Pléiade, 1948–1961.

Serré de Rieux, Jean de. *La Musique.* Paris, 1714.

_____ . *Les Dons des enfants de Latone.* Paris, 1734.

Sévigné, Madame de. *Correspondance.* Paris: La Pléiade, 1972–1978. Ed. A. Edward Newton. *The Letters of Madame de Sévigné.* 7 vols. English trans. Carnavalet Edition. Philadelphia: J. P. Horn, 1927.

Spannheim, Ézéchiel. *Relation de la Cour de France en 1690.* Mercure de France, 1973.

Titon du Tillet. *Description du Parnasse Français* (Description of the French Parnassus). Paris, 1727, 1760.

Trévoux, A. *Mémoires pour l'histoire des Sciences et des Beaux-Arts.* November 1704, August 1709.

WORKS WRITTEN AFTER 1800

This bibliography includes some editions of Charpentier's works which have appeared after the publication of H. Wiley Hitchcock's *Catalogue raisonné.* Nevertheless, one is advised to refer to Hitchcock's catalog for a complete overview of the publications, still few in number. A facsimile of Charpentier's manuscripts is planned in the future by the Éditions Minkoff, in Geneva.

Anthony, James R. *French Baroque Music from Beaujoyeulx to Rameau.* Rev. ed. New York: W. W. Norton, 1978. New revision. Portland: Amadeus Press, 1995.

Antoine, Michel. *Henry Desmarest (1661–1741): Biographie critique.* Paris, 1965.

Bachelin, Henri. *Les noëls français.* Paris, 1927.

Barber, Clarence H. *The Liturgical Music of Marc-Antoine Charpentier: the Masses, Motets, Leçons de ténèbres.* Diss. Harvard University, 1955.

_____ . "Les oratorios de Marc-Antoine Charpentier." *Recherches sur la musique française classique* 3 (1963): 91–130.

Barthélemy, Maurice. *André Campra, sa vie et son oeuvre (1660–1744).* Paris, 1957.

_____ . "Notes sur M.-A. Charpentier à propos d'un article du M.G.G." *Revue belge de musicologie* 7 (1953): 51–53.

Beaussant, Philippe. "Molière et l'Opéra." *Europe* 523–524 (1972): 155–168.

Beechey, Gwilym. "Guillaume Gabriel de Nivers (1632–1714) and His *Litanies de la Sainte Vierge.*" *Recherches sur la musique française classique* 15 (1975): 80–90.

Benoit, Marcelle. *Les musiciens du roi de France (1661–1733).* Que sais-je? 2048. Paris: Presses universitaires de France, 1982.

———. *Musiques de Cour, Chapelle, Chambre, Écurie: Recueil de documents inédits (1661–1733).* Paris: Picard, 1971.

———. *Versailles et les musiciens du roi: Étude institutionnelle et sociale (1661–1733).* Paris: Picard, 1971.

Biver, Paul, and Marie-Louise Biver. *Abbayes, monastères et couvents de femmes à Paris, des origines à la fin du XVIIIe siècle.* Paris, 1975.

Blanchard, Roger. *Marc-Antoine Charpentier, Miserere des Jésuites/Dies irae.* Paris: CNRS, 1984.

Bluche, François. *Louis XIV.* Paris, 1986.

———. *La vie quotidienne au temps de Louis XIV.* Paris, 1984.

Bonnassies, Jules. *La musique à la Comédie-Française.* Paris: Baur, 1874.

Boquet, Guy. "Naissance d'une troupe, naissance d'un répertoire." *Revue d'histoire du théâtre* 32/2 (1980–1982): 105–126.

Borrel, Eugène. "La vie musicale de Marc-Antoine Charpentier d'après le Mercure Galant (1678–1704)." *XVIIe siècle* 21–22 (1954): 433–441.

Boysse, Ernest. *Le théâtre des Jésuites.* Paris, 1880.

Brenet, Michel. "Charpentier." *Le Guide musical* 49–52 (December 1892): 345–347, 359–360, 372–373, 383–384.

———. *Les concerts en France sous l'Ancien Régime.* Paris, 1900.

———. "Marc-Antoine Charpentier." *La Tribune de Saint-Gervais* 6 (1900): 65–76.

———. *Les musiciens de la Sainte-Chapelle du Palais.* Paris, 1910. Geneva: Minkoff, 1973.

———. "Note sur *Le Jugement de Salomon* et son auteur M.-A. Charpentier." *La Tribune de Saint-Gervais* 20 (1914): 128–130.

Brossard, Yolande de. *Musiciens de Paris (1535–1792): Actes d'état civil d'après le fichier Laborde.* Paris, 1965.

———. *Sébastien de Brossard, théoricien et compositeur, 1655–1730.* Paris, 1987.

Bukofzer, Manfred F. *Music in the Baroque Era, from Monteverdi to Bach.* New York: W. W. Norton, 1947.

Burke, John. "The Early Works of Marc-Antoine Charpentier." Diss. University College Oxford, 1985.

Cessac, Catherine. "Éléments pour une biographie." *L'Avant-scène opéra* 68 (October 1984): 6.

Champigneulle, Bernard. *L'âge classique de la musique française.* Paris: Aubier, 1946.

Charpentier, Marc-Antoine. *Médée. L'Avant-scène opéra* 68 (October 1984): 6.

Chevalley, Sylvie. "Le vieux Corneille et la jeune Comédie-Française." *Europe* (April–May 1974): 174–185.

Choron, Alexandre, and François Fayolle. *Dictionnaire historique des musiciens*. Paris, 1810. Trans. by John S. Sainsbury, under the title *A Dictionary of Musicians from the Earliest Times*. New York: Da Capo Press, 1966.

Chouquet, Gustave. *Histoire de la musique dramatique en France*. Paris, 1873.

Les Cisterciens à Paris, catalogue of the exhibition at the Musée Carnavalet. Paris, 1986.

Crussard, Claude. "Marc-Antoine Charpentier théoricien." *Revue de musicologie* 24 (1945): 49–68.

——. *Un musicien français oublié: Marc-Antoine Charpentier (1634–1704)*. Paris: Librairie Floury, 1945. New York: AMS Press, 1978.

——. "Qui était Marc-Antoine Charpentier?" *Journal musical français* (April 1954).

Dainville, François de. *L'éducation des Jésuites (XVIe–XVIIIe siècles)*. Paris, 1978.

——. "Lieux de théâtre et salles des actions dans les collèges de jésuites de l'ancienne France." *Revue d'histoire du théâtre* 2 (1950): 185–190.

Delmas, Christian, ed. *Pierre Corneille, Andromède, tragédie*. Paris: Librairie Marcel Didier, 1974.

Desautels, Andrée. "Un manuscrit autographe de M.-A. Charpentier à Québec." *Recherches sur la musique française classique* 21 (1983): 118–127.

De Smidt, J. R. H. *Les Noëls et la tradition populaire*. Amsterdam, 1932.

Despois, Eugène. *Le théâtre français sous Louis XIV*. Paris: Hachette, 1874.

Despois, Eugène, and Paul Mesnard, eds. *Oeuvres de Molière*. Paris: Hachette, 1873–1900. 11 vols.

Douchain, Olivier. "Les organistes laïques du diocèse de Toul aux XVIIe et XVIIIe siècles." Part 3. *Recherches sur la musique française classique* 22 (1984): 160–218.

Ducrot, Ariane. "Les représentations de l'Académie Royale de Musique à Paris au temps de Louis XIV (1671–1715)." *Recherches sur la musique française classique* 10 (1970): 19–55.

Dufourcq, Norbert. "Le disque et l'histoire de la musique. Un exemple: Marc-Antoine Charpentier." *Recherches sur la musique française classique* 3 (1963): 207–220.

——. *La musique française*. Paris: Picard, 1970.

Dumesnil, René. "Un ouvrage inédit de Marc-Antoine Charpentier . . . : *Le jugement de Salomon*." *Mercure de France* (15 September 1939): 703–704.

Dunn, James Platte. "The *Grands Motets* of Marc-Antoine Charpentier (1634–1704)." Diss. Iowa State University, 1962.

Dupont-Ferrier, Gustave. *La vie quotidienne d'un collège parisien pendant plus de 350 ans: du collège de Clermont au lycée Louis-le-Grand (1563–1920)*. Paris, 1921.

Duron, Jean. "L'année musicale 1688." *XVIIe siècle* 139 (1983): 229–241.

——. "Les deux versions de la messe *Assumpta est Maria* de Marc-Antoine Charpentier." *Revue de musicologie* 70/1 (1984): 83–85.

————. *Marc-Antoine Charpentier, David et Jonathas*. Paris: CNRS, 1981.

————. "L'orchestre de Marc-Antoine Charpentier." *Revue de musicologie* 72/1 (1986): 23–65.

Écorcheville, Jules. *Catalogue du fonds de musique ancienne de la Bibliothèque Nationale* (Catalogue of the old music collection of the Bibliothèque Nationale), vol. 4. Paris, 1910–1914. 2–74.

————. *Corneille et la musique*. Paris, 1906.

Fétis, François-Joseph. *Biographie universelle des musiciens et bibliographie générale de la musique*. Brussels, 1837–1844; Paris, 1877–1878.

Flicoteaux, Dom. E. *Fêtes de gloire: Avent, Noël, Épiphanie*. Paris, 1951.

Forster, Donald H. "The Oratorio in Paris in the 18th Century." *Acta Musicologica* 47 (January–June 1975): 67–133.

Froberville, J. de. "L'*Actéon* de Marc-Antoine Charpentier." *Revue de musicologie* 26 (1928): 75–76.

Fülop-Miller, René. *Les Jésuites et le secret de leur puissance. Histoire de la Compagnie de Jésus. Son rôle dans l'histoire de la civilisation*. Paris, 1933.

Gastoué, Amédée. *L'église et la musique*. Paris, 1936.

————. "La musique à Avignon et dans le Comtat du XIVe au XVIIIe siècle." *Revista Musicale Italiana* 12 (1905): 768–777.

————. "Notes sur les manuscrits et sur quelques oeuvres de Marc-Antoine Charpentier." *Mélanges de musicologie offerts à M. Lionel de La Laurencie*. Paris, 1933. 153–164.

Gérold, Théodore. "L'art du chant au XVIIe siècle." Diss. Strasbourg, 1921.

Girdlestone, Cuthbert. *La tragédie en musique (1673–1750) considérée comme genre littéraire*. Geneva: Droz, 1972.

Gofflot, L. V. *Le théâtre au collège*. Paris, 1907.

Gossip, C. J. "Le décor de théâtre au collège des Jésuites à Paris au XVIIe siècle." *Revue d'histoire du théâtre*. 33/1 (1981): 26–38.

Grand, Cécile. *Un opéra jésuite: David et Jonathas de Marc-Antoine Charpentier*. Paris: Conservatoire national supérieur de musique, 1983. (Essay not available to general public).

Guiffrey, Jules. "Testament et inventaire de Mademoiselle de Guise." *Nouvelles archives de l'art français*, 3rd series, 12 (1896): 200–233.

Guy-Lambert. "Charpentier, Marc-Antoine." *Dictionnaire de la musique*. Ed. Marc Honegger. Paris, 1970.

Hellouin, Frédéric. "Le Noël musical français." *Le Guide musical*. 50 (December 1905).

Hitchcock, Hugh Wiley. "Charpentier, Marc-Antoine." *The New Grove Dictionary of Music and Musicians*, vol. 4. Ed. Stanley Sadie. London: Macmillan, 1980.

————. "Charpentier, Marc-Antoine." *Dictionnaire de la musique en France aux XVIIe et XVIIIe siècles*. Ed. Marcelle Benoit. Paris: Fayard, 1992.

————. "Charpentier's *Médée*." *The Musical Times* (London) 125/1700 (October 1984): 562–567.

————. "Deux 'nouveaux' manuscrits de Marc-Antoine Charpentier." *Revue de musicologie* 58/2 (1972): 253–255.

————. "The Instrumental Music of Marc-Antoine Charpentier." *The Musical Quarterly* 47/1 (1961): 58–72.

_____. *The Latin Oratorios of Marc-Antoine Charpentier*. 3 vols. Diss., University of Michigan, 1955.

_____. "The Latin Oratorios of Marc-Antoine Charpentier." *The Musical Quarterly* 41 (1955): 41–65.

_____, ed. *L'oeuvre complète de Marc-Antoine Charpentier*. Geneva: Editions Minkoff, 1990–.

_____. *Marc-Antoine Charpentier*. Oxford Studies of Composers. London: Oxford University Press, 1977.

_____. "Marc-Antoine Charpentier." *The New Grove French Baroque Masters*. Ed. Stanley Sadie. London: Macmillan, 1986. 71–116.

_____. "Marc-Antoine Charpentier and the Comédie-Française." *Journal of the American Musicological Society* 24/2 (Summer 1971): 225–281.

_____. *Marc-Antoine Charpentier, Judicium Salomonis*. New Haven: A. R. Editions, 1964.

_____. "Marc-Antoine Charpentier, Mémoire et Index." *Recherches sur la musique française classique* 23 (1985): 5–44.

_____. *Marc-Antoine Charpentier, Pestis Mediolanensis*. University of North Carolina Press, 1979.

_____. *Marc-Antoine Charpentier, Prologue et intermèdes du Malade imaginaire de Molière*. Geneva: Minkoff, 1973.

_____. "*Médée*, le chef-d'oeuvre d'un musicien 'savant'." *Médée / Marc Antoine Charpentier*. Caen: Théâtre de Caen et Actes Sud, 1993. 47–52.

_____. *Médée*, le chef-d'oeuvre d'un musicien 'savant'." *Marc Antoine Charpentier Médée*. Ivry-sur-Seine: Imprimerie Jourdan [pour l'Opéra-Comique de Paris], 1993, 51–59.

_____. *Les oeuvres de Marc-Antoine Charpentier: Catalogue raisonné*. Paris: Picard, 1982.

_____. "Les oeuvres de Marc-Antoine Charpentier: Postscriptum à un catalogue." *Revue de musicologie* 70/1 (1984): 37–50.

_____. "Problèmes d'édition de la musique de Marc-Antoine Charpentier pour *Le Malade imaginaire*." *Revue de musicologie* 58/1 (1972): 3–15.

_____. "Some Aspects of Notation in an *Alma Redemptoris Mater* by M.-A. Charpentier." *Notations and Editions*. Ed. Edith Borroff. Dubuque, IA: W. C. Brown, 1974. Rpt. New York: Da Capo Press, 1979. 127–141.

Jal, A. *Dictionnaire critique de biographie et d'histoire*. Paris, 1872.

Johnson, Martha N. "Ten Magnificats by Marc-Antoine Charpentier." M.A. Thesis, North Carolina University, 1967.

Jurgens, Madeleine, and Elizabeth Maxfield-Miller. *Cent ans de recherche sur Molière, sur sa famille et sur les comédiens de sa troupe*. Paris: S.E.V.P.E.N., 1963.

Käser, Theodor. *Die Leçons de ténèbres im 17. und 18. Jahrhundert*. Publikationen der Schweizerischen Musikforschenden Gesellschaft. Series 2, vol. 12. Bern: Verlag Paul Hapt, 1966.

Kolneder, Walter. "Die *Règles de composition* von Marc-Antoine Charpentier." *Müller-Blattau (Joseph), Mélanges zum 70. Geburtstag von Joseph Müller-Blattau*. Kassel, 1966.

Labelle, Nicole. *L'oratorio*. Que sais-je? 2119. Paris: Presses universitaires de France, 1983.

La Gorce, Jérôme de. "L'Académie Royale de Musique en 1704, d'après des documents inédits." *Revue de musicologie* 65.2 (1979): 160–191.

————. *Berain, Dessinateur du Roi Soleil.* Paris, 1986.

La Laurencie, Lionel de. "Un opéra inédit de M.-Antoine Charpentier: *La Descente d'Orphée aux enfers.*" *Revue de musicologie* 10 (1929): 184–193.

Launay, Denise. "A propos de quelques motets polyphoniques en l'honneur de saint Martin: Contribution à l'histoire du motet aux XVIe et XVIIe siècles." *Revue de musicologie* 47 (1961): 67–80.

————. "A propos d'une messe de Charles d'Helfer: le problème de l'exécution des messes réputées *a capella* en France aux XVIIe et XVIIIe siècles." *Colloques de Wégimont* 4 (1957): 177–200.

————. "Charpentier (Marc-Antoine)." *Larousse de la musique.* Paris, 1957.

————. "Charpentier (Marc-Antoine)." *Die Musik in Geschichte und Gegenwart.* Kassel, 1952.

————. "Les deux versions musicales d'*Andromède:* une étape dans l'histoire du théâtre dans ses rapports avec la musique." *Colloque Pierre Corneille.* Rouen: Université de Basse-Normandie, October 1984. 413–441.

————. "L'enseignement de la composition dans les maîtrises en France aux XVIe et XVIIe siècles." *Revue de musicologie* 68 (1982): 79–90.

————. *Marc-Antoine Charpentier, Te Deum pour deux choeurs et deux orchestres.* "Le Pupitre." Paris: Heugel, 1969.

————. "Les motets à double choeur en France au début du XVIIe siècle." *Revue de musicologie* 40 (1957): 173–195.

Lavignac, Albert, and Lionel de La Laurencie. *Encyclopédie de la musique et dictionnaire du conservatoire.* Paris, 1913–31.

Lebeau, Élisabeth. "La musique des cérémonies célébrées à la mort de Marie-Thérèse, reine de France, 1683." *Colloques de Wégimont* 4 (1957): 200–219.

Lebègue, Raymond. "Les ballets des Jésuites." *Revue des cours et conférences* April–May 1936: 127–140, 209–222, 321–330.

————. "Les Jésuites et le théâtre." *Études sur le théâtre français* (1936): 165–207.

Lejeaux, Jeanne. "Les décors de théâtre dans les collèges de Jésuites." *Revue d'histoire du théâtre* 7:3–4 (1955): 305–315.

Lemaître, Edmond. *Marc-Antoine Charpentier, Médée.* Paris: CNRS, 1987.

————. *Marc-Antoine Charpentier, Neuf leçons de ténèbres.* Paris: CNRS, 1983.

————. "L'orchestre dans le théâtre lyrique français chez les continuateurs de Lully, 1687–1713." *Recherches sur la musique française classique* 24 (1986): 107–127.

Le Moël, Michel. "Un foyer d'italianisme à la fin du XVIIe siècle: Nicolas Mathieu, curé de Saint-André-des-Arts." *Recherches sur la musique française classique* 3 (1963): 43–48.

Lowe, Robert W. *Marc-Antoine Charpentier et l'opéra de collège.* Paris: G.-P. Maisonneuve & Larose, 1966.

————. "Marc-Antoine Charpentier, compositeur chez Molière." *Les Études classiques* 32 (1965): 34–41.

_____ . "Marc-Antoine Charpentier, compositeur pour la maison professe des Jésuites à Paris." *Études* (January 1959): 88–93.

_____ . "Marc-Antoine Charpentier, compositeur pour la Sainte-Chapelle de Paris." *XVIIᵉ siècle* 56 (1962): 37–43.

_____ . "Les représentations en musique au Collège Louis-le-Grand, 1650–88." *Revue d'histoire du théâtre* 10/1 (1958): 21–34.

_____ . "Les représentations en musique dans les collèges de Paris et de province (1632–1757)." *Revue d'histoire du théâtre* 15/2 (1963): 119–126.

Massenkeil, Günther. "Marc-Antoine Charpentier als Messenkomponist." *Colloquium Amicorum: Jos. Schmidt-Görg zum 70. Geburtstag.* Bonn: Beethoven-Haus, 1967. 228–238.

Masson, Chantal. "Journal du marquis de Dangeau." *Recherches sur la musique française classique* 2 (1961–1962): 197–226.

Maurice-Amour, Lila. "Les musiciens de Corneille 1650–99." *Revue de musicologie* 27 (1955): 43–75.

_____ . "Rythme dans les comédies-ballets de Molière." *Revue d'histoire du théâtre* 26:2 (1974): 118–131.

Mélèse, Pierre. *Répertoire analytique des documents contemporains concernant les théâtres à Paris sous Louis XIV, 1659–1715.* Paris: Droz, 1934.

_____ . *Le théâtre et le public à Paris sous Louis XIV.* Paris: Droz, 1934.

Mittman, Barbara G. "Les Spectateurs sur la scène: quelques chiffres tirés des registres du XVIIᵉ siècle." *Revue d'histoire du théâtre* 32/3 (1980): 199–215.

_____ . *Spectators on the Paris Stage in the Seventeenth and Eighteenth Centuries.* Theater and Dramatic Studies 25. Ann Arbor: UMI Research Press, 1984.

Mongrédien, Georges. *Les comédiens français du XVIIᵉ siècle: dictionnaire biographique, suivi d'un inventaire des troupes: 1590–1710, d'après les documents inédits.* Paris: CNRS, 1981.

_____ . "Molière et Lully." *XVIIᵉ siècle* 98–99 (1973): 3–15.

_____ . *Recueil des textes et documents du XVIIᵉ siècle relatifs à Molière.* 2 vols. Paris: CNRS, 1965.

_____ . *La vie quotidienne des comédiens au temps de Molière.* Paris, 1966. Trans. by Claire Eliane Engel, under the title *Daily Life in the French Theatre at the Time of Molière.* Daily Life Series 16. London: George Allen and Unwin Ltd., 1969.

Monval, Georges. "Documents inédits: Perrin, Molière, Lully." *Le Moliériste* 3 (1881–1882): 168–169.

Nef, Karl. "Das Petrus Oratorium von Marc-Antoine Charpentier und die Passion." *Jahrbuch der Musikbibliothek Peters für 1930.* Leipzig: Peters, 1931. 24–31.

Nielson, Bodil Ellerup. "Les grands oratorios bibliques de Marc-Antoine Charpentier." *Dansk arsbog for musikforskning, 1966–1967.* Copenhagen, 1968. 29–61.

Nuitter, Charles, and Ernest Thoinan. *Les origines de l'opéra français.* Paris: Plon, 1886.

Oliver, A. Richard. "Molière's Contribution to the Lyric Stage." *The Musical Quarterly* 33 (1947): 350–364.

Paillard, Jean-François. *La musique française classique.* Que sais-je? 878. Paris: Presses universitaires de France, 1973.

Parmley, Andrew. "The Secular Stage Works of Marc-Antoine Charpentier." Diss. Royal Holloway, London, n.d. (Not available.)

Pellisson, Maurice. *Les comédies-ballets de Molière.* Paris, 1914. Éditions d'aujourd'hui, Les Introuvables, 1976.

Philips, J. H. "Le théâtre scolaire dans la querelle du théâtre au XVIIᵉ siècle." *Revue d'histoire du théâtre* 35/2 (1983): 190–221.

Picard, Évelyne. "Liturgie et musique à Sainte-Anne-la-Royale au XVIIᵉ siècle." *Recherches sur la musique française classique* 20 (1981): 249–254.

Powell, John S. "Charpentier's Music for Molière's *Le Malade imaginaire* and Its Revisions." *Journal of the American Musicological Society* 39/1 (Spring 1986): 87–142.

———. *Marc-Antoine Charpentier, Music for Molière's Comedies.* Madison: A. R. Editions, Inc., 1988.

———. *Marc-Antoine Charpentier, Vocal Chamber Music.* Madison: A. R. Editions, Inc., 1986.

———. *Music in the Theater of Molière.* Diss. University of Washington, 1982.

———. "Music and the Self-fulfilling Prophecy in Molière's *Le Mariage forcé.*" *Early Music* 21: 2 (May 1993): 213–230

Prunières, Henry. *L'opéra italien en France avant Lully.* Paris, 1913. Paris: Champion, 1975.

Quittard, Henri. *Henry Du Mont (1610–1684).* Paris, 1906.

———. "*La Couronne de fleurs* de M.-A. Charpentier sur des vers inconnus de Molière." *Revue musicale* 8 (1908): 482–491.

———. "Notes sur un ouvrage inédit de Marc-Antoine Charpentier." *Zeitschrift des internationalen Musikgesellschaft* 6 (1905): 323–330.

———. "*Orphée descendant aux enfers.*" *Revue musicale* 4 (1904): 495–496.

———. "Un prologue inédit de Molière pour *Le Malade imaginaire.*" *Journal des débats politiques et littéraires,* no. 194, supplément (14 July 1905).

Ranum, Orest. *Paris in the Age of Absolutism.* New York: Wiley, 1968.

Ranum, Patricia M. "Étienne Loulié (1654–1702n): Musicien de Mlle de Guise, pédagogue et théoricien." *Recherches sur la musique française classique* 25 (1987) and 26 (1988).

———. "Mademoiselle de Guise ou les défis de la quenouille." *XVIIᵉ siècle* 144 (July–September 1984): 221–231.

———. "A Sweet Servitude: A Musician's Life at the Court of Mlle de Guise." *Early Music* 15/3 (August 1987): 346–360.

———. "Un portrait présumé de Marc-Antoine Charpentier." *Bulletin de la Société de Marc-Antoine Charpentier* 4 (January 1991).

———. "Titon du Tillet: le premier 'biographe' de Marc-Antoine Charpentier." *Bulletin de la Société Marc-Antoine Charpentier* 6 (January 1992): 9–19.

Raugel, Félix. "Marc-Antoine Charpentier." *Festschrift Karl Gustav Fellerer.* Ed. Heinrich Hüschen. Regensburg: Gustav Bosse Verlag, 1962. 417–420.

_____. "Marc-Antoine Charpentier." *Musik-revy, Nordisk tidskrift för musik och gramofon* 10/1 (1955): 21–23.

_____. *L'oratorio.* Paris, 1948.

Reboud, René-Marie. "Messire Arthus Aux Cousteaux, maître de musique de la Sainte-Chapelle du Palais (1590–1654)." *XVIIe siècle* 21–22 (1954): 403–417.

Reynes, Geneviève. *Couvents de femmes.* Paris, 1987.

Roskseth, Yvonne. "Un Magnificat de Marc-Antoine Charpentier." *Journal of Renaissance and Baroque Music* 1 (1946): 192–199.

Ruff, Lillian M. "Marc-Antoine Charpentier's *Règles de composition.*" *The Consort* 24 (1967): 233–270.

Sadie, Julie Anne. "Charpentier and the Early French Ensemble Sonata." *Early Music* 7/3 (July 1979): 330–335.

Saint-Paul Saint-Louis, les jésuites à Paris. Catalogue of the exhibition at the Musée Carnavalet. Paris, 1985.

Saint-Saëns, Camille. "Un contemporain de Lully." *Au courant de la vie.* Paris, n.d. 7–9.

Smither, Howard E. "The Oratorio in the Baroque Era: Italy, Vienna, Paris." *A History of the Oratorio.* Vol. 1. Chapel Hill, 1977.

Solnon, Jean-François. *La Cour de France.* Paris, 1987.

Spycket, Sylvie. "Thomas Corneille et la musique." *XVIIe siècle* 21–22 (1954): 442–455.

Stein, Henri. *Le Palais de Justice et la Sainte-Chapelle de Paris: Notice historique et archéologique.* Paris, 1912.

Taiz-Destouches, Danièle. "Jean Mignon (1640–1710), maître de chapelle de Notre-Dame de Paris: Contribution à une histoire de la messe polyphonique au XVIIe siècle." *Recherches sur la musique française classique* 14 (1974): 82–153.

Tapié, Victor-Lucien. *Baroque et classicisme.* Paris, 1980. Trans. by A. Ross Williamson, under the title *The Age of Grandeur: Baroque Art and Architecture.* New York: Praeger, 1961.

Taveneaux, René. *La vie quotidienne des jansénistes.* Paris, 1973.

Thierry, Édouard. *Documents sur Le Malade imaginaire.* Paris, 1880.

Tiersot, Julien. *La musique dans la comédie de Molière.* Paris: La Renaissance du livre, 1922.

_____. "La musique des comédies de Molière à la Comédie-Française." *Revue de musicologie* 3 (1922): 20–28.

Tunley, David. "The Emergence of the Eighteenth-Century French Cantata." *Studies in Music* 1 (1967): 67–88.

Wilhelm, Jacques. *La vie quotidienne du Marais au XVIIe siècle.* Paris, 1966.

_____. *La vie quotidienne des Parisiens au temps du Roi-Soleil, 1660–1715.* Paris, 1977.

Index of Names

Index of Music

Numbers in parentheses correspond to numbers assigned to Charpentier's compositions by H. Wiley Hitchcock in *Les oeuvres de Marc-Antoine Charpentier: Catalogue raisonné* (1982).